Lecture Notes in Computer Science 11633

Commenced Publication in 1973
Founding and Former Series Editors:
Gerhard Goos, Juris Hartmanis, and Jan van Leeuwen

More information about this series at http://www.springer.com/series/7410

Xingming Sun · Zhaoqing Pan ·
Elisa Bertino (Eds.)

Artificial Intelligence and Security

5th International Conference, ICAIS 2019
New York, NY, USA, July 26–28, 2019
Proceedings, Part II

Editors
Xingming Sun
Nanjing University of Information
Science and Technology
Nanjing, China

Zhaoqing Pan
Nanjing University of Information
Science and Technology
Nanjing, China

Elisa Bertino
Purdue University
West Lafayette, IN, USA

ISSN 0302-9743 ISSN 1611-3349 (electronic)
Lecture Notes in Computer Science
ISBN 978-3-030-24264-0 ISBN 978-3-030-24265-7 (eBook)
https://doi.org/10.1007/978-3-030-24265-7

LNCS Sublibrary: SL4 – Security and Cryptology

This Springer imprint is published by the registered company Springer Nature Switzerland AG
The registered company address is: Gewerbestrasse 11, 6330 Cham, Switzerland

Preface

The 5th International Conference on Artificial Intelligence and Security (ICAIS 2019), formerly called the International Conference on Cloud Computing and Security (ICCCS), was held during July 26–28, 2019, at New York University, New York, USA. Over the past four years, ICAIS has become a leading conference for researchers and engineers to share their latest results from research, development, and applications in the fields of artificial intelligence and information security.

We used the Microsoft Conference Management Toolkits (CMT) system to manage the submission and review processes of ICAIS 2019. We received 1529 submissions from 20 countries and regions, including USA, Canada, UK, Italy, Ireland, Japan, Russia, France, Australia, South Korea, South Africa, India, Iraq, Kazakhstan, Indonesia, Vietnam, Ghana, China, Taiwan, and Macao, etc. The submissions cover the areas of artificial intelligence, big data, cloud computing and security, information hiding, IoT security, multimedia forensics, encryption and cybersecurity, and so on. We thank our Technical Program Committee members and external reviewers for their efforts in reviewing papers and providing valuable comments to the authors. From the total of 1,529 submissions, and based on at least three reviews per submission, the Program Chairs decided to accept 230 papers, yielding an acceptance rate of 15%. The volume of the conference proceedings contains all the regular, poster, and workshop papers.

The conference program was enriched by a series of keynote presentations, and the keynote speakers included: Nasir Memon, New York University, USA; Edward Colbert, Virginia Tech Hume Center for National Security and Technology, USA; Quanyan Zhu, New York University, USA; Zhihua Xia, Nanjing University of Information Science and Technology, China; Tom Masino, TradeWeb, USA; etc. We thank them for their wonderful speeches.

There were 45 workshops organized at ICAIS 2019, covering all the hot topics in artificial intelligence and security. We would like to take this moment to express our sincere appreciation for the contribution of all the workshop chairs and their participants. We would like to extend our sincere thanks to all authors who submitted papers to ICAIS 2019 and to all Program Committee members. It was a truly great experience to work with such talented and hard-working researchers. We also appreciate the external reviewers for assisting the Program Committee members in their particular areas of expertise. Moreover, we want to thank our sponsors: Nanjing University of Information Science and Technology, Springer, New York University, IEEE Broadcast Technology Society (BTS) Nanjing Chapter, ACM China, Michigan State University, Taiwan Cheng Kung University, Taiwan Dong Hwa University, Taiwan Providence University, Nanjing University of Aeronautics and Astronautics, State Key Laboratory of Integrated Services Networks, and the National Nature Science Foundation of China.

May 2019

Xingming Sun
Zhaoqing Pan
Elisa Bertino

Organization

General Chairs

Yun Q. Shi	New Jersey Institute of Technology, USA
Mauro Barni	University of Siena, Italy
Xingang You	China Information Technology Security Evaluation Center, China
Elisa Bertino	Purdue University, USA
Quanyan Zhu	New York University, USA
Xingming Sun	Nanjing University of Information Science and Technology, China

Technical Program Chairs

Aniello Castiglione	University of Salerno, Italy
Yunbiao Guo	China Information Technology Security Evaluation Center, China
Suzanne K. McIntosh	New York University, USA
Zhihua Xia	Nanjing University of Information Science and Technology, China
Victor S. Sheng	University of Central Arkansas, USA

Publication Chair

Zhaoqing Pan	Nanjing University of Information Science and Technology, China

Workshop Chair

Baowei Wang	Nanjing University of Information Science and Technology, China

Organization Chairs

Edward Wong	New York University, USA
Zhangjie Fu	Nanjing University of Information Science and Technology, China

Technical Program Committee

Saeed Arif	University of Algeria, Algeria
Anthony Ayodele	University of Maryland University College, USA

Chuan Qin	University of Shanghai for Science and Technology, China
Jiaohua Qin	Central South University of Forestry and Technology, China
Yanzhen Qu	Colorado Technical University, USA
Zhiguo Qu	Nanjing University of Information Science and Technology, China
Kui Ren	State University of New York, USA
Arun Kumar Sangaiah	VIT University, India
Zheng-guo Sheng	University of Sussex, UK
Robert Simon Sherratt	University of Reading, UK
Yun Q. Shi	New Jersey Institute of Technology, USA
Frank Y. Shih	New Jersey Institute of Technology, USA
Biao Song	King Saud University, Saudi Arabia
Guang Sun	Hunan University of Finance and Economics, China
Jiande Sun	Shandong Normal University, China
Jianguo Sun	Harbin University of Engineering, China
Jianyong Sun	Xi'an Jiaotong University, China
Krzysztof Szczypiorski	Warsaw University of Technology, Poland
Tsuyoshi Takagi	Kyushu University, Japan
Shanyu Tang	University of West London, UK
Xianping Tao	Nanjing University, China
Jing Tian	National University of Singapore, Singapore
Yoshito Tobe	Aoyang University, Japan
Cezhong Tong	Washington University in St. Louis, USA
Pengjun Wan	Illinois Institute of Technology, USA
Cai-Zhuang Wang	Ames Laboratory, USA
Ding Wang	Peking University, China
Guiling Wang	New Jersey Institute of Technology, USA
Honggang Wang	University of Massachusetts-Dartmouth, USA
Jian Wang	Nanjing University of Aeronautics and Astronautics, China
Jie Wang	University of Massachusetts Lowell, USA
Jing Wang	Changsha University of Science and Technology, China
Jinwei Wang	Nanjing University of Information Science and Technology, China
Liangmin Wang	Jiangsu University, China
Ruili Wang	Massey University, New Zealand
Xiaojun Wang	Dublin City University, Ireland
Xiaokang Wang	St. Francis Xavier University, Canada
Zhaoxia Wang	A-Star, Singapore
Sheng Wen	Swinburne University of Technology, Australia
Jian Weng	Jinan University, China
Edward Wong	New York University, USA
Eric Wong	University of Texas at Dallas, USA

Q. M. Jonathan Wu	University of Windsor, Canada
Shaoen Wu	Ball State University, USA
Shuangkui Xia	Beijing Institute of Electronics Technology and Application, China
Lingyun Xiang	Changsha University of Science and Technology, China
Shijun Xiang	Jinan University, China
Yang Xiang	Deakin University, Australia
Yang Xiao	The University of Alabama, USA
Haoran Xie	The Education University of Hong Kong, SAR China
Naixue Xiong	Northeastern State University, USA
Xin Xu	Wuhan University of Science and Technology, China
Wei Qi Yan	Auckland University of Technology, New Zealand
Aimin Yang	Guangdong University of Foreign Studies, China
Ching-Nung Yang	Taiwan Dong Hwa University, Taiwan, China
Chunfang Yang	Zhengzhou Science and Technology Institute, China
Fan Yang	University of Maryland, USA
Guomin Yang	University of Wollongong, Australia
Ming Yang	Southeast University, China
Qing Yang	University of North Texas, USA
Yuqiang Yang	Bohai University, USA
Ming Yin	Purdue University, USA
Xinchun Yin	Yangzhou University, China
Shaodi You	Australian National University, Australia
Kun-Ming Yu	Chung Hua University, Taiwan, China
Yong Yu	University of Electronic Science and Technology of China, China
Gonglin Yuan	Guangxi University, China
Mingwu Zhang	Hubei University of Technology, China
Wei Zhang	Nanjing University of Posts and Telecommunications, China
Weiming Zhang	University of Science and Technology of China, China
Xinpeng Zhang	Fudan University, China
Yan Zhang	Simula Research Laboratory, Norway
Yanchun Zhang	Victoria University, Australia
Yao Zhao	Beijing Jiaotong University, China
Linna Zhou	University of International Relations, China

Organizing Committee

Xianyi Chen	Nanjing University of Information Science and Technology, China
Yadang Chen	Nanjing University of Information Science and Technology, China
Beijing Chen	Nanjing University of Information Science and Technology, China

Huajun Huang	Central South University of Forestry and Technology, China
Jielin Jiang	Nanjing University of Information Science and Technology, China
Zilong Jin	Nanjing University of Information Science and Technology, China
Yan Kong	Nanjing University of Information Science and Technology, China
Yiwei Li	Columbia University, USA
Yuling Liu	Hunan University, China
Lirui Qiu	Nanjing University of Information Science and Technology, China
Zhiguo Qu	Nanjing University of Information Science and Technology, China
Guang Sun	Hunan University of Finance and Economics, China
Huiyu Sun	New York University, USA
Le Sun	Nanjing University of Information Science and Technology, China
Jian Su	Nanjing University of Information Science and Technology, China
Lina Tan	Hunan University of Commerce, China
Qing Tian	Nanjing University of Information Science and Technology, China
Yuan Tian	King Saud University, Saudi Arabia
Zuwei Tian	Hunan First Normal University, China
Xiaoliang Wang	Hunan University of Science and Technology, China
Lingyun Xiang	Changsha University of Science and Technology, China
Lizhi Xiong	Nanjing University of Information Science and Technology, China
Leiming Yan	Nanjing University of Information Science and Technology, China
Hengfu Yang	Hunan First Normal University, China
Li Yu	Nanjing University of Information Science and Technology, China
Zhili Zhou	Nanjing University of Information Science and Technology, China

Contents – Part II

Artificial Intelligence

Big Data

Cloud Computing and Security

Artificial Intelligence

CCNET: Cascading Convolutions for Cardiac Segmentation

Chao Luo[1], Xiaojie Li[1(✉)], Yucheng Chen[2], Xi Wu[1], Jia He[1], and Jiliu Zhou[1]

[1] Chengdu University of Information Technology, No. 24 Block 1, Xuefu Road, Chengdu 610225, China
lixj@cuit.edu.cn

[2] West China Hospital, Sichuan University, Chengdu, China

Abstract. Myocardial segmentation plays a pivotal role in the clinical diagnosis of cardiac diseases. The difference in size and shape of the heart poses an extensive challenge to the clinical diagnosis. Being specific, the large amount of noise generated by the cardiac magnetic resonance (CMR) images also gives rise to substantial interference in the clinical diagnosis. Inspired by associated tasks, we put forward a network for the myocardium segmentation. In the proposed methodology, at first, we establish numerous sub-sampling layers in a bid to attain the high-level features, together with fusing the feature information of different visual fields by assuming different convolution kernel sizes. Thereafter, high-level features coupled with initial input features are merged by means of a plurality of cascaded convolution layers. It is capable of directly improving the performance of myocardium segmentation. We perform an assessment of our approach on 165 CMR T1 mapping images with lower PSNR, and the results demonstrate that our architecture outperforms previous approaches.

Keywords: Myocardial segmentation · Cascaded convolution

1 Introduction

Both the assessment and early diagnosis of cardiac function have emerged as a primary point in contemporary health issues for the high incidence of cardiovascular disease and mortality [1,2]. Moreover, the analysis of the cardiac function plays a pivotal role in the clinical cardiology for not only the patient management, but also the disease diagnosis, risk evaluation, and therapy decision [3–5]. Owing to the digital imagery, different medical imaging modalities, for instance, magnetic resonance imaging (MRI) and positron emission tomography (PET), provide highly identified information by showing the difference between normal and diseased soft tissues (and organs) [6,7]. MRI is capable of obtaining the native three-dimensional cross-sectional imaging, besides being capable of obtaining multi-directional images without a reconstruction [8,9].

X. Sun et al. (Eds.): ICAIS 2019, LNCS 11633, pp. 3–11, 2019.
https://doi.org/10.1007/978-3-030-24265-7_1

Accordingly, the location and extent of the lesion and the relationship with surrounding tissues and organs can be shown for the determination of the lesion [10,11]. That is why it offers exclusive advantages for the qualitative localization and quantitative diagnosis of many lesions [12]. Furthermore, MRI offers the advantages of a high contrast resolution and soft tissue resolution [13,14]. Accordingly, MRI images are mostly put to use as a basis for the diagnosis in clinical diagnosis and treatment. In particular, in the diagnosis of heart disease, the MRI image of the heart is quite critical [15–17]. Nonetheless, CMR images require doctors to manually label soft tissue areas, which has the potential to lead to lots of work, together with being likely to result into the inaccurate labeling because of doctors′ different experiences [18,19].

For the purpose of solving the above issues, numbers of computer algorithm-based auxiliary methodologies have been put forward and applied [20–23]. Recently, automatic segmentation algorithms, which are based on the machine learning, have been put forward in the literature successfully solved different medical image segmentation tasks [24–26]. For instance, Olaf Ronneberger, together with his team, put forward the Unity Network (U-net) for Biomedical Image Segmentation, a full-convolution network that does not have any fully connected layer [27]. The attribute of the network suggests that it still retains numerous feature channels in the up-sampling stage, making the network capable of transmitting the environmental information to higher resolution layers. Besides, U-Net is designed for the classification of each pixel, so that it could attain a higher segmentation accuracy [28,29]. Nonetheless, it is not possible to use U-Net directly for myocardial segmentation tasks [30]. It has been clearly identified: (1) The accuracy of the receptive field and positioning cannot be enhanced simultaneously. When the receptive field selection is comparatively larger, the reduction dimension of the corresponding pool layer is expected to increase, which is expected to lead to the lower positioning accuracy. Likewise, in the case of a small field of receptive, the positioning accuracy is also expected to decrease. (2) There is more noise in the myocardial image. The contrast between the myocardium and the surrounding tissue is quite poor, substantially lowering the accuracy of the segmentation. (3) The redundancy of using U-net for image segmentation tasks is excessively large [27,31]. Owing to the fact that each pixel takes a patch, the similarity of patches of two adjacent pixels is quite high, resulting into an extensive amount of redundancy, making the network training very slow [32,33].

Aimed at addressing the above issues, in the current work, we put forward a network for the analysis of the myocardium. In the proposed methodology, a productive cascading convolution is established for fusing multi-scale features. Our method makes following contributions: (1) We put forward an effective end-to-end segmentation task network, which has the potential to input a completely original image, together with outputting a segmented prediction map directly. (2) We establish a productive cascading convolution for fusing multi-scale features with various receptive fields. Through the use of convolution kernels of different sizes, we have the option of obtaining multi-scale features, in addition to the hierarchical contextual information regarding the myocardium. We verified our approach on 165 T1-mapping CMR images. As the results reveal, our network outperforms previous methodologies.

2 Segmentation Task Using Cascading Convolutions (CCNET)

2.1 Network Architecture

Our network has been presented in Fig. 1. In each of the down-sampling stages, we firstly make use of multiple convolutions for the purpose of obtaining the high-level feature. In each convolution block, convolution kernels of different sizes and numbers are developed for the extraction of the multi-scale information and hierarchical context information. Besides that, we add the output and input features of the layer as the input of the next layer, which has the potential to enhance the reuse of features, in addition to improving the accuracy of segmentation. In the up-sampling stage, aimed at restoring the size of the original image and fully utilizing the original features, we combine the output features of each layer with the output features in the down-sampling.

For the purpose of making it certain that the size of the picture, following the convolution, is the same as the size prior to the convolution, zero padding is employed in each of the convolutional layers. In our experiments, the Relu activation function is put to use in the network. Each convolution block contains a convolutional layer, coupled with an activation layer, a batch normalization layer and a pool layer. A convolution with filter size 1×1 is put to use for the generation of the final segmentation map and reduction of the number of feature maps prior to the deconvolution, whereas other convolutions make use of filters of different sizes in the network.

The network structure is capable of adequately extracting and learning the characteristics of the input data. And by fully combining the characteristics of the original input, the network can make full use of the original features without loss. Therefore, the network can achieve very good segmentation effects.

2.2 Cascading Features

We establish a productive cascading convolution for fusing features with various receptive fields. In this network, seven 1×1 convolutions are employed for capturing the high-level features, and the feature resolution is enhanced with the increase in the amount of computation. Thereafter, we spliced the three down-sampled convolution features and the three up-sampled features as multi-scale features, followed by fusing the global contextual information. Thereafter, a kernel size of 1×1 convolutional layer is adopted for the reduction of the number of feature maps.

Owing to the cascading multi-scale nature, our network is capable of capturing different features with different filter sizes. Moreover, cascaded convolutions have multi-scale features, hierarchies, and semantic information, effectively segmenting different sizes of myocardium.

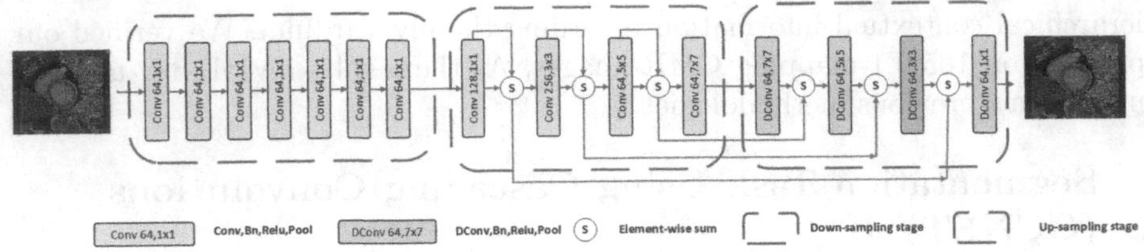

Fig. 1. The network structure proposed in this paper.

2.3 Loss Function

Cross entropy is mostly employed for the classification or segmentation loss function of deep neural networks. Herein, we make use of the cross entropy as the loss function of the myocardial segmentation.

$$H(y, y') = -\sum_{i}^{n} y_i' log y_i, \tag{1}$$

where H is a representation of the loss value, y indicates the predicted probability distribution, y_i denotes the true probability, and n suggests the number of samples. Furthermore, the cross entropy loss function is put to a frequent use in classification networks. In the current paper, we employ the classification methodology for the purpose of segmenting tasks. We take into consideration the myocardial circle to be segmented as a category and the background as a category.

3 Experiment and Results

3.1 Dataset, Pre-processing and Evaluation Metrics

In this experiment, CMR T1-mapping images of 165 myocardial sections from the same hospital were both trained and tested. The ground truth of the training and the testing samples of images with the myocardial are manually annotated by an experienced cardiologist. The pixel size of each CMR image amounts to 1.406 × 1.406 mm having a size ranging between 192 × 256 and 224 × 256. Taking into consideration the fact that the size of the myocardium is small and surrounded by substantial amount of noise, we first resample the resolution of the image to 1 × 1 × 1 and subsequently, each image is cut into a fixed image size of 128 × 128. Eventually, the intensity range of the T1-mapping images is normalized to [0–255].

We make use of four indicators for the purpose of judging the performance of the network, which includes the dice similarity coefficient (DSC), area under the curve (AUC), jaccard similarity coefficient (JSC), and F1-score are employed for the assessment of the segmentation accuracy. The DSC is mostly employed for the calculation of the overlap metric between the results of segmentation and the ground truth. The dice coeficient for bit vectors is defined as:

$$DSC = \frac{2||PG||_2}{|P|_2^2 + |G|_2^2} \quad (2)$$

where PG is the element-wise product of the prediction (P) and the ground truth (G), and $||x||_2$ is the L2-norm of X. The AUC is a probability value. The greater the AUC value, the better the performance. The AUC score was computed with a closed-form formula:

$$AUC = \frac{S_0 - n_0(n_0+1)/2}{n_0 n_1} \quad (3)$$

where n_0 is the number of pixel that belong to the ground truth, n_1 is the opposite and $S_0 = \sum_{i=1}^{n_0 r_i}$, where r_i is the rank given by the predict model of the ground truth to the ith pixel in the CMR image. The F1 score is the harmonic average of precision and recall, wherein an F1 score reaches its best value at one (perfect precision and recall) and the worst at zero. The JSC is put to use for the improvement of similarities and differences between finite sample sets. The larger the JSC value, the higher the sample similarity.

3.2 Implementation Details and Parameter Settings

Train Strategy: Owing to the fact that the amount of data is not quite extensive, we employ a 5-fold cross-validation methodology. There are an aggregate of 165 images, 132 images for training, 33 images for verification, and verification results as our test results.

Learning Rate Strategy: We conducted several trials with different learning rates, and the results showed that the learning rate of *0.001* was the most appropriate. If the learning rate is too high, it will lead to over-fitting, and the network cannot learn the feature information correctly. If the learning rate is too low, the network fitting speed is very slow. Therefore we set the learning rate to *0.001*, the initial learning rate is exponentially degraded every 10 iterations at a learning rate decay rate of 0.9.

Experiment Configurations: To ensure the consistency of the experiment, we use accuracy as the quantization metric, *100* epochs are trained for each experiment (*batch_size* = 3). All experiments are implemented in python2.7 by using Tensorflow and Keras framework. We train the networks on a NVIDIA Tesla M40 GPU and the model that performs the best on test data set are saved for further analysis.

3.3 Results

Aimed at verifying the performance of our network, we compared it with two classic segmentation methodologies (U-Net and Deeplabv3). In this experiment,

Table 1. Experimental results of 3 different networks. The table shows the average of the four indicators.

Model	DSC	AUC	F1-score	JSC
U-Net	0.7306	0.8757	0.7397	0.5863
Deeplabv3	0.7133	0.8421	0.7245	0.5084
CCNet	0.7512	0.8951	0.7581	0.6152

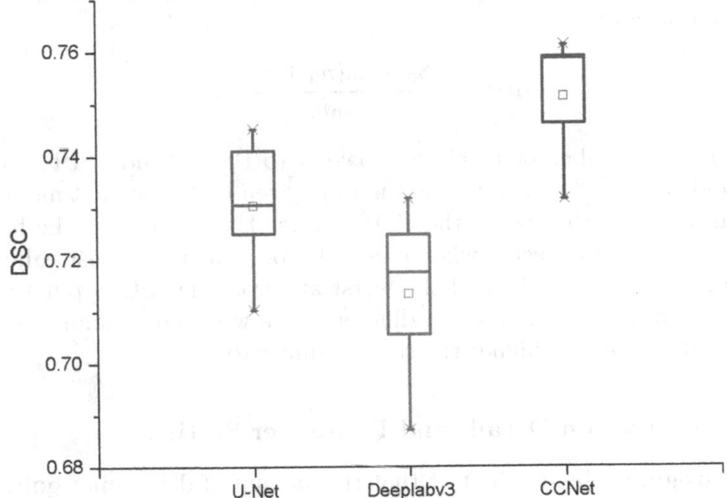

Fig. 2. Box diagram of DSC for three different networks. Each network performs 5 experiments, and the box plot was drawn based on the DSC value of each experimental result.

we implemented U-Net and Deeplabv3 on the basis of tensorflow, and parameters were set to be the same as that of our network.

Table 1 sheds light on the segmentation results for each network. As evident from Table 1, among the four indicators, the network we put forward manifests the best performance. The average DSC value of our proposed network has the potential to reach 0.7512, the average AUC value can reach 0.8951, the F1-score can reach 0.7581, and JSC value is 0.6152. The performance of our proposed network is better in comparison with that of U-Net and Deeplabv3, considering the four indicators.

Furthermore, Fig. 2 reveals a box diagram of the DSC values for the three networks. As evident to find out from Fig. 2, despite the fact that U-Net and Deeplabv3 are capable of attaining better results, the overall performance of the proposed network is better as compared with that of the other two networks.

It is quite evident to observe from Fig. 3 that the proposed network is capable of segmenting the myocardial circle efficiently. Through the comparison of the segmentation results with U-Net and Deeplabv3, we can figure it out that the

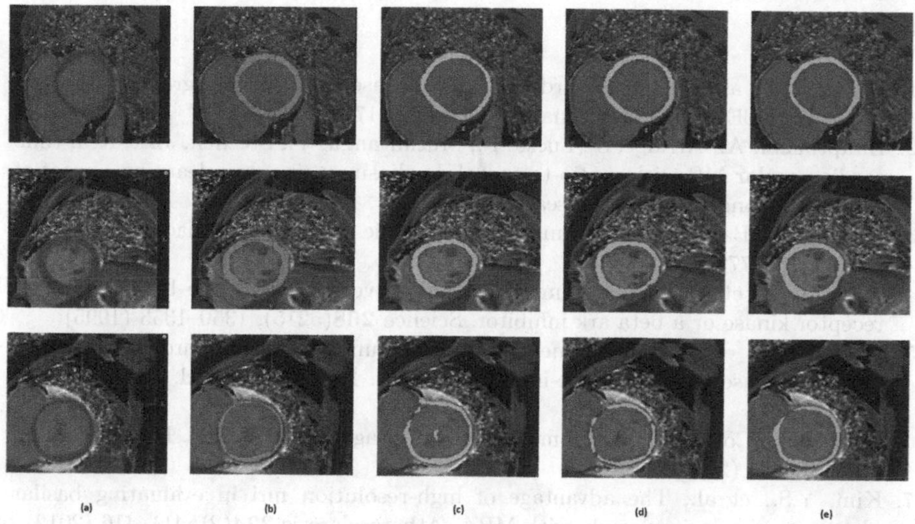

Fig. 3. Segmentation results of three different samples in different networks. The first column shows the original CMR image, and the second column shows the ground truth. (a) Raw, (b) Ground truth, (c) U-Net, (d) Deeplabv3, (e) CCNet.

segmentation result of our network is not only less noisy but also closer to the ground truth. In particular, through the comparison of results of both the second and third rows, we can see that U-Net and Deeplabv3 are going to produce a substantial amount of noise to interfere with the myocardial segmentation, while the myocardial portion of our network segmentation is quite smooth as well as noiseless.

4 Conclusion

In this paper, we put forward a CNN network with cascading convolutions for the myocardial segmentation. The cascading convolutions have the ability of perceiving multi-scale features of myocardial as well as hierarchical semantic and contextual information. In order to prove the effectiveness of our proposed network, we performed its comparison with two segmentation networks. The proposed methodology was found to be superior to all other networks, in terms of three indicators. Experiments reveal the fact that the proposed network is capable of substantially improving the segmentation performance. The network is also suitable for the segmentation tasks of other medical images, and we are going to make use of this network for different medical images.

Acknowledgment. This work was supported by the National Natural Science Foundation of China (Grant No. 61602066) and the Scientific Research Foundation (KYTZ201608) of CUIT and the major Project of Education Department in Sichuan (17ZA0063 and 2017JQ0030), and partially supported by the Sichuan international science and technology cooperation and exchange research program (2016HH0018).

References

1. Wang, J., et al.: Detecting cardiovascular disease from mammograms with deep learning. IEEE Trans. Med. Imaging **PP**(99), 1172–1181 (2017)
2. Hauptmann, A., Arridge, S., Lucka, F., Muthurangu, V., Steeden, J.A.: Real-time cardiovascular MR with spatio-temporal de-aliasing using deep learning - proof of concept in congenital heart disease (2018)
3. Kelly, R.A., Balligand, J.L., Smith, T.W.: Nitric oxide and cardiac function. Life Sci. **81**(10), 779–793 (1996)
4. Koch, W.J., et al.: Cardiac function in mice overexpressing the beta-adrenergic receptor kinase or a beta ark inhibitor. Science **268**(5215), 1350–1353 (1995)
5. Frustaci, A., et al.: Improvement in cardiac function in the cardiac variant of Fabry's disease with galactose-infusion therapy. N. Engl. J. Med. **345**(1), 25–32 (2001)
6. Jadvar, H., Colletti, P.M.: Competitive advantage of PET/MRI. Eur. J. Radiol. **83**(1), 84–94 (2014)
7. Kim, Y.S., et al.: The advantage of high-resolution mri in evaluating basilar plaques: a comparison study with MRA. Atherosclerosis **224**(2), 411–416 (2012)
8. Lau, L.U., Thoeni, R.F.: Case report. Uterine lipoma: advantage of mri over ultrasound. Br. J. Radiol. **78**(925), 72 (2005)
9. Andica, C., et al.: The advantage of synthetic MRI for the visualization of early white matter change in an infant with sturge-weber syndrome. Magn. Reson. Med. Sc. **15**(4), 347–348 (2016)
10. Avendi, M.R., Kheradvar, A., Jafarkhani, H.: A combined deep-learning and deformable-model approach to fully automatic segmentation of the left ventricle in cardiac MRI. Med. Image Anal. **30**, 108–119 (2016)
11. Golkov, V., et al.: q-space deep learning for twelve-fold shorter and model-free diffusion MRI scans. IEEE Trans. Med. Imaging **35**(5), 1344–1351 (2016)
12. Beets-Tan, R.G.: MRI in rectal cancer: the T stage and circumferential resection margin. Colorectal Dis. **5**(5), 392–395 (2010)
13. Giedd, J.N., et al.: Brain development during childhood and adolescence: a longitudinal MRI study. Nat. Neurosci. **10**(10), 861–863 (1999)
14. Biswal, B., Yetkin, F.Z., Haughton, V.M., Hyde, J.S.: Functional connectivity in the motor cortex of resting human brain using echo-planar MRI. Magn. Reson. Med. **34**(4), 537–541 (2010)
15. Luo, G., An, R., Wang, K., Dong, S., Zhang, H.: A deep learning network for right ventricle segmentation in short-axis MRI. In: Computing in Cardiology Conference (2017)
16. Kramer, C.M., Barkhausen, J., Flamm, S.D., Kim, R.J., Nagel, E.: Standardized cardiovascular magnetic resonance imaging (cmr) protocols, society for cardiovascular magnetic resonance: board of trustees task force on standardized protocols. J. Cardiovasc. Magn. Reson. **10**(1), 35–35 (2008). Official Journal of the Society for Cardiovascular Magnetic Resonance
17. Pennell, D.J., et al.: Clinical indications for cardiovascular magnetic resonance (CMR): consensus panel report. J. Cardiovasc. Magn. Reson. **25**(21), 727–765 (2004)
18. Moon, J.C., et al.: Myocardial T1 mapping and extracellular volume quantification: a society for cardiovascular magnetic resonance (SCMR) and CMR working group of the european society of cardiology consensus statement. J. Cardiovasc. Magn. Reson. **15**(1), 92–92 (2013)

19. Singh, P., et al.: Cine-CMR partial voxel segmentation demonstrates increased aortic stiffness among patients with marfan syndrome. J. Thorac. Dis. **9**(Suppl 4), S239 (2017)
20. Arbelaez, P., Maire, M., Fowlkes, C., Malik, J.: Contour detection and hierarchical image segmentation. IEEE Trans. Pattern Anal. Mach. Intell. **33**(5), 898–916 (2011)
21. Yang, L., Zhang, Y., Chen, J., Zhang, S., Chen, D.Z.: Suggestive annotation: a deep active learning framework for biomedical image segmentation. In: Descoteaux, M., Maier-Hein, L., Franz, A., Jannin, P., Collins, D.L., Duchesne, S. (eds.) MICCAI 2017. LNCS, vol. 10435, pp. 399–407. Springer, Cham (2017). https://doi.org/10.1007/978-3-319-66179-7_46
22. Fang, S., et al.: Feature selection method based on class discriminative degree for intelligent medical diagnosis. CMC: Comput. Mater. Continua **55**(3), 419–433 (2018)
23. Fang, W., Zhang, F., Sheng, V.S., Ding, Y.: A method for improving CNN-based image recognition using DCGAN. CMC: Comput. Mater. Continua **57**(1), 167–178 (2018)
24. Charles, R.Q., Su, H., Mo, K., Guibas, L.J.: Pointnet: Deep learning on point sets for 3D classification and segmentation, pp. 77–85 (2016)
25. Wang, G., et al.: Interactive medical image segmentation using deep learning with image-specific fine-tuning. IEEE Trans. Med. Imaging **PP**(99) (2017)
26. Gaonkar, B., Hovda, D., Martin, N., Macyszyn, L.: Deep learning in the small sample size setting: cascaded feed forward neural networks for medical image segmentation. In: Medical Imaging 2016: Computer-Aided Diagnosis, p. 97852I (2016)
27. Ronneberger, O., Fischer, P., Brox, T.: U-Net: convolutional networks for biomedical image segmentation. In: Navab, N., Hornegger, J., Wells, W.M., Frangi, A.F. (eds.) MICCAI 2015. LNCS, vol. 9351, pp. 234–241. Springer, Cham (2015). https://doi.org/10.1007/978-3-319-24574-4_28
28. Dong, H., Yang, G., Liu, F., Mo, Y., Guo, Y.: Automatic brain tumor detection and segmentation using U-Net based fully convolutional networks. In: Valdés Hernández, M., González-Castro, V. (eds.) MIUA 2017. CCIS, vol. 723, pp. 506–517. Springer, Cham (2017). https://doi.org/10.1007/978-3-319-60964-5_44
29. Tong, Q., Ning, M., Si, W., Liao, X., Qin, J.: 3D deeply-supervised U-Net based whole heart segmentation. In: Pop, M., et al. (eds.) STACOM 2017. LNCS, vol. 10663, pp. 224–232. Springer, Cham (2018). https://doi.org/10.1007/978-3-319-75541-0_24
30. Ronneberger, O.: Invited talk: U-Net convolutional networks for biomedical image segmentation. Bildverarbeitung für die Medizin 2017. I, p. 3. Springer, Heidelberg (2017). https://doi.org/10.1007/978-3-662-54345-0_3
31. Basu, A., Buch, V., Vogels, W., Eicken, T.V.: U-Net: a user-level network interface for parallel and distributed computing. ACM Sigops Oper. Syst. Rev. **29**(5), 40–53 (1995)
32. Iglovikov, V., Shvets, A.: Ternausnet: U-net with vgg11 encoder pre-trained on imagenet for image segmentation (2018)
33. Brua, R.B., Culp, J.M., Benoy, G.A.: Comparison of benthic macroinvertebrate communities by two methods: Kick- and u-net sampling. Hydrobiologia **658**(1), 293–302 (2011)

A Deep Belief Networks Based Prediction Method for Identification of Disease-Associated Non-coding SNPs in Human Genome

Rong Li[1], Feng Xiang[2], Fan Wu[3], and Zhixin Sun[1](✉)

[1] Telecommunication and Networks National Laboratory, Nanjing University of Posts and Telecommunications, Nanjing 210003, People's Republic of China
sunzx@njupt.edu.cn

[2] YuanTong Express Co., Ltd., Shanghai 201705, People's Republic of China

[3] Department of Computer Science, Tuskegee University, Tuskegee, AL 36088, USA

Abstract. Single nucleotide polymorphisms (SNPs), as one kind of the most common genetic variations, are responsible for individual differences. Furthermore, SNPs are found to be closely associated with many major kinds of diseases that could affect human health, such as hypertension, diabetes, cancer and mental illness. To accurately distinguish functionally related variants from the mass background genetic variations is a significant challenge facing biology and computer scientists and the challenge becomes more severe when dealing with variants in non-coding human genome. In this study, we present a deep belief networks (DBNs) based prediction method to identify candidate disease-associated non-coding SNPs in human genome. For feature extraction, we propose a digital coding based method to convent the nucleotide sequences of SNPs into numerical vectors directly as the input of DBNs. Then the DBNs with 10 layers are used to build the prediction model. 10-fold cross-validation result shows that the proposed method can achieve accuracy with the sensitivity of 73.48% and specificity of 74.31%. Since there is no any artificial feature needed, our approach can get rid of the dependence on huge amounts of genome annotation data which used by other traditional methods.

Keywords: SNPs · Deep belief networks · Imbalanced data

1 Introduction

Single nucleotide polymorphisms (SNPs) are one base (A, T, C or G) changes occurred in human genome, and they are among the most common variations in human genome [1]. Currently, SNPs in the coding sequences have drawn vast attention, since they could change the protein products and structures directly and thus being readily detectable [2]. While findings of the Genome Wide Association Studies (GWAS) [3] indicate that most significant variants lie in non-coding regions of the human genome, where sequences have much higher evolutionary turnover and lower conservation than coding sequences [4], thus are difficult to interpret.

X. Sun et al. (Eds.): ICAIS 2019, LNCS 11633, pp. 12–24, 2019.
https://doi.org/10.1007/978-3-030-24265-7_2

Functionally relevant variants are known to be responsible for phenotypic differences, and their detection is in urgent demand for patient stratification, therapeutic interventions, drug development and especially precision medicine [5, 6]. A variety of methods to predict the effect of a coding variant on protein function have been proposed over the last decades, such as SIFT [7] and PolyPhen [2]. These two methods are largely based on quantifying constraint on the affected residues from a multiple-sequence alignment. Compared to protein coding sequences, the non-coding sequences are much less conservative and their functions remain poorly understood, so prediction of functionally relevant non-coding variants are much more challenging. Recent progress on prioritizing functional non-coding variants has been made by integrating various genomic annotations and evolutionary conservation at the position of interest. Funseq2 builds an organized data context by processing large-scale genomics and cancer resources into small-scale informative data and then uses them to annotate and prioritize noncoding regulatory variants in cancer [8]. GWAVA predicts the functionality of non-coding variants by integrating various genomic and epigenomic annotations, largely from ENCODE and GENCODE [9]. CADD prioritizes functional, deleterious, and pathogenic variants by objectively integrating many diverse annotations into a single, quantitative score, which is called the C-score [10]. FDSP uses regulatory elements annotation data, mainly chromatin states, conservative features and histone modifications, to develop the pipeline to predict novel susceptibility SNPs [11].

We are targeted at the prediction of disease-associated non-coding SNPs. In this work, an effective computational method based on deep belief networks (DBNs) for identification of disease associated non-coding SNPs is presented. As the deep learning network can automatically learn the high-level abstract features of the target object [12, 13]. So, for feature extraction, we propose a digital coding based method to convent the nucleotide sequences of SNPs into numerical vectors directly as the input of DBNs, thus no artificial features are needed. In addition, a random under-sampling strategy is adopted to deal with unbalanced data, and then the proposed algorithm is tested on a set of documented disease-associated SNPs and nonfunctional background SNPs. Cross-validation result shows that our proposed method achieves better performance than GWAVA and the method we previously proposed on data we collected.

2 Materials and Methods

2.1 Datasets

The disease-associated SNPs we used to build the identification model were from GWAS Catalog [14]. GWAS Catalog is a publicly available manually curated collection of published GWAS research productions and provided by the National Human Genome Research Institute of the USA. SNPs collected in GWAS Catalog are highly SNP-trait correlated SNPs with association significance $p < 1 \times 10^{-5}$. There are 24,263 disease-associated SNPs in GWAS Catalog currently. However, SNPs in GWAS Catalog is collected from different research literature that carried out in different ages. While, with the development of the next generation sequencing technology, SNPs data is constantly updated. Therefore, to ensure the accuracy of all the disease-associated

SNPs, we mapped them to dbSNP (dbSNP 146, Human Genome Build GRCh38) [15], and all those SNPs that couldn't match the records in dbSNP were picked away. In addition, SNPs in GWAS Catalog are not confined to the non-coding human genome, so the 17,700 SNPs located in non-coding sequences were finally leaved as the positive samples for building our prediction model.

To the control set, first, as the method Ritchie et al. [16] used in their work to prioritize functionally relevant non-coding variants, all common SNPs (SNP with minor allele frequency MAF > 0.05) in the 1 kb surrounding each of the disease-associated variants were downloaded from dbSNP (dbSNP 146) and 201,329 SNPs were obtained at this stage. The control set built by this way was described as the most stringent control set by Ritchie et al. Then, we put forward a three-step procedure to further reduce any potential functional SNPs in our negative dataset. That is: (1) SNPs in strong linkage disequilibrium (LD) with any disease-associated SNPs ($\gamma^2 \geq 0.8$) were removed. The LD data was obtained from HapMap [17] (all populations in HapMap release 27, phases I + II + III) [12]; (2) Any SNP with annotated functions in Ensemble variation database [18] (release 84) was picked away; (3) SNPs with association p-values less than 0.01 in GWAS Central [19] were removed. After the three-step procedure, 157,057 SNPs were ultimately kept as the negative samples.

2.2 Deep Belief Networks

The concept of deep learning originates from the study of artificial neural networks, whose motivation is to build neural networks that can simulate the analysis and learning behavior of the human brain [20, 21]. Deep belief network (DBN) is a kind of deep learning model proposed by Hinton in 2006 [22]. DBN is a network structure formed by the stacking of multilayer Restricted Boltzmann Machines (RBMs) [23].

Restricted Boltzmann Machines. RBM is a stochastic neural network structure based on statistics. The RBM network has only two layers (see Fig. 1). The first layer is known as the visible layer that composed of m visible neurons, and the second layer is the hidden layer that composed of n hidden neurons. The neurons in RBM only have two states (0 and 1), indicating whether the neurons are activated or not. And when all the values of the visible neurons are known, each hidden neuron is irrelevant, that is:

$$P(h|v) = \prod_{j=1}^{n} P(h_j|v) \tag{1}$$

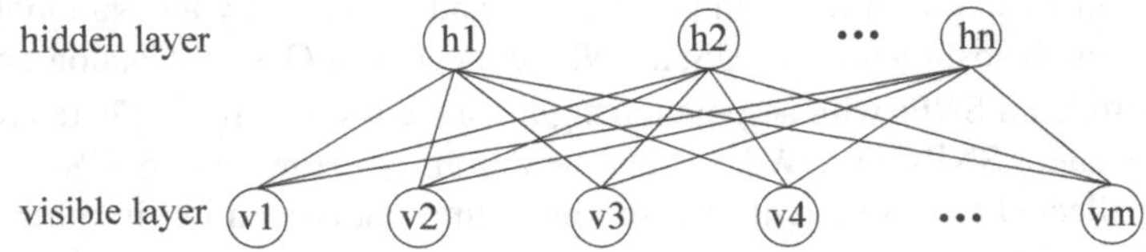

Fig. 1. The diagram of the structure of RBM network model

Similarly, all visible neurons are conditional independent when all hidden neurons are known, that is:

$$P(v|h) = \prod_{j=1}^{m} P(v_j|h) \tag{2}$$

The purpose of RBM training is to obtain the connection weight matrix $W\left(w_{ij}(1 \le i \le m, 1 \le j \le n)\right)$ between the visible layer and the hidden layer. When the input data $V = \left(v_1, v_2, \cdots, v_m\right)$ is assigned to the visible layer, the RBMs will decide whether to open or close the hidden neurons according to the weight matrix W. The detailed calculation procedure is as follows: first, the activation value of the hidden neuron h_j is calculated as:

$$E_{h_j} = WV = \sum_{i=1}^{m} w_{ij}v_i + b_j \tag{3}$$

where b_j is the bias corresponding to the j-th hidden neuron. Then, the probability of the hidden neuron h_j in open state (represented by 1) is given as:

$$P\left(h_j = 1|V\right) = \sigma\left(E_{h_j}\right) = 1/\left(1 + e^{-E_{h_j}}\right) \tag{4}$$

where $\sigma(x)$ is the activation function and $\sigma(x) = 1/(1 + e^{-x})$. Given the hidden layer, the calculation method for the visible layer is as the same. The RBM model based on energy is defined as:

$$E(v, h|\theta) = -\sum_{i=1}^{n} a_i v_i - \sum_{j=1}^{m} b_j h_j - \sum_{i=1}^{n} \sum_{j=1}^{m} v_i w_{ij} h_j \tag{5}$$

where $\theta = \left\{w_{ij}, a_i, b_j\right\}$ is the set of parameters in the RBM, and a_i, b_j are biases corresponding to the i-th visible neuron and the j-th hidden neuron respectively. The joint distribution formula of the neuron states can be further deduced as follows:

$$P(v, h|\theta) = e^{-E(v,h|\theta)}\Big/Z(\theta),\ Z(\theta) = \sum_{v,h} e^{-E(v,h|\theta)} \tag{6}$$

The distribution probability of the input data is calculated by the likelihood function as follows:

$$P(v|\theta) = \sum_{h} e^{-E(v,h|\theta)}\Big/Z(\theta) \tag{7}$$

It is difficult to solve the parameters $w_{i,j}$, a_i, b_j directly, so according to the characteristic that the neurons states within the same layer of RBM is conditionally independent, Eq. (8) can be obtained.

$$P\left(h_j = 1|v, \theta\right) = \sigma\left(a_i + \sum_{i} v_i w_{i,j}\right);\ P(v_i = 1|h, \theta) = \sigma\left(b_j + \sum_{j} w_{ij} h_j\right) \tag{8}$$

The parameter set θ can be determined by performing a stochastic gradient descent on the negative loglikelihood probability of the training data as follows:

$$L(\theta) = \sum_{t=1}^{T} \log P\left(v^{(t)}|\theta\right)$$
$$= \sum_{t=1}^{T} \log \sum_h \exp\left[-E\left(v^{(t)}, h|\theta\right)\right] - \log \sum_v \sum_h \exp[-E(v,h)|\theta]; \tag{9}$$
$$\partial L/\partial\theta = \sum_{t=1}^{T} \left(<\partial\left(-E\left(v^{(t)}, h|\theta\right)\right)/\partial\theta >_{P(h|v^{(t)},\theta)} - <\partial(-E(v,h|\theta))/\partial\theta >_{P(v,h|\theta)}\right)$$

where $< * >_P$ denotes an expectation operation. Gibbs sampling [24] is used to obtain the approximation to the gradient in Eq. (9). Hinton proposed a learning algorithm called contrast divergence (CD) to calculate the value of each parameter [25].

Deep Belief Networks. DBN is a probabilistic neural network formed by stacking of multi-layer RBMs. Figure 2 shows the structure of the DBN, where v is the input data for the visible layer, and $\boldsymbol{h_1} \sim \boldsymbol{h_2}$ are n hidden layers. The training process of each layer in DBN is reconstructing the input data of the previous layer by activating or suppressing the neurons in present layer, and then assign the outputs to be inputs of the next layer.

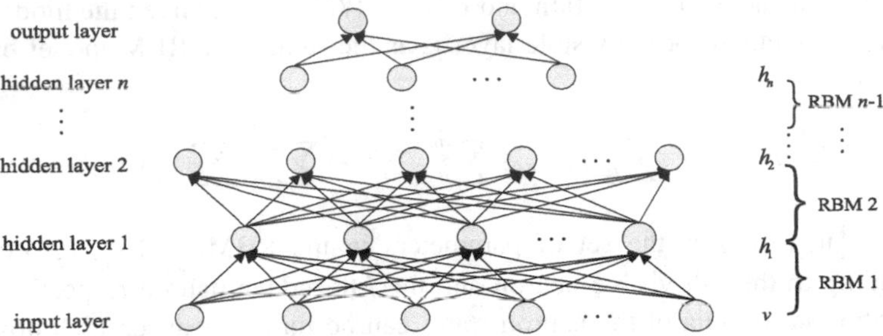

Fig. 2. The sketch of the structure of DBN model

The probability distribution of the DBN model $P(v, h_1, h_2, \cdots, h_n)$ can be expressed by the formula:

$$P(v, h_1, h_2, \cdots, h_n) = P(v|h_1)\left(\prod_{k=1}^{n-2} P(h_k|h_{k+1})\right)P(h_{n-1}, h_n) \tag{10}$$

where $P(h_k|h_{k+1})$ is the conditional probability distribution of h_k when h_{k+1} is given, and $P(h_k|h_{k+1})$ is the joint probability distributions of h_k and h_{k+1}.

The training process of DBNs consists of two steps: pre-training and fine-tuning. In pre-training step, from the bottom up, every two layers of the DBN form an RBM model, and the parameters of the RBM model is obtained by the contrast divergence algorithm. After all hidden layers have been trained, an output layer is added for the real-valued output. Then the fine-tuning step is performed using the back-propagation algorithm.

2.3 Feature Extraction

The deep learning network can automatically learn the high-level abstract features of the target object [27], so we consider using DBNs to learn the related features of DNA sequences directly. In this work, we proposed a digital coding based method to convert the nucleotide composition of SNP sequences into corresponding numerical representation.

As all DNA sequences are composed of four fundamental bases (A, C, G and T), so if a numerical number is assigned to each base, for example, base A assigned 0, base C assigned 1, base G assigned 2, base T assigned 3, then any DNA sequence fragment can be transformed to a set of numerical vector. Similarly, for the 16 dinucleotides (AA, AC, AG,…TT), integral number 0–15 can be assigned; and integral number 0–63 can be assigned to the 64 trinucleotides (AAA, AAC, AAG,…TTT). By this way, the *k*-mer base composition of the DNA sequence can be converted into a numerical vector, which can be directly used as the input of the DBNs. Thus, we propose a digital coding based sequence feature transformation algorithm to transform DNA sequence fragments into the feature form that can be used as an input of the deep network model. For a given DNA sequence, denoted as $b_n^u \cdots b_2^u b_1^u v_{ref}/v_{alt} b_1^d b_2^d \cdots b_n^d$, the corresponding numerical feature F_d is:

$$F_d = \Big[\left(b_n^u \cdots b_1^u v_{ref} b_1^d \cdots b_n^d\right)_{1-mer} \left(b_n^u \cdots b_1^u v_{ref} b_1^d \cdots b_n^d\right)_{2-mer} \left(b_n^u \cdots b_1^u v_{ref} b_1^d \cdots b_n^d\right)_{3-mer} \left(v_{alt}\right)_{1-mer} \left(b_1^u v_{alt} b_1^u\right)_{2-mer} \left(b_2^u b_1^u v_{alt} b_1^d b_2^d\right)_{3-mer} \Big] \tag{11}$$

where b_i^u is the nucleotide in the *i*-th position upstream the SNP location, and the superscript lowercase letter u represents upstream; b_j^d is the nucleotide in the *j*-th position downstream the SNP location, the superscript lowercase letter d represents downstream; v_{ref} and v_{alt} are the two SNP nucleotides; $(*)_{k-mer}$ mean to convert the DNA sequence in parentheses into values by *k*-mer mode, that is, change base A, T, C, G to number 0, 1, 2, 3 respectively for 1-mer mode, change base AA, AT, …, AG to number 0, 1, 2, …15 respectively for 2-mer mode, and follow suit.

The quality of deep learning model is partly related to whether the input data be normalized or not. So normalization is employed to deal with each feature with equation:

$$x_i^* = y_{lower} + \left(y_{upper} - y_{lower}\right)\left(x_i - x_{\min}\right)/\left(x_{\max} - x_{\min}\right) \tag{12}$$

where x_i and x_i^* are the feature data before and after normalization; $\left(y_{lower}, y_{upper}\right)$ is the normalization scale, namely all data are mapped to a range from y_{lower} to y_{upper}, with $(0, 1)$ chosen; x_{min} and x_{max} are the maximum and minimum value for each type of feature in the training dataset.

2.4 Prediction Model Building

DBNs Training. In our DBNs based prediction model of disease-associated SNPs, we use back propagation (BP) neural network to fine-tune the parameters and to predict the final classification results. The procedures for RBMs and DBNs training are shown in Tables 1 and 2, and the significance of the parameters in the two tables are discussed later.

Table 1. The procedure of RBMs training

Name: RBMtrain ( )
Input: training sample X, number of hidden neurons m, learning rate α, momentum k, weight attenuation coeffcient λ, capacity of batches *Batchsize*, maximum training period T.
Output: weight matrix W; bias vector of hidden layer b; bias vector of visible layer c.

Training:
Parameter initialization: $W \sim N(0, 0.01)$ (Gaussian Distribution with mean value 0 and variance 0.01), b and c are both initialized to 0.
For $t = 1, 2, \cdots T$
  Split the training dataset x into S (sample size/Batchsize) subsets randomly, namely $X = \{x_1, x_2, \cdots, x_s\}$
  For $s = 1, 2, \cdots, S$
    Set the initial state of the visible layer $v_1 = x_s$ 。
    For $j = 1, 2, \cdots, m$
      Calculate $P(h_{1j} = 1 | v_1) = sigm\left(b_j + \sum_i v_{1i} W_{ij}\right)$
      Sample $h_{1j} \in \{0,1\}$ from $P(h_{1j} | v_1)$
    EndFor
    For $i = 1, 2, \cdots, n$
      Calculate $P(v_{2i} = 1 | h_1) = sigm\left(a_i + \sum_j W_{ij} h_{1j}\right)$
      Sample $v_{2i} \in \{0,1\}$ from $P(v_{2i} | h_1)$
    EndFor
    For $j = 1, 2, \cdots, m$
      Calculate $P(h_{2j} = 1 | v_2) = sigm\left(b_j + \sum_i v_{2i} W_{ij}\right)$
    EndFor
    Update each parameter:

$$\begin{cases} \Delta W = k\Delta W + \alpha\left(\left(v_1' P(h_{1.} = 1 | v_1) - v_2' P(h_{2.} = 1 | v_2)\right) / Batchsize - \lambda W\right) \\ \Delta b = k\Delta b + \alpha(v_1 - v_2) / Batchsize \\ \Delta c = k\Delta c + \alpha\left(h_1 - P(h_{2.} = 1 | v_2)\right) / Batchsize \\ W = W + \Delta W; b = b + \Delta b; c = c + \Delta c \end{cases}$$

  EndFor
EndFor

Parameter Setting. The selection of parameters has a great influence on the training effects of DBNs. So, we will discuss the key parameters listed in Tables 1 and 2 here.

The Number of the Hidden Layers. The number of hidden layers in DBNs, also called the depth of the network, can affect the fitting accuracy of the data. In theory, the more layers the network has, the stronger its ability to fit the data. However, the higher the network depth is, the more difficult the network training would be. In order to select the ideal network depth parameters, we use the method of experimental test to study the

Table 2. The procedure of DBNs training

```
Name: DBNtrain( )
Input: input sample X, sample label Y, number of hidden layers L.
Output: weight matrix W, bias vector of hidden layer b, bias vector of visible layer c.
Training:
Set h^0 = X
For l = 1,2,···,L
    Calculate h^l = P(h^l = 1 | h^{l-1});
    RBMtrain(h^{l-1}, α, W^k, b^k, c^k)
EndFor
According to the input h^L and sample label Y, train BP neural network to obtain the final
weight vector w^{L+1} between the last hidden layer and the output layer;
Fine-tune the weight matrix W:
For l = L+1, L,···,2,1
    If l = L+1
        Δw^l = -(Y - P(h^{L+1} = 1 | h^L)).×h^L.×(1 - h^L)
    else
        d^l = (d^{l+1} W^l).×(h^l.×(1 - h^l))
        ΔW^l = d^{l+1} h^l
    EndIf
    W^l = W^l - ΔW^l
EndFor
```

effect of different network depth (1–8) on the accuracy of our recognition model of disease-associated SNPs.

The Number of the Hidden Neurons. When DBNs being used as a discriminant model, the value of the number of hidden neurons in each layer has a great influence on the recognition accuracy of the built model. In our experiment, we test the effect of different number of hidden neurons (from 100 to 1000) on the prediction accuracy of the model. For training convenience, we set the number of hidden neurons in each layer to be the same, but actually the number can be different.

The Initialization of Weight and Bias. Although a large initial weight W can reduce the training time, it may also lead to miss the optimal parameters. Therefore, in our model, the initial weight matrix W is randomly selected from the Gaussian distribution with the mean value of 0 and the variance of 0.01. The biases of both the hidden layer and the visible layer are initialized to 0.

The Batch and Its Capacity. DBNs training needs a lot of computing. So, training the input sample set in batches will obviously improve the computational efficiency of DBNs model. The capacity of the small batches is called Batchsize. The ideal Batchsize should be equal to the number of sample categories, and each batch should contain at least one sample of all categories [28]. In our experiment, the training data is imbalanced, with 17,700 disease-associated SNPs and 157,057 neutral SNPs. Before modeling, random under-sampling method is used to sample the positive and negative samples to a balanced 1: 1 dataset. So, the number of training set samples is a multiple of 177, therefore we set the Batchsize to 177.

The Learning Rate. The learning rate is closely related to the training speed and training result of RBMs model, so the choice of learning rate is very important. In our prediction model, the learning rate is initialized to 0.001, and at each iteration, the learning rate is updated according to: $\Delta\alpha = \alpha - 0.9 \times i/T\alpha$, where $\Delta\alpha$ is the updated learning rate; i represents the i-th iteration; T is the maximum training period.

Momentum. To avoid falling into the local optimum, Hinton added the coefficient called momentum to the parameter iteration equation as follows:

$$W = W + k\Delta W + \alpha\partial L(\theta)/\partial W,$$

where k is the momentum; α is the learning rate; and $\partial(\theta)/\partial W$ is the gradient of the likelihood function according to Eq. (9).

Weight Decay. To avoid overfitting when training DBNs, a penalty function is usually added to the gradient to punish the larger parameter value, that is, known as the weight decay strategy. $\lambda/2\sum_i\sum_j w_{ij}^2$ is the simplest penalty function. Also, to avoid the optimization objective function changes with the change of learning rate, the penalty item should be multiplied by the learning rate. At this time, the updated equation of the weight W is: $W = W + k\Delta W + \alpha(\partial L(\theta)/\partial W - \lambda W)$, where λ is the weight decay coefficient, and is set to 0.1; ΔW is calculated as: $\Delta W = k\Delta W + \alpha(\partial L(\theta)/\partial W - \lambda W)$.

2.5 Result Evaluation

For our imbalanced training data, Sensitivity (Sn), specificity (Sp) and Matthews correlation coefficient (MCC) are used to quantitatively evaluate the performance of the prediction method.

$$\begin{aligned} Sn &= TP/(TP + FN); Sp = TN/(TN + FP) \\ MCC &= (TP \times TN - FP \times FN)\Big/\sqrt{(TP + FP)(TP + FN)(TN + FP)(TN + FN)} \end{aligned} \tag{13}$$

where TP is true positive; TN is true negative; FN is false negative; FP is false positive.

3 Results and Discussion

3.1 Performance of Our Method

To get a relatively objective result, 10-fold cross-validation is employed to achieve the final performance of our proposed method. The training data we collected is imbalanced with 17,700 positive samples and 157,057 negative samples, so random under-sampling strategy is used to balance the positive and negative samples.

In our DBNs based prediction model, we investigate the prediction effect of the DBN with the network depth from 1 to 8 (when the network depth is 1, the DBN equals to a BP neural network) and the number of hidden neurons from 100 to 1000 $(100, 200, 300, \cdots 1000)$. The maximum of parameter iterations in the RBM training stage and the maximum fine-tuning times in the BP neural network are both set to 200. A SNP is actually a change nucleotide, so it has only one base. When building the prediction model for functional SNPs, we will extend the SNP sequence forward and backward to a certain length. In our work, we choose the SNP sequence with length 201 (the 100 bases upstream the SNP location plus the 100 bases downstream the SNP location) to build our prediction model. As the feature extraction method given by Eq. (11), a 606-dimension feature vector is obtained for each SNP sample. The result of our proposed method is shown in Fig. 3. It can be seen from Fig. 3 that the prediction results of the DBNs based model are greatly affected by the two parameters. When the number of hidden layers is 7 and each layer has 1000 hidden neurons, the model achieves the relatively best prediction result with MCC of 0.412. At this point, the corresponding *Sn* is 73.48% and the *Sp* is 74.31%.

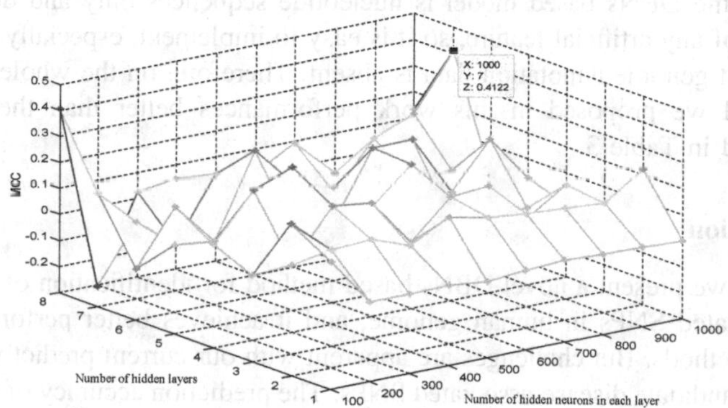

Fig. 3. The result of our proposed method for prediction non-coding disease-associated SNPs.

3.2 Compared to Other Methods

We have compared our proposed method with GWAVA [16] and the method of our previous work (denoted as dissnp_predict) [29]. GWAVA offers a web server which provides pre-computed scores for all known variants from the Ensembl variation database [18]. GWAVA provides three different prediction scores (range from 0–1 with higher scores indicating variants predicted as more likely to be functional.) corresponding to three different versions of classifiers respectively, which are denoted as unmatched score, TSS score and region score. Table 3 shows the comparison results.

GWAVA achieves the lowest sensibility while its specificity is very high. We though reasons for this phenomenon could be that GWVAV haven't do any operation to deal with their imbalance data, therefore the prediction model will maximize the whole classification accuracy. In other words, GWAVA intends to predict a sample as the majority category to achieve more higher whole recognition accuracy. The data GWAVA used to build the prediction model is imbalanced, while we haven't seen any operation to deal with this problem in their article.

Table 3. Comparison of our DBNs based method with other methods.

Method		Evaluation Indicator		
		Sn	Sp	MCC
GWAVA	Region score	10.79%	98.94%	0.208
	TSS score	11.08%	96.76%	0.121
	Unmatched score	12.75%	92.67%	0.061
dissnp_predict		71.32%	72.34%	0.395
Our DBNs based method		73.48%	74.31%	0.412

Compared to the method of our previous work - dissnp_predict, the method based on DBNs achieves better result with both the sensibility and specificity increased by 2% approximately. In addition, the advantage of the DBNs based method is obvious. The input of the DBNs based model is nucleotide sequences only and doesn't need participation of any artificial feature, so it is easy to implement, especially in situation where relevant genome annotation data is absent. Therefore, on the whole, the DBNs based method we proposed in this work performances better than the other two methods listed in Table 3.

3.3 Discussion

In this paper, we present a novel DBNs based method for identification of non-coding disease-associated SNPs in human genome, and it achieves better performance than some other methods. But challenges are apparent with our current predictive approach to prioritize candidate disease-associated SNPs. The prediction accuracy of it is still not very satisfactory. And to simplify the training process, we set the number of hidden neurons in DBNs to be the same, while the optimal model for disease-associated SNPs may not be acquired with the same number of hidden neurons. While different number of hidden neurons will certainly increase the computation complexity. How to find the optimal parameter for our model is very challenging and will be part of our work in future.

Acknowledgment. We are grateful to the National Engineering Laboratory for Logistics Information Technology, YuanTong Express co. LTD.

Funding. This work was supported by grants from the Scientific Research Foundation of Nanjing University of Posts and Telecommunications (No. NY218143).

References

1. Zhang, K., Deng, M., Chen, T., et al.: A dynamic programming algorithm for haplotype block partitioning. Proc. Natl. Acad. Sci. U.S.A. **99**(11), 7335–7339 (2002)
2. Adzhubei, I.A., Schmidt, S., Peshkin, L., et al.: A method and server for predicting damaging missense mutations. Nat. Methods **7**(4), 248–249 (2010)
3. McCarthy, M.I., Abecasis, G.R., et al.: Genome-wide association studies for complex traits: consensus, uncertainty and challenges. Nat. Rev. Genet. **9**(5), 356–369 (2008)
4. Hindorff, L.A., Sethupathy, P., Junkins, H.A., et al.: Potential etiologic and functional implications of genome-wide association loci for human diseases and traits. Proc. Natl. Acad. Sci. U.S.A. **106**(23), 9362–9367 (2009)
5. Kaiser, J.: NIH opens precision medicine study to nation. Science **349**(6255), 1433 (2015)
6. Shrager, J.: Precision medicine: fantasy meets reality. Science **353**(6305), 1216–1217 (2016)
7. Kumar, P., Henikoff, S., Ng, P.C.: Predicting the effects of coding non-synonymous variants on protein function using the SIFT algorithm. Nat. Protoc. **4**(7), 1073–1081 (2009)
8. Fu, Y., Liu, Z., Lou, S., et al.: FunSeq2: a framework for prioritizing noncoding regulatory variants in cancer. Genome Biol. **15**(10), 480 (2014)
9. Consortium, T.E.P.: An integrated encyclopedia of DNA elements in the human genome. Nature **489**(7414), 57–74 (2014)
10. Kircher, M., Witten, D.M., Jain, P., et al.: A general framework for estimating the relative pathogenicity of human genetic variants. Nat. Genet. **46**(3), 310–315 (2014)
11. Dong, S.S., Guo, Y., Yao, S., et al.: Integrating regulatory features data for prediction of functional disease-associated SNPs. Brief. Bioinform. **20**(1), 26–32 (2017)
12. Li, C., Jiang, Y., Cheslyar, M.: Embedding Image through generated intermediate medium using deep convolutional generative adversarial network. CMC: Comput. Mater. Continua **56**(2), 313–324 (2018)
13. Fang, W., Zhang, F., Sheng, V.S., et al.: A method for improving CNN-based image recognition using DCGAN. CMC: Comput. Mater. Continua **57**(1), 167–178 (2018)
14. MacArthur, J., Bowler, E., Cerezo, M., et al.: The new NHGRI-EBI Catalog of published genome-wide association studies (GWASCatalog). Nucleic Acids Res. **45**, D896–901 (2017)
15. Sherry, S.T., Ward, M.H., Kholodov, M., et al.: dbSNP: the NCBI database of genetic variation. Nucleic Acids Res. **29**(1), 308–311 (2011)
16. Ritchie, G.R., Dunham, I., Zeggini, E., et al.: Functional annotation of noncoding sequence variants. Nat. Methods **11**(3), 294–296 (2014)
17. International HapMap, C.: The international HapMap project. Nature **426**(6968), 789–796 (2003)
18. Yates, A., Akanni, W., Amode, M.R., et al.: Ensembl 2016. Nucleic Acids Res. **44**, D710–D716 (2016)
19. Beck, T., Hastings, R.K., Gollapudi, S., et al.: GWAS Central: a comprehensive resource for the comparison and interrogation of genome-wide association studies. Eur. J. Hum. Genet. **22**(7), 949–952 (2014)
20. Sun, Z.J., Xue, L., Xu, Y.M., et al.: Overview of deep learning. Appl. Res. Comput. (China) **29**(8), 2806–2810 (2012)
21. Schmidhuber, J.: Deep learning in neural networks: an overview. Neural Netw. **61**, 85–117 (2015)
22. Hinton, G.E., Osindero, S., Teh, Y.W.: A fast learning algorithm for deep belief nets. Neural Comput. **18**(7), 1527–1554 (2006)

23. Fischer, A., Igel, C.: An introduction to restricted boltzmann machines. In: Alvarez, L., Mejail, M., Gomez, L., Jacobo, J. (eds.) CIARP 2012. LNCS, vol. 7441, pp. 14–36. Springer, Heidelberg (2012). https://doi.org/10.1007/978-3-642-33275-3_2
24. Geman, S., Geman, D.: Stochastic relaxation, gibbs distributions, and the bayesian restoration of images. IEEE Trans. Pattern Anal. Mach. Intell. **6**(6), 721–741 (1984)
25. Hinton, G.E.: Training products of experts by minimizing contrastive divergence. Neural Comput. **14**(8), 1771 (2002)
26. Roux, N.L., Bengio, Y.: Representational power of restricted boltzmann machines and deep belief networks. Neural Comput. **20**(6), 1631 (2008)
27. Bengio, Y.: Learning deep architectures for AI. Found. Trends Mach. Learn. **2**(1), 1–55 (2009)
28. Hinton, G.E.: A practical guide to training restricted boltzmann machines. Momentum **9**(1), 599–619 (2012)
29. Han, J.Q., Li, R., Zhang, X.M., et al.: A computational method for identification of disease-associated non-coding SNPs in human genome. In: IEEE/ACIS 16th International Conference on Computer and Information Science, pp. 125–129 (2017)

On Human-Like Performance Artificial Intelligence – A Demonstration Using an Atari Game

Seng-Beng Ho(✉), Xiwen Yang, Therese Quieta, Gangeshwar Krishnamurthy, and Fiona Liausvia

AI Progamme a*STAR, Singapore, Singapore
hosengbeng@gmail.com, Yang_Xiwen@scei.a-star.edu.sg, {therese_quieta, gangeshwar_krishnamurthy, liausviaf}@ihpc.a-star.edu.sg

Abstract. Despite the progress made in AI, especially in the successful deployment of deep learning for many useful tasks, the systems involved typically require a huge number of training instances, and hence a long time for training. As a result, these systems are not able to rapidly adapt to changing rules and constraints in the environment. This is unlike humans, who are usually able to learn with only a handful of experiences. This hampers the deployment of, say, an adaptive robot that can learn and act rapidly in the ever-changing environment of a home, office, factory, or disaster area. Thus, it is necessary for an AI or robotic system to achieve human performance not only in terms of the "level" or "score" (e.g., success rate in classification, score in Atari game playing, etc.) but also in terms of the *speed* with which the level or score can be achieved. In contrast with earlier DeepMind's effort on Atari games, in which they demonstrated the ability of a deep reinforcement learning system to learn and play the games at human level in terms of score, we describe a system that is able to learn causal rules rapidly in an Atari game environment and achieve human-like performance in terms of both *score* and *time*.

Keywords: Causal learning · Human-like performance AI · Atari game playing · Space invaders game playing · Problem solving

1 Introduction

Artificial intelligence (AI) has taken great strides in many domains of applications. However, there has been realization that even though many AI systems can perform certain tasks very well that normally require human intelligence, and sometimes even superseding human abilities in those tasks, their performance is not "human-like" in some aspects. For example, when deep learning is applied to pattern classification and recognition, the accuracy is very high and sometimes outstrips human performance. However, humans usually require only a few instances of training examples to learn to classify and recognize the objects involved with high accuracy, whereas deep learning systems typically require many orders of magnitude of the number of training examples needed by humans. Thus, we can distinguish two aspects of judging the capability of an

X. Sun et al. (Eds.): ICAIS 2019, LNCS 11633, pp. 25–37, 2019.
https://doi.org/10.1007/978-3-030-24265-7_3

intelligent system, human or artificial. There is the *level* of performance, which is often a percentage score on the success on some tasks, such as classification, and the other is the *time* taken to learn. Human-like performance means the system must perform well on both measures. Currently AI systems largely satisfy only the "level" aspect.

One notable example recently is the DeepMind's seemingly successful attempt in using deep reinforcement learning to play Atari games, in which it was purported that the system is a general learning system that is applicable to a wide domain of applications [1]. The claim of generality stems from the fact that the one same algorithm, namely the deep reinforcement learning algorithm, was used quite successfully (in some cases more successfully than others) to play a slew of more than 50 Atari games with a large variety of game scenarios. Their measure of success in playing these games focuses on the "score" measure – i.e., is the system able to score well, at human (novice or expert) score levels? By that measure of score, they succeeded reasonably well - in more than 50% of the games involved, the system was able to score higher than that of humans. However, by the measure of *time*, DeepMind's system plays at a speed many orders of magnitudes slower than that of human players. Tsividis also pointed out this large discrepancy between the time performance of DeepMind's system and that of human players [2].

As for DeepMind's approach and achievement vis-à-vis AlphaGO [3], we observe that a human Go (or for that matter chess) player only has the ability to search a vastly smaller state space compared to that searched by AlphaGo when playing the game, and yet is still able to perform at Grand Master level, despite the recent losses to AlphaGo. Relatively speaking, despite the fact that mechanisms are in place to reduce the search space (e.g., Monte Carlo search mechanisms), AlphaGo still employs basically relatively brute-force search with the aid of super powerful computers. Obviously, the mental processing mechanisms employed by human players on the one hand and AlphaGo on the other are vastly different.

As Go and chess are relatively complicated in terms of the mental processing mechanisms in the human player's mind, which have not been fully understood, we believe human players use the learning and understanding of causality to learn how to play Atari games. Ho and Zhu's groups have developed a framework and method to learn causality from visual input [4–11]. We have applied the method to the Atari game, Space Invaders, and have been able to demonstrate that a framework based on learning of causal rules from the visual environment together with an AI problem solving framework can produce a system that achieves human-like performance *both* in terms of level (score) and time taken. Below we first describe the basic principles behind the causal learning and problem solving framework and then describe the application to Space Invaders.

To understand why this is important for AI and robotics, imagine the situations typically faced by a robot if it is to learn and perform tasks on a day to day basis such as operating a toaster or a washing machine. To operate a toaster, a robot is expected to learn that there is a causal connection between the pressing down of the lever on the toaster and the heating up of the toaster, hence the toasting of the bread. If a robot is to function satisfactorily as a house-help, it has to learn this at most within a small handful of demonstrations. Similarly, for a washing machine, a robot is expected to observe the process of loading clothes into a washing machine and then turning it on to wash the clothes, and learning this process perhaps within one or two demonstrations. Similarly, there are many rapid learning scenarios such as these with the various machines normally found in the offices, factories, disaster areas, and many other places in which a generally adaptive robot is expected to rapidly learn the causalities between actions and effects to be able to function effectively. Thus, human-like performance is indispensable. Deep reinforcement learning is not able to handle this kind of demands.

This paper attempts to use the example of the Atari game, Space Invaders, to firstly illustrate and define what it really means to achieve human-like performance for AI, and secondly demonstrate the mechanisms that enable human-like performance for an AI system.

2 A Causal Learning and Problem Solving Framework

2.1 Basic Idea Behind Causal/Temporal Learning

Judea Pearl has recently announced in his book that causality is now a legitimate domain of study [12]. The reason why the study of causality and hence causal learning has been hampered in the past was that there has been an often chanted "mantra" that "correlation is not causality." However, in the domain of statistics, a method for scientific cause-effect discovery has long been established, and it is basically to uncover the correlation between an intervention (such as the administering of a drug) and an effect (such as the curing of a disease) observed later, with other variables randomized (e.g., age, gender, nationality of the patients involved, etc.) [13–15]. Statistics takes a conservative stance with regards to correlations without intervention. E.g., if there is correlation in the data between smoking and lung cancer, one should not immediately conclude that smoking causes lung cancer because there could be a gene that predisposes people to smoking and at the same time it predisposes people to develop lung cancer later in life (some tobacco companies have used this to their defense when facing lawsuits). This is the source of the mantra "correlation is not causality."

Yang and Ho [16] take the stance that both causality and temporal correlations are important for AI's purposes. If one can establish the correlation between an intervention/action and a subsequent effect, thus establishing the causality between the action and effect, one can use it for (i) prediction – if the action is taken, the effect is expected; and (ii) problem solving – to achieve the effect, one can take the action. On the other hand, if a temporal correlation is observed between two events, none of which is an intervention/action taken by the system/human, then the temporal correlation is useful only for prediction – if the first event is observed, the second event is likely to follow. Thus, whether there is a gene that causes both smoking and the subsequent lung cancer is not important for prediction – if there is indeed a correlation between the two events, then observing someone smoking is sufficient to conclude that lung cancer may follow, notwithstanding whether there is an underlying gene that is ultimately causally responsible for both.

In the following discussion, most of the concepts and constructs are applicable to both causality and temporal correlation as defined above. In some cases where they differ, we will highlight it explicitly, otherwise it can be assumed that the mechanisms work for both situations.

2.2 Diachronic vs Synchronic Causal Condition for Causal/Temporal Rule Learning

In the framework of causal/temporal learning set up by Ho's group [6, 7, 16], a distinction is made between *diachronic* vs *synchronic* causal/temporal conditions. (As mentioned above, as the following discussion is applicable to both causality and temporal correlation, we will omit the "temporal" portion sometimes henceforth.) Figure 1 illustrates the distinction with an example.

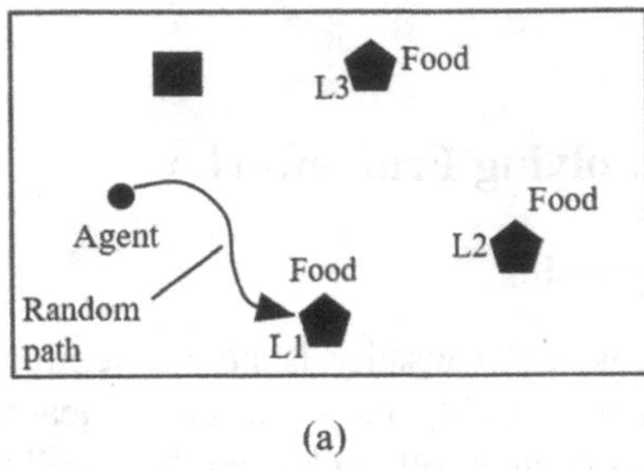

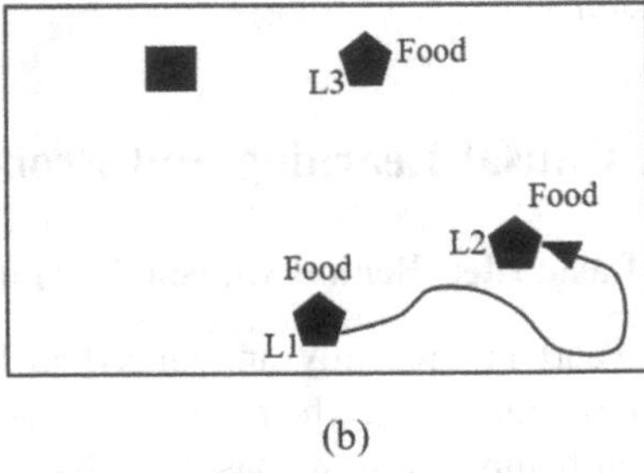

Fig. 1. (a) An Agent wanders around in the environment and *Touches* a piece of Food and experiences *Energy_Increase*. (b) The Agent encounters another experience of *Energy_Increase*.

In Fig. 1(a) it is shown that an Agent explores around in an environment and accidentally *Touches* a piece of Food at time *T1* and at location *L1* and it finds itself experiencing an increase in energy. A causal rule can be learned as such: *At(Agent, L1, T1) & Touch(Agent, Food, L1, T1) → Energy_Increase(Agent, L1, T1).* This is a *specific* causal rule: it says as currently understood, the *Energy_Increase* can take place if the Agent *Touches* the Food at location *L1* and time *T1*.

The action part of the causal rule, *Touch(Agent, Food, L1, T1),* is the *diachronic* causal condition. The "background" or "context" part of the rule, *At(Agent, L1, T1),* is the *synchronic* causal condition. The synchronic causal condition is an "enabling" condition – it enables the diachronic preconditional "cause" - *Touch(Agent, Food, L1, T1)* to give rise to the "effect" - *Energy_Increase(Agent, L1, T1).*

Now, suppose the Agent then wanders to another location *L2* and *Touches* another piece of Food at time *T2* and also experiences an increase in energy. Another specific causal rule can be learned: *At(Agent, L2, T2) & Touch(Agent, Food, L2, T2) → Energy_Increase(Agent, L2, T2).* At this stage, a general causal rule can be induced from the two specific instances: *At(Agent, Any L, Any T) & Touch(Agent, Food, Any same L, Any same T) → Energy_Increase(Agent, Any same L, Any same T),* meaning that the exact values of location and time are not important for the *Touching* action to give rise to *Energy_Increase* (but they must be the same in the three predicates), but the *Touching* action itself is necessary.

We term this process of unsupervised learning in which the causal rules are picked up, learned, and encoded from observation carried out on the environment the process of *causal learning* (of causal rules). The process is similar for *temporal correlation rule* learning – as we mentioned above. If the first event is not an action effected by the agent (in this case, *Touch*), and instead it is just an event observed in the environment, then it would be just a temporal correlation rule useful for prediction but not problem solving (because the first event, not being an action, cannot be effected by the agent). Similar concepts of diachronic vs synchronic preconditions apply to temporal correlation rules.

2.3 The Atari Game Space Invaders

In this section, we describe the basic features of the Space Invaders game. Figure 2(a) shows a screen shot of the game. Basically, the game consists of a bunch of "Space Invaders" coming from the top part of the screen, moving horizontally and then slowly downward, toward a Player at the bottom of the screen. Bullets are fired by the Space Invaders toward the Player. The Player has three actions available to her: move left, move right, or fire a bullet upward to destroy the Space Invaders. Every time an Invader gets hit, the Score for the Player will increase. The Player gets "destroyed" when it is hit. It has three "lives" and when those are expended, the game is over. If the Player can destroy all the Invaders before all three lives are expended, the game proceeds to the next level. There are barriers lined up near the bottom of the screen between the Invaders and Players that can shield the bullets from either side.

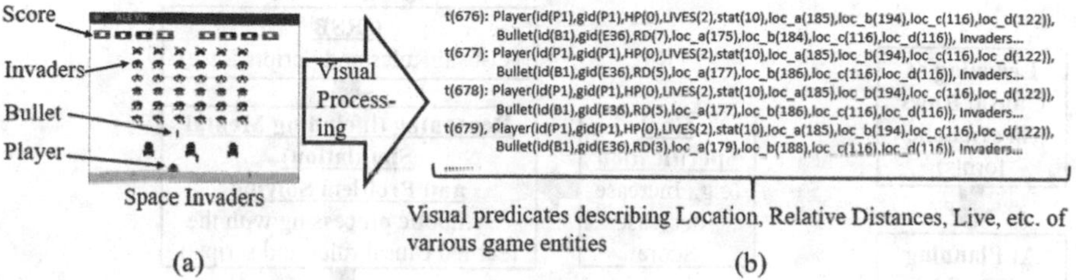

Fig. 2. (a) The Space Invaders game. (b) The symbolic predicates extracted from the scene.

In Fig. 2(b), we show the symbolic predicate description of the scene of the Space Invaders game. The data is organized in a temporal form: at each time frame, there is a description of every entity and their associated parameters, much like the predicate description associated with the discussion in Fig. 1. So, for example, the description of a few of the Space Invaders and the Player at time frame *Time(t1)* could be: *Time(t1) - Invader(ID = 10, LocationX = x1, LocationY = y1), Invader(ID = 11, LocationX = x2, LocationY = y2)... Player(LocationX = x10)....* If there are bullets in the corresponding time frames, they will be included. We encoded a "vision module" to extract this information from every time frame of the Space Invaders game scene generated by the Atari game engine.

2.4 A System for Causal/Temporal Learning, Reasoning, and Problem Solving

In traditional AI, there was a sub-domain of study on problem solving in which there was an attempt to formulate a General Problem Solver (GPS) that has general problem solving mechanisms for all situations. The GPS can act on the facts and knowledge involved in particular domains to derive solutions for particular situations [17]. Our approach is similar here, except that the knowledge, in the form of causal rules, is learned from causal/temporal learning, while in traditional AI research associated with GPS, the knowledge involved was typically hand-coded. Figure 3(a) shows this basic structure.

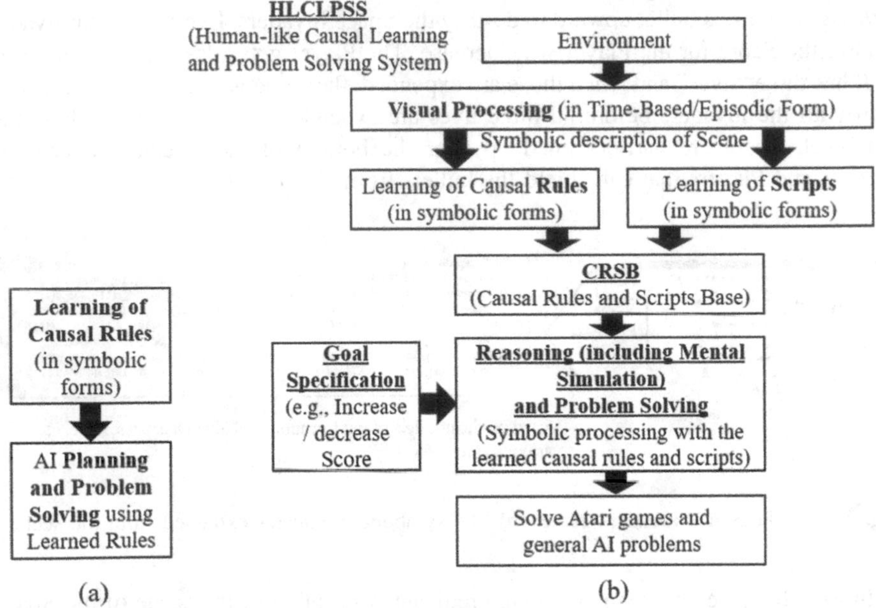

Fig. 3. (a) The basic overall causal learning and problem solving framework. (b) The detailed processing modules of the Human-like Causal Learning and Problem Solving System (HLCLPSSS).

In Fig. 3(b), we show the further detail on the various modules in the system. The processing begins with the Environment, which for Space Invaders would be the Space Invaders' visual scene. A Visual Processing module converts that to a time-based, episodic form as described above (Fig. 2(b)).

Next, causal rules, much like those discussed in connection with Fig. 1 are learned and encoded. A "clean" causal rule extracted could be something like: *At(Player, Any Location, Any Time) & Contact(Player, Invader_Bullet, Any Same Location, Any Same Time) → Destroyed(Player, Any Same Location, Any Same Time + 1)*. (In the system we implemented, typically, very "clean" rules – meaning rules that do not have "unwanted" predicates - such as that above are not always easily obtained through the unsupervised causal learning process. However, the mechanism sufficed for the subsequent problem solving processes that yielded the results that we could use to demonstrate the idea of human-like performance for AI). A small handful of visual predicates, such as *Contact*, *Destroyed*, etc. are built-in recognition mechanisms which we assume a typical visual system, natural or artificial, should provide.

In order to facilitate problem solving, the system also learns and encodes Scripts, as shown in Fig. 3(b). Scripts are basically longer chains of actions. E.g., a sequence of movements of a bullet from the starting point to the ending point could be a "Movement Script". Currently, in this system, sequences of any 5 actions observed in the environment are stored as Scripts. This vastly cuts down the search space of the problem solving process.

The Problem Solving process of the system (Fig. 3(b)) basically uses the traditional backward chaining process of AI – given a Goal specification, what are the rules and scripts from the Causal Rules and Script Base (CRSB) that can be assembled to concoct a solution. As will be described below, there are two kinds of Goals – Goal to achieve a desired state (Increase of Score) and Goal to avoid an undesired state (Destruction of Player). As part of the Reasoning process, Mental Simulation is carried out to determine if there is any undesired state – e.g., the movement rules and scripts of the Invader's bullet can be used to project into the future to see if they might hit the Player, much like a human mentally imagining the sequences of known event changes that lead to a certain consequence.

2.5 Goal-Directed Problem Solving

As mentioned above, there are two kinds of goals - Goal to achieve a desired state (Increase of Score) and Goal to avoid an undesired state (Destruction of Player). These are described as follows:

Goal to Achieve a Desired State and the Associated Learning Process
Figure 4 illustrates a typical situation in Space Invaders in which there is a desired Goal to achieve.

In Fig. 4(a), it is shown that the Player is not in a position to fire a bullet to destroy an Invader. The Player carries out a backward chained problem solving process and obtains a solution – move to a location at which the Invader is in the direct line of fire and fire a bullet to destroy the Invader.

The learning process proceeds as follows. In an initial "exploration phase" (much like the exploration phase of reinforcement learning), the Player fires at random, and occasionally a bullet would hit an Invader and destroy the Invader. After a few instances of similar experience, a causal rule such as this is learned: *At(Player_Bullet, Any Location, Any Time) & Contact(Player_Bullet, Invader(Any ID), Any Same Location, Any Same Time)* $\rightarrow$ *Destroyed(Invader(Any Same ID), Any Same Location, Any Same Time + 1)*. (As mentioned above, in our implemented system, the learned rules may not look as "clean", as there are other "noisy" diachronic and synchronic conditions that "creep" into the rule, but they suffice for problem solving purposes and

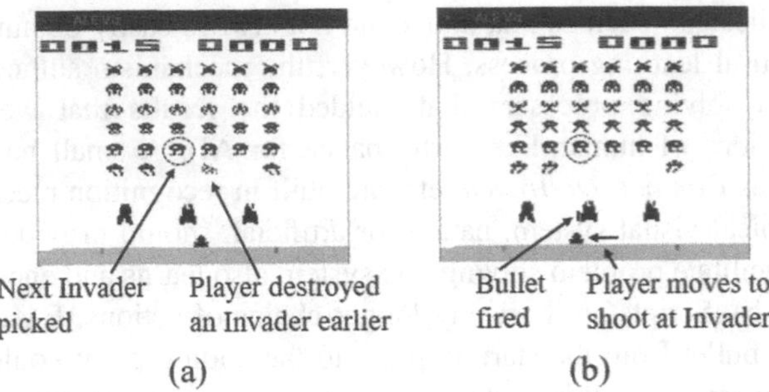

Fig. 4. To achieve a desired goal in Space Invaders: Player finds a solution to destroy an Invader. (a) Player is not in the correct position to destroy the Invader. (b) Player moves to the correct position as directed by the solution of a problem solving process.

this clean rule is good for illustrating the basic idea.). When an Invader is destroyed, the Score goes up, and that is a desired Goal.

After all these causal rules have been learned, the system is ready to carry our backward chained problem solving. At all times, the system is in the mode of looking for ways to achieve a desired Goal, and in this case, it would be *Increase_Score* or *Destroyed(Invader(Any ID, Any Location, Any Time))*. So, the above rules are then used in a backward chained process – in order to achieve destruction of an (any) Invader, a *Player_Bullet* must be made in *Contact* with it. In order for a *Player_Bullet* to be made in *Contact* with it, the *Player_Bullet* must be fired from a certain position (encoded in the scripts learned earlier in an unsupervised learning process), in order for the *Player_Bullet* to be fired at a certain position the Player must *Move* to a certain location, etc. Thus, the solution shown in Fig. 4(b) is obtained. The Invader target can be selected at random or the nearest one to the Player is selected.

The above process closely simulates the problem solving processes carried out by a human player rapidly in her mind about what to do to achieve the Goal of increasing the Score, and also simulates the rapid learning process for a human player to reach some decent level of score performance.

Goal to Avoid an Undesired State and the Associated Learning Process

Figure 5 illustrate a typical situation in Space Invaders in which there is an undesired Goal to avoid.

In Fig. 5(a), it is shown that an Invader fires a bullet at the Player. Using *mental simulation* based on the earlier learned, known rules of the bullet's behavior, the system knows that some time in the future the bullet will hit the Player (because it is in the bullet's path) and the Player will be destroyed. The system therefore concocts a plan to *prevent* this from happening. The solution is to move left a little bit as shown in Fig. 5(b). In Fig. 5(c) it is shown that the bullet and hence the destruction of the player is successfully avoided.

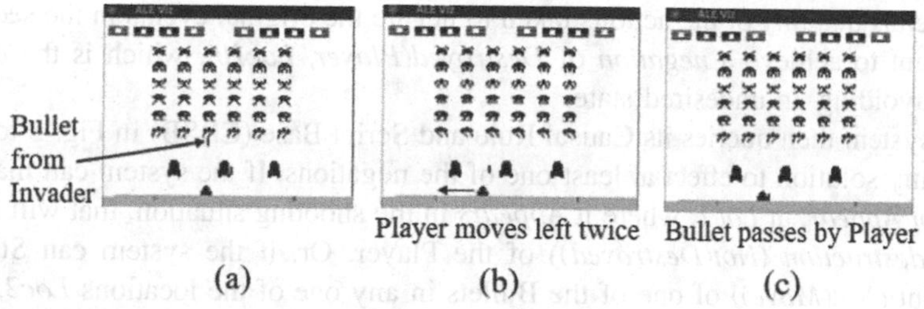

Fig. 5. Player avoids an undesired Goal of being destroyed by a bullet from an Invader. (a) A bullet is fired from an Invader toward the Player, and in mental simulation, the system knows that the Player will get hit. (b) The system concocts a plan after some problem solving process to avoid the bullet. (c) The bullet is avoided.

The learning of this process capitalizes on the idea of contrapositivity in logic. Consider the following logical statement:

$$A \text{ and } B \text{ and } C \text{ and } D \ldots \rightarrow E \tag{1}$$

The contrapositive of the above is:

$$\text{Not } E \rightarrow \text{Not } A \text{ or Not } B \text{ or Not } C \text{ or Not } D \ldots \tag{2}$$

This contrapositive reasoning process is built into the system and used in the process of reasoning out a way to avoid an unnecessary goal. For example, in the beginning of the Space Invaders game, the situation of experiencing the undesired goal is first learned in a few instances in which the Invaders fire bullets and they destroy the Player (this is not random – the game engine deliberately does that). The entire script containing the following sequence of events is learned: a bullet (i) appearing, (ii) moving step by step toward the Player, (iii) contacting the Player, and then (iv) destroying the Player:

$$\begin{aligned} &Appear(Bullet, Loc1)\ \mathbf{and}\ Move(Bullet, Loc2)\ \mathbf{and}\ Move(Bullet, Loc3)\ \mathbf{and}\ldots \\ &Contact(Bullet, Player, Loc10) \rightarrow Destroyed(Player, Loc10) \end{aligned} \tag{3}$$

This sequence is a *conjunction* of a series of events that must happen for the player to be destroyed. (After the system has encountered more instances of (3), a generalized version with "any location" in the location parameters will be learned.)

Applying the contrapositive reasoning process, this is converted into:
Not(Destroyed(Player, Loc10) →
Not(Appear(Bull Appear(Bullet, Loc1) ***or***
Not(Move(Bullet, Loc2) ***or***
Not(Move(Bullet, Loc3) ***or***
Not(Contact(Bullet, Player, Loc10))

which means that *any* of the actions taken to negate the original events in the sequence is sufficient to achieve a *negation* of *Destroyed(Player, Loc10),* which is the desired Goal of avoiding an undesired state.

The system then queries its Causal Rule and Script Base (CRSB) in Fig. 3 to see if there is any solution to effect at least one of the negations. If the system can make the Bullet *not Appear*, at *Loc1*, where it *Appears* in the shooting situation, that will lead to the *non-destruction* (*Not(Destroyed)*) of the Player. Or, if the system can Stop the Movement *(Not(Move))* of one of the Bullets in any one of the locations *Loc2*, *Loc3*, etc., it will also be able to prevent the destruction of the Player (it is like a super-hero being able to stop a bullet in mid-flight). The last choice is to achieve a *Not(Contact (Bullet, Player, Loc10)).* It turns out for the Space Invaders game, the only action available is to move the Player right or left, or to fire a bullet from the Player, none of which actions can immediately achieve any of the above negations. When the system encounters this situation of no available solutions from the CRSB, it will nevertheless try to emit *any* action at its disposal (this is built-in as a general *"try anything to see if there is a solution"* procedure). It turns out that in this case by randomly emitting a sequence of left and right movements of the Player, a *Not(Contact(Bullet, Player, Loc10))* can be achieved – typically by moving left or right by a few pixels. This involves a search process with a small state space.

Therefore, in general, causal learning, unlike the traditional AI search processes, when used in problem solving, can arrive at problem solutions very rapidly. Though there may still be some search processes involved like in our example above, the search space is miniscule compared to those typically effected by traditional AI search processes, such as the A* search process.

3 Results of Human-Like Performance Space Invaders Game Playing System

The various causal learning, reasoning, and problem solving processes, including internal mental simulations processes (Fig. 3(b)), have been implemented and tested on the Space Invaders game. The results are shown in Fig. 6.

In Fig. 6, the results from 3 trials, starting from the beginning of a typical Space Invaders game, are shown along with (i) human novice performance; and (ii) DeepMind's deep reinforcement learning results, as reported in their paper [1], time-scaled based on the total number of video frames needed before certain performance is achieved (video frame is 30 frames per second). We also executed DeepMind's publicly accessible code to obtain its performance in the early part of the game – up to 20 h of play time. There is a level of score, about 200, when the Player shoots at random with no goal-directed behavior, and it is shown as a line labeled "Avg Random Play".

In the first two rounds of the game for the HLCLPSS, the actions generated by the Player are turned off to facilitate the learning of the basic causal rules (like an "observation phase"), so meaningful score data for HLCLPSS begins at around the 6 min time point. For the next four rounds of the game, the HLCLPSS carries out Player actions at random (moving and shooting), corresponding to an "exploration phase"

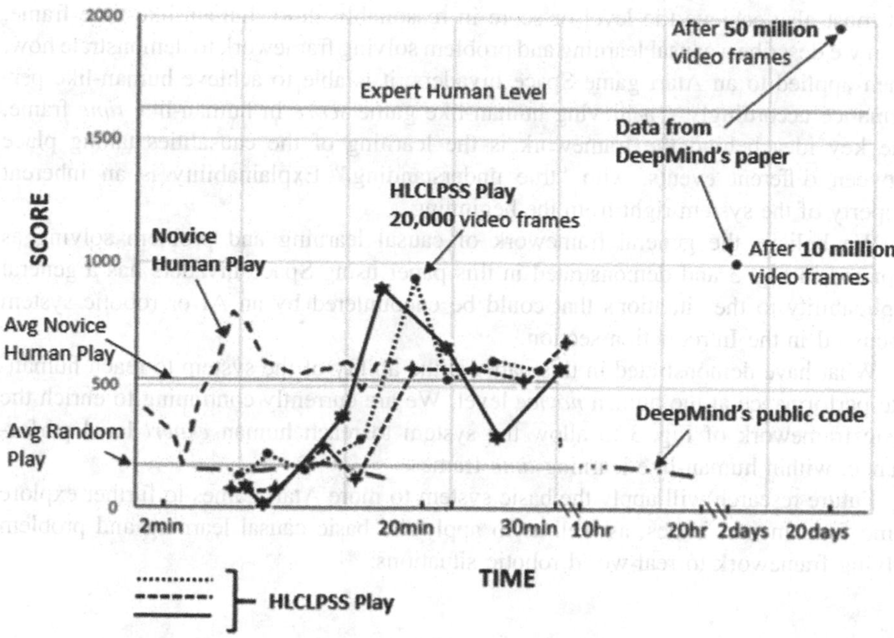

Fig. 6. The results of the Human-like Causal Learning and Problem Solving System (HLCLPSS) applied to the Space Invaders game (3 trials), along with DeepMind's results (as reported in their paper [1]) for comparison.

(in the same spirit as the exploration phase in reinforcement learning). At the end of these four rounds, typically enough "good" causal rules and scripts are learned to play a successful game. Therefore, from round seventh onward (typically around the 15 min time point), the random action process is turned off and the HLCLPSS begins the process of problem solving and planning using the learned causal rules and scripts (the "exploitation" phase), and it can be seen in Fig. 6 that the score levels reach that of the novice player quite rapidly after that.

It can be seen that our system's speed of learning is close to the order of magnitude of that of the human novice. In contrast with human novice though, we began with no prior knowledge of the game. Humans typically would have some fundamental prior knowledge relevant to the game when they begin to play it, thus they are able to learn at an even faster rate – typically in fewer than a few minutes.

Compared to DeepMind's deep reinforcement learning though, the HLCLPSS's speed of learning is obviously faster by many orders of magnitude.

4 Conclusion

In this paper, we first define what we mean by human-like performance AI, which is a system that is not only able to achieve human performance in terms of "level" or "score" (like the percentage accuracy in classification or the game score in a computer game), but must also achieve the level or score in reasonably short, human-like time frame. Then we describe a causal learning and problem solving framework to demonstrate how, when applied to an Atari game Space Invaders, it is able to achieve human-like performance accordingly – achieving human-like game *score* in human-like *time* frame. The key idea behind the framework is the learning of the causalities taking place between different events, with “true understanding.” Explainability is an inherent property of the system right from the beginning.

We believe the general framework of causal learning and problem solving as depicted in Fig. 3 and demonstrated in this paper using Space Invaders has a general applicability to the situations that could be encountered by an AI or robotic system discussed in the Introduction section.

What have demonstrated in this paper is the ability of the system to reach human-like performance at the human *novice* level. We are currently continuing to enrich the basic framework of Fig. 3 to allow the system to reach human *expert* level performance, within human-like learning *time* frames.

Future research will apply the basic system to more Atari games to further explore some fundamental issues, as well as to apply the basic causal learning and problem solving framework to real world robotic situations.

References

1. Mnih, V., et al.: Human-level control through deep reinforcement learning. Nature **518**, 529–533 (2015)
2. Tsividis, P.A., Pouncy, T., Xu, J.L., Tenenbaum, J.B., Gershman, S.J.: Human learning in Atari. In: AAAI Spring Symposium Technical Report, pp. 643–646. AAAI, Palo Alto (2017)
3. Silver, D., et al.: Mastering the game of Go with deep neural networks and tree search. Nature **529**(28), 484–489 (2016). https://doi.org/10.1038/nature16961
4. Fire, A., Zhu, S.-C.: Learning perceptual causality from video. ACM Trans. Intell. Syst. Technol. **7**(2), 23 (2012)
5. Fire, A., Zhu, S.-C.: Inferring hidden statuses and actions in video by causal reasoning. In: IEEE Conference on Computer Vision and Pattern Recognition Workshops, pp. 9–16. IEEE Press, Piscataway, New Jersey (2017)
6. Ho, S.-B.: On effective causal learning. In: Goertzel, B., Orseau, L., Snaider, J. (eds.) AGI 2014. LNCS (LNAI), vol. 8598, pp. 43–52. Springer, Cham (2014). https://doi.org/10.1007/978-3-319-09274-4_5
7. Ho, S.-B.: Principles of Noology: Toward a Theory and Science of Intelligence. SC, vol. 3. Springer, Cham (2016). https://doi.org/10.1007/978-3-319-32113-4
8. Ho, S.-B.: Deep thinking and quick learning for viable AI. In: Proceedings of the Future Technologies Conference, pp. 156–164. IEEE Press, Piscataway (2016)
9. Ho, S.-B.: The role of synchronic causal conditions in visual knowledge learning. In: IEEE Conference on Computer Vision and Pattern Recognition Workshops, pp. 9–16. IEEE Press, Piscataway (2017)
10. Ho, S.-B., Liausvia, F.: A ground level causal learning algorithm. In: Proceedings of the IEEE Symposium Series on Computational Intelligence for Human-like Intelligence, pp. 110–117. IEEE Press, Piscataway (2016)

11. Ho, S.-B., Liausvia, F.: On inductive learning of causal knowledge for problem solving. In: Technical Reports of the Workshops of the 31st AAAI Conference on Artificial Intelligence, pp. 735–742. AAAI, Palo Alto, California (2017)
12. Pearl, J.: The Book of Why: The New Science of Cause and Effect. Basic Books, New York (2018)
13. Neyman, J.: Sur les applications de la theorie des probabilites aux experiences agricoles: Essai des principes. Master's Thesis. Excerpts reprinted in English, Statistical Science, vol. 5, pp. 463–472 (1923). (D. M. Dabrowska, and T. P. Speed, Translators.)
14. Rubin, D.: Causal inference using potential outcomees. J. Am. Stat. Assoc. **100**(496), 321–322 (2005). https://doi.org/10.1198/016214504000001880
15. Ho, S.-B., Edmonds, M., Zhu, S.-C.: Actional-perceptual causality: concepts and inductive learning for ai and robotics. Presented at the workshop on perspectives on robot learning: imitation and causality, robotics: science and systems conference, Carnegie Mellon University, Pittsburgh, Pennsylvania (2018)
16. Yang, X., Ho, S.-B.: Learning correlations and causality through an inductive bootstrapping process. In: IEEE Symposium on Computational Intelligence. IEEE Press, Piscataway, (2018)
17. Newell, A., Shaw, J.C., Simon, H.A.: Report on a general problem-solving program. In: Proceedings of the International Conference on Information Processing, pp. 256–264 (1959)

Implementation of Multiplicative Seasonal ARIMA Modeling and Flood Prediction Based on Long-Term Time Series Data in Indonesia

Sri Supatmi[1,2(✉)], Rongtao Huo[1], and Irfan Dwiguna Sumitra[3]

[1] School of Computer and Software, Nanjing University of Information Science and Technology, Nanjing, Jiangsu, China
sri.supatmi@email.unikom.ac.id

[2] Computer Engineering Department, Universitas Komputer Indonesia, Bandung, West Java, Indonesia

[3] Postgraduate of Information System Department, Universitas Komputer Indonesia, Bandung, West Java, Indonesia

Abstract. Time series modeling and prediction has fundamental importance in the various practical field. Thus, a lot of productive research works is working in this field for several years. Many essential methods have been proposed in publications to improve the accuracy and efficiency of time series modeling and prediction. This research aims to present the proposed prediction model namely Multiplicative seasonal ARIMA model (MSARIMA) based on non-stationary time series data to predicting the flood event. In this paper, we have described the performance of the ARMA model, the ARIMA model, and MSARIMA model to predict the flood event in the Region over Indonesia in 42 years (1976–2017). We have used the two performance measures respectively (MAPE, and RMSPE) to evaluate prediction accuracy as well as to compare different models fitted to a time series data. The result has shown the proposed predicting model has the best performance accuracy than the others model in this research.

Keywords: Flood · Prediction model · Data time series · Non-stationary data · ARMA · ARIMA · MSARIMA

1 Introduction

High rainfall [1] is one of the crucial factors in the flood event in Indonesia. Rainfall forecasting effectively is essential to avoid flood and drought control. Moreover, to improve water and soil conservation as well as protection of life and property.

The traditional researches of meteorological and hydrological prediction are mainly focused on linear parametric methods and time series forecasting. In the basic models, a time series data can have many patterns and illustrate different randomly determined processes. The basic models which widely used linear time series models in literature are two types such as Autoregressive (AR) [2–4, 6, 7] and Moving Average (MA) [3, 5, 7] models. The Autoregressive Moving Average (ARMA) [3–7] and Autoregressive

X. Sun et al. (Eds.): ICAIS 2019, LNCS 11633, pp. 38–50, 2019.
https://doi.org/10.1007/978-3-030-24265-7_4

Integrated Moving Average (ARIMA) [2–4, 6, 7] are the combinings of AR and MA. A variety of ARIMA in seasonal times series forecasting namely the Seasonal Autoregressive Integrated Moving Average (SARIMA) [2–4, 6, 8] models is used. ARIMA model and its different variety are based on the famous Box-Jenkins principle [3–6, 9–11] and broadly known as the Box-Jenkins methods. The linear time series models are based on the assumption that the influence of the lagged rainfall is linear [8].

Hence the goal of this paper is to find out if there exists a possibility for improving the accuracy of flood prediction using proposed flood event prediction model (Multiplicative Seasonal ARIMA/MSARIMA) which was not favored in prior attempts by the ARMA and ARIMA model.

In this study, we examine the monthly data variables of rainfall and temperature in Bandung of Indonesia from January 1976 to December 2017, which pattern a series of 504 experiments. These data are available from the Bandung of Meteorological, Climatology and Geophysics Bureau in Indonesia [12].

2 Related and Previous Work

There are many researchers concern in flood forecasting used the time series data from short-term to long-term data: the related and previous works described in this chapter as below.

Previous researches [8, 13–19] studied commonly techniques of spectrum analysis used in conjunction with time series of investigating periodicities. In [20, 21], presented the rainfall predictions used spectral analysis method. Shi et al. [8] studied the monthly rainfall forecasting model employing the hidden periodicities time series. This research concerns the monthly rainfall in Nantong of China for 27 years (1989–2005) historical data which forms a set of 204 experiments. Wang et al. [22] studied the precipitation forecast for monthly precipitation at Lanzhou precipitation station in Lanzhou, China. The result of this study obtains 79% accuracy of precipitation forecast employing the ARIMA model. In 1998 [23], and 1999 [24, 25] published a paper in which they described the analysis of hydrological process devoid examining the influences of seasonal factors [21]. The other researchers employing the ARIMA model to neglected stationary test and the effects from cross-monthly variety within a year [22, 26–28]. In 2012, Yulianti et al. [29] demonstrated that the transfer function model is a better prediction model than ARIMA model of water discharge in the Katulampa dam in Indonesia. The transfer function model gets MAPE 15.43%, and the ARIMA model achieves MAPE 56.43%. In the 2017s authors pointed that the ARIMA modeling using to water level forecasting in the Middle Reach of the Yangtse River and obtain good accuracy of error [30].

David and co-workers proposed a hybrid approach for multi-step-ahead wind speed forecasting in Brazil. The hybrid approach using SARIMA and neural network as combining. The result of hybrid approach obtained error MAE 0.141, RMSE 0.316, and MAPE 1.862%. This result is better than SARIMA, SARIMA+WAVELET, and neural network as a compared model for hybrid approach [31]. In [32–35] the authors published the SARIMA model to rainfall forecasting in some Regions in Ghana with a similar value of rainfall prediction. In [36–44] also forecasting the rainfall in their countries employing the SARIMA model.

3 Study Area

Figure 1 illustrates the region of Bandung city, West Java Province of Indonesia. The location of Bandung city is the longitude 107°36′ on East and Latitude 6°55′ on South. Bandung city is located at an altitude of 791 m above sea level (masl). The highest point is in the North with an altitude of 1,050 m above sea level, and the lowest point is in the South with an altitude of 675 m above sea level. The area surrounded by mountains forms the city of Bandung into a kind of basin (Bandung Basin). The climate of the surrounding mountains influences the environment of Bandung city. Based on the historical databases, the temperature varies from 17.2 °C to 29.9 °C, and the rainfall ranges from 5 mm to 81.5 mm throughout the year of 1976 to 2017 [12], shown in Figs. 2 and 3 (Table 1).

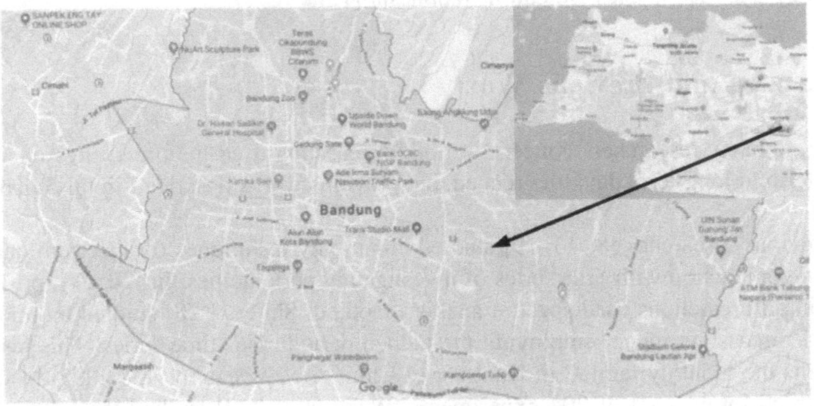

Fig. 1. The location of the flood forecasting area in Bandung city, Indonesia

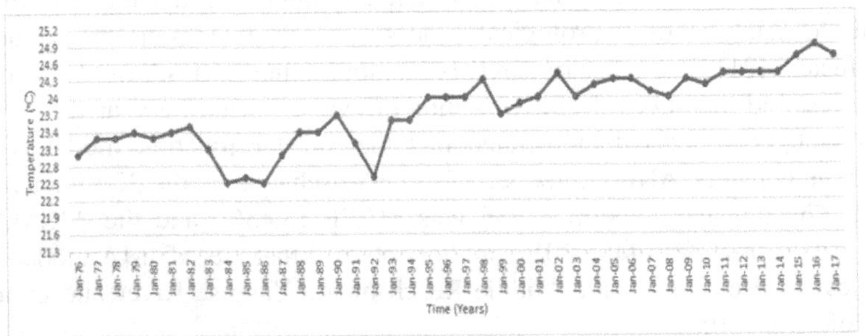

Fig. 2. The historical data of ambient temperature series (1976 to 2017) from Bandung city

Table 1. Parameters summary statistic of Bandung city

Parameter	Min	Mean	Max
Temperature (°C)	17.2	23.76	29.9
Rainfall (mm)	5	25.195	45.39

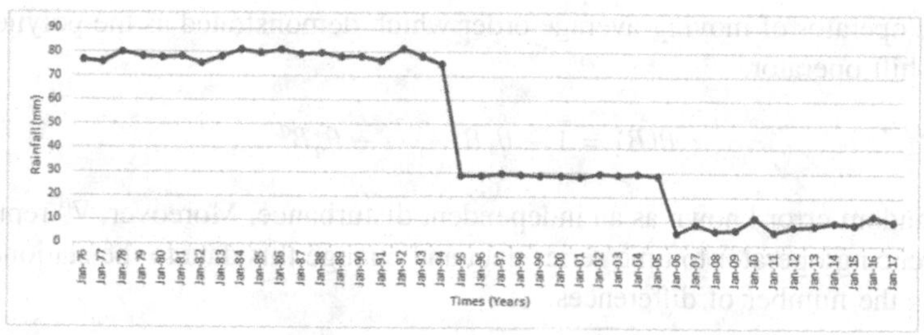

Fig. 3. The historical data of rainfall series (1976 to 2017) from Bandung city

4 Material and Modelling

4.1 ARMA Model Overview

Autoregressive moving average known as ARMA is the combining model of autoregressive (AR) and moving average (MA). This model is a useful class of time series model. Generally, ARMA (p, q) model is denoted as [3, 5, 7]:

$$Z_t = \alpha + \sum\nolimits_{i=1}^{p} \emptyset_i Z_{t-i} + \sum\nolimits_{j=1}^{q} \theta_j \varepsilon_{t-j} + \varepsilon_t \tag{1}$$

Where p is the model order of the autoregressive (AR) terms, sometimes called a number of time lags of AR. and q is the model order of moving average (MA) terms. The expectation of MA is represented as α, which equal to zero ($\alpha \cong 0$). In addition, ε_t is the error terms.

4.2 ARIMA Model Overview

ARIMA or autoregressive integrated moving average model is ARMA model generalization and denoted as [45] ARIMA (p, d, q). Where p is autoregressive order, d is the differencing order which is the number of data time series have had the previous values subtracted (needs more than two number), and the moving-average process represents as q.

The ARIMA model is written as

$$\emptyset(B)\nabla^d Z_t = \theta(B)\varepsilon_t \tag{2}$$

B is the operator of the backshift, denoted as:

$$BZ_t = Z_{t-1} \tag{3}$$

$\emptyset(B)$ is the operator of AR which illustrated polynomial in the operator of back-shift.

The $\emptyset(B)$ also can be written as

$$\emptyset(B) = 1 - \emptyset_1 B - \cdots - \emptyset_p B^p \tag{4}$$

θ(B) is the operator of moving-average order which demonstrated as the polynomial in the back-shift operator.

$$\theta(B) = 1 - \theta_1 B - \cdots - \theta_q B^q \tag{5}$$

εt is the random error known as an independent disturbance. Moreover, ∇^d represented as a differencing operator to time series data and change this data to the stationary data series, *d* is the number of differences.

4.3 Proposed Forecasting Model (MSARIMA) Approach

Multiplicative seasonal ARIMA (MSARIMA) is a more straightforward approach and one which works well in practice which is to model the regular and seasonal dependence separately, and then construct the model incorporating both multiplicatively.

The multiplicative seasonal autoregressive moving average (MSARIMA) is an extension of the ARIMA model proposed in [2, 4, 5]. In the most typical case is that we can get a rainfall time series has seasonal varieties, MSARIMA model is adapted from [2, 4, 5]. Due to the varieties of the data in this paper, we can integrate seasonality into the ARIMA model multiplicatively.

MSARIMA model can be denotated as $MSARIMA(p, d, q)x(P, D, Q)_S$.

The principal structure of the proposed flood forecasting approach based on MSARIMA model is illustrated in Fig. 4. This architecture is structured by MSARIMA and balancing procedure in MSARIMA multi-step block.

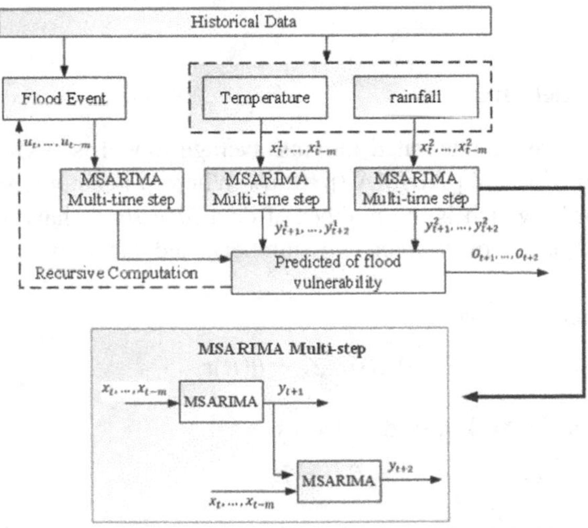

Fig. 4. Structure of proposed MSARIMA model approach

The main steps for the MSARIMA model are as follows. The first step has created a database from historical data in [12], as the observed data. The observed data selection is implemented. The MSARIMA model used a linear predictor to forecast the future values of the observed data. The dimension of the output data from MSARIMA model is reduced through the balancing procedure, accorded to Fig. 4. The balancing procedure aims to reduces the dimension of a large data set with correlated variables into a smaller set with uncorrelated variables and to avoid the unbalanced data [46, 47]. The MSARIMA model is employed to forecast flood event series based on the past values of a flood event and the data from the previous step.

The multi-step forward predicting is obtained recursively by inserting input variables with the predicted outputs. Principally, the model combines two identical one-step forward linear models to deliver a series of predictions. Since the observed data are received to one-step forward (12 years), it is employed as input for two-step forward prediction (24 years), and these steps are repeated until observed data of the next 42 years is predicted. The same recursive method is implemented for flood even prediction as additional input information for the further forecast until 42 years is forecasted.

The multiplicative seasonal ARIMA (MSARIMA) is denoted as below

$$\Phi_P(B^s)\phi_p(B)\nabla_s^D\nabla^d Z_t = \theta_q(B)\Theta_Q(B^s)\alpha_t \tag{6}$$

Where the autoregressive side in the seasonal AR order P, the moving-average side in seasonal MA order Q, the regular AR order p, the regular MA order q, the seasonal differentiating operator in order D, and the regular differentiating operator in order d described as

$$\Phi_P(B^s) = 1 - \Phi_1(B^s) - \Phi_2(B^{2s}) - \Phi_3(B^{3s}) - \cdots - \Phi_P(B^{sP}) \tag{7}$$

$$\phi_p(B) = 1 - \phi_1(B) - \phi_2(B^2) - \phi_3(B^3) - \cdots - \phi_p(B^p) \tag{8}$$

α_t is the white noise process, and s is the period of seasonal ($s > 1$).

If we substitute the Eqs. 7 and 8 into Eq. 6, the MSARIMA model can be written as

$$\Phi_P(B^s)\phi_p(B)(1 - B^s)^D(1 - B)^d Z_t = \theta_q(B)\Theta_Q(B^s)\alpha_t \tag{9}$$

If we are applying the Eq. 9 in this research where the seasonal s = 12 years, 24 years, 36 years, and 42 years, the equation can be written as

For the one-step forward (s = 12 years)

$$\left(1 - \Phi_1 B^{12} - \cdots - \Phi_P B^{12P}\right)\left(1 - B^{12}\right)^D Z_t = 1 - \Theta_1\left(B^{12}\right) - \cdots - \Theta_Q\left(B^{12Q}\right)\alpha_t \tag{10}$$

For the multi-step forward (s = 24 years)

$$\left(1 - \Phi_1 B^{24} - \cdots - \Phi_P B^{24P}\right)\left(1 - B^{24}\right)^D Z_t = 1 - \Theta_1\left(B^{24}\right) - \cdots - \Theta_Q\left(B^{24Q}\right)\alpha_t \tag{11}$$

For the multi-step forward (s = 36 years)

$$\left(1 - \Phi_1 B^{36} - \cdots - \Phi_P B^{36P}\right)\left(1 - B^{36}\right)^D Z_t = 1 - \Theta_1\left(B^{36}\right) - \cdots - \Theta_Q\left(B^{36Q}\right)\alpha_t \tag{12}$$

For the multi-step forward (s = 42 years)

$$\left(1 - \Phi_1 B^{42} - \cdots - \Phi_P B^{42P}\right)\left(1 - B^{42}\right)^D Z_t = 1 - \Theta_1\left(B^{42}\right) - \cdots - \Theta_Q\left(B^{42Q}\right)\alpha_t \quad (13)$$

Where t = *1, 2, 3, ...,* T and the MSARIMA model is formulated in B^{12}, B^{24}, B^{36}, B^{42} since we are relating years from different years.

The prediction models can be developed employing only previous values of flood event series or fetching data in historical account data of other variables such as temperature, and rainfall [12]. The strength inputs to flood event forecasting considering three variables such as flood event in the previous values, air temperature, and rainfall. Table 2 present the correlation matrix to Bandung city database. The result shows a stronger relationship between air temperature and rainfall with flood event (0.572 and 0.553).

Table 2. Correlation matrix of Observed variables to Bandung city

	Temperature	Rainfall	Flood event
Temperature	1		
Rainfall	−0.413	1	
Flood event	−0.572	−0.553	1

5 Forecasting Performance Metrics

In this research, the forecasting performance measures employing two models respectively the mean absolute percentage error (MAPE) and the root mean square percentage error (RMSPE). In each for the forthcoming definitions, R_t is the real value, P_t is the forecasted value, $E_t = R_t - P_t$, and n is the number of the test set.

5.1 The Mean Absolute Percentage Error (MAPE)

This calculation is given by [3, 4, 9, 24, 26] denoted below:

$$MAPE = \frac{1}{n}\sum\nolimits_{i=1}^{n} |E_t| \times 100 \quad (14)$$

5.2 The Root Mean Square Percentage Error (RMSPE)

Mathematically, RMSE [3, 9, 26] written as below

$$RMSE = \sqrt{\frac{1}{n}\sum\nolimits_{i=1}^{n} E_t^2} \quad (15)$$

Also, the percentage of RMSE can be written as the equation below:

$$RMSPE = \sqrt{\frac{1}{n}\sum_{i=1}^{n} E_t^2} \times 100 \quad (16)$$

6 Result and Discussion

The discussion of the result begins with the explanation of the performance of the proposed flood forecasting model (MSARIMA). MSARIMA model implemented in one-step forward forecasting (12 years) and continued performed in the multi-step forward prediction (up to 42 years). The MSARIMA model was applied in some Region in Bandung city. The forecasting model is implemented employing MATLAB 2017. The detailed results are described as below.

6.1 Forecasting Result: One-Step Forward

This part describes the forecasting results obtaining the proposed MSARIMA approach for the one-step forward. Parameters of ARMA, ARIMA, and MSARIMA model automatically obtained by MATLAB 2017 software which aims to obtain the identifying the best model to each historical data series using autocorrelation function (ACF), and partial autocorrelation function (PACF). For the statistic measures employing MAPE and RMSPE. Table 3 shows the best ARMA, ARIMA, and MSARIMA model obtained to each observed variable. In that case, the proposed MSARIMA model approach presented in part 4 was applied, and flood event forecasting was obtained.

Table 3. ARMA, ARIMA, and MSARIMA model to observed variables

	ARMA	ARIMA	MSARIMA
Temperature	ARMA (1, 1)	ARIMA (1, 1, 1)	MSARIMA $(0, 0, 0) \times (0, 1, 1)_{12}$
Rainfall	ARMA (1, 1)	ARIMA (1, 0, 1)	MSARIMA $(0, 0, 0) \times (1, 1, 1)_{12}$

The proposed MSARIMA model was compared with other commonly used techniques such as ARMA, and ARIMA. This compare aims to evaluate the performance of the proposed MSARIMA model approach. Table 4 shows the forecasting errors for ARMA, ARIMA, and proposed MSARIMA model. It is mean that the proposed MSARIMA model reduced the forecasting error from the ARMA and ARIMA model which considerable in Bandung city.

Table 4. One-step forward forecasting errors to Bandung

	ARMA	ARIMA	MSARIMA
MAPE (%)	0.6462	0.9247	**0.0236**
RMSPE (%)	2.2385	3.2033	**0.0818**

The flood event observed and forecasted values presented in Fig. 5(a) and (b). The proposed MSARIMA model outperforms the other models, and the forecasted values almost same or similar the trend of flood event variety.

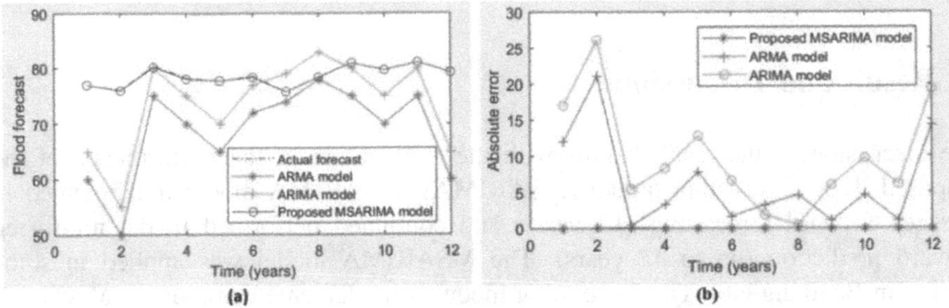

Fig. 5. (a) Observed flood series and one-step forward forecasting in Bandung (b) Absolute error for one-step forward forecasting in Bandung

6.2 Forecasting Result: Multi-step Forward

This part illustrates multi-step forward predicting results obtained with the proposed MSARIMA model. The model was considered to 2-step (24 years), 3-step (36 years), and 4-step (42 years).

Figure 6 presents the performance of ARMA, ARIMA, and MSARIMA model on multi-step forward (up to 42 years). It shows the MSARIMA model obtained the best absolute error compared with other models.

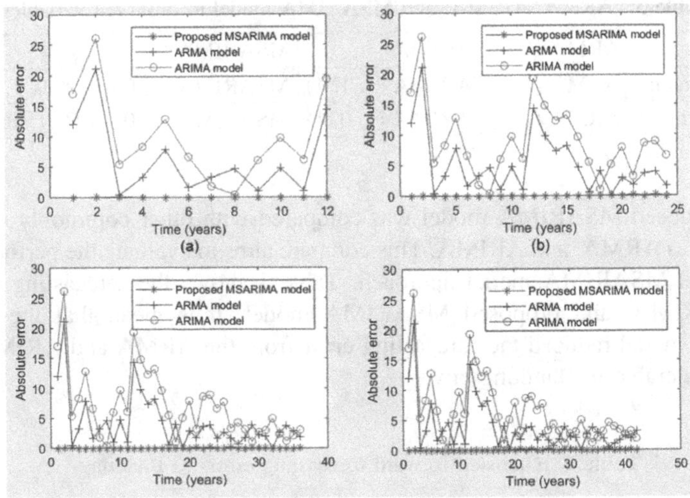

Fig. 6. Absolute error for one-step forward forecasting (a) 12 years and multi-step forward forecasting (b) 24 years (c) 36 years (d) 42 years in Bandung

The histogram in Fig. 7 indicates that the proposed MSARIMA model performs better than other models for all analyzed, presenting the lowest MAPE, and RMSPE errors. The proposed MSARIMA model approach illustrates its effectiveness being a robust approach when applied for one-step forward and multi-step forward forecasting in Bandung city.

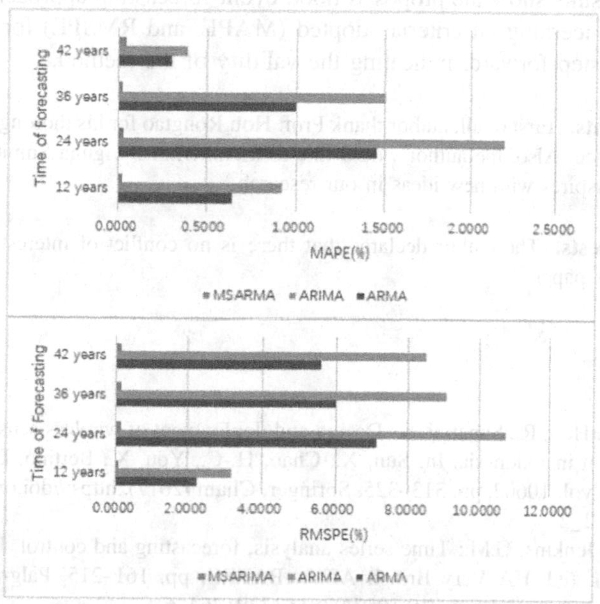

Fig. 7. Performance for one-step forward forecasting (12 years) and multi-step forward forecasting (24 years, 36 years, 42 years) in Bandung employing ARMA, ARIMA, and Proposed MSARIMA respectively: MAPE, and RMSPE

According to MAPE and RMSPE values in Table 4 and Fig. 7 for the proposed MSARIMA model, the accuracy obtained more than 99%. The proposed MSARIMA model approach give reliable flood event forecasting comparing with the other model presented in literature employing other databases. In [22] the accuracy obtained 79% for precipitation forecast in monthly precipitation. In [29] MAPE for water level forecasting obtained 15.43% for transfer function model and 56.43% for ARIMA model. In [32], studied forecasting of monthly rainfall obtained 95% accuracy.

7 Conclusions

A flood forecasting model approach is proposed for multi-step forward flood event forecasting based on multiplicative seasonal ARIMA (MSARIMA). This model consists of seasonal ARIMA algorithms which are capable of learning stationary and nonstationary system behavior, respectively. Observed variables are first predicted and thereupon to forecast flood event series. Recursively performance is employing to multi-step forward forecasting variables. The performance consists of one-step forward (12 years), two-step forward (24 years), three-step forward (36 years), and four-step forward (42 years). The experiment is applied using real meteorological data from some region in Bandung city. The proof of the proposed MSARIMA model performance is achieved by comparing results with other basic models used such as ARMA, ARIMA. The results show the proposed flood event forecasting approach outperforms these models concerning all criteria adopted (MAPE, and RMSPE) for one-step forward and multi-step forward, indicating the validity of the method.

Acknowledgements. First of all, author thank Prof. Hou Rongtao for his thoroughness, valuable advice, and patience. Also, the author would like to thank Irfan Dwiguna Sumitra who always encourages and inspires with new ideas in our research.

Competing Interests. The author declares that there is no conflict of interests regarding the publication of this paper.

References

1. Sumitra, I.D., Hou, R., Supatmi, S.: Design and deployment of wireless sensor networks for flood detection in Indonesia. In: Sun, X., Chao, H.-C., You, X., Bertino, E. (eds.) ICCCS 2017. LNCS, vol. 10602, pp. 313–325. Springer, Cham (2017). https://doi.org/10.1007/978-3-319-68505-2_27
2. Box, G.E.P., Jenkins, G.M.: Time series analysis, forecasting and control. In: Box, G.E.P., Jenkins, G.M. (eds.) A Very British Affair. PATEC, pp. 161–215. Palgrave Macmillan, London (2013). https://doi.org/10.1057/9781137291264_6
3. Hipel, K.W., McLeod, A.I.: Time Series Modelling of Water Resources and Environmental Systems. Elsevier, New York (1994)
4. Box, G.E.P., Jenkins, G.: Time Series Analysis, Forecasting and Control. Holden-Day, San Fransisco (1970)
5. Lee, J.: Univariate time series modeling and forecasting (BOX-Jenkins Methods), Econ 413, Lecture 4 (2008)
6. Adhikari, R., Agrawal, R.K.: An Introductory on Time Series and Forecasting. LAP Lambert Academic Publishing, January 2013. https://doi.org/10.13140/2.1.2771.8084
7. Cochrane, J.H.: Time series for Macroeconomic and Finance, Graduate School of Business, University of Chicago, Spring (1997)
8. Shi, C., Wang, H., Yin, F.: Monthly rainfall forecasting model with hidden periodicities. In: The 6th International Forum on Strategic Technology, pp. 1239–1242. IEEE (2011)
9. Zhang, G.P.: Time series forecasting using a hybrid ARIMA and neural network model. Neurocomputing **50**, 159–175 (2003)
10. Cheng, J., Xu, R., Tang, X., Sheng, V.S., Cai, C.: An abnormal network flow feature sequence prediction approach for DDoS attacks detection in big data environment. CMC: Comput. Mater. Continua **55**(1), 095–119 (2018)
11. Wang, B., et al.: Research on hybrid model of garlic short-term price forecasting based on big data. CMC: Comput. Mater. Continua **57**(2), 283–296 (2018)
12. Bandung of Meteorological, Climatology and Geophysics Bureau. http://data.bandung.go.id/dataset/laporan-iklim-kota-bandung-tahun-1976-2017. Accessed 21 May 2018

13. Anderson, T.W.: The Statistical Analysis of Time Series. Wiley, New York (1971)
14. Bloomfield, P.: Fourier Analysis of Time Series: An Introduction, 2nd edn. Wiley, New York (2000)
15. Brillinger, D.R.: Time Series Data Analysis and Theory. Rinehart and Winston, Holt, New York (1975)
16. Chatfield, C.: The Analysis of Time Series: An Introduction, 4th edn. Chapman and Hall, London (1989)
17. Kay, S.M.: Modern Spectral Estimation: Theory and Application, Englewood Cliffs. Prentice Hall, New York (1998)
18. Koopmans, E.H.: The Spectral Analysis of Time Series, 2nd edn. Academic Press, San Diego (1995)
19. Priestley, M.B.: Spectral Analysis and Time Series. Academic Press, London (1981)
20. Tabony, R.C.: A principal component and spectral analysis of European rainfall. J. Climatol. **1**, 283–294 (1981)
21. Kottegoda, N.T., Natale, L., Raiteri, E.: Some considerations of periodicity and persistence in daily rainfalls. J. Hydrol. **296**, 23–37 (2004)
22. Wang, H.R., Wang, C., Lin, X., Kang, J.: An improved ARIMA model for precipitation simulations. Nonlinear Process. Geophys. **21**, 1159–1168 (2014). https://doi.org/10.5194/npg-21-1159-2014
23. Niua, X.-F., Edmiston, H.L., Bailey, G.O.: Time series model for salinity and other environmental factors in the Apalachicola estuarine system. Estuar. Coast. Shelf Sci. **46**, 549–563 (1998)
24. Jin, J.L., Ding, J., Wei, Y.M.: Threshold autoregressive model based on genetic algorithm and its application to forecasting the shallow groundwater level. Hydraul. Eng. **17**, 51–55 (1999)
25. Toth, E.A., Montanari, A., Bath, A.: Real-time flood forecasting via combined use of conceptual and stochastic models. J. Phys. Chem. Earth Part B: Hydrol. Occans Atmos. (1999). https://doi.org/10.1016/S1464-1909(99)00082-9
26. Ahmad, S., Khan, I.H., Parida, B.P.: Performance of stochastic approaches for forecasting river water quality. Water Res **35**, 4261–4266 (2001)
27. Lehmann, A., Rode, M.: Long-term behavior and cross-correlation water quality analysis of the River Elbe. J. Water Res. **35**, 2153–2160 (2001)
28. Qi, W., Zhen, M.P.: Winters and ARIMA model analysis of the lake level of Salt Lake Zabuye, Tibetan Plateau. J. Lake Sci. **18**, 21–28 (2006). https://doi.org/10.18307/2006.0103
29. Yulianti, H., Mariza, H., Hilda, Z.: Flood prediction using transfer function model of rainfall and water discharge approach in Katulampa dam. In: The 3rd International Conference on Sustainable Future for Human Security SUSTAIN 2012, pp. 317–326. Elsevier (2012)
30. Yu, Z., Jiang, Z., Lei, G., Liu, F.: ARIMA modelling and forecasting of water level in the middle reach of the Yangtze River. In: 4th International Conference on Transportation Information and Safety (ICTIS) 2017, Banff, Canada, 8–10 August. IEEE (2017)
31. David, B.A., Carolina, M.A., Roberto, C.L.O., Jose C.R.F.: Hybrid approach combining SARIMA and neural networks and multi-step ahead wind speed forecasting in Brazil. IEEE Access **XX** (2017)
32. Afrifa-Yamoah, E., Saeed, B.I.I., Karim, A.: SARIMA modelling and forecasting of monthly rainfall in the Brong Ahafo Region of Ghana. J. World Environ. **6**(1), 1–9 (2016). http://journal.sapub.org/env
33. Abdul-Aziz, A.R., Anoyke, M., Kwame, A., Munyakazi, L., Nsowah-Nuamah, N.N.N.: Modelling and forecasting rainfall pattern in Ghana as a seasonal ARIMA process: the case of Ashanti Region. Int. J. Hum. Soc. Sci. **3**(3), 224–233 (2013)

34. Wideru, S., Nasiru, S., Asamoah, Y.G.: Proposed seasonal autoregressive integrated moving average model for forecasting rainfall pattern in the Navrongo municipality of Ghana. J. Environ. Earth Sci. **3**(12), 80–85 (2013)
35. Ampaw, E.M., Akuffo, B., Opoku, L.S., Lartey, S.: Time series modelling of rainfall in new Juaben municipality of the eastern region of Ghana. Contemp. Res. Bus. Soc. Sci. **4**(8), 116–129 (2013)
36. Tariq, M.M., Abbasabd, A.I.: Time series analysis of Nyala rainfall using ARIMA method. SUST J. Eng. Comput. Sci. **17**(1), 5–11 (2016)
37. Papalaskaris, T., Theologos, P., Pantrakis, A.: Stochastic monthly rainfall time series analysis, modeling and forecasting in Kavala City, Greece, North-Eastern Mediterranean Basin. In: International Conference on Efficient and Sustainable Water System Management Toward Worth Living Development, 2nd EWaS 2016 (2016). Proc. Eng. **162**, 254–263
38. Pekavora, P., Onderka, M., Pekar, J., Roncak, P., Miklanek, P.: Prediction of water quality in the Danube River under extreme hydrological and temperature conditions. J. Hydrol. Hydromech. **1**(57), 254–263 (2009)
39. Valipour, M.: Long-term runoff study using SARIMA and ARIMA models in the Unites States. J. Meteorol. Appl. **22**(3), 592–598 (2015)
40. Ali, S.M.: Time series analysis of Baghdad rainfall using SARIMA method. Iraqi J. Sci. **54**(4), 1136–1142 (2013)
41. Chang, X., Gao, M., Wang, Y., Hou, X.: Seasonal Autoregressive integrated moving average model for precipitation of time series. J. Math. Stat. **8**(4), 500–505 (2012)
42. Gautam, R., Sinha, A.K.: Time series analysis of reference crop evapotranspiration for Bokaro District, Jharkhand, India. J. Water Land Dev. **30**, 51–56 (2011). https://doi.org/10.1515/jwld-2016-0021
43. Janhabi, M., Jha, R.: Time-series analysis of monthly rainfall data for the Mahanadi River Basin, India. J. Sci. Cold Arid Reg. **5**(1), 73–84 (2013)
44. Tadesse, K.B., Dinka, M.O.: Application of SARIMA model to forecasting monthly flows in Waterval River, South Africa. J. Water Land Dept. **35**, 229–236 (2017). https://doi.org/10.1515/jwld-2017-0088
45. Yanming, Y., Haiyan, Z., Ruili, Z.: Prediction and analysis of aircraft failure rate based on SARIMA model. In: The 2nd IEEE International Conference on Computational Intelligence and Applications. IEEE (2017)
46. Jollife, I.T.: Principal Component Analysis, 2nd edn. Springer, New York (2002). https://doi.org/10.1007/b98835
47. Moniz, N., Branco, P., Torgo, L.: Resampling strategies for imbalanced time series. In: Proceeding IEEE International Conference on Data Science and Advanced Analytics, pp. 282–291. IEEE (2016)

Improved Bayesian Method with Collision Recovery for RFID Anti-collision

Chu Chu[1(✉)], Guangjun Wen[1], Zhong Huang[1], Jian Su[2], and Yu Han[1]

[1] University of Electronic Science and Technology of China, Chengdu, Sichuan, People's Republic of China
chuchu_824@163.com

[2] Nanjing University of Information Science and Technology, Nanjing, Jiangsu, People's Republic of China

Abstract. In a radio-frequency identification (RFID) systems, Aloha Based Protocols is widely adapted to solve the anti-collision problem. Currently, the problem of anti-collision can be divided into two parts. The first part is how to estimate the tags accurately. The other part is how to improve system efficiency. In this paper, the existing tag estimation method in physical layer is used to improve Bayesian Method for tag estimation in slot Aloha protocol, and the tag access probability for each slot based on collision recovery method is designed to maximize the system efficiency. The simulation shows that the posterior probability distribution of number of tags can adapt quickly to concentrate around the true value in few slots and the system throughput can close to the theoretical limit of the slotted Aloha system.

Keywords: Slotted aloha · Collision recovery method · Bayesian method · Anti-collision protocol

1 Introduction

Radio Frequency Identification (RFID) is a kind of wireless identification technology, which is widely used in various fields [2–5]. An RFID system consists of at least one readers and multiple tags which have their own unique identification number. During tag recognition, when the reader sends a query command, multiple tags may return signals at the same time to cause collisions. Therefore, anti-collision algorithm is employed in readers to avoid collisions between tags and improve system efficiency (read rate).

The existing anti-collision algorithms mainly focus on the MAC layer, which is mainly divided into tree-based and ALOHA-based categories [3–14]. Tree-based algorithms resolve collisions by muting subsets of tags that are involved in a collision. Successively muting larger subsets finally leads to successful transmission of a tag's identification. The tree-based algorithms have been studied extensively in the literature [1, 7–9]. On the other hand, one of the most popular anti-collision algorithm is the ALOHA based algorithm. In [10, 11], the authors proposed tag estimate methods for RFID anti-collision using framed ALOHA. Based on Schoute's analysis [12], if the

X. Sun et al. (Eds.): ICAIS 2019, LNCS 11633, pp. 51–61, 2019.
https://doi.org/10.1007/978-3-030-24265-7_5

frame length is assumed to be the number of tags, the expected value of collision tags is 2.39C, where C is the number of collision slots. However, the assumption is difficult to confirm and may cause some errors which decrease the system efficiency. In [13], Vogt presents two tag estimation functions, denoted as Vogt-I and Vogt-II. The author proposed an estimate function using the distance between the read result and the expected value vector to estimate the tag quantity. The available frame lengths are limited to powers of 2 and results in lower throughput. Chen et al. [14] proposes a simple but relatively accurate method (FEIA) for tag backlog estimation. The procedures of the estimation and frame size adjustment should be performed at every time slot, which causes a heavy loading for a mobile reader with limited computation capability. Moreover, the FEIA is constrained by the scenario that the initial slot should not be idle during a frame.

However, there are relatively few studies on slotted Aloha [20, 21]. The advantage of the slotted ALOHA is that it is very simple. These tags transmit their RN16 to reader in a slot, and if there is a collision, they simply retransmit. Hence, if the access probability can be well estimated, the number of remaining tags can be estimated in a few slots, and the theoretical upper limit of system throughput can be reached in less slots.

On the other hand, the conventional anti-collision algorithm is only a medium access control (MAC) layer protocol. In these algorithm, when multiple tags transmit in one slot, the collision slot will be discarded, especially the number of tags is large, which will cause a great waste of time slots. If the useful tag information can be separated from the collision signal, the collision slot can be transformed into a useful slot, which greatly improves the system efficiency. Therefore, the study of physical layer collision signal recovery method has aroused wide interest. Khasgiwale et al. [15] utilise information from tag collisions on the physical layer to estimate the number of tags involved in that specific collision slot. Ou et al. [16] presented a BiGroup method, which utilized the collided tag transmissions at both time domain and constellation domain to separate different kinds of tags. Angerer et al. [17] present a physical layer signal recovery model with both single antenna and multiple antenna systems. Xi Tan et al. [18] use smooth filter to find the center of the cluster to obtain the amplitude histogram. An algorithm for detecting the number of collision tags and signal recovery is also proposed.

In this paper, we improve the bayesian method by combining the collision recovery method to estimate the tags. Unlike previous study, we consider the combination of cross-layer methods to improve system efficiency and the accuracy of tag estimation. Through the tag estimation method in physical layer, the feedback in each slot can be divided into idle slots, successful slots, collision slots of 2 tags, collision slots of 3 tags and collision of more tags. Hence, the posterior probability distribution of number of tags is derive by improving the Bayesian method. We also derive the optimal tag access probability for each slot considering the ability of collision recovery in physical layer to maximize the system throughput.

The rest of this paper is organized as follows, Sect. 2 introduces the RFID system model based on slot ALOHA protocol and Bayesian method. Section 3 describe the flow of estimating the number of tags by Bayesian method combined with collision signal recovery method, and the adjustment of access probability after each slot is discussed; The simulation results are discussed in Sect. 4; The conclusion and future work are presented in Sect. 5.

2 Preliminaries

2.1 System Model

As we can see in Fig. 1, in slotted ALOHA protocol, the reader initiates a read cycle by broadcasting a request command to all tags under its coverage. In each slot, unrecognized tags within the reader's coverage send RN16 to the reader with a certain access probability. If the reader successfully receives the RN16 data returned by a tag, the ACK command containing the RN16 is fed back to complete the tag recognition. Since the number of tags is unknown, there are three possible situations in a slot: idle, successful, and conflicting. Idle slot means that there is no label in this slot to return their identification number. Successful slot means that only one tag in the slot wants the reader to send an identification number and is successfully identified by the reader. A collision occurs when multiple tags return their identification number to the reader in the same slot, which is called a collision slot. If there is a collision, tags re-transmit after a random delay. The collision occurs at slots boundary only, hence there are no partial collisions.

For slotted ALOHA protocol, it is important to assign appropriate access probabilities to tags that reduce the slot used to identify all tags, and the setting of the access probability depends on the accurate estimate of the number of tags before the start of each time slot. Furthermore, in slotted ALOHA protocol, the collision tags will be discarded. If it is possible to recovery the tag's information in collision slots, the collision slots will be convert to "useful time slots". All of these will improve the system efficiency.

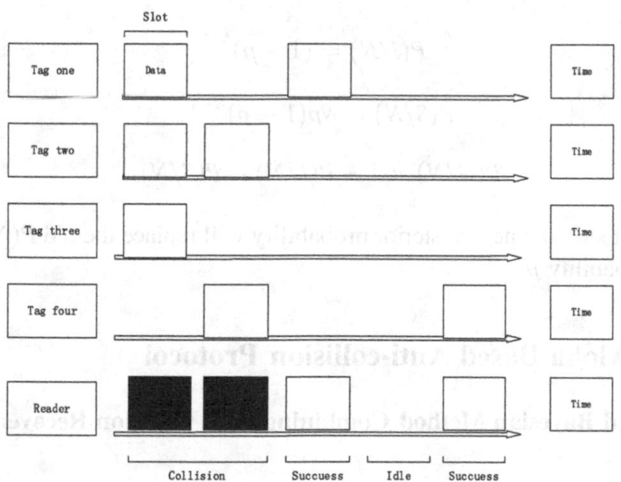

Fig. 1. Schematic diagram of slot ALOHA protocol

2.2 Tag Number Estimation Based on Bayesian Method

In [19], the author apply Bayesian method to estimate the number of remaining tags and determine the access probability of each slot in MAC layer. The specific Bayesian estimation method is shown below:

1. Set N_{real} as the value of the true label number involved in the tag recognition process.
2. Then, set $N_{\max}$ as the maximum of the distribution and assume that the number of labels is a random variable with a prior probability $P(N)$ obeying a uniform distribution of $N - (0, N_{\max})$. $P(N)$ takes part in the Bayesian estimation process as the initial value and updates with the estimated number of each round.
3. The access probability p of each tag is calculated by the reader in each slot according to the result of the previous slot, and is broadcast to the tag. All remaining unrecognized tags will adaptively adjust the probability p to access the next slot.

In these work, ternary feedback is assumed that informs the result of tags access in a slot whether it is idle (I), success(S), or collision(C). According to the given N, the posterior probability distribution defined is defined as:

$$P(N/outcome) = \frac{P(outcome/N)P(N)}{P(outcome)} \tag{1}$$

Where $P(outcome) = \sum_{N} P(outcome/N)P(N)$ and $\sum_{N} P(N/outcome) = 1$

The likelihood function according to the outcome (I, S, C) of the previous slot for any given N:

$$P(I/N) = (1 - p)^{N} \tag{2}$$

$$P(S/N) = Np(1 - p)^{N-1} \tag{3}$$

$$P(C/N) = 1 - P(I/N) - P(S/N) \tag{4}$$

For the next slot, the new posterior probability will replace the old $P(N)$ for finding the access probability p.

3 Slotted Aloha Based Anti-collision Protocol

3.1 Improved Bayesian Method Combining with Collision Recovery Method

In slotted ALOHA protocol, according to the outcome of the previous slot, we can use Bayesian estimation method to estimate the number of remaining unrecognized tags [14]. Divides the outcome into three Intervals (I, S, C). However, when collision happen, the number of tags in the collision slots is not known. If the access probability is set too large at the beginning, the accuracy of the tag estimation will decrease.

Tag estimation method in physical layer will obtain the number of tags in the collision slot. Hence, the interval of collision slot (C) can be divided into more. In each interval, the likelihood function corresponding to the number of collision tags can be derive and used to calculate the posterior probability.

By using the method of [11], Collision signals in the time domain can be mapped onto the constellation domain. There will be 2^m cluster which m is the number of tags in the collision slot. If SNR is larger than 25 dB, Clusters can be well identified in the scenario 2 or 3 tags. Hence, we assumed that the tags in collision can be estimated successfully when $m = 2\, or\, 3$.

As a result, we can further divide the collision slot into three states: C_2, C_2 and C_{more}, and the likelihood function of three states can be obtained according to the previous slot for any given N:

$$P(C_2/N) = C_{NP}^2 p^2 (1-p)^{(N-2)} \tag{5}$$

$$P(C_3/N) = C_{NP}^3 p^3 (1-p)^{(N-3)} \tag{6}$$

$$P(C_{more}/N) = P(C/N) - P(C_2/N) - P(C_3/N) \tag{7}$$

Finally, we divide the outcome into five intervals $(I, S, C_2, C_3, C_{more})$.

In collision slots, we find the starting time and bit boundaries of each tag, then the bipartite grouping algorithm is use to divide the clusters into “H” and “L”. The algorithm outputs a sequence of binary states that represents the transmitted signal of that tag. In our method, we assumed that the sequence of one tag can be recovery correctly when two or three tags collision.

Hence, In the process of tag identification. For the above three situations (C_2, C_3, S), $P(N/C_2)$, $P(C_2/N)$, $P(N/S)$ should be shifted one step down to the left, which means that the tag that is successfully identified will not take part in the next time slot recognition process. Then, we calculated the posterior probability $P(N/outcome)$ for any given N to replace the old $P(N)$ for finding the access probability p.

3.2 Calculation of Access Probability Combined with Collision Recovery Method

In slotted ALOHA system, a tag will leave the identification process in the next slot if it is successfully identified. So the access probability of the tag is crucial for the performance of slotted ALOHA. If the access probability is set too small, there will be many idle slots since only a small number of tags will send RN16 in the slot which result in wasting excessive identification time. On the other hand, many collision slots will be generated because of the large access probability.

To obtain the access probability of each tag in the next slot, we first need to calculate the number of remaining tags. By calculating the mean number of tags, the number of remaining tags p_{opt} can be estimated as: $N_0 = \sum NP(N)$. In [14], the access probability is set to: $p = {}^1\!/_{N_0}$. However, it only considers maximizing the probability of successful slots. If it is possible to recover from a slot with $R \leq M$ colliding tags, we only encounter an unreadable slot if more than M tags transmit in the same slot ($J = 1$). In [12], the Maximum system throughput of this case is shown in Fig. 2:

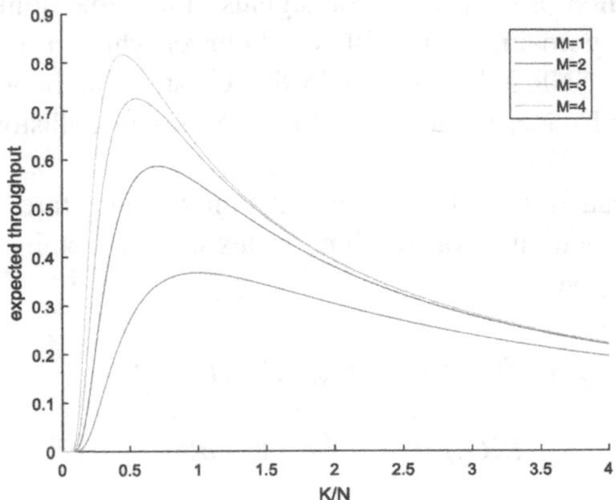

Fig. 2. Expected throughput for $J = 1$ depending on frame size to tag ratio K/N.

Where K is the frame size and N is the tag population size in frame slotted aloha. In our method, we consider the case where the reader selects one of these tags and confirms the single tag while the other received tag responses are discarded ($M = 3$). It can be seen from Fig. 2 that theoretical limit of throughput is 70.7%.

Given the probability distribution of number of tags, the average probability of success, collision of two tags and three tags (we call them "useful slots") over N becomes:

$$\overline{P(S/p)} = E[P(S/N,p)] = \sum_{N} Np(1-p)^{N-1}P(N) \tag{8}$$

$$\overline{P(C_2/p)} = E[P(C_2/N,p)] = \sum_{N} C_N^2 p^2(1-p)^{(N-2)}P(N) \tag{9}$$

$$\overline{P(C_3/p)} = E[P(C_3/N,p)] = \sum_{N} C_N^3 p^3(1-p)^{(N-3)}P(N) \tag{10}$$

The total average probability of three cases is given:

$$\overline{P(Total/p)} = \overline{P(S/p)} + \overline{P(C_2/p)} + \overline{P(C_3/p)} \tag{11}$$

In order to maximize the average probability of three cases, the optimal p_{opt} of each slot can readily be derived by solving the following equation:

$$\frac{d}{dp}\overline{P(Total/p)} = P(N) \times \left(\sum_N \frac{d}{dp} Np(1-p)^{N-1} + \sum_N \frac{d}{dp} C_N^2 p^2 (1-p)^{(N-2)} + \sum_N \frac{d}{dp} C_N^3 p^3 (1-p)^{(N-3)}\right) = 0 \tag{12}$$

Based on the improvement of above two points, the algorithm is shown below:

Algorithm 1

1. Initialize all parameters and start tag identification.
2. Determine the outcome of last slot, calculate the value of likelihood function corresponding the outcome using Eq.2-Eq.7 for any given N with $N:(0, N_{max})$
3. Calculate the posterior probability distribution of each given N using Eq.1. For the case of outcome (C_2, C_3, S), $P(N/Outcome)$ should be shifted one step down to the left, and the value of N_{max} is subtracted by 1.
4. Decide the access probability p for each tag to participate in the next slot by solving the Eq.12.
5. Repeat steps 2-4 until there is no tag to be identified.

4 Simulation Results and Discussion

In this section, we compare the performance differences between the Bayesian estimation of MAC layer and the Bayesian estimation combined with collision tag estimation and recovery method in different cases. These three scheme are mentioned later and the tags identification process is in accordance with the slot ALOHA protocol.

At the beginning of the simulation, $P(N)$ is set as uniformly distributed from 2 to N_{max}, N_{max} is set to 200, 1000 and N_{real} is set to 100. So we can get the relationship between the number of remaining tags and the slot index as shown in Figs. 3 and 4.

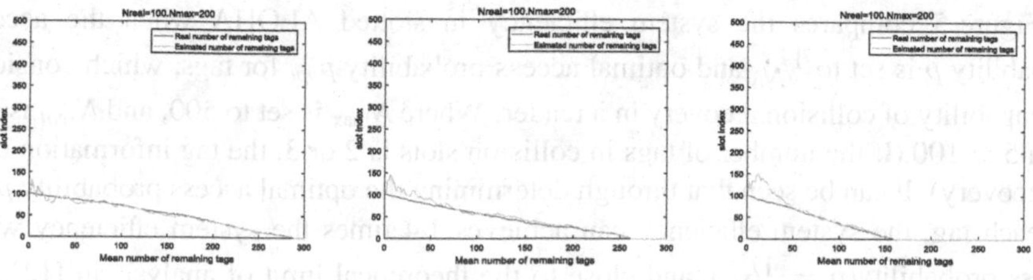

Fig. 3. Evolution of the probability distribution in three cases with $N_{real} = 100$, $N_{max} = 200$

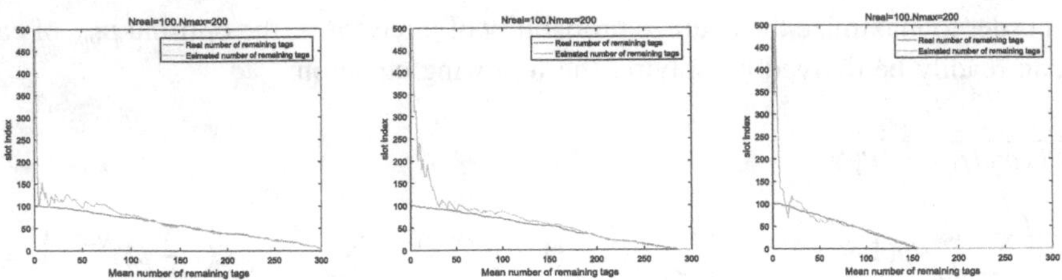

Fig. 4. Evolution of the probability distribution in three cases with $N_{real} = 100$, $N_{\max} = 1000$

As can be seen, in the early slots the estimated N_0 decreases rapidly from $N_{real}/2$ and reaches the real number of remaining tags with different values of $N_{\max} =$ 200,1000. Especially, when collision tag number estimation and collision tag signal recovery method are adopted, the number of estimated tags can approach the real number of remaining tags in a shorter time slot, and the N_{real} number of all tags can be identified using a shorter time slot. This is because Bayes estimation is more accurate if we can estimate the tags in the collision slot. If the tag information in the collision slot can be further recovery, the time slot needed for tag identification will be further reduced significantly.

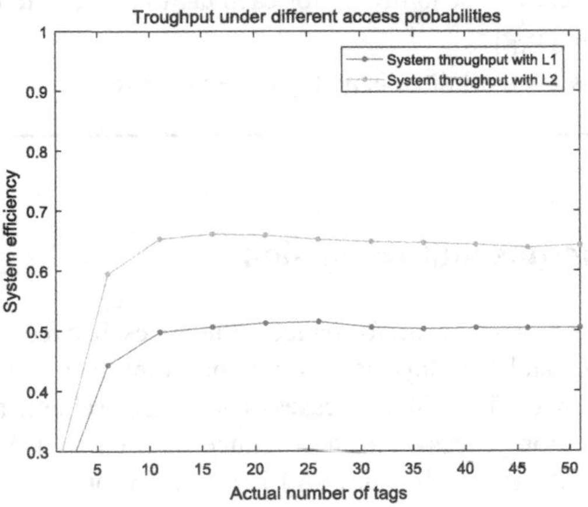

Fig. 5. Performance comparison under different access probability

Figure 5 compares the system efficiency in slotted ALOHA when the access probability p is set to $1/N_0$ and optimal access probability p_{opt} for tags, which consider the capability of collision recovery in a reader. Where $N_{\max}$ is set to 500, and N_{real} is set from 5 to 100.(If the number of tags in collision slots is 2 or 3, the tag information can be recovery). It can be seen that through determining the optimal access probability p_{opt} for each tag, the system efficiency can achieves 1.4 times the system efficiency with access probability($p = 1/N_0$), and close to the theoretical limit of analysis in [12].

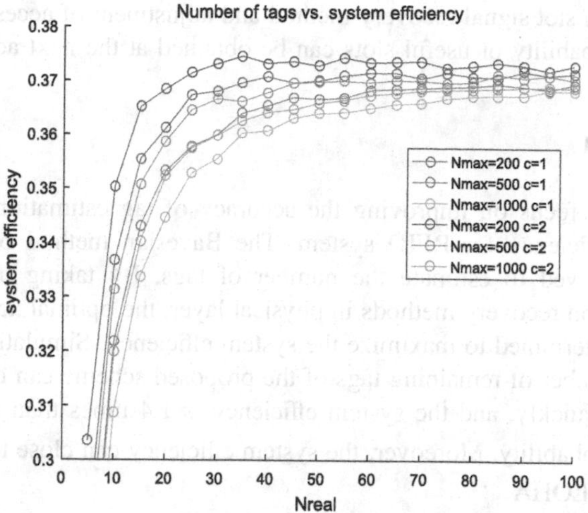

Fig. 6. Comparison between Schemes 1 and 2

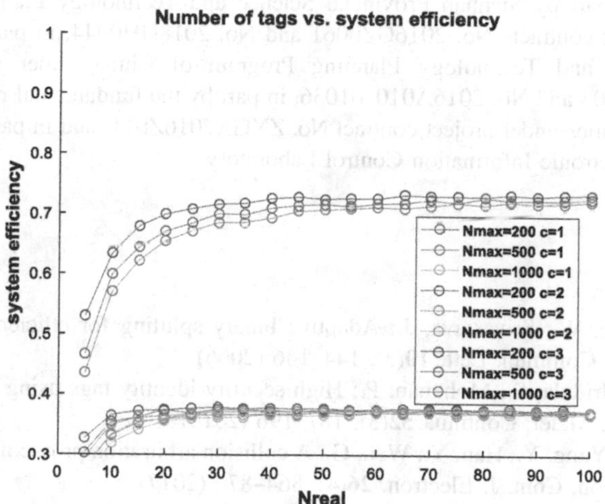

Fig. 7. System efficiency of the three schemes

Figure 6 compares the system efficiency of Schemes 1 and 2 under different N_{real}. When N_{real} reaches a certain value, both Schemes 1 and 2 can reach the theoretical limit of 36.8% of the ideal slotted aloha. However, when N_{real} is small, only the Scheme 2 can reach the theoretical. Therefore, Scheme 2 can achieve higher system efficiency. This is because by subdividing conflict slots into three intervals, we can estimate the actual number of tags more accurately, and hence, reduce the time slots needed for tag identification. Figure 7 compares the system efficiency of three scheme. Scheme 3 can achieve 36.8% even if the N_{real} is small. Finally, the system efficiency close to 70.7%. This is because collision slots can be converted into useful slots by means of collision slot signal recovery method and adjustment of access probability p, and a greater probability of useful slots can be obtained at the next access.

5 Conclusion

In this paper, we focus on improving the accuracy of tag estimation and achieving higher system efficiency for RFID system. The Bayesian method based on slotted ALOHA is improved to estimate the number of tags. By taking into account the benefits of collision recovery methods in physical layer, the optimal access probability for each tag is determined to maximize the system efficiency. Simulation results show that the mean number of remaining tags of the proposed scheme can converges to the real value more quickly, and the system efficiency is 1.4 times than the system with $^1/_{N_0}$ as access probability. Moreover, the system efficiency can close to the theoretical limit of slotted ALOHA.

Acknowledgment. This work was supported in part by the National Natural Science Foundation of China under project contracts 61601093, No. 61791082, No. 61701116 and No. 61371047, in part by Sichuan Provincial Science and Technology Planning Program of China under project contracts No. 2016GZ0061 and No. 2018HH0044, in part by Guangdong Provincial Science and Technology Planning Program of China under project contracts No. 2015B090909004 and No. 2016A010101036, in part by the fundamental research funds for the Central Universities under project contract No. ZYGX2016Z011, and in part by Science and Technology on Electronic Information Control Laboratory.

References

1. Myung, J., Lee, W., Srivastava, J.: Adaptive binary splitting for efficient RFID tag anti-collision. IEEE Commun. Lett. **10**(3), 144–146 (2006)
2. Pradeep, A., Mridula, S., Mohanan, P.: High security identity tags using spiral resonators. CMC: Comput. Mater. Continua **52**(3), 187–196 (2016)
3. Su, J., Xie, L., Yang, Y., Han, Y., Wen, G.: A collision arbitration protocol based on specific selection function. Chin. J. Electron. **26**(4), 864–870 (2017)
4. Chen, H., Liu, K., Ma, C., Han, Y., Su, J.: A novel time-aware frame adjustment strategy for RFID anti-collision. CMC: Comput. Mater. Continua **57**(2), 195–204 (2018)
5. Su, J., Zhao, X., Luo, Z., Chen, H.: Q-value fine-grained adjustment based RFID anti-collision algorithm. IEICE Trans. Commun. **99**(7), 1593–1598 (2016)
6. Su, J., Sheng, Z., Xie, L., Li, G., Liu, A.X.: Fast splitting based tag identification algorithm for anti-collision in UHF RFID system. IEEE Trans. Commun. **67**, 1 (2018)
7. Kaplan, M., Gulko, E.: Analytic properties of multiple-access trees. IEEE Trans. Inf. Theory **31**(2), 255–263 (2003)
8. Law, C., Lee, K., Siu, K.Y.: Efficient memoryless protocol for tag identification (extended abstract). In: International Workshop on Discrete Algorithms and Methods for Mobile Computing and Communications, pp. 75–84. ACM (2000)

9. Nanjundaiah, M., Chaudhary, V.: Improvement to the anticollision protocol specification for 900 MHz Class 0 radio frequency identification tag. In: International Conference on Advanced Information Networking and Applications, pp. 616–620. IEEE Computer Society, Taiwan (2005)
10. Cha, J.R., Kim, J.H.: Novel anti-collision algorithms for fast object identification in RFID system. In: International Conference on Parallel & Distributed Systems-Workshops, pp. 63–67. IEEE Computer Society, Fukuoka (2005)
11. Floerkemeier, C., Zurich, E.: Transmission control scheme for fast RFID object identification. In: IEEE International Conference on Pervasive Computing & Communications Workshops. IEEE, Pisa (2006)
12. Schoute, F.: Dynamic frame length ALOHA. Mob. Commun. **31**(4), 565–568 (1983)
13. Vogt, H.: Multiple object identification with passive RFID tags. Pervasive Comput. **3**(3), 98–113 (2002)
14. Chen, W.T.: A feasible and easy-to-implement anticollision algorithm for the EPC global UHF class-1 generation-2 RFID protocol. IEEE Trans. Autom. Sci. Eng. **11**(2), 485–491 (2014)
15. Khasgiwale, R.S., Adyanthaya, R.U., Engels, D.W.: Extracting information from tag collisions. In: 2009 IEEE International Conference on RFID, pp. 131–138. IEEE, Florida (2009)
16. Ou, J., Li, M., Zheng, Y.: Come and be served: parallel decoding for COTS RFID tags. IEEE/ACM Trans. Networking **25**(3), 500–511 (2015)
17. Angerer, C., Langwieser, R., Rupp, M.: RFID reader receivers for physical layer collision recovery. IEEE Trans. Commun. **58**(12), 3526–3537 (2011)
18. Tan, X., Wang, H., Fu, L.: Collision detection and signal recovery for UHF RFID systems. IEEE Trans. Autom. Sci. Eng. **15**(1), 239–250 (2016)
19. Annur, R., Srichavengsup, W., Nakpeerayuth, S.: Bayesian method of slotted aloha based anti-collision protocol for RFID systems. In: IEEE Twelfth International Symposium on Autonomous Decentralized Systems, pp. 87–90. IEEE, Taiwan (2015)

Multi-step Attack Scenarios Mining Based on Neural Network and Bayesian Network Attack Graph

Jianyi Liu(✉), Bowen Liu, Ru Zhang, and Cong Wang

School of Cyberspace Security, Beijing University of Posts and Telecommunications, Beijing 100876, China
liujy@bupt.edu.cn

Abstract. In order to find attack patterns from a large number of redundant alert logs, build multi-step attack scenarios, and eliminate the false alerts of the alert logs, this paper proposes a new multi-step attack scenario construction model, which is divided into two parts: offline mode and online mode. In the offline mode, the known real attack alert log is used to train the neural network for removing error alerts, and eventually to generate a Bayesian network attack graph by alert aggregation processing and causal association attack sequence. In the online mode, a large number of online alert logs are used to update the neural network and the Bayesian network attack graph generated by the previous offline mode, so that the iterative attack graph is more complete and accurate. In the end, we extract a variety of multi-step attack scenarios from the Bayesian network attack graph to achieve the purpose of eliminating false alerts in the redundant IDS alert logs. In order to verify the validity of the algorithm, we use the DARPA 2000 dataset to test, and the results show that the algorithm has higher accuracy.

Keywords: IDS log analysis · Neural network · Causal association analysis

1 Introduction

Today, the Internet plays a very important role in our lives. At the same time, cyber attacks are also increasing, which makes the cyber security field face severe challenges and even threatens national security [1].

Typical attack behaviors include botnet attacks, distributed denial of service, and worm attacks. Most of the cyber attacks are not done in one step, but need a purposeful and step-by-step process to complete. IDS cannot detect and identify these multi-step attacks. Therefore, if we can reconstruct the attack scenario and understand the attack mode and attack intention of the attacker, we will identify the multi-step attack mode, which eliminates the IDS error alert logs and ensures the efficiency of network attack detection.

This paper combines the fully connected neural network and the Bayesian network attack graph to multiple attack scenarios, and uses the DARPA 2000 dataset to test and compare it with the previous papers. It has found advantages such as higher accuracy for correct alert screening and faster calculation of algorithms.

X. Sun et al. (Eds.): ICAIS 2019, LNCS 11633, pp. 62–74, 2019.
https://doi.org/10.1007/978-3-030-24265-7_6

The rest of this paper is organized as follows: the next section will briefly review the related work in this area. The third section describes the proposed alert correlation method in the offline mode and the online mode. The fourth section tests the model on the DARPA 2000 and gives the experimental results. The last section concludes the paper.

2 Related Work

In recent years, a large number of literatures have been researched on IDS [2, 3], analysis of the association between IDS alert logs is mainly divided into four categories: alert correlation analysis based on causal logic, alert correlation analysis based on scene, alert correlation analysis based on similarity and alert correlation analysis based on data mining [4].

The method based on causal logic assumes a causal relationship between consecutive anomalous events from the same threat behavior, and the latter anomaly is performed on the premise that the previous anomaly event is valid. The basic idea is to give the reasons for the occurrence of various types of alarms and the consequences after they occur, and then complete the causal association by matching the causes and results between the warnings to reconstruct the cyber threat behavior.

Zali et al. [5] used a causal association graph model to define the causal relationship between alerts. In this paper, a threat behavior sequence is established through the forward queue tree construction process, and the backward queue tree construction process is used to detect whether there is a false positive or a false negative.

In the real-time intrusion alert-related RIAC proposed by Lin [6], an alert type is expanded to a triple: alert type description, antecedent event, and consequence event. By matching the cause and effect of each alert type, the causal relationship between each alert type and the characteristic conditions that need to be matched are obtained. Based on this, causal correlation matching is performed on the alert data, and the associated alert sequence fragments are obtained, and then these fragments are connected to form a complete threat behavior.

The basic idea of the scenario-based method is to abstract all known threat behaviors into rule knowledge in advance, and then match the pending alert data with the defined rules, Reproduce the cyber threat behavior scenario based on the matching result. The rule knowledge describes the process of threat behavior and the conditions that each step needs to meet. The scenario-based method is not very different, and the main difference is the way in which threat behavior is described.

Liu et al. [7] proposed an alert correlation model based on finite automatic state machine, which contains three key description scenarios: the process key scenarios, the attacker key scenarios, and the victim key scenarios.

The similarity-based method assumes that there is a certain similarity between alerts from the same threat behavior. The basic idea is to determine whether to correlate alerts based on the similarity between alerts. By uniformly abstracting the attribute information of the alert data into a vector mode, the distance between the function calculation vectors and the cluster vector are defined to complete the alert association.

The key to the similarity-based algorithm is the definition of the vector distance calculation function. The typical method [8–11] is to define a similarity calculation function for each attribute of the alert in advance, and then obtain the similarity between the alerts by weighted summation. If the similarity exceeds a predetermined threshold, an association operation is performed. The main difference is that the definition of the attribute calculation function is different.

Literature [8] defines an attribute similarity calculation function for each attribute characteristic, and literature [9] expresses the similarity between alerts by defining and calculating the entropy of each alert. Literature [10] adds the context information of the alert to the clustering process, and effectively removes the redundant alert data while improving the clustering accuracy.

The method based on data mining assumes that there is a certain relationship between alerts from the same network threat behavior. The basic idea is to use data mining algorithms to discover the relationship hidden behind the data distribution and reconstruct the threat behavior sequence according to the association information. Frequent sequence mining is one of the commonly used data mining methods for alert correlation [12–14]. This method believes that there is a certain relationship between alert data appearing in a short time interval. According to the time window, the alert sequence is decomposed into multiple sub-sequences, and then the frequent items are mined for these sub-sequences, and the obtained alerts in the frequent itemsets can be considered as having an association relationship.

Vasilomanolakis et al. [15] introduced the geographical location information of the event into the two-dimensional data analysis.

Ge Lin et al. [16] proposed a multi-dimensional data analysis method based on the distributed power set Apriori algorithm, respectively mining the frequent itemsets in each dimension, and then conducting comprehensive association analysis.

The method based on causal logic and the method based on data mining have the ability to identify unknown threat behaviors, and the correlation ability is relatively high. The based on scene method can be matched with the rule knowledge base, and the correlation precision is relatively high. The based on similarity method is calculated. The complexity is relatively small, so the correlation efficiency is relatively high.

3 Our Approach

This paper presents a model for continuous learning. The model builds a multi-step associated attack graph model based on a supervised learning neural network and an improved Bayesian network. The main problems solved are:

1. There are a large number of low-level error alerts in IDS;
2. Many multi-step association methods directly relate to the original IDS alert, which leads to a large number of errors and redundancy in the results.

In this paper, the model is mainly divided into two parts, offline mode and online mode. The offline mode of the model is to input the offline alerts into the neural network for training, remove the false alerts and redundant alerts, and then use the Bayesian network to generate the alert attack graph to discover the multi-step attack mode.

In online mode, a large number of real-time IDS logs are used to iterate the offline mode method, update neural network parameters and Bayesian network attack graphs to improve the accuracy of the model and achieve eliminating false positives. The process structure diagram of the method is shown in Fig. 1.

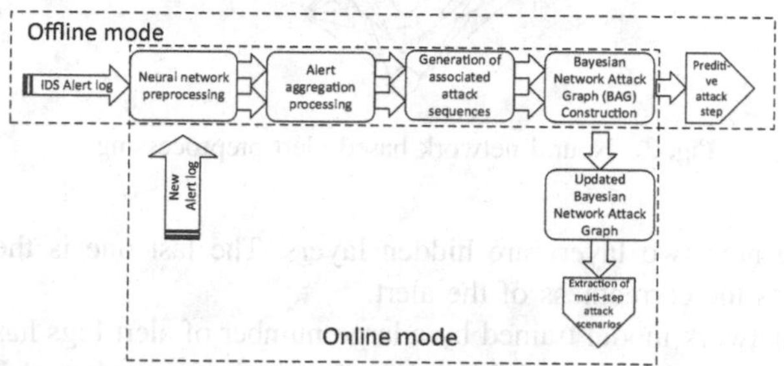

Fig. 1. Multi-step attack scene mining based on Bayesian network attack graph

3.1 Offline Mode

Figure 2 is a structural flow chart of the offline mode. The mode is divided into four steps: alert pre-processing based on neural network, alert aggregation processing, causal-related attack sequence generation, Bayesian network attack graph construction.

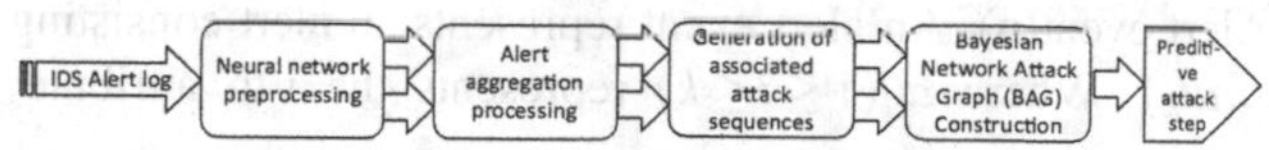

Fig. 2. Flowchart of offline mode

Neural Network Based Alert Preprocessing

The number of IDS alert logs is very large. In this paper, IDS alerts caused by normal or non-malicious network activities are called error alerts. The presence or absence of these alerts is directly related to the accuracy of the multi-step attack scenarios we generate later. This step is mainly to screen and filter the false alerts. By analyzing a large number of alert logs, the following three characteristics are obtained:

1. The number of related alerts
2. Alert density
3. Alert periodicity.

The three characteristics of different alert logs are taken as input. The authenticity of the alert is the label. A three-layer neural network is constructed, and the output result is the authenticity of the alert. Neural network graph based on alert preprocessing is shown in Fig. 3.

Figure 3 shows the neural network structure in the alert pre-processing stage. The input layer has three inputs: The number of related alerts, Alert density, and Alert

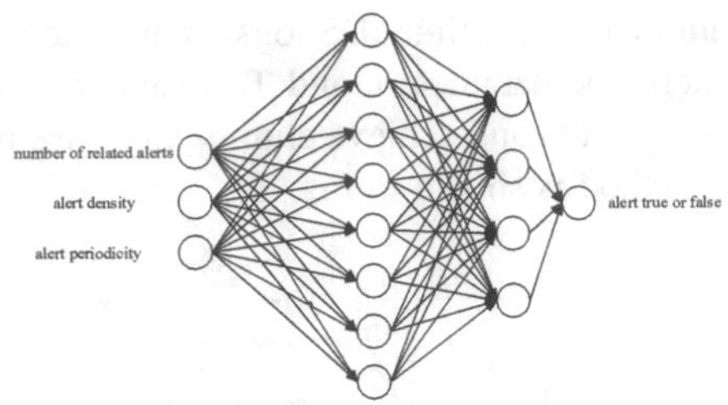

Fig. 3. Neural network based alert preprocessing

periodicity. The next two layers are hidden layers. The last one is the output layer which determines the correctness of the alert.

The neural network model trained by a large number of alert logs has the ability to distinguish between real alerts and false alerts from a large number of IDS alert logs, providing a basis for constructing a multi-step attack scenario. However, the neural network only through the offline mode is not very effective, and it is necessary to continuously update the online mode to achieve the optimal effect. The specific update method is shown in Fig. 3.

Alert Aggregation Processing

We need to aggregate these similar alert logs to get more streamlined data, reducing the complexity of the next calculation.

To illustrate this section clearly, the concepts involved are as follows:

Definition 1: Alert event(**a**). An alert event represents an alert consisting of a k-tuple $(at_1, at_2, at_3, \ldots, at_k)$. Where $at_i (1 \leq i \leq k)$ represents the i-th attribute of the alert event.

Definition 2: Meta-alerts(**ma**). All alerts with the same alert type (which conform the predefined time condition $\mathbf{\Delta t}$) are merged together. The combination of these alerts forms a meta alert. There is an alert set $\{at_1, at_2, at_3, \ldots . at_j\}$ in one time interval, if

$$at_1[alertType] = at_2[alertType] = \ldots = at_n[alertType](timestamp \notin alertType)$$

These similar alerts form a meta alert [17]. The timestamp attribute of the meta-alert takes the timestamp of the first occurrence of alert event a, and the number of meta-alerts is smaller than the number of original alert events.

Definition 3: Alert sequence (**AS**). A set of chronologically ordered meta-alerts is called an alert sequence, denoted AS, $AS = \{ma_1, ma_2, ma_3, \ldots, ma_n\}$, And satisfy:

$$ma_i.timestamp \leq ma_j.timestamp (1 \leq i \leq j \leq n)$$

The specific method steps of alert aggregation processing are as follows:

1. For a large number of alerts, we sort by the time stamp of each alarm event. According to setting time parameter T, we take T hours as a batch and divide all alerts into L batches. Each batch is recorded as $b_i (1 \leq i \leq L)$.

2. Divide the time window by Δt for all batches, as shown in Fig. 4. The length of the time window is determined by the variable parameters Δt.

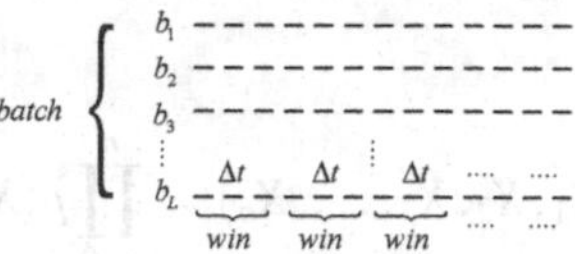

Fig. 4. Batch and Time window

3. Traverse all the windows in each bi ($1 \leq$ i $\leq$ L), and convert all the alert events in each window into the **ma** according to the Definition 2 to reduce the number of alerts.
4. Extract all the meta alerts from bi ($1 \leq$ i $\leq$ L), and generate L alert sequence $\{AS_1, AS_2, AS_3, \ldots, AS_L\}$ according to Definition 3.

The alert sequences AS are generated after the alert aggregation process where a full or partial multi-step attack in attack scenario will exist.

Generation of Causal Association Attack Sequences

Definition 4: Attack scenario association sequence (**ASS**). When an attacker completes a multi-step attack, the alert sequence generated by triggering IDS is called an attack scenario sequence, which is recorded as ASS, where $ASS = \{ma_1, ma_2, \ldots, ma_k\}$, $ma_i(1 \leq i < j \leq k)$ represents the i-th meta alert, and satisfies $ma_i.\,timestamp < ma_j.\,timestamp(1 \leq i \leq j \leq k)$.

After the alert aggregation process, L alert sequences (AS) are obtained. We generate several ASS from each AS according to the following causal association rules.

Set two different meta alerts, A and B. If A and B meet the alert causality, one of the following rules must be observed:

1. $\left\{ \begin{array}{l} A[srcIPs] = B[srcIPs], A[dstIPs] = B[dstIPs], \\ A[srcPorts] = B[srcPorts], A[dstPorts] = B[dstPorts] \end{array} \right\}$
2. $\{A[dstIPs] = B[srcIPs], A[dstPort] = B[srcPort]\}$

After filtering L ASs by causal association rules, m ASSs are generated. $M = \{ASS_1, ASS_2, \ldots, ASS_m\}$, A Bayesian network attack graph model for the M set will be constructed to improve the accuracy and robustness of the prediction.

Construction of Bayesian Network Attack Graph (BAG)

A Bayesian network is a directed acyclic graph in which a node is a random variable, and the edges of the connected nodes refer to the interdependencies between the nodes. The classification of nodes in a Bayesian network mainly includes: parent node, child node, leaf node, root node, and neighbor node.

Each node corresponds to a Conditional Probability Table (CPT). The root node does not depend on any node which is called the prior probability distribution table.

The probability that other nodes occur depends on the conditional probability distribution table composed of the values of their parent nodes.

Ω is a set of given random variables (S1, S2, S3… , Sn) whose joint probability is given by a chain rule, following the formula (1) where all the parent nodes of the variable are $pa(s_i)$.

$$p(\Omega) = p(X_1, X_2, X_3, \ldots, X_n) = \prod_{i=0}^{n} p(X_i/pa(X_i)) \tag{1}$$

Definition 5: The Bayesian Attack Diagram (BAG) is a 4-tuple (S, τ, ε, P) [18], where:

a. S represents all nodes in the attack graph
b. τ represents the reachability between two nodes, which means whether there is an attack path. The parent node of node Si is defined as formula (2)

$$Pa[S_i] = \{S_j \in S | (S_j, S_i) \in \tau\} \tag{2}$$

c. ε represents the relationship between the node and its parent, broken down into a binary group $<S_j, d_j>$, $d_j \in \{AND, OR\}$. $d_j = AND$ represents that an attack of state S_j needs to satisfy all the parent nodes whose state is 1, which means $S_j = 1 \rightarrow \forall S_i \in Pa[S_j], S_i = 1$, $d_j = OR$ represents that an attack of state S_j satisfies that one of the parent nodes has a state of 1, which mean $S_j = 1 \rightarrow \exists S_i \in Pa[S_j], S_i = 1$.
d. P represents a set of conditionally independent probability distribution functions, each of which has a Local Conditional Probability Distribution (LCPD).

Definition 6: (LCPD function) Assume that BAG = (S, τ, ε, P) is a Bayesian network attack graph, and S_j is a node in BAG. Assume that v_i is the probability of attacking S_j through S_i successfully. The conditional probability of node S_j depends on the ε relationship between the node S_j and all parent nodes. Such as formula (3) and formula (4).

When

$$d_j = AND, \Pr(S_j | Pa[S_j]) = \begin{cases} 0, \exists S_i \in Pa[S_j] | S_i = 0 \\ \Pr(\bigcap_{S_i=1} v_i), other \end{cases} \tag{3}$$

When

$$d_j = OR, \Pr(S_j | Pa[S_j]) = \begin{cases} 0, \forall S_i \in Pa[S_j] | S_i = 0 \\ \Pr(\bigcup_{S_i=1} v_i), other \end{cases} \tag{4}$$

3.2 Online Mode

The online mode is optimized and supplemented for the offline model. Due to the large number of IDS alert logs, we can't get a complete and efficient attack scenario correlation model through one modeling. The online model is a method of continuous iteration to perfect the optimization of the model, the structure of which is shown in Fig. 5.

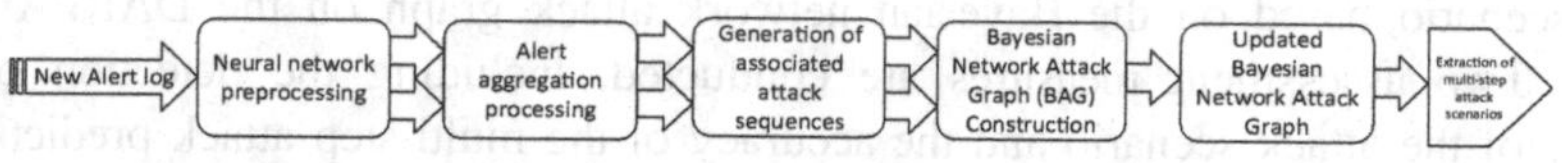

Fig. 5. Flowchart of online mode

The online mode is mainly for two aspects, one is the parameter update of the neural network in the data preprocessing stage, and the other is to update the overall Bayesian network attack graph (BAG).

Neural Network Parameter Update

The specific steps for parameter update are as follows:

1. For IDS alert logs in online mode, screen out the logs with no tag and incomplete alert attribute.
2. For the neural network, set the hyper-parameter of the network, such as: the learning rate of the network, the size of the network input (batch-size), and so on.
3. The alert log data is sent to the network in batches as batch-size, and the parameters are updated by the gradient descent method.
4. After the parameters are updated, the accuracy of the neural network is improved which makes it more accurately to track the real alert logs.

Bayesian Network Attack Graph Update

The online alert logs remove a large number of false alerts after passing through the neural network. After the alert aggregation and the causal attack sequence generation operation, a new ASS and an AS are obtained.

The newly generated ASS and AS are merged with the existing ASS and AS, and the 4-tuple (S, τ, ε, P) is updated respectively. Process is as follows:

1. For S, if a new element appears in the new AS sequence, the node represented by S in the BAG is updated.
2. For τ, update the attack path for the BAG graph nodes corresponding to the multi-step attack sequences in the new ASS.
3. For ε, update the dual group <Sj, dj> of the relationship between the node and its parent in the BAG.
4. For P, the probability of each alert node is affected by the probability of its parent node, and the posterior probability of the parent node corresponding to each node is updated, thereby updating the Conditional Probability Table (CPT) of the corresponding node.

After the iteration and update of the model by the online mode, the root node and the leaf node in the BAG are fixed, and finally all possible multi-step attack scenarios are found.

4 Experiment

This section presents the experimental results obtained by the proposed multi-step attack scenario based on the Bayesian network attack graph on the DARPA 2000 dataset. Two assessment measures are conducted, including the detection of the integrity of the attack scenario and the accuracy of the multi-step attack prediction.

For this model, we set the hyper parameters which are shown in Table 1.

Table 1. The parameters of our model for experiments

Parameter name	Parameter value
Neural Network batch-size	128
Neural Network learning-rate	0.01
Neural Network epoch	100
T	1 h
Time Window	5 min

The case of generating mete-Alert after passing through the neural network is shown in Table 2.

Table 2. Alert information

Sum Alerts	3964
After neural network remaining alarms	1129
Meta-Alerts	221

Divide the meta-Alert in Table 2 into different phases, which are shown in Table 3.

Table 3. Different step in Multi-step attack

Step1	IPSweep, ICMP PING, ICMP Echo Reply
Step2	Sadmind Ping, RCP portmap sadming port query udp request, RPC portmap sadmind request UDP
Step3	Admind, RPC sadmind query with root credentials attempt UDP
Step4	RPC sadmind UDP NETMGT_PROC_SERVICE CLIENT_DOMAIN overflow attempt
Step5	RSERVICES rsh root

In the first step, the attacker first probes the surviving host in the network and generates a large number of Echo requests. The second step attacker sends an RCP request to the victim. The third step attacker attempts to establish a UDP connection. The fourth step performs a buffer overflow attack, and the fifth step attempts to obtain root privileges. After the fifth step, the attacker remotely logs in to install the mstream daemon preparing for DDos, and finally initiates a DDos attack. During the experiment, analyze the flow in the data after the fifth step of the attack referring to [19–22], add in the BAG and replace the process with a dotted line. The result is shown in Fig. 6.

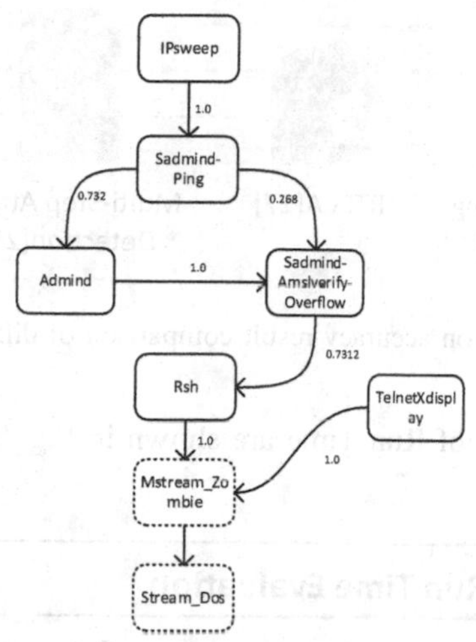

Fig. 6. BAG of the LLDDoS from DARPA 2000

Extract the possible multi-step attack scenarios from Fig. 6 which are shown in Fig. 7.

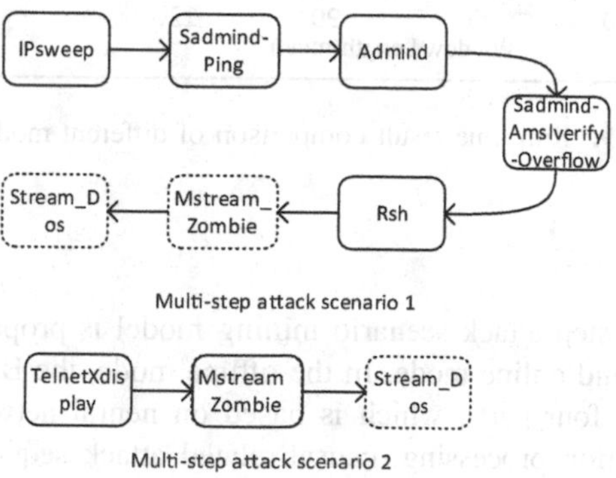

Fig. 7. Multi-step attack scenario results

Comparative Results:
Use the Predictive accuracy and Run Time as evaluation indicators, The comparison results of Prediction Accuracy are shown in Fig. 8.

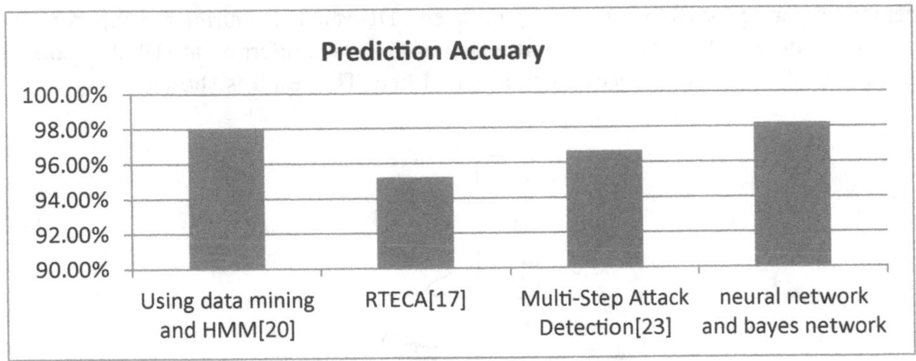

Fig. 8. Prediction accuracy result comparison of different models

The comparison results of Run Time are shown in Fig. 9.

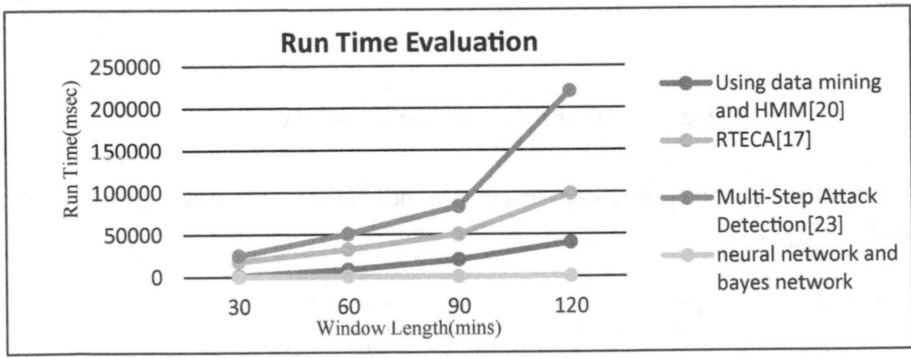

Fig. 9. Run time result comparison of different models

5 Conclusion

In this paper, a multi-step attack scenario mining model is proposed, which has two modes: offline mode and online mode. In the offline mode, the BAG for the IDS alert logs is constructed in four parts, which is based on neural network-based alert processing, alert aggregation processing, causal-related attack sequence generation, and Bayesian network attack graph (BAG) construction. The neural network-based alert pre-processing is to extract the real alerts from the original alert logs of the IDS mixed with the false alerts by using the trained neural network. the alert aggregation processing is to convert the true alert into a meta-alert and alert sequence in batches to reduce the number of alerts. Causal-related attack sequence generation is to generate a correlation sequence based on the association rule for the meta-alert in each alert sequence, and finally generate BAG. In the online mode, we use the online IDS alert logs to iterate and update the neural network and improve the BAG. After multiple online modes, a multi-step attack scenario that may occur is extracted from the complete BAG. After comparison experiments, it is concluded that the accuracy of the extracted multi-step attack scenario is over 98%. And in the case of higher accuracy, the running time is greatly shortened compared to [17, 20, 23].

Acknowledgements. This work was supported by The National Key Research and Development Program of China under Grant 2016YFB0800903, the NSF of China (U1636112, U1636212).

References

1. Zhang, R., Liu, G., Liu, J., et al.: Analysis of message attacks in aviation data-link communication. IEEE Access **6**, 455–463 (2018)
2. Cheng, J., Xu, R., Tang, X., Sheng, V.S., Cai, C.: An abnormal network flow feature sequence prediction approach for DDoS attacks detection in big data environment. CMC Comput. Mater. Continua **55**(1), 095–119 (2018)
3. Cheang, C.F., Wang, Y., Cai, Z., Xu, G.: Multi-VMs intrusion detection for cloud security using dempster-shafer theory. CMC Comput. Mater. Continua **57**(2), 297–306 (2018)
4. Wang, Y., Cheng, L., Ma, X.: A survey of threat behavior detection techniques using alert correlation. J. Natl. Univ. Def. Technol. **39**(5) (2017)
5. Valeur, F., Vigna, G., Kruegel, C., Kemmerer, R.: Comprehensive approach to intrusion detection alert correlation. IEEE Trans. Dependable Secur. Comput. **1**(3), 146–169 (2004)
6. Lin, Z.W., Li, S., Ma, Y.: Real-time intrusion alert correlation system based on prerequisites and consequence. In: Proceedings of Wireless Communications Networking and Mobile Computing, pp. 1–5 (2010)
7. Liu, L., Zheng, K.F., Yang, Y.X.: An intrusion alert correlation approach based on finite automata. In: Proceedings of Communications and Intelligence Information Security, pp. 80–83 (2010)
8. Wang, C.H., Yang, J.M.: Adaptive feature-weighted alert correlation system applicable in cloud environment. In: Proceedings of Asia Joint Conference on Information Security, pp. 41–47 (2013)
9. Ghasemi Gol, M., Ghaemi-Bafghi, A.A.: New alert correlation framework based on entropy. In: Proceedings of International Conference on Computer and Knowledge Engineering, pp. 184–189 (2013)
10. Shittu, R., Healing, A., Ghanea-Hercock, R., et al.: Intrusion alert prioritisation and attack detection using post-correlation analysis. Comput. Secur. **50**, 1–15 (2015)
11. Zhang, R., Huo, Y., Liu, J., et al.: Constructing APT attack scenarios based on intrusion kill chain and fuzzy clustering. Secur. Commun. Netw. **2017**(2), 1–9 (2017)
12. Elshoush, H.T., Osman, I.M.: Alert correlation in collaborative intelligent intrusion detection systems-a survey. Appl. Soft Comput. **11**(7), 4349–4365 (2011)
13. Mei, H., Gong, J., Zhang, M.: Research on discovering multi-step attack patterns based on clustering IDS alert sequences. J. Commun. **32**(5), 63–69 (2011). (in Chinese)

14. Tian, Z., Zhang, Y., Zhang, W., et al.: An adaptive alert correlation method based on pattern mining and clustering analysis. J. Comput. Res. Dev. **46**(8), 1304–1315 (2009). (in Chinese)
15. Xiao, S., Zhang, Y., Liu, X., et al.: Alert fusion based on cluster and correlation analysis. In: Proceedings of the International Conference on Convergence and Hybrid Information Technology, Daejeon, South Korea, pp. 163–168 (2008)
16. Yu, Y., Zhang, S., Lv, L.: Information security alert multi-level fusion model. Comput. Eng. Appl. **42**(29), 154–156 (2006)
17. Ramaki, A.A., Amini, M., Atani, R.E.: RTECA: real time episode correlation algorithm for multi-step attack scenarios detection. Comput. Secur. **49**, 206–219 (2015)
18. Poolsappasit, N., Dewri, R., Ray, I.: Dynamic security risk management using bayesian attack graphs. IEEE Trans. Dependable Secur. Comput. **9**(1), 61–74 (2012)
19. GhasemiGol, M., Ghaemi Bafghi, A.: E correlator: an entropy based alert correlation system. Secur. Commun. Netw. **8**(5), 822–836 (2015)
20. Farhad, H., AmirHaeri, M., Khansari, M.: Alert correlation and prediction using data mining and HMM. ISC Int. J. Inf. Secur. **3**(2), 77–101 (2011)
21. Fredj, O.B.: A realistic graph based alert correlation system. Secur. Commun. Netw. **8**, 2477–2493 (2015)
22. Ahmadinejad, S.H., Jalili, S., Abadi, M.: A hybrid model for correlating alerts of known and unknown attack scenarios and updating attack graphs. Comput. Netw. **55**(9), 2221–2240 (2011)
23. Soleimani, M., Ghorbani, A.: Multi-layer episode filtering for the multi-step attack detection. Comput. Commun. **35**, 1368–1379 (2012)

A Comparative Study of Machine Learning Classifiers for Network Intrusion Detection

Farrukh Aslam Khan[1](✉) and Abdu Gumaei[2]

[1] Center of Excellence in Information Assurance, King Saud University, Riyadh, Saudi Arabia
fakhan@ksu.edu.sa

[2] Department of Computer Science, College of Computer and Information Sciences, King Saud University, Riyadh, Saudi Arabia
abdugumaei@gmail.com

Abstract. The network intrusion detection system (NIDS) has become an essential tool for detecting attacks in computer networks and protecting the critical information and systems. The effectiveness of an NIDS is usually measured by the high number of detected attacks and the low number of false alarms. Machine learning techniques are widely used for building robust intrusion detection systems, which adapt with the continuous changes in the network attacks. However, a comparison of such machine learning techniques needs more investigation to show their efficiency and appropriateness for detecting sophisticated malicious attacks. This study compares the most popular machine learning methods for intrusion detection in terms of accuracy, precision, recall, and training time cost. This comparison can provide a guideline for developers to choose the appropriate method when developing an effective NIDS. The evaluation of the adopted baseline machine learning classifiers is conducted on two public datasets, i.e., KDD99 and UNSW-NB15. The time taken to build a model for each classifier is also evaluated to measure their efficiency. The experimental results show that the Decision Tree (DT), Random Forests (RF), Hoeffding Tree (HT), and K-Nearest Neighbors (KNN) classifiers show higher accuracy with reasonable training time in the 10-fold cross validation test mode compared to other machine learning classifiers examined in this study.

Keywords: Network intrusion detection · Machine learning techniques · Computer networks · KDD99 dataset · UNSW-NB15 dataset

1 Introduction

The network intrusion detection system (NIDS) is the second line of defense in computer networks and the Internet. It follows up and works together with other security tools such as firewall and popular data encryption algorithms [1] (See Fig. 1). The effort to develop a robust NIDS for detecting network attacks and malicious activities is still the focus of attention for many researchers and developers. A number of techniques and methods have been proposed in the past few years for protecting networks against malicious activities, threats, and security attacks. For example, Gong and Sarac [2], Murugesan

X. Sun et al. (Eds.): ICAIS 2019, LNCS 11633, pp. 75–86, 2019.
https://doi.org/10.1007/978-3-030-24265-7_7

et al. [3], and Song and Perrig [4] proposed some techniques for IP trace back. Crotti et al. [5], Nguyen and Armitage [6], and Callado et al. [7] proposed some techniques for IP traffic classification. Zhou and Lang [8], Dharmapurikar and Lockwood [9], Chen and Leneutre [10], Das et al. [11], Hu et al. [12], and Mabu et al. [13] implemented and discussed a set of different methods for network intrusion detection studying advantages and disadvantages with the performance of these methods. Hadlington [14] addressed and explained the human factors that cause some issues of cybersecurity violations. However, the continuous changes of attack patterns make machine learning

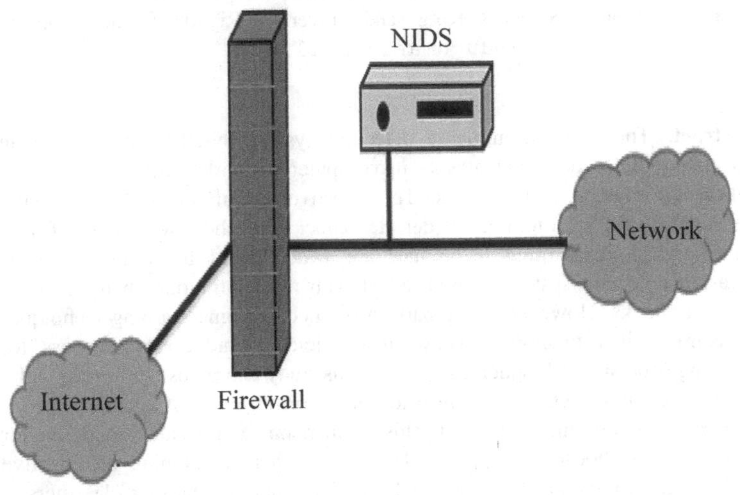

Fig. 1. NIDS as a second line of defense.

techniques appropriate to adapt for detecting the variants of sophisticated attacks.

In recent years, machine learning techniques have been utilized to detect network attacks, malicious executables, and threats [15, 16]. Machine learning algorithms are able to give computer applications the capability to learn patterns of attacks from historical network traffic and detect the modified or even unknown patterns of attacks in network traffic [17].

Customarily, machine learning approach is used as a data analysis tool to develop automatic methods for classification [18, 19], prediction [20], decision making [21], and forecasting [22]. In this context, several studies have investigated the ability of machine learning techniques for the problem of network intrusion detection. Solanki and Dhamdhere [23] measured the accuracy of support vector machine (SVM) and decision tree (C4.5) methods. They tested the two methods on a dataset of four different attacks and found that the accuracy of C4.5 was better than that of SVM. In [24], the authors proposed a study to compare a set of machine learning classifiers for detecting the most popular network attacks and determining the best classifier for each class of attacks. They found that most classifiers have a good accuracy for detecting the denial of service (DoS) attack. Gao et al. [25] proposed a method for analyzing normal and abnormal network traffic using hidden Markov model to detect intrusions. They conducted different experiments achieving 63.2% of the detection accuracy. In [8], the authors proposed an approach to use a Fourier transform method to classify periodic patterns of network traffic into normal or abnormal for detecting intrusions and abnormal behaviors. Another method was proposed by Gomez and Dasgupta [26] for network intrusion detection using fuzzy logic.

Ye et al. [27] proposed a multiple audit technique using frequency occurred in network data traffic. Unfortunately, the data used for testing in this study was pure, simple and did not consider real situations of network traffic. Furthermore, Goonatilake et al. [28] applied a Chi-square test to detect abnormal activities of network traffic and developed a network intrusion detection system. The work proposed in [29] compared five architectures of neural networks for network intrusion detection and analyzed their performance. This work shows that the conjugate gradient descent and quasi-Newton achieved better results in terms of detection rates. The authors in [30–33] used swarm intelligence with machine learning techniques to detect network intrusions.

Few comparative studies on some machine learning methods have been introduced for botnet detection [34, 35] and network defense [36]. However, the effectiveness of machine learning methods on network intrusion detection still needs more investigation in terms of accuracy and time cost of training. In this work, we test and compare the most popular machine learning techniques for network intrusion detection on two public datasets, i.e., KDD99 [37] and UNSW-NB15 [38]. Our goal and contribution is to use a set of measures to evaluate the performance of these techniques for network intrusion detection in order to guide researchers and developers to select the appropriate technique based on its accuracy and efficiency. This study differs from all previous comparative studies in that it provides a comprehensive investigation to show the ability of the most popular machine learning classifiers to detect both the old and new network attacks.

The remainder of the paper is organized as follows: Sect. 2 explains the main phases and steps of the proposed methodology. Experiments and discussion on the results are presented in Sect. 3. Finally, a conclusion of the proposed work is presented in Sect. 4.

2 Proposed Methodology

The proposed methodology for benchmarking machine learning classifiers for intrusion detection consists of two main phases: training phase and testing phase. In both phases, two key steps are basically used before applying the classifier models. The inputs of the methodology are the training and testing datasets of network traffic features. The outputs are the results of evaluation metrics for both 10-fold cross validation test mode and supplied test mode. Figure 2 shows the phases and steps of the proposed methodology.

The following subsection describes the main steps in both phases of the proposed methodology.

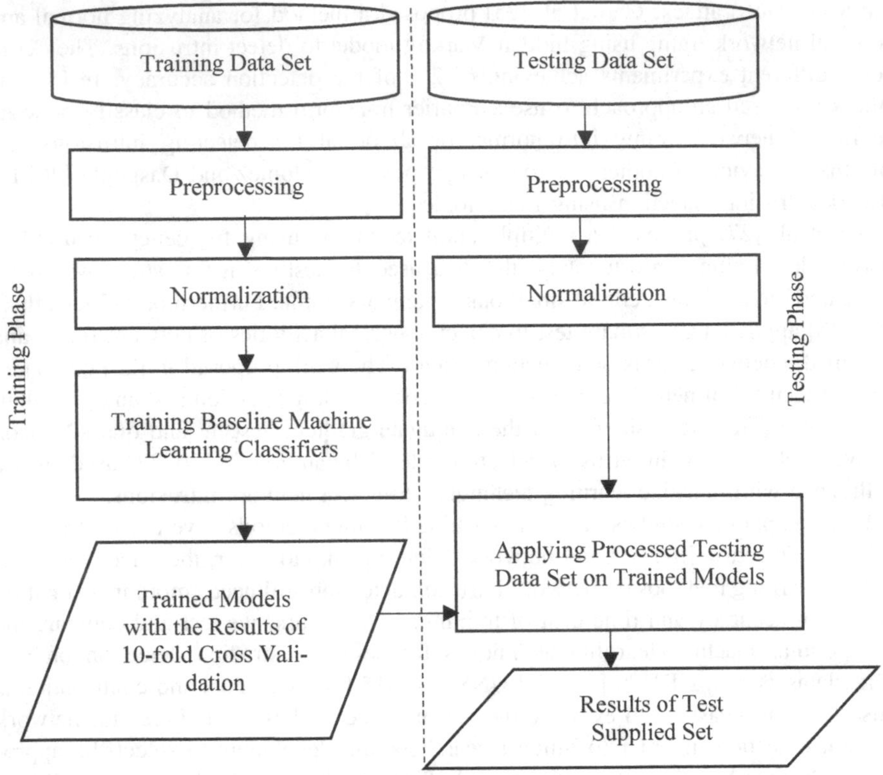

Fig. 2. Proposed methodology.

2.1 Preprocessing

Preprocessing of network traffic features play an essential role for the intrusion detection task. It is the initial step in many data mining applications. This step consists of two main tasks: the nominal-to-numeric feature conversion and the feature redundancy removal. First, the nominal-to-numeric data conversion is applied on the used datasets. Then, the redundant records of the dataset features are removed. The reason of using this step is to convert the feature values into numeric format, which is acceptable for classifiers, and eliminate the effects of redundant features on the performance of these classifiers.

In our methodology, KDD99 and UNSW-NB15 datasets are subjected to the preprocessing step. The KDD99 dataset contains 494,021 records for training and 73269 records for testing; both of them contain 38 numeric features, 3 non-numeric features, and 1 non-numeric value that represents the normality of the traffic (normal or abnormal). The UNSW-NB15 dataset consists of 175341 records for training and 82332 records for testing. These records consist of 3 non-numeric features, 39 numeric features, and 1 feature for the type of traffic (normal or abnormal). After applying this step, the redundant records in the KDD99 dataset are removed and these records are reduced to 145,586 instances. The non-numeric features of both the datasets are converted into numeric features.

2.2 Normalization

Normalization of traffic features is also important to transform the independent feature values into a specific range. In the fields of data analyzing and data mining, it is known as feature normalization. Since the features extracted from network traffic have very large values, the normalization step is used to suppress the effect of these values. A min-max normalization technique is utilized to normalize these values linearly in the range between 0 and 1, which can be computed as:

$$d_{i,j} = \frac{d_{i,j} - \min(d_{i,j})}{\max(d_{i,j}) - \min(d_{i,j})} \quad (1)$$

where $d_{i,j}$ represents the feature value in the row i and column j of the dataset d.

2.3 Training Machine Learning Classifiers

In this step, we train a set of baseline classifiers with different kernel functions to achieve the goal of our study. These classifiers are K-Nearest Neighbors (KNN), Naïve Bayes (NB), Naïve Bayes with Kernel Estimator (NB-KE), Support Vector Machine with Polynomial function kernel (SVM-POLY), Support Vector Machine with Radial Basis Function kernel (SVM-RBF), Sequential Minimal Optimization (SMO) for training the SVM classifier, Decision Tree (DT), Decision Stump (DS), Hoeffding Tree (HT), and Random Forests (RF). For training, the adopted classifiers are trained on the training datasets to build trained models, which will be used in the next step.

2.4 Testing Machine Learning Classifiers

This step is responsible for testing the trained models on the unseen test dataset. It is a straightforward step performed to determine the success of machine learning classifiers used in our study. For each input network traffic feature, there is an actual class label.

First, we input the feature values of a test example from the testing dataset into the trained classifier models to get the classification results; then we compare the actual class label with the classified label. If they match, then we sign it as correctly classified and move to another test example. If they do not match, then we sign it as incorrectly classified. During this step, we setup a set of performance metrics for the network intrusion detection problem.

3 Experiments and Discussion

The experiments are conducted using a popular machine learning tool called Weka (Waikato Environment for Knowledge Analysis) [39], on a laptop with a 64-bit Windows 10 operating system, an Intel CPU processor of 2.0 GHz Core i7-4510U, and a RAM of 8 GB. The public KDD99 and UNSW-NB15 datasets are used as input to the proposed methodology in our experiments. As mentioned above, the KDD99 dataset has 145,586 records for training and 73,269 records for testing, while the

UNSW-NB15 dataset consists of 175,341 records for training and 82,332 for testing. Tables 1 and 2 show the distribution of the training dataset according to traffic's behavior, which may be normal or abnormal, and the type of attacks. In order to test and evaluate the adopted machine learning classifiers, these classifiers are first trained on the training datasets, and then the testing datasets are used for evaluation in the experiments.

Table 1. The distribution of attacks in the KDD99 training dataset.

Class name	No. of instances	Percentage (%)
Normal	87,832	60.33
Abnormal	57,754	39.67
Total	145,586	100

Table 2. The distribution of attack types in the UNSW-NB15 training dataset.

Class name	No. of instances	Percentage (%)
Normal	56,000	31.94
Abnormal	119,341	68.06
Total	175,341	100

The experimental results are evaluated based on three metrics. These three metrics are the accuracy, precision, and recall (sensitivity).

$$Accuracy = \frac{(TP + TN)}{(TP + TN + FP + FN)} \tag{2}$$

$$Precision = \frac{TP}{(TP + FP)} \tag{3}$$

$$Recall = \frac{TP}{(TP + FN)} \tag{4}$$

where TP and TN are the true positive and true negative values; FP and FN are the false positive and false negative values, respectively.

After preparing the training and testing datasets for evaluating the baseline machine learning classifiers, the accuracy, precision, and recall are computed for both training and testing phases.

3.1 Results of 10-Fold Cross Validation Test Mode

The 10-fold cross validation test mode is utilized to evaluate the model's performance in the training phase. Here, we divide the training dataset into 10-folds. Each fold is used for testing and the other 9-folds are used for training. The results of these 10-folds are averaged to get the final result. Table 3 shows the results of evaluation metrics on the KDD99 dataset to classify the normal and abnormal behaviors of network traffic based on the 10-fold cross validation test mode. In all the tables, the bold font indicates the top four highest results achieved by the evaluated classifiers.

Table 3. Results of evaluation metrics of 10-fold cross validation for classifying normal and abnormal traffic of KDD99 dataset.

Classifier model	Accuracy (%)	Weighted average of precision	Weighted average of recall
KNN	**99.8393**	**0.998**	**0.998**
NB	96.589	0.966	0.966
NB-KE	97.337	0.974	0.973
SVM-POLY	97.214	0.973	0.972
SVM-RBF	98.4367	0.984	0.984
SMO	98.8289	0.988	0.988
DT	**99.8661**	**0.999**	**0.999**
DS	95.7757	0.960	0.958
HT	**99.2293**	**0.992**	**0.992**
RF	**99.9437**	**0.999**	**0.999**

Table 4 illustrates the time taken to build models of classifiers in the training phase for normal and abnormal classification of KDD99 dataset.

Table 4. Time taken to build a classifier model in the training phase for normal and abnormal classification of KDD99 dataset

Classifier model	Time taken to build a classifier model (in seconds)
KNN	0.06
NB	1.03
NB-KE	1.01
SVM-Poly	228.88
SVM-RBF	198.69
SMO	789.77
DT	40.78
DS	2.15
HT	5.5
RF	128.51

Table 5 shows the results of evaluation metrics of 10-fold cross validation on the UNSW-NB15 dataset to classify normal and abnormal traffic.

Table 5. Results of evaluation metrics of 10-fold cross validation for classifying normal and abnormal traffic of UNSW-NB15 dataset.

Classifier model	Accuracy (%)	Weighted average of precision	Weighted average of recall
KNN	**93.7134**	**0.937**	**0.937**
NB	75.749	0.831	0.757
NB-KE	79.9157	0.848	0.799
SVM-POLY	70.44	0.707	0.704
SVM-RBF	81.708	0.817	0.817
SMO	83.588	0.837	0.836
DT	**95.5413**	**0.955**	**0.955**
DS	92.0629	0.928	0.921
HT	**93.5349**	**0.935**	**0.935**
RF	**96.0791**	**0.961**	**0.961**

Table 6 illustrates the time taken to build a classifier model for normal and abnormal classification of UNSW-NB15 dataset in the training phase.

Table 6. Time taken to build a classifier model for normal and abnormal classification of UNSW-NB15 dataset in the training phase.

Classifier model	Time taken to build a classifier model (in Seconds)
KNN	0.18
NB	1.84
NB-KE	3.06
SVM-Poly	793.48
SVM-RBF	748.36
SMO	531.11
DT	76.13
DS	3.95
HT	8.27
RF	542.97

3.2 Results of Supplied Test Set Mode

In this section, we evaluate the benchmark classifiers on the testing datasets as supplied test sets. Tables 7 and 8 show the results of normal and abnormal classification using the supplied KDD99 and UNSW-NB15 test sets of the testing phase.

The values of precision for each classifier in Tables 3, 5, 7, and 8 evaluate the percentage of network traffic intrusions that were correctly classified, whereas the value of recall evaluates the percentage of actual intrusions in the network traffic that were

Table 7. Results of evaluation metrics for normal and abnormal classification using supplied KDD99 test set of the testing phase.

Classifier model	Accuracy (%)	Weighted average of precision	Weighted average of recall
KNN	**96.0065**	**0.962**	**0.960**
NB	94.6799	0.947	0.947
NB-KE	94.4287	0.948	0.944
SVM-Poly	94.0411	0.943	0.940
SVM-RBF	94.9474	0.951	0.949
SMO	**95.1125**	**0.952**	**0.951**
DT	**96.218**	**0.962**	**0.962**
DS	93.9811	0.944	0.940
HT	92.6586	0.926	0.927
RF	**96.7926**	**0.969**	**0.968**

Table 8. Results of evaluation metrics for normal and abnormal classification using supplied UNSW-NB15 test set of the testing phase.

Classifier model	Accuracy (%)	Weighted average of precision	Weighted average of recall
KNN	**84.4872**	0.855	**0.845**
NB	76.3907	0.782	0.764
NB-KE	76.2219	0.768	0.762
SVM-Poly	68.3379	0.689	0.683
SVM-RBF	83.2216	0.835	0.832
SMO	**85.3411**	**0.863**	**0.853**
DT	**84.554**	**0.864**	**0.846**
DS	76.6324	0.835	0.766
HT	59.4423	0.763	0.594
RF	**83.6333**	**0.869**	**0.836**

correctly classified. From all tables, the results reveal that DT, RF, HT, and KNN classifiers achieve high results in the 10-fold cross validation test mode of both datasets compared to the other classifiers, while the DT, RF, SMO, and KNN achieve high results in the supplied test mode of both datasets compared to the other classifiers.

4 Conclusion

In this paper, a comprehensive comparative study of machine learning classifiers for network intrusion detection is presented. The adopted classifiers in this study were KNN, NB, NB-KE, SVM-POLY, SVM-RBF, SMO, DT, DS, HT, and RF. The aim of this study was to evaluate the performance of these classifiers for network intrusion detection, thereby guiding the researchers and developers to select the appropriate technique based on its accuracy and efficiency. The proposed methodology consists of two phases: training and testing. In both phases, two main steps are used before applying the classifier models. The inputs of the methodology are the training and testing datasets of network traffic features, and the outputs are the results of evaluation metrics for both 10-fold cross validation test mode and supplied test set mode. The evaluation of the adopted classifiers is conducted with two publicly available datasets, i.e., KDD99 and UNSW-NB15. The results show that the accuracy results obtained by DT, RF, HT and KNN classifiers are the highest with reasonable time cost of building the classifier model in the 10-fold cross validation test mode, while the DT, RF, SMO, and KNN classifiers achieve high results in the supplied test mode of both datasets compared to the other machine learning classifiers.

References

1. Li, G., Yan, Z., Fu, Y., Chen, H.: Data fusion for network intrusion detection: a review. Secur. Commun. Netw. **2018**, 16 pages (2018)
2. Gong, C., Sarac, K.: A more practical approach for single-packet IP traceback using packet logging and marking. IEEE Trans. Parallel Distrib. Syst. **19**(10), 1310–1324 (2008)
3. Murugesan, V., Shalinie, M., Neethimani, N.: A brief survey of IP traceback methodologies. Acta Polytech. Hung. **11**(9), 197–216 (2014)
4. Song, D.X., Perrig, A.: Advanced and authenticated marking schemes for IP traceback. In: Proceedings of IEEE Conference on Computer Communications (INFOCOM 2001), Anchorage, Alaska, USA, pp. 878–886 (2001)
5. Crotti, M., Gringoli, F., Pelosato, P., Salgarelli, L.: A statistical approach to IP-level classification of network traffic. In: Proceedings of 2006 IEEE International Conference on Communications (ICC 2006), Istanbul, Turkey, pp. 170–176 (2006)
6. Nguyen, T.T., Armitage, G.: A survey of techniques for internet traffic classification using machine learning. IEEE Commun. Surv. Tutorials **10**(4), 56–76 (2008)
7. Callado, A., et al.: A survey on internet traffic identification. IEEE Commun. Surv. Tutorials **11**(3), 37–52 (2009)
8. Zhou, M., Lang, S.-d.: Mining frequency content of network traffic for intrusion detection. In: Proceedings of IASTED International Conference on Communication, Network and Information Security (CNIS 2003), New York, USA, pp. 101–107 (2003)
9. Dharmapurikar, S., Lockwood, J.W.: Fast and scalable pattern matching for network intrusion detection systems. IEEE J. Sel. Areas Commun. **24**(10), 1781–1792 (2006)
10. Chen, L., Leneutre, J.: A game theoretical framework on intrusion detection in heterogeneous networks. IEEE Trans. Inf. Forensics Secur. **4**(2), 165–178 (2009)
11. Das, A., Nguyen, D., Zambreno, J., Memik, G., Choudhary, A.: An FPGA-based network intrusion detection architecture. IEEE Trans. Inf. Forensics Secur. **3**(1), 118–132 (2008)
12. Hu, W., Hu, W., Maybank, S.: AdaBoost-based algorithm for network intrusion detection. IEEE Trans. Syst. Man Cybern. Part B Cybern. **38**(2), 577–583 (2008)
13. Mabu, S., Chen, C., Lu, N., Shimada, K., Hirasawa, K.: An intrusion-detection model based on fuzzy class-association-rule mining using genetic network programming. IEEE Trans. Syst. Man Cybern. Part C Appl. Rev. **41**(1), 130–139 (2011)
14. Hadlington, L.: Human factors in cybersecurity; examining the link between internet addition, impulsivity, attitudes towards cybersecurity, and risk cybersecurity behaviors. Heliyon **3**(7), e00346 (2017)

15. Kolter, J.Z., Maloof, M.A.: Learning to detect and classify malicious executables in the wild. J. Mach. Learn. Res. **7**, 2721–2744 (2006)
16. Siddiqui, S., Khan, M.S., Ferens, K., Kinsner, W.: Detecting advanced persistent threats using fractal dimension based machine learning classification. In: Proceedings of the 2016 International Workshop on Security and Privacy Analytics (IWSPA 2016), New Orleans, Louisiana, USA, pp. 64–69 (2016)
17. Mukkamala, S., Janoski, G., Sung, A.: Intrusion detection using neural networks and support vector machines. In: Proceedings of the 2002 International Joint Conference on Neural Networks, IJCNN 2002, vol. 2, pp. 1702–1707. IEEE (2002)
18. Gumaei, A., Sammouda, R., Al-Salman, A.M., Alsanad, A.: An effective palmprint recognition approach for visible and multispectral sensor images. Sensors **18**(5), 1575 (2018)
19. Gumaei, A., Sammouda, R., Al-Salman, A.M.S., Alsanad, A.: An improved multispectral palmprint recognition system using autoencoder with regularized extreme learning machine. Comput. Intell. Neurosci. **2018**, 13 pages (2018)
20. Weiss, S.M., Kulikowski, C.A.: Computer Systems That Learn: Classification and Prediction Methods from Statistics, Neural Nets, Machine Learning, and Expert Systems. Morgan Kaufmann Publishers Inc., San Francisco (1991)
21. Pal, S.K., Skowron, A.: Rough-Fuzzy Hybridization: A New Trend in Decision Making. Springer, Singapore (1999)
22. Alsanad, A.: Forecasting daily demand of orders using random forest classifier. Int. J. Comput. Sci. Netw. Secur. **18**(4), 79–83 (2018)
23. Solanki, M., Dhamdhere, V.: Intrusion detection system using means of data mining by using C 4.5 algorithm. Int. J. Appl. Innov. Eng. Manag. (IJAIEM) **4**(5), 2319–2484 (2015)
24. Nguyen, H.A., Choi, D.: Application of data mining to network intrusion detection: classifier selection model. In: Ma, Y., Choi, D., Ata, S. (eds.) Challenges for Next Generation Network Operations and Service Management (APNOMS 2008). LNCS, vol. 5297, pp. 399–408. Springer, Heidelberg (2008). https://doi.org/10.1007/978-3-540-88623-5_41
25. Gao, B., Ma, H.-Y., Yang, Y.-H.: HMMs (Hidden Markov models) based on anomaly intrusion detection method. In: Proceedings of 2002 International Conference on Machine Learning and Cybernetics, Beijing, China (2002)
26. Gomez, J., Dasgupta, D.: Evolving fuzzy classifiers for intrusion detection. In: Proceedings of the 2002 IEEE Workshop on Information Assurance, New York, USA (2001)
27. Ye, N., Li, X., Chen, Q., Emran, S., Xu, M.: Probabilistic techniques for intrusion detection based on computer audit data. IEEE Trans. Syst. Man Cybern. Part A Syst. Hum. **31**, 266–274 (2001)
28. Goonatilake, R., Herath, A., Herath, S., Herath, S., Herath, J.: Intrusion detection using the chi-square goodness-of-fit test for information assurance, network, forensics and software security. J. Comput. Sci. Coll. **23**(1), 255–263 (2007)
29. Dao, V.N., Vemuri, V.R.: Computer network intrusion detection: a comparison of neural network methods. Differ. Equ. Dyn. Syst. **10**(1&2), 201–214 (2002)
30. Malik, A.J., Khan, F.A.: A hybrid technique using binary particle swarm optimization and decision tree pruning for network intrusion detection. Cluster Comput. (2017). https://doi.org/10.1007/s10586-017-0971-8
31. Malik, A.J., Shahzad, W., Khan, F.A.: Network intrusion detection using hybrid binary PSO and random forests algorithm. Secur. Commun. Netw. **8**(16), 2646–2660 (2015)
32. Malik, A.J., Khan, F.A.: A hybrid technique using multi-objective particle swarm optimization and random forests for PROBE attacks detection in a network. In: IEEE Conference on Systems, Man, and Cybernetics, Manchester, UK, 13–16 October 2013 (2013)

33. Malik, A.J., Shahzad, W., Khan, F.A.: Binary PSO and random forests algorithm for PROBE attacks detection in a network. In: IEEE Congress on Evolutionary Computation (CEC 2011), New Orleans, USA, 5–8 June 2011 (2011)
34. Ryu, S., Yang, B.: A comparative study of machine learning algorithms and their ensembles for Botnet detection. J. Comput. Commun. **6**(05), 119 (2018)
35. Bansal, A., Mahapatra, S.: A comparative analysis of machine learning techniques for botnet detection. In: Proceedings of the 10th International Conference on Security of Information and Networks, pp. 91–98. ACM, October 2017
36. Ali, A., Hu, Y.H., Hsieh, C.C.G., Khan, M.: A comparative study on machine learning algorithms for network defense. Va. J. Sci. **68**(3), 1 (2017)
37. KDD Cup 1999 Data. *Kdd.ics.uci.edu* (2018). https://kdd.ics.uci.edu/databases/kddcup99/kddcup99.html. Accessed 23 Mar 2018
38. UNSW-NB15 Dataset: UNSW Canberra at the Australian Defense Force Academy, Canberra, Australia (2015). https://www.unsw.adfa.edu.au/australian-centre-for-cybersecurity/cybersecurity/ADFA-NB15-Datasets/. Accessed 23 Mar 2018
39. WEKA: Data Mining Software in Java (2018). http://www.cs.waikato.ac.nz/ml/weka. Accessed 25 Sept 2018

On True Language Understanding

Seng-Beng Ho[1(✉)] and Zhaoxia Wang[1,2]

[1] Institute for High Performance Computing, A*STAR, Singapore, Singapore
hosengbeng@gmail.com, wangz.ihpc@gmail.com
[2] Nanjing University of Information Science and Technology, Nanjing, China

Abstract. Despite the relative successes of natural language processing in providing some useful interfaces for users, natural language *understanding* is a much more difficult issue. Natural language processing was one of the main topics of AI for as long as computers were put to the task of generating intelligent behavior, and a number of systems that were created since the inception of AI have also been characterized as being capable of natural language understanding. However, in the existing domain of natural language processing and understanding, a definition and consensus of what it means for a system to "truly" understand language do not exist. For a system to understand an idea, firstly it has to ground the meaning of the concepts in the idea that it manipulates - the concepts that are associated with the words it inputs and outputs. However, there has not been any standardized consensus on what constitutes adequate semantic grounding. This paper presents a spatio-temporal representational method as a basis for a specification of what constitutes adequate semantic grounding, particularly in connection with certain words and concepts related to grounding of physical concepts and mental constructs. This research has critically important implication for learning – true language understanding will usher in an era of learning through language instruction, which is how humans learn, to rapidly accumulate a vast amount of knowledge critical to the propagation of the species and the advancement of its civilization.

Keywords: Natural language understanding · Semantic grounding · Spatio-temporal representation · Grounding of physical concepts · Grounding of mental constructs

1 Introduction

Even though natural language processing (NLP) has been a bourgeoning field in artificial intelligence (AI), and has scored successes in many applications [1–4], natural language *understanding* (NLU), on the other hand, has not been satisfactorily addressed. With respect to certain NLP applications, such as question-answering, an NLP system is typically able to give reasonably satisfactory answers in many instances. Despite this, from the "understanding" point of view, scientists engaged in NLU research still believe that the system involved does not really "understand." What does it really mean to understand? "To understand" seems to require more than generating a string of language tokens (words) in the output. But what is this extra ability that a language understanding system should have to qualify it as having "truly" understood a

X. Sun et al. (Eds.): ICAIS 2019, LNCS 11633, pp. 87–99, 2019.
https://doi.org/10.1007/978-3-030-24265-7_8

language input? What true language understanding is still an unsolved problem and an un-answered question. This paper provides the answer and presents a specification for true language understanding.

2 The Importance of Semantic Grounding

2.1 The Problems with Dictionary Definitions

First, we would like to explore the issue of concept or semantic grounding. Let us begin with a simple concept "Move." Often we refer to the dictionary for "meanings" of words. Here, we would like to show that the dictionary cannot supply the "meaning" for true understanding. The definition of *Move* in Merriam Webster is:

Move: To *go* from one place or position to another

So, for a language processing system to understand the meaning of any concept or word, it has to understand the meaning of the constituents of its definition. Let us next retrieve the definition of a key constituent of the above definition, "Go":

Go: To *move* on a course

Thus, there is circularity in the definitions: *Move* is defined in terms of *Go* and *Go* is defined in terms of *Move*. One has a feeling that the system does not "really understand" other than to rephrase a series of words with another series of words [5].

2.2 The Proposed Spatio-Temporal Representations

What is *really* the meaning of the concept *Move*? We submit that it is a spatio-temporal concept that is better represented in a "pictorial" manner as shown in Fig. 1.

In Fig. 1(a) one can see that there is an axis representing the time dimension and three other axes representing the spatial dimensions. Different from the three spatial dimensions, time is a unique and special dimension sensed by humans. The "blob" is an object A. The object A changes its location over time. Figure 1(b) shows a simplified spatio-temporal representation of the concept *Move* in which the object A changes one unit of elemental location over one unit of time. This is a reduction of a three-dimensional representation (x, y, z) of space (Fig. 1(a)) to a two-dimensional representation (x = 0, y, z) of space for the purpose of simplification without compromising the concepts involved.

In Fig. 1(c) there is a more general representation. The gray "bars" represent "any number of units in between." Therefore, the representation in Fig. 1(c) says that the object A changes *any* amount of space location over *any* amount of time.

Combining the representational schemes of Figs. 1(a), (b) and (c), we define a new space variable l and spatial change Δl, and we leverage the unique and special dimension of time t to represent *Move*. The gray "bars" represent "any number of units in between." Therefore, the representation in Fig. 1(d) says that the object A changes *any* amount of location over any amount of time. This, we submit, is the definition of *Move* in its most grounded and general form.

Of course, pictures such as those in Fig. 1 have to be operated on by some processes to render them fully operational. Therefore, we posit that there are processes that operate on these representations as follows:

(i) RECOGNITION: Firstly, there is the process of recognition. In order to determine whether an instance of *Move* has occurred in the environment with respect to some objects, a system would check if the object has indeed changed location with respect to time, as stipulated by Fig. 1(d)

(ii) ACTION/GENERATION: Secondly, if a system, endowed with the definition of *Move* as stipulated in Fig. 1, is asked to "move the object," it would act to change the object's location over time, as stipulated by Fig. 1(d).

We posit that both (i) and (ii) suffice to demonstrate that the system "truly understands" the concept *Move* as stipulated in the representations of Fig. 1.

Of course, the representation of the concept *Move* need not be pictorial as shown in Fig. 1. One can also use logic language to represent it as follows:

$$\forall \text{Object}, x, y, z, t \quad Location(Object, x, y, z, t) \wedge Location(Object, x+\Delta x, y+\Delta y, z+\Delta z, t+\Delta t) \rightarrow Move(Object) \tag{1}$$

To make the representation simpler and more general, we use l to represent spatial location and Δl to represent spatial location changes, and Eq. (1) can be then represented as:

$$\forall \text{Object}, l, t \quad Location(Object, l, t) \wedge Location(Object, l+\Delta l, t+\Delta t) \rightarrow Move(Object) \tag{2}$$

which states exactly the same thing as the pictorial representations of Fig. 1, which is that if the Object is at location l at time t and then at location $l + \Delta l$ at time $t + \Delta t$, it is deemed to have *Moved*, if $\Delta l \neq 0$. This logic representation, when acted on with some processes, would also be able to render the concept fully operational with respect to the RECOGNITION and ACTION/GENERATION requirements as described above. The critical issue is not whether the fundamental representation that leads to "true" understanding is pictorial or logical. The issue is that space and time are fundamental ad "atomic" with respect to our understanding of the world and only by defining concepts such as *Move*, which is spatio-temporal in nature, in its most fundamental spatio-temporal form, can the true understanding of these concepts be achieved.

2.3 Other Examples of Spatio-Temporal Representations of Physical Concepts

In Fig. 2 we show some other related atomic, ground level concepts represented in spatio-temporal forms.

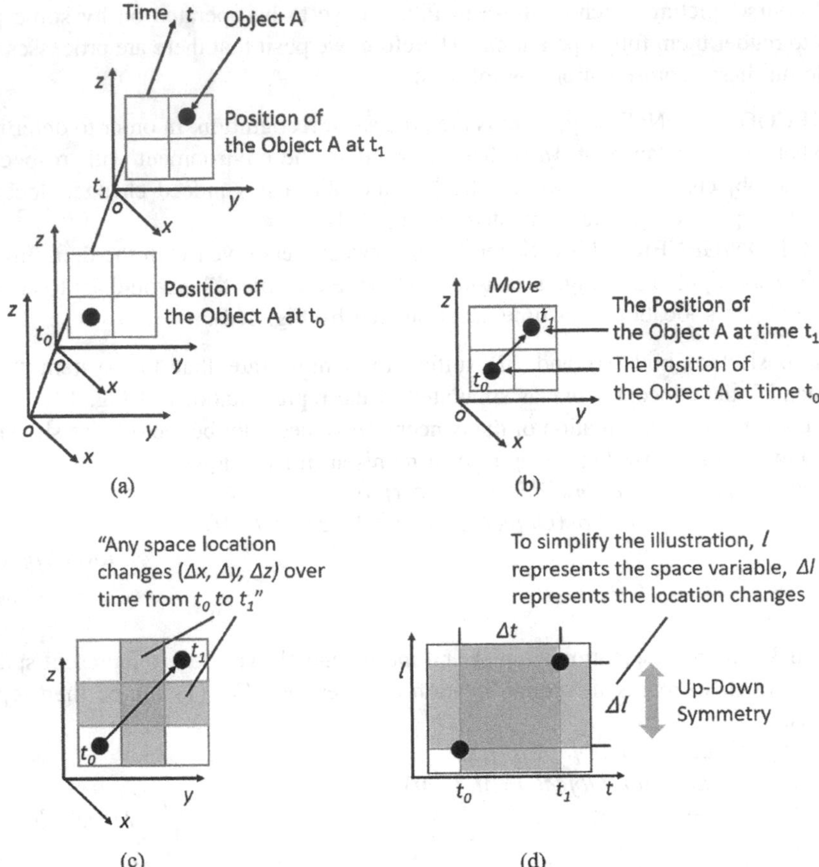

Fig. 1. (a) A spatio-temporal representation of a specific instance of the concept *Move* in which the object A changes one elemental location in both y and z dimensions over time from t_0 to t_1. In order to make the illustration simple, we assume that there is no location change in the x dimension. (b) A simplified representation of the spatio-temporal representation of the concept *Move* in which the Object A changes *one* unit of elemental location in both y and z dimensions over time from t_0 to t_1. (c) A spatio-temporal representation of a general concept *Move* in which the object A changes *any* number of elemental locations in both y and z dimensions over time from t_0 to t_1. (d) After l is leveraged to represent the space dimension and Δl to represent spatial dimensional changes, a spatio-temporal representation of a general concept *Move* in which an Object changes *any* number of elemental locations Δl over *any* amount of time Δt. The "Up-Down Symmetry" indicator specifies that the template has an up-down symmetry – it encodes both the "upward" (i.e., +ve space direction) as well as the "downward" (−ve space direction). Based on [5, 6].

Figure 2(a) shows the concept of "Materialization," in which, at time frame t_1, there is no object in the corresponding location but there is an act of *Materialization*, represented by an "exploding" shape. Then, at time frame t_2, an Object appears. Figure 2(b) shows the concept of "Stay", in which the Object does not change location over time.

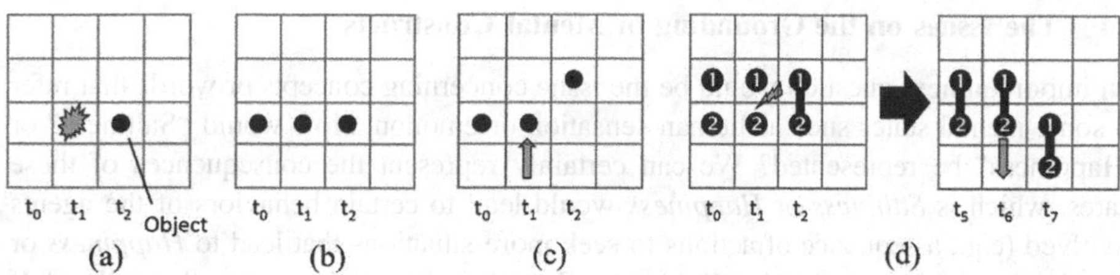

Fig. 2. Spatio-temporal representations of (a) *Materialization*. (b) *Stay*. (c) *Push and Make Move*. (d) *Attach* – the left figure showing the *Attach* action and the right figure showing the consequence – later, if a force is applied to one of them in the direction away from the other, both Objects would move together. The vertical dimension is space and the horizontal one is time. Based on [5, 6].

Figure 2(c) shows the concept of "Push and Make Move" in which at time frame t_1, a force appears and acts on the Object involved, and in the next time frame t_2, the Object changes location by one unit. Figure 2(d) shows the concept of "Attach", in which an *Attach* action is performed at time frame t_1 between two Objects, and in time frame t_2, the two Objects acquire a new property (in a sense a "change of state") which is shown as a bar connecting them. Later, suppose a force is acted on one of them to move it in the direction away from the other, the other will follow. This is the grounded meaning of *Attach* [5, 6].

These are specific instances much like Fig. 1(a). Corresponding generalized versions of these such as that in Fig. 1(b) would allow a system to achieve (i) RECOGNITION and (ii) ACTION/GENERATION as stipulated above. There are other atomic concepts discussed in Ho [5, 6] and we posit that something akin to a set of ground and atomic concepts like this is necessary to achieve semantic grounding for a language system to bring about true language understanding, at least with respect to various physical aspects of the environment. (There are other "mental" aspects such as the various concepts and words referring to the various emotions and sensations experienced by humans that will be discussed below.)

In cognitive linguistics, there has also been some investigations into grounded language understanding. For example, in Fig. 3, the representations of the concepts of "Before" and "After" are demonstrated.

Cognitive linguistics [7] defines *landmark* (lm) as the "focus" of the sentence and *trajector* (tr) as something that is "in reference to the focus." In Fig. 3, it is shown that *Before* and *After* both involve two temporal time frames in a sequence. In the concept of *After*, the earlier event is the *lm* and the later event is the *tr*, and vice versa for *Before*.

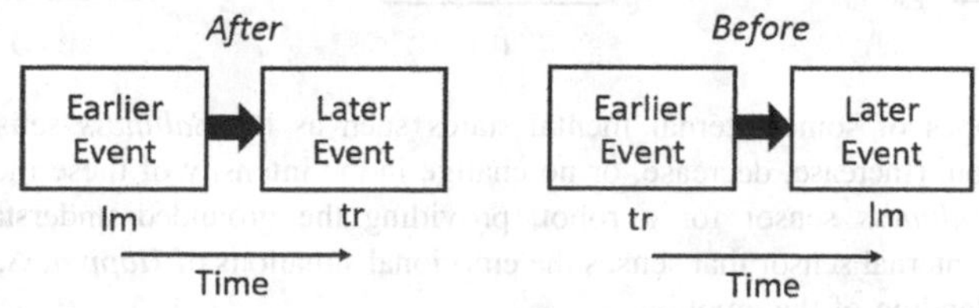

Fig. 3. Cognitive linguistic representation of the concepts of Before and After [7].

2.4 The Issues on the Grounding of Mental Constructs

An important next question would be the issue concerning concepts or words that refer to some mental states such as human sensation or emotion. How would "Saltiness" or "Happiness" be represented? We can certainly represent the consequences of these states, which is *Saltiness* or *Happiness* would lead to certain behaviors of the agents involved (e.g., a sequence of actions to seek more situations that lead to *Happiness* or situations to avoid experiencing *Saltiness*). But what about the concepts themselves? If a human says "I want to *move*," a natural language understanding system can use the above spatio-temporal representation in Fig. 1 to expect a certain spatio-temporal behavior of the human, and hence "truly" understands what he means. However, if he were to say "I am *happy*", and if the system simply responds, "I don't know how it feels to be happy, but I know what you will be doing in the state of happiness," the system can still be a good companion, but the human may then respond, "You don't really understand me."

In Ho [5], it has been demonstrated that it is possible to represent the *changes* of these internal mental states in a system. Consider mental parameters such as *Saltiness* (a kind of sensation) or *Happiness* (a kind of emotion). Their changes can be representation as shown in Fig. 4(a). These changes are in turn describable by the earlier spatio-temporal concepts such as *Move* in the upward direction, which corresponds to *Increase* in the intensity, or *Stay* – no change in intensity.

One can imagine there is a *Saltiness* sensor installed in a robotic system as shown in Fig. 4(b), and the output of the sensor may fluctuate like in Fig. 4(a). Then, the robotic system could output something like, "After consuming salty food, I detect an increase in *Saltiness* in my food receptacle." And if both human and the robotic system agree to the labeling of this particular sensory impression arising from the salty food as "Saltiness", then the robotic system can be said to also "truly" understand the meaning of *Saltiness*. The meaning of *Saltiness* is grounded in the input to the robotic system from the *Saltiness* sensor.

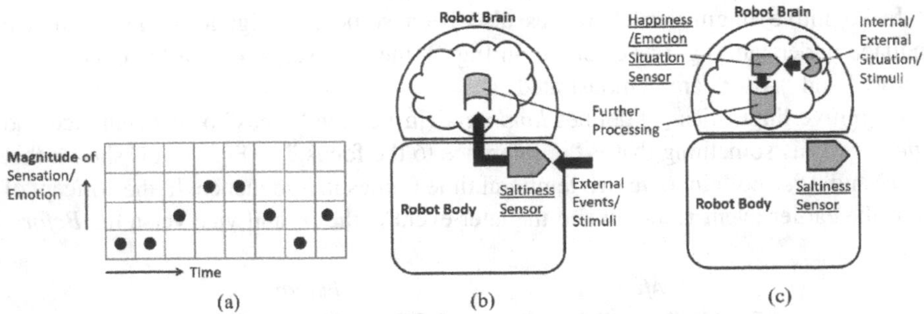

Fig. 4. (a) Changes of some internal mental states such as the *Saltiness* sensation and the *Happiness* emotion. (Increase, decrease, or no change in the intensity of these mental states are shown.) (b) A *Saltiness* sensor for a robot, providing the grounded understanding of the sensation. (c) An internal sensor that senses the emotional situations of *Happiness*, providing the grounded understanding of the emotion.

For the issue of emotions such as *Happiness*, one could imagine that there is an internal mental "Happiness" sensor in a robotic brain, as shown in Fig. 4(c). When certain internal states arises in the brain (e.g., the imagining, recall or sensing of "happy" situations), this sensor detects them and outputs certain signals to signify such a state representing a *Happiness* situation exists. The robot can then be said to understand *Happiness* in the same way that a human does, in parallel with the situation of the understanding of the concept of *Saltiness*. The concept of *Happiness* is grounded in the "output" of the internal "sensor" (not from an external sensor like the *Saltiness* sensor) to the rest of the processing system (i.e., some parts of the brain that processes this further). (We ignore the "qualia" problem for now – i.e., the "subjective quality" of the sensation and emotion involved – and instead focus on specifying the *functional* aspects of these sensations and emotions in the systems described in Figs. 4(b) and (c).)

Thus in the case of understanding of certain sensation, the issue cannot be divorced from the presence and availability of certain sensors converting certain external stimuli to internal signal (i.e., if a robot does not have a *Saltiness* sensor, it will never be able to truly understand *Saltiness*, much like a human who is color blind, which means she does not have the corresponding sensors of certain colors, can never truly understand the sensation of these colors). In the case of understanding certain emotions such as *Happiness*, the system must have an "internal sensor" that can sense those corresponding situations (whether currently sensed from the external world or imagined from past experiences), and generate a signal to some other parts of the system that process it like the processing of sensations like *Saltiness*. It is through the detection of this signal that the robot "truly" understands the emotion involved.

2.5 An Example to Demonstrate True Language Understanding

In Ho [5], it has been shown how some instructions can be given to a language understanding system to construct a tool and use it for some purpose. In Fig. 5, we use a simplified 1D (one dimensional) space and 1D time representation to illustrate the process (this should readily generalize to 3D space and 1D time).

In Fig. 5 there is a sequence of actions specified by a stream of linguistic instructions (left side of the figure) and we show the corresponding "understood" actions to be performed (right side of the figure). *We posit that systems like this demonstrate true and deep understanding of the language involved.*

In the figure, the situation begins with an Agent (❶) situated some distance away from an Object (✪) she wishes to retrieve out from a certain Confinement Area. There is a constraint here that the Agent cannot move more than 2 pixel distance from her point of origin (corresponding to the situation that a person may only use her hand to reach out to a certain distance), and the confine is defined as the 3 pixel (1D) space within the current location of the object as shown in the figure. Firstly, it is shown that an elemental object (❷) is being *Materialized* next to the Agent (see Fig. 2 for this operation), effected by the Agent. (In our 3D real world, this could correspond also to the Agent bringing a piece of material to a location for the subsequent construction purposes.) Then, another *Materialization* action is given to materialize another elemental object (❸). Following this, an *Attach* action is generated to attach these two elemental objects together. Subsequently another object (❹) is materialized and

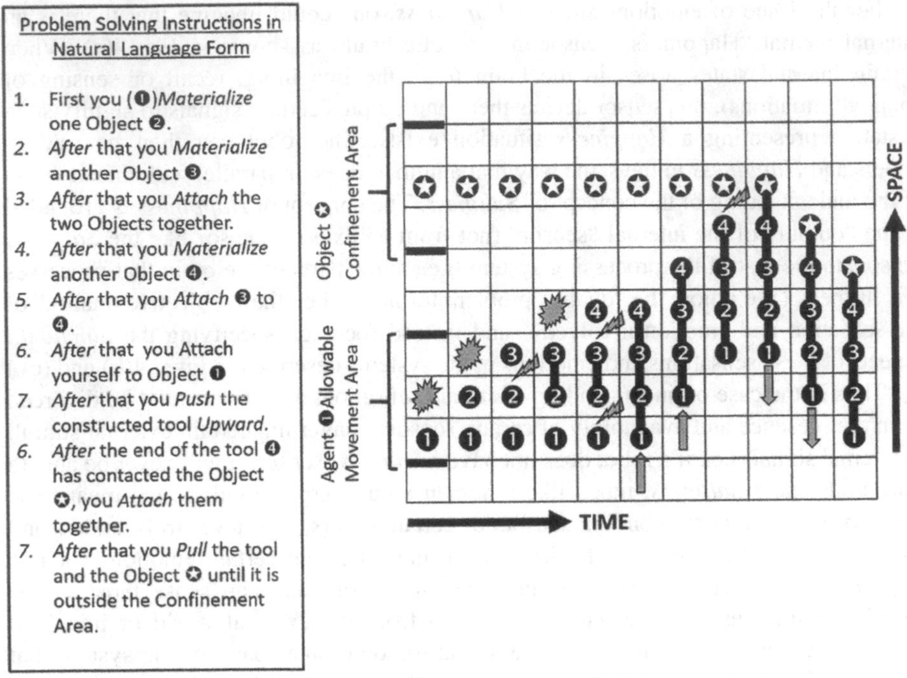

Problem Solving Instructions in Natural Language Form
1. First you (❶)Materialize one Object ❷.
2. After that you Materialize another Object ❸.
3. After that you Attach the two Objects together.
4. After that you Materialize another Object ❹.
5. After that you Attach ❸ to ❹.
6. After that you Attach yourself to Object ❶
7. After that you Push the constructed tool Upward.
6. After the end of the tool ❹ has contacted the Object ✪, you Attach them together.
7. After that you Pull the tool and the Object ✪ until it is outside the Confinement Area.
Object ✪ Confinement Area
Agent ❶Allowable Movement Area
TIME
SPACE

Fig. 5. The understanding of some natural language instructions in a system, which carries out the correct actions accordingly, reflecting its "true" understanding. All the grounded constructs discussed earlier such as *Move*, *Materialize*, *Attach*, *Push*, *After* are brought to bear here. Based on [5].

attached to object ❸. At this point the agent has constructed a long enough tool to reach the desired Object (✪). Under the language instruction, she then *Pushes* the tool "forward" to touch the desired Object, *Attaches* the tool to the Object (in 3D space, the corresponding action could be "grabbing" the object), then *Pulls* the object back toward her initial location. The Object is hence moved out of the Confinement Area.

Through this example, one can see that every part of the language instruction plays a part in instructing the system what to do, and the system "fully understands" in that it carries out the actions accurately. In a sense, *understanding* is *understanding how to act*.

There is another level of the true language understanding system in Fig. 5 that we did not describe, which is the *syntactic* level of understanding – how to convert the English sentences to correctly interpret the overall meaning from the meaning of its parts. We assume that there is a method to do this correctly. What is demonstrated in Fig. 5 is the *semantic* aspect - how the *meaning* of each of the parts of the language instructions on the left side of the figure can be interpreted at the ground level – at the level in which the understanding of the words' meanings lead to specific actions.

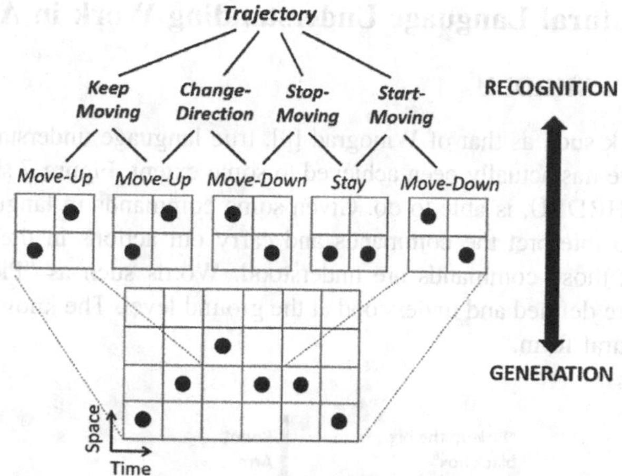

Fig. 6. The higher level concept *Trajectory* defined in terms of lower level and ground level concepts. This is a *specific* instance of the concept of *Trajectory*. It could be suitably generalized like in the case of Fig. 1(b). RECOGNITION and GENERATION of the concept are quite straight forward. Based on [5, 6].

2.6 Higher Level Concepts Are Grounded Through Lower Ones

Concepts such as *Move* are at the ground level in that they have *direct* spatio-temporal correspondences. There are concepts that are at much higher levels that are built upon these concepts. For example, "Change-Direction" can be defined in terms of *Move-Up* and *Move-Down* as shown in Fig. 6. At a higher level, there is the concept of "Trajectory." Figure 6 is a *specific* instance of *Trajectory* [5, 6]. Something akin to the general version of *Move* in Fig. 1(d) can be concocted for *Trajectory* as well and it can be defined as a sequence of "*any number of Moves, any number of Changes of Directions, any number of steps of Stay, in any combination.*" But its meaning is grounded in the ground level constructs of *Move*, *Stay*, etc. Thus, higher, more abstract levels of concepts are grounded through intermediate and ground level concepts.

Figure 6 also shows the construct can be used to RECOGNIZE as well as GENERATE the concept of *Trajectory* in a very straight forward manner.

The basic dictionary definition of Trajectory (Merriam-Webster) is:

Trajectory: The curve that a body (such as a planet or comet in its orbit or a rocket) describes in space.

Compared to the representation in Fig. 6, the representation in Fig. 6 is grounded in the sense that it satisfies the RECOGNTIION and ACTION criteria above in a very straight forward manner, and allows a system to directly operate on it.

3 Earlier Natural Language Understanding Work in AI

3.1 Winograd's SHRDLU

In earlier AI work such as that of Winograd [8], true language understanding such as that posited above has actually been achieved to some extent. Figure 7 shows what his system, called SHRDLU, is able to do. Given some commands in language form, the system is able to interpret the commands and carry out actions in the real world to demonstrate that those commands are understood. Words such as "Pick-up," "big," "black," "box" are defined and understood at the ground level. The knowledge is hand-coded in procedural form.

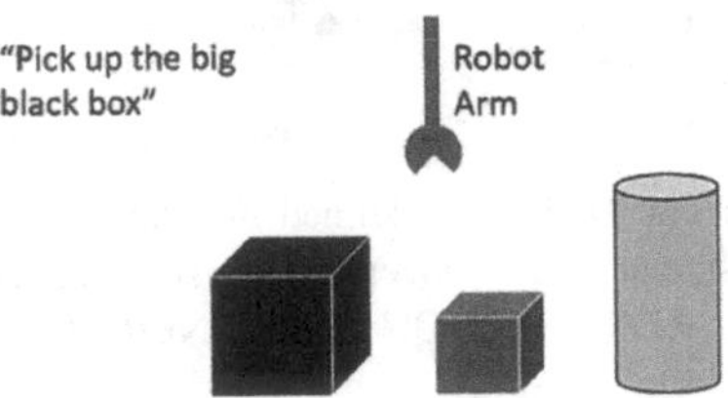

Fig. 7. SHRDLU – an earlier natural language understanding effort. Based on [8].

3.2 Schank's Script Representation

Another work in earlier AI by Roger Schank and Robert Abelson [9] used "scripts" to encode deep understanding. Figure 8 is an example of a "Restaurant Script" in which all the activities that take place in a restaurant together with the corresponding goals and intentions of the participants are encoded (Fig. 8 is a vastly stripped-down version of the script. Please refer to [9] For the full detailed version).

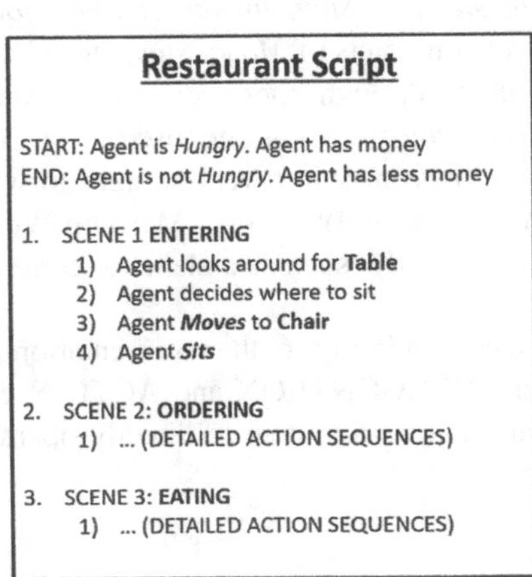

Fig. 8. Schank and Abelson's [9] Restaurant Script (a stripped-down version of a figure in [9]).

With this deep representation, their question answering system can respond to statements such as "I went to the restaurant yesterday. I didn't leave a tip." The expected human-like response would be "Oh, was the service bad?" Now, a typical dictionary definition of the concept of a restaurant is "a business establishment where meals or refreshments may be purchased" (Merriam Webster). With this kind of shallow, ungrounded definition and representation, the above human-like response would not be possible.

3.3 Relationships Between the Earlier Effort and Ours

The difference between our proposed true language understanding representations as demonstrated in Figs. 1, 2, 3, 4, 5 and 6 and that of Winograd and Schank is: our is at an even deeper ground or atomic level representation. For example, the "block" in Winograd's SHRDLU system or the Table in Schank's Restaurant Script have further detailed structures that are not captured in their representations. But in spirit, our system is similar to theirs.

The research in language understanding such as that represented by the work of Winograd and Schank fizzled out because their systems were not scalable. There were no computer vision and machine learning at that time (the 1970's) and the knowledge involved was hand-coded. If an AI system is endowed with computer vision and learning capabilities, deep knowledge structures such as the Restaurant Script can be learned by bringing the system (say, a "child" robot) to a restaurant and let it observe and learn the activities inside. As the robot moves about in an environment, it will be able to pick up scripts of all kinds of activities. These scripts will then form the knowledge basis for deep and true language understanding.

Pei et al. and Si et al. [10, 11] have demonstrated just such a computer vision capability. Through video observation of the activities in a room carried out by various human agents, their system is able to construct a causal spatio-temporal AND-OR graph that encodes all the possible observed sequences of long range human behavior in the scene. This is akin to the scripts of Schank and Abelson, except that this also represents both the learning and encoding of grounded information about the real world. This will set the stage for the acquisition of knowledge for true language understanding.

4 Summary and Conclusion

In this paper we first showed that dictionary-like definitions, i.e., definitions of words in terms of other words, are not sufficient for a language processing system to achieve true language understanding because these definitions are ultimately circular. To achieve true understanding of various concepts and words, these concepts and words must be grounded, either directly or indirectly, through other intermediate concepts to some ground level representations that are directly tied to the physical or mental constructs to which they refer. We presented the idea that for physical concepts, there is a set of spatio-temporal descriptions that can suffice to provide the ground level representations (e.g., *Move*, *Materialize*, etc.). We posited that there is probably a limited, small set of these "atomic" basic concepts that are sufficient to ground all the concepts related to physical concepts in the human lexicon, and this is consistent with previous work.

For mental constructs such as sensation and emotion, we posited that an intelligent system needs to have the corresponding external and internal sensors akin to those humans possess to be able to truly understand the corresponding concepts or words in a natural language discourse.

We also specified the conditions of being able to use these concepts both to recognize instances of them in the real world and to act on the real world to be the conditions for "true" understanding. Thus understanding, in a sense, is understanding of how to recognize and act. We reviewed two former natural language understanding systems from the early days of AI, namely that of Winograd and Schank and Abelson, to demonstrate that similar ideas have been propounded before but were forgotten in AI because those systems were not scalable. We also mentioned that armed with the new tools of computer vision and machine learning, systems like these may become scalable and therefore we should revisit this issue of natural language understanding.

Future research would focus on (i) further ascertaining a sufficient set of grounded concepts for most if not all concepts/words in the human mental lexicon to be grounded on; (ii) elucidating on how other complex concepts can be grounded accordingly; (iii) demonstrating an AI or robotic system that can really benefit from true language understanding – either in carrying out complex instructions by humans correctly, or through language, learning a vast amount of knowledge necessary for its functioning, much like how the vast majority of a human's knowledge is learned.

This will usher in an era of machine learning akin to that of human learning, in which most complex knowledge is learned rapidly through language instruction. This kind of machine learning will be set totally apart from the slow and restricted kinds of machine learning today – the supervised and unsupervised learning methods applied to pattern recognition, or the reinforcement learning method applied to action sequence learning.

References

1. Ferrucci, D., et al.: Building Watson: an overview of the DeepQA project. AI Mag. **31**(3), 59–79 (2010)
2. Ganegedara, T.: Natural Language Processing with TensorFlow: Teach Language to Machines Using Python's Deep Learning Library. Packt Publishing, Birmingham (2018)
3. Manning, C.D., Schutze, H.: Foundations of Statistical Natural Language Processing. MIT Press, Cambridge (1999)
4. Wang, Z., Chong, C.S., Lan, L., Yang, Y., Ho, S.-B., Tong, J.C.: Fine-grained sentiment analysis of social media with emotion sensing. In: IEEE Future Technologies Conference 2016 (FTC 2016), San Francisco, United States, 6–7 December 2016
5. Ho, S.-B.: Principles of Noology: Toward a Theory and Science of Intelligence. Springer, Cham (2016). https://doi.org/10.1007/978-3-319-32113-4
6. Ho, S.-B.: The atoms of cognition: a theory of ground epistemics. In: Proceedings of the 34th Annual Meeting of the Cognitive Science Society, pp. 1685–1690. Cognitive Science Society, Austin (2012)

7. Langacker, R.W.: Foundation of Cognitive Grammar, vol. I. Stanford University Press, Stanford (1987)
8. Winograd, T.: A Procedural Model of Language Understanding. In: Schank, R., Colby, K.M. (eds.) Computer Models of Thought and Languag. W. H. Freeman & Company, San Francisco (1973)
9. Schank, R., Abelson, R.: Scripts, Plans, Goals, and Understanding. Lawrence Erlbaum Associates, Hillsdale (1977)
10. Pei, M., Jia, Y., Zhu, S.-C.: Parsing video events with goal inference and intent prediction. In: International Conference on Computer Vision. IEEE, New Jersey (2011)
11. Si, Z., Pei, M., Yao, B., Zhu, S.-C.: Unsupervised Learning of AND-OR grammar and semantics from video. In: International Conference on Computer Vision. IEEE, New Jersey (2011)

The $\ell_{2,1}$-Norm Stacked Robust Autoencoders via Adaptation Regularization for Domain Adaptation

Shuai Yang[1], Yuhong Zhang[1(✉)], Yi Zhu[1], Han Ding[1], and Xuegang Hu[1,2]

[1] Hefei University of Technology, Hefei 230601, Anhui, China
yangs@mail.hfut.edu.cn, {zhangyh,jsjxhuxg}@hfut.edu.cn

[2] Anhui Province Key Laboratory of Industry Safety and Emergency Technology, Hefei 230601, Anhui, China

Abstract. Domain adaption aims to promote the learning tasks in target domain by using the knowledge from source domain whose data distribution is different from target domain. How to reconstruct more robust and high-level feature space to reduce the discrepancy between source and target domains is the crucial problem in domain adaptation. Recently, deep learning methods have shown promising results on learning new representations. However, in most of the previous work, the local geometry structure of data is not taken into account, which is benefit for constructing more robust feature space. Therefore, we propose a novel algorithm termed $\ell_{2,1}$-norm stacked robust autoencoders via adaptation regularization (SRAAR) to learn better feature representations for domain adaptation. More specifically, we incorporate an effective manifold regularization into the objective function to preserve the local geometry structure of data. In addition, label information is used to compute the maximum mean discrepancy (MMD) in order to reduce the distance between source and target domains. Experimental results show the effectiveness of proposed approach.

Keywords: Domain adaption · $\ell_{2,1}$-norm · Manifold regularization · MMD

1 Introduction

Domain adaptation aims at training a classifier on labeled data of source domain to classify unseen or unlabeled data of target domain. In recent years, lots of domain adaptation approaches have been studied [1–3]. Recently, deep learning has been applied in learning robust representations and achieved significant effect [4–8] in domain adaptation.

Glorot et al. [9] proposed stacked denoising autoencoders (SDA), which is an unsupervised model based on deep learning framework. SDA learns high-level feature space on raw input by stacking multiple layers of denoising autoencoders. Chen et al. [10] proposed the marginalized stacked denoising autoencoders (mSDA). mSDA is more efficient than SDA in representation learning,

X. Sun et al. (Eds.): ICAIS 2019, LNCS 11633, pp. 100–111, 2019.
https://doi.org/10.1007/978-3-030-24265-7_9

since it optimized the structure and parameters with liner approach instead of the expensive iteration process. In addition, Csurka et al. [11] proposed an extended framework for marginalized domain adaptation with a domain regularization, which minimizes the maximum mean discrepancy (MMD) [12] between source and target domains to learn robust feature space. Jiang et al. [13] proposed $\ell_{2,1}$-norm stacked robust autoencoders ($\ell_{2,1}$-SRA) to learn effective representations for domain adaptation tasks.

Although many methods based on autoencoders has been successfully applied in feature learning, they do not explicitly consider the geometry structure of data and pay little attention to the domain divergence that may arise in the new feature space. Therefore, in this paper, we propose a new method called $\ell_{2,1}$-norm stacked robust autoencoders via adaptation regularization (SRAAR) to learn more effective representations, which uses manifold regularization to keep the local geometry structure of data, and minimizes the divergence between source and target domains by MMD. The main contributions of SRAAR are summarized as follows:

(1) Manifold regularization is introduced to preserve the local geometry data structure, which makes similar samples in the raw feature space stay close in the reconstructed space.
(2) The maximum mean discrepancy (MMD) is designed in our framework to learn more powerful feature representations. We first obtain the pseudo label of instances of target domain, and then compute MMD with the label information from both domains to measure the distance between the means of corresponding classes.

2 Related Work

The goal of cross-domain classification is to reduce the performance degradation of classifier between source domain and target domains. Recent work has mainly investigated two techniques for alleviating the difference: learning joint feature representations [14–18] and learning robust feature space with deep learning models [9,10,13,19]. This paper belongs to the second one.

Many researchers have used autoencoders as a powerful tool for automatic extraction of nonlinear features. Glorot et al. [9] trained stacked denoising autoencoders (SDA) to reconstruct the input vectors on the union of the source and target data, and extracted features from partial and random corruption for domain adaptation. The denoiseres can be stacked into deep learning architectures. Chen et al. [10] proposed the marginalized denoising autoencoders (mSDA) that addresses two crucial limitations of SDA: high computational cost and the lack of scalability to high-dimensional features. mSDA marginalized noise and adopted the liner denoiser to learn parameters instead of the stochastic gradient descent algorithm. In addition, there are some variant models based on SDA and mSDA. Based on the work of Ganin and Lempitsky [20], Clinchant et al. [21] proposed an unsupervised regularization method for mSDA, which can get invariant features between domains and make the adaptation easier. Ziser et al. [22] proposed a neural network model that marries two ideas together: SCL [14] and auto-encoder neural networks. The model is a three-layer neural network that encode the non-pivot features of input example into low dimensional representations, so that the existence of pivot features in the example can be decoded. Zhu et al. [23] proposed transfer learning with stacked reconstruction independent component analysis (SRICA). In this algorithm, the proposed stacked reconstruction independent component analysis is a semi-supervised deep learning method and it is proven to be effective. Jiang et al. [13] proposed $\ell_{2,1}$-norm stacked robust autoencoders, which uses $\ell_{2,1}$-norm as a measure of reconstruction error to reduce the effect of outliers. In their work, feature variance is introduced into the regularization term to ensure that the contribution of each feature is equal.

3 Proposed Algorithm

In this section, we first give some basic concepts used in this paper, and then give the details of our SRAAR algorithm.

3.1 Notation

The definitions and notations used frequently in this paper as follows. For a matrix $V \in \Re^{m\times n}$, V_{ij} is the (i,j)-th entry of V, V_i is the i-th row of V, and V_j is the j-th column of V. And the $l_{2,1}$-norm of matrix V is denoted as $\|V\|_{2,1} = \sum_i \|V_i\|_2$.

Given a labeled source domain D_s and an unlabeled target domain D_t, where $D_s = \{(x_i^s, y_i^s)\}_{i=1}^{n_s}$ and $D_t = \{(x_j^t)\}_{i=1}^{n_t}$. Where n_s and n_t is the number of instances in the source and target domain respectively; x_i^s and x_j^t is the i-th, j-th instance in the source and target domain respectively; y_i^s is the label of the i-th instance in the source domain D_s. The goal of our method is to learn the feature representation, on which a classifier can be learned to predict the labels of samples from the target domain D_t.

3.2 SRAAR Framework

We propose the SRAAR based on deep learning method with adaptation regularization to learn more robust feature representations. Our SRAAR takes three factors into consideration for feature representations learning. The first term is the reconstruction error J_1, which aims at learning good feature representations from the input data. The second term is manifold regularization R_g, which can preserve local geometry structure of data to optimize the representation space. The last term is the maximum mean discrepancy R_m, which can reduce the distance between source domain and target domains. The objective function to be minimized in our model can be written as Eq. 1:

$$J = J_1 + \beta R_g + \gamma R_m \tag{1}$$

where parameters $\beta > 0$ and $\gamma > 0$ are used to balance the regularization terms.

The first term is the reconstruction error. We use the $\ell_{2,1}$-norm as a measure of reconstruction error for our robust autoencoder to reduce the effect of outliers. And feature variance is introduced into the regularization term to ensure that the contribution of each feature is equal. The objective function can be written as Eq. 2:

$$J_1 = \min_W \|X - XW\|_{2,1} + \lambda tr(W^T \Lambda W) \quad (2)$$

where $X = [x_1^s, \cdots x_{n_s}^s, x_1^t, \cdots x_{n_t}^t]^T \in \Re^{n \times d}$ is the centered data matrix in $D_s \cup D_t$, Λ is a diagonal matrix and $\Lambda_{ii} = X_{i.} X_{i.}^T$.

The second term is manifold regularization. Both labeled instances and unlabeled instances are taken into account in manifold regularization. In this subsection, we use samples from both domains to build a graph with n vertices where each vertex corresponds to a sample in two domains. The similarity of vertices in matrix M is defined as Eq. 3:

$$M_{ij} = \begin{cases} exp(\frac{\|x_i - x_j\|^2}{-2\sigma^2}), x_i \in N_k(x_j) \quad or \quad x_j \in N_k(x_i) \\ 0, \qquad\qquad\qquad\qquad otherwise \end{cases} \quad (3)$$

where $N_k(x_i)$ is the set of k nearest neighbors of x_i and σ is a width parameter. We hope to preserve local geometry structure of data by minimizing the following equation, as shown in Eq. 4:

$$R_g = \frac{1}{2} \min_W \sum_{i,j=1}^{n_s+n_t} \|x_i W - x_j W\|_2^2 M_{ij} = \min_W tr(W^T X^T L X W) \quad (4)$$

where L is the graph Laplacian, which can be obtained by $L = D - M$. D is a diagonal matrix with $D_{ii} = \sum_j M_{ij}$.

The third term of the objective function is MMD. Most previous work uses MMD as a regularizer for the cross-domain classifier learning [11,24]. In the work of [25], MMD does not need labels and can be calculated between all available source instances and all target instances. In our method, in order to minimize the distance between two centroids of corresponding classes in both domains, the label of instances from source domain and the pseudo label of instances from target domain are used. Due to the label of instance from the target domain are unknown, we use logistic regression (LR) to train a classifier in source domain, and then use this classifier to obtain the pseudo label of instances from target domain. And the MMD with the linear kernel is used. The corresponding loss as shown in Eq. 5.

$$R_m = tr(W^T X^T C X W) \quad (5)$$

$$C_{ij} = \begin{cases} \frac{1}{N_s^c N_s^c}, if \quad X_i, X_j \in D_s, \quad y_i = y_j = c \\ \frac{1}{N_t^c N_t^c}, if \quad X_i, X_j \in D_t, \quad y_i = y_j = c \\ \frac{-1}{N_s^c N_t^c}, if \quad X_i \in D_s, X_j \in D_t, \quad y_i = y_j = c \\ \frac{-1}{N_t^c N_s^c}, if \quad X_i \in D_t, X_j \in D_s, \quad y_i = y_j = c \\ 0, \qquad otherwise \end{cases} \quad (6)$$

where N_s^c denotes the number of source instances from the class c and N_t^c denotes the number of target instances from the class c.

3.3 Solution of Our Framework

By integrating manifold regularization term and the maximum mean discrepancy term, the objective function J is shown as Eq. 7.

$$J = \|X - XW\|_{2,1} + \lambda tr(W^T \Lambda W) + \beta tr(W^T X^T LXW) + \gamma tr(W^T X^T CXW) \quad (7)$$

The objective of our proposed SRAAR is a convex problem with a non-smooth loss function and smooth regularization. By setting the derivative of Eq. 7 w.r.t. W to zero, the above equation becomes

$$\nabla_W J = -2X^T GX + 2X^T GXW + 2\lambda\Lambda W + 2\beta X^T LXW + 2\gamma X^T CXW = 0 \quad (8)$$

$$G_{ii} = \frac{1}{2\|x_i - x_i W\|_2 + \varepsilon} \quad (9)$$

where ε is a very small positive number.

Because G is dependent on X, we update G and W alternatively to solve this problem. If G is given, W could be calculated by

$$W = (X^T GX + \lambda\Lambda + \beta X^T LX + \gamma X^T CX)^{-1} X^T GX \quad (10)$$

We alternatively update W and G by Eqs. (9 and 10) until convergence to solve the problem Eq. 1. The whole process of our SRAAR model is summarized in Algorithm 1.

Following the same strategy adopted by other autoencoders based on deep learning methods, we also learn the new representations layer by layer greedily. To apply SRAAR to domain adaptation, firstly, we learn feature representations in both domains, and the nonlinearly is injected through the nonlinear encoder function $tanh()$. Then the original features h^0 ($h^0 = X^0$) are combined with the output of all layers to form new representations. Finally, a linear support vector machine (SVM) is trained based on the new feature representations.

4 Experiments

In this section, we perform a comprehensive experimental study on domain adaption problem to evaluate both the effectiveness and scalability of the proposed SRAAR models, including sentiment polarity prediction, email spam filtering, newsgroups content classification.

Algorithm 1. $\ell_{2,1}$-Norm Stacked Robust Autoencoders via Adaptation Regularization (SRAAR)

Input: labeled source domain D_s, unlabeled target domain data D_t, number of the layer l, number of nearest neighbors k, parameter α, λ , β and γ
Output: hidden representation of l layer X^l
Initialize $X^0 = h^0 = [x_1^s, \cdots x_{n_s}^s, x_1^t, \cdots x_{n_t}^t]^T$;
Initialize $G_{ii} = 1 \quad for \quad i = 1, \cdots, d$;
for $z \leftarrow 1$ to l do
  Construct a weighted graphic M by KNN on the whole set h^{z-1} with Eq. 3;
  Compute the graph Laplacian L;
  Compute C with Eq. 6;
  repeat
    Update W by Eq. 10
    Update G by Eq. 9
  until convergence
  Computer $h^z = tanh(\alpha h^{z-1} W)$;
  Define $X^z = [X^{z-1}, h^z]$;
end
return X^l

4.1 Data Sets

Amazon Review Dataset[1]. The Amazon review dataset contains the collection of product reviews from Amazon.com about four product domains: Books (B), DVDS (D), Electronics (E) and Kitchen appliances (K). And we can construct 12 cross-domain tasks. For each domain, there are 1000 positive and 1000 negative reviews. As $\ell_{2,1}$-SRA and mSDA focus on feature learning, we use the raw bag-of-words (bow) features as their input, and the 5000 most frequent common features selected for each adaptation task with TF-IDF as weight.

Email Spam Filtering Dataset[2]. There are 4000 labeled training instances which are collected from publicly available sources (source domain) in this dataset, and half of them are spam and the other half are non-spam. The testing instances were collected from 3 different user inboxes (target domains), each of them consists of 2500 samples. We also chose the 5000 most frequent terms as features.

20 Newsgroups Classification Dataset[3]. There are 18774 news documents with 61188 features on the 20 Newsgroups dataset. It is a hierarchical structure with 6 main categories and 20 subcategories. It contains four largest main categories, including comp, rec, sci, and talk. In our experiments, the largest category comp is selected as the positive class and one of the three other categories is chosen as the negative class for each setting. The settings of this dataset are listed in Table 1.

[1] http://www.cs.jhu.edu/mdredze/datasets/sentiment/.
[2] http://www.ecmlpkdd2006.org/challenge.html.
[3] http://qwone.com/~jason/20Newsgroups/.

Table 1. Description of data generated from 20 Newsgroups.

Setting	Source domain	Target domain
comp vs rec	comp.windows.x rec.sport.hockey	comp.sys.ibm.pc.hardware rec.motorcycles
comp vs sci	comp.windows.x sci.crypt	comp.sys.ibm.pc.hardware sci.med
comp vs talk	comp.windows.x talk.politics.mideast	comp.sys.ibm.pc.hardware talk.politics.guns

4.2 Compared Methods

We compare our approach with several state-of-the-art methods to test our work's effectiveness: the standard Logistic Regression (LR), standard Support Vector Machine (SVM), Marginalized Stacked Denoising Autoencoders (mSDA)[4] [10], Regularization Denoising Autoencoders (MDA-TR)[5] [25] and $\ell_{2,1}$-Norm Stacked Robust Autoencoders ($\ell_{2,1}$-SRA) [13].

Parameter Setting: In our experiments, we set the number of nearest neighbors k as 10 on all datasets, and the number of layers l in SRAAR is 5, 3, 3, α is 2, 20, 5 for Amazon Review, Spam and 20 Newsgroups. In the method of mSDA, the best parameters will be shown in the experiment. For MDA-TR, we use the default parameters as reported in [25]. For $\ell_{2,1}$-SRA, the number of layers is 5, 3 and 3 for Amazon Review, Spam and 20 Newsgroups. The parameter α is 2 for Amazon Review, 20 for Spam and 5 for 20 Newsgroups. And the parameter λ is 0.5, 10 and 5 for Amazon Review, Spam and 20 Newsgroups.

4.3 Classification Accuracy

Table 2 show the experimental results on three data sets. The best results in each settling have been marked in bold. And both SVM and LR are traditional approaches, those accuracy are the lower limits. We have the following observations from experimental results. (1) SRAAR, $\ell_{2,1}$-SRA and mSDA performs better than MDA-TR, which shows deep learning methods usually learn better representations than shallow learning methods. (2) Our SRAAR performs better than $\ell_{2,1}$-SRA and mSDA, which shows that SRAAR overcome the shortcoming of most exiting domain adaptation methods which focus only one aspect of the data. (3) Compared with $\ell_{2,1}$-SRA, the performance is improved, especially in the task of B→E, B→K, D→E, and Public→U0, Public→U1, and comp vs. sci, the accuracy is best, which verifies that it is necessary to preserve local geometry structure of data. (4) Moreover, we can observe that SRRAR performs quite well on the Spam dataset than the other two datasets. The reason might be that SRAAR can obtain more robust representations on the Spam dataset. It seems

[4] http://www.cse.wustl.edu/~mchen.

[5] http://github.com/sclincha/xrce_msda_da_regularization.

Table 2. Performance (accuracy %) on three datasets.

Task	SVM	LR	MDA-TR	mSDA	$\ell_{2,1}$-SRA	SRAAR
B→ D	80.65	81.23	83.32	84.36	84.72	**84.74**
B→ E	72.58	73.38	75.29	76.43	76.06	**81.82**
B→ K	75.44	77.41	82.86	82.46	84.32	**85.38**
D→ B	78.59	79.4	83.20	83.49	83.65	**83.76**
D→ E	72.82	75.37	80	82.05	80.64	**83.75**
D→ K	76.40	79.19	86.14	87.38	**87.55**	**87.55**
E→ B	70.48	70.97	78.66	79.37	78.99	**79.73**
E→ D	72.36	73.42	79.14	79.34	**80.12**	**80.12**
E→ K	86.19	86.41	86.16	**88.46**	88.07	88.44
K→ B	71.49	72.47	79.06	79.13	79.35	**79.39**
K→ D	74.40	76.1	79.39	79.39	79.95	**80.39**
K→ E	84.49	85.7	87.33	87.38	**87.64**	**87.64**
Average	76.32	77.51	81.71	82.44	82.59	**83.56**
Public → U0	72.79	72.71	82.55	78.00	81.99	**88.99**
Public → U1	73.94	74.86	85.87	85.12	85.99	**89.75**
Public → U2	78.64	80.08	85.92	90.44	**91.36**	**91.36**
Average	75.12	75.88	84.78	84.52	86.45	**90.03**
comp vs. rec	77.13	79.82	80.32	80.78	82.61	**83.32**
comp vs. sci	74.77	75.38	73.86	76.45	79.35	**80.26**
comp vs. talk	92.69	92.85	94.01	**94.17**	92.74	93.06
Average	81.53	82.68	82.68	83.80	84.90	**85.54**

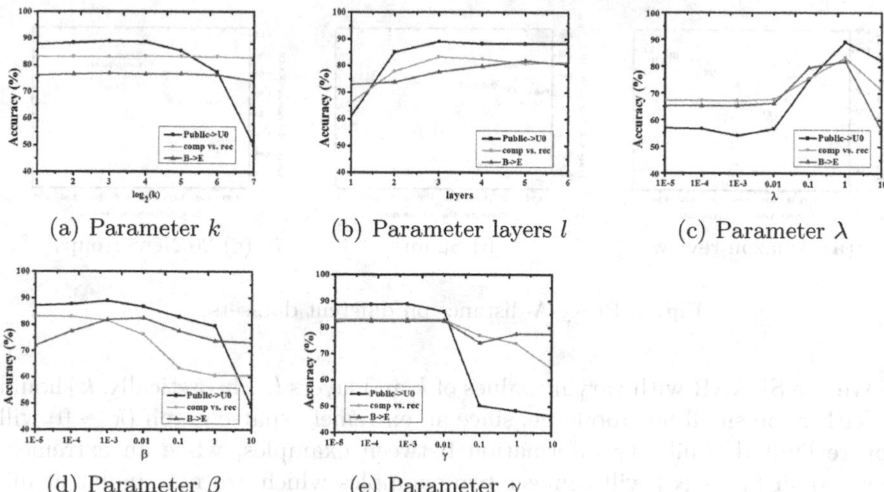

(a) Parameter k (b) Parameter layers l (c) Parameter λ

(d) Parameter β (e) Parameter γ

Fig. 1. Parameter sensitivity study for SRAAR on selected datasets

that domain adaptation on the spam dataset is easier than that on the Amazon dataset and 20 Newsgroups dataset.

4.4 Parameter Sensitivity

We conduct empirical parameter sensitivity analysis, which validates that SRAAR can achieve optimal performance under wide range of parameter values. There are six parameters in our method: the number of nearest neighbor k, the number of layers l, parameter α, shrinkage regularization λ, manifold regularization β and MMD regularization γ. In this section, we mainly discuss five parameters: k, l, λ, β and γ. We randomly select one generated dataset from Amazon review, Spam and 20 Newsgroups, and discuss the results. When one parameter is changed, the other parameters are fixed in the experiments.

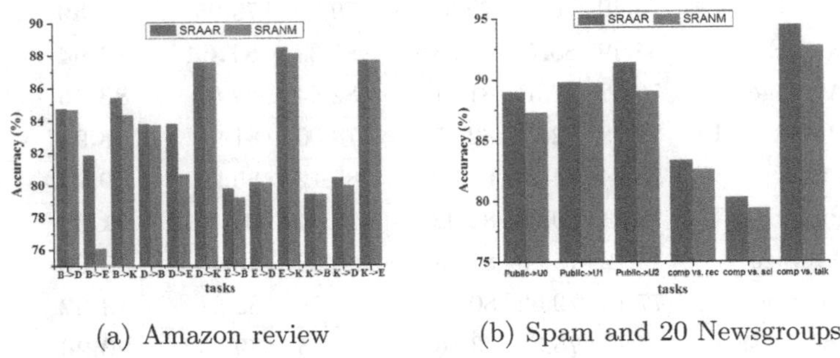

(a) Amazon review (b) Spam and 20 Newsgroups

Fig. 2. Comparison of SRANM and SRAAR

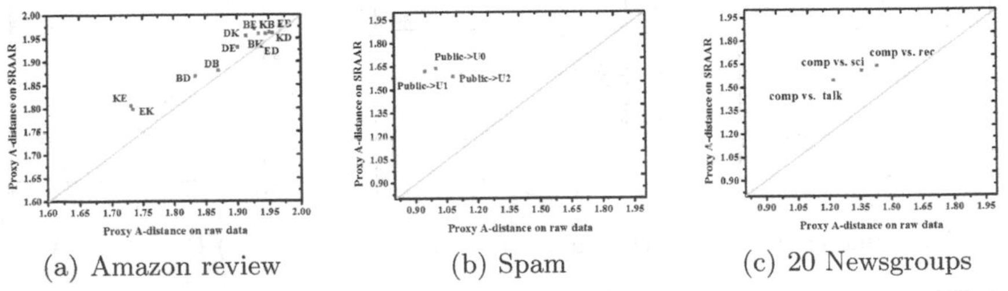

(a) Amazon review (b) Spam (c) 20 Newsgroups

Fig. 3. Proxy-A-distance on different datasets

We run SRAAR with varying values of k and layers l. Theoretically, k should be neither too small nor too large, since an extremely sparse graph ($k \to 0$) will capture limited similarity information between examples, while an extremely dense graph ($k \to \infty$) will connect two examples which are not similar at all. We plot the classification accuracy w.r.t. different values of k in Fig. 1(a), which indicates a wide range $k \in [4,32]$ for optimal parameter values. We also studied the effect of the number of layers. We plotted the accuracies with different number of layers on the same datasets as above, which are shown in Fig. 1(b). We can see that our method usually performs the best with 3–5 layers. According to these observations from Fig. 1(b), the number of layers l are 5, 3, 3 for Amazon review, Spam and 20 Newsgroups respectively.

We also run SRAAR with varying values of parameter λ, β, and γ. We tune parameter λ, β, and γ by a "grid-search" strategy from {1E-05, 1E-04, 1E-03, 0.01, 0.1, 1, 10} and record the best result, and all the results are reported in Fig. 1. From Fig. 1(c)–(e), We find that SRAAR is sensitive to the selection of λ, β, γ, and if the value of λ, β, and γ is large enough, the performance of SRAAR is very poor. According to these observations, $\lambda \in [0.1, 1]$, $\beta \in$ [1E-4, 0.01], $\gamma \in$ [1E-5, 1E-3] are the optimal parameter values.

4.5 The Manifold Regularization

In order to validate the manifold regularization in our SRAAR is efficient, we compare our SRAAR to SRANM (not taking manifold regularization into account). And the experimental results are showed in Fig. 2. It can be seen from Fig. 2(a), (b), our SRAAR perform better than SRANM in all tasks. Especially in the tasks of B→E, B→K and D→E, Public→U2 and comp vs. talk, the performance is significantly improved, which verifiers that is necessary to preserve the local geometry structure of data. Therefore, we can conclude that taking manifold regularization into account for domain adaptation is efficient.

4.6 Transfer Distance

Ben-David et al. [26] suggested using the proxy-A-distance to measure the similarity between two domains. A proxy-A-distance is defined as $d_A = 2(1 - 2\epsilon)$, where ϵ is the generalization error of a classifier (a linear SVM in our case) trained on the binary classification problem to discriminate source domain and target domain. Fig. 3 shows the proxy-A-distance before and after SRAAR is applied. Surprisingly, the distance increases in the new representation on all the datasets, which means that the new representation are suitable for both sentiment analysis tasks and text classification tasks. We can observe that the distance on Spam dataset and 20 Newsgroups dataset are increased more than others. It seems that domain adaptation on Amazon dataset is more difficult than others.

5 Conclusion

In this paper, we proposed a domain adaptation algorithm for learning feature representations with a deep learning architecture, referred to as $\ell_{2,1}$-norm stacked robust autoencoders via adaptation regularization for domain adaptation (SRAAR). There are two components in our method, the first one is a manifold regularization, which preserves the local geometry structure of data that makes similar sample more close. The other one is the maximum mean discrepancy (MMD), which is used to minimize the discrepancy between source and target domains. Experimental results demonstrate the effectiveness of our proposed SRAAR.

Acknowledgments. This work is supported in part by the National Key Research and Development Program of China under grant (2016YFC0801406) and the Natural Science Foundation of China under grants (61503112, 61673152, 61503116).

References

1. Pan, S.J., Yang, Q.: A survey on transfer learning. IEEE Trans. Knowl. Data Eng. **22**(10), 1345–1359 (2010)
2. Daumé III, H., Marcu, D.: Domain adaptation for statistical classifiers. CoRR abs/1109.6341 (2011)
3. Sagha, H., Cummins, N., Schuller, B.W.: Stacked denoising autoencoders for sentiment analysis: a review. Wiley Interdisc. Rev. Data Min. Knowl. Discov. **7**(5), e1212 (2017)
4. Cao, S., Yang, N., Liu, Z.: Online news recommender based on stacked autoencoder. In: 16th IEEE/ACIS International Conference on Computer and Information Science, ICIS 2017, Wuhan, China, 24–26 May 2017, pp. 721–726 (2017)
5. Eyiokur, F.I., Yaman, D., Ekenel, H.K.: Domain adaptation for ear recognition using deep convolutional neural networks. IET Biometrics **7**(3), 199–206 (2018)
6. Deng, H., Zhang, L., Shu, X.: Feature memory-based deep recurrent neural network for language modeling. Appl. Soft Comput. **68**, 432–446 (2018)
7. Zhao, X., Wu, J., Zhang, Y.: Fault diagnosis of motor in frequency domain signal by stacked de-noising auto-encoder. Comput. Mater. Continua **57**, 223–242 (2018)
8. Tu, Y., Lin, Y., Wang, J.: Semi-supervised learning with generative adversarial networks on digital signal modulation classification. Comput. Mater. Continua **55**, 243–254 (2018)
9. Glorot, X., Bordes, A., Bengio, Y.: Domain adaptation for large-scale sentiment classification: a deep learning approach. In: Proceedings of the 28th International Conference on Machine Learning, ICML 2011, Bellevue, Washington, USA, 28 June 2 July 2011, pp. 513–520 (2011)
10. Chen, M., Xu, Z.E., Weinberger, K.Q., Sha, F.: Marginalized denoising autoencoders for domain adaptation. In: Proceedings of the 29th International Conference on Machine Learning, ICML 2012, Edinburgh, Scotland, UK, 26 June–1 July 2012 (2012)
11. Csurka, G., Chidlovskii, B., Clinchant, S., Michel, S.: An extended framework for marginalized domain adaptation. CoRR abs/1702.05993 (2017)
12. Borgwardt, K.M., Gretton, A., Rasch, M.J., Kriegel, H., Scholkopf, B., Smola, A.J.: Integrating structured biological data by kernel maximum mean discrepancy. In: Proceedings of the 14th International Conference on Intelligent Systems for Molecular Biology, Fortaleza, Brazil, 6–10 August 2006, pp. 49–57 (2006)
13. Jiang, W., Gao, H., Chung, F., Huang, H.: The l2,1-norm stacked robust autoencoders for domain adaptation. In: Proceedings of the Thirtieth AAAI Conference on Artificial Intelligence, 12–17 February 2016, Phoenix, Arizona, USA, pp. 1723–1729 (2016)

14. Blitzer, J., McDonald, R.T., Pereira, F.: Domain adaptation with structural correspondence learning. In: Proceedings of the 2006 Conference on Empirical Methods in Natural Language Processing, EMNLP 2007, 22–23 July 2006, Sydney, Australia, pp. 120–128 (2006)
15. Xue, G., Dai, W., Yang, Q., Yu, Y.: Topic-bridged PLSA for cross-domain text classification. In: Proceedings of the 31st Annual International ACM SIGIR Conference on Research and Development in Information Retrieval, SIGIR 2008, Singapore, 20–24 July 2008, pp. 627–634 (2008)
16. Pan, S.J., Ni, X., Sun, J., Yang, Q., Chen, Z.: Cross-domain sentiment classification via spectral feature alignment. In: Proceedings of the 19th International Conference on World Wide Web, WWW 2010, Raleigh, North Carolina, USA, 26–30 April 2010, pp. 751–760 (2010)
17. Daumé III, H.: Frustratingly easy domain adaptation. CoRR abs/0907.1815 (2009)
18. Bollegala, D., Weir, D.J., Carroll, J.A.: Cross-domain sentiment classification using a sentiment sensitive thesaurus. IEEE Trans. Knowl. Data Eng. **25**(8), 1719–1731 (2013)
19. Zhuang, F., Cheng, X., Luo, P., Pan, S.J., He, Q.: Supervised representation learning: transfer learning with deep autoencoders. In: Proceedings of the Twenty-Fourth International Joint Conference on Artificial Intelligence, IJCAI 2015, Buenos Aires, Argentina, 25–31 July 2015, pp. 4119–4125 (2015)
20. Ganin, Y., Lempitsky, V.S.: Unsupervised domain adaptation by backpropagation. In: Proceedings of the 32nd International Conference on Machine Learning, ICML 2015, Lille, France, 6–11 July 2015, pp. 1180–1189 (2015)
21. Clinchant, S., Csurka, G., Chidlovskii, B.: A domain adaptation regularization for denoising autoencoders. In: Proceedings of the 54th Annual Meeting of the Association for Computational Linguistics, ACL 2016, 7–12 August 2016, Berlin, Germany, Volume 2: Short Papers (2016)
22. Ziser, Y., Reichart, R.: Neural structural correspondence learning for domain adaptation. In: Proceedings of the 21st Conference on Computational Natural Language Learning (CoNLL 2017), Vancouver, Canada, 3–4 August 2017, pp. 400–410 (2017)
23. Zhu, Y., Hu, X., Zhang, Y., Li, P.: Transfer learning with stacked reconstruction independent component analysis. Knowl.-Based Syst. **152**, 100–106 (2018)
24. Long, M., Cao, Y., Wang, J., Jordan, M.I.: Learning transferable features with deep adaptation networks. In: Proceedings of the 32nd International Conference on Machine Learning, ICML 2015, Lille, France, 6–11 July 2015, pp. 97–105 (2015)
25. Csurka, G., Chidlowskii, B., Clinchant, S., Michel, S.: Unsupervised domain adaptation with regularized domain instance denoising. In: Hua, G., Jégou, H. (eds.) ECCV 2016, Part III. LNCS, vol. 9915, pp. 458–466. Springer, Cham (2016). https://doi.org/10.1007/978-3-319-49409-8_37
26. Ben-David, S., Blitzer, J., Crammer, K., Pereira, F.: Analysis of representations for domain adaptation. In: Proceedings of the Twentieth Annual Conference on Neural Information Processing Systems, Vancouver, British Columbia, Canada, 4–7 December 2006, pp. 137–144 (2006)

Molecular Dynamics Simulation Optimization Based on GROMACS on Sunway TaihuLight

Xudong Tang, Tao Wu, Tiejun Wang(✉), and Jiliang Wu

Chengdu University of Information Technology,
Chengdu 610225, Sichuan, China
tjw@cuit.edu.cn

Abstract. Compared with gene research, human proteomics research is relatively rare. There is less research, that is protein dynamic structure in the cross-disciplinary field. For precision medicine, proteomics research is necessary. This article starts with software and aims to speed up the protein simulation process and reduce the experimental cycle. In order to reduce the time-consuming of protein simulation and non-biopolymer simulation process and improve the performance of GROMACS software. This paper optimized the performance of GROMACS by using manual vectorization to optimize its hotspots on Sunway TaihuLight System, and designed several test cases. The experiment was simulated and evaluated for performance testing. The final optimization effect is remarkable, reaching a speedup ratio of about 136%.

Keywords: GROMACS · Protein simulation · Manual vectorization · Performance optimization

1 Introduction

Precision medicine has been playing an increasingly important role in tailoring medical treatment to the individual characteristics of each patient and classifying individuals into subpopulations that differ in their susceptibility to a particular disease. It leverages medical frontier technologies, such as genome and proteome, to analyze, identify and validate specific biomarkers from large sample populations to accurately find out the causes and treatment targets. Compared to genes, proteins have been relatively understudied in human blood, even though they are the 'effectors' of human biology, are disrupted in many diseases, and are the targets of most medicines. The very limited study of mesoscale problems between the two boundary scales on each of the four levels, molecular biology, cellular biology, histology, and systems biology, results in bottleneck problems in non-coding ribonucleic acid (RNA) and dynamic protein structure, organelle regulation, and tissue and functional systems, respectively, and which have become the unresolved focal problems in modern biological and medical research [1]. Deep understanding of material basis of life phenomena at the molecular level would help explore the law of life activities in essence, understand the mechanisms of diseases and develop new drugs [2].

The functions and effects of protein molecules are closely related to their spatial structure. It is continuous movement of protein molecules that leads to different protein

X. Sun et al. (Eds.): ICAIS 2019, LNCS 11633, pp. 112–123, 2019.
https://doi.org/10.1007/978-3-030-24265-7_10

structures such as folding, stretching, binding ligand and substrate, and which determine different functions and effects of protein molecules. Therefore, not only should we study the order of amino acids and the 3D structure of proteins, but also the correspondence between the structure and function of proteins and to simulate the binding process of ligands and receptors. In order to research proteins at atomic level, the simulation of protein molecules has begun to be thoroughly and systematically studied. With the rapid development of molecular dynamics simulation, some relatively full-function simulation software for biology have been developed, such as GROMACS [3], NAMD [4], LAMMPS [5], Desmond [6], and etc. Especially, the former two are most widely used to simulate protein molecules. In 1999, Wright et al. [7] proposed the unstructured nature of intrinsically disordered proteins in solution. Subsequent studies predicted that one-third of eukaryotic cells in the organism contain unordered sequences [8], nearly 25% of the proteins encoded by human gene are completely random, and 40% of the proteins contain a unstructured domain of at least 30 amino acid residues in length [9, 10]. Although solid disordered proteins are unstructured in solution, when they bind with ligands they will fold into ordered 3D conformation at some moment, and which is extremely short. In order to verify the two hypotheses - the Induced fit model [11] and the Structured selection model [12], molecular-level simulations are necessarily required. However, the time scale of the process of the binding and folding of inherent disordered protein is often in the range from microsecond to millisecond. It is difficult to simulate the process taken place in microsecond or millisecond directly using traditional molecular dynamics simulation technologies [1]. With the rise of large computing centers such as supercomputing, the molecular dynamics simulations at microsecond or millisecond level have been applied gradually. But, it is still time-consuming.

In this paper, we proposed a method to optimize the performance of the non-bond force calculation process using GROMACS molecular simulation running on the Sunway TaihuLight System by using the SIMD programming interface of Sunway CPU. Firstly, we introduce the GROMACS system and the algorithm flow. Then we demonstrate the experimental process considering to the composition of SW26010 processor.

Finally, we run the performance tests and the results show that the parallel optimization of the molecular dynamics simulation reduces the experimental period of simulating abiotic polymer and improves the efficiency of molecular dynamics simulation partly. It not only reduces the time required by the simulation process, but also saves the manpower and resources.

2 Model and System Introduction

2.1 GROMACS Introduction

GROMACS is short for Groningen Machine for Chemical Simulations, and which is a free and open source software. GROMACS is a computational engine for molecular dynamics simulation and energy minimization. Biochemical molecules that can be used for simulation studies using GROMACS include proteins, lipids, nucleic acids, and even molecules of non-biological origin, polymers, and etc. In this subject, the iterative process of GROMACS mainly includes three parts: adjacency table construction, force calculation, and state update. In the adjacency table structure, the atomic group is constructed and the adjacency table used in the potential is generated. The force calculation part calculates the short-range force and the long-range force. Short-range force uses spatially similar atomic calculations to calculate bubble repulsion, van der Waals force, etc. While long-range force mainly needs to solve the calculation of Coulomb force under long distance, mainly using particle grid (PME) or reaction in the field (RF) method. The state update part is to update the speed and position of the atom according to the force after calculating the stress state of each atom, and adjust the constant temperature or constant pressure or constant volume according to the configuration of the example.

2.2 GROMACS Simulation Algorithm Flow

The purpose of molecular dynamics simulation is to simulate the structural evolution of the macromolecular configuration system over time. The GROMACS simulation algorithm (see Fig. 1) can be roughly divided into two parts, one is the PP process for calculating the short-range force, and the other is the PME process for calculating the long-range force. First, enter the initial conditions. Assuming that the potential energy of the atomic position function is system V, the input includes the coordinates r of all atoms, and an initial velocity v for each atom in a given system to initialize the simulation process. Calculate short-range and long-range forces. Calculate the electrostatic field force and van der Waals force of all atoms in the V system, electrostatic potential energy (1).

$$U = \frac{k}{2}\sum\nolimits_{n} \cdot \sum\nolimits_{i=1}^{N} \sum\nolimits_{j=1}^{N} \frac{q_i q_j}{r_{ij,n\,i}} \tag{1}$$

$$F_i = m_i \frac{\partial^2 \gamma_i}{\partial t^2}, i = 1, \cdots N \tag{2}$$

$$F_i = \sum F_{ij} \tag{3}$$

This force is equal to the non-bond interaction force between the atoms, (2), then plus the bonding force between the atoms and plus the constraints sums or external forces. Potential energy, kinetic energy and pressure tensor may also need to be calculate here. Update the configuration. Solving Newton's equation of motion by numerical method (3) simulate the motion of atoms. Output position, speed, energy, temperature, pressure, etc. When simulation is long-term, update the data and then iterate through the whole process.

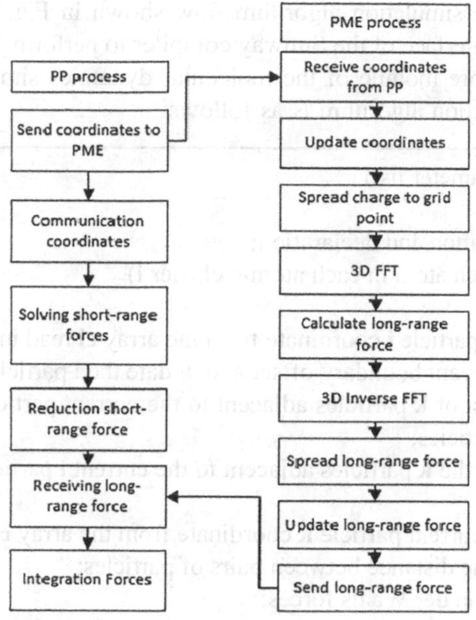

Fig. 1. Molecular dynamics flow chart

3 Experimental Design

The development of drugs requires a lot of manpower, material resources and plenty of time. Our goal is to reduce the blindness of the experiment by improving the performance of the protein molecular simulation tool GROMACS. Including protein simulation, abiotic polymer simulation, drug screening and drug design simulation are implemented efficiently on the Sunway TaihuLight system. To improve the simulation efficiency when performing molecular dynamics simulation experiments to save manpower, material resources and time.

The experimental environment of this subject is the multi-core architecture of the SW26010 processor in the Sunway TaihuLight supercomputer, located in Wuxi, China. A SW26010 chip contains 4 computing core groups, each core group contains 1 computing control core called master core and 64 computing cores called 64 slave cores. These 64 slave cores have 64 KB high-speed cache (LDM), it is also the high technology of Sunway. The synergy between the control core and the computing cores can greatly improve the performance of various applications. In the SW26010, both the computational control core and the computing cores extend the SIMD vectorization support. For the sake of power consumption and application requirements, the control core and computing cores of the SW 26010 all support the SIMD extension structure of the same width with 256-bit SIMD designed.

First, after hotspot analysis, the GROMACS protein molecular simulation process hotspot function is called nbnxn_kernel_(), and the hotspot module is nbnxn_kernel_ref_inner.h. Corresponding to the short-range force internal iterative solution part shown in the program simulation algorithm flow shown in Fig. 1. We designed the SIMD programming interface of the Sunway compiler to perform manual vectorization optimization on the core module of the molecular dynamics simulation algorithm in GROMACS. The function algorithm is as follows:

```
nbnxn_kernel_ (parameter list)
{
   Variable initialization and declaration;
   for (traversing each atom in each atomic cluster i)
   {
      Obtaining the particle i coordinate from the array ci read in the input file;
      Obtain the relevant boundary offset and update the i particle coordinates;
      Obtaining a list of k particles adjacent to the current particle i from an array
      of adjacent particles;
      for (traversing the k particles adjacent to the current i particle)
      {
         Obtain the current particle k coordinate from the array ci;
         Calculate the distance between pairs of particles;
         Calculate van der Waals forces;
         Updating the three-dimensional force vector of the current particle k;
         Calculate the resultant force of the i particles;
      }
   Updating the three-dimensional force vector of the i particle;
   Updating the boundary force vector of the i particle;
   Updating the potential energy value of the van der Waals energy group in
   which the i particle is located;
   }
}
```

The SIMD programming interface of the master core of SW26010 chip supports 256-bit data for single-instruction and multi-data parallelism. It can process 4 single-precision or double-precision floating-point operations in one operation, or can handle 8 32-bit fixed-point operations in one operation. Or directly handle a 256-bit long integer operation in one operation. In the non-vectorized code, the two-loop iterative calculation inside the short-range force is the real hotspot of the whole simulation software. We designed a global manual vectorization of the inner loop of a two-layer loop of internal iterations of short-range forces. In order to improve the GROMACS simulation performance, we have made the following design: (1) firstly perform single-precision local precision reduction processing in the short-range force calculation part. (2) global manual vectorization of inner-layer loop, SIMD ban inner layer loop Calculation. (3) The macro defines the expansion of the function, and puts the conditional macro definition of the corresponding function in the .h file into the inner layer iteration and performs vectorization expansion to facilitate the overall vectorization calculation. (4) There are several standard library functions in the inner layer iterative calculation, such as exp, sqrt, etc. This topic applies the SIMD programming interface of the Sunway TaihuLight System, and the design rewrites the standard library function. (5) Inner layer iteration and optimization design of memory access during the entire short-range force calculation process.

Then, in order to test the molecular dynamics simulation tool GROMACS optimization effect, we prepared two media for large molecule simulation of different atomic numbers to verify the optimization effect of the tool. Medium 1 is a molecular dynamics simulation in a xylem fiber channel that uses 3 million atoms for simulation. Medium 2 is a molecular dynamics simulation in an ion channel. This experiment used 140,000 atoms for simulation calculations. In order to make the parallel effect, we have set different process numbers to verify the simulation of the xylem fiber channel. For molecular dynamics simulation in xylem fiber channels we designed 64 processes and 512 processes to verify the effects separately.

4 Simulation Results

Both the molecular dynamics simulation of ion channels and xylem fiber channels are shown here. The pictures shown in Sect. 4 are from the *. gro file (molecular structural model file) generated by GROMACS. These *. gro files are based on the molecular structure model of GROMACS after the last iteration step is completed after 1000 steps (xylem fiber channels) or 10000 steps (ion channels) of molecular dynamics simulation. Then we analyze the data and get the following graphs through VMD (Visual Molecular Dynamics) simulation software. After analysis and comparison, the molecular space structure of the optimized code simulation is basically the same as the optimized molecular space structure, and the same simulation effect output is achieved.

The Figs. 2, 3 and 4 are the final structure model obtained by optimizing the ion channel model of the first 140,000 particles.

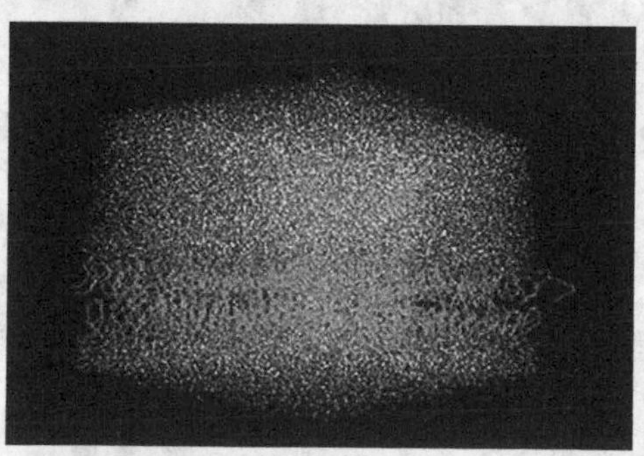

Fig. 2. Ion channels spatial structure

This is the final structure model of the optimized 140,000-particle ion channel model. Comparing the following three graphs (Figs. 5, 6 and 7) with the above Figs. 2, 3 and 4, we can find that the final molecular structure is basically the same. The difference in color is something we do specifically to distinguish between the pre-optimization and the optimized.

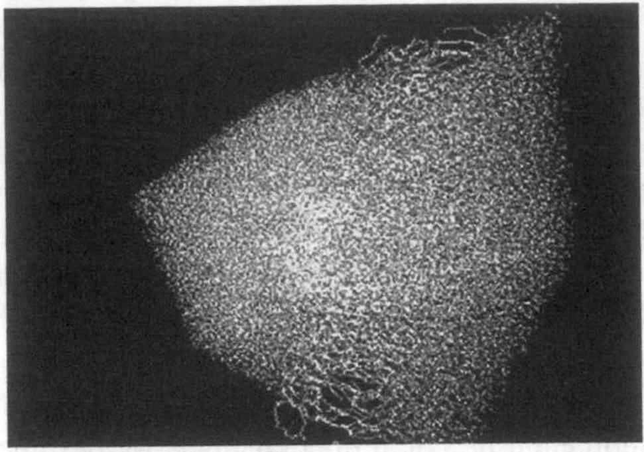

Fig. 3. Ion channels side of space structure

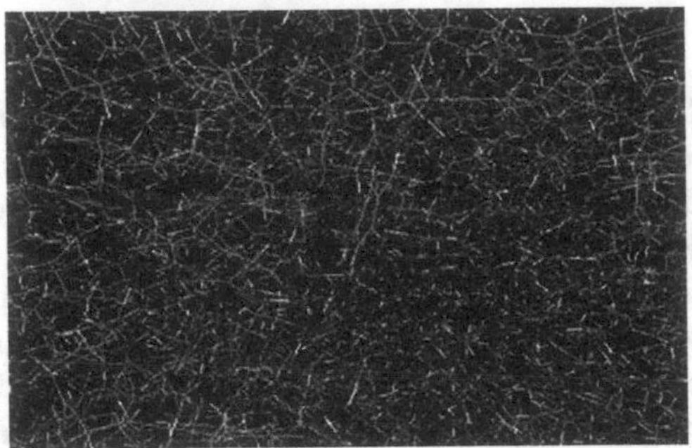

Fig. 4. Chemical bond

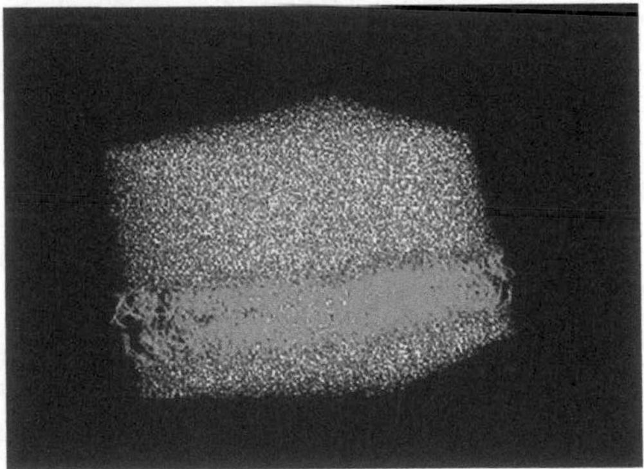

Fig. 5. Ion channels side of space structure

Following is the final structural model of xylem fiber channel with 3 million particles before program be optimized (Figs. 8, 9 and 10).

Following is the final structural model of xylem fiber channel with 3 million particles after program be optimized (Figs. 11, 12 and 13).

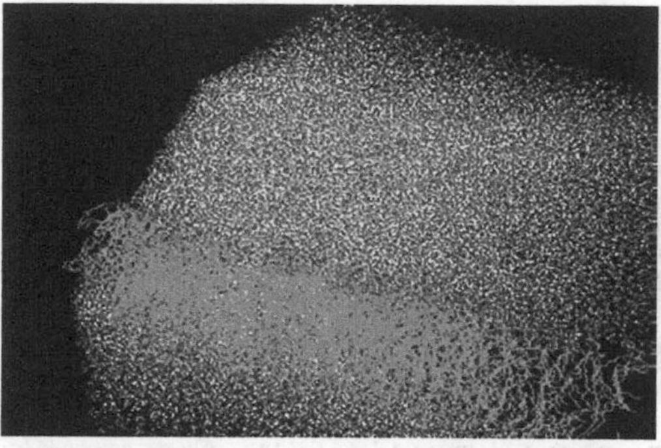

Fig. 6. Ion channels spatial structure

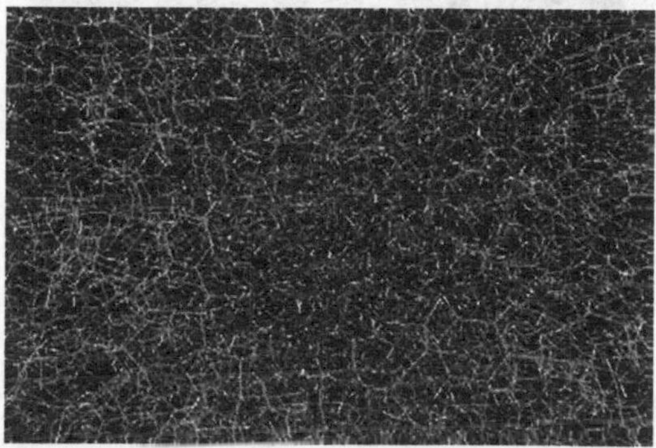

Fig. 7. Chemical bond

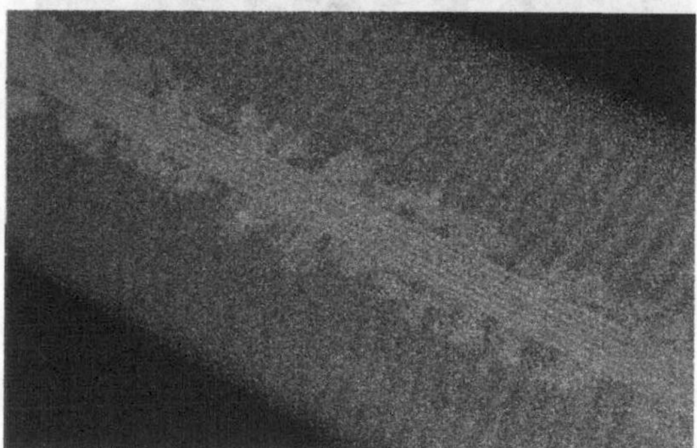

Fig. 8. Xylem fiber channels spatial structure

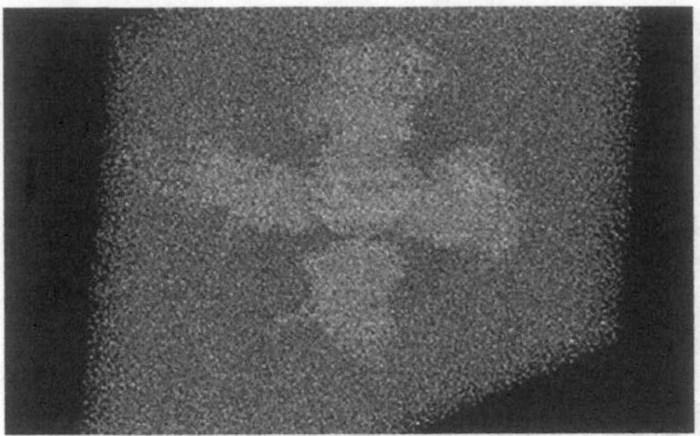

Fig. 9. Xylem fiber channels side of space structure

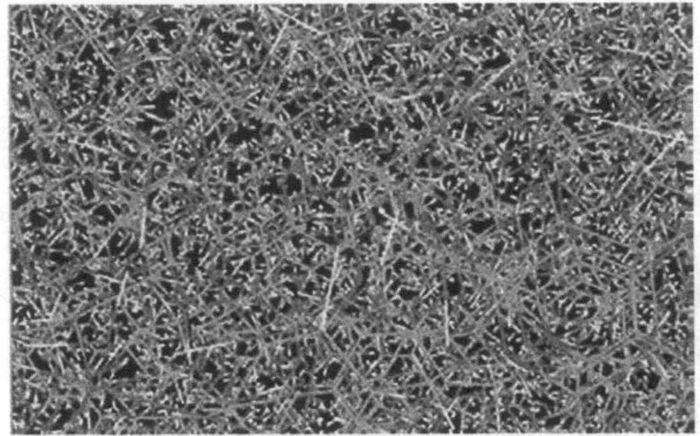

Fig. 10. Chemical bond

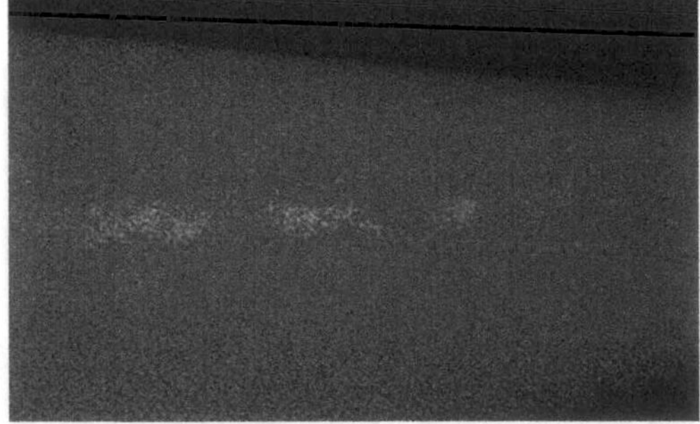

Fig. 11. Xylem fiber channels spatial structure

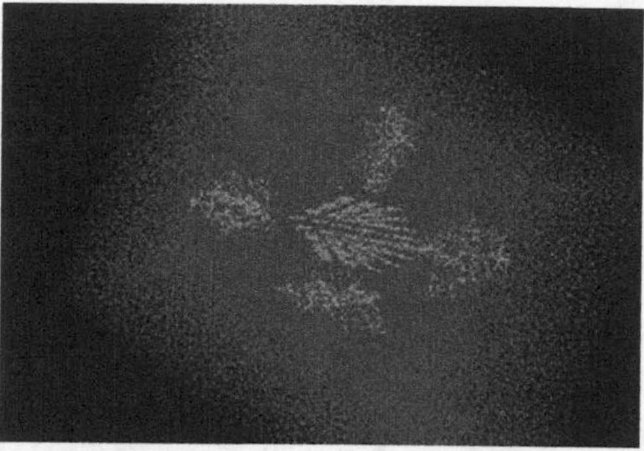

Fig. 12. Xylem fiber channels side of space structure

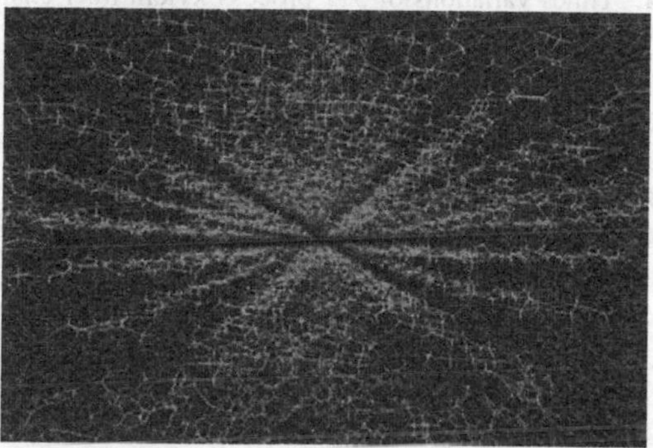

Fig. 13. Chemical bond

5 Performance Test and Evaluation

In the following diagram the optimization steps of 1–5 corresponds to the optimization design of Sect. 3 (Figs. 14 and 15).

After testing on the Sunway TaihuLight System, the above test results are shown as following. In the case of simulation using a 64-process in xylem fiber medium, it (see Table 3) takes 3800 s before optimization, and the time after optimization is 2760 s, and the speedup ratio reaches 137.68% (see Table 1). When using the 512 process to simulate in xylem fiber medium (see Table 2), the pre-optimization code took 583 s, the optimized code took 428 s, the speedup ratio reached 136.21%, and the simulation process did not optimize the code when using the 16 process using ion media simulation. It (see Table 1) takes 6500 s to go down, and in the case of optimized code, it takes 4800 s, and you can see a significant performance improvement with a speedup ratio of 135.42%.

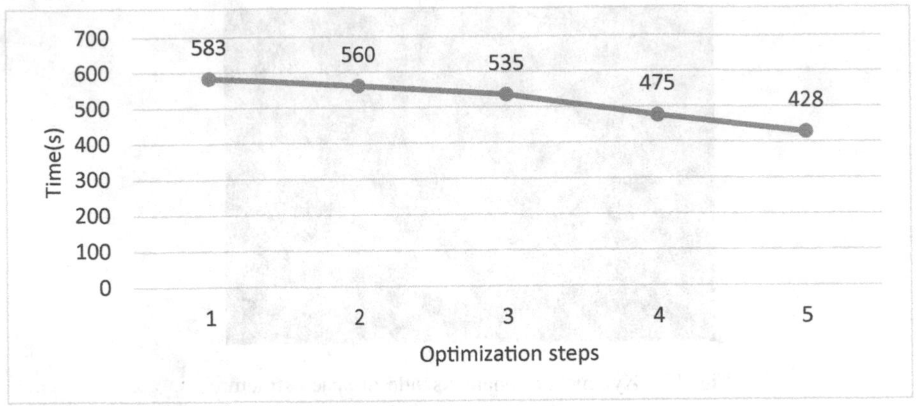

Fig. 14. Times variations of 512 process xylem fiber channels

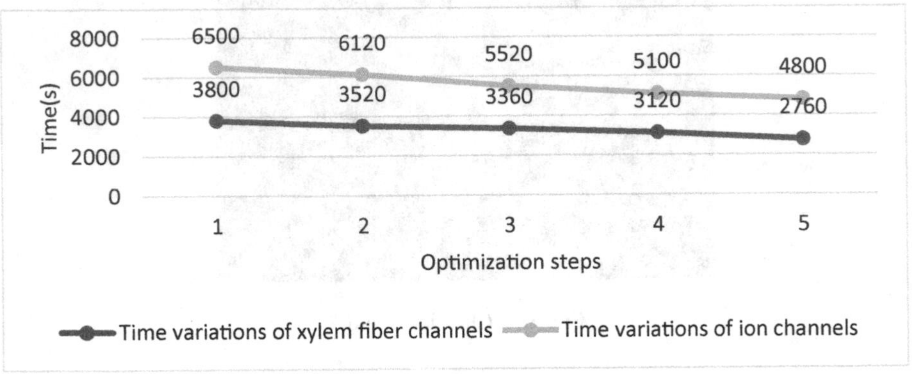

Fig. 15. 64 process xylem fiber channels and 16 process ion channels

Table 1. Test case time change and speedup

Test case	Before optimization	Optimized	Speedup
16 process ion channel medium	6500	4800	135.42%
64 process xylem fiber channels medium	3800	2760	137.68%
512 process xylem fiber channels medium	583	428	136.21%

6 Conclusions

Proteomics research is crucial for the future of smart medical care. This article reduces the time spent on protein simulation and non-biopolymer simulation by improving the performance of the GROMACS software. This paper based on the Sunway TaihuLight System, the hotspot part of the molecular dynamics simulation process of GROMACS is optimized by the manual vectorization optimization, which reduced the time spent on

GROMACS molecular dynamics simulation. In the 64-process xylem fiber cases, the speedup ratio is 137.68%. The speedup ratio is 135.42% in the 16-process ion channel, and the speedup ratio is 136.21% reached in the 512-process xylem fiber cases. There are also some shortcomings in this paper. Sunway TaihuLight's greatest advantage lies in 64 slave cores. But we don't deeply analyze the data structure of GROMACS program, and we don't take advantage of the 64 slave cores. If we can use 64 slave cores, the simulation performance will be doubled improved.

Acknowledgements. This research is jointly supported by the Science and Technology Support Program of Sichuan Province (Grant NO. 2017JQ0030). The authors also thank the reviewers for their time and efforts during the review process.

References

1. Li, J.H.: Exploring the logic and landscape of the knowledge system: multilevel structures, each multiscaled with complexity at the mesoscale. Engineering **2**(3), 276–285 (2016)
2. Ren, Y., Xu, J.: Frontiers of molecular dynamics simulations of protein systems reexamine from the meso-science perspective. Chin. J. Process. Eng. **18**, 1126–1137 (2018)
3. Hess, B., Kutzner, C., van der Spoel, D., et al.: Gromacs 4: algorithms for highly efficient, load-balanced, and scalable molecular simulation. J. Chem. Theory Comput. **4**(3), 435–447 (2008)
4. Phillips, J.C., Braun, R., Wang, W., et al.: Scalable molecular dynamics with NAMD. J. Comput. Chem. **26**(16), 1781–1802 (2005)
5. Plimpton, S.: Fast parallel algorithms for short-range molecular dynamics. J. Comput. Phys. **117**(1), 1–19 (1995)
6. Bowers, K.J., Chow, E., Xu, H.F., et al.: Scalable algorithms for molecular dynamics simulations on commodity clusters. In: IEEE Conference on Supercomputing (SC 2006), p. 43 (2006)
7. Wright, P.E., Dyson, H.J.: Intrinsically unstructured proteins: re-assessing the protein structure-function paradigm. J. Mol. Biol. **293**(2), 321–331 (1999)
8. Pancsa, R., Tompa, P.: Structural disorder in eukaryotes. Plos One **7**(4), e34687 (2012)
9. Oldfield, C.J., Cheng, Y., Cortese, M.S., et al.: Comparing and combining predictors of mostly disordered proteins. Biochemistry **44**(6), 1989–2000 (2005)
10. Uversky, V.N., Dunker, A.K.: Understanding protein non-folding. Biochim. Biophys. Acta Proteins Proteomics **1804**(6), 1231–1264 (2010)
11. Huang, Y., Liu, Z.R.: Kinetic advantage of intrinsically disordered proteins in coupled folding binding process: a critical assessment of the "fly-casting" mechanism. J. Mol. Biol. **393**(5), 1143–1159 (2009)
12. Espinoza-Fonseca, L.M.: Reconciling binding mechanisms of intrinsically disordered proteins. Biochem. Biophys. Res. Commun. **382**(3), 479–482 (2009)
13. Wang, T., Tao, W., Ashrafzadeh, A.H., He, J.: Crowdsourcing-based framework for teaching quality evaluation and feedback using linguistic 2-tuple. CMC Comput. Mater. Continua **57**(1), 81–96 (2018)
14. Wang, S., Zhang, Y., Zhang, L., Cao, N., Pang, C.: An improved memory cache management study based on spark. CMC Comput. Mater. Continua **56**(3), 415–431 (2018)

A Review of Network Representation Learning

Dan Xu, Le Wang, Jing Qiu(✉), and Hui Lu(✉)

Cyberspace Institute of Advance Technology, Guangzhou University, Guangzhou 510006, China
2382290823@qq.com, {wangle,qiujing,luhui}@gzhu.edu.cn

Abstract. With the development of the technology, social software such as Facebook, Twitter, YouTube, QQ, WeChat has also achieved great development. According to the existing data, in the first quarter of 2018, WeChat's monthly number has reached 1 billion [1]. At the same time, these large-scale nodes also carry a large amount of external information such as texts and pictures, forming a complex information network. Information networks are widely used in real life and have enormous academic and economic value. Academically, artificial intelligence, big data, deep learning and other technologies are developing rapidly. Large and complex neural networks and complex information networks urgently need to make a reasonable analysis of data [2]. In terms of application value, information networks and social networks also have a wide range of application scenarios, such as recommendation systems, community discovery and other tasks [3]. Therefore, the research and application of complex information networks is a hot issue in the field of artificial intelligence, and it is necessary to study it.

Keywords: Big data · Complex information network · Representation

1 Background

In the conventional representation method, we generally express the graph using an adjacency matrix, an adjacency list, and the like [4]. Let a network be denoted as G = (V, E), where V denotes a set of nodes and E denotes a set of edges. The edge $e = (v_i, v_j) \in E$ represents an edge between the node v_i and the node v_j. The adjacency matrix of the network can be defined as $A \in R\hat{}(|V| * |V|)$, where $A_{ij} = 1$, if $(v_i, v_j) \in E$, otherwise $A_{ij} = 0$. The adjacency matrix is a very simple network data [5]. Intuitive expression, each row in matrix A can represent the link relationship between a node and other nodes, so it can be regarded as a representation of the corresponding node, The adjacency matrix method is simple and straightforward, but it has huge problems. Each matrix A will occupy the storage space of $|V| * |V|$. This is unacceptable when the data size is huge and exceeds one million [6]. Due to the sparsity of the adjacency matrix, when the dimension is 10, we need to cover 80% on each axis to capture 10% of the data. This problem can be described as a dimensional disaster. In addition, when the amount of data without correlation increases exponentially with time, the computing power also increases exponentially. When there is a correlation between the data, the computational power requirement can even reach double

X. Sun et al. (Eds.): ICAIS 2019, LNCS 11633, pp. 124–132, 2019.
https://doi.org/10.1007/978-3-030-24265-7_11

exponential growth, which will be the existing computing power. Ask a huge challenge. This problem can be described as a big data challenge. Therefore, finding new representations has become an urgent issue

2 Introduction

In order to cope with and solve the shortcomings of traditional adjacency matrix notation, researchers began to find new representations for nodes in the network. The main idea is to achieve the purpose of dimensionality reduction through the form of vectors, thus developing a number of network learning representation algorithms. These algorithms achieve the goal of dimensionality reduction by transforming network information from traditional high-dimensional, sparse forms into low-dimensional, dense vector forms, and use them for the input of existing machine learning algorithms [7]. At the same time, the vector representation of the node can be provided as a feature to a device such as an SVM support vector machine, or can be converted to spatial coordinates for visualization tasks [8]. These algorithms achieve the goal of dimensionality reduction through different means, so that they can better study and analyze the connections between nodes in complex information networks, find common methods to solve various practical problems in the context of information networks, and effectively integrate them [10]. The network structure and the external information of the node achieve a more effective representation and have far better performance than the adjacency matrix expression [11].

3 Unsupervised Network Embedding

3.1 Word2vec

Word2vec is characterized by the use of word vectors to represent words. It uses CBOW and Skip-Gram to train the model and get the word vector, but it does not use the traditional DNN model [12]. The first optimized data structure is to use the Huffman tree instead of the hidden layer and the output layer [13]. The leaf nodes of the Huffman tree act as output layer neurons, and the leaf nodes represent the size of the vocabulary. Play the role of hidden layer neurons.

The algorithm uses a three-layer neural network, which is the input layer-hidden layer-output layer. The core technology is to use Huffman coding according to the frequency of occurrence of words, so that the content of the word hidden layer activated by all word frequencies is basically the same. The higher the frequency of words, the fewer the number of hidden layers they activate, which effectively reduces the calculation. the complexity. This three-layer neural network itself models the language model, but at the same time obtains a representation of a word in vector space. Obtaining the representation of words in vector space is the real goal of Word2vec.

Word2vec uses the co-occurrence relationship of words to map words to low-dimensional vectors, and retains the rich information in the corpus, and has successfully applied in the text, which has set off a wave of vectorization [14].

3.2 DeepWalk

DeepWalk is an article in KDD 2014. The idea of the algorithm is very simple. The graph starts from a node and performs a random walk to generate sequence data similar to text. Then the node id is used as a 'word', and the skip gram is used to train the word vector. This seemingly simple idea actually makes sense. The algorithm is equivalent to Matrix Factorization, and DeepWalk also inspired a series of subsequent work [15]. The DeepWalk algorithm makes full use of the information of the random walk sequence in the network structure. There are two advantages to using the information of the random walk sequence: First, The random walk sequence relies only on local information, so it can be applied to distributed and online systems. When using the adjacency matrix, all information must be stored in memory for processing, which faces high computation time and space consumption. Second, Modeling the random walk sequence can reduce the variance and uncertainty of the modeling 0–1 binary adjacency matrix.

Advantages:

(1) Compared with the traditional cluster and dimensionality reduction methods, the advantage of this method is that it can be debugged, which means that this thing can pile data, so it is applied in the knowledge map on social networks.
(2) Compared with the traditional cluster, you can learn the dimensions and make further use.
(3) Compared with the dimension reduction ratio, there is no advantage, but the graph structure itself has nothing normal and has a dimension reduction method that can be used on a large scale.

3.3 Node2vec (Scalable Feature Learning for Networks)

This is an algorithm based on the development of the DeepWalk algorithm. Based on DW, it redefines the strategy of generating a Bias random walk. It also needs to use skip gram for training [16]. The paper analyzes the two traversal methods of BFS and DFS, and the network structure information they retain is not the same. In DeepWalk, random walks are performed according to the weight of the edge, and node2vec adds a weight adjustment parameter α: t is the previous node, v is the latest node, and x is the candidate next node. d(t, x) is the minimum hop count from t to the candidate node. Different p and q parameter settings are used to preserve different information. When both p and q are 1.0, it is equivalent to DeepWalk [17].

The following table summarizes the analogy between the DeepWalk algorithm and word2vec (Table 1).

Table 1. The comparison between Deep Walk and word2vec

Model	Target	Input	Output
Word2vec	Words	Sentences	Word embeddings
DeepWalk	Nodes	Node sequences	Node embeddings

3.4 LINE (Large Scale Information Network Embedding)

The LINE algorithm proposes two unique concepts, first-order similarity and second-order similarity. The first-order similarity is that two points are directly connected, and the larger the edge weight is, the two points are similar; the second-order similarity is that many neighbors are shared between the two points, and their similarity is very high [18]. As shown below (Fig. 1).

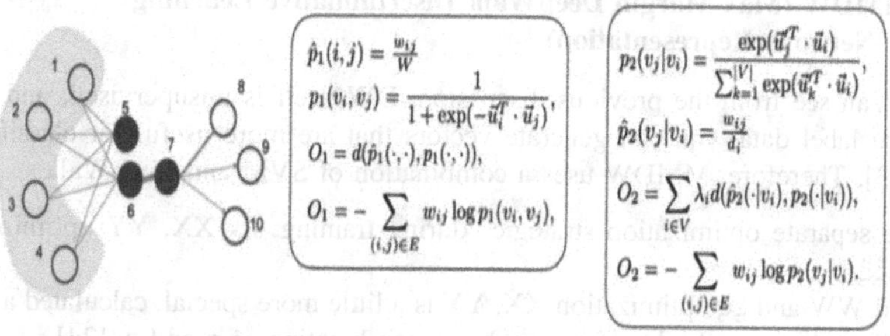

Fig. 1. The basic principle of the LINE algorithm

For the above example, there is a strong direct relationship between nodes 6 and 7, so we think there is a high first-order proximity between them. Although nodes 5 and 6 are not directly connected, they have as many as 4 common sub-nodes. It is not objective to think that nodes 5 and 6 are not related to each other, and at the same time, in order to solve the sparsity problem caused by using only thc first-order proximity. The LINE algorithm introduces the concept of second-order proximity and considers that there is a strong second-order proximity between nodes 5 and 6. At the same time, the above figure shows the calculation formula and function optimization method used in the two similarities [19].

The algorithm also constructs an objective function in a very simple way to retain the information of both at the same time, and selects the KL divergence as the distance measurement function to obtain the final loss function O1. In addition, the effect of directly using SGD when sampling the edge of the algorithm is not good, so it will be sampled according to the weight of the edge, and each edge is calculated as binary.

3.5 GraRep (Learning Graph Representations with Global Structural Information)

The LINE algorithm has a good description and learning effect on the relationship between two adjacent contacts, or nodes separated by one node, but is not good at capturing the relationship between distant nodes, for example, there is a path between two nodes. When the number of intermediate nodes is greater than 2, the LINE algorithm is somewhat weak [20]. Therefore, Shaosheng Cao from Xidian University proposed the GraRep algorithm, which can well capture the relationship between distant nodes on the one hand, and matrix decomposition to learn the node representation on the other hand [21].

This algorithm still uses the idea of matrix decomposition to analyze the different k-steps (the number of steps in the random walk), the information depicted is also different, so you can decompose the matrix of each step, and finally The vectors obtained in each step are stitched together as the final result [22].

4 Expected Network Embedding Method

4.1 MMDW (Max-Margin DeepWalk Discriminative Learning of Network Representation)

As you can see from the previous discussion, DW itself is unsupervised, and if you introduce label data, you can generate vectors that are more useful for classification tasks [23]. Therefore, MMDW uses a combination of SVM and DeepWalk.

1. Take separate optimization strategies during training, fix XX, YY optimize WW and ξξ
2. Fixed WW and ξξ optimization XX, YY is a little more special, calculated a biased Gradient, because the loss function has a combination of x and w [24].

In this way, both the discrimination and the representation are optimized in the training to achieve a good result.

$$\frac{\min}{X,Y} L_{DW} = \frac{\min}{X,Y} ||M - (X^T Y)||_2^2 + \frac{\lambda}{2}(||X||_2^2 + ||Y||_2^2),$$

$$\frac{\min}{X,Y,W,\xi} L = \frac{\min}{X,Y,W,\xi} L_{DW} + \frac{1}{2}||W||_2^2 + C\sum_{i=1} \xi_i$$

$$\text{s.t.} \quad \mathrm{w}_{l_i}^T x_i - w_j^T x_i \geq \mathrm{e}_i^j = \xi_i, \forall i,j$$

For a vertex i ∈ T, the gradient becomes $\frac{\partial L}{\partial \mathrm{X}_i} + \eta \sum_{j=1}^{m} \alpha_i^j (w_{l_i} - w_j)^T$, which is named Biased Gradient. Here, η balances the primal gradient and the bias [25].

4.2 TADW (Network Representation Learning with Rich Text Information)

In the actual information network, some nodes often have text information. Therefore, in the matrix decomposition framework, if the text is directly added as a sub-matrix, the learned vector will contain more information. The text matrix is the SVD dimensionality reduction result for the TFIDF matrix [26].

The traditional method is to find the vector and text vector of the node and then stitch it into a 2K vector. TADW performs matrix decomposition on an M vector. The M_{ij} in the M vector represents the probability of random walks of nodes i to j. Then M is decomposed, and the text vector matrix of the network node is added in the process of decomposition [27]. Using the inductive matrix completion technique to decompose the vector M. TADW algorithm is a very good algorithm, using matrix decomposition to simulate the DW algorithm. You can also add other network property views. This idea can be extended to add multiple view features [28].

4.3 NEU (Fast Network Embedding Enhancement via High Order Proximity Approximation)

The algorithm was proposed in 2017 and published on IJCAI. This is a very tricky way to analyze some of the Embedding methods that can be considered matrix decomposition (Table 2):

Table 2. The comparison between SC, DeepWalk and GraRep

	SC	DeepWalk	GraRep
Proximity matrix	L	$\sum_{K=1}^{K} \frac{A^k}{K}$	$A^k, k = 1 \cdots K$ Word embeddings
Computation	Accurate	Approximate	Accurate
Scalability	Yes	Yes	No
Performance	Low	Middle	High

The above figure compares the four aspects of these three algorithms, including the Proximity Matrix, Computation, Scalability, and Performance aspects [29].

It is concluded that if the matrix decomposition f(A) = RCf(A) = RC can more accurately include higher-order information, the effect will be better, but the result is that the computational complexity of the algorithm is higher [30].

So the article uses a very clever way to update the results of the (low-order low-order) matrix decomposition to obtain higher order decomposition results, so that the final vector effect is better. Applicable to multiple algorithms.

4.4 SDNE (Structural Deep Network Embedding)

This is an algorithm that can map network data to deep nonlinear low-dimensional space and has better robustness. At the same time, this is the first network representation algorithm that uses deep learning [31].

The SDNE model combines first-order similarity and second-order similarity to construct a semi-supervised depth model. Among them, the first-order similarity preserves the local structure information of the network, and the loss function is defined by Laplacian Eigenmaps. The second-order similarity preserves the global structure information of the network, and the adjacent vector of the pair is reconstructed by two self-encoders. It is worth noting that when the self-encoder reconstructs the input contiguous vector, a B is added to the original self-encoder loss function, which can be regarded as a kind of "weight" to solve the network structure reconstruction process. The adjacent vector is too sparse (the number of zero elements is much larger than the number of non-zero elements). This seems to be more common, and can be used for reference in future model design.

In this algorithm, a new semi-supervised deep model is proposed, which integrates the first-order and second-order similarities in the network. Therefore, the low-dimensional network obtained by the model indicates that the local and overall characteristics of the network can be well represented [32]. The proposed algorithm verifies the two application problems (multi-label classification, visualization) in five real data sets. The results show that for data with few network labels, we have improved by at least 20% over other benchmark methods [33]. In some cases, we only need 60% or less of the training data, and we can get good results.

5 Summary and Outlook

This article describes some of the existing network representation algorithms, but there are some algorithms that are not limited by the length. In the current practical application, taking the LINE algorithm as an example, it is possible to complete the embedding of millions of nodes and billions of edges in a single learning machine within a few hours, and the efficiency and performance are far superior to the traditional representation. These emerging network representation algorithms have very important academic significance and wide application value [4, 35–37].

Although the network representation research has achieved fruitful results, it also faces enormous challenges:

1. The existing network representation learning model does not consider external knowledge information such as knowledge maps, but the external knowledge information is extremely rich, and can provide reasoning ability for network representation learning and its subsequent applications [38].
2. The existing network representation learning model supports a scale that is still not large enough [39]. The size of the social network in the actual scene can easily reach hundreds of millions of nodes, indicating that storage and training efficiency are under heavy pressure [40].
3. Network Representation Learning Model The training process generally causes the node to fit the real structure of the network as much as possible, but ignores subsequent applications [41]. Therefore, how to improve the existing model with purpose is the huge challenge that the network represents learning in application [42, 43].

Acknowledgement. This research was funded in part by the National Natural Science Foundation of China (61871140, 61872100, 61572153, U1636215), the National Key research and Development Plan (Grant No. 2018YFB0803504).

References

1. Tang, M., Zhu, L., Zou, X.: A document vector representation based on Word2Vec. Comput. Sci. **43**(06), 214–217+269 (2016)
2. Zhou, L.: The working principle and application of Word2vec. Sci. Technol. Inf. Dev. Econ. **25**(02), 145–148 (2015)
3. Feng, W., Zhu, F., Liu, S.: Label discovery community discovery algorithm based on deep walk model. Comput. Eng. **44**(03), 220–225+232 (2018)
4. Li, J., Zhao, Y., Wang, L.: A network representation method with multiple structures and text fusion. Comput. Sci. **45**(07), 38–41+77 (2018)

5. Cao, S.: Graph node feature vector learning algorithm based on global information. Xidian University (2016)
6. Tang, J., Qu, M., Wang, M., et al.: LINE: large-scale information network embedding. In: International World Wide Web Conferences Steering Committee, pp. 1067–1077 (2015)
7. Ding, J., Huang, T., Wang, J., Hu, W., Liu, J., Liu, Y.: Virtual network em-bedding through node connectivity. J. China Univ. Posts Telecommun. **22**(01), 17–23+56 (2015)
8. Wang, L., Qu, H., Zhao, J.: Virtual network embedding algorithm for load balance with various requests. Chin. J. Electron. **23**(02), 382–387 (2014)
9. Chen, W., Zhang, Y., Li, X.: Netw. Represent. Learn. Big Data **1**(03), 8–22+7 (2015)
10. Gong, S., Chen, J., Huang, C., Zhu, Q.: Trust-aware secure virtual network mapping algorithm. Trans. Commun. **36**(11), 180–189 (2015)
11. Liu, S., Liu, H., He, C., Chao-bo, H.E.: Link prediction algorithm based on network representation learning and random walk. J. Comput. Appl. **37**(08), 2234–2239 (2017)
12. Tu, C., Yang, C., Liu, Z., Sun, M.: Review of network representation learning. Sci. China Inf. Sci. **47**(08), 980–996 (2017)
13. Cao, H., Qu, Z., Xue, Y., Yang, L.: Efficient virtual network embedding algorithm based on restrictive selection and optimization theory approach. China Commun. **14**(10), 39–60 (2017)
14. Yang, Z., Guo, Y.: An exact virtual network embedding algorithm based on integer linear programming for virtual network request with location constraint. China Commun. **13**(08), 177–183 (2016)
15. Xing, X., Wu, T.: Knowledge mapping and network representation learning. Ind. Technol. Forum **15**(17), 61–62 (2016)
16. Hu, H., Zhang, F., Mao, Y., Wang, Z.: A forwarding map mapping algorithm based on regional topology information. Front. Inf. Technol. Electron. Eng. **18**(11), 1854–1867 (2017)
17. Cao, H., Hu, H., Qu, Z., Yang, L.: Heuristic solutions of virtual network embedding: a survey. China Commun. **15**(03), 186–219 (2018)
18. Chen, L., Zhu, Y., Qian, T., Zhu, H., Zhou, J.: Network representation learning model based on edge sampling. J. Softw. **29**(03), 756–771 (2018)
19. Chai, Y., Liu, W., Si, Y., Qiu, J.: A review of research on knowledge semantic modeling technology for big data. Inf. Technol. Cyber Secur. **37**(04), 11–17 (2018)
20. Liu, J., Wang, J., Wang, W.: Research and application of text network representation. China Sci. Technol. Pap. Online **10**, 755–760 (2007)
21. Wang, W., Huang, W., Wu, L., Ke, W., Tang, W.: Network representation learning algorithm based on improved random walk. Comput. Appl. 1–6 (2018). http://kns.cnki.net/kcms/detail/51.1307.TP.20180929.0951.024.html
22. A new algorithm based on the proximity principle for the virtual network embedding problem. J. Zhejiang Univ. Sci. C (Comput. Electron.) **12**(11), 910–918 (2011)
23. Wu, B.: Virtual network embedding algorithm based on resource locality index. In: Proceedings of 2016 2nd Workshop on Advanced Research and Technology in Industry Applications (WARTIA 2016), p. 8. International Society of Engineering and Engineering (2016)
24. Gong, S.: Energy-efficient virtual network embedding for heterogeneous networks. In: Proceedings of 2016 First IEEE International Conference on Computer Communication and the Internet (ICCCI 2016), p. 6. IEEE Huazhong Normal University (2016)
25. Lai, M.: Research on algorithm for virtual network embedding based on integer programming. In: Proceedings of 2015 3rd International Conference on Machinery, Materials and Information Technology Applications (ICMMITA 2015), p. 4. International Informatization and Engineering Associations, Atlantis Press (2015)

26. Liang, N.N.: Dynamic virtual network embedding based on auction-game theory. In: Proceedings of 2015 International Conference on Advances in Mechanical Engineering and Industrial Informatics (AMEII 2015), p. 6. International Society for Information and Engineering (2015)
27. Lin, R.: Virtual network embedding in flexi-grid optical networks. In: Proceedings of 2017 17th IEEE International Conference on Communication Technology (ICCT 2017), p. 6. IEEE Beijing Section, Sichuan Institute of Electronics (2017)
28. Zhu, Q.: Heuristic survivable virtual network embedding based on node migration and link remapping. In: Proceedings of 2014 IEEE 7th Joint International Information Technology and Artificial Intelligence Conference, p. 5. IEEE Beijing Section (2014)
29. Qin, Z.: Knowledge representation and its application based on semantic neural network. In: Proceedings of Global Manufacturing Advanced Forum and 21st Century Simulation Technology Seminar, p. 4. China System Simulation Society, Guizhou University, Guizhou Provincial Economic and Trade Commission, Guizhou Provincial Department of Science and Technology, Guizhou Provincial Information Industry Department, Guizhou Provincial Science and Technology Association, Guiyang Municipal People's Government (2004)
30. Zheng, D.: Reasoning strategy of knowledge representation of expert system based on pattern recognition and neural network. In: 1995 China Control Conference Proceedings (Part 2), p. 4. China Automation Society Control Theory Professional Committee (1995)
31. Qi, J., Liang, X., Li, Z., Chen, Y., Xu, Y.: Large-scale complex information network representation learning: concepts, methods and challenges. Chin. J. Comput. **41**(10), 2394–2420 (2018)
32. Wu, S., Zhang, Z., Qian, Q.: Research on text representation model based on language network. Inf. Sci. **31**(12), 119–125 (2013)
33. Lu, B., Huang, T., Sun, X., Chen, J., Liu, Y.: Dynamic recovery for survivable virtual network embedding. J. China Univ. Posts Telecommun. **21**(03), 77–84 (2014)
34. Cao, S., Lu, W., Xu, Q.: GraRep: Learning graph representations with global structural information. In: Proceedings of the 24th ACM International on Conference on Information and Knowledge Management (CIKM 2015), pp. 891–900. ACM, New York (2015). https://doi.org/10.1145/2806416.2806512
35. Liu, Z., Ma, H., Liu, S., Yang, Y., Li, X.: A network representation learning algorithm based on node text attribute information. Comput. Eng. **44**(11), 165–171 (2018)
36. Xie, S.: Research on cross-network node association based on node representation. University of Electronic Science and Technology (2018)
37. Wen, W., Huang, J., Cai, R., Hao, Z., Wang, L.: A graph representation learning method based on prior information of nodes. J. Softw. **29**(03), 786–798 (2018)
38. Tu, C., Yang, C., Liu, Z., Sun, M.: A review of network representation learning. Sci. Sin. Inf. Sci. **47**(08), 980–996 (2017)
39. Zhao, S., Chen, J., Gong, S.: Virtual SDN network mapping algorithm based on particle swarm optimization. Comput. Eng. **42**(12), 84–90 (2016)
40. Xiong, Z., Shen, Q., Wang, Y., et al.: Paragraph vector representation based on word to vector and CNN learning. CMC Comput. Mater. Contin. **55**, 213–227 (2018)
41. Wang, C., Feng, Y., Li, T., et al.: A new encryption-then-compression scheme on gray images using the markov random field. Comput. Mater. Contin. **56**(1), 107–121 (2018)
42. Gao, Z., Xia, S., Zhang, Y., et al.: Real-time visual tracking with compact shape and color feature. Comput. Mater. Contin. **55**(3), 509–521 (2018)
43. Chen, Y., Yin, B., He, H., et al.: Reversible data hiding in classification-scrambling encrypted-image based on iterative recovery. CMC Comput. Mater. Contin. **56**(2), 299–312 (2018)

A Two-Stage Deep Neural Network for Sequence Labeling

Yongmei Tan[1(✉)], Lin Yang[2], Shaozhang Niu[1], Hao Zhu[1], and Yongheng Zhang[1]

[1] School of Computer Science, Beijing University of Posts and Telecommunications, Beijing 100876, China
{ymtan, szniu, hzhu, zhangyongheng}@bupt.edu.cn
[2] Beijing Sankuai Online Technology Co., Ltd., Beijing, China
wximo@live.com

Abstract. State-of-the-art sequence labeling systems require large amounts of task-specific knowledge in the form of handcrafted features and data pre-processing, and those systems are established on news corpus. English as second language (ESL) corpus is collected from articles written by English-learner. The corpus is full of grammatical mistakes, and then it is much more difficult to do sequence labeling. We propose a two-stage deep neural network architecture for sequence labeling, which enable the higher-layer to make use of the coarse-grained labeling information of the lower-level. We evaluate our model on three datasets for three sequence labeling tasks—Penn Treebank WSJ corpus for part-of-speech (POS) tagging, CoNLL 2003 corpus for named entity recognition (NER) and CoNLL 2013 corpus for grammatical error correction (GEC). We obtain state-of-the-art performance on three datasets 97.60% accuracy for POS tagging, 91.38% F1 for NER and 38% F1 for determiner error correction of GEC and 28.89% F1 for prepositional error correction of GEC. We also evaluate our system on ESL corpus PiGai for POS tagging and obtain 96.73% accuracy. The implementation of our network is publicly available.

Keywords: POS · NER · CONLL · GEC · LSTM · BLSTM · GRU · RNN · RCNN · CNN

1 Introduction

It is well recognized the importance of sequence labeling in natural language processing like POS tagging and NER. Traditional methods have achieved the state-of-art performance in sequence labeling tasks, such as Expectation Maximization (EM) (Owoputi et al. 2013), Conditional Random Field (CRF) (Passos et al. 2014) and Support Vector Machines (SVM) (Luo et al. 2015). Those models require lots of high qualified hand-crafted features, but such task-specific knowledge is costly to develop (Ma and Hovy 2016).

Deep Learning has achieved great success in a number of tasks in natural language processing (NLP). These include, but are not limited to the following. Recurrent neural network (RNN) (Goller and Kuchler 1996) extract more features and has shown great

X. Sun et al. (Eds.): ICAIS 2019, LNCS 11633, pp. 133–144, 2019.
https://doi.org/10.1007/978-3-030-24265-7_12

advantage of modeling sequential data. Long-short term memory (LSTM) (Hochreiter and Schmidhuber 1997), bidirectional long-short term memory (BLSTM) (Graves et al. 2005) and gated recurrent unit (GRU) (Cho et al. 2014) have out-performed classic RNN in modeling sequential data by setting cells and gates to control the data flow.

Along this line of research on using deep learning works for sequence labeling, we propose a RNN architecture by combining BLSTM, recurrent convolutional neural network (RCNN) and residual network for sequence labeling. We first use CNN (LeCun et al. 1989) to encode the character-level information and feed it into the first BLSTM. Then the word-level information is concatenated with the output of the first BLSTM before feeding them into the second BLSTM. The whole process is split into two steps: (1) coarse-grained labeling, (2) fine-grained labeling. Coarse tags (see Sect. 3.3) and fine tags (see Sect. 3.4) are used to train the model separately in POS tagging and NER.

The contributions of this work are as follows:

- We propose a new neural network architecture for sequence labeling.
- Our system achieves competitive results on both news and ESL corpus for POS, NER and GEC tasks.

2 Related Work

Many deep learning approaches have proven to be effective in a variety of NLP tasks. Collobert et al. (2011) used a CNN over a sequence of word embeddings with a CRF layer on top. More recently, Huang et al. (2015) presented a LSTM-CRF model, but using hand-crafted spelling features. Dos Santos et al. (2014) used CNN to extract character-lever features for sequence labeling. However, their model focuses more on words themselves and ignores sequential information. Lample et al. (2016) presented a hybrid tagging architecture - LSTM-CRF Model. Ma and Hovy (2016) proposed a BLSTM-CRF model and combined both word-level and character-level representations. Tan et al. (2017) separated tagging processing into two stages and used simple feed-forward neural network. ELMo (Peters et al. 2018), used tasks-specific architectures that include the pre-trained representations as additional features.

GEC task is challenging since for many error types, current GEC systems do not achieve high performance and much research is still needed. Among all the error types, determiners and prepositions are the most frequent errors made by English learners (Ng et al. 2013). UIUC built a multi-class averaged perceptron with corpus web-1T and Gigaword for articles or determiners and got F1 33.40% (Rozovskaya et al. 2013). NARA proposed a phrase-based statistical machine translation model with Lang-8 multilingual corpus for preposition errors and got f1 17.53% (Ippei et al. 2013).

Based on those work, we use label tags to train the model and change the way of combining information. Experimental results show that our system achieves competitive results for all of the three different tasks, demonstrating that using coarse- and fine-grained labeling is more important than handling them in the same layer.

3 Recurrent Neural Network for Sequence Labeling

We introduce a hybrid tagging architecture and its detailed implementation in this section. This architecture is similar to the ones presented by Lample et al. (2016) and Ma and Hovy (2016).

As shown in Fig. 1, we use CNN to encode the character-level representations and then feed it into the first BLSTM while we design coarse-grained labeling to label sequence roughly. Then we combine the word-level representations and the output of first BLSTM before feeding them into the second BLSTM while we label the sequence by fine-grained tags.

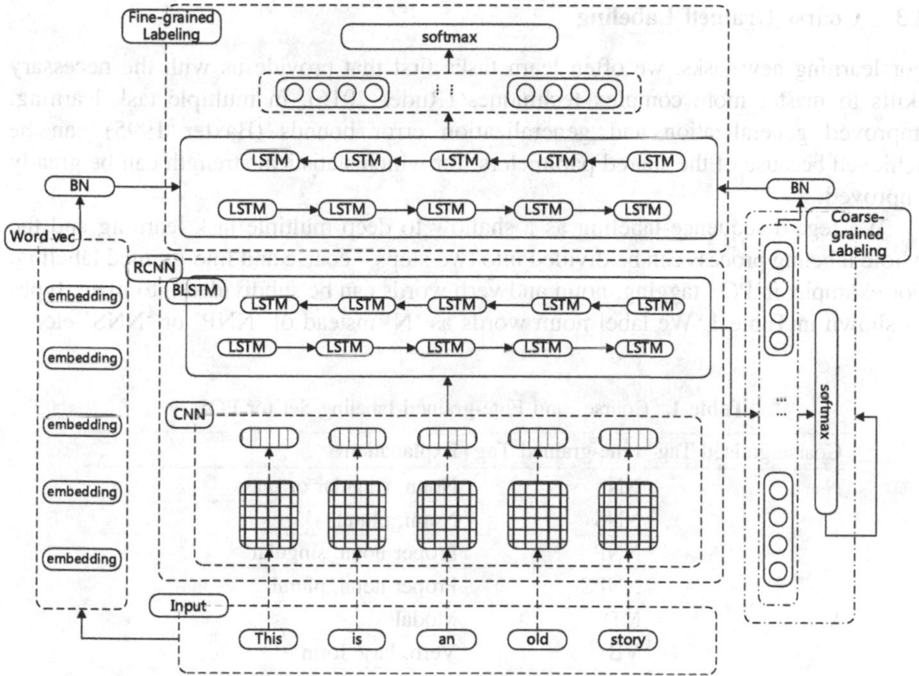

Fig. 1. Overview of a sequence labeling architecture with deep bi-directional RNNs.

3.1 CNN for Character-Lever Information

Previous studies (Santos and Zadrozny 2014; Chiu and Nichols 2015) have shown that CNN is an effective approach to extract morphological information (like the prefix or suffix of a word) from characters of words and encode it into neural representations.

Firstly, we encode character-level information of a word into its character-level representation. Then we map words into vectors. For example, in Fig. 1, when given word 'this', we split this word into characters. Every character can be mapped into a vector and we concatenate those vectors into a matrix. Secondly, we feed this matrix into CNN. After convolution and pooling processes, we fetch the character-level information.

3.2 BLSTM for Sequential Information

We use RNN to extract sequential information. However, the ability of classic RNN is limited by the length of the sequence. When the sequence is getting longer, the gradient vanishing or gradient exploding problem occurs during training (Kolen and Kremer 2001), (Bengio et al. 1994), and it's hard to train the model.

LSTM can avoid those gradient problems. By setting input gate, output gate, forget gate and cell, LSTM can control the data flow. LSTM can fetch only the information before time t and the posterior information doesn't affect the output at time t while BLSTM (Graves et al. 2005) has been proven to be an effective solution and it combines the information preceding part and following part at time t.

3.3 Coarse-Grained Labeling

For learning new tasks, we often learn tasks first that provide us with the necessary skills to master more complex techniques (Ruder 2016). In multiple task learning, improved generalization and generalization error bounds (Baxter 1995) can be achieved because of the shared parameters, for which statistical strength can be greatly improved.

We regard sequence labeling as a shallow to deep multiple task learning and the whole labeling process can be divided into two steps – coarse and fine-grained labeling. For example, in POS tagging, noun and verb words can be subdivided into many types as shown in Table 1. We label noun words as 'N' instead of 'NNP' or 'NNS' etc.

Table 1. Coarse- and Fine-grained labeling Set for POS.

Coarse-grained Tag	Fine-grained Tag	Explanation
N	NN	Noun, singular or mass
	NNS	Noun, plural
	NNP	Proper noun, singular
	NNPS	Proper noun, plural
V	MD	Modal
	VB	Verb, base form
	VBD	Verb, past tense
	VBG	Verb, gerund or present participle
	VBN	Verb, past participle
	VBP	Verb, non-3rd person singular present
	VBZ	Verb, 3rd person singular present

3.4 Fine-Grained Labeling

After fine-grained labeling, original information has been selected and some is ignored through the neural network layers. While a residual neural network sets gates to build information path and then allows information to transmit cross some layers (Srivastava et al. 2015). We use the residual network to build information path. Information path takes an important effect in gradient back propagation (Veit et al. 2016) instead of connecting layers by layers and reduces the complexity in training model.

In a classic feed-forward neural network, the i-th layer is updated by:

$$y_i = f(y_{i-1}) \tag{1}$$

where y_{i-1} is the input of (i-1)-th layer and y_i is the output.

In a residual neural network, we calculate y_i by:

$$y_i = f(y_{i-1}) + y_{i-1} \tag{2}$$

When training deep neural networks, the distribution of each layer's input changes as the parameters of the previous layer are changed (Ioffe and Szegedy 2015), which leads to gradient vanishing or gradient exploding problem. So that we need to slow down the training speed and lower learning rates and carefully initializes parameters. Batch normalization (Ba et al. 2016), (Cooijmans et al. 2016), (Laurent et al. 2015) uses mini-batch statistics to standardize features, significantly reducing training time, faster convergence and improved generalization.

While word-level information crosses the coarse-grained labeling layer, we combine output of first BLSTM and word-level representations. We use batch normalization to normalize them and feed them into second BLSTM.

4 Experiments

This section presents the method we use to train our models, the results we obtained on various tasks and the impact of our networks' configuration on model performance.

4.1 Data Sets

POS Tagging. We use WSJ (Marcus et al. 1993) and English-learner articles (PiGai[1] corpus). WSJ corpus has 45 kinds of tags and we follow the standard split for the training (section 0–18), development (section 19–21) and test (section 22–24) sets (Manning 2011; Søgaard 2016). PiGai corpus has 44 kinds of tags. This corpus has 13,762 sentences and we follow Tan et al. (2017) the training (sentence 1–10,000), development (10,001–12,416) and test (12,417–13,761) sets.

NER. The CoNLL 2003 setup,[2] is a NER benchmark data set based on Reuters data. The contest provides training, validation and testing sets. This dataset contains four different types of named entities: "PERSON", "LOCATION", "ORGANIZATION", and "MISC".

[1] http://www.pigai.org

[2] http://www.cnts.ua.ac.be/conll2003/ner

GEC. For GEC, we use the corpus of CoNLL 2013 shared task,[3], this dataset contains five different types of grammatical errors and we evaluate on determiner and preposition words errors to test our sequence labeling model.
The corpora statistics are shown in Table 2.

Table 2. Corpora statistics. SENT and TOKEN refer to the number of sentences and tokens in each dataset. ArtOrDet and Prep refer to article or determiner error and preposition error separately.

Dataset		POS		NER	GEC		
		WSJ	PiGai	CoNLL2003	CoNLL2013		
					ArtOrDet	Prep	All
Train	SENT	38,219	10,000	14,987	6,658	2,404	45,106
	TOKEN	912,344	241,178	204,567	/	/	/
Dev	SENT	5,527	2,416	3,466	/	/	/
	TOKEN	131,768	56,684	51,578	/	/	/
Test	SENT	5,462	1,346	3,684	690	312	3,470
	TOKEN	129,654	32,987	46,666	/	/	/

4.2 Parameter Initialization

Stanford's publicly available GloVe,[4] 100-dimensional embedding trained on 6 billion words from Wikipedia and web text (Pennington et al. 2014) is used in our model. Character embedding is initialized with uniform samples between 0 and 1.

To encourage the model to depend on both character-level embeddings and pre-trained word representations (Lample 2016), we use dropout training (Hinton et al. 2012), applying a dropout mask before inputting to the first and second BLSTM in Fig. 1. Dropout rate is set to 0.5.

Some other hyper-parameters are shown in Table 3. For example, in our BLSTM, the size of hidden units is 200. We use Adam optimizer (Kingma and Ba 2014) to train our model. The batch is fixed at 10 and learning rate η_0 is initialzed at 0.01. Learning rate of each training epoch is updated as follows:

$$\eta_t = \frac{\eta_0}{(1+\rho t)} \tag{3}$$

where decay rate ρ is 0.2 and t is the number of epoch completed.

[3] http://www.comp.nus.edu.sg/~nlp/conll13st.html

[4] http://nlp.stanford.edu/projects/glove/

Table 3. Hyper-parameters for all experiments.

Layer	Hyper-parameter	POS/NER/GEC
CNN	Window size	5*5
	Number of filters	1
LSTM	State size	200
	Initial state	0.0
	peepholes	false
	Batch size	10
	Initial learning rate	0.01
	Decay rate	0.2
	Gradient clipping	/
Word Embedding	Dimension	100

4.3 Experimental Results

POS Tagging. We run experiments to dissect the effectiveness of each component (layer) of our neural network architecture by ablation studies and compare the performance with three baseline models.

BLSTM-Rsd. We use word-level information as the input of first BLSTM and then combine word-level information and the output of the first BLSTM to feed them into the second BLSTM. The loss of the final outputs and the fine-grained labels are used to update the parameters of the whole model.

BLSTM-Rsd-2StageLearning. We combine word-level information and the output of the first BLSTM with the different distribution to feed them into the second BLSTM. In the first stage, RCNN is trained by the loss of its outputs and coarse-grained labels. In the second stage, the whole model is trained by the final loss.

BLSTM-Rsd-2StageLearning-BN. We import the batch normalization to normalize the inputs of two BLSTM.

BLSTM-RCNN-Residual-2StageLearning-BN. We use RCNN to replace the first BLSTM to improve the capacity of our model by training model to extract the character-level information.

Table 4 shows the results of our model in comparison to the results reported in state-of-the-art literature. BLSTM-RCNN-Residual-2StageLearning-BN model significantly outperforms the BLSTM-Rsd-2StageLearning-BN model, showing that character-level representations are important for linguistic sequence labeling task. This is consistent with results reported by previous work (Santos and Zadrozny 2014; Chiu and Nichols 2015; Ma and Hovy 2016). Our system outperforms Ma and Hovy (2016). Meta BiLSTM (Bohnet et al. 2018) outperforms our system.

We also perform experiments on the ESL corpus. Although POS tagging on ESL corpus is a difficult task, there are several models proposed to resolve it. As shown in Table 5, our system outperforms Ma and Hovy (2016). Tan et al. (2017) use a multiple

Table 4. POS tagging accuracy of our model on both the development and test sets from WSJ corpus, together with one baseline models.

Model	Dev (Acc)	Test (Acc)
BRNN-CNN-CRF (Ma and Hovy 2016)	97.46	97.55
Meta BiLSTM (Bohnet et al. 2018)	\	97.96
BLSTM-Residual	96.12	96.21
BLSTM-Residual-2StageTraining	96.46	96.48
BLSTM-Residual-2StageTraining-BN	96.68	96.73
BLSTM-RCNN-Residual-2StageTraining-BN	97.53	97.60

layers feed-forward neural network and obtain 95.63% accuracy on PiGai corpus. Our model also performs considerably better than Tan et al. (2017) (95.63%). Senna,[5] use CNN to extract character information and use feed-forward neural network to label sequential data, when it comes to PiGai corpus, model can obtain 95.32% accuracy.

Table 5. POS tagging accuracy on PiGai corpus, together with two baseline models.

Model	Test (Acc)
Senna (Collobert et al. 2011)	95.32
Tan et al. (2017)	95.63
BLSTM-RCNN-Residual-2StageLearning-BN	**96.78**

NER. Table 6 shows the precision, recall and F1 scores of previous models for NER on the data sets from CoNLL-2003 shared task. For the purpose of comparison, we list their results together with ours. Similar to the observations of POS tagging, our model achieves improvements over BRNN-CNN-CRF (Ma and Hovy 2016) and LSTM-CRF (Lample et al. 2016). ELMo (Peters et al. 2018), uses tasks-specific architectures that include the pre-trained representations as additional features.

Table 6. NER P, R and F1 scores of our model on both the development and test sets from CoNLL 2003, together with two baseline models.

Model	Dev			Test		
	P	R	F1	P	R	F1
LSTM-CRF (Lample et al. 2016)	\	\	\	\	\	90.94
BRNN-CNN-CRF (Ma and Hovy 2016)	**94.8**	**94.6**	**94.7**	91.3	**91.0**	91.21
ELMo (Peters et al. 2018)	\	\	\	\	\	92.22
BLSTM-Residual	85.3	74.5	79.5	83.3	77.2	80.20
BLSTM-Residual-2StageLearning	90.2	84.7	87.3	87.1	86.2	86.66
BLSTM-Residual-2StageLearning-BN	90.7	84.6	87.6	88.3	85.1	86.69
BLSTM-RCNN-Residual-2StageLearning-BN	93.4	88.7	91.0	**92.0**	90.7	91.38

[5] http://ronan.collobert.com/senna/

GEC. The GEC problem can be resolved by sequence labeling model. For example, the following sentence is (formatted as "word_tag"):

"Some_DT 0_CD institutions_NNS are_VBP part_NN of_IN the_DT pension_NN fund_NN ._.".

We replace prepositions with "*TO*":

"Some_DT 0_CD institutions_NNS are_VBP part_NN TO_of the_DT pension_NN fund_NN ._.".

Then we use our model to label the word "TO" and give the exact preposition as a tag.

Table 7 illustrates the results of our model for GEC, together with two previous top performance models for comparison. Our model significantly outperforms UIUC (Ng et al. 2013) and NARA (Yoshimoto et al. 2013).

Table 7. GEC P, R and F1 scores of our model on data set from CoNLL 2013, together with one baseline models.

Error types	Model	P	R	F1
ArtOrDet	UIUC (Ng et al. 2013)	0.4784	0.2565	0.3340
	BLSTM-RCNN-Residual-2StageLearning-BN	0.3315	0.4464	**0.3805**
Prep	NARA (Yoshimoto et al. 2013)	0.1254	0.2910	0.1753
	BLSTM-RCNN-Residual-2StageLearning-BN	0.1921	0.5820	**0.2889**

4.4 Parameters Selection

If a model is excessively complex, such as having too many parameters, it will have poor predictive performance as it overreacts to minor fluctuations in the training data. We use dropout method to mitigate this problem. As shown in Table 8, dropout is quite effective and we set dropout 0.5 for all dropout layers through all the experiments.

Table 8. POS tagging accuracy of our model on the training, development and test sets from WSJ corpus, with dropout and without dropout.

Dropout	Train (Acc)	Dev (Acc)	Test (Acc)
–	97.22	95.67	95.24
0.5	98.32	97.53	**97.60**

We use the GloVe word vectors to initialize word embedding. As shown in Table 9, the best result is dimensions are set to 100 and we use it in the following experiments.

Table 9. POS tagging accuracy of our model on the test set from WSJ corpus, with the different embedding.

Embedding	Test (Acc)
GloVe 50	97.21
Glove 300	97.14
Random	96.72
GloVe 100	**97.60**

5 Discussion

We investigate the effectiveness of our model in detail. The experiments show that our model has several appealing properties.

First, our model is effective in dealing with sequence labeling tasks. As shown in Tables 4 and 6, coarse-grained labeling and CNN part can improve the performance of our model on POS tagging, NER and GEC tasks.

Second, our model has high generality in doing different sequence labeling tasks. As shown in Tables 4, 5, 6 and 7, our model can handle a variety of sequential tasks such as POS, NER and GEC.

Third, our model is applicable to dealing with ESL corpus. As shown in Tables 5 and 7, our model is pretty good at dealing with the ESL corpus with grammatical errors.

6 Conclusion

In this paper, we introduce a two-stage deep neural network architecture for sequence labeling by using bidirectional LSTM, RCNN and residual network. We first use CNN to encode character-level information and feed it into first BLSTM. Meanwhile, we combine word-level information with the information from the first BLSTM to feed them into second BLSTM. Based on coarse- and fine-grained labeling, our model achieves state-of-art or competitive results on both news and ESL corpus for POS, GEC and NER tasks.

Acknowledgments. The authors would like to thank the anonymous reviewers for the constructive comments.

References

Ba, J.L., Kiros, J.R., Hinton, G.E.: Layer Normalization (2016)

Baxter, J.: Learning internal representations. In: 8th Conference on Computational Learning Theory, pp. 311–320. ACM (1995)

Bengio, Y., Simard, P., Frasconi, P.: Learning long-term dependencies with gradient descent is difficult. IEEE Trans. Neural Netw. **5**(2), 157–166 (1994)

Bohnet, B., McDonald, R., Simoes, G., Andor, D., Pitler, E., Maynez, J.: Morphosyntactic tagging with a Meta-BiLSTM model over context sensitive token encodings. In: Proceedings of the 56th Annual Meeting of the Association for Computational Linguistics, pp. 2642–2652 (2018)

Cai, R., Zhang, X., Wang, H.: Bidirectional recurrent convolutional neural network for relation classification. In: Proceedings of the 54th Annual Meeting of the Association for Computational Linguistics, pp. 756–765 (2016)

Caruana, R.A.: Multitask connectionist learning. In: Connectionist Models Summer School, pp. 372–379 (1995)

Chang, C.H., Chen, C.D.: HMM-based Part-of-Speech Tagging for Chinese Corpora (1993)

Chung, J., Ahn, S., Bengio, Y.: Hierarchical Multiscale Recurrent Neural Networks (2016)

Cho, K., Merrienboer, B.V., Bahdanau, D., Bengio, Y.: On the properties of neural machine translation: encoder-decoder approaches. Comput. Sci. (2014)

Collobert, R., Weston, J., Bottou, L., Karlen, M., Kavukcuoglu, K., Kuksa, P.: Natural language processing (almost) from scratch. J. Mach. Learn. Res. **12**, 2493–2537 (2011)

Cooijmans, T., Ballas, N., Laurent, C., Gülçehre, Ç., Courville, A.: Recurrent Batch Normalization (2016)

Enez, J.U.G., Arquez, L.S.M.: SVMTool: A general POS tagger generator based on Support Vector Machines. Report on the geology of Trinidad: Part I. of the West Indian survey (2004)

Graves, A., Schmidhuber, J.: Special issue: framewise phoneme classification with bidirectional LSTM and other neural network architectures. Neural Networks **18**(5–6), 602–610 (2005)

Hinton, G.E., Srivastava, N., Krizhevsky, A., Sutskever, I., Salakhutdinov, R.R.: Improving neural networks by preventing co-adaptation of feature detectors. Comput. Sci. **3**(4), 212–223 (2012)

Hochreiter, S.: Untersuchungen zu Dynamischen Neuronalen Netzen (1991)

Hochreiter, S., Bengio, Y., Frasconi, P., Schmidhuber, J.: Gradient flow in recurrent nets: the difficulty of learning long-term dependencies. In: Kremer, S.C., Kolen, J.F. (eds.) A Field Guide to Dynamical Recurrent Neural Networks. IEEE Press (2001)

Hochreiter, S., Schmidhuber, J.: Long short-term memory. Neural Comput. **9**(8), 1735–1780 (1997)

Huang, Z., Xu, W., Yu, K.: Bidirectional LSTM-CRF models for sequence tagging. Comput. Sci. (2015)

Ioffe, S., Szegedy, C.: Batch normalization: accelerating deep network training by reducing internal covariate shift. Comput. Sci. (2015)

Kingma, D.P., Ba, J.: Adam: a method for stochastic optimization. Comput. Sci. (2014)

Lample, G., Ballesteros, M., Subramanian, S., Kawakami, K., Dyer, C.: Neural architectures for named entity recognition. In: Proceedings of NAACL (2016)

Laurent, C., Pereyra, G., Brakel, P., Zhang, Y., Bengio, Y.: Batch normalized recurrent neural networks. Comput. Sci. (2015)

Luo, G., Huang, X., Lin, C.Y., Nie, Z.: Joint entity recognition and disambiguation. In: Conference on Empirical Methods in Natural Language Processing, pp. 879–888 (2015)

Ma, X., Hovy, E.: End-to-end Sequence Labeling via Bi-directional LSTM-CNNs-CRF (2016)

Marcus, M.P., Marcinkiewicz, M.A., Santorini, B.: Building a large annotated corpus of English: the penn treebank. Comput. Linguist. **19**(2), 313–330 (1993)

Mikolov, T., Chen, K., Corrado, G., Dean, J.: Efficient estimation of word representations in vector space. Comput. Sci. (2013)

Ng, H.T., Wu, S.M., Wu, Y.B., Hadiwinoto, C., Tetreault, J.: The CoNLL-2013 shared task on grammatical error correction. In: Proceedings of the 17th Conference on Computational Natural Language Learning, pp. 1–12 (2013)

Passos, A., Kumar, V., Mccallum, A.: Lexicon infused phrase embeddings for named entity resolution. Comput. Sci. (2014)

Pennington, J., Socher, R., Manning, C.: Glove: global vectors for word representation. In: Conference on Empirical Methods in Natural Language Processing, pp. 1532–1543 (2014)

Peters, M.E., et al.: Deep contextualized word representations (2018)

Sang, E.F.T.K.: Introduction to the CoNLL-2003 shared task: language-independent named entity recognition. In: Proceedings of the 7th conference on Natural language learning at HLT-NAACL (2003)

Santos, C.N.D., Zadrozny, B.: Learning character-level representations for part-of-speech tagging. In: International Conference on Machine Learning, pp. 1818–1826 (2014)

Srivastava, R.K., Greff, K., Schmidhuber, J.: Highway networks. Comput. Sci. (2015)

Søgaard, A., Goldberg, Y.: Deep multi-task learning with low-level tasks supervised at lower layers (2016)

Tan, Y.M., Yang, L., Hu, D.: A part-of-speech tagging algorithm for essay written by chinese english learner. J. Beijing Univ. Posts Telecommun. **40**(2), 30–34 (2017)

Veit, A., Wilber, M., Belongie, S.: Residual Networks Behave Like Ensembles of Relatively Shallow Networks (2016)

Wen, Y., Zhang, W., Luo, R., Wang, J.: Learning text representation using recurrent convolutional neural network with highway layers (2016)

Yoshimoto, I., et al.: NAIST at 2013 CoNLL grammatical error correction shared task. In: Proceedings of the Seventeenth Conference on Computational Natural Language Learning: Shared Task, pp. 26–33 (2013)

Reinforcement Learning Based Content Push Policy for HetNets with Energy Harvesting Small Cells

Yi Zhang(✉), Yifei Wei, Da Guo, and Mei Song

School of Electronic Engineering,
Beijing University of Posts and Telecommunications,
Beijing, People's Republic of China
{zzyy,weiyifei,guoda,songm}@bupt.edu.cn

Abstract. In order to utilize renewable energy and save traditional energy, many literatures in recent years have drawn attention to content caching in wireless communications. In this article, we focus on content push and cache to increase green energy utilization and save traditional energy. The state transition probability and future rewards in the mobile environment are unknown. Therefore, we use reinforcement learning to solve the problem of green energy distribution and the content push. Q-Learning is a model-free enhanced learning technology that can find an optimal action selection strategy in the MDP question. The Boltzmann distribution method is used to update the strategy. Finally, we can find the desired action based on the current state and the optimal strategy. SBS selects actions according to the Boltzmann strategy and then iteratively updates the Q-tables to get the best action in each state. Through numerical simulation, we prove the validity of the model and get the regularity of SBS's decision.

Keywords: Content push · Renewable energy · Q-learning · Reinforcement learning

1 Introduction

Due to the rapid growth of multimedia services and the dramatic increase in carbon dioxide emissions. Green communication is an effective measure to solve such problems. There are many ways of green wireless access, such as energy harvesting (EH), multicast, and heterogeneous networks. EH technology using natural energy such as solar energy, wind energy, kinetic energy, etc. can greatly reduce the power consumption of wireless communication of conventional power supplies, thereby reducing carbon dioxide emissions [1]. It is considered one of the candidate technologies for implementing green communication [2].

Supported by the National Natural Science Foundation of China (61871058).

X. Sun et al. (Eds.): ICAIS 2019, LNCS 11633, pp. 145–156, 2019.
https://doi.org/10.1007/978-3-030-24265-7_13

Wireless multicast achieves enormous energy benefits by simultaneously providing multimedia content that is usually of interest to multiple users while broadcasting a single data stream to different users, which avoids repeated retransmissions of the same content [3]. Heterogeneous networks use densely deployed small base stations (SBS) to provide higher user rates by reducing the distance between users and base stations. However, each technology has its limitations.

Since the battery capacity is limited, energy and traffic arrival mismatches may occur, resulting in energy waste or shortage [4]. On the other hand, in order to achieve wireless multicast, some user requests need to be delayed in order to wait for concurrent transmissions, which may seriously impair the quality of service of early needs [5]. Finally, because the deployment of micro base stations is not flexible enough, the cost of deploying support for power lines and high-speed backhaul links is relatively high [6]. Heterogeneous wireless networks may become a network architecture in which small transmit power small cell base stations (SBSs) are responsible for small areas to improve overall performance [7]. SBS deployment and operating costs can be reduced through renewable energy [8,9]. Macro base stations powered by traditional energy sources provide services for users when energy is insufficient. However, because the battery capacity is limited and the arrival of green energy is random, when the energy arrives and the user's request does not match, it will cause resource shortage and waste. Content push of SBS and content caching of end users effectively avoid duplicate transmission of content, so the consumption of traditional energy sources is reduced, and the efficiency of responding to user requests is improved [10]. Based on the EH status and content popularity distribution, SBS actively caches and pushes content earlier than it actually needs [11].

In this article, we focus on content push and cache to increase green energy utilization and save traditional energy. The Markov model has been widely applied to the optimization of energy consumption. Most models now assume that Markov's state transition probability and expected rewards are known. Due to the random nature of user requests for arrival and renewable energy to capture, this assumption often does not hold in the actual environment.

Therefore, we use reinforcement learning to solve the problem of green energy distribution [12]. Q-Learning is a model-free enhanced learning technology that can find an optimal action selection strategy in the MDP question [13,14]. It learns through an action-value function. Ultimately, it can give the desired action based on the current state and the optimal strategy.

This paper is organized as follows. The system models and the optimization objectives are described in Sect. 2. Section 3 provides the Q-learning analysis and the Boltzmann distribution policy iteration algorithm to find the optimal policy. Some numerical results are presented in Sect. 5. Finally, we conclude this study in Sect. 6.

2 System Models

The system model is assumed to be a two-tiered heterogeneous network consisting of a macro base station (MBS) and multiple small green energy base stations, as shown in the figure. The macro base station is completely powered by the traditional energy. Small base station is entirely powered by green energy. Each SBS provides services to users within its coverage area and treats other SBS data transmissions as background interference. Due to SBS intensive deployment, the sum interference per user is considered the same. And Because all SBSs operate in the same way, we only focus on one SBS strategy formulation in the model. The SBS connects to the MBS through a wired/wireless backhaul link to acquire content and store it in a cache to reduce congestion in the core network. This article assumes that the entire content is stored in the core network. The process of obtaining content from the MBS to the core network is negligible. We assume that the time and energy consumption for acquiring content are negligible, so we only focus on the content transfer from SBS to users (Fig. 1).

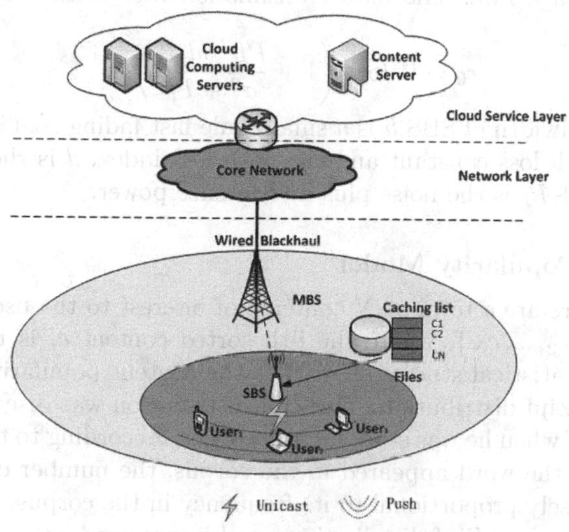

Fig. 1. Two-tiered heterogeneous network.

Data transmission in each small cell is through a single channel. The SBS and the macro cell BS are connected through a wireless backhaul link, and the SBS can quickly obtain the required content from the macro base station. When SBS has enough energy, it can unicast the required content to the user who sent the request, or push the popular content to all users in its coverage area. When the battery power is insufficiently transmitted, the BS enters a sleep mode and passes the user request to the macro BS. Even if the battery is adequately transported, SBS can choose to sleep. In this way, more energy will be available later. On the user side, if the desired content is in the user's cache, the content in the cache can be used directly without the need for transmission by the base station. In this article, we focus on designing push policies to make full use of the green energy in SBS.

The model is divided by the time slot T_p and the request Q_t is generated from the user side in each time slot. The small base station selects the corresponding action according to the battery status and request content, consumes U_t energy, and captures A_t energy at the same time. On the user side, each user accepts and saves the push content list C_t. The detailed description of the model is as follows:

The user request is assumed to follow the Bernoulli distribution, with content requests with a probability of $p_u \in [0,1]$ in each T_p. The request position obeys uniform distribution. Due to the limited green energy, new energy small base stations are mostly deployed in areas with less traffic. So there is at most one user request in a time slot. The total number of user requests for base station follows a binomial distribution. Due to the dense deployment of SBS, the Poisson distribution can be used for fitting. In each T_p, each content is transmitted at the same average rate. The data transmission rate of each content can be calculated as

$$r_0 = W\log_2\left(1 + \frac{Ph^2\beta d^{-\alpha}}{\sigma^2 + P_I}\right). \tag{1}$$

W is the bandwidth of SBS,h is a small-scale fast fading coefficient. α and β represent the path loss constant and the path loss index. d is the transmission distance and $\sigma^2 + P_I$ is the noise plus interference power.

2.1 Content Popularity Model

Assume that there are a total of N contents of interest to the user, represented by list $C = \{c_1, c_2, ..., c_N\}$, where the i-th sorted content c_i is requested with probability f_i. Statistical studies show that the content popularity distribution conforms to the Zipf distribution. The Zipf distribution was discovered by Harvard linguist Zipf when he was studying the corpus. According to the order of the number of times the word appeared in the corpus, the number of words in the word list is inversely proportional to its frequency in the corpus, or the product of the two is a constant.Zipf distribution can be expressed as

$$P(r) = \frac{c}{r^v}. \tag{2}$$

where r denotes the ranking of the frequency of occurrence of a word, and $P(r)$ denotes the frequency of occurrence of the word ranked r. The word frequency distribution c is equal to about 0.1.

Therefore, the popularity of content c_i can be expressed as

$$f_i = \frac{1/r^v}{\sum_{j=1}^{N} 1/j^v}. \tag{3}$$

The user's interest content will change over time, and over time, some popular content will be replaced. In this model, the content itself is not concerned, so the process of updating the popular content is not considered. According to the model, the user is always pushed the most popular content currently stored in the small base station. Pushed content can be represented as $C_t = \{c_1, c_2, ..., c_k\}$. The remaining unpush list can be represented as $\overline{C_t} = \{c_{k+1}, ..., c_{N-1}, c_N\}$.

2.2 Optimization Objective

In general, SBS acts according to the updated system status, sleep, unicast, or push. When the SBS chooses to sleep or push due to certain factors, or the user's request is not in the SBS push list, at this time, our user request needs to be handled by the macro base station. The macro base station needs to consume traditional energy while processing user requests. Our goal is to minimize the consumption of traditional energy sources and increase the utilization of green energy over a long period of time. Our optimization goal can be expressed as

$$E_M = \sum_{t=0}^{T=\infty} P_{mt}(d)T_p \tag{4}$$

where P_m is the transmit power of the macro base station.

3 Problem Formulation

In order to achieve this optimization goal, we need to determine the behavior of SBS in each period. Due to the state transition probability is unknown, we can use the reinforcement learning method to achieve the goal of energy saving. This problem can be modeled as a deep learning optimization problem. We adopt the Q-learning algorithm and regard SBS as an agent. Several elements need to be explained.

3.1 State Space

The basis for an agent's ability to choose the best action is to first define the state space. The agent can perceive the different state set of its environment S system state is represented by $S_t = (E_t, C_t, X_t, Y_t)$. E_t: the current power of the SBS. C_t: a current push state. X_t: the energy consumption of the SBS unicast. Y_t represents the energy consumption of the MBS unicast. For a user request generated at distance from SBS, $X_t = P_{st}(d_{st})T_p$, P_{st} can be solved by (1) equation. Similarly, $Y_t = P_{mt}(d_{mt})T_p$, P_{mt} can be solved by (1) equation.

This makes the problem very difficult because the battery level and the user request location is a continuous state space. So we discretize the continuous state space S. Energy is measured by each energy unit E_{unit} and $B_{\max} = k \cdot E_{unit}$. Then the energy state is $E_t \in \{0, 1, 2, ..., k\}$. We select a series of d_s to satisfy the following formula $P_s(d_s)T_p = X_t E_{unit}$ and X_t is a positive integer. $X_t = 0$ represents no unicast request. The discretization of Y_t is the same as X_t, and we will not describe it here.

3.2 Action Space

Consider adding a pure green energy-powered access point with caching function to the macro base station. The access point selects its own behavior according to the current power level, cached content, and user requests. SBS's action collection is

$$A = \{a_0, a_1, a_2, a_3\}. \tag{5}$$

a_0 is sleep, at which point the user requests service from the macro base station; a_1 indicates the action which unicast to the user directly; a_2 represent the action which request content from the BS, update the cache and deliver it; a_3 push the most popular content.

The BS may not be able to take all the three actions. When SBS has enough energy, it can unicast the content according to the request, or push the hot content to all users in the coverage. When the content requested by the user is not in the SBS cache list, there are two ways to send the content to the user. The SBS requests the content from the macro base station, updates the buffer and delivers it, or the SBS requests the macro base station to send the content directly to the user. The SBS can also choose to enter sleep mode for energy storage, at which point the content request will be completely handled by the MBS. When taking a push operation, SBS always pushes the most popular content to the user. Minimize the number of duplicate data transmissions.

3.3 Reward

The reward function is designed based on the amount of conventional energy consumed by the system's system. It is hoped that the amount of traditional energy consumed by the system will be minimal, and the prescribed return function $R(s, a)$ will be negative. $R(s, a)$ can be expressed as

$$R(s,a) = \begin{cases} -P_m(d)T_p & a = a_0, a_3 \\ -P_{ms}T_p & a = a_2 \\ 0 & a = a_1 \end{cases} \tag{6}$$

3.4 Policy and Value Function

Watkins defines the value of the state-action pair as a Q-value expressed as Q(s, a). The Q-value is a predictive estimate of the reward value, which refers to the discount award obtained by the strategy constructed by the sequence of actions executed in the current state. Because the higher reward value in the subsequent state can also make the current Q value high, the low reward value in the current state does not necessarily mean that its Q value is low.

4 Solution with Q-Learning

4.1 Boltzmann Distribution Policy

In the interactive process between the agent and the environment, it is possible to dynamically change the selection of the action value function by means of a value function, so as to achieve a balance between exploration and utilization. The introduced Boltzmann distribution is as follows

$$p(a_t = a|s_t = s) = \frac{e^{Q(s,a)/T}}{\sum\limits_{a_k \in A} e^{Q(s,a_k)/T}} \tag{7}$$

where T stands for temperature.

The Boltzmann distribution is used to indicate the degree of random exploration in the control exploration strategy. It is easy to see from Boltzmann that the state selection function is continuously attenuated as the Q value of the learning process increases. Consistent with the idea of tactical reinforcement for reinforcement learning. At the beginning, the agent knows little about the environmental information. At this time, it is suitable for random exploration with a large probability. After the agent has a certain understanding of the environment, the agent needs to increase the use of existing knowledge based on the existing knowledge so that the algorithm can quickly converge to an optimal level.

In the beginning of reinforcement learning, because the agent knows little about the external environment, it is more suitable to perform a random exploration process at this time. As the learning process continues to deepen, the agent has more and more knowledge of the external environment. Depending on the existing knowledge, agents need to strengthen the use process so that the reinforcement learning process eventually converges.

4.2 Q-Learning Algorithm

Watkins defines the value of the state-action pair as a Q-value expressed as Q(s, a). The Q-value is a predictive estimate of the reward value, which refers to the discount award obtained by the strategy constructed by the sequence of actions executed in the current state. Because the higher reward value in the subsequent state can also make the current Q value high, the low reward value in the current state does not necessarily mean that its Q value is low. Q-learning iteration formula is as follows

$$Q(s_t, a_t) = Q(s_t, a_t) + \alpha_t(r_{t+1} + \gamma \max_a Q(s_{t+1}, a) - Q(s_t, a_t)). \tag{8}$$

When the Q value is continuously iteratively updated, when n approaches a positive infinity, $Q(s_t, a_t)$ will converge to the optimal value, then the formula can be obtained at this time.

$$Q(s_t, a_t) = r_{t+1} + \gamma \max_a Q(s_{t+1}, a) \tag{9}$$

5 Numerical Simulations

In our simulation, we consider one SBS equipped with solar panels is implemented in the coverage area of a traditional MBS and The arrival of energy meets the Poisson distributionwith average arrival rate 0.75 units of energy.

Table 1. Q-learning algorithm

Initialize: $Q(s,a),\forall s \in S, a \in A(s)$
Repeat:(for each episode)
  Draw initial state s_0
  Choose A from S using $BoltzmannDistribution$ policy derived from Q
  Repeat:(for each step of episode)
    take action A ,observe $R, S^{'}$
    Choose $A^{'}$ from $S^{'}$ using $BoltzmannDistribution$ policy derived from Q
    $Q(S,A) \leftarrow Q(S,A) + \alpha(r + \gamma \max Q(S^{'}, A^{'}) - Q(S,A))$
    $S \leftarrow S^{'}, A \leftarrow A^{'}$
  Until S is terminal
End

MBS is entirely powered by traditional energy sources. We set delivery spectrum efficiency $r_0/W = 1.5\,\text{bps/Hz}$, the pathloss parameters $\beta = 10\,\text{dB}$ and $\alpha = 2$, $T_p = 1\,\text{s}$, $N = 10$, SBS cell radius $R_s = 50\,\text{m}$. The battery capacity is Emax = 15, and we set $M = 4$, $P(R_s) = 1\,\text{W}$. The channel coefficient h follows Rayleigh fading, whose mean value and the interference plus noise power $\sigma^2 + P_I$ are set so that holds for $r = r_0$, $d = R$, $P_t s = P_s(R_s)$. Since the model has too many dimensions, we will discretize the energy requested by the macro base station according to the energy unit standard formulated by SBS in the simulation (Table 1).

In order to more easily demonstrate the decision made by the SBS as an agent, we assume that the SBS stores all the contents, that is, only three actions of a_0, a_1, and a_3 are performed. It is represented by 0, 1, and 3 respectively. First of all, we can find that the more the promotion content, the smaller the system decides to promote. No content are pushed when $C_k = 0$. In addition to the user's proximity to the BS, the BS will promote popular content in most states. Second, for users close to BS, SBS tends to choose thinness. Since these users consume a very small amount of unicast energy and can also enjoy higher communication quality, it is more advantageous than transmitting a request to a macro BS. According to the Q-table, we can find out the rules that SBS presents when making optimal decisions. Therefore, it can be applied in practical application scenarios. p_u is the user request probability, which we will set later (Figs. 2 and 3).

For energy, we use unicast and full priority push as a reference. Then we evaluate the quality of the push mechanism. Figures 4 and 5 show that in a single time slot T_p, the user's request probability is $p_u = 0.5$, $p_u = 0.9$. As shown in Figs. 4 and 5. Unicast-Only Policy is a unicast-first strategy. The system performs a push operation when there is no unicast request. Push-Only is the policy with push as the highest priority. The system preferentially performs push operations on each time slot. When all popular content is pushed, unicast operations are

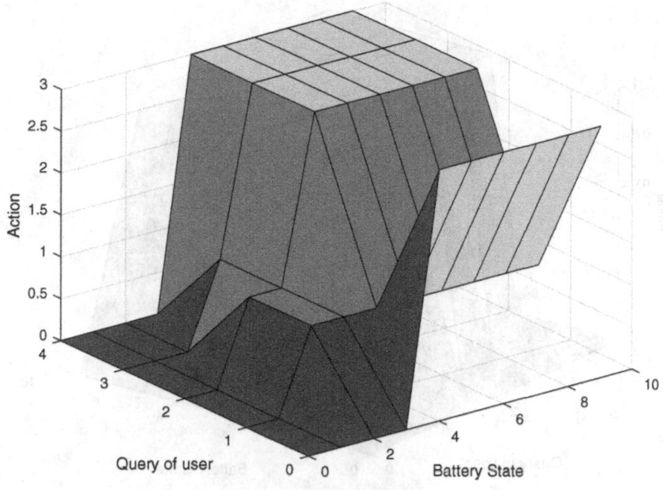

Fig. 2. Q-learning action ($C_k = 0$).

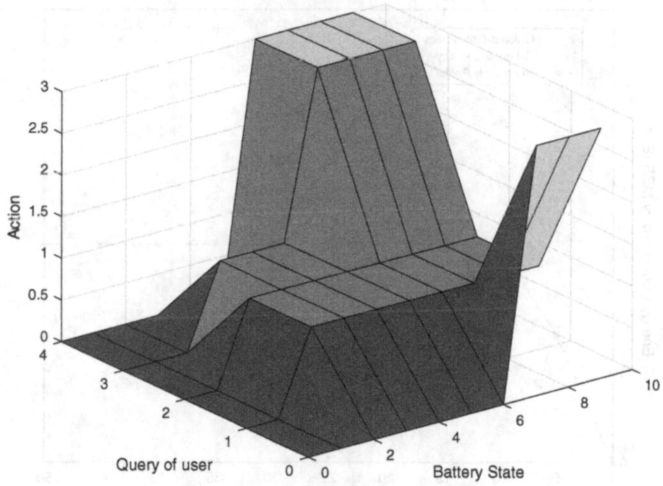

Fig. 3. Q-learning action ($C_k = 5$).

performed. The results show that compared to the push-only strategy, the push strategy learned through Q-Learning takes more time to push out the content in the content list, but consumes the least amount of energy. The Push-Only policy can quickly push the content list to the user at the expense of rejecting unicast requests from previous users, but the overall energy consumption is high. The preferential unicast strategy shows a large difference in the amount of user requests. When each slot user request probability is close to 1, SBS basically has no chance to perform a push operation. When the user request probability is 0.5, when there is no user request, the SBS may perform a push operation. At the

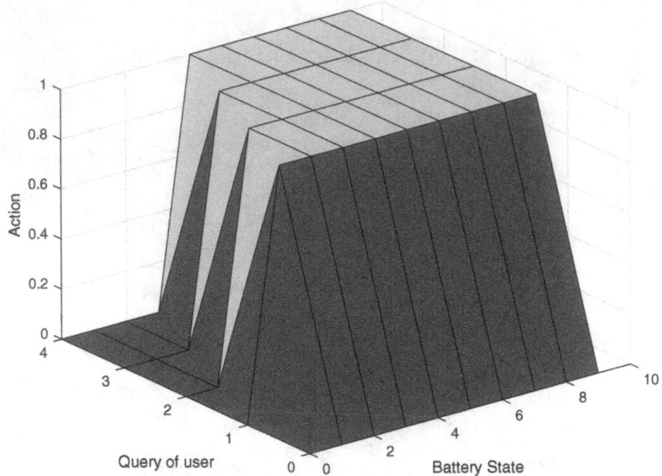

Fig. 4. Q-learning action ($C_k = 10$).

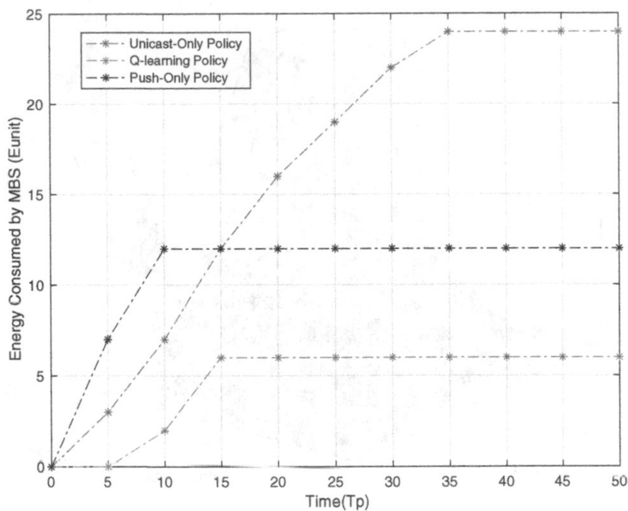

Fig. 5. Energy consumed by MBS (Eunit) ($p_u = 0.5$).

later stage, the content list may be completely pushed and basically no longer consume energy. Therefore, the performance of Unicast-Only strategy has a lot to do with the number of users. In general, after a period of learning, Q-learning performs actions according to the Q-table to get the best results (Fig. 6).

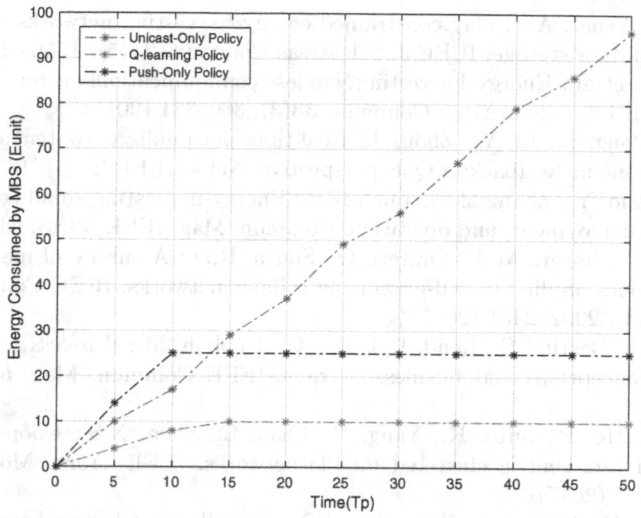

Fig. 6. Energy consumed by MBS (Eunit) ($p_u = 0.9$).

6 Conclusions

In this article, we focus on content push and cache to increase green energy utilization and save traditional energy. The Markov model has been widely applied to the optimization of energy consumption. Due to the random nature of user requests for arrival and renewable energy to capture, this assumption often does not hold in the actual environment. We use reinforcement learning to solve the problem of green energy distribution. Q-Learning is a model-free enhanced learning technology that can find an optimal action selection strategy in the MDP question. It learns through an action-value function. The Boltzmann distribution method is used to update the strategy. Ultimately, it can give the desired action based on the current state and the optimal strategy. Simulation results have been given to demonstrate that the algorithm can improve the utilization of green energy.

Acknowledgment. This work was supported by the National Natural Science Foundation of China (61871058).

References

1. Ku, M.L., Li, W., Chen, Y., Liu, K.J.R.: Advances in energy harvesting communications: past, present, and future challenges. IEEE Commun. Surv. Tutor. **18**(2), 1384–1412 (2017)
2. Jha, R., Gandotra, P., Jain, S.: Green communication in next generation cellular networks: a survey. IEEE Access **PP**(99), 1–1 (2017)
3. Peng, H., Liu, Y., Wang, J.: Verifiable diversity ranking search over encrypted outsourced data. CMC: Comput. Mater. Continua **55**(1), 037–057 (2018)

4. Varan, B., Yener, A.: Delay constrained energy harvesting networks with limited energy and data storage. IEEE J. Sel. Areas Commun. **34**(5), 1550–1564 (2016)
5. Ulukus, S., et al.: Energy harvesting wireless communications: a review of recent advances. IEEE J. Sel. Areas Commun. **33**(3), 360–381 (2015)
6. Tao, X., Dong, L., Li, Y., Zhou, J.: Real-time personalized content catering via viewer sentiment feedback: a QoE perspective. Netw. IEEE **29**(6), 14–19 (2015)
7. Mao, Y., Luo, Y., Zhang, J., Letaief, K.B.: Energy harvesting small cell networks: feasibility, deployment, and operation. Commun. Mag. IEEE **53**(6), 94–101 (2015)
8. Klaine, P.V., Imran, M.A., Onireti, O., Souza, R.D.: A survey of machine learning techniques applied to self-organizing cellular networks. IEEE Commun. Surv. Tutor. **19**(4), 2392–2431 (2017)
9. Paschos, G., Bastug, E., Land, I., Caire, G., Debbah, M.: Wireless caching: technical misconceptions and business barriers. IEEE Commun. Mag. **54**(8), 16–22 (2016)
10. Zhang, S., He, P., Suto, K., Yang, P., Zhao, L., Shen, X.S.: Cooperative edge caching in user-centric clustered mobile networks. IEEE Trans. Mob. Comput. **PP**(99), 1–1 (2017)
11. Ma, Y., Li, Y., Huang, Z., Wen, G.: acSB: anti-collision selective-based broadcast protocol in CR-AdHocs. CMC: Comput. Mater. Continua **56**(1), 35–46 (2018)
12. Zhang, Q., Lin, M., Yang, L.T., Chen, Z., Li, P.: Energy-efficient scheduling for real-time systems based on deep Q-learning model. IEEE Trans. Sustain. Comput. **PP**(99), 1–1 (2017)
13. Van Hasselt, H., Guez, A., Silver, D.: Deep reinforcement learning with double Q-learning. Comput. Sci. (2015)
14. Li, Y.: Deep reinforcement learning: an overview (2017)

A Comparative Research on Open Source Edge Computing Systems

Jiayue Liang, Fang Liu(✉), Shen Li, and Zhenhua Cai

Sun Yat-sen University, Guangzhou 510006, China
{liangjy77,lish286,caizhh8}@mail2.sysu.edu.cn,
liufang25@mail.sysu.edu.cn

Abstract. With the development of edge computing, open source communities have put forward several edge computing systems. This paper discussed about edge computing and its current situation, then presented typical open source edge computing systems such as EdgeX Foundry, Azure IoT Edge, CORD, Apache Edgent and Akraino Edge Stack, and gave a comparison about them on their characteristics. A comparison study on their characteristics were given to help users to understand these open source edge computing systems and make choices.

Keywords: Edge computing systems · Open source

1 Introduction

Cloud computing is the dominated computing paradigm in the past decade, providing efficient, centralized computing platform for big data. Recently, with the development of Internet of Things (IoT) [1] and the popularization of 4G/5G, massive devices are connected into the network, and a huge amount of data are generated all the time, which challenges the linearly increasing capability of cloud computing. Meanwhile, many applications of IoT demand lower response time and improved security, and the cloud computing cannot meet the requirements. Under this background, edge computing [2] is put forward to solve these problems. Edge computing takes advantage of the compute resources of edge nodes to perform computation so that the data can be processed at the edge. Several software systems for edge computing have been designed to help the popularization of edge computing, such as cloudlet [3] and Firework [4]. Open source communities began to develop open source systems such as EdgeX Foundry [5] and Apache Edgent [6]. However, there is no public literature to help users to select and use these open source edge computing systems. In this paper, our research analyzes several open source systems for edge computing to provide an overview of these systems.

The remaining parts of this paper are organized as follows. In Sect. 2, we discuss the current situation of edge computing. In Sect. 3, we present five open source edge computing systems. In Sect. 4, we give a comparison about these open source systems. Finally, Sect. 5 summarizes our conclusions.

X. Sun et al. (Eds.): ICAIS 2019, LNCS 11633, pp. 157–170, 2019.
https://doi.org/10.1007/978-3-030-24265-7_14

2 Edge Computing

Edge computing is a new paradigm and it calls for technologies to enable computation to be performed at the edge of the network in close proximity to data sources. W. Shi et al. gave their definition on "edge" as "any computing and network resources along the path between data sources and cloud data centers" [2]. Edge computing is expected to solve problems that challenge cloud computing. One problem is the pressure of bandwidth. Not all the data from the IoT objects are necessary to be sent to the cloud for processing, and most of them can be processed at the edge. Edge computing performs computing tasks on edge devices to process part of the data so as to reduce the data volume sent to the cloud and the pressure of bandwidth. Another problem is the latency. Centralized processing in the cloud may not meet the need of real-time processing for IoT applications. Edge computing processes data at the edge so as to get a shorter response time. The third problem is security and privacy [7]. In many cases, the data are not expected to share due to privacy concern and a local solution is needed. Edge computing provides support to process data at the edge without sending them to the cloud. Edge computing has a wide application area such as smart city, smart home, intelligence manufacturing and lots of other use cases in IoT.

Edge computing has obtained a rapid development. In 2015, the Open Edge Computing initiative [8] was published by Vodafone, Intel, Huawei and Carnegie Mellon University. Then the Open Fog Consortium [9] was established by Cisco, Microsoft, Intel, Dell, ARM and Princeton University. In 2016, the Edge Computing Consortium (ECC) [10] was established in Beijing by Huawei, Chinese Academy of Sciences, Intel, ARM, etc. What's more, software systems developed specifically for edge computing were launched gradually such as Cloudlet, ParaDrop [11] and Firework. A cloudlet is a small-scale cloud datacenter at the edge of the network, which provides compute resources to support running interactive mobile applications provided by mobile devices with low latency [3]. ParaDrop, as an edge computing framework, leverages the computing resource of wireless gateways or access points at the edge for developers to create and run services. Firework focus on the data sharing problem among the applications for the Internet of Everything (IOE), and put forward a computing framework to enable distributed data processing and sharing among multiple stakeholders such as edge nodes or the cloud in the hybrid cloud-edge environment [4]. As for commercial companies, especially cloud service providers, Amazon published AWS Greengrass [12], which can deploy applications to local devices for data processing with the help of the AWS Cloud capabilities such as deployment and management. Microsoft and Alibaba Cloud published solutions namely Azure IoT Edge [13] and Link IoT Edge [14] respectively, which are similar to AWS Greengrass with the concept "hybrid cloud-edge analytics". Open source communities also launched several open source edge computing systems, and we present them in Sect. 3.

Open source edge computing systems, supported by multiple companies with latest technologies, accelerate the development of edge computing. It is meaningful to perform a study on these systems so as to help users to understand these systems. In this paper, we studied five of these systems in detail.

3 Open Source Edge Computing Systems

The Linux Foundation published two projects, EdgeX Foundry in 2017 and Akraino Edge Statck [15] in 2018. The Open Network Foundation (ONF) launched a project namely CORD (Central Office Re-architected as a Datacenter) [16]. The Apache Software Foundation published Apache Edgent. Microsoft published Azure IoT Edge in 2017 and announced it was available and open source in 2018.

Among these open source edge computing systems, EdgeX Foundry and Apache Edgent focus on IoT, they try to solve problems which bring difficulties to practical application of edge computing in IoT. Azure IoT Edge provides with hybrid cloud-edge analytics, which helps to migrate cloud solutions to IoT devices. CORD and Akraino Edge Stack focus on providing edge cloud services.

3.1 EdgeX Foundry

EdgeX Foundry is a standardized interoperability framework for IIoT edge computing, whose sweet spots are edge nodes such as gateways, hubs, routers [5]. It can connect with various sensors and devices via different protocols, manage them and collect data from them, and export the data to a local application at the edge or the cloud for further processing. IIoT, where a huge amount of data are produced all the time, has urgent need for combination with edge computing. However, the diversity of hardware, software and communication protocols among sensors and devices in IIoT brings a great difficulty on managing them and collecting data from them. EdgeX Foundry is such a framework to provide interoperability to solve this problem, aiming to simplify and standardize the foundation of computing architectures in the IIoT market, and create an ecosystem of interoperable components. EdgeX is designed to be agnostic to hardware, CPU, operating system, and application environment. It can run natively or run in docker containers.

Figure 1 [5] shows the architecture of EdgeX Foundry. "South side" at the bottom of the figure includes "all IoT objects, within the physical realm, and the edge of the network that communicates directly with those devices, sensors, actuators, and other IoT objects, and collects the data from them" [5]. Relatively, "north side" at the top of the figure includes "the Cloud (or Enterprise system) where data are collected, stored, aggregated, analyzed, and turned into information, and the part of the network that communicates with the Cloud" [5]. EdgeX Foundry connects these two sides regardless of the differences of hardware, software and network. EdgeX tries to unify the manipulation method of the IoT objects from South Side to a common API, so that those objects can be manipulated in the same way by the applications of North Side.

EdgeX uses a Device Profile to describe a south side object. A Device Profile defines the type of the object, the format of data that the object provides, the format of data to be stored in EdgeX and the commands used to manipulate this object. Each Device Profile involves with a Device Service, which is a service that converts the format of the data, and translates the commands into instructions that IoT objects know how to execute. EdgeX provides SDK for developers to create Device Services, so that it can support for any combination of device interfaces and protocols by programming.

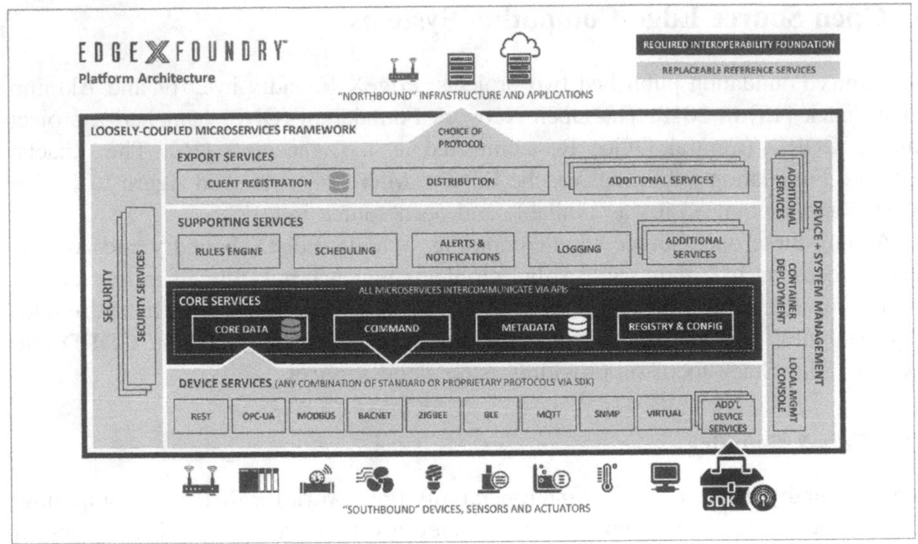

Fig. 1. Architecture of EdgeX Foundry

EdgeX consists of a collection of microservices, which allows services to scale up and down based on device capability. These microservices can be grouped into four service layers and two underlying augmenting system services as depicted in Fig. 1. The four layers are Device Services Layer, Core Services Layer, Supporting Services Layer and Export Services Layer. Two underlying augmenting system services are System Management and Security. Each layer consists of several components and all of these components use a common Restful API for configuration.

Device Services Layer. This layer consists of Device Services. According to the Device Profiles, Device Service Layer converts the format of the data, sends them to Core Services Layer, and translates the command requests from Core Services Layer.

Core Services Layer. This layer consists of four components Core Data, Command, Metadata, Registry and Configuration. Core Data is a persistence repository as well as a management service. It stores and manages the data collected from the south side objects. Command is a service to offer the API for command requests from north side to Device Services. Metadata is a repository and management service for metadata about IoT objects. For example, the Device Profiles are uploaded and stored in Metadata. Registry and Configuration provides centralized management of configuration and operating parameters for other microservices.

Supporting Services Layer. This layer is designed to provide edge analytics and intelligence [5]. Now the Rules Engine, Alerting and Notification, Scheduling and Logging microservices are implemented. We can set a target range of data to trigger a specific device actuation as a rule and Rules Engine helps to realize by monitoring the incoming data. Alerting and Notifications can send notifications or alerts to another system or person by email, REST callback or other methods when a urgent actuation or a service malfunction happens. Scheduling can set up a timer to regularly clean up the stale data. Logging is used to record the running information of EdgeX.

Export Services Layer. This layer connects EdgeX with North Side and consists of Client Registration and Export Distribution. Client Registration enables clients like a specific Cloud or a local application to register as recipients of data from Core Data. Export Distribution distributes the data to the Clients registered in Client Registration.

System Management and Security. System Management provides with management operations including installation, upgrade, start, stop and monitoring as EdgeX is scalable and can be deployed dynamically. Security is designed to protect the data and command of IoT objects connected with EdgeX Foundry.

EdgeX is designed for use cases which deal with multitudes of sensors or devices, such as automated factories, machinery systems and lots of other cases in IoT. Now EdgeX Foundry is in the rapid update phase, more features will be added in future release. An EdgeX UI is in development as a web-based interface to add and manage the device.

3.2 Azure IoT Edge

Azure IoT Edge, provided by Microsoft Azure as a cloud service provider, tries to move cloud analytics to edge devices. These edge devices can be routers, gateways or other devices which can provide compute resources. The programming model of Azure IoT Edge is the same as that of other Azure IoT services [17] in the cloud, which enables user to move their existing application from Azure to the edge devices for lower latency. The convenience simplifies the development of edge applications. In addition, Azure services like Azure Functions, Azure Machine Learning and Azure Stream Analytics can be used to deploy complex tasks on the edge devices such as machine learning, image recognition and other tasks about artificial intelligence.

Azure IoT Edge consists of three components: IoT Edge modules, IoT Edge runtime and a cloud-based interface as depicted in Fig. 2. The first two components run on edge devices, the last one is an interface in the cloud. IoT Edge modules are containerized instances running the customer code or Azure services. IoT Edge runtime manages these modules. The cloud-based interface is used to monitor and manage the former two components, in other words, monitor and manage the edge devices.

IoT Edge modules are the places that run specific applications as the units of execution. A module image is a docker image containing the user code. A module instance, as a docker container, is a unit of computation that running the module image. If the resources of edge devices supports, these modules can run the same Azure services or custom application as in the cloud because of the same programing model. In addition, these modules can be deployed dynamically as Azure IoT Edge is scalable.

IoT Edge runtime acts as a manager on the edge devices. It consists of two modules, IoT Edge hub and IoT Edge agent. IoT Edge hub acts as a local proxy for IoT Hub which is a managed service as a central message hub in the cloud, and is responsible for communication. As a message broker, IoT Edge hub helps modules communicate with each other, and transport data to IoT Hub. IoT Edge agent is used to deploy and monitor the IoT Edge modules. It receives the deployment information

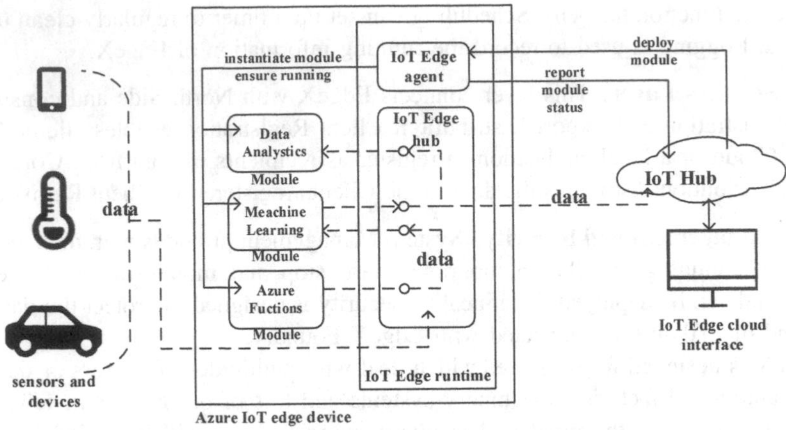

Fig. 2. Diagram of Azure IoT Edge

about modules from IoT Hub, instantiates these modules, and ensures they are running, for example, restarts the crashed modules. In addition, it reports the status of the modules to the IoT hub.

IoT Edge cloud interface is provided for device management. By this interface, users can create edge applications, then send these applications to the device and monitor the running status of the device. This monitoring function is useful for use cases with massive devices, users can deploy applications to devices on a large scale and monitor these devices.

A simple deployment procedure for applications is that, users choose a Azure service or write their own code as an application, then build it as an IoT Edge module image, and deploy this module image to the edge device with the help of the IoT Edge interface. Then the IoT Edge runtime receives the deployment information, pulls the module image and instantiates the module instance.

Azure IoT Edge has wide application area, now it has application cases on intelligent manufacturing, irrigation system, drone management system and so on. It's worth noting that Azure IoT Edge is open-source but the Azure services charge for fee.

3.3 CORD

CORD is an open source project of ONF initiated by AT&T and is designed for network operators. Current network infrastructure is built with closed proprietary integrated systems provided by network equipment providers. Due to the closed property, the network capability cannot scale up and down dynamically. And the lack of flexibility results in inefficient utilization of the compute and networking resources. CORD plans to reconstruct the edge network infrastructure to build datacenters with SDN [18], NFV [19] and Cloud technologies. It attempts to slice the compute, storage and network resources so that these datacenters can act as clouds at the edge, providing agile services for end-user customers.

CORD is an integrated system built from commodity hardware and open source software. Figure 3 [16] shows the hardware architecture of CORD. It uses commodity servers that are interconnected by a Fabric of White-box switches. These commodity servers provide with compute, storage resources and the fabric of switches is used to build the network. This switching fabric is organized to a Spine-Leaf topology rather than traditional three-tier network topology, because it can provide scalable throughput for greater East-to-West network traffic. In addition, specialized access hardware is required to connect subscribers. The subscribers can divided into three categories for different use cases, mobile subscribers, enterprise subscribers and residential subscribers. Each category demands different access hardware due to different access technology. In terms of software, Fig. 4 [16] shows the software architecture of CORD. Based on the servers and the fabric of switches, OpenStack provides with IaaS capability for CORD, it manages the compute, storage and networking resources as well as creating virtual machines and virtual networks. Docker is used to run services in containers for isolation. ONOS (Open Network Operating System) is a network operating system which is used to manage network components like the switching fabric and provide communication services to end-users. XOS provides a control plane to assemble and compose services. Other software projects provide with component capabilities, for example, vRouter (Virtual Router) provides with virtual routing functionality.

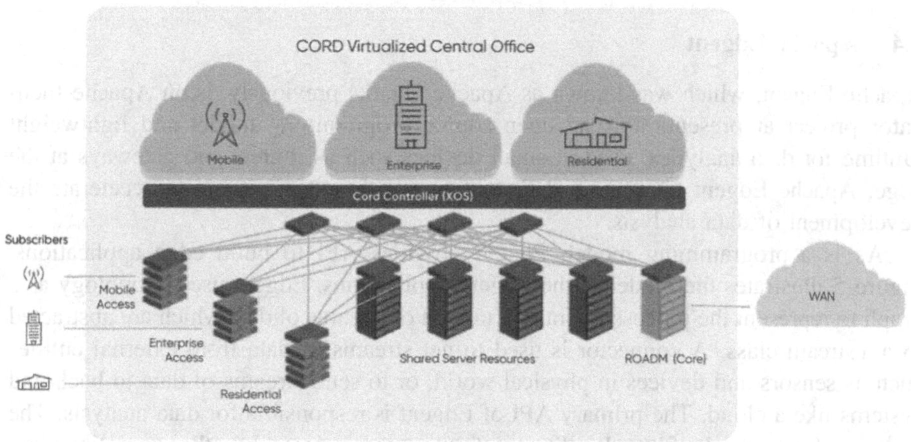

Fig. 3. Hardware architecture of CORD

The edge of the operator network is a sweet spot for edge computing because it connects customers with operators and is close to customers' applications as data sources. CORD takes edge computing into consideration and moves to support edge computing as a platform to provide edge cloud services from the 4.1 release version. CORD can be deployed into three solution, M-CORD (Mobile CORD), R-CORD (Residential CORD) and E-CORD (Enterprise CORD) for different use cases. M-CORD focus on mobile network, especially 5G network, it plans to disaggregate and virtualize cellular network functions to enable services be created and scaled dynamically.

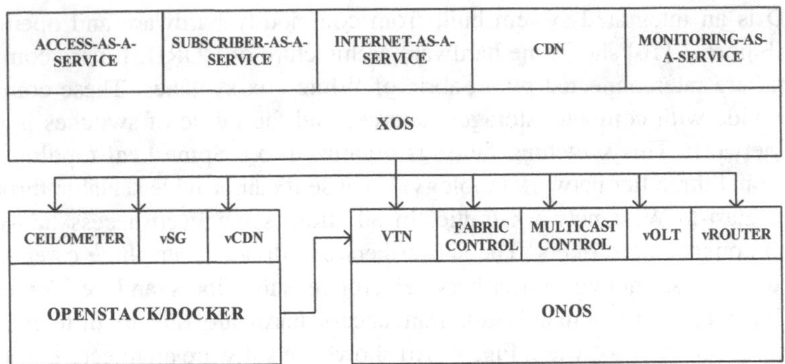

Fig. 4. Software architecture of CORD

This agility helps to provide multi-access edge services for mobile applications. For those use cases like driverless cars or drones, users can rent the edge service to run their edge applications. Similarly, R-CORD and E-CORD are designed to be agile service delivery platforms but for different users, residential and enterprise user relatively.

So far, deployment of CORD is still in test among network operators, and it needs more researches to combine CORD with edge applications.

3.4 Apache Edgent

Apache Edgent, which was known as Apache Quarks previously, is an Apache Incubator project at present. It is an open source programming model and lightweight runtime for data analytics, used in small devices such as routers and gateways at the edge. Apache Edgent focuses on data analytics at the edge, aiming to accelerate the development of data analysis.

As is a programming model, Edgent provides API to build edge applications. Figure 5 illustrates the model of the Edgent applications. Edgent uses a topology as a graph to represent the processing transformation of streams of data which are abstracted to a Tstream class. A connector is used to get streams of data from external entities such as sensors and devices in physical world, or to send streams of data to back-end systems like a cloud. The primary API of Edgent is responsible for data analysis. The streams of data can be filtered, split, transformed or processed by other operations in a topology. Edgent use a provider to act as a factory to create and execute topologies. To build an Edgent applications, user should firstly get a provider, then create a topology and add the processing flow to deal with the streams of data, and finally submit the topology. The deployment environments of Edgent are Java 8, Java 7 and Android.

Edgent provides API for sending data to back-end systems and now supports MQTT, IBM Watson IoT Platform, Apache Kafka and custom message hubs. Edgent applications analyze the data from sensors and devices, and send the essential data to the back-end system for further analysis. For IoT use cases, Edgent helps to reduce the cost of transmitting data and provide local feedback.

Edgent is suitable for use cases in IoT such as intelligent transportation, automated factories and so on. In addition, the data in Edgent applications are not limited to sensor

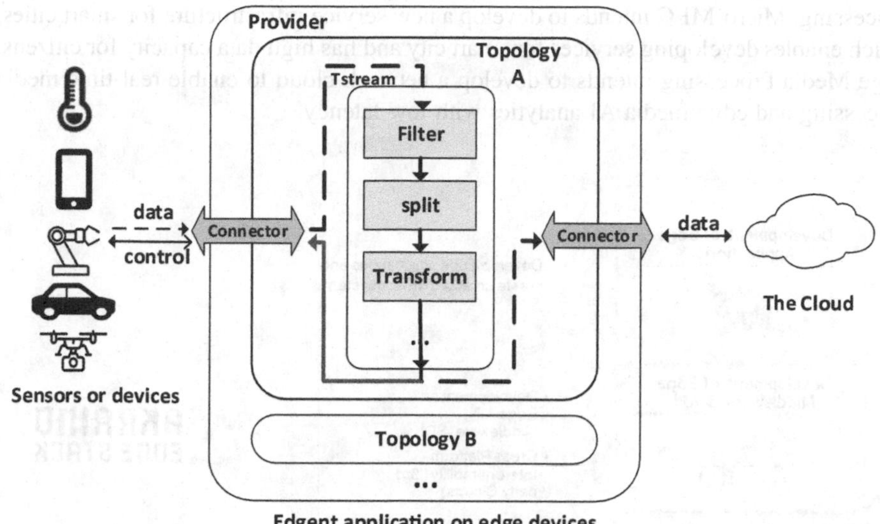

Fig. 5. Model of the Edgent applications

readings, they can also be files or logs. Therefore, Edgent can be applied to other use cases. For example, it can perform local data analysis when embedded in application servers, where it can analyze error logs without impacting network traffic [6].

3.5 Akraino Edge Stack

Akraino Edge Stack, initiated by AT&T and now hosted by Linux Foundation, is a project to develop a holistic solution for edge infrastructure so as to support high-availability edge cloud service [15]. An open source software stack, as the software part of this solution, is developed for carrier to facilitate optimal networking and workload orchestration for underlying infrastructure in order to meet the need of edge computing such as low latency, high performance, higher availability, scalability and so on.

To provide a holistic solution, Akraino Edge Stack has a wide scope from infrastructure layer to application layer. Figure 6 [15] shows the scope with three layers. In the application layer, Akraino Edge Stack wants to create an app/VNF ecosystem and calls for edge applications. The second layer consists of middleware which supports applications in the top layer. In this layer, Akraino Edge Stack plans to develop Edge API and framework for interoperability with 3rd party Edge projects such as EdgeX Foundry. At the bottom layer, Akraino Edge Stack intends to develop an open source software stack for the edge infrastructure in collaboration with upstream communities. It interfaces with and maximize the use of existing open source projects such as Kubernetes, OpenStack and so on. Akraino Edge Stack provides different edge use cases with blueprints, which are declarative configurations of entire stack including hardware, software, point of delivery, etc. [15] The application domains of these blueprints start from Telco industry, will expend to more domains like Enterprise and industrial IoT. Now Akraino Edge Stack has put forward several blueprints such as Micro-MEC and Edge Media

Processing. Micro-MEC intends to develop a new service infrastructure for smart cities, which enables developing services for smart city and has high data capacity for citizens. Edge Media Processing intends to develop a network cloud to enable real-time media processing and edge media AI analytics with low latency.

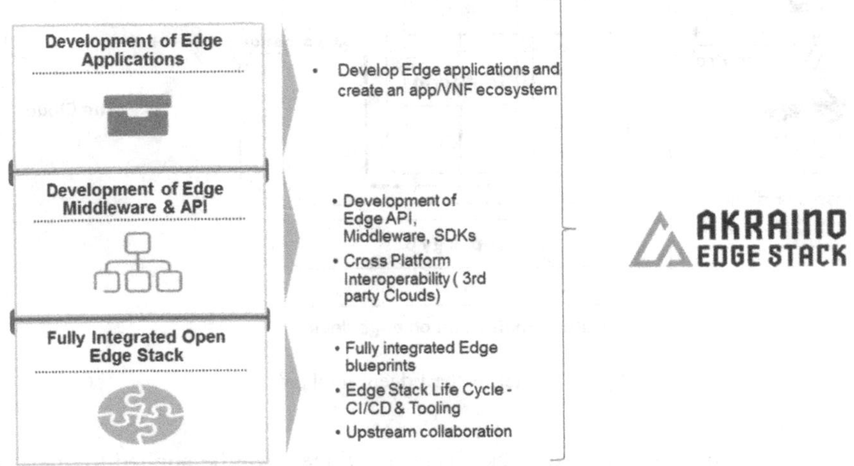

Fig. 6. Akraino Edge Stack's scope

As an emerging project, Akraino Edge Stack moved to execution since August 2018, thus more researches need to be done with the development of this project.

4 Comparative Study

In this section, we summarize the features of the systems discussed above in Table 1. Then compare these open source edge computing systems under different aspects as shown in Table 2. These aspccts includes: the main purpose of the systems, the application area, target user, the virtualization technology, system characteristic and limitation. We believe they are of importance on giving a better understanding of these systems. Finally, we discuss some use scenarios to help to choose a suitable system for researchers.

4.1 Main Purpose

The main purpose shows the target problem that a system tries to fix. It is a key factor for us to choose a suitable system to run edge applications. Therefore, we choose main purpose as the first aspect we use to compare.

As an interoperability framework, EdgeX Foundry aims to communicate with any sensor or device in IoT. And this ability is necessary for edge applications with data from various sensors and devices. Azure IoT Edge offers an efficient solution to move

Table 1. Features of open edge systems

Feature	EdgeX Foundry	Azure IoT Edge	Apache Edgent	CORD	Akraino Edge Stack
Scalability	Scalable	Scalable	Not scalable	Scalable	Scalable
User access interface	Restful API or EdgeX UI	Web service, Command-line	API	API or XOS-GUI	N/A
Deployment	Dynamic	Dynamic	Static	Dynamic	Dynamic
OS support	Various OS	Various OS	Various OS	Ubuntu	Linux
Programming Framework	Not provides	Java, .NET, C, Python, etc.	Java	Shell script, python	N/A

Table 2. Comparison of open edge system characteristics

Aspect	EdgeX Foundry	Azure IoT Edge	Apache Edgent	CORD	Akraino Edge Stack
Main purpose	Provide with Interoperability for IoT edge	Support hybrid cloud-edge analytics	Accelerate the development process of data analysis	Transform edge of the operator network into agile service delivery platforms	Support edge clouds with an open source software stack
Application area	IoT	Unrestricted	IoT	Unrestricted	Unrestricted
Target user	General users	General users	General users	Network operators	Network operators
Virtualization technology	Container	Container	JVM	Virtual Machine and Container	Virtual Machine and Container
System characteristic	A common API for device management	Powerful Azure services	APIs for data analytics	Widespread edge clouds	Widespread edge clouds
Limitation	Lack of programable interface	Azure Services is chargeable	Limited to data analytics	Unable to be offline	Unable to be offline

the existing applications from cloud to edge, and to develop edge applications in the same way with the cloud applications. Apache Edgent helps to accelerate the development process of data analysis in IoT use cases. CORD aims to reconstruct current edge network infrastructure to build datacenters so as to provide agile network services for end-user customers. From the view of edge computing, CORD provides with multi-access edge services. Akraino Edge Stack provides an open source software stack to support high-availability edge clouds.

4.2 Application Area

This subsection discusses about the suitable application area of these systems, considering that some systems are created to meet the need of specific application area.

EdgeX Foundry and Apache Edgent both focus on IoT edge, and EdgeX Foundry is good at communication with various sensors and devices, while Edgent is good at data analysis. They are suitable for intelligent manufacturing, intelligent transportation and smart city where various sensors and devices generate data all the time. Azure IoT Edge can be thought as the expansion of Azure Cloud. It have an extensive application area but depends on the compute resources of edge devices. Besides, it is very convenient to deploy edge applications about artificial intelligence such as machine learning and image recognition to Azure IoT Edge with the help of Azure services. CORD and Akraino Edge Stack support edge cloud services, which has no restriction on application area. If the edge devices of users don't have sufficient computing capability, these two systems are suitable for users to run resource-intensive and interactive applications in connection with operator network.

4.3 Target User

Though these open source systems focus on edge computing, but their target user are not the same. EdgeX Foundry, Azure IoT Edge and Apache Edgent have no restriction on target users. Therefore, every developer can deploy them into local edge devices like gateways, routers and hubs. Differently, CORD and Akraino Edge Stack are created for network operators because they focus on edge infrastructure.

4.4 Virtualization Technology

Virtualization technologies are widely used nowadays [20]. Virtual machine technology can provide better management and higher utilization of resources, stability, scalability and other advantages. Container technology can provide services with isolation and agility but with negligible overhead, which can be used in edge devices [21]. Using OpenStack and Docker as software components, CORD and Akraino Edge Stack use both of these two technologies to support edge cloud.

Different edge devices may have different hardware and software environment. For those edge systems which are deployed on edge devices, container is a good technology for services to keep independence in different environment. Therefore, EdgeX Foundry and Azure IoT Edge choose to run as docker containers. As for Edgent, Edgent applications run on JVM.

4.5 System Characteristic

System characteristics show the unique features of the system, which may help user to develop, deploy or monitor their edge applications. It will save lots of workload and time if making good use of these characteristics. EdgeX Foundry provides with a common API to manage the devices, and this brings great convenience to deploying and monitoring edge applications in large scale. Azure IoT Edge provides powerful

Azure services to accelerate the development of edge applications. Apache Edgent provides a series of functional APIs for data analytics, which lowers the difficulty and reduces the time on developing edge analytic applications. CORD and Akraino Edge Stack provide with multi-access edge services on edge cloud, we only need to keep connection with operator network, then we can apply for these services without the need to deploy an edge computing system on edge devices by ourselves.

4.6 Limitation

This subsection discusses the limitation of the latest version of them to deploy edge applications. The latest version of EdgeX Foundry has not provided a programmable interface in its architecture for developers to write their own application. Although EdgeX allows us to add custom implementations, but it demands more workload and time. As for Azure IoT Edge, though it is open-source and free, but Azure services are chargeable as commercial software. For Apache Edgent, it is lightweight and it focuses on only data analytics. As for CORD and Akraino Edge Stack, these two systems demand stable network between data sources and the operators because the edge applications are running on the edge of operator network rather than local devices.

4.7 Scenarios

Based on the differences of aspects discussed above, now we can discuss where and when each system should be chosen from the view of edge application.

In the first scenario, suppose we want to run edge applications on local area network, and use local enterprise system as back end system with no need for third-party clouds. In this case, we can choose EdgeX Foundry or Apache Edgent. Further, suppose we want a good device management ability with various and devices added in this system, we should choose EdgeX Foundry because it provides APIs to manage and control the devices. If we focus on data analysis, a best approach would be to use Apache Edgent because it helps to accelerate the development of edge analytic applications.

Then suppose we want to build edge applications about artificial intelligence. In this case, Azure IoT Edge can reduce the difficulty of development by providing powerful Azure services like Azure Machine Learning, as well as commercial support.

At last, suppose we want to run mobile edge applications on drones or autonomous cars. In this case, we should choose edge cloud services with wireless access, so CORD or Akraino Edge Stack are the best choice.

5 Conclusions

In this paper, we presented five open source edge computing systems, EdgeX Foundry, Azure IoT Edge, CORD, Apache Edgent and Akraino Edge Stack. We also listed features of them, gave a comparative study about them and described user scenarios. We hope this paper can give the readers a better understanding of their characteristic and help readers to choose an appropriate systems according to their requirement.

Acknowledgments. This work is supported by the National Key Research and Development Program of China under Grant No. 2016YFB1000302 and the National Natural Science Foundation of China under Grant Nos. 61832020.

References

1. Morabito, G.: The internet of things: a survey. Comput. Netw. **54**(15), 2787–2805 (2010)
2. Shi, W., Cao, J., Zhang, Q., Li, Y., Xu, L.: Edge computing: vision and challenges. IEEE Internet Things J. **3**(5), 637–646 (2016)
3. Satyanarayanan, M., Bahl, P., Caceres, R., Davies, N.: The case for VM-based cloudlets in mobile computing. IEEE Pervasive Comput. **8**(4), 14–23 (2009)
4. Zhang, Q., Zhang, Q., Shi, W., Zhong, H.: Firework: data processing and sharing for hybrid cloud-edge analytics. IEEE Trans. Parallel Syst. **29**(9), 2004–2017 (2018)
5. EdgeX Foundry Homepage. https://www.edgexfoundry.org. Accessed 16 Nov 2018
6. Apache Edgent Homepage. http://edgent.apache.org. Accessed 16 Nov 2018
7. Cui, J., Zhang, Y., Cai, Z., Liu, A., Li, Y.: Securing display path for security-sensitive applications on mobile devices. Comput. Mater. Contin. **55**(1), 17 (2018)
8. Open Edge Computing initiative Homepage. http://openedgecomputing.org. Accessed 16 Nov 2018
9. The Open Fog Consortium. https://www.openfogconsortium.org. Accessed 16 Nov 2018
10. Edge Computing Consortium. http://www.ecconsortium.org. Accessed 16 Nov 2018
11. Willis, D., Dasgupta, A., Banerjee, S.: ParaDrop: a multi-tenant platform to dynamically install third party services on wireless gateways. In: ACM Workshop on Mobility in the Evolving Internet Architecture. ACM (2014)
12. AWS Greengrass. https://aws.amazon.com/greengrass. Accessed 16 Nov 2018
13. Azure IoT Edge. https://azure.microsoft.com/zh-cn/services/iot-edge. Accessed 16 Nov 2018
14. Link IoT Edge. https://www.aliyun.com/product/iotedge?spm=5176.224200.loT.7.34666e-d6dQ8fjt. Accessed 16 Nov 2018
15. Akraino Edge Statck Homepage. https://www.akraino.org. Accessed 16 Nov 2018
16. CORD Homepage. https://www.opennetworking.org/cord. Accessed 16 Nov 2018
17. Azure IoT Homepage. https://azure.microsoft.com/en-us/overview/iot/. Accessed 16 Nov 2018
18. Nunes, B.A.A., Mendonca, M., Nguyen, X.N., Obraczka, K., Turletti, T.: A survey of software-defined networking: past, present, and future of programmable networks. IEEE Commun. Surv. Tutor. **16**(3), 1617–1634 (2014)
19. Hawilo, H., Shami, A., Mirahmadi, M., Asal, R.: NFV: state of the art, challenges, and implementation in next generation mobile networks (vEPC). IEEE Netw. **28**(6), 18–26 (2014)
20. Xie, X., Yuan, T., Zhou, X., Cheng, X.: Research on trust model in container-based cloud service. Comput. Mater. Contin. **56**(2), 273–283 (2018)
21. Morabito, R.: Virtualization on Internet of Things edge devices with container technologies: a performance evaluation. IEEE Access **5**, 99 (2017)

Weather Forecasting Using Artificial Neural Network

Md. Tanvir Hasan[1(✉)], K. M. Fattahul Islam[2], Md. Sifat Rahman[3], and Song Li[1]

[1] Beihang University, Beijing, China
tanvir89@gmail.com, songli.faprl@buaa.edu.cn
[2] Military Institute of Science and Technology, Dhaka, Bangladesh
fattahulislam@gmail.com
[3] Stamford University Bangladesh, Dhaka, Bangladesh
mdsifat.r@gmail.com

Abstract. Weather forecasting is a blessing of modern technology. It enables us to understand the nature of the atmosphere. Precise weather forecasting is one of the greatest challenges in the modern world. Unlike traditional methods, modern weather forecasting involves a combination of computer models, observation (by use of balloons and satellites) and patterns recognition along with various trends. Forecasting can be made accurately and precisely by the proper application of these methods. For forecasting various kinds of computer methods are used and these methods are related to various complex formulas. Researchers have done many things to establish a relationship of recent (input) data and target data which is linear. But practically the relationship is nonlinear. After establishing the nonlinearity, many models have been made to get future weather data. As the weather data is nonlinear, Artificial Neural Network (ANN) has become an effective way of predicting weather data precisely and accurately. Neural Network is a system that can be trained with certain input and output. It creates its own structure based upon how it is trained. In this paper we predicted weather data for a particular month of a season and compared the result for different functions and training method of ANN.

Keywords: Mean square error · Forecasting · Artificial neural network

1 Introduction

Weather forecasting is such a blessing of modern technology which predict the atmospheric condition for a specific location. Weather forecasts depend on proper collection of quantitative data regarding the current state of the atmosphere. Those data help us to predict how the atmosphere will be after a period using various methods.

Because of the nature of the atmosphere an enormous computational power is required to solve the equations. The equation which describes the atmosphere error related to measure the initial conditions and an incomplete understanding of atmospheric processes suggest that forecasting becomes less accurate because of timing. There is a multiplicity of end uses to weather forecasts.

X. Sun et al. (Eds.): ICAIS 2019, LNCS 11633, pp. 171–180, 2019.
https://doi.org/10.1007/978-3-030-24265-7_15

2 Ease of Use

2.1 Broad Objective

- To observe sharp change in predicted data with respect to previous data available.
- To predict whether the weather condition is normal or there is any chance of natural calamities.
- To distinguish among various seasons.

2.2 Specific Objective

- To become familiar with weather radar principle and prediction process.
- To understand relation between various parameters in weather radar equations.
- To understand the concept of neural network & how it works.
- To predict four different weather parameters.
- Compare predicted data with actual data.
- To observe neural network training state and training error.
- Data analysis and prediction for a season.

3 Background

Weather Forecasting has been playing a vital role in our day to day life since the birth of human race. Various kinds of warnings are important because they are accustomed to protect our lives and properties. Forecasting is so useful in the field of agriculture through various parameters like rain, temperature etc. Therefore, it also has a significant effect in the service markets. Utility companies use forecasting to calculate demand for the future. On an everyday basis, people use weather forecasts to determine clothing on a given day. Outdoor activities are severely condensed by rain, snow fall and the wind speed. So, forecasts can be used to plan activities around these events and to plan ahead and survive them. In order to forecasting Weather, the methods which are being used worldwide have shown below:

3.1 Persistence Method

The first method is the Persistence Method. It is the simplest way of producing a forecast. It assumes that the conditions at the time of the forecast will remain unchanged. This method seems to work very well when there is very little change in the weather [1]. If weather conditions change significantly from day to day, the persistence method usually breaks down. Then it is not the best method of forecasting.

3.2 Climatology Method

Through the climatology method we can simply forecast the weather. This method includes averaging weather statistics data which has been accumulated over many years to make the forecast. The climatology method only works well when the weather pattern is similar to that expected for the chosen time of year [1]. If the pattern is quite unusual for the given time of year, this method will often fail.

3.3 Analog Approach Method

The analog method is a complicated method of forecasting. It examines present weather condition and tries to relate it with the scenario of a past when weather conditions were so close (an analog). If the weather conditions match then the forecaster can make a prediction. But in reality, it is almost not possible to find a perfect analog. Different weather parameters rarely align themselves in the same locations as they were in the past. As a result, small differences between the analog and current time can lead to different results [1]. However, as time passes and more weather data is archived, the chances of finding a perfect match for the current weather condition should improve and so should analog forecasts.

3.4 Numerical Weather Prediction

Numerical Weather Prediction (NWP) uses the power of computers for forecasting. Complex computer programs which are known as forecasting models. These models help to predict various parameters like pressure, wind speed, humidity, temperature etc. The interaction required to produce weather information by predicted value of various parameters is done by the forecaster. This prediction is not truly precise. It contains some error.

4 Forecasting Procedure for Numerical Models

4.1 Analysis Phase

Taking observations and providing an initial state to the model.

4.2 Prediction Phase

Solve basic equations to predict the future states of atmosphere.

4.3 Post-processing Phase

It includes the production of a series of maps, model output statistics etc. Among various numerical prediction methods, we have chosen ANN (Artificial Neural Network) tool which can be processed and implemented using MATLAB (Fig. 1).

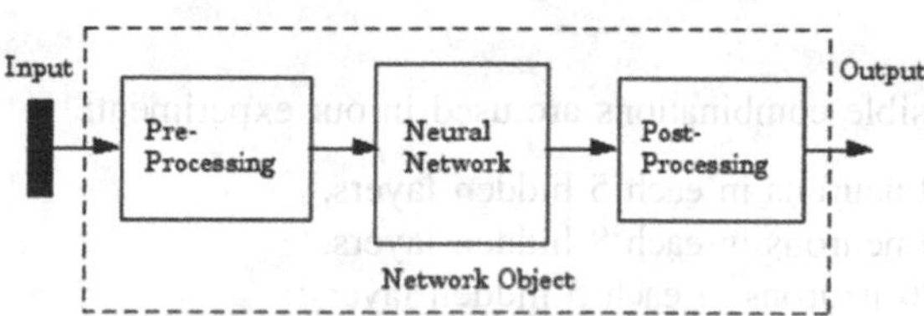

Fig. 1. Multilayer processing [2]

5 Reasons Behind Choosing ANN Over Conventional Computing

For better understanding of artificial neural computing it is important to know how a conventional computer and various software of this computer process information. A regular computer has a central processor that can address an array of memory locations where various kinds of data and instructions are stored. For computation the processor needs to read an instruction. It also requires help from the memory address section. After that the instruction is then executed and results are saved in a specified memory location as per requirement. In a serial system the computational steps are done sequentially and logically. In comparison neural networks are not as complex as the computer [8]. In neural network we don't have a processor but many parts which only can take the weight from the input. Rather than executing instructions neural networks responds according to the pattern of inputs presented to it. There are also no separate memory addresses for storing data. Instead, information is contained in the overall activation phase of the network. Proper knowledge is thus represented by the network itself. The represented knowledge is quite literally more than the sum of its individual components.

6 Figures and Tables

A typical feed forward back propagation network that we have used in our experiment should have three different layers (input, hidden, output). For training the network we have used different combinations of neuron and hidden layer. We have first analyzed the effect of number of neurons (50, 80 and 100) and the transfer function (tan-sigmoid/pure-linear) on mean square error i.e. performance (Fig. 2).

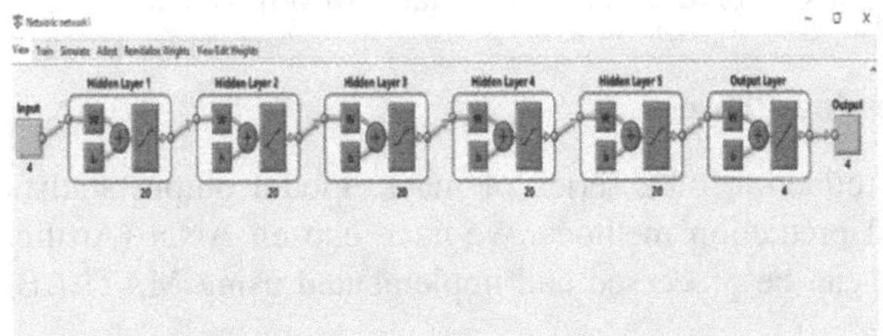

Fig. 2. Five hidden layer model

Following possible combinations are used in our experiment:

50 neurons: 10 neurons in each 5 hidden layers.
80 neurons: 10 neurons in each 8 hidden layers.
100 neurons: 20 neurons in each 5 hidden layers.

In the experiment we used tan-sigmoid function as a transfer function and pure-linear transfer function in the last extra hidden layer. We used two different training functions (TRAINGDX/TRAINLN) in this experiment. Comparisons of different methods of neural network for January data and training performance are given below (Table 1):

Table 1. Training performance

Serial	No. of neurons	Performance/MSE	Training function	Training algorithm
1	50	20.511	TRAINGDX	Gradient descent with momentum and adaptive LR
2	50	7.32	TRAINLM	Levenberg-Marquardt
3	80	15.54	TRAINGDX	Gradient descent with momentum and adaptive LR
4	80	6.547	TRAINLM	Levenberg-Marquardt
5	100	13.2298	TRAINGDX	Gradient descent with momentum and adaptive LR
6	100	5.92	TRAINLM	Levenberg-Marquardt

As we predict weather data for January, for training we have used the data of 2013 as an input and data of 2014 as target for the certain month. Sample data of January 2013 is given below (Table 2):

Table 2. Training

Serial	Temperature (deg, cel)	Dew point (deg, cel)	Humidity (percentage)	Pressure (hpa)
1	11.001	11.258	99.18	1012.258
2	11.0021	11.36	99.48	1012.44
3	11.3125	11.154	99.47852	1012.215
4	11.265	11.854	99.47	1012.48
5	11.365	11.468	99.82	1012.25
6	11.398	11.48	100.002	1012.396
7	11.45	11.478	99.8452	1012.35
8	11.89	11.665	99.284	1012.482
9	11.364	11.25	99.634	1012.4788
10	11.62	11.84	99.258	1012.255

Data is taken as half an hour interval from January 1 to January 31 (Total 4 * 1488 data).

We use January data of 2014 as target for training. Sample data of January 2014 is as below (Table 3):

Table 3. Training

Serial	Temperature (deg, cel)	Dew point (deg, cel)	Humidity (percentage)	Pressure (hpa)
1	13.29	11.35	8.3251	1018.48
2	13.285	11.88	81.38	1017.124
3	13.255	11.6	81.5	1017
4	13.158	11.28	82.4	1017.85
5	13.29	11.78	81.14	1017.855
6	13.245	11.88	81.221	1017.239
7	13.55	11.9	81.8541	1019.158
8	13.47	11.585	81.358	1017.482
9	13.96	11.58	81.78	1017.25
10	13.2	12.001	81.28	1017.30

Predicted weather data of January is given below (Figs. 3, 4 and Table 4):

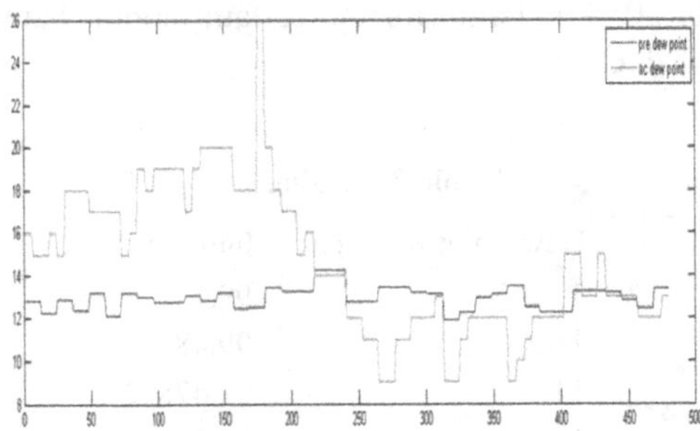

Fig. 3. Graphical representation of actual dew point and predicted dew point of January 2015

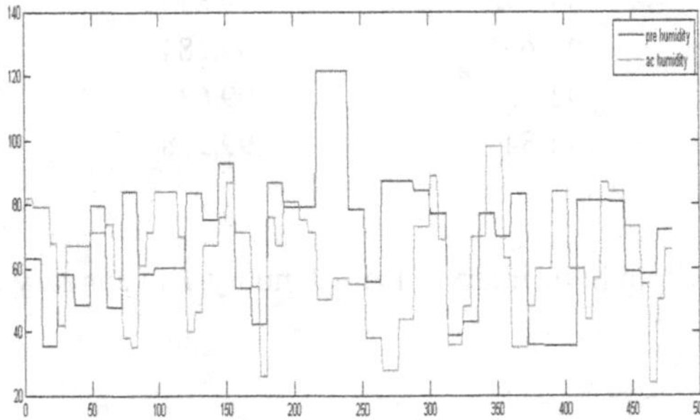

Fig. 4. Graphical representation of actual humidity and predicted humidity of January 2015

Table 4. Predicted January data

Serial	Temperature (deg, cel)	Dew point (deg, cel)	Humidity (percentage)	Pressure (hpa)
1	19.07705	12.85081	62.94053	1018.147
2	19.07705	12.85081	62.94053	1018.147
3	19.07705	12.85081	62.94053	1018.147
4	19.07705	12.85081	62.94053	1018.147
5	19.07705	12.85081	62.94053	1018.147
6	19.07705	12.85081	62.94053	1018.147
7	19.07705	12.85081	62.94053	1018.147
8	19.07705	12.85081	62.94053	1018.147
9	19.07705	12.85081	62.94053	1018.147
10	19.07705	12.85081	62.94053	1018.147

Actual data of January 2015 is given below (Table 5):

Table 5. actual data

Serial	Temperature (deg, cel)	Dew point (deg, cel)	Humidity (percentage)	Pressure (hpa)
1	19.002	16.008	82.33	1015.75
2	19.047	16.0003	82.2225	1014.98
3	19.007	16.339	82.255	1015.84
4	19.229	16.22	82.36	1015.8
5	19.1721	16.001	82.17	1015.87
6	19.0002	16.0225	82.852	1015.8
7	18.896	15.2225	79.96	1014.78
8	18.788	15.325	79.92	1014.85
9	18.958	15.336	79.78	1014.78
10	18.9871	15.005	79.008	1014.035

The variation was observed by graph for each parameter (Figs. 5, 6).

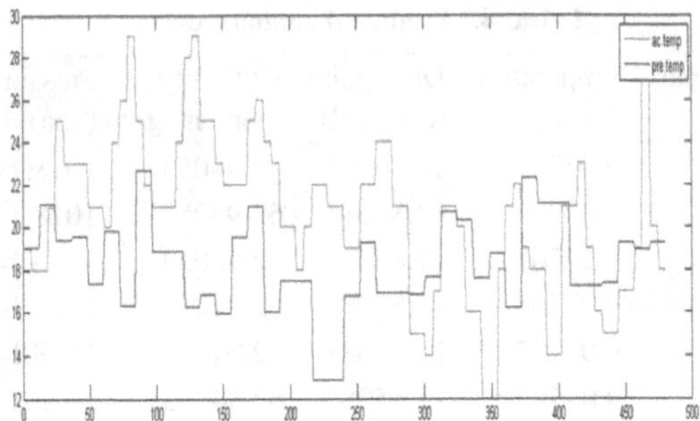

Fig. 5. Graphical representation of actual temperature and predicted temperature of January 2015

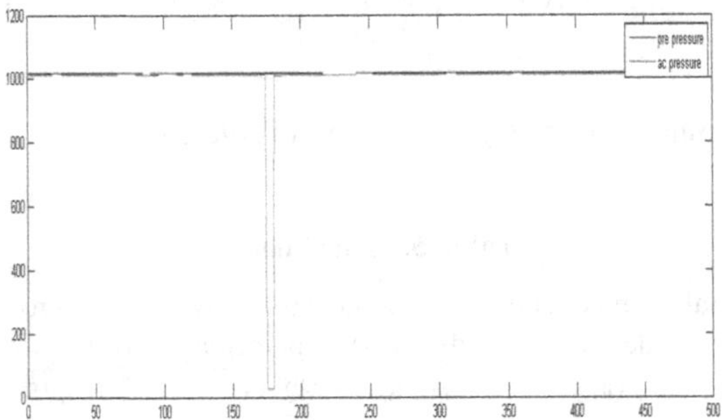

Fig. 6. Graphical representation of actual pressure and predicted pressure of January 2015

7 Observation

For different sets of operation shown we have learned the following factors which affect the performance of Artificial Neural Network:

- As we increase the number of neurons, decreases the mean square error i.e. increases the performance.
- For the same number of neurons TRAINLM transfer function gives better performance than TRAINGDX though the training time is more for TRAINLM than TRAINGDX transfer function.
- We use training target data as sample for the prediction of certain month's weather data.

8 Limitations

- The process of weather data analysis and prediction is done only for one month.
- Our prediction is only quantitative.
- We can't predict the possibility of any kind of natural calamities.
- Analysis and prediction of four weather parameters are done.

- Predicted values did not properly match the actual values but it was close.
- Back propagation neural networks are in a sense the ultimate 'black boxes'. We don't need to define any particular structure for the network. We only collect data, prepare them to feed as input and target. In the process we can only see the network to be trained and wait for the output.
- Actually, in back propagation we almost don't know what we are doing. Learning is done by the network automatically as time progresses.
- As the final product instead of getting an equation with coefficients, we get a trained network.
- Back propagation network sometimes requires thousands of epochs.
- As a result, sometimes, it takes so much time to be trained.

9 Recommendation for Future Improvement

Networks can be connected to sensors so that data is automatically stored. The training error can be minimized. The prediction can be done more precisely to minimize the difference between the actual value and the predicted value. Additional post processing system can be introduced to predict possibility of natural calamities.

10 Concluding Remarks

This paper presents a survey that using artificial neural network (ANN) approach for weather forecasting yields good results. As a result, it can be considered as an alternative to traditional metrological approaches. This study describes the capabilities of artificial neural network in predicting several weather parameters like temperature, humidity, dew point and atmospheric pressure. It presents a survey of existing literature to examine how neural networks have been used to generate both regression and classification forecasts.

Neural-networks-based ensemble models were developed and applied for half hourly weather forecasting of Dhaka, Bangladesh. The experimental results show that the networks can be trained effectively without excessively compromising the performance.

For prediction Artificial Neural Network tool of Matlab was used. Feed-Forward back propagation type network was used for training because it has given the desired predicted value.

The mean square error was plotted and in the paper. It has been shown that how MSE changes with respect to number of hidden layers, neuron, learning function etc. The Combination for which the MSE was the minimum was used for the prediction purpose. The appearance of various stopping criteria has also shown in here.

For checking the validation of our prediction predicted values was plotted along with actual value to observe the variation. This was done separately for each parameter. Three different networks having multiple layers for a month were developed and shown in the paper.

References

1. Aguado, Burt: Understanding Weather and Climate. Chap. 13-Weather Forecasting and Analysis. http://www.atmo.ttu.edu/schroeder/ATMO_1300/Notes/chapter13.pdf
2. Methods of interpreting numerical weather prediction output for aeronautical meteorology, by the CAeM working group on advanced techniques applied to aeronautical meteorology, 2nd edn., technical note no. 195. http://projects.knmi.nl/geoss/wmo/RRR/AeroMet/WMO-770.pdf
3. Beale, M.H., Hagan, M.T., Demuth, H.B.: Neural Network Toolbox™ User's Guide. https://www.mathworks.com/help/pdf_doc/nnet/nnet_ug.pdf
4. A Basic Introduction to Neural Networks. http://pages.cs.wisc.edu/~bolo/shipyard/neural/local.html
5. https://en.wikipedia.org/wiki/Mean_squared_error
6. Weather underground, Meteorological Data for January and for year 2013, 2014, 2015 of Dhaka city
7. http://www.extremetech.com/extreme/215170-artificial-neural-networks-arechanging-the-world-what-are-they
8. Christos Stergiou and Dimitrios Siganos: Neural Networks. http://www.doc.ic.ac.uk/~nd/surprise_96/journal/vol4/cs11/report.html#. What is a Neural Network
9. https://en.wikipedia.org/wiki/Artificial_neural_network
10. https://deepmind.com/blog/enabling-continual-learning-in-neural-networks/
11. Zeng, D., Dai, Y., Li, F., Sherratt, R.S., Wang, J.: Adversarial learning for distant supervised relation extraction. CMC Comput. Mater. Contin. **55**(1), 121–136 (2018)
12. Cui, Q., McIntosh, S., Sun, H.: Identifying materials of photographic images and photorealistic computer generated graphics based on deep CNNs. CMC Comput. Mater. Contin. **055**(2), 229–241 (2018)

A New Quantitative Evaluation Method for Fuzzing

Tiantian Tan[1(✉)], Baosheng Wang[1(✉)], Haitao Zhang[2(✉)], Guangxuan Chen[2(✉)], Junbin Wang[2(✉)], Yong Tang[1(✉)], and Xu Zhou[1(✉)]

[1] National University of Defense Technology, Changsha 410073, China
happinesschild@126.com, wangbaosheng@126.com, {ytang, zhouxu}@nudt.edu.cn

[2] People's Public, Security University of China, Beijing 100038, China
happinesschild@126.com, happinesschild@126.com, 2335371229@qq.com

Abstract. In order to ensure the network system security, many fuzzing strategies have been proposed recently, how to formally measure the performance of various fuzzing strategies, and choose the optimal strategy to improve the efficiency and effectiveness of vulnerabilities mining are becoming more and more important, this paper designed a fuzzing strategy evaluation framework, generated the taint data graph by the tracker, generated semantic tree by the parser, constructed a mapping from the taint data graph to semantic tree, quantitative calculated strategy performance using effective value and entropy value, selected optimal strategy according to evaluation value. The experiment proved that this method is reasonable and feasible, and optimal strategy selected by it can effectively improve the code coverage and vulnerability exploration effectiveness.

Keywords: The fuzzing evaluation · Taint data graph · Mapping · Semantic tree · Backtracking

1 Introduction

With the wide application of information technology in all walks of life, the security of huge amount of network data becomes more and more important to the development of all fields. Many efficient security mechanisms have been proposed, for some examples, Cai et al. [1] proposed a multi-monitor joint detection mechanism with lower communication overhead; Liu et al. [2] designed more robust DDoS detection mechanism based on Conditional Random Fields model; Cai et al. [3] proposed a distributed Ternary Content Addressable Memory (TCAM) coprocessor architecture for Longest Prefix Matching (LPM), Policy Filtering (PF), and Content Filtering (CF); Shengqun Fang et al. proposed a feature selection method based on class discriminative degree for intelligent medical diagnosis [4]; Menghua et al. designed a method using imbalanced triangle synthetic data for machine learning anomaly detection [5]; Jinhua et al. designed a security display path for security sensitive application on mobile devices [6].

X. Sun et al. (Eds.): ICAIS 2019, LNCS 11633, pp. 181–190, 2019.
https://doi.org/10.1007/978-3-030-24265-7_16

The vulnerability exists in the implementation of security mechanisms above, which is the basis for the security of huge amount of network data [7]. Fuzzing, the most widely used automatic software testing technology [8], has become a hot spot in the field of vulnerability exploration at home and abroad. Although more and more fuzzing strategies have been proposed, some problems exist in fuzzing.

- A lack of a common systematic evaluation method. In various fuzzing studies, fuzzing has various measure indexes and there is a lack of a systematic method to evaluate the effectiveness and efficiency suit for every fuzzing strategy.
- A lack of systematic evaluation mechanism during fuzzing process. The current fuzzing architecture lacks systematic evaluation mechanism. It will waste a lot of time to statistic and analyze the effectiveness and efficiency of fuzzing manually.
- A lack of optimal fuzzing strategy selection method. How to select optimal fuzzing strategy among many fuzzing strategies lacks systematic theoretical support [9, 10].

Aim to above problems, this paper proposed a new method to measure the effectiveness and efficiency of fuzzing during fuzzing process, the contributions of this paper include:

- It proposed a new quantitative evaluation method for fuzzing, introduced two measure indicators, effective value and entropy value, to provide a standard and universal framework for various fuzzing evaluation, the evaluation score can be used to select optimal fuzzing strategy for improving the efficiency of vulnerability exploration.
- It designed a method to quantitative compute the effective score of fuzzing during the test process, provide the effectiveness of fuzzing test case generation strategy during the process of fuzzing, the effectiveness score can be used to measure effectiveness of fuzzing.
- It designed a method to quantitative compute the efficiency score of fuzzing during the process of fuzzing, provide the efficiency of fuzzing test case generation strategy during the process of fuzzing, the efficiency score can be used to measure efficiency of fuzzing.

2 Relevant Research

Focus on the research of fuzzing, researchers at home and abroad have made a significant progress. Combining mutation technology and generation technology, reference [11] proposed a test case generation method to improve the effectiveness and efficiency, simplified the complexity of test case construction, and improved the degree of automation. Reference [12, 13] has made more standardized fuzzing engine modules, enhanced code reusability and the flexibility of the fuzzing architecture, and improved the generalization ability of testing for multiple target programs. In reference [14], log function is added to the fuzzing tool for recording the context and the input causing the exception, it can assist in further locating the exception, and recover the error. References [15, 16] added analysis module to the fuzzing tool to statistic result information, such as code coverage. The evaluation indicators of fuzzing in studies above are various and there is a lack of a systematic method to evaluate the effectiveness of fuzzing. The current fuzzing architecture lacks systematic evaluation mechanism, and the method of optimal strategy selection, it lacks systematic theoretical support [9, 10].

Based on this background, this paper proposed a method to evaluate the effect of fuzzing during fuzzing process, included the code coverage rate of the test case, introduced two measure indicators, effective value and entropy value, to quantitative calculate the evaluation score of fuzzing strategy, the evaluation score is beneficial to select optimal fuzzing strategy for improving the efficiency of vulnerability exploration.

3 Fuzzing Evaluation Framework

The fuzzing is a software test method which constructs test cases randomly or according to format specification to input target program and monitor if target program goes to a crash or exception. For various fuzzing strategy effectiveness evaluation, this paper has designed the fuzzing evaluation framework, as shown in Fig. 1, its first step is to input the initial test case set into the target program, and generate taint data graph through taint data traced by tracker. At the same time, the test case input set is parsed by parser and generated a semantic tree, then construct a mapping from the taint data graph to corresponding semantic tree, which can indicate the type of information field and the legal value that has been processed. Combined with mapping and backtracking data, the effective value and efficiency value of the strategy are quantitative to calculate the overall evaluation value of the strategy. According to the ascending order of the evaluation score, the strategy which is improved to a stable larger score can be selected from the strategy set.

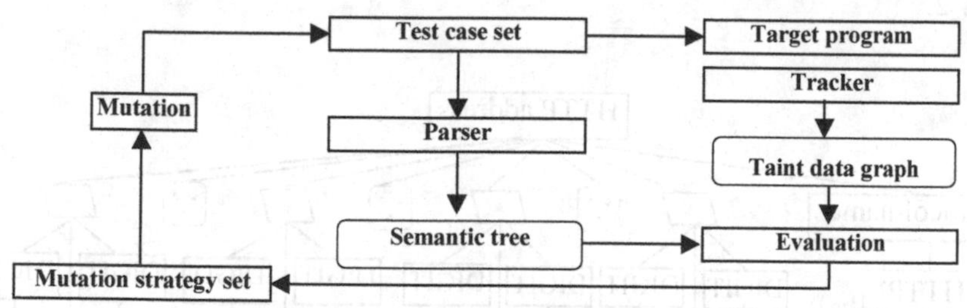

Fig. 1. The framework for fuzzing evaluation.

3.1 The Main Modules of Evaluation Framework

The main modules of the framework include tracker, parser, taint data graph.

Tracker is used to trace library function calls. The C language and binary parsing use memory manipulation functions such as strcpy and memcpy to extract different fields. The tracker intercepts and records calls of these functions. Establish the corresponding taint data graph by reading system calls from files or sockets.

The parser provides the ability to parse protocol request and response messages, transform each input data into a semantic tree, and provides the ability to traverse the semantic tree.

The taint data graph can be used to represent the change of the taint data in the form of a directed graph $GT = (VGT, EGT)$ and a triplet to represent each node $V_i = (a_i, s_i, c_i)$, where: a_i represents the memory address of the node buffer; S_i indicates the size of the buffer; C_i represents the binary string of the buffer. The directed edge which (v_i, v_j) connects node $v_i = (a_i, s_i, c_i)$ and node $v_j = (a_j, s_j, c_j)$, represents the process of function call in which the taint data is transferred from memory address a_i to address a_j. Since the data is usually copied from the middle position, the content size of S_j is usually a part of that of S_i [17, 18].

3.2 Backtracking Method

A backtracking (an abstract memory stack representation) represents the corresponding path in the taint data graph, namely a chain of function calls in the thread. Backtracking is implemented through stack expansion, which uses the ELF library function to parse DWARF debugging information and reads the information stored in the stack frame. This process is repeated until the entire stack is traversed by getting the return address of the stack and the pointer to the next stack.

3.3 Semantic Tree Generation and Representation

Hierarchical clustering algorithm is widely used in the generation of semantic tree. Methods in reference [19] are used to generate semantic tree. In this paper, the input information of fuzzing engine will be represented in a semantic tree structure. For example, for an ip address, the semantic tree representation of the input data is shown in Fig. 2.

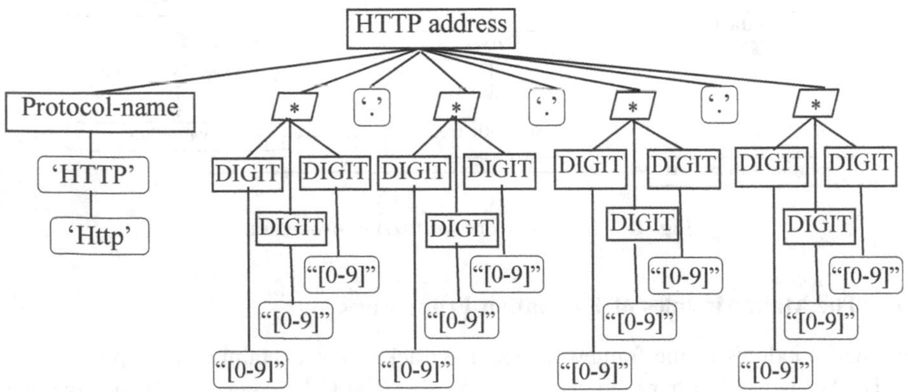

Fig. 2. An ip address's semantic tree representation.

3.4 Mapping Construction from Taint Data Graph to Semantic Tree

Tracker creates a taint data graph for each information of message received by the target program. In Fig. 3, each node represents a section of the starting input information. Connect the nodes of each taint data graph to the corresponding nodes of the semantic tree to define the relationship between the taint data and the semantic tree. Therefore, the semantics of each value can be inferred from the semantic tree to establish a comprehensive description of its architecture [20]. The mapping between the taint data graph and the semantic tree is shown in Fig. 3 (double arrows represent the mapping).

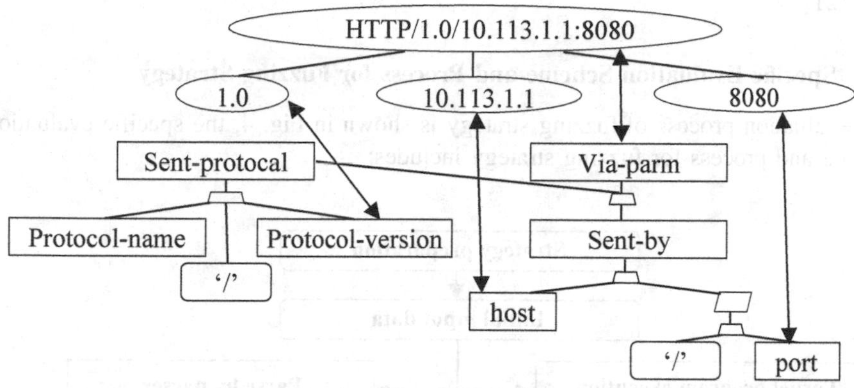

Fig. 3. The mapping from taint data graph to semantic tree.

4 The Process of Fuzzing Evaluation

4.1 Quantification and Evaluation of Fuzzing Process

A taint data graph was created for each input, and Euclidean spatial equation was used to define the effective parameter *Power* for each strategy:

$$Power\ (q) = \frac{1}{m}\sqrt{\sum\nolimits_{i=1}^{m} q_i^2} \tag{1}$$

where q_i represents the number of different backtracks performed on mapping i, and m represents the number of mappings.

Corresponding to instantaneous input q_t, the average effect equation is defined.

$$Power\ (q_t) = \frac{1}{t}\sqrt{\sum_{i=1}^{m} q_{i,t}^2} \tag{2}$$

where the vector $q_{i,t}$ represents the different amounts of backtracking in the mapping i within t time, and m represents the number of mappings.

At the same time, measure the overall distribution of backtracking, entropy of a test case q is defined as Eq. (3).

$$H(q) = -\sum_{i=1}^{m} r_i \log(r_i) \tag{3}$$

Where $r_i = \frac{q_i}{\sum_{i=1}^{m} q_i}$.

The entropy of the test case can better reflect the code coverage, and the higher the entropy value, the more values are executed by backtracking. The performance of the fuzzing strategy can be evaluated through the entropy value and effective value index, and the input with higher entropy value and effective value is selected as the new test case [21].

4.2 Specific Evaluation Scheme and Process for Fuzzing Strategy

The evaluation process of fuzzing strategy is shown in Fig. 4, the specific evaluation scheme and process for fuzzing strategy includes:

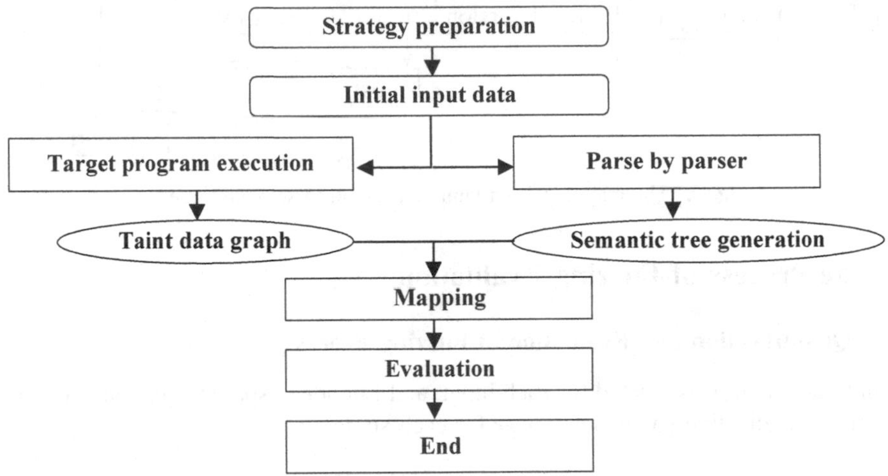

Fig. 4. Evaluation process of fuzzing strategy.

(1) Enter initial test case set of some strategy, inject target program and monitor target program execution.
(2) Generate the taint data graph by tracker and record the number of backtracking.
(3) Establish the mapping relationship between the taint data graph and the semantic tree.
(4) Calculate the number of mapping of taint data graph and semantic tree.
(5) Each strategy was scored based on a tuple (P_i, H_i).

5 Experiments and Evaluation

The tests in this article are based on PROTOS (a well-known SIP security test suite), and the tracker is based on ELF [21].

5.1 Scientific and Effective Verification of Measure Index

Higher entropy value means higher code coverage rate, namely larger number of backtracking and corresponding variable values. To verify the scientific evaluation method by comparing the entropy value and effective value of PROTOS and normal input, the result is shown in Fig. 5. The entropy value and effective value of PROTOS are larger than normal input. Figure 6 shows that messages with higher entropy score and effective score can find more backtracking and variable values, as well as higher effective code coverage rate.

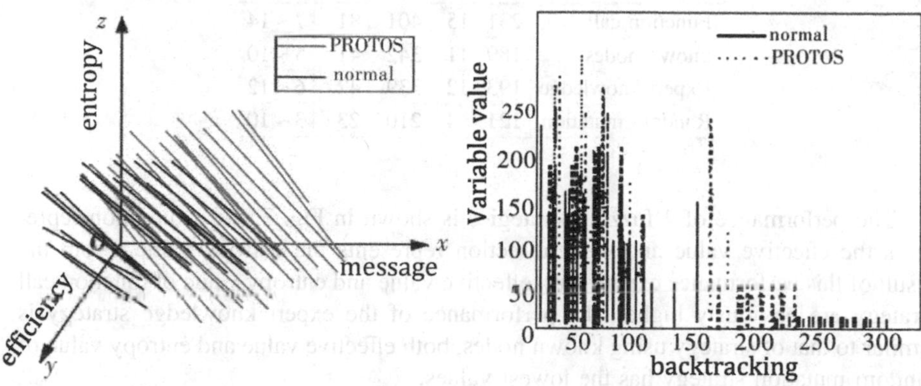

Fig. 5. Comparison of entropy value

Fig. 6. Comparison of backtracking and effective value and variable value.

5.2 Strategy Evaluation

Four fuzzing strategies in strategy selection module are used as the samples to be evaluated:

(1) Random mutation. A simple mutation technique randomly modifies data to generate test cases.
(2) Expert knowledge. Based on the mutation method of the expert template, the expert manually defines the fields which need to be modified for test data generation.
(3) Using known nodes. It can identify the fields that have been parsed by the target program and evaluate the effect of every node in the semantic tree, its effect is depend on the number of nodes in its connected backtracking.

(4) Using function calls. Track and analyze program function calls, such as strcpy, to replace non-keyword parts of test case by the data which can cause buffer overflows and be used as a long field during mutation.

Each strategy S_i corresponds to a tuple (P_i, H_i), *Pi* represents the average effective value, and H_i represents the average entropy value [22, 23]. Calculate the evaluation value of each strategy.

This paper selected to test lighttpd to the HTTP server, the statistical test results is shown as Table 1, among them, the TN represents nodes of a taint data graph, EN represents the number of merged nodes, the STN represents the number of semantic tree nodes, MN represents the number of mapping, BS represents the range of backtracking values, all this value is the average value of injection messages.

Table 1. Statistics result of four fuzzing strategies.

Variation strategy	TN	EN	STN	MN	BS
Function call	231	15	401	81	7~14
known nodes	189	11	342	41	5~10
Expert knowledge	193	12	339	42	6~12
Random mutation	121	4	210	23	3~10

The performance of 4 fuzzing strategies is shown in Fig. 7, the y direction represents the effective value and the x direction represents the entropy value. From the result of this performance experiment, effective value and entropy value of function call strategy are obviously higher, the performance of the expert knowledge strategy is similar to that of strategy using known nodes, both effective value and entropy value of random mutation strategy has the lowest values.

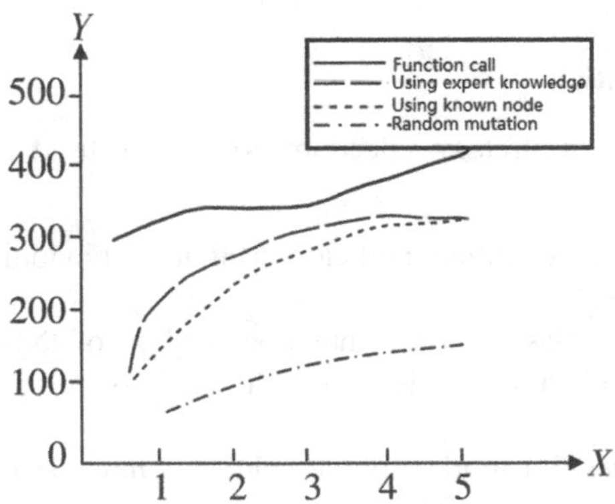

Fig. 7. Effective and entropy distribution of 4 strategies.

Table 2 shows the statistics result of 4 strategies, the number of discovered vulnerabilities is in the table, it can verify vulnerability detection effect of different strategies and confirm this strategy evaluation is scientific and reasonable.

Table 2. Vulnerability detection results using four strategies.

Type	Function call	Known nodes	Expert knowledge	Random mutation
DoS	5	1	2	1
Separator overload	4	1	1	1
Buffer overflow	6	3	3	2
Integer overflow	4	0	2	1
Port consumption	3	1	1	0
Line break error	3	0	0	0

6 Conclusion

In this paper proposed an evaluation framework of fuzzing strategy, gave the evaluation indicators and quantitative calculation method, verified the scientific and validity of this evaluation method using 4 fuzzing strategies. The evaluation framework of fuzzing strategy can provide a semi-automatic mechanism for fuzzing strategy evaluation during fuzzing, save manual time and effort consumption, and made it convenient to select the most optimal fuzzing strategy to improve the effectiveness and efficiency of fuzzing. The future work is to further improve the automatic level and efficiency.

References

1. Cai, Z., Chen, M., Chen, S., Qiao, Y.: Searching for widespread events in large networked systems by cooperative monitoring. In: International Conference on Network Protocols, pp. 123–133. IEEE, Francisco (2015)
2. Liu, Y., Cai, Z.-P., Zhong, P.: Detection approach of DDoS attacks based on conditional random fields. J. Softw. **22**(8), 1897–1910 (2011)
3. Cai, Z., Wang, Z., Zheng, K.: A distributed TCAM coprocessor architecture for integrated longest prefix matching, policy filtering, and content filtering. IEEE Trans. Comput. **62**(3), 417–427 (2015)
4. Fang, S., et al.: Feature selection method based on class discriminative degree for intelligent medical diagnosis. Comput., Mater. Continua **55**(3), 419–433 (2018)
5. Luo, M., Ke, W., Cai, Z., Liu, A., Li, Y., Cheang, C.F.: Using imbalanced triangle synthetic data for machine learning anomaly detection. Comput., Mater. Continua **55**(7), 15–26 (2018)
6. Cui, J., Zhang, Y., Cai, Z., Liu, A., Li, Y.: Security display path for security sensitive application on mobile devices. Comput., Mater. Continua **55**(1), 17–35 (2018)
7. Tiantian, T., Baosheng, W., Zhou, X., Yong, T.: The new progress in the research of binary vulnerability exploits. In: Xingming, S., Zhaoqing, P., Elisa, B. (eds.) Conference 2018, LNCS, vol. 11064, pp. 277–286. Springer, Heidelberg (2018)

8. Tiantian, T., Baosheng, W., Zhou, X., Yong, T.: The new progress in the research of binary vulnerability analysis. In: Xingming, S., Zhaoqing, P., Elisa, B. (eds.) Conference 2018, LNCS, vol. 11064, pp. 265–276. Springer, Heidelberg (2018)
9. Jianjun, X., Sun Lechang, W., Zhiyong, W.H., Jingjv, L.: PNG vulnerability exploiting technique based on fuzzing. Comput. Digit. Eng. **27**(8), 2811–2812 (2010)
10. Lanzi, A., Martignoni, L., Monga, M., et al.: A smart fuzzer for x86 executables. In: Proceeding of the 3rd International Workshop on Software Engineering for Secure Systems, p. 7. IEEE Computer Society, Washington (2007)
11. Miller, C., Petersonzn, J.: Analysis of mutation and generation based fuzzing. http://securityevaluators.com/files/papers/analysisfuzzing.pdf 01 March 2007
12. Peach. http://www.peachFuzzer.com 01 June 2009
13. Lin, S., Xiao-song, Z., Enbiao, S.: New method of software vulnerability detection based on fuzzing. Appl. Res. Comput. **2**(5), 99–110 (2016)
14. Zhiyong, W., Hongchuan, W.: Survey on fuzzing. Appl. Res. Comput. **27**(3), 1086–1088 (2010)
15. Vuagnoux, M.: Autodafe: an act of software torture. http://autodafe.sourceforge.net/docs/autodafe.pdf 05 August 2006
16. SPIKE proxy. http://www.immunitysec.com/recources-freesoftware.html June 2009
17. Xu, H., Chapin, S.: Address-space layout randomization using code islands. J. Comput. Secur. **17**(3), 331–362 (2009)
18. Ho, A., Fetterman, M., Clark, C., et al.: Practical taint-based protection using demand emulation. In: Proceedings of the 1st ACM SIGOPS/EuroSys European Conference on Computer Systems, pp. 29–41. ACM Press, New York (2006)
19. Brooks, C.H., Montanez, N.: Improved annotation of the blogosphere via autotagging and hierarchical clustering. In: Proceedings of the 15th Intenational Conference on World Wide Web, pp. 625–632. ACM Press, New York (2006)
20. Howard, M., Lipner, S.: Inside the windows security push. IEEE Secur. Priv. **1**(1), 57–61 (2003)
21. Kaksonen, R.: A Functional Method for Assessing Protocol Implementation Security. University of Oulu, Finland (2001)
22. Home FTP server's SITE INDEX' command remote denial of service vulnerability, http://www.securityfocus.com/bid/37033. 16 November 2009
23. XM easy personal FTP server file/folder remote denial of service vulnerability. http://www.securityfocus.com/bid/37112. 24 November 2009

Classification of ECG Arrhythmia Using CNN, SVM and LDA

Jian Liu[1(✉)], Shuang Song[1], Guozhong Sun[2], and Yu Fu[3]

[1] School of Computer and Communication Engineering, University of Science and Technology Beijing, Beijing 100083, People's Republic of China
liujian@ustb.edu.cn, huxin3518@163.com

[2] Dawning Information Industry Chengdu Co., Ltd., Chengdu 610213, People's Republic of China
sungzh@sugon.com

[3] Southwest Minzu University, Chengdu 610041, Sichuan, China
40976900@qq.com

Abstract. Nowadays heart disease is one of the serious diseases threatening human health, and a robust and efficient method is needed to achieve a real-time analysis and help doctors to diagnose. In this paper, we mainly propose an ECG arrhythmia classification algorithm based on convolutional neural network (CNN). Specifically we compare different CNN models, and then use them to raise the correct rate of classification combining linear discriminant analysis (LDA) and support vector machine (SVM). All cardiac arrhythmia beats are derived from MIT-BIH Arrhythmia Database, which are divided into five types according to the standard developed by the Association for the Advancement of Medical Instrumentation (AAMI). The training set and the testing set come from different people and the correction of classification is greater than 90%.

Keywords: Electroencephalography · Convolutional neural network (CNN) · Support vector machine (SVM) · Linear discriminant analysis (LDA)

1 Introduction

Electrocardiograph (ECG) is an important medical diagnosis for cardiovascular diseases. It is a hot spot for domestic and international scholars to analyze ECG signals automatically by using computers, which is of great significance for doctors to diagnose and prevent diseases at early stage.

ECG signal is a kind of non-stationary periodic signal, of which a single heart beat can reveal vital disease information. All cardiac arrhythmia beats that we used are derived from MIT-BIH Arrhythmia Database. MIT-BIH Arrhythmia Database is the most representative [1] in all databases used in analyzing ECG signals. This database

This work is supported by Intelligent Manufacturing Standardization Program of Ministry of Industry and Information Technology (No. 2016ZXFB01001).

X. Sun et al. (Eds.): ICAIS 2019, LNCS 11633, pp. 191–201, 2019.
https://doi.org/10.1007/978-3-030-24265-7_17

contains 48 records of heartbeats at 360 Hz for approximately 30 min of 47 different patients. According to the work of de Chazal et al. [2], the standard of performance evaluation can be defined for two kinds: inter-patient scenario (training and test ECG beats are extracted from different patients) and intra-patient scenario (heartbeats from the same patient in the training and test).

The classification methods in intra-patient scenario often have a higher accuracy, since the training set and test set are all from the same person, intra-patient scenario search algorithm reveals application limitations on real-time diagnoses. Some studies on the classification in inter-patient scenario also have satisfactory results. Many researches divide the training set and test set according to the work of de Chazal et al. [2]. The first set is composed of all heart-beats of records: 101, 106, 108, 109, 112, 114, 115, 116, 118,119, 122, 124, 201, 203, 205, 207, 208, 209, 215, 220, 223 and 230, called Dataset 1 (DS1) as training set, while the second is composed of all heartbeats of records: 100, 103, 105, 111, 113, 117, 121, 123, 200, 202, 210, 212, 213, 214, 219, 221, 222, 228, 231, 232, 233 and 234, called Dataset 2 (DS2) as test set.

Most of methods like deep neural network [3], reservoir computing with logistic regression [4] and domain transfer SVM [5] need complex feature extraction and complicated network structure, so they are time consuming approaches for real-time diagnoses. As the rise of convolution neural network on face recognition and image processing, similar methods are put into use on ECG classification. Kiranyaz et al. [6,7] propose a 1-D convolution neural network (CNN) to classify ECG beats. The network has 5 layers and the accuracy of VEB and SVEB are 99% and 99.6%, respectively. Zubair et al. [8] take a similar structure and the accuracy is 92.7%. Acharya et al. use more complex CNN networks, a 11-layer CNN [9] and a 9-layer CNN [10], and the accuracy of these two models is about 93%. However, these CNN methods are all in intra-patient scenario and the performance will be easily affected when the signal comes from new individuals. Hence, in order to improve the performance of above CNN methods, we propose a classification method in inter-patient scenario based on convolution neural network. The SVM and LDA features are used to optimize the algorithm.

2 Methodology and Model

2.1 Pre-processing

In this paper, the MIT-BIH arrhythmia database is used. According to the recommendation of Advancement of Medical Instrumentation (AAMI) [8], each ECG beat is classified into the following five heart beat types: N (normal beats), S (supraventricular ectopic beats), V (ventricular ectopic beats), and F (fusion beats), and Q (unclassifiable beats). As the last class Q has too few beats to train, we consider the first four classes. We take DS1 as training set and DS2 as test set. There are totally 50969 heart beats in training set and 49661 heart beats in test set.

Since the R position of each ECG signal is labelled in MIT-BIH database, we segment each sample into single beats according to the R position. We take samples from both sides of R waves. After segmentation, since amplitudes of beats from different people have big differences, all beats need to be normalized, separately. One single beat has about 200 samples which are down sampled into 64 points so that it is convenience to put these signals into the network.

2.2 Convolution Neural Network

Convolution neural network (CNN) has great advantages in feature extraction and classification [10], especially in analyzing pictures.

Four types of ECG beats are shown in Fig. 1. The first class is normal beats. The atrial premature beat in second class has earlier P wave so that the R interval of this kind of beat is often longer than others. The premature ventricular contraction beat in third class has earlier wide QRS wave without P wave. Therefore, there are huge differences between these four classes of ECG beats and it is possible to use CNN to classify. CNN is usually made of two parts: automatic feature extraction and fully connected multilayer perceptron. The feature extraction part generally includes convolution layers and pooling layers. These layers are convolved with their respective kernel size and then put into an activation function. The result of convolution layers is defined as

$$x_j^l = f\Big(\sum_{i \in M_j} x_i^{l-1} * k_{ij}^l + b_j^l\Big) \tag{1}$$

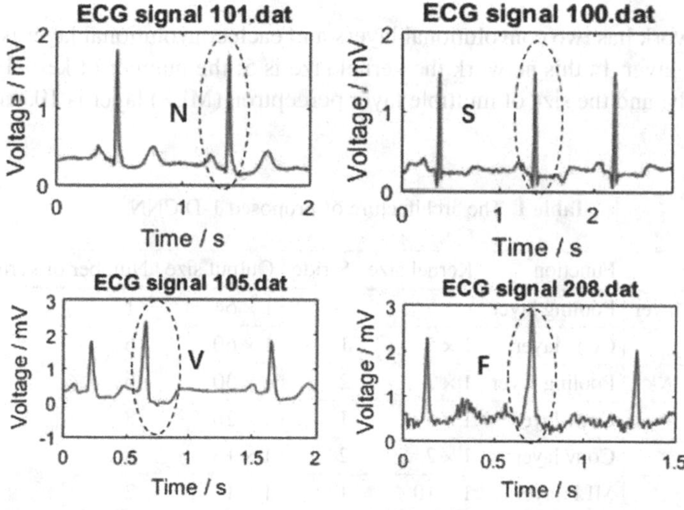

Fig. 1. Four types of ECG beats

where l represents the number of layer and x_i^{l-1} is the input of l layer, k_{ij}^l is the kernel from the ith neuron at layer l-1 to the jth neuron at layer l, b is the bias and f is the activation function. This layer is used to extract features from the signal by using different kernels.

Pooling layer has the function similar to down sampling, which is defined as

$$x_j^l = f(\beta_j^l down(x_i^{l-1}) + b_j^l) \quad (2)$$

where $down(*)$ represents down sampling and the pool size is usually 2; b is the bias; β is the weight. In this layer, the number of output signal is not changed and the size becomes half of the input signal.

After initializing b and β, we can get the results of the network. When we compare results with real labels, we can calculate loss of each layer by back-propagation algorithm and optimize the network structure by gradient descent. After an extended series of repeated experiments over a long period we can get a better structure of the network as is shown in Fig. 2 and Table 1.

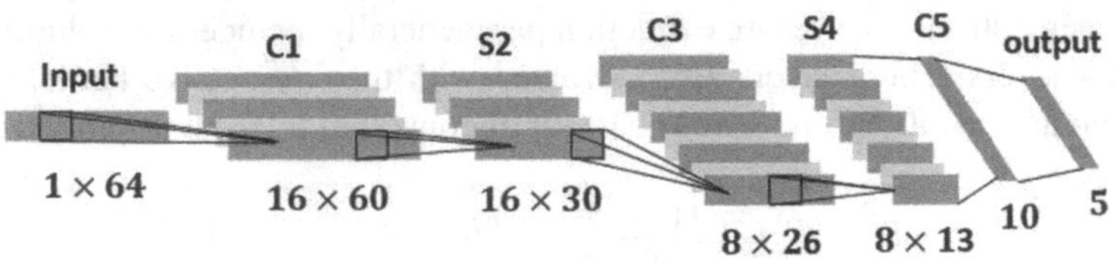

Fig. 2. The architecture of the proposed 1-D CNN

This network has two convolutional layers and each convolutional layer is followed by a pooling layer. In this network the kernel size is 5; the number of kernel is 16 and 8, respectively, and the size of multiple layer perceptron (MLP) layer is 10, as is shown in Table 1.

Table 1. The architecture of proposed 1-D CNN

Name	Function	Kernel size	Stride	Output size	Number of kernel
Input layer	Pooling layer	-	-	1 × 64	1
C1	Conv layer	1 × 5	1	1 × 60	16
M1	Pooling layer	1 × 2	2	1 × 30	16
C2	Conv layer	1 × 5	1	1 × 26	8
M2	Conv layer	1 × 2	2	1 × 13	8
FC1	MLP layer	1 × 10	1	1 × 1	2

2.3 Linear Discriminant Analysis

To find the internal characteristic of ECG signal, we use LDA to improve the accuracy of classification. LDA can project high dimensional pattern samples to the best discriminant vector space, which is beneficial to extract information of classification and compress the dimension of feature space. After the projection of LDA, we can get the largest class distance and the minimum intra class distance of model samples so that the signals can get the best separability in this space.

We can calculate m_k which represents the average of the data in class K as

$$m_k = \frac{1}{N_k}\sum_{n \in C_k} x_n \tag{3}$$

where x_n is the data; K is the number of classes; N_k is the data number of class C_k.

So, we can get the within-class scatter matrix S_w as,

$$S_w = \sum_{k=1}^{K} S_k \tag{4}$$

where

$$S_k = \sum_{n \in C_k} N_k(x_n - m_k)(x_n - m_k) \tag{5}$$

We can also calculate the average m of all data as,

$$m = \frac{1}{N}\sum_{n=1}^{N} x_n = \frac{1}{N}\sum_{n=1}^{K} N_k m_k \tag{6}$$

So, the between-class scatter matrix S_B is,

$$S_B = \sum_{k=1}^{K} N_k(m_k - m)(m_k - m)^T \tag{7}$$

and total covariance matrix S_T is defined as,

$$S_T = S_W + S_B \tag{8}$$

The discriminant function $J(W)$ is defined as

$$J(W) = \frac{W^T S_B W}{W^T S_W W} \tag{9}$$

where W is the projection matrix, we can get the projection matrix through maximize the discriminant function

$$W = arg_w max\{(W^T S_W W)^{-1}(W^T S_B W)\} \tag{10}$$

The output of LDA is computed as

$$y = W^T x \tag{11}$$

We use LDA method to optimize the networks. This method is called NNLDA and the architecture is shown in Fig. 3. In this method, the dimension of each beat is reduced into five points by LDA. The first ECG segmentation method and one-dimension network are also adopted in this method. The input data and structure are the same as the first method, while the input of MLP layer is added with the five points calculated by LDA.

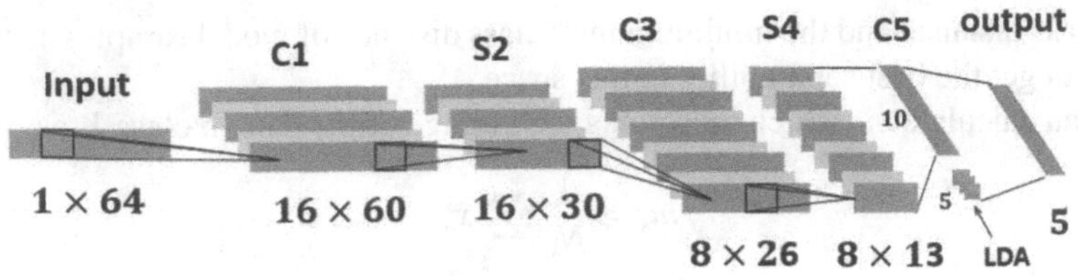

Fig. 3. Thearchitecture of the proposed CNN combined with LDA

2.4 Support Vector Machine

Support vector machine is a widely used classification method [11], and it is also a supervised machine learning method. A group of planes or infinite dimensional spaces are created to realize classification and regression tasks in SVM. Define two classes as −1 and 1, and assume that the data is linearly separable. So we can define the hyperplane as

$$w^T x + b = 0 \tag{12}$$

where w is the coefficient of this hyperplane and b is the maximum distance between the hyperplane and support vector. We can search the optimal hyperplane by changing these two variables. The loss function can be defined as,

$$\phi(w, \xi) = \frac{1}{2}\|w\|^2 + c\sum_{i=1}^{N} \xi_i \tag{13}$$

where ξ_i is the slack variable and different penalty factors such as C are assigned to the sample data of different importance, and the trade-off can be determined between training errors and model complexity $\|w\|^2$.

In order to compare classification performance of CNN and SVM, we design three kinds of method. The first one called SVM in which we only use SVM classifier. The input is a single beat of 64 points and the output are five labels (Fig. 4).

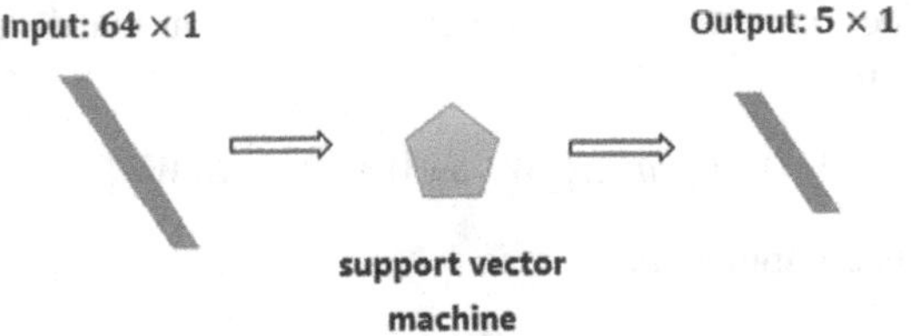

Fig. 4. ECGSVM: The architecture of SVM classifier

In second method, we combine CNN model with SVM classifier. We use above-mentioned one-dimension CNN model, and replace MLP layer with SVM classifier. This method is called CNNSVM and the model is shown in Fig. 5.

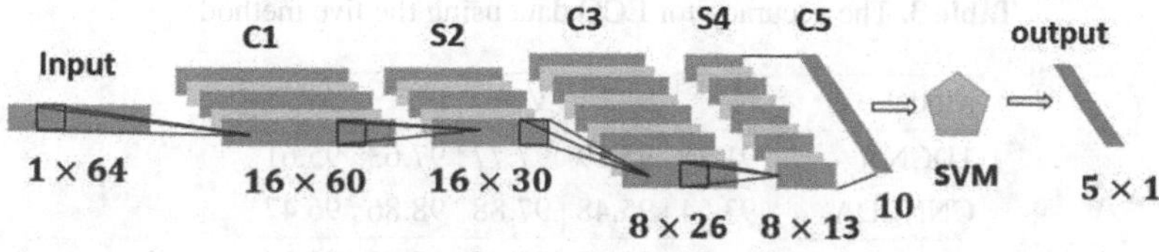

Fig. 5. CNNSVM: The architecture of the proposed CNN combined with SVM classifier

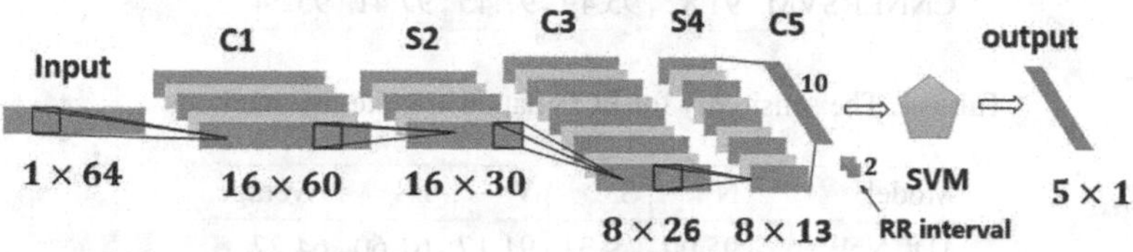

Fig. 6. CNNLRSVM: The architecture of the CNN combined with RR interval features

When we segment the heart beats, the interval between R wave is ignored. Therefore, we design the method called CNNLRSVM. This method is based on the method SVM and the input of SVM is added with the left interval and right interval of R peak. The structure of this method is shown in Fig. 6.

3 Result

As is mentioned above, we propose five methods which are based on one-dimension CNN model. In order to improve the these two major methods, we use S1 data set as training set and S2 data set as test set. There are totally 49661 heart beats from 22 samples in the test set, and the distribution is shown in Table 2.

Classification performance is measured using the four standard metrics found in the literature [6]: classification accuracy (Acc), sensitivity (Sen), specificity (Spe), and positive predictivity (Ppr). Four standard metrics for ECG data using above five methods are shown in Tables 3, 4, 5 and 6.

We use LDA method to extract inner features of ECG beats and combine with CNN structure and this method is called CNNLDA. From the tables we can see that, the method of CNNLDA has a higher accuracy. It has a balanced result in these four classes and the average accuracy is up to 96.47%.

Table 2. The distribution of four classes in training set and test set

Class	N	S	V	F
Train count	45824	943	3788	414
Test percent	89.90%	1.85%	7.43%	0.81%
Test count	44218	1836	3219	388
Test percent	89.04%	3.70%	6.48%	0.78%

Table 3. The accuracy for ECG data using the five methods

Model	N	S	V	F	Average
1DCNN	91.75	95.29	97.77	97.63	95.61
CNNLDA	93.64	95.48	97.88	98.86	96.47
SVM	87.71	95.19	92.48	97.76	93.29
CNN10SVM	89.47	94.63	97.45	95.78	94.33
CNNLRSVM	91.82	95.49	97.45	97.41	95.54

Table 4. The sensitivity for ECG data using the five methods

Model	N	S	V	F	Average
1DCNN	95.00	9.31	91.17	61.60	64.27
CNNLDA	97.39	11.49	85.78	25.77	55.11
SVM	90.72	7.46	84.93	18.30	50.35
CNN10SVM	91.55	27.4	89.23	64.43	68.15
CNNLRSVM	94.06	33.12	90.2	40.72	64.53

Table 5. The specificity for ECG data using the five methods

Model	N	S	V	F	Average
1DCNN	65.43	98.73	91.17	97.91	88.31
CNNLDA	63.23	98.78	85.78	99.44	86.81
SVM	63.27	98.87	84.93	98.39	86.36
CNN10SVM	72.61	97.38	89.23	96.02	88.81
CNNLRSVM	73.65	98.00	90.20	97.85	89.93

Table 6. The positive predictivity for ECG data using the five methods

Model	N	S	V	F	Average
1DCNN	95.71	22.74	78.78	18.86	54.02
CNNLDA	95.55	26.95	83.46	26.53	58.12
SVM	95.25	21.68	47.67	8.20	43.20
CNN10SVM	96.44	29.94	77.29	11.32	53.75
CNNLRSVM	96.66	39.87	76.51	12.99	56.51

There are three methods using SVM. In the first method called SVM, we only use SVM to classify the ECG beats and the sensitivity of all classes are not high. In the second method called CNN10SVM, there is a great improvement in accuracy of the sensitivity of class S and class F. In the second method called CNNLRSVM, we add the R wave intervals into the input features of SVM and the average accuracy is up to 95.54%, in addition the sensitivity of class S is also improved. While we compare these two methods, the sensitivity of class F in method CNNLRSVM is little lower than method CNNSVM. However, the performance of method CNNLRSVM is the best among all kinds of classification accuracy.

Comparing the methods mentioned above, we can see that these methods have different strength in different area. All in all, the method which combines CNN structure and SVM classifier has a better performance in the classification of these four classes.

4 Discussion

The accuracy of these five methods in Fig. 7 shows that the CNN has a better strength in extracting waveform characteristic compared with SVM. Comparing the method CNN10SVM with CNNLRSVM, we can see that the result is better when we consider the RR intervals between each ECG beat. The method which uses CNN combined with LDA has the highest accuracy, and the average accuracy of these four classes is up to 96.47%. The comparison of the inter-patient scheme with the existing works of class S and class V is presented in Table 7.

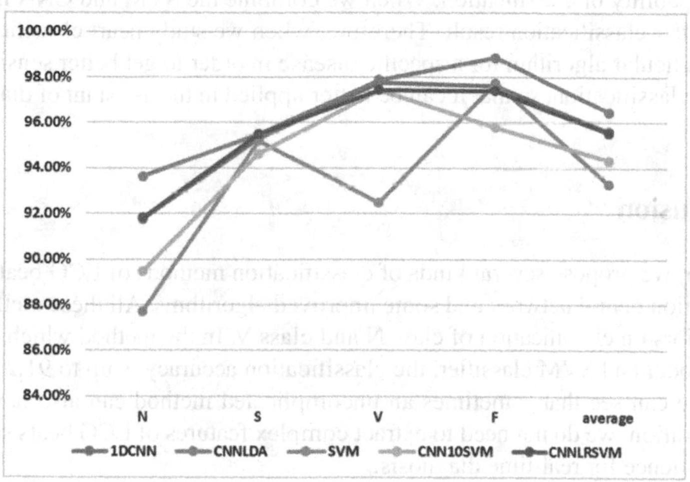

Fig. 7. The accuracy of these five methods

It can be observed from Table 7 that the proposed method exhibits superior performance for distinguishing V class from various other classes of signals in comparison with the existing methodologies presented in literatures. The method CNNLDA has the highest accuracy while the method CNNLRSVM has higher sensitivity and positive predictivity of these two classes.

Comparing the five methods mentioned above, we can see that the results are quite different. In conclusion, CNN method has a more prominent performance in classification of morphological features; linear discriminant analysis can extract the deep

Table 7. Comparison of ECG beat classification methods on MIT BIH arrhythmia database

Method	VEB				SVEB			
	Acc	Sep	Spe	Ppr	Acc	Sep	Spe	
Jiang et al. [12]	98.1	86.6	99.3	93.3	96.6	50.6	98.8	67.9
Ince et al. [13]	97.6	83.4	98.1	87.4	96.1	62.1	98.5	56.7
Ye et al. [14]	N/A	81.5	N/A	63.1	N/A	60.8	N/A	52.3
Shadmand et al. [15]	98.0	87.4	98.8	88.6	97.4	58.6	99.0	71.3
Raj et al. [16]	N/A	87.9	N/A	61.9	N/A	63.4	N/A	60.7
CNN	97.8	91.2	91.2	78.8	95.3	09.3	98.7	22.7
CNNLDA	97.9	85.8	85.8	83.5	95.5	11.5	98.8	27.0
SVM	92.5	84.9	84.9	47.7	95.2	7.5	98.9	21.7
CNN10SVM	97.4	89.2	89.2	77.2	95.2	27.4	97.3	29.9
CNNLRSVM	97.4	90.2	90.2	76.5	95.4	33.1	98.0	39.8

information from the data in reduction dimension and support vector machine has an excellent capability of classification. When we combine the SVM and CNN model, we can get a better classification result. Therefore, when we study heart classification, we can use a particular algorithm for a specific disease in order to get better sensitivity and accuracy of classification, so that it can be better applied in the assistant of diagnosis by doctors.

5 Conclusion

In this paper, we propose several kinds of classification methods of ECG beats, and we use convolution neural network and some improved algorithms. All these methods have good behaviors on classification of class N and class V. In the method which combines the CNN model and SVM classifier, the classification accuracy is up to 91.29%. From the result we can see that sometimes an uncomplicated method can also have a good result. In addition, we do not need to extract complex features of ECG beats so that it is more convenience for real-time diagnosis.

References

1. Moody, G.B., Mark, R.G.: The impact of the MIT-BIH arrhythmia database. IEEE Eng. Med. Biol. Mag. Quart. Mag. Eng. Med. Biol. Soc. **20**(3), 45 (2001)
2. De Chazal, P., Dwyer, M.O., Reilly, R.B.: Automatic classification of heart beats using ECG morphology and heartbeat interval features. IEEE Trans. Bio-Med. Eng. **51**(7), 1196–206 (2004)
3. Rahhal, M.M.A., et al.: Deep learning approach for active classification of electrocardiogram signals. Inform. Sci. Int. J. **345**(C), 340–354 (2016)
4. Escalona-Morn, M.A., et al.: Electrocardiogram classification using reservoir computing with logistic regression. IEEE J. Biomed. Health Inform. **19**(3), 892 (2015)

5. Bazi, Y., et al.: Domain adaptation methods for ECG classification. In: International Conference on Computer Medical Applications, pp. 1–4. IEEE (2013)
6. Kiranyaz, S., Ince, T., Gabbouj, M.: Real-time patient-specific ECG classification by 1-D convolutional neural networks. IEEE Trans. Biomed. Eng. **63**(3), 664 (2016)
7. Kiranyaz, S., et al.: Convolutional neural networks for patient-specific ECG classification, pp. 2608–2611 (2015)
8. Zubair, M., Kim, J., Yoon, C.: An automated ECG beat classification system using convolutional neural networks. In: International Conference on IT Convergence and Security, pp. 1–5. IEEE (2016)
9. Hu, Y.H., Palreddy, S., Tompkins, W.J.: A patient-adaptable ECG beat classifier using a mixture of experts approach. IEEE Trans. Bio-Med. Eng. **44**(9), 891–900 (1997)
10. Zhang, Y., et al.: Sentiment classification based on piecewise pooling convolutional neural network. Comput. Mater. Contin. **56**, 285–297 (2018)
11. Shi, J., et al.: New method for computer identification through electromagnetic radiation. CMC-Comput. Mater. Contin. **57**(1), 69–80 (2018)
12. Jiang, W., Kong, S.G.: Block-based neural networks for personalized ECG signal classification. IEEE Trans. Neural Netw. **18**(6), 1750–1761 (2007)
13. Ince, T., Kiranyaz, S., Gabbouj, M.: A generic and robust system for automated patient-specific classification of ECG signals. IEEE Trans. Biomed. Eng. **56**(5), 1415–1426 (2009)
14. Ye, C., Kumar, B., Coimbra, M.: Heartbeat classification using morphological and dynamic features of ECG signals. IEEE Trans. Biomed. Eng. **59**(10), 2930–2941 (2012)
15. Shadmand, S., Mashoufi, B.: A new personalized ECG signal classification algorithm using block-based neural network and particle swarm optimization. Biomed. Signal Process. Control. **25**, 12–23 (2016)
16. Raj, S., Ray, K.C., Shankar, O.: Cardiac arrhythmia beat classification using DOST and PSO tuned SVM. Elsevier North-Holland (2016)

Discrete Similarity Preserving Hashing for Cross-modal Retrieval

Mingyang Li[1], Xiangwei Kong[2(✉)], Tao Yao[3], and Yujia Zhang[4]

[1] School of Information and Communication Engineering, Dalian University of Technology, Dalian 116024, China
myli@mail.dlut.edu.cn

[2] Department of Data Science and Management Engineering, Zhejiang University, Hangzhou 310058, China
kongxiangwei@zju.edu.cn

[3] Department of Information and Electrical Engineering, Ludong University, Yantai 264025, China
yaotaoedu@ldu.edu.cn

[4] School of Engineering and Applied Science, University of Pennsylvania, Philadelphia, PA 19104-6391, USA
yjzhang7@seas.upenn.edu

Abstract. Hashing methods have attracted great attention for cross-modal retrieval due to the low memory requirement and fast computation. Cross-modal hashing methods aim to transform the data from different modalities into a common Hamming space. However, most existing cross-modal hashing methods ignore the restrictions on the Hamming distance between dissimilar instances. Besides, most cross-modal hashing methods relax discrete constraints and then quantize the continuous values to obtain suboptimal solutions as hash codes, which causes quantization error and low retrieval performance. To address above problems, we propose a novel supervised cross-modal hashing method, termed Discrete Similarity Preserving Hashing (DSPH). DSPH simultaneously preserves inter-modality and intra-modality similarity. Specifically, DSPH puts restrictions on both the similar and dissimilar instances to learn more discriminative hash codes. Moreover, we present a discrete gradient descent algorithm to solve the discrete optimization problem. Extensive experiments conducted on Wiki and NUS-WIDE datasets show that DSPH improves retrieval performance compared with several state-of-the-art cross-modal hashing methods.

Keywords: Cross-modal hashing · Retrieval · Similarity preservation · Discrete optimization

1 Introduction

With the development of Internet and information technology, the multimedia information existing in different media types on the Internet presents

X. Sun et al. (Eds.): ICAIS 2019, LNCS 11633, pp. 202–213, 2019.
https://doi.org/10.1007/978-3-030-24265-7_18

explosive increasing. Explosive multimedia information brings challenges to data management and information security [24]. Meanwhile, to adapt to the multimedia information development trend, cross-modal retrieval becomes an important problem, which attracts the attention of quite a few researchers. The typical application scenario of cross-modal retrieval is that given a query from one modality, similar instances from another modality are retrieved. Hashing is very popular in recent years. It aims to embed data into compact binary codes. In this way, we can use smaller storage space to save data and measure the similarity between different modalities via Hamming distance, which can be calculated rapidly by bit-wise XOR operations. Such binary-based strategy has been integrated for direct binary search [22].

Recently, researchers have proposed many unimodal hashing methods, such as [4,5,11,12,18,23,25]. Because of the heterogeneous gap, these unimodal hashing methods cannot directly work in cross-modal retrieval. Over the last decade, many cross-modal hashing methods have been proposed. According to whether labels or semantic affinities of training data are used, existing cross-modal hashing methods are generally grouped into unsupervised methods [3,10,20] and supervised methods [1,7,13,21]. Due to the use of supervised information, supervised methods usually perform better than unsupervised methods.

Similarity preservation is one of the most important things in cross-modal hashing methods. Most existing methods focus on inter-modality similarity. But intra-modality similarity is also significant, which has been shown in [14,21]. SMFH [21] utilize graph Laplacian regularization to preserve intra-modality similarity. However, SMFH only concentrates on instances in the set of k-nearest neighbors, whereas the weights of the instances outside the k-nearest neighbors are set to 0 in the affinity matrices. In this way, similar instances in the original feature space will share similar hash codes, but dissimilar instances may not necessarily have dissimilar hash codes due to the lack of restriction.

Besides, hash codes learning is a discrete optimization problem, which is generally NP-hard. The most widely adopted strategy is to relax the original discrete constraints into continuous constraints to optimize the objective functions. Then quantize the obtained continuous values as binary codes. However, this strategy generates quantization error, and the methods proposed in [6,17] have verified that this strategy has adverse impact on retrieval performance.

In addition, most cross-modal hashing methods combine hash codes learning and hash functions learning in a joint objective function. Then optimize it iteratively. In this way, hash functions are difficult to extend to other forms due to the tight combination with optimization process.

To address the above challenges, we propose a novel supervised cross-modal hashing method named Discrete Similarity Preserving Hashing (DSPH). DSPH simultaneously preserves the inter-modality and intra-modality similarity. We reconstruct the inter-modality similarity matrix via the inner product between hash codes and keep intra-modality similarity via two graph regularization terms for image and text modality, respectively. Different from SMFH [21], we take the instances outside the k-nearest neighbors into consideration when designing the affinity matrix. Thus the dissimilar instances have dissimilar hash codes after they are mapped into the Hamming space, and the similar instances have similar hash codes. In particular, we present a discrete gradient descent algorithm to deal with the NP-hard discrete optimization problem. Inspired by the unimodal hashing method proposed in [8], we use a two-step learning strategy for DSPH. The first step is to learn hash codes. The second step is to learn hash functions according to the learnt hash codes. This two-step strategy can avoid the close coupling of the optimization process and the form of hash functions, so hash functions can be easily extended to other forms. Furthermore, two-step optimization can make the algorithm easier to optimize.

The main contributions of this paper are as follows.

- Our method simultaneously preserves the inter-modality and intra-modality similarity. Especially for intra-modality similarity, we design a novel affinity matrix which has restrictions on both the similar and dissimilar instances. In this way, dissimilar instances have dissimilar hash codes, and vice versa.
- We propose a discrete gradient descent algorithm to handle the discrete optimization problem.
- Extensive experiments on two datasets show that our DSPH outperforms the compared state-of-the-art methods.

2 Discrete Similarity Preserving Hashing

In this section, we present our proposed DSPH method and give the optimization process.

The illustration of the framework is given in Fig. 1. In the training phase, DSPH follows the two-step learning strategy. The first step is to learn hash codes by discrete optimization while preserving inter-modality and intra-modality similarity. The second step is to learn hash functions according to the learnt hash codes. In the testing phase, when a query comes from one modality, it will be projected to hash codes by the learnt modality-specific hash function.

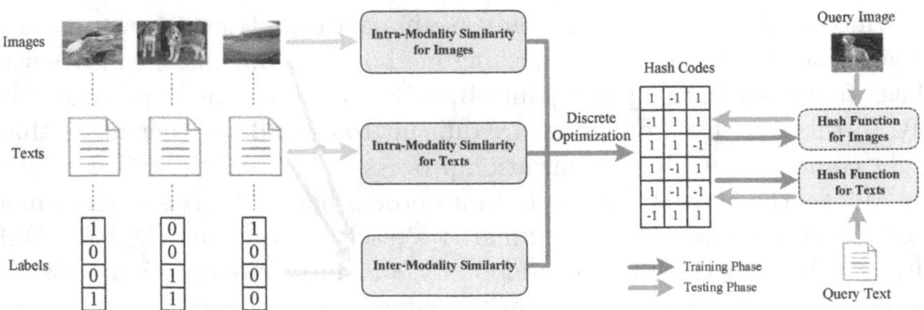

Fig. 1. The framework of the proposed DSPH.

2.1 Problem Formulation

Suppose that we have a training set containing n instances with two modalities. $\mathbf{X}^{(1)} = [x_1^{(1)}, x_2^{(1)}, \ldots, x_n^{(1)}] \in \mathbb{R}^{d_1 \times n}$ and $\mathbf{X}^{(2)} = [x_1^{(2)}, x_2^{(2)}, \ldots, x_n^{(2)}] \in \mathbb{R}^{d_2 \times n}$ represent the feature matrices of two different modalities respectively, where $x_i^{(m)} \in \mathbb{R}^{d_m}$ is the feature vector for the i-th instance in the m-th modality. Class label matrix is defined as $\mathbf{Y} = \{0,1\}^{c \times n}$, where c denotes the class number of the training set. For single-label datasets, each instance belongs to only one category, whereas for multi-label datasets, each instance may belong to more than one category.

The hash functions can be many different kinds of forms. For simplicity, we adopt the linear regressions to form hash functions. Compared with non-linear hash functions, the linear hash functions are easier and can save training time. The hash function for the m-th modality is written as:

$$h_m(x_i^{(m)}) = \text{sign}(\mathbf{P}_m^T x_i^{(m)}), m = 1, 2, \tag{1}$$

where sign$(\cdot)$ is the sign function. $\mathbf{P}_m \in \mathbb{R}^{k \times d_m}$ is the projection matrix, where k is the length of hash codes. So the corresponding hash codes matrix of the m-th modality is $\mathbf{B}_m = \text{sign}(\mathbf{P}_m^T \mathbf{X}^{(m)})$, where $\mathbf{B}_m \in \{-1,1\}^{k \times n}$.

2.2 Inter-modality Similarity Preservation

In order to preserve the inter-modality similarity, the same instance should have the same hash codes in different modalities, that is:

$$\mathbf{B}_1 = \mathbf{B}_2 = \mathbf{B} \tag{2}$$

In addition, we leverage the label matrix $\mathbf{Y}$ to calculate the cosine distance between the label vectors to construct the similarity matrix $\mathbf{S}$. In order to keep the inter-modality similarity, the inner product between hash codes is expected to approximate the similarity matrix $\mathbf{S}$. This model has been used in some hashing methods, such as [10,16]. The object function of inter-modality similarity preservation is given as:

$$\mathcal{L}_{inter} = \left\|\mathbf{B}^T\mathbf{B} - k\mathbf{S}\right\|_F^2 \tag{3}$$

2.3 Intra-modality Similarity Preservation

Inspired by [21], we utilize graph Laplacian regularization to preserve the similarity within each modality. The object function of intra-modality similarity preservation for the m-th modality can be written as:

$$\begin{aligned}\mathcal{L}_{intra_m} &= \tfrac{1}{2}\sum_{i,k} \mathbf{W}_{i,k}^{(m)} \left\|b_i - b_k\right\|^2 \\ &= tr(\mathbf{B}(\mathbf{D}^{(m)} - \mathbf{W}^{(m)})\mathbf{B}^T) \\ &= tr(\mathbf{B}\mathbf{L}_m\mathbf{B}^T)\end{aligned} \tag{4}$$

where $\mathbf{L}_m$ is the Laplacian matrix for the m-th modality, and $\mathbf{L}_m = \mathbf{D}^{(m)} - \mathbf{W}^{(m)}$. $\mathbf{D}^{(m)}$ is a diagonal matrix where $\mathbf{D}_{ii}^{(m)} = \sum_k \mathbf{W}_{i,k}^{(m)}$. $\mathbf{W}^{(m)}$ is the affinity matrix which will be described in the following paragraph.

Our method differs from [21] in that we take the instances outside the k-nearest neighbors into consideration. Hence, the entry $\mathbf{W}_{i,k}^{(m)}$ in $\mathbf{W}^{(m)}$ is defined as:

$$\mathbf{W}_{i,k}^{(m)} = \begin{cases} e^{-\frac{\left\|x_i^{(m)} - x_k^{(m)}\right\|^2}{\sigma^2}}, \text{if } x_i^{(m)} \in \mathbb{K}_1(x_k^{(m)}) \text{ or } x_k^{(m)} \in \mathbb{K}_1(x_i^{(m)}) \\ -\mu e^{\frac{\left\|x_i^{(m)} - x_k^{(m)}\right\|^2}{\sigma^2}}, \text{if } x_i^{(m)} \in \mathbb{K}_2(x_k^{(m)}) \text{ or } x_k^{(m)} \in \mathbb{K}_2(x_i^{(m)}) \\ 0, \text{else} \end{cases} \tag{5}$$

where $\mathbb{K}_1(x_k^{(m)})$ denotes the set of k_1 nearest neighbors of $(x_k^{(m)})$, and $\mathbb{K}_2(x_k^{(m)})$ denotes the set of k_2 farthest neighbors of $(x_k^{(m)})$. μ is a trade-off parameter. In this way, the Hamming distance between dissimilar instances will be far, and the Hamming distance between similar instances will be near.

2.4 Overall Objective Function and Optimization

Combining the inter-modality similarity preservation as in (3) and intra-modality similarity preservation as in (4), our overall objective function of hash codes learning is given as:

$$\begin{aligned} &\min_{\mathbf{B}} \mathcal{L}(\mathbf{B}) = \alpha \left\|\mathbf{B}^T\mathbf{B} - k\mathbf{S}\right\|_F^2 + \sum_{m=1}^{2} \beta_m tr(\mathbf{B}\mathbf{L}_m\mathbf{B}^T) \\ &s.t.\ \mathbf{B} \in \{-1, 1\}^{k \times n} \end{aligned} \tag{6}$$

where α, β_1, β_2 are trade-off parameters.

Due to the discrete constraint, solving (6) is a NP-hard problem. Here we do not relax the discrete constraints. We present a discrete optimization method, called discrete gradient descent algorithm. The main idea is to use the gradient descent algorithm iteratively and quantize the valuc by sign($\cdot$) to obtain $\mathbf{B}^{(j)}$ at each iteration. And then use $\mathbf{B}^{(j)}$ for the next iteration. Specifically, we first compute the gradient of $\mathcal{L}(\mathbf{B})$:

$$\nabla\mathcal{L}(\mathbf{B}) = 4\alpha\mathbf{B}\mathbf{B}^T\mathbf{B} - 4\alpha k\mathbf{B}\mathbf{S} + 2\beta_1\mathbf{B}\mathbf{L}_1 + 2\beta_2\mathbf{B}\mathbf{L}_2 \tag{7}$$

Suppose that we have got the discrete code result $\mathbf{B}^{(j)}$ at the j-th iteration. Then the iterative formula to update $\mathbf{B}$ for the $(j+1)$-th iteration is:

$$\mathbf{B}^{(j+1)} = \text{sign}(\mathbf{B}^{(j)} - \lambda\nabla\mathcal{L}(\mathbf{B}^{(j)})) \tag{8}$$

where λ is learning rate. In fact, this discrete optimization method resonates with the iterative formula of DPLM proposed in [19], but we think about the solution from another perspective.

2.5 Hash Functions Learning

Here we utilize the linear hashing functions as in (1) for simplicity. That is, we should learn two projection matrices $\mathbf{P}_1$ and $\mathbf{P}_2$. So the objective function of hash functions learning is showed as:

$$\begin{aligned}\min_{\mathbf{P}_1,\mathbf{P}_2} \mathcal{G} = \left\|\mathbf{B} - \mathbf{P}_1^T\mathbf{X}^{(1)}\right\|_F^2 + \left\|\mathbf{B} - \mathbf{P}_2^T\mathbf{X}^{(2)}\right\|_F^2 \\ + \gamma\mathcal{R}(\mathbf{P}_1, \mathbf{P}_2)\end{aligned} \tag{9}$$

where $\mathcal{R}(\cdot) = \|\cdot\|_F^2$ is the regularization term to resist overfitting, and γ is a trade-off parameter.

Let $\frac{\partial\mathcal{G}}{\partial\mathbf{P}_1} = 0, \frac{\partial\mathcal{G}}{\partial\mathbf{P}_2} = 0$,then we can obtain:

$$\mathbf{P}_1 = (\mathbf{X}^{(1)}\mathbf{X}^{(1)T} + \gamma\mathbf{I})^{-1}\mathbf{X}^{(1)}\mathbf{B}^T \tag{10}$$

$$\mathbf{P}_2 = (\mathbf{X}^{(2)}\mathbf{X}^{(2)T} + \gamma\mathbf{I})^{-1}\mathbf{X}^{(2)}\mathbf{B}^T \tag{11}$$

where $\mathbf{I}$ is a identity matrix.

2.6 Complexity Analysis

Here we analyze the complexity of our proposed method. In the training phase, the computational cost of updating $\mathbf{B}$ is $O((k^2n + k^2n^2 + kn^2)T)$, where T is the number of iterations. The computational cost of computing $\mathbf{P}_m$ is $O(d_m^3 + d_m^2k + d_m^2n + d_mkn)$. Due to $k, d_m \ll n$, the overall complexity for training DSPH is approximately $O((k^2 + k)n^2T)$. Furthermore, for each online query, the time complexity for mapping it to hash codes is $O(dk)$.

3 Experiments

In this section, we evaluate our proposed DSPH on two cross-modal datasets. We compare DSPH with several state-of-the-art cross-modal hashing methods on two cross-modal retrieval tasks: image query to text database and text query to image database. Then we present the analysis of experiment results.

3.1 Datasets

Wiki [15] dataset is collected from Wikipedia, containing 2,866 image-text pairs, which are classified into 10 categories. Images are represented by 128-dimensional SIFT feature vectors and texts are represented by 10-dimensional topic vectors. This dataset is a single-label dataset. We randomly take out 2,173 pairs as the training set and the rest 693 pairs as the test set.

NUS-WIDE [2] dataset is downloaded from Flickr. Images and corresponding tags are regarded as image-text pairs. Following [3,9], the top 10 largest concepts containing 186,577 pairs are selected to form the experimental dataset. Images are represented by 500-dimensional SIFT feature vectors, and texts are represented by 1,000-dimensional bag-of-words feature vectors. This dataset is a multi-label dataset. Here we select 2,000 pairs as the test set and the rest as the training set.

3.2 Experimental Settings

We take unsupervised ones IMH [20], CMFH [3], and FSH [10], and supervised ones CVH [7], SMFH [21], and DASH [13] as baselines, where DASH has two cases, i.e. DASH_i and DASH_t. On NUS-WIDE dataset, in order to reduce the computational resource of these methods and make fair comparisons with baselines, we randomly select 5,000 samples as the training set. All the codes of baselines are provided by the authors. In DSPH, we empirically set $\alpha = 0.5$, $\beta_1 = \beta_2 = 1$, $k_1 = 300$, $k_2 = 200$, $\mu = 0.5$, and $\gamma = 0.001$. We take the test set as the query set and the training set as the retrieval set. To be more practical, we discard the learnt hash codes in the training phase and use hash functions to generate hash codes of all instances for our DSPH and baselines. The experimental results are averaged after 5 runs. All our experiments are performed on a workstation which has a 2.60 GHZ Intel Xeon E5-2650 CPU and 128.0 GB RAM.

We measure the cross-modal retrieval performance by mean Average Precision (mAP) and precision-recall (PR) curves.

3.3 Experimental Results

Results on Wiki: The mAP results on Wiki dataset are reported in Table 1. From Table 1, we can observe that DSPH achieves higher mAP results than baselines regardless of image to text and text to image. In addition, DSPH obtains better mAP results with longer hash codes. The reason might be that longer codes can encode more information.

In order to further verify the global retrieval performance of DSPH, we plot the precision-recall curves at 32 bits hash codes, and the results are shown in Fig. 2. From the PR curves in Fig. 2, we have two observations. First, on text to image task, DSPH outperforms all the baselines. Second, on image to text task, the precision of DSPH is better than baselines when the recall is low, but the precision of DSPH is slightly lower when the recall is high. This phenomenon does not doubt the effectiveness of our DSPH because it is applicable in practice. In reality, users always pay more attention to the instances in the top of the returned list, i.e. in the case of low recall.

Results on NUS-WIDE: The mAP results on NUS-WIDE dataset are also reported in Table 1. We can see that DSPH significantly outperforms all the baselines. Specially, on image to text task, the maximum improvement of DSPH enhances 6.69% compared with the second best method.

The precision-recall curves at 32 bits hash codes are also plotted in Fig. 2. From the PR curves, we can see that DSPH achieves the best performance on both of the two tasks, which demonstrates that our DSPH has great global retrieval performance and DSPH ourperforms baselines.

3.4 Effect of Graph Laplacian Regularization Term

One of the contributions in DSPH is that in graph Laplacian regularization term, we puts restrictions on dissimilar instances. In order to measure its effect, we give

Table 1. MAP@100 results on two datasets for different tasks.

Image to Text	Wiki				NUS-WIDE			
Methods	16 bits	32 bits	64 bits	128 bits	16 bits	32 bits	64 bits	128 bits
CVH	0.1865	0.1737	0.1563	0.1534	0.3668	0.3708	0.3726	0.3730
IMH	0.1984	0.1668	0.1591	0.1395	0.3861	0.3814	0.3818	0.3840
CMFH	0.2295	0.2397	0.2528	0.2518	0.4046	0.4096	0.4121	0.4110
SMFH	0.2411	0.2437	0.2486	0.2489	0.4046	0.4105	0.4140	0.4132
DASH_i	0.2156	0.2099	0.2093	0.1995	0.4680	0.4676	0.4604	0.4427
DASH_t	0.2384	0.2440	0.2524	0.2600	0.4699	0.4544	0.4385	0.4150
FSH	0.2408	0.2503	0.2582	0.2608	0.3819	0.3929	0.4035	0.4138
DSPH	**0.2455**	**0.2586**	**0.2643**	**0.2660**	**0.4824**	**0.4814**	**0.4926**	**0.5096**
Text to Image	Wiki				NUS-WIDE			
Methods	16 bits	32 bits	64 bits	128 bits	16 bits	32 bits	64 bits	128 bits
CVH	0.2621	0.2193	0.1836	0.1786	0.3622	0.3684	0.3692	0.3728
IMH	0.2369	0.2050	0.1875	0.1480	0.3759	0.3732	0.3741	0.3749
CMFH	0.3479	0.3793	0.3997	0.4193	0.3825	0.3848	0.3837	0.3857
SMFH	0.3658	0.3907	0.4076	0.4161	0.3801	0.3789	0.3810	0.3842
DASH_i	0.3477	0.3397	0.3490	0.3455	0.4157	0.4104	0.4106	0.4070
DASH_t	0.3881	0.3992	0.4172	0.4117	0.3997	0.3961	0.3896	0.3840
FSH	0.3871	0.4145	0.4317	0.4440	0.3681	0.3760	0.3843	0.3886
DSPH	**0.4086**	**0.4198**	**0.4390**	**0.4468**	**0.4160**	**0.4113**	**0.4192**	**0.4199**

a variant of DSPH, which is called DSPH_nd. This variant removes the weights for instances outside the k-nearest neighbors, i.e. $\mu = 0$ in (5). We compare their mAP results at 16 bits hash codes, and the results are reported in Table 2.

From Table 2, we can see that DSPH performs better than DSPH_nd, which proves the effectiveness of the proposed restrictions on dissimilar instances. In addition, SMFH [21] also preserves inter-modality and intra-modality similarity. Obviously, DSPH performs best in Table 2. Except for image to text task on Wiki dataset, DSPH_nd achieves significantly higher mAP results than SMFH, although DSPH_nd does not concentrate on the instances outside the k-nearest neighbors, which is similar to SMFH. The reason is that overall objective functions are different and our objective function of hash codes learning is optimized via a discrete algorithm. These results testify the superiority of our method.

3.5 Parameter Analysis

Here we analyze parameters of the proposed DSPH. We test one parameter while fixing the rest of the parameters.

We first conduct experiments to analyze the effect of k_1 and k_2. Parameter k_1 controls the number of similar instances included in the calculation of graph

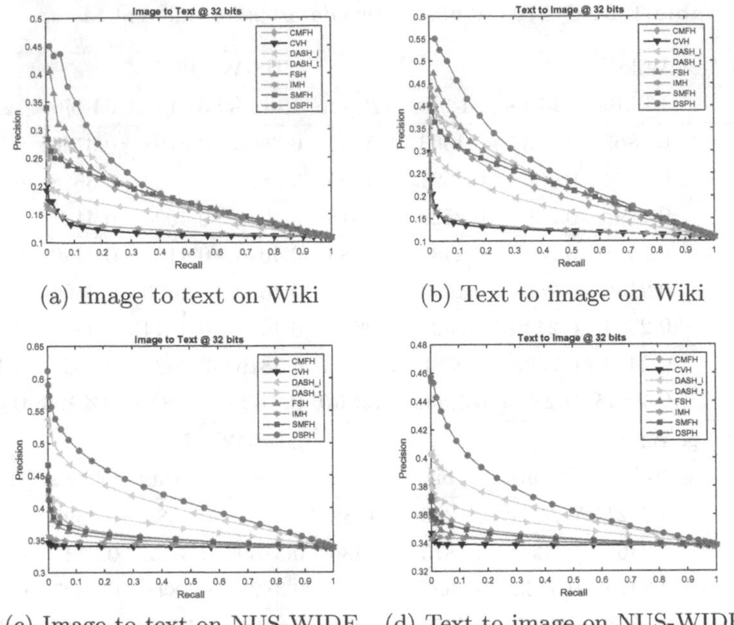

(a) Image to text on Wiki (b) Text to image on Wiki

(c) Image to text on NUS-WIDE (d) Text to image on NUS-WIDE

Fig. 2. Precision-recall curves on two dataset at 32 bits hash codes.

Table 2. MAP@100 results of different graph Laplacian regularization terms.

Image to Text	Wiki	NUS-WIDE
SMFH	0.2411	0.4046
DSPH_nd	0.2408	0.4633
DSPH	0.2455	0.4824
Text to Image	Wiki	NUS-WIDE
SMFH	0.3658	0.3801
DSPH_nd	0.3987	0.4094
DSPH	0.4086	0.4160

Laplacian regularization terms, and parameter k_2 controls the number of dissimilar instances. The results on Wiki dataset are plotted in Fig. 3, with code length varying from 16 bits to 128 bits. From Fig. 3, we have the following observations. When $k_1 \leq 300$, a larger value of k_1 conduces to better comprehensive performance under consideration of various hash bits. When $k_2 \leq 200$, a larger value of k_2 also conduces to better comprehensive performance. Fortunately, DSPH performs well with a comparatively small k_1 such as $k_1 = 300$ and a comparatively small k_2 such as $k_2 = 200$. When the value is too large, the comprehensive performance does not get better. These properties help to reduce training cost.

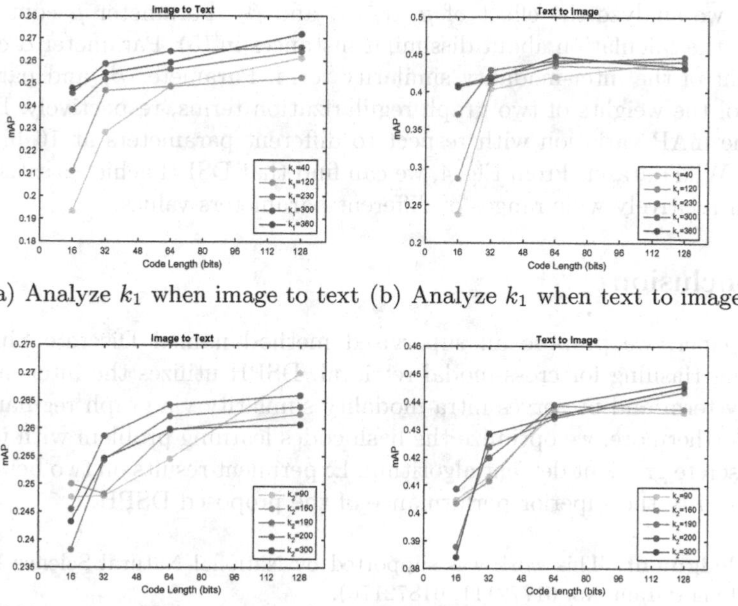

(a) Analyze k_1 when image to text (b) Analyze k_1 when text to image

(c) Analyze k_2 when image to text (d) Analyze k_2 when text to image

Fig. 3. The analysis of k_1 and k_2 on Wiki dataset with code length varying from 16 bits to 128 bits.

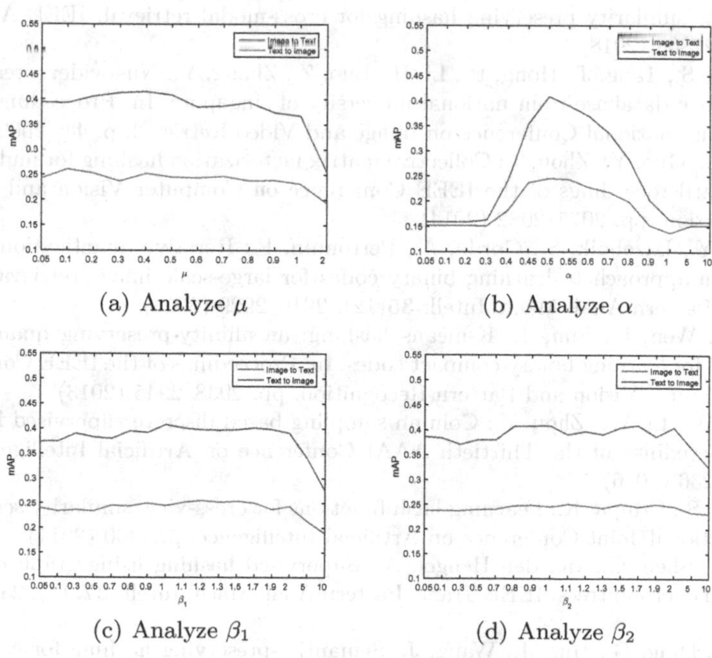

(a) Analyze μ (b) Analyze α

(c) Analyze β_1 (d) Analyze β_2

Fig. 4. The analysis of different parameters on Wiki dataset at 16 bits hash codes.

Then we analyze the effect of μ, α, β_1, and β_2. Parameter μ controls the weight of the calculation about dissimilar instances in (5). Parameter α controls the weight of the inter-modality similarity term. Parameter β_1 and parameter β_2 control the weights of two graph regularization terms, respectively. Figure 4 shows the mAP variation with respect to different parameters at 16 bits hash codes on Wiki dataset. From Fig. 4, we can find that DSPH achieves satisfactory results in relatively wide ranges of different parameters values.

4 Conclusion

In this paper, we propose an supervised method named Discrete Similarity Preserving Hashing for cross-modal retrieval. DSPH utilizes the inter-modality similarity term and preserves intra-modality similarity via graph regularization terms. Furthermore, we optimize the hash codes learning problem with the proposed discrete gradient descent algorithm. Experiment results on two benchmark datasets verify the superior performance of the proposed DSPH.

Acknowledgment. This work was supported by National Natural Science Foundation of China (Grant No. 61772111, 61872170).

References

1. Chen, Z., Zhong, F., Min, G., Leng, Y., Ying, Y.: Supervised intra- and inter-modality similarity preserving hashing for cross-modal retrieval. IEEE Access **6**, 27796–27808 (2018)
2. Chua, T.S., Tang, J., Hong, R., Li, H., Luo, Z., Zheng, Y.: Nus-wide: a real-world web image database from national university of singapore. In: Proceedings of the ACM International Conference on Image and Video Retrieval, p. 48 (2009)
3. Ding, G., Guo, Y., Zhou, J.: Collective matrix factorization hashing for multimodal data. In: Proceedings of the IEEE Conference on Computer Vision and Pattern Recognition, pp. 2075–2082 (2014)
4. Gong, Y., Lazebnik, S., Gordo, A., Perronnin, F.: Iterative quantization: a procrustean approach to learning binary codes for large-scale image retrieval. IEEE Trans. Pattern Anal. Mach. Intell. **35**(12), 2916–2929 (2013)
5. He, K., Wen, F., Sun, J.: K-means hashing: an affinity-preserving quantization method for learning binary compact codes. In: Proceedings of the IEEE Conference on Computer Vision and Pattern Recognition, pp. 2938–2945 (2013)
6. Kang, W., Li, W., Zhou, Z.: Column sampling based discrete supervised hashing. In: Proceedings of the Thirtieth AAAI Conference on Artificial Intelligence, pp. 1230–1236 (2016)
7. Kumar, S., Udupa, R.: Learning hash functions for cross-view similarity search. In: International Joint Conference on Artificial Intelligence, p. 1360 (2011)
8. Lin, G., Shen, C., van den Hengel, A.: Supervised hashing using graph cuts and boosted decision trees. IEEE Trans. Pattern Anal. Mach. Intell. **37**(11), 2317–2331 (2015)
9. Lin, Z., Ding, G., Hu, M., Wang, J.: Semantics-preserving hashing for cross-view retrieval. In: Proceedings of the IEEE Conference on Computer Vision and Pattern Recognition, pp. 3864–3872 (2015)

10. Liu, H., Ji, R., Wu, Y., Huang, F., Zhang, B.: Cross-modality binary code learning via fusion similarity hashing. In: Proceedings of the IEEE Conference on Computer Vision and Pattern Recognition, pp. 6345–6353 (2017)
11. Liu, W., Wang, J., Ji, R., Jiang, Y.G., Chang, S.F.: Supervised hashing with kernels. In: Proceedings of the IEEE Conference on Computer Vision and Pattern Recognition, pp. 2074–2081 (2012)
12. Liu, W., Wang, J., Kumar, S., Chang, S.F.: Hashing with graphs. In: International Conference on Machine Learning, pp. 1–8 (2011)
13. Ma, D., Liang, J., Kong, X., He, R.: Frustratingly easy cross-modal hashing. In: Proceedings of the 2016 ACM on Multimedia Conference, pp. 237–241 (2016)
14. Masci, J., Bronstein, M.M., Bronstein, A.M., Schmidhuber, J.: Multimodal similarity-preserving hashing. IEEE Trans. Pattern Anal. Mach. Intell. **36**(4), 824–830 (2014)
15. Rasiwasia, N., et al.: A new approach to cross-modal multimedia retrieval. In: Proceedings of the 18th ACM International Conference on Multimedia, pp. 251–260 (2010)
16. Shen, F., Liu, W., Zhang, S., Yang, Y., Tao Shen, H.: Learning binary codes for maximum inner product search. In: Proceedings of the IEEE International Conference on Computer Vision, pp. 4148–4156 (2015)
17. Shen, F., Shen, C., Liu, W., Tao Shen, H.: Supervised discrete hashing. In: Proceedings of the IEEE Conference on Computer Vision and Pattern Recognition, pp. 37–45 (2015)
18. Shen, F., Shen, C., Shi, Q., van den Hengel, A., Tang, Z., Shen, H.T.: Hashing on nonlinear manifolds. IEEE Trans. Image Process. **24**(6), 1839–1851 (2015)
19. Shen, F., Zhou, X., Yang, Y., Song, J., Shen, H.T., Tao, D.: A fast optimization method for general binary code learning. IEEE Trans. Image Process. **25**(12), 5610–5621 (2016)
20. Song, J., Yang, Y., Yang, Y., Huang, Z., Shen, H.T.: Inter-media hashing for large-scale retrieval from heterogeneous data sources. In: Proceedings of the 2013 ACM SIGMOD International Conference on Management of Data, pp. 785–796 (2013)
21. Tang, J., Wang, K., Shao, L.: Supervised matrix factorization hashing for cross-modal retrieval. IEEE Trans. Image Process. **25**(7), 3157–3166 (2016)
22. Wang, Y., Ni, R., Zhao, Y., Xian, M.: Watermark embedding for direct binary searched halftone images by adopting visual cryptography. Comput., Mater. Continua **55**(2), 255–265 (2018)
23. Weiss, Y., Torralba, A., Fergus, R.: Spectral hashing. In: Advances in Neural Information Processing Systems, pp. 1753–1760 (2009)
24. Yang, Z., Huang, Y., Li, X., Wang, W.: Efficient secure data provenance scheme in multimedia outsourcing and sharing. Comput., Mater. Continua **56**(1), 1–17 (2018)
25. Zhang, L., Zhang, Y., Gu, X., Tang, J., Tian, Q.: Scalable similarity search with topology preserving hashing. IEEE Trans. Image Process. **23**(7), 3025–3039 (2014)

Classification of Vitiligo Based on Convolutional Neural Network

Jian Liu[1(✉)], Jianwei Yan[1], Jie Chen[2], Guozhong Sun[3], and Wei Luo[4]

[1] School of Computer and Communication Engineering, University of Science and Technology Beijing, Beijing 100083, China
liujian@ustb.edu.cn, g20178686@xs.ustb.edu.cn

[2] Department of Breast Surgery, West China Hospital, Sichuan University, Chengdu 610041, People's Republic of China
chenjiedoctor@126.com

[3] Dawning Information Industry Chengdu Co, Ltd, Chengdu 610213, People's Republic of China
sungzh@sugon.com

[4] Department of Dermatology, Air Force Medical Center, PLA, Beijing 100142, China

Abstract. Vitiligo is one of the most intractable skin disease in the world. According to incomplete statistics, there is about 0.5–2% incidence of vitiligo in the world, and the number is still growing, so the early diagnosis of vitiligo is very important. In recent years, deep learning has been successfully applied to medical image classification and has achieved outstanding performance, which helps achieve vitiligo intelligent diagnosis. In this paper, we propose a method base on probability-average value of three convolutional neural network (CNN) models which are same structures, and trained with three different color-space images (RGB, HSV, and YCrCb) for the same vitiligo dataset. The applied strategy is found to achieve the classification performance of 94.2% area under the roc curve (AUC), 87.8% accuracy, 91.9% precision, 90.9% sensitivity, 80.2% specificity which outperforms the individual networks.

Keywords: Vitiligo · Convolutional neural network · Color-space · Probability-average · Classification

1 Introduction

The body's largest organ is the human skin, accounting for about 15% of the total body weight in adult humans [1]. The internal part of the body is separated from the outside environment by the skin, so the skin is an important defense line of the body. It can prevent fungal infection, bacteria, allergies, viruses and body temperature control. Many skin diseases, such as vitiligo, acne, psoriasis, eczema, melanoma, etc. can also affect your appearance and health. Therefore, it is necessary to treat skin diseases very seriously and identify and prevent the spread

This work is supported by Intelligent Manufacturing Standardization Program of Ministry of Industry and Information Technology (No. 2016ZXFB01001).

X. Sun et al. (Eds.): ICAIS 2019, LNCS 11633, pp. 214–223, 2019.
https://doi.org/10.1007/978-3-030-24265-7_19

of skin diseases at an early stage. In the process of medical image processing, traditional image recognition can identify these diseases by segmentation edges and feature extraction. [2] design of a segmentation system based a Bayesian model and extraction a total of 859 features, use the combination of SVM and FDR was revealed a psoriasis classification accuracy of 99.84%. In [3], proposed a texture characteristic and the k-means algorithm based effectively detection of hand eczema. Alam et al. [4] use the color-based segmentation method based on k-means clustering, combined with morphological image processing techniques segment accurately eczema lesion region, resulted in a 90% accuracy with SVM. [5] through some feature selection method can improve the accuracy and reduce the FNR compare to the traditional feature selection methods, and the multi-label classification framework have better accuracy and lower FNR than the traditional expert system.

However, the traditional segmentation and feature extraction methods are highly dependent on threshold, which requires a lot of expert experience, and the poor generalization ability leads to unsatisfactory classification results. When Convolution Neural Network (CNN) [6] appears, image recognition achieves breakthrough development. CNN has a strong ability of feature extraction and image classification. [7] design a CNN model to detect photographic images (PI) and average detection accuracy of 98%. Pal et al. [8] use a U-shaped fully convolutional neural network (FCN) is trained to segment psoriasis images, which more effect than traditional methods was achieved the RCPC and Jaccard value of 88%, 88.5%. Shen et al. [9] use the pre-trained VGG16 neural network to train acne dataset, the accuracy is up to 92.8%. In [10], Yu et al. use a deep residual network discriminate skin cancer. The system consists of two networks. One is the Complete Convolutional Residual Network (FCRN). Which is used to segment skin lesions. The other network is a very deep residual network aim to classification. The proposed framework was obtained the high classification accuracy of 94.9%. Acne, psoriasis and melanoma have begun to use deep learning to identify disease, have achieved good results, especially in the recognition of melanoma has exceeded the correct rate of doctor diagnosis [11].

Obviously, CNN is of great importance in the identification of skin diseases. However, there is almost no research on intelligent diagnosis and recognition of vitiligo. According to incomplete statistics, the incidence of vitiligo in the world is about 0.5–2% [12,13]. The vitiligo is a common pigmented skin disease characterized by local or generalized loss of pigmentation and white spot formation. When vitiligo is still at an early stage, the number of vitiligo spots is small, the treatment effect is significant, the harm to human body is small, the treatment cost is low. Early diagnosis of vitiligo is very important, so automatic diagnosis of vitiligo is of great significance. In this paper, we propose a method base on three identical CNN models, trained with three different color-space images (RGB, HSV, and YCrCb) for the same vitiligo dataset. The result is better than a single model. The rest of the paper is organized as follows. In Sect. 2 the proposed method is presented. Experimentation and Results are explained in Sect. 3. Finally, conclusions are discussed in Sect. 4.

2 Method

In this paper we use the vitiligo dataset from a hospital, there is a total of 38677 images and each image is 768 × 576 size. The dataset is composed of two classes of vitiligo (positive) and normal (negative) as is shown in Fig. 1. Individual image have Red, Green, Blue (RGB) color channels.

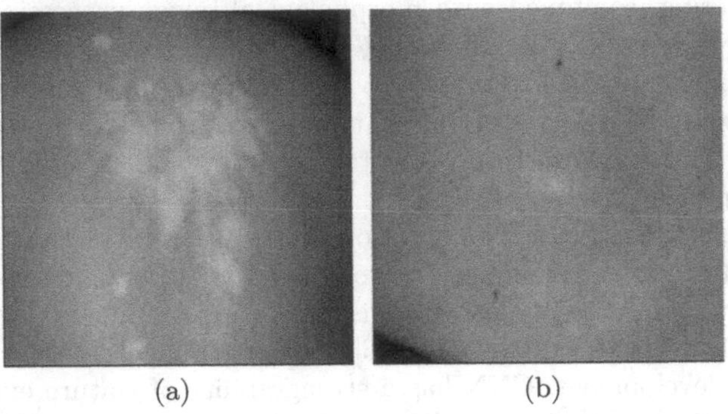

Fig. 1. Representative vitiligo (a) and normal skin (b). (Color figure online)

2.1 Dataset Processing

Images are resampled into 224 × 224 size using bilinear interpolation as provided in OpenCV [14]. Next, normalizing the dataset, 30000 images are used to training and 8677 images for evaluation. The formula of normalization as follows:

$$x^* = \frac{x - \mu}{\sigma} \tag{1}$$

Where μ and σ represent the mean and variance of training set respectively. And then adopt rotating, vertical and horizontal flipping, shifting. The previous work has demonstrated the effectiveness of data augmentation through simple techniques. The RGB images transform to HSV and YCrCb keeps some HIS [15] in high-contrast segmentation as demonstrated in Fig. 2. Therefore, the use of CNN in HSV and YCrCb for lesion detection is also effective, to some extent, the three color-space images are complementary, combined to analysis lesion detection will be better. We developed tools in Python to aid in handling batch conversion to array files containing 38677 224px × 224px, 3-channel images with their corresponding labels. The order of images and labels are identical across the transformations.

2.2 CNN Classifier

CNN usually consists of two parts: automatic feature extraction and full connection layer, in which feature extraction includes convolution layer and pooling layer. We can get a good classification model without through to manually

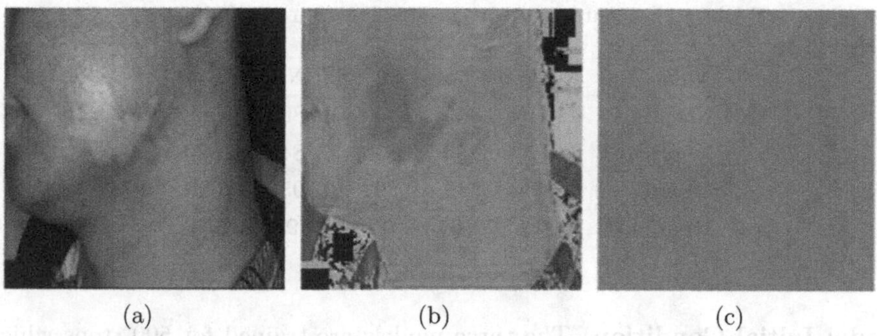

Fig. 2. Example color-space transformations of a vitiligo image from RGB (a) to HSV (b) and YCrCb (c).

selecting features, this is the advantage of CNN. The Keras-Framework [16] is used in this experiment. It has many pre-trained models, which can shorten the development time. This framework shows the powerful function of CNN and its simplicity. We choose four commonly (Resnet50, Vgg16, Xception, Iceptionv3) [17] used CNN models. After preliminary experiments, the Resnet50 has many indicators are better than other models, which is more suitable for classification of vitiligo data as shown in Table 1. This is because Resent model has residual module which can make the whole structure converge in the direction of identical mapping and ensure that the final error rate does not become worse and worse as the depth increases. Therefore, Resnet50 is used as the basline model which is shown in Fig. 3. The formula of residual module as follows:

$$f = W_i \varphi(W_{i-1}x) \tag{2}$$

$$y = f(x, W_i) + x \tag{3}$$

Where φ represent the relu function, W_i represent the weight layer.

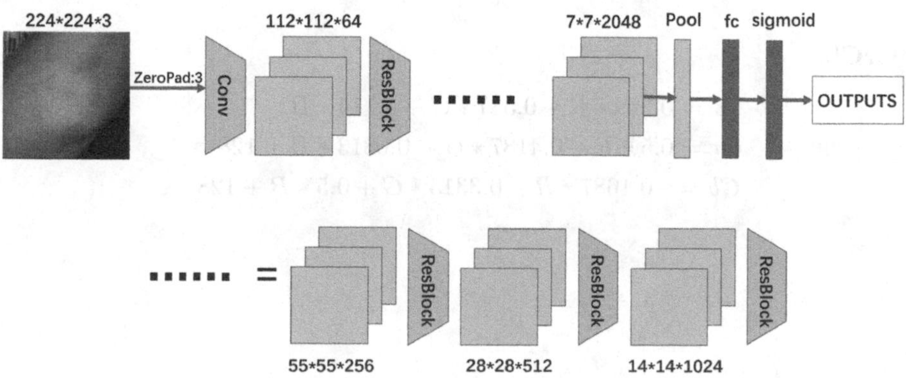

Fig. 3. The structure of Resnet50 model.

Table 1. Percentage of correct classification (RGB image).

Name	AUC	ACC	PPV	SEN	SPE
Xception	0.911	0.845	0.900	0.880	0.758
Iceptionv3	0.912	0.846	0.899	0.884	0.752
Vgg16	0.917	0.849	0.892	0.895	0.732
Resnet50	**0.922**	**0.861**	**0.908**	**0.896**	**0.775**

Model Initial Condition. The three models are trained for 500 steps which take approximately a week. 30000 images are used to training and 8677 images for evaluation. The initialization of training is setting as follows.
Original image size = 768 × 576
Resize image size = 224 × 224
Data Augmentation = Rotating, Flipping, Shifting
Learning rate = 0.001
Batch size = 32
Loss function and Optimizer = binary cross entropy and Adam
Model weights and biases = Pretrain-Resnet50
Framework = Keras
Hardware = NVIDIA GeForce TITAN XP

Recognition Flow of Vitiligo Disease. The predictive value of vitiligo is averaged from the output probabilities of the three models (see Fig. 4), the vitiligo recognition algorithm in detail as follows.
Step 1: Read the input RGB image as Array file, and the corresponding label are made into one-hot encoding.
Step 2: Convert the RGB image into HSV and YCrCb image using the formula:

$$r = \frac{R}{255}, g = \frac{G}{255}, b = \frac{B}{255}, Max = max(r, g, b), Min = min(r, g, b)$$

YCrCb:

$$\begin{aligned} Y &= 0.299 * R + 0.587 * G + 0.114 * B \\ Cr &= 0.5 * R - 0.4187 * G - 0.0813 * B + 128 \\ Cb &= -0.1687 * R - 0.3313 * G + 0.5 * B + 128 \end{aligned} \tag{4}$$

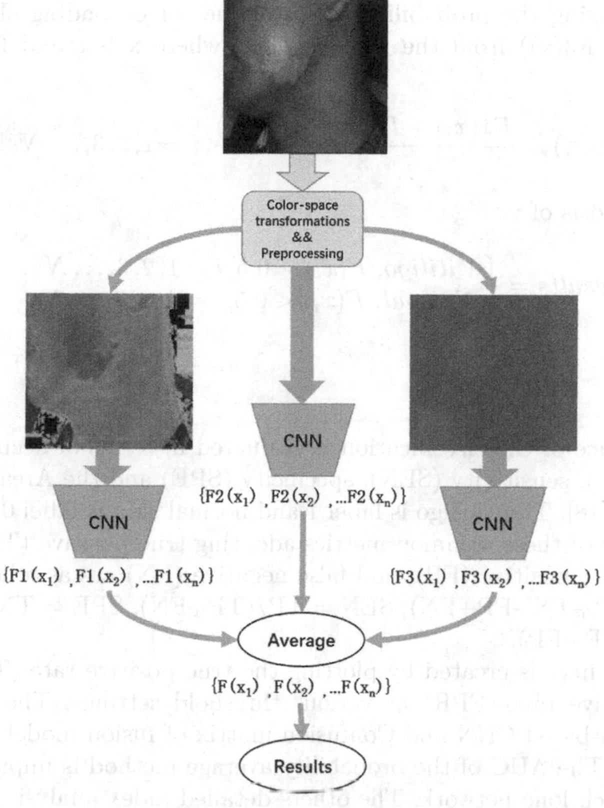

Fig. 4. Recognition flow of vitiligo disease.

HSV:

$$
H = \begin{cases} 0^\circ & , Max = Min \\ 60^\circ * \dfrac{g-b}{Max-Min} + 0^\circ & , Max = r \, and \, g \geq b \\ 60^\circ * \dfrac{g-b}{Max-Min} + 360^\circ & , Max = r \, and \, g < b \\ 60^\circ * \dfrac{b-r}{Max-Min} + 120^\circ & , Max = g \\ 60^\circ * \dfrac{r-g}{Max-Min} + 240^\circ & , Max = b \end{cases}
$$
$$
S = \begin{cases} 0 & , Max = 0 \\ \frac{Max-Min}{Max} & , Otherwise \end{cases} \tag{5}
$$
$$
V = Max
$$

Step 3: Data preprocessing and trained with three identical Keras-Resnet50 models.

Step 4: Averaging the probability values of the corresponding classes output (F1(x), F2(x), F3(x)) from the three models, where x is stand for the input data.

$$F(x_i) = \frac{F1(x_i) + F2(x_i) + F3(x_i)}{3}, i = 1, 2, 3, \dots N \tag{6}$$

Step 5: Diagnosis of vitiligo.

$$Results = \begin{cases} Vitiligo, F(x_i) \geq 0.5, i = 1, 2, 3, \dots N \\ Normal, F(x_i) < 0.5, i = 1, 2, 3, \dots N \end{cases} \tag{7}$$

3 Results

The performance of the classification is evaluated in terms of accuracy (ACC), precision (PPV), sensitivity (SEN), specificity (SPE) and the Area Under ROC Curve (AUC) [18]. The vitiligo is label 1 and normal skin is label 0. The respective definitions of these common metrics adopting true positive (TP), true negative (TN), false positive (FP), and false negative (FN) are as follows: ACC = (TP+TN)/(TP+TN+FP+FN), SEN = TP/(TP+FN), SPE = TN/(TN+ FP), PPV= TP/(TP+FP).

The ROC curve is created by plotting the true positive rate (TPR) against the false positive rate (FPR) at various threshold settings. The ROC of the transformation-based CNN and Confusion matrix of fusion model are shown in Figs. 5 and 6. The AUC of the probability-average method is improve to 94.2% better than each lone network. The others detailed index analysis are shown in

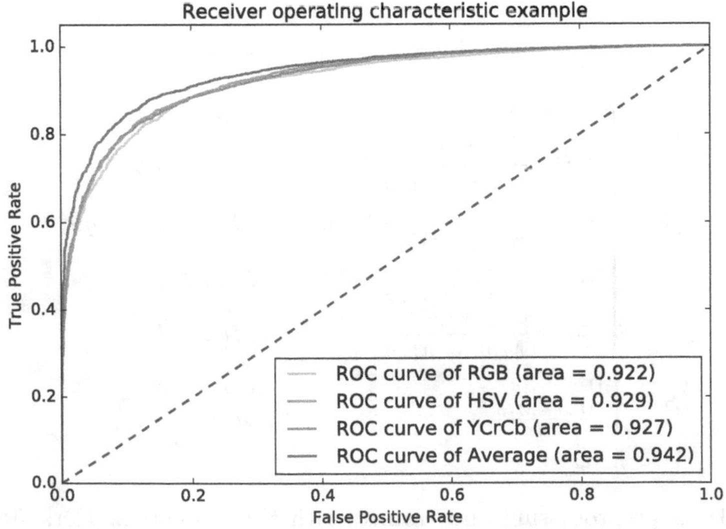

Fig. 5. The ROC of two vitiligo-and-normal-skin binary-classifier models.

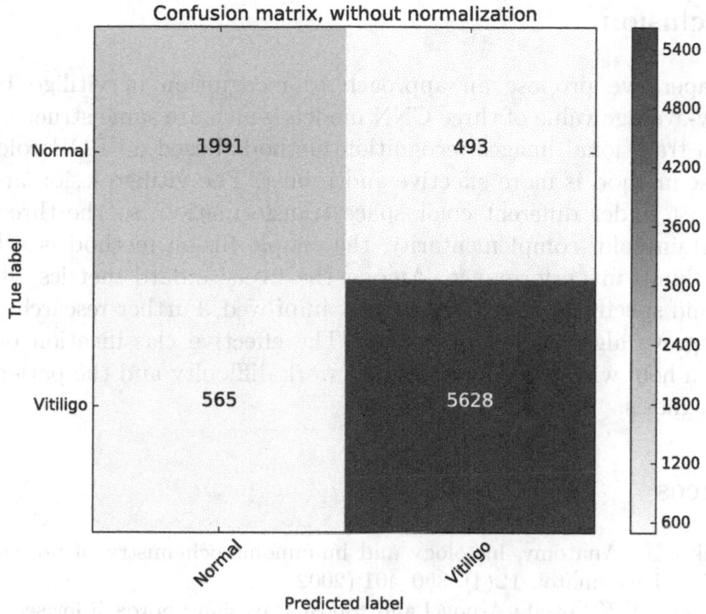

Fig. 6. The confusion matrix of probability-average model.

Table 2. We can see that the specificity of these three models is very low, no more than 80%, however the combination of different color spaces reach 80.2%. The vitiligo is a pigmented disease, and lesion areas have high contrast under different color space transformation, the fusion method can effectively recognition effect of lesion areas, reduce the misdiagnosis rate. At the same time, the accuracy, precision and sensitivity are improved to 87.8%, 91.9%, 90.9% respectively. In conclusion, our method is simple effective and low-complexity, that can be better applied in the assistant of doctor's diagnosis, also can provide a research idea for other pigmented diseases.

Table 2. Performance of transformation-based CNN.

Name	AUC	ACC	PPV	SEN	SPE
RGB	0.922	0.861	0.908	0.896	0.775
HSV	0.929	0.863	0.910	0.896	0.780
YCrCb	0.927	0.860	0.913	0.889	0.789
Average	**0.942**	**0.878**	**0.919**	**0.909**	**0.802**

4 Conclusion

In this paper, we propose an approach to recognition of vitiligo based on probability-average value of three CNN models which are same structures, compared with traditional images recognition methods based on RGB color space, the propose method is more effective and robust. The vitiligo lesion areas have high contrast under different color space transformation, so the three models have a certain color-complementarity, the simple fusion method is achieved a significant jump in performance. Among the five-standard metrics, the AUC, accuracy and specificity have been greatly improved. Further research is underway to improve algorithm performance. The effective classification of vitiligo diseases can help with the doctors reduce work difficulty and the patients carry out self-diagnosis.

References

1. Kanitakis, J.: Anatomy, histology and immunohistochemistry of normal human skin. Eur. J. Dermatol. **12**(4), 390–401 (2002)
2. Shrivastava, V.K., et al.: A novel and robust Bayesian approach for segmentation of psoriasis lesions and its risk stratification. Comput. Methods Programs Biomed. **150**, 9–22 (2017)
3. Suter, C., et al.: Detection and quantification of hand eczema by visible spectrum skin pattern analysis. In: Proceedings of the Twenty-first European Conference on Artificial Intelligence. IOS Press (2014)
4. Alam, M.N, et al.: Automatic detection and severity measurement of eczema using image processing. In: 2016 38th Annual International Conference of the IEEE Engineering in Medicine and Biology Society (EMBC). IEEE (2016)
5. Fang, S., et al.: Feature selection method based on class discriminative degree for intelligent medical diagnosis. CMC: Comput. Mater. Continua **55**(3), 419–433 (2018)
6. Krizhevsky, A., Sutskever, I., Hinton, G.E.: Imagenet classification with deep convolutional neural networks. In: Advances in Neural Information Processing Systems (2012)
7. Cui, Q., McIntosh, S., Sun, H.: Identifying materials of photographic images and photorealistic computer generated graphics based on deep CNNs. CMC: Comput. Mater. Continua **055**(2), 229–241 (2018)
8. Pal, A., et al.: Psoriasis skin biopsy image segmentation using deep convolutional neural network. Comput. Methods Programs Biomed. **159**, 59–69 (2018)
9. Shen, X., et al.: An automatic diagnosis method of facial acne vulgaris based on convolutional neural network. Sci. Rep. **8**(1), 5839 (2018)
10. Yu, L., et al.: Automated melanoma recognition in dermoscopy images via very deep residual networks. IEEE Trans. Med. Imaging **36**(4), 994–1004 (2017)
11. Esteva, A., et al.: Dermatologist-level classification of skin cancer with deep neural networks. Nature **542**(7639), 115 (2017)
12. Krüger, C., Schallreuter, K.U.: A review of the worldwide prevalence of vitiligo in children/adolescents and adults. Int. J. Dermatol. **51**(10), 1206–1212 (2012)
13. Lotti, T., D'Erme, A.M.: Vitiligo as a systemic disease. Clin. Dermatol. **32**(3), 430–434 (2014)

14. Bradski, G., Kaehler, A.: Learning OpenCV: Computer Vision with the OpenCV Library. O'Reilly Media Inc, New York (2008)
15. Pentland, A.P.: Perceptual organization and the representation of natural form. In: Readings in Computer Vision, pp. 680–699 (1987)
16. Chollet, F.: Keras: The python deep learning library. Astrophysics Source Code Library (2018)
17. Litjens, G., et al.: A survey on deep learning in medical image analysis. Med. Image Anal. **42**, 60–88 (2017)
18. Powers, D.M.: Evaluation: from precision, recall and F-measure to ROC, informedness, markedness and correlation (2011)

Big Data

Multi-scale and Hierarchical Embedding for Polarity Shift Sensitive Sentiment Classification

Qian Li(✉), Qiang Wu, and Xiaofei Liu

University of Technology Sydney, Sydney, Australia
{Qian.Li-7,Xiaofei.Liu}@student.uts.edu.au, Qiang.Wu@uts.edu.au

Abstract. Appropriate paragraph embedding is critical for sentiment classification. However, the embedding for paragraph with polarity shift is very challenging and insufficiently explored. In this paper, a MUlti-Scale and Hierarchical embedding method, MUSH, is proposed to learn a more accurate paragraph embedding for polarity shift sensitive sentiment classification. MUSH adopts CNN with multi-size filters to reveal multi-scale sentiment atoms and utilizes hierarchical multi-line CNN-RNN structures to simultaneously capture polarity shift in both sentence level and paragraph level. Extensive experiments on four large real-world data sets demonstrate that the MUSH-enabled sentiment classification significantly enhances the accuracy compared with three state-of-the-art and four baseline competitors.

Keywords: Paragraph embedding · Sentiment analysis · Polarity shift

1 Introduction

Sentiment classification refers to determining the polarity of a given paragraph. One of the most popular and efficient ways for the above work is using a machine learning based approach. This kind of approach can significantly reduce the hand-work cost for building sentiment lexicon and can capture more complex representation structures compared with lexicon rules. A fundamental task of the machine learning based approach is to embed the paragraph into a suitable vector space, in which a classifier can be learned to analyze the sentiment polarity.

The paragraph embedding is critical yet challenge for sentimental classification since the embedded representation determines the classifier quality but comprehensively revealing the complex relationships in a paragraph is difficult. Currently, lots of paragraph embedding methods for sentiment classification have been proposed to reveal hierarchical relationships in a paragraph from the word level to sentence and paragraph level. These relationships are finally embedded into a vector space to represent the meaning of paragraph for sentiment analysis. Although a variety of relationships have been studied, three kinds of relationships attracted the most of the focus. (1) The context information where context

X. Sun et al. (Eds.): ICAIS 2019, LNCS 11633, pp. 227–238, 2019.
https://doi.org/10.1007/978-3-030-24265-7_20

refers to the content surrounded a word, sentence, and/or a paragraph. Several context-aware embedding methods have been proposed, such as the methods [1,3,9,16,22,23,25]. (2) The sequential relationship that contains the order of word and/or sentence in a paragraph. The sequential-aware method, including the works [11,14,17,18], reveals the sequential relationships to capture different meanings of word and/or sentence in different place. (3) The relationship between paragraph and sentiment. This is the most direct relationship for the sentiment analysis task. The sentiment-aware methods include the work of [12,19,20]. The above three relationships reflect the key paragraph characteristics for sentiment analysis. Actually, the current methods captured one or more relationships in the paragraph, however, none of these methods captures all of these relationships.

Although significant progress has been made in paragraph embedding, most of the current methods overlook the *sentiment polarity shift*, which means the sentiment polarity is slightly or extremely changed by some indicator words or expressions. The sentiment polarity shift is very important for sentiment classification but is hard to be captured. For example, the negative words, such as *not*, can change the sentiment polarity of word *happy* from positive to negative at sentence level. Similarly, the turning words, such as *however*, will cause a sentiment polarity turnover at sentence level. Obviously, the embedding methods that ignore the sentiment polarity shift may deviate the sentiment polarity of a paragraph in its representation. Taking bag-of-words embedding as an example, which presents a paragraph as the frequency of each word. The bag-of-words embedding enables a downstream sentiment classifier by providing the proportion and frequency of emotional words. However, when the negative words like *not* or turning words like *however* exist, the sentiment polarity of a paragraph may be changed but the bag-of-words embedding cannot reflect this change for the classifier. As a result, the classifier may fail to distinguish different sentiment polarity.

The limited efforts for polarity shift sensitive paragraph embedding can be categorized into three paradigms: (1) counting sentiment words with reversing human labeled polarity-shifted words, e.g. the work in [2]; (2) splitting the paragraph via machine learning determined polarity-shifted words, and embedding the separated paragraph, e.g. the work in [10] and [5]; and (3) the combination of the previous methods, e.g. the work in [6] and [21]. Although these methods consider the words that will cause polarity shift, they may still fail when facing the following challenges: (1) the polarity shift is with multiple forms; and (2) the polarity shift exists in both sentence and paragraph level with complex long-term dependence. For the first challenge, polarity shift may be caused by multiple forms, including the explicit negative and/or turning words and implicit tone and/or context. It is hard for existing methods to simultaneously capture these explicit and implicit polarity shift factors. For the second challenge, the above methods of polarity shift sensitive paragraph embedding do not model the hierarchical and sequential structure of a paragraph, thus, is difficult to embed the polarity shift correctly.

In this paper, we propose a MUlti-Scale and Hierarchical embedding method, MUSH, to learn a more accurate embedding for a paragraph with sentiment polarity shift. MUSH is a hierarchical model that leverages sentiment information from sentence level to paragraph level to embed the sentiment of a paragraph into a vector space. At sentence level, MUSH adopts convolutional neural networks (CNN) with multi-size filters to reveal multi-scale sentiment atoms based on word embedding. Upon these sentiment atoms, a bidirectional gated recurrent neural network (RNN) is used to capture the inter-atoms couplings. At paragraph level, to reveal the polarity shift among sentences, a similar multi-scale CNN-RNN structure is utilized. This structure can recognize the multi-scale sentence-level sentiment segment by CNN and exploit their dependence by RNN. It should be noted that MUSH captures both context, sequential and sentiment information in a paragraph, and the representation ability of MUSH is largely lifted by simultaneously disentangling the multi-forms and hierarchical polarity shift compared with existing methods.

The key contributions made in this work are summarized as follows:

- *Learning polarity shift with multiple forms.* The CNN with multi-size filters is learned to revealing the multi-scale sentiment atoms and sentiment segment. This learning model leverages multi-scale local information around a word or a sentence, thus, comprehensively reveals the polarity shift with different forms.
- *Learning hierarchical polarity shift with complex dependence.* A hierarchical CNN-RNN structure is proposed to capture the polarity shift at both sentence level and paragraph level. The local dependence is learned by multi-layer CNN, and the long-term dependence is captured by bidirectional gated RNN upon the CNN learned abstractions. The co-working of CNN and RNN in a hierarchical way effectively disentangles complex of polarity shifts and embeds them into a vector space.
- *An end-to-end paragraph embedding model for polarity shift sensitive sentiment classification.* The embedding model MUSH is proposed to learn an end-to-end paragraph embedding that not only considers the context and sequential information, but also captures the polarity shift catering for complex real-world sentiment analysis tasks.

We compare MUSH with state-of-the-art methods on four large real-world data sets with various characteristics. The experimental results demonstrate MUSH significantly improves the sentiment classification performance.

The rest of paper is organized as follows. Section 2 details the proposed MUSH. Then, Sect. 3 illustrates the MUSH performance by comparing it with state-of-the-art methods in real-world data sets. Finally, Sect. 4 concludes this paper and discusses the further challenges and opportunities.

2 Embedding for Paragraph with Polarity Shift

In this section, we first systematically analyze the characteristics of sentiment polarity shift. Following the analyzing result, we propose a multi-scale and hierarchical embedding model, namely MUSH, and discuss each component in this model.

2.1 Sentiment Polarity Shift Analysis

In this paper, we mainly consider two characteristics of sentiment polarity shift that bring major challenges for paragraph embedding: (1) the polarity shift is with multi-forms; and (2) the polarity shift hierarchically exists in a paragraph. Here, we analyze these two characteristics shift separately.

The Multi-forms of Polarity Shift. The polarity shift may be caused by both explicit indicators and implicit descriptions. The explicit indicators are the words or terms that can cause a consistent or contrary polarity changes. Typical explicit indicators include negative words and conjugation words. Different from the explicit indicators, implicit descriptions may not involve any indicator in the paragraph, however, the polarity is changed by a sequential combination of specific words or sentences.

Although current efforts have been tried to capture the explicit indicators, most of them fail to simultaneously capture the implicit and explicit polarity shift. In this paper, we propose MUSH to tackle this problem. Specifically, MUSH captures such multi-forms polarity shift by a CNN-RNN structure, which will be detailed in the Sect. 2.2.

The Hierarchical of Polarity Shift with Long-Term Dependence. The polarity shift hierarchically exists in a paragraph from sentence level to paragraph level. This hierarchy brings a serial of challenges in sentiment analysis. Regarding inter-level polarity shift interactions, with both word polarity shift and sentence polarity shift, it is hard to figure out the final polarity. Regarding intra-level polarity shift interactions, another challenge is induced by the long-term dependence of words or sentences. Here, the long-term dependence means the polarity at the end of a sentence may depend on the words at the beginning of the sentence.

The hierarchical of polarity shift with long-term dependence makes the global sentiment representation hard to infer. In this paper, we propose MUSH to disentangle these intra- and inter-level polarity shift interactions via a hierarchical neural network structure as described in Sect. 2.2.

2.2 Paragraph Embedding

We propose a multi-scale and hierarchical embedding method, MUSH, for polarity shift sensitive paragraph embedding. The structure of MUSH is shown in Fig. 1. MUSH is a hierarchical neural network constructed by sentence-level and paragraph-level embedding modules, each of which is a multi-scale CNN-RNN structure. The sentence-level embedding module captures the context information, sequential information, and multi-forms sentence-level polarity shift. The paragraph-level embedding module reveals the sentiment segments and multi-forms paragraph-level polarity shift. MUSH learns paragraph embedding through an end-to-end training process guided by a specific sentiment classification task to further capture the sentiment information. MUSH preserves the distribution properties of paragraphs in the embedding space, and explicitly models the polarity shift.

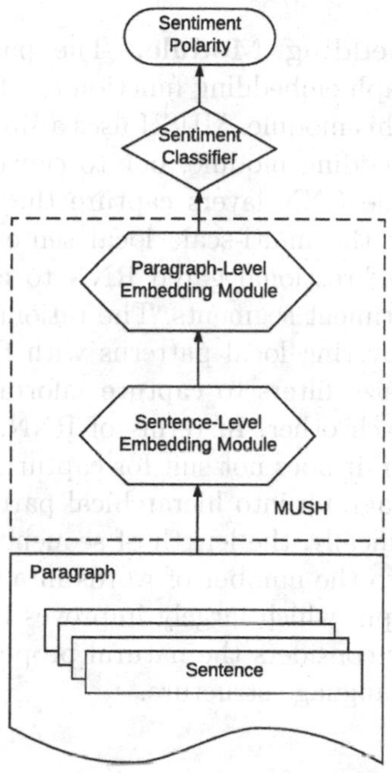

Fig. 1. MUSH structure: MUSH is a multi-scale and hierarchical neural network that constructed by two modules, i.e. sentence-level embedding module and paragraph-level embedding module. MUSH learns paragraph embedding for polarity shift sensitive classification through an end-to-end training process guided by a specific task.

Sentence-Level Embedding Module. The sentience-level embedding module learns the word embedding function e_w and sentence embedding function e_s. The structure in the module is shown in Fig. 2. The first layer of the module is a word embedding layer. In MUSH, this word embedding layer should be pre-trained by unsupervised method, such as skip-gram [15], to capture the word context information. Although the context-based word embedding may not provide significant information for sentiment polarity discrimination, it reflects the local structure in a paragraph that contributes to the generalization ability of the final paragraph embedding. To capture the multi-scale sentiment atoms, MUSH adopts the CNN layers with multi-size filters. The multi-scale local patterns revealed by CNN similar to the n-gram features that used by traditional NLP methods. However, the CNN based features are more sensitive to the patterns with high utility to the final task, i.e. the sentiment atom, compared to n-gram features which treat each feature makes the same contribution. For each

CNN layer, a bidirectional gated RNN layer is used to leverage the dependence of sentiment atoms. It captures the polarity shift in each scale. The outputs of RNN layers are merged by fully connected layers, which reveal the relationships among multi-scale polarities.

Paragraph-Level Embedding Module. The paragraph-level embedding module learns the paragraph embedding function e_d. The structure in the module is shown in Fig. 3. In this module, MUSH uses a similar CNN-RNN structure in the sentence-level embedding module, but to capture different information. Specifically, the multi-scale CNN layers capture the sentiment segments in a paragraph, which reflects the multi-scale local sentence polarity dependence. Then, MUSH adopts a bidirectional gated RNN to capture the polarity shift in the CNN captured sentiment segments. The rationale is as follows. In terms of CNN, it suits for discovering local patterns with fixed receive field. MUSH adopts CNN with multi-size filters to capture information in different receive fields that complement each other. In terms of RNN, although it can capture the sequential information, it does not suit for capturing long-term dependence. MUSH decomposes a paragraph into hierarchical parts to cut down the length of a sequence. More specifically, the length of sequence drops from the number of words in a paragraph to the number of words in a sentence and the number of sentences in a paragraph, which largely improves the RNN performance. In this way, MUSH not only considers the natural properties of polarity shift but also fits the paragraph's language structure.

3 Experiments

In the experiments, we evaluate the MUSH embedding performance through its enabled sentiment classification accuracy, compared with three state-of-the-art methods and four baseline methods on four large real-world data sets.

3.1 Data Sets

The data sets used in the experiments include *IMDB movie review*, *Yelp 2013*, *Yelp 2014*, and *Yelp 2015* data sets. They are widely used as benchmarks to evaluate sentiment classification performance.

The first *IMDB movie review* data set was collected by Diao et al. [4]. It involves 348,415 movie reviews with sentiment rating levels ranging from 1 to 10. The *Yelp 2013*, *Yelp 2014*, and *Yelp 2015* data sets are provided by Yelp challenge in 2013, 2014, 2015, respectively. They contain public hotels and restaurants comments with 335,018, 1,125,457, and 1,569,264 reviews in each year. The rating levels are ranging from 1 to 5. The details of these four data sets are shown in Table 1.

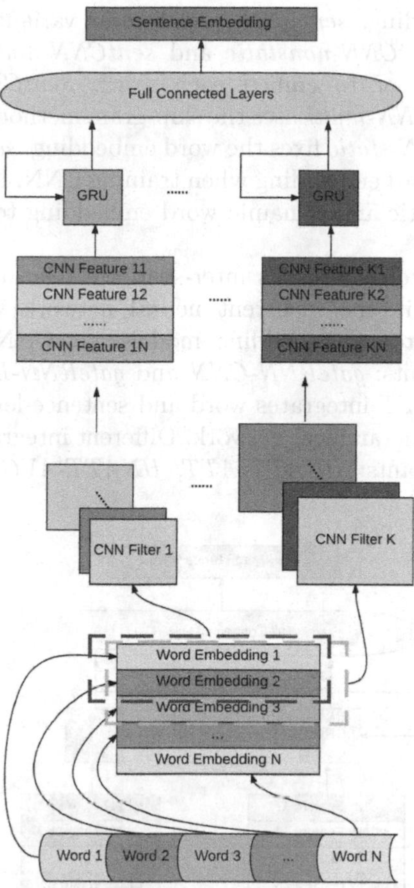

Fig. 2. The structure of sentence-level embedding module: the first layer of the module is a word embedding layer. Then, several CNN layers with multiple filter size are connected to the word embedding layer. For each CNN layer, a corresponding RNN layer is followed. The end of the module is fully connected layers that merge the outputs of RNN layers to a sentence embedding.

3.2 Experiments Setting

To evaluate the performance of our proposed MUSH, we compared it with four baseline methods and three state-of-the-art methods. The baseline methods include bag-of-words (BOW), bag-of-words with term frequency-inverse document frequency (BOW-TFIDF), ngram, and ngram with term frequency-inverse document frequency (ngram-TFIDF). The embedding of these methods is fed into logistic regression to construct the sentiment classifier. The state-of-the-art embedding methods and their variants include:

- *SentCNN* [7]. This method captures neighbourhood relationships among words by feeding word embedding into CNN. According to the trainability

of the word embedding, *sentCNN* derives four variants: *sentCNN-random*, *sentCNN-static*, *sentCNN-nonstatic* and *sentCNN-multi*. *SentCNN-random* uses a random vector to embed each word. *SentCNN-static*, *sentCNN-nonstatic* and *sentCNN-multi* uses the skip-gram method [15] for word embedding. While *sentCNN-static* fixes the word embedding, *sent-nonStatic* dynamically adjusts the word embedding when training CNN. In contrast, *sentCNN-multi* uses both static and dynamic word embedding to learn text representation.
- *GateRNN* [17]. GateRNN learns inter-sentence relationships based on sentence embedding via the recurrent neural network with gated recurrent units. Different sentence embedding models, i.e. CNN and LSTM, induce two *gateRNN* variants: *gateRNN-CNN* and *gateRNN-LSTM*.
- *HNATT* [24]. *HNATT* integrates word and sentence-level sequential characteristics through a hierarchical network. Different integrating methods induce three *HNATT* variants: *HNATT-ATT*, *HNATT-AVG* and *HNATT-MAX*.

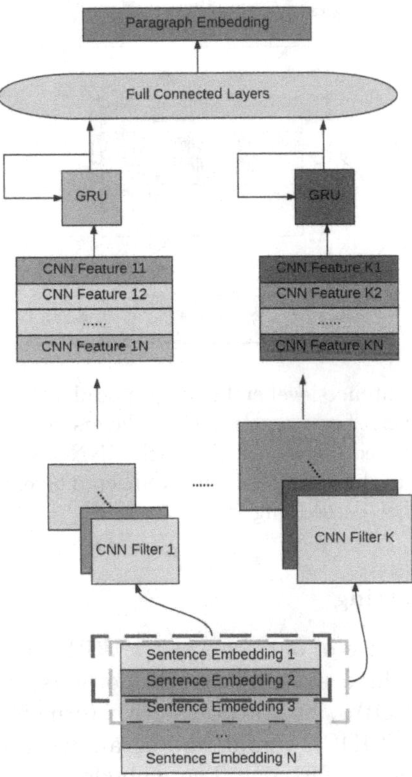

Fig. 3. The structure of paragraph-level embedding module: the CNN layers with multiple filter size followed by bidirectional gated RNN layers are used to capture multi-scale polarity shift. The fully connected layers that merge the outputs of RNN layers to a paragraph embedding.

Table 1. Characteristics of data sets in the experiments: #v refers to the number of vocabulary, #s and #w refers to the number of sentence and word, respectively.

Data set	#class	#reviews	average #s	max #s	average #w	max #w	#v
IMDB	10	348,415	14.0	1,484	325.6	2,802	115,831
Yelp 2013	5	335,018	8.9	151	151.6	1,184	211,245
Yelp 2014	5	1,125,457	9.2	151	156.9	1,199	476,191
Yelp 2015	5	1,569,264	9.0	151	151.9	1,199	612,636

HNATT-ATT uses attention mechanism to weighted sum words and sentences embedding. *HNATT-AVG* and *HNATT-MAX* adopt the averaged and max value of words/sentences embedding, respectively.

The pre-processing method for a paragraph is following the setting in [24]. The Stanford's CoreNLP [13] is used to split a paragraph into sentences and tokenize each sentence. The word embedding is initially set according to the pre-training via skip-gram model [15].

In the experiments, the word embedding dimension is set as 100. Regarding MUSH, the CNN with 2×100 and 3×100 filter sizes are used to capture the 2-gram and 3-gram features. In the sentence-level embedding module, the number of filters in CNN layers, the number of gated recurrent unit (GRU), and the number of node in a fully connected layer is set as 32, 64, and 64, respectively. In the paragraph-level embedding module, these settings are 64, 128 and 128, respectively. In the training process, the batch normalization is used after every layer, and the dropout with keeping probability 0.5 is adopted after fully connected layers. We set the batch size as 64 and use Adam algorithm [8] to optimize the MUSH.

3.3 MUSH-Enabled Sentiment Classification Results

The MUSH embedding is fed into a single layer feed-forward neural network (SLFN) with softmax as the output layer to make the sentiment classification. The results are compared with the competitors as shown in Table 2.

As can been seen in Table 2, the MUSH-enabled sentiment classification achieves the best results in all four data sets. The performance lift is mainly benefited by (1) hierarchical modeling the paragraph, and (2) capturing the polarity shift. From the results, MUSH is significantly better than all competitors instead of HNATT. It is because HNATT is also a hierarchical model that share some same strengths as MUSH. In addition, HNATT uses attention mechanism to capture the important information in a paragraph that to some extent can focus on polarity shift indicators. However, MUSH adopts a direct way to model and capture the polarity shift. It provides a better understanding of polarity shift complexities. Therefore, MUSH gets a better embedding performance than HNATT.

Table 2. Embedding performance in terms of sentiment classification accuracy

Methods	IMDB	Yelp 2013	Yelp 2014	Yelp 2015
BOW	15.5	20.2	29.4	31.8
BOW-TFIDF	21.3	31.6	36.0	38.9
ngram	25.1	36.6	41.3	44.5
ngram-TFIDF	27.3	39.1	43.2	45.7
sentCNN-random	29.4	55.6	57.9	58.9
sentCNN-static	29.2	53.5	58.2	59.2
sentCNN-nonstatic	24.6	47.1	52.6	52.2
sentCNN-multi	29.4	53.3	58.3	58.7
gateRNN-CNN	40.6	61.4	62.7	63.2
gateRNN-LSTM	41.7	63.5	66.9	67.8
HNATT-ATT	42.5	63.2	67.3	68.1
HNATT-AVG	42.2	63.8	66.8	67.7
HNATT-MAX	42.9	63.7	66.8	68.0
MUSH	**43.2**	**64.3**	**67.5**	**68.9**

4 Conclusion

In this paper, we propose a multi-scale and hierarchical embedding method, MUSH, for polarity shift sensitive sentiment classification. The MUSH uses an end-to-end learning method to embed paragraph into vector space that recognizes the polarity shift and maintains the context information, sequential information, and sentiment information in paragraph space. The experimental results support the performance merits of the MUSH compared with the state-of-the-art methods. MUSH captures the sentiment features in an implicit process. In the future, the explicit sentiment information and features will be considered to combine with the implicit MUSH features to construct more powerful sentiment representation.

Compliance with Ethical Standards

Conflict of Interest

The authors declare that they have no conflict of interest.

Ethical Approval

This article does not contain any studies with human participants or animals performed by any of the authors.

References

1. Arora, S., Liang, Y., Ma, T.: A simple but tough-to-beat baseline for sentence embeddings. In: International Conference of Learning Representations (2017)
2. Asghar, M.Z., Khan, A., Ahmad, S., Qasim, M., Khan, I.A.: Lexicon-enhanced sentiment analysis framework using rule-based classification scheme. PLoS One **12**(2), e0171649 (2017)
3. Chen, M.: Efficient vector representation for documents through corruption. In: International Conference of Learning Representations (2017)
4. Diao, Q., Qiu, M., Wu, C.Y., Smola, A.J., Jiang, J., Wang, C.: Jointly modeling aspects, ratings and sentiments for movie recommendation (JMARS). In: Proceedings of the 20th ACM SIGKDD International Conference on Knowledge Discovery and Data Mining, pp. 193–202. ACM (2014)
5. Ikeda, D., Takamura, H., Okumura, M.: Learning to shift the polarity of words for sentiment classification. Trans. Jpn. Soc. Artif. Intell. **25**, 50–57 (2010)
6. Kennedy, A., Inkpen, D.: Sentiment classification of movie reviews using contextual valence shifters. Comput. Intell. **22**(2), 110–125 (2006)
7. Kim, Y.: Convolutional neural networks for sentence classification. arXiv preprint arXiv:1408.5882 (2014)
8. Kingma, D., Ba, J.: Adam: a method for stochastic optimization. arXiv preprint arXiv:1412.6980 (2014)
9. Le, Q., Mikolov, T.: Distributed representations of sentences and documents. In: Proceedings of the 31st International Conference on Machine Learning, pp. 1188–1196 (2014)
10. Li, S., Lee, S.Y.M., Chen, Y., Huang, C.R., Zhou, G.: Sentiment classification and polarity shifting. In: Proceedings of the 23rd International Conference on Computational Linguistics, pp. 635–643. Association for Computational Linguistics (2010)
11. Lin, Z., et al.: A structured self-attentive sentence embedding. In: International Conference of Learning Representations (2017)
12. Maas, A.L., Daly, R.E., Pham, P.T., Huang, D., Ng, A.Y., Potts, C.: Learning word vectors for sentiment analysis. In: Proceedings of the 49th Annual Meeting of the Association for Computational Linguistics, pp. 142–150. Association for Computational Linguistics (2011)
13. Manning, C.D., Surdeanu, M., Bauer, J., Finkel, J.R., Bethard, S., McClosky, D.: The stanford CoreNLP natural language processing toolkit. In: ACL (System Demonstrations), pp. 55–60 (2014)
14. Margarit, H., Subramaniam, R.: A batch-normalized recurrent network for sentiment classification. In: Advances in Neural Information Processing Systems, pp. 2–8 (2016)
15. Mikolov, T., Sutskever, I., Chen, K., Corrado, G.S., Dean, J.: Distributed representations of words and phrases and their compositionality. In: Advances in Neural Information Processing Systems, pp. 3111–3119 (2013)
16. Ren, Y., Zhang, Y., Zhang, M., Ji, D.: Context-sensitive Twitter sentiment classification using neural network. In: AAAI, pp. 215–221 (2016)
17. Tang, D., Qin, B., Liu, T.: Document modeling with gated recurrent neural network for sentiment classification. In: EMNLP, pp. 1422–1432 (2015)
18. Tang, D., Qin, B., Wei, F., Dong, L., Liu, T., Zhou, M.: A joint segmentation and classification framework for sentence level sentiment classification. IEEE/ACM Trans. Audio Speech Lang. Process. **23**(11), 1750–1761 (2015)

19. Tang, D., Wei, F., Qin, B., Yang, N., Liu, T., Zhou, M.: Sentiment embeddings with applications to sentiment analysis. IEEE Trans. Knowl. Data Eng. **28**(2), 496–509 (2016)
20. Vo, D.T., Zhang, Y.: Target-dependent twitter sentiment classification with rich automatic features. In: International Joint Conference on Artificial Intelligence, pp. 1347–1353 (2015)
21. Xia, R., Xu, F., Yu, J., Qi, Y., Cambria, E.: Polarity shift detection, elimination and ensemble: a three-stage model for document-level sentiment analysis. Inform. Process. Manag. **52**(1), 36–45 (2016)
22. Xiang, L., Li, Y., Hao, W., Yang, P., Shen, X.: Reversible natural language watermarking using synonym substitution and arithmetic coding. CMC: Comput. Mater. Contin. **55**(3), 541–559 (2018)
23. Xiong, Z., Shen, Q., Wang, Y., Zhu, C.: Paragraph vector representation based on word to vector and CNN learning. CMC: Comput. Mater. Contin. **55**(2), 213–227 (2018)
24. Yang, Z., Yang, D., Dyer, C., He, X., Smola, A.J., Hovy, E.H.: Hierarchical attention networks for document classification. In: HLT-NAACL, pp. 1480–1489 (2016)
25. Zhuang, Y., et al.: Bag-of-discriminative-words (BoDw) representation via topic modeling. IEEE Trans. Knowl. Data Eng. **29**(5), 977–990 (2017)

Trade-off Between Energy Consumption and Makespan in the Mapreduce Resource Allocation Problem

Xiaolu Zhang, Xi Liu, Weidong Li, and Xuejie Zhang(✉)

School of Information Science and Engineering, Yunnan University, Kunming, China
{zxl,weidong,xjzhang}@ynu.edu.cn, lxghost@126.com

Abstract. Minimizing energy consumption when executing Mapreduce jobs is a significant challenge for data centers; however, it traditionally conflicts with the system performance. This paper aims to address this problem by making a trade-off between energy consumption and performance. In this paper, we design an integer linear bi-objective optimization model and propose a two-phase heuristic allocation algorithm to find a high-quality feasible solution. By adopting Non-dominated Sorting Genetic Algorithm II with the feasible solution, we obtain a set of Pareto optimal solutions to minimize both energy consumption and makespan. Finally, we perform experiments on several real workloads to evaluate the solutions produced by our proposed algorithm and analyze the trade-off relationship between energy and makespan. The results show that the Pareto optimal solutions are close to the lower bound obtained by the relaxation of the integer linear bi-objective optimization model and can also assist system manager to make intelligent resource allocation decisions for Mapreduce applications based on the energy efficiency and performance needs of the system.

Keywords: Energy consumption · Makespan · Mapreduce · NSGA-II · Resource allocation

1 Introduction

Mapreduce [1] is an open-resource distributed programming framework that is designed to process big data on the Hadoop platform [2]. Owing to its easy-to-programming, built-in data distribution and fault tolerance, Mapreduce has been widely utilized by many applications. Recently, many researchers have studied to reduce Mapreduce energy consumption or achieve high performance through hardware and software methods. Wirtz et al. [3] used an intelligent DVFS scheduling that adjusts the CPU frequency based on the workloads' computational needs to achieve significant energy savings. Goiri et al. [4] proposed a Mapreduce framework for scheduling jobs to maximize green-energy consumption by delaying a large number of computations within the job's bounded time and suggested building a data center that uses renewable sources instead of electricity. Johnson et al. [5] proposed an approach that migrates a job at lower-priced energy locations of execution. Liao et al. [6] presented a data placement

X. Sun et al. (Eds.): ICAIS 2019, LNCS 11633, pp. 239–250, 2019.
https://doi.org/10.1007/978-3-030-24265-7_21

policy to decrease energy consumption of task waiting and minimum resource allocation algorithms to improve energy utilization rate of Mapreduce jobs by the deadline constraints. As for performance, Zaharia et al. [7] designed a simple robust scheduling algorithm (LATE) to increase the response time in Mapreduce. Their approach uses estimated completion time to predict the execution time of the tasks. Xiao et al. [8] presented an improved mini batch K-means algorithm based on simulated annealing algorithm for calculating the number of clusters and reducing the number of iterations in order to reduce the Mapreduce computation time. Ren et al. [9] proposed a job-scheduling algorithm that extends job priorities to guarantee rapid responses for small jobs to optimize the completion time of small Mapreduce jobs. Zhang et al. [10] used the classification of machine learning to model the cloud resource allocation and proposes two resource allocation prediction algorithms based on linear and logistic regressions to increase the resource utilization for Mapreduce. Chen et al. [11] considered the online Mapreduce scheduling problem of minimizing the makespan, and devised a 1-competitive online algorithm. Unfortunately, the goal of energy efficiency often conflict with the goal of achieving high performance. The least execution time typically requires the most energy consumption, and the least energy consumption usually results in a significantly reduced performance. It is important to find a set of solutions that trade-off energy consumption and performance to fit the needs of the Mapreduce system.

The trade-off problem has been one of the active research topics in resource allocation problem in need of guaranteeing energy efficiency and performance. Friese et al. [12] formulated a bi-objective resource allocation problem to analyze the trade-off between energy consumption and makespan in a heterogeneous resource allocation problem. Tarplee et al. [13] presented a scalable scheduling algorithm for the energy consumption and makespan bi-objective optimization problem in the HPC environment. Lin et al. [14] studied the impact of job features and parallel execution capabilities on the job completion reliability and job energy consumption of a Mapreduce cluster. We observe that existing solutions are not effective to deal with Mapreduce workloads that consist of map/reduce tasks with lower energy consumption and faster response time requirements.

In a recent work, Mashayekhy et al. [15] studied the map/reduce-level energy efficiency of a Mapreduce job and proposed a minimization model on the energy consumption that requires the execution time of the job to meet the deadline constraint. Our research is closely related to this work. In our previous work [16], we proposed a profit maximum model that minimizes the cost of energy consumption while maintaining the minimization makespan and adopts a weight b-matching rounding algorithm to get a complete resource allocation for Mapreduce. Li et al. [17, 18] proposed polynomial-time algorithms for the energy-aware profit maximizing scheduling problem and proved the worst-case performance ratio is close to 2 based on task types, respectively. We refer this idea and divide map/reduce tasks into different task types and divide map/reduce slots into different slot types due to the similarity of the energy consumption and makespan of tasks on slots in big-data processing to reduce the computational cost. In this paper, we model the static Mapreduce resource allocation (SMRA) problem as a bi-objective optimization based on task types and slot types. The first objective is to minimize the total energy consumption of slots in the Mapreduce cluster. The second objective is to minimize the makespan, which is the maximum completion time of all Mapreduce tasks. We design a novel technique that utilizes a feasible solution produced by a heuristic algorithm as the initial population, then adopts Non-dominated Sorting Genetic algorithm II (NSGA-II) [19] to find a set of high-quality solutions that represent the trade-off between energy consumption and makespan. In summary, the contributions of this paper are:

(1) model the SMRA problem as a bi-objective optimization on both energy consumption minimization and makespan minimization;
(2) design a two-phase heuristic allocation algorithm to find a feasible solution;
(3) adopt a well-known multi-objective genetic algorithm to find a set of Pareto optimal solutions (called Pareto front).

2 Bi-objective Optimization Model

We consider a Mapreduce job consisting of a set of map/reduce tasks, which are executed on sets of map/reduce slots. Let $\boldsymbol{M}$ be the set of map task types and $\boldsymbol{R}$ be the set of reduce task types. Let $\boldsymbol{A}$ be the set of map slot types and $\boldsymbol{B}$ be the set of reduce slot types. Let MT_i be the number of map tasks of type $i \in \boldsymbol{M}$ and RT_i be the number of reduce tasks of type $i \in \boldsymbol{R}$. Let AS_j be the number of map slots of type $j \in \boldsymbol{A}$ and BS_j be the number of reduce slots of type $j \in \boldsymbol{B}$, and the number of tasks are more than the number of slots under normal condition. Let x_{ij} be the number of map tasks of type i assigned to map slots of type j and y_{ij} be the number of reduce tasks of type i assigned to reduce slots of type j. Let $\boldsymbol{EEC}$ be a matrix with entries e_{ij}, where e_{ij} is the *estimated energy consumption* for a task of type $i \in \{\boldsymbol{M}, \boldsymbol{R}\}$ executed on a slot of type $j \in \{\boldsymbol{A}, \boldsymbol{B}\}$. Similarly let $\boldsymbol{EPT}$ be a matrix with entries p_{ij}, where p_{ij} is the *estimated processing time* of a task of type $i \in \{\boldsymbol{M}, \boldsymbol{R}\}$ executed on a slot of type $j \in \{\boldsymbol{A}, \boldsymbol{B}\}$. For a given resource allocation, the total energy consumption is the sum of the energy consumed by all map/reduce tasks. The amount of energy consumed by a task type is dependent upon the slot type on which that task is executed. Therefore, the total energy consumption, denoted by *EC*, of a Mapreduce job is given by Eq. 1. The makespan, denoted by *MS*, is determined by the maximum completion time of map/reduce tasks executed on slot types, and is given by Eq. 2.

$$EC = \sum_{j \in A} \sum_{i \in M} e_{ij} \cdot x_{ij} + \sum_{j \in B} \sum_{i \in R} e_{ij} \cdot y_{ij} \tag{1}$$

$$MS = \max_{\forall j \in A} \frac{\sum_{i \in M} p_{ij} \cdot x_{ij}}{AS_j} + \max_{\forall j \in B} \frac{\sum_{i \in R} p_{ij} \cdot y_{ij}}{BS_j} \tag{2}$$

We formulate the SMRA problem as an integer linear programming model (ILP) as follows:

$$\underset{x_{ij},y_{ij}}{\text{Minimize}}(EC, MS) \tag{3}$$

Subject to:

$$\sum_{j \in A} x_{ij} = MT_i, \forall i \in \boldsymbol{M} \tag{4}$$

$$\sum_{j \in B} y_{ij} = RT_i, \forall i \in \boldsymbol{R} \tag{5}$$

$$x_{ij} \in \boldsymbol{Z}^+ \cup \{0\}, \forall i \in \boldsymbol{M}, \forall j \in \boldsymbol{A} \tag{6}$$

$$y_{ij} \in \boldsymbol{Z}^+ \cup \{0\}, \forall i \in \boldsymbol{R}, \forall j \in \boldsymbol{B} \tag{7}$$

The objective function is to minimize *EC* and *MS*, where x_{ij} and y_{ij} are the decision variables. Constraint 4 ensures that all of the map tasks of a single type are assigned to some map slot type(s) for execution. Constraint 5 ensures that all of the reduce tasks of a single type are assigned to some reduce slot type(s) for execution. Constraints 6 and 7 ensure the non-negativity and integrality of the decision variables.

3 A Two-Phase Heuristic Allocation Algorithm

As we know, finding the optimal solutions of the Bi-objective optimization is NP-hard. Therefore, we first design a two-phase heuristic allocation algorithm called TPHA (including TPHA-I and TPHA-II) to find a feasible solution for the ILP model. The TPHA-I phase combines the two objectives and finds the solutions of the ILP. The TPHA-II phase determines a detailed allocation of all map/reduce tasks to specific map/reduce slots. The two phases are presented in the next subsections. First, we define the PE metric to characterize the energy consumption and makespan of each task type as follows:

$$pe_i^m = \min_{\forall j \in A} \frac{e_{ij} \cdot AS_j}{p_{ij}}, \forall i \in \boldsymbol{M} \tag{8}$$

$$pe_i^r = \min_{\forall j \in B} \frac{e_{ij} \cdot BS_j}{p_{ij}}, \forall i \in \boldsymbol{R} \tag{9}$$

Where pe_i^m and pe_i^r represent the energy consumption rates of map task type i and reduce task type i, respectively.

3.1 TPHA-I Algorithm

The TPHA-I algorithm to find the integer solutions x_{ij} and y_{ij} is given in Algorithm 1. TPHA-I builds two priority queues, Q^m and Q^r, to store the orders of the map/reduce task types, respectively, based on the PE metric. In each iteration of the while loop, the algorithm chooses the task type with the maximum pe_i^m (or pe_i^r) from the priority queues and assigns the task type to the slot types with the minimum processing time. The assignment procedure of reduce task types to reduce slot types is similar to the map assignment procedure.

Algorithm 1 TPHA-I Algorithm

Input: $\boldsymbol{EEC}$, $\boldsymbol{EPT}$

Output: $\boldsymbol{X}$, $\boldsymbol{Y}$

1: create an empty priority queue Q^m
2: create an empty priority queue Q^r
3: **for all** $i \in \boldsymbol{M}$ **do**
4: $pe_i^m = \min_{\forall j \in A} e_{ij} \cdot AS_j / p_{ij}$
5: Q^m.equeue(i, pe_i^m)
6: **for all** $i \in \boldsymbol{R}$ **do**
7: $pe_i^r = \min_{\forall j \in B} e_{ij} \cdot BS_j / p_{ij}$
8: Q^r.equeue(i, pe_i^r)
9: $p_j^m = 0, \forall j \in \boldsymbol{A}$
10: **while** Q^m is not empty **do**
11: $i^m = Q^m$.extractmax( )
12: $k = 0$
13: **while** $k < MT_{i^m}$ **do**
14: $j^m = \arg\min_{j \in A} p_j^m$
15: $x_{i^m j^m} = x_{i^m j^m} + 1$
16: $p_{j^m}^m = p_{j^m}^m + p_{i^m j^m}$
17: $k = k + 1$
18: **end while**
19: Q^m.remove($i^m, pe_{i^m}^m$)
20: **end while**
21: **while** Q^r is not empty **do**
22: assign the reduce task types to reduce slot types (The code is similar to lines 10-20)
23: **end while**

Algorithm 2 TPHA-II Algorithm

Input: $\boldsymbol{EPT}$, $\boldsymbol{X}$, $\boldsymbol{Y}$

Output: slot scheduling

1: {assign map tasks to map slots}
2: **for all** $j \in \boldsymbol{A}$ **do**
3: create an empty queue Q^j
4: **for all** $i \in \boldsymbol{M}$ **do**
5: **for** $k = 1$ **to** x_{ij} **do**
6: Q^j.equeue($X_{ij}[k]$)
7: **end for**
8: **end for**
9: z = sort descending by $\boldsymbol{EPT}(Q^j)$
10: $P_s^m = 0, \forall s \in A_j$
11: **for** $\lambda = 1$ **to** $\| z \|$ **do**
12: $j^m = \arg\min_{s \in A_j} P_s^m$
13: assign task $z[\lambda]$ to slot j^m
14: $P_{j^m}^m = P_{j^m}^m + p_{\tau(z[\lambda])\gamma(j^m)}$
15: **end for**
16: **end for**
17: {assign reduce tasks to reduce slots}
18: (The code is similar to lines 2-16)

3.2 TPHA-II Algorithm

After assigning task types to slot types, the algorithm must find a feasible method to schedule the tasks already assigned to each slot type to specific slots. This problem is known as scheduling a set of heterogeneous tasks onto a set of identical slots. The longest processing time (LPT) algorithm [20] can be used to solve this scheduling problem and independently schedule each slot type. The TPHA-II algorithm using LPT is given in Algorithm 2. We create an empty queue Q^z to contain tasks of each task type. Let the function $\tau(m)$ return the task type of task m, and let the function $\gamma(s)$ return the slot type of slot s. Let X_{ij} be the array of tasks that belong to task type i and slot type j. The tasks are sorted in descending order according to the ***EPT***. The algorithm loops over this sorted list to assign each task to the slot that has the minimum processing time at a time.

4 NSGA-II Adopted for SMRA

The above two-phase heuristic allocation algorithm is validated empirically to find a feasible solution for SMRA. In this section, we use the feasible solution from TPHA as part of the initial population of NSGA-II to produce a set of Pareto optimal solutions that trade off between energy consumption and makespan. NSGA-II is an adaptation of the Genetic Algorithm (GA) to find a Pareto front of a multi-objective optimization problem. Similar to all GAs, the NSGA-II uses crossover and mutation operators to evolve the populations of chromosomes into better solutions over time. For our problem, we modify NSGA-II to meet the constraints of the bi-objective optimization model, including the encoding and decoding methods, crossover operator, and mutation operator.

A. Encoding and Decoding Methods

Based on the feasible solution obtained by TPHA, we adopt integer coding to initialize the population. Within a gene there is a single integer number representing the slot on which the task will be executed. Provided that there are $m + r$ map/reduce tasks to be processed, we use the vector $\boldsymbol{S} = \{s_1, s_2,.., s_m, s_{m+1}, s_{m+2}, \ldots, s_{m+r}\}$ as an individual chromosome to represent a feasible solution. Each gene represents a map/reduce slot and the sequence of all reduce genes follows all map genes. The decoding method allocates each map/reduce task to a specific map/reduce slot.

B. Crossover Operator

We perform the crossover operator by adopting a two-point crossover operator for the evolution of individual chromosomes. In each population, two chromosomes are selected on the basis of crossover probability and genes are swapped between two indices which are selected randomly as the crossover points within the map/reduce gene interval, respectively, of that chromosome.

C. Mutation Operator

We use a single-point mutation operator for the evolution of individual chromosomes. Chromosomes are selected from crossover offspring according to the mutation probability. Within a chromosome, a map gene and a reduce gene are randomly selected and replaced by a new map slot and a new reduce slot that are arbitrarily selected within the specified range of slots respectively.

After the crossover and mutation operating, we present the overall NSGA-II algorithm in Algorithm 3. The NSGA-II algorithm first initializes the population from the TPHA solution, random solutions and other heuristic seeding solutions. The new offspring population is created by applying the crossover and mutation operators, as shown in line 4. After that, the NSGA-II adopts an elitist algorithm, which keeps the best chromosomes from the previous generation and allows them to be evaluated in the current generation. In line 5, we combine parent and offspring populations into a single meta-population of size 2*N*. Line 6 performs the fast non-dominated sorting approach [19], which ranks the solutions within the population based on dominance. Dominance is defined that one solution is better than another solution in at least one objective and better than or equal to the other objectives. In our research, we use the minimum energy consumption and minimum makespan as the bi-objective function to find the domination ranks. The next parent population is created by lines 7–17. If the size of the next parent population is more than *N*, we take a subset of solutions from the highest rank, based on the crowding distance metric method [19], which calculates the proximity measure between two chromosomes. The process continues until the stopping condition is satisfied.

Algorithm 3 NSGA-II Algorithm

Input: the initial solutions
Output: the final population
1: create initial population of N chromosomes: P_0
2: **while** termination $t \neq 0$ **do**
3: O_t = create-new-offspring(P_t)
4: {crossover(P_t), mutation(P_t)}
5: $C_t = P_t \cup O_t$
6: $\Re$ =fast-non-dominated-sort(C_t)
7: $P_{t+1} = \varnothing$ and $i = 1$
8: **while** $\| P_{t+1} \| + \| \Re_i \| \leq N$ **do**
9: $P_{t+1} = P_{t+1} \cup \Re_i$
10: $i = i + 1$
11: **end while**
12: **if** $\| P_{t+1} \| + \| \Re_i \| > N$ **then**
13: crowding-distance($\Re_i$)
14: sort-descending($\Re_i$)
15: $P_{t+1} = P_{t+1} \cup \Re_i[1:(N - \| P_{t+1} \|)]$
16: $t = t + 1$
17: **end if**
18: **end while**

5 Experimental Results

5.1 Experimental Setup

We perform simulations on Terasort [21] workloads to construct a Pareto front and analyze the trade-off between energy consumption and makespan. The workloads include the number of tasks, task types and slot types, as presented in Table 1. There are 5 map/reduce task types, 10 map/reduce slot types and a total of 60 slots. The real historical ***EEC*** and ***EPT*** data sets are gathered from the literature [15]. In each simulation, the NSGA-II algorithm consists of 50 chromosomes and is set to execute for

5000 iterations. For the initial population, we use the chromosomes generated by TPHA, random chromosomes and other chromosomes generated by the minimum energy consumption algorithm which assigns map/reduce tasks to the slots that have the lowest energy consumption and the min-min makespan algorithm based on the min-min algorithm [22] which assigns map/reduce tasks to the slots with the minimum completion time (MCT).

Table 1. Experiment workload

Workload	Map tasks	Reduce tasks	Task types	Slot types
(48M, 48R)	48	48	5	10
(48M, 64R)	48	64	5	10
(64M, 48R)	64	48	5	10
(64M, 64R)	64	64	5	10

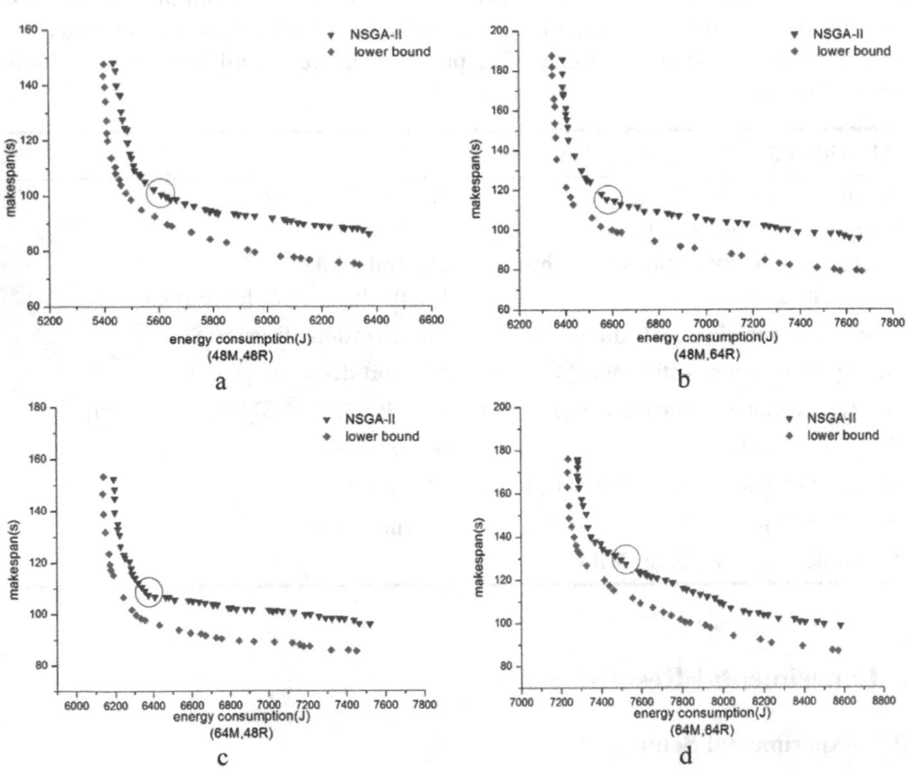

Fig. 1. Pareto fronts and lower bounds

5.2 Analysis of Results

We analyze the performance of NSGA-II for four Mapreduce workloads, as presented in Table 1. Figure 1 shows the Pareto fronts and lower bounds of four workloads. In each plot, the lowest green points represent the lower bound on the Pareto front, which is obtained by solving the ILP relaxation of the assignment of individual tasks to individual slots by Matlab. The Pareto front generated by the NSGA-II algorithm after 5000 iterations is shown by the blue points. There is a set of points along the Pareto front, and each point represents a complete resource allocation solution. In these figures, we circle a set of points. On the left of such points, a small increase in energy consumption results in a large decrease in makespan. On the right of such points, a small decrease in makespan results in a large increase in energy consumption. As shown in these figures, we note that the curve obtained by NSGA-II is close to the lower bound, which implies that there is very little room for improvement of the Pareto front after 5000 iterations, and the TPHA provides the solutions to converge in the lower-left corner in a relatively short number of iterations and a reasonable run time. For example, the average total time to run 5000 iterations for the workload (48M, 48R) is 248 s.

To further understand how points in the Pareto front differ from one another, we select 5 points along the final Pareto front of the workload (48M, 48R) and analyze the individual energy consumptions and makespans, as shown in Figs. 2 and 3. Figure 2 includes 5 subplots (a–e), and each subplot presents the energy consumption of each point in more detail. On the x-axis of each subplot, the slots are sorted by energy consumption in descending order. On the y-axis, we have the energy consumption of each slot. Note that each figure has different values along the y-axis. In Fig. 2e, the solution provides the lowest makespan, and the energy consumptions for all slots are unbalanced. This is because tasks are going to run on the slots that use more energy to reduce the system makespan. From Fig. 2d to Fig. 2a, we can see that the energy consumption becomes increasingly more balanced with respect to the makespan. In these cases, the NSGA-II algorithm focuses on trying to minimize the energy consumed, and thus, the makespan is compromised. As we see in the corresponding makespan subplots, from Fig. 3a to e, the makespan becomes increasingly more balanced with respect to the energy consumption. That is because each task has an affinity for the specific slot that minimizes its energy consumption.

6 Conclusion and Future Work

With the increasing need for big-data processing in Mapreduce clusters, improving Mapreduce performance while reducing energy cost has become a challenging problem. In this paper, we formulate this trade-off problem as a bi-objective optimization of energy consumption and makespan and first propose a two-phase heuristic allocation algorithm to find a feasible solution, which is then used as part of the initial population for the NSGA-II algorithm to construct the Pareto front for Mapreduce resource allocation problem. By performing experiments on real workloads, the results show that both of the proposed algorithms provide very fast and high quality Pareto optimal

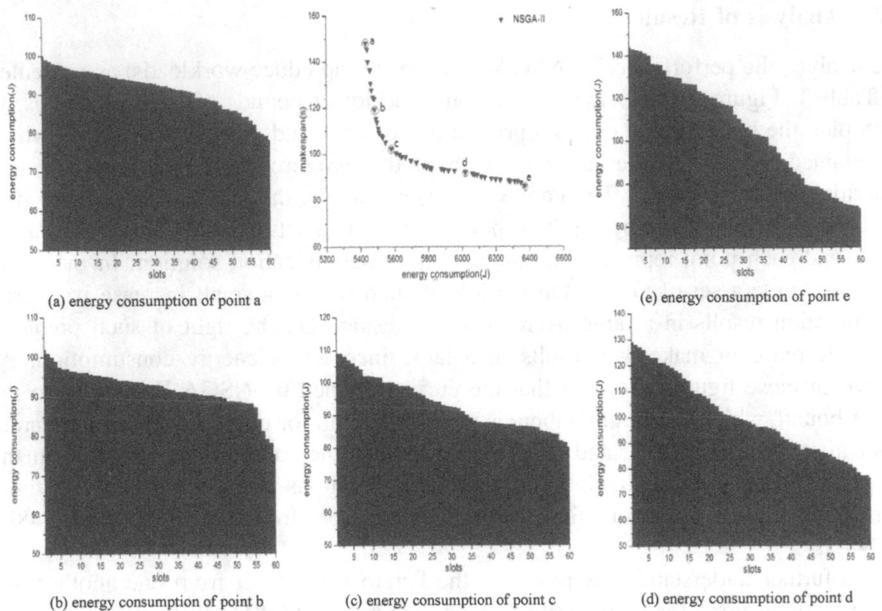

Fig. 2. Energy Consumptions in the Pareto front of workload (48M, 48R)

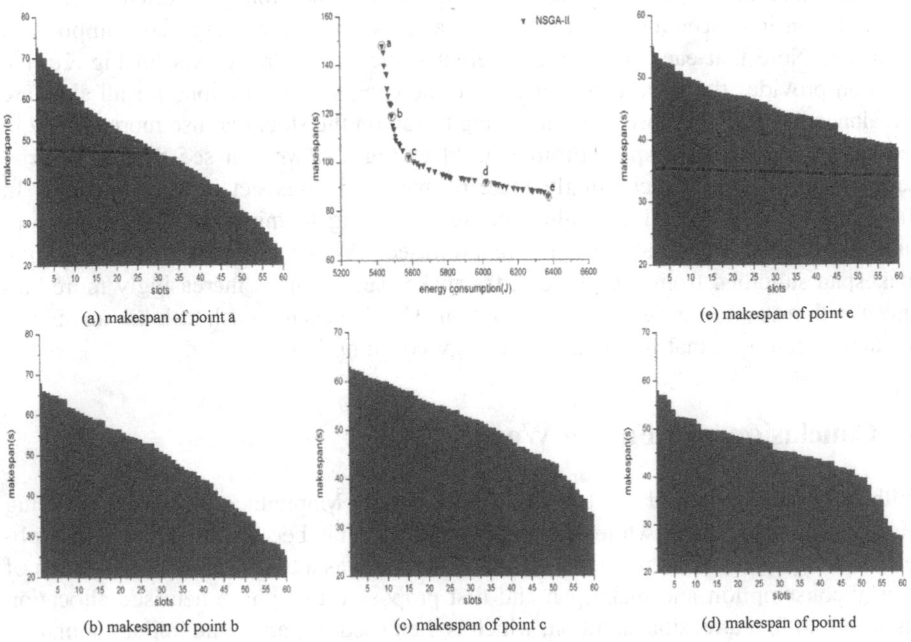

Fig. 3. Makespans in the Pareto front of workload (48M, 48R)

solutions, making them suitable for Mapreduce applications. Given these solutions, a system manager can be allowed to select an appropriate resource allocation solution from the Pareto front that balances the energy and performance needs of the system.

Acknowledgments. This paper was supported by the National Natural Science Foundation of China (Nos. 61762091, 61662088), the Natural Science Foundation of Yunnan Province of China (No. 2017ZZX228), Program for Excellent Young Talents of Yunnan University, and Training Program of National Science Fund for Distinguished Young Scholars.

References

1. Dean, J., Ghemawat, S.: MapReduce: simplified data processing on large clusters. Commun. ACM **51**(1), 107–113 (2008)
2. Hadoop: http://Hadoop.apache.org/. Accessed 15 Nov 2017
3. Wirtz, T., Ge, R.: Improving Mapreduce energy efficiency for computation intensive workloads. In: Proceedings on the Green Computing Conference and Workshops, pp. 1–8. IEEE, Orlando (2011)
4. Goiri, Í., Le, K., Nguyen, T.D., Guitart, J., Torres, J., Bianchini, R.: GreenHadoop: leveraging green energy in data-processing frameworks. In: 7th ACM European conference on Computer Systems, pp. 57–70. ACM, New York (2012)
5. Johnson, C., Chiu, D.: Hadoop in flight: migrating live MapReduce jobs for power-shifting data centers. In: 9th International Conference on Cloud Computing, pp. 92–99. IEEE (2017)
6. Liao, B., Tao, Z., Yu, J., Yin, L.T., Guo, G., Guo, B.L.: Energy consumption modeling and optimization analysis for MapReduce. J. Comput. Res. Dev. **53**(9), 2107–2131 (2016)
7. Zaharia, M., Konwinski, A., Joseph, A.D., Katz, R.H., Stoica, I.: Improving MapReduce performance in heterogeneous environments. In: 8th USENIX Symposium on Operating Systems Design and Implementation, p. 7. USENIX, San Diego (2008)
8. Xiao, B., Wang, Z., Liu, Q., Liu, X.D.: SMK-means: an improved mini batch K-means algorithm based on Mapreduce with big data. Comput. Mater. Continua **56**(3), 365–379 (2018)
9. Ren, Z.J., Wan, J., Shi, W.S., Xu, X.H., Zhou, M.: Workload analysis, implications, and optimization on a production hadoop cluster: a case study on taobao. IEEE Trans. Serv. Comput. **7**(2), 307–321 (2014)
10. Zhang, J.X., Xie, N., Zhang, X.J., Yue, K., Li, W.D., Kumar, D.: Machine learning based resource allocation of cloud computing in auction. Comput. Mater. Continua **56**(1), 123–135 (2018)
11. Chen, C., Xu, Y.F., Zhu, Y.Q., Sun, C.Y.: Online MapReduce scheduling problem of minimizing the makespan. J. Comb. Optim. **33**(2), 590–608 (2017)
12. Friese, R., Brinks, T., Oliver, C., Siegel, H.J., Maciejewski, A.A.: Analyzing the trade-offs between minimizing makespan and minimizing energy consumption in a heterogeneous resource allocation problem. In: 2nd International Conference on Advanced Communications and Computation, pp. 81–89. IARIA XPS, Venice (2012)
13. Tarplee, K., Friese, R., Maciejewski, A., Siegel, H.J., Chong, E.K.P.: Energy and makespan tradeoffs in heterogeneous computing systems using efficient linear programming techniques. IEEE Trans. Parallel Distrib. Syst. **27**(6), 1633–1646 (2016)
14. Lin, J.C., Leu, F.Y., Chen, Y.: Impact of MapReduce policies on job completion reliability and job energy consumption. IEEE Trans. Parallel Distrib. Syst. **26**(5), 1364–1378 (2015)

15. Mashayekhy, L., Nejad, M.M., Grosu, D., Zhang, Q., Shi, W.S.: Energy-aware scheduling of Mapreduce jobs for big data applications. IEEE Trans. Parallel Distrib. Syst. **26**(10), 2720–2733 (2015)
16. Zhang, X., Li, W., Liu, X., Zhang, X.: A profit-maximum resource allocation approach for Mapreduce in data centers. In: Au, M.H.A., Castiglione, A., Choo, K.-K.R., Palmieri, F., Li, K.-C. (eds.) GPC 2017. LNCS, vol. 10232, pp. 460–474. Springer, Cham (2017). https://doi.org/10.1007/978-3-319-57186-7_34
17. Li, W.D., Liu, X., Zhang, X.J., Cai, X.B.: A Task-type-based algorithm for the energy-aware profit maximizing scheduling problem in heterogeneous computing systems. In: 15th IEEE/ACM International Symposium on Cluster, Cloud and Grid Computing (CCGrid), pp. 1107–1110. IEEE, Shenzhen (2015)
18. Li, W.D., Liu, X., Cai, X.B., Zhang, X.J.: Approximation algorithm for the energy-aware profit maximizing problem in heterogeneous computing systems. J. Parallel Distrib. Comput. **124**, 70–77 (2019)
19. Deb, K., Pratap, A., Agarwal, S., Meyarivan, T.: A fast and elitist multiobjective genctic algorithm: NSGA-II. IEEE Trans. Evol. Comput. **6**(2), 182–197 (2002)
20. Graham, R.L.: Bounds on multiprocessing timing anomalies. SIAM J. Appl. Math. **17**(2), 416–429 (1969)
21. Huang, S., Huang, J., Dai, J.Q., Xie, T., Huang, B.: The HiBench benchmark suite: characterization of the MapReduce-based data analysis. In: 26th International Conference on Data Engineering Workshops, pp. 41–51. IEEE, Long Beach (2010)
22. Braun, T.D., et al.: A comparison of eleven static heuristics for mapping a class of independent tasks onto heterogeneous distributed computing systems. J. Parallel Distrib. Comput. **61**(6), 810–837 (2001)

FSampleJoin: A Fixed-Sample-Based Method for String Similarity Joins Using MapReduce

Decai Sun[1,2(✉)] and Xiaoxia Wang[1]

[1] College of Information Science and Technology, Bohai University, Jinzhou 121013, China
{sdecai,wxxsdc}@163.com
[2] Key Laboratory of Big Data in Digital Publishing, SAPPRFT, Jinzhou, China

Abstract. Data integration and data cleaning have received significant attention in the last three decades, and similarity joins is a basic operation in these areas. In this paper, a new fixed-sample-based algorithm, called FSampleJoin, is proposed to do string similarity joins using MapReduce. Our algorithm employs a filter-verify based framework. In filter stage, a fixed-sample partition scheme is adopted to generate high-quality signatures without losing any true pairs. In verify stage, a secondary filter is employed to eliminate the dissimilar string pairs further, and the remaining candidate pairs are verified with length-aware verification method. Experimental results show that our algorithm outperforms state-of-the-art approaches though they are similar in condition of edit distance zero.

Keywords: String similarity joins · MapReduce · Data integration · Big data

1 Introduction

Data integration and data cleaning are essential techniques in big data processing, and they have received significant attention in the last three decades. The similarity joins [1–4] is a basic operation in many applications, such as data integration and cleaning, near duplicate detection, entity resolution, document clustering, cloud data searching, and so on. It can find all similar string pairs from sets quickly. In literature, many similarity functions have been proposed to quantify the similarity between two strings, such as edit distance [5, 6], hamming distance, Jaccard similarity, Cosine similarity, Dice similarity, and so on. The edit distance between two strings is the minimum number of single character insertions, deletions and replacements required to transform one string into another. In this paper, we focus on string similarity joins with edit distance constraints.

Existing methods to address similarity joins can be broadly classified into two categories [7], in-memory algorithms and parallel algorithms. MapReduce is a famous framework proposed by Google to facilitate processing large-scale data in parallel. The MapReduce programs run on a large cluster with multiple nodes. MapReduce framework [7–9] is widely used to design parallel similarity joins algorithms. PassJoinKMR [6] is a self-join (only one set) algorithm based on MapReduce, but its verification time is a little longer. MassJoin [7] is an efficient two sets similarity joins algorithm using MapReduce, and it supports both set-based and character-based similarity joins. However, MassJoin

X. Sun et al. (Eds.): ICAIS 2019, LNCS 11633, pp. 251–262, 2019.
https://doi.org/10.1007/978-3-030-24265-7_22

generates a large numbers of signatures in filtration stage, which incur on more filtration time although some signatures are reduced in its merge algorithm. To accelerate string similarity joins with edit distance constraints, we devise a novel MapReduce based string similarity joins algorithm and some effective techniques are developed to accelerate string similarity joins. To summarize, we make the following contributions.

(1) We devise a fixed-sample-based string similarity joins algorithm using MapReduce, called FSampleJoin, which can find all similar string pairs between two sets.
(2) In our algorithm's filter stage, a fixed-sample partition scheme is adopted to generate high-quality signatures without losing any true pairs. Then the optimal functions between fixed-sample length and edit distance for three real-world datasets are obtained.
(3) We propose a Standard-Match filter to filtrate the dissimilar string pairs in filter stage and a secondary filter to filtrate dissimilar sting pairs further in verify stage.

The rest of this paper is organized as follows. Section 2 introduces the problem formulation and related works. Section 3 provides a partition scheme with fixed-samples. Section 4 details our algorithm's framework. Section 5 provides the experimental results and the conclusion is made in Sect. 6.

2 Preliminary

2.1 Problem Formulation

In this paper, we focus on string similarity joins between two string sets with edit distance constraints. The problem to be solved is formalized as follows.

Definition 1 (String Similarity Joins with Edit Distance Constraints). *Given two string sets R, S and an edit distance threshold τ, a string similarity join finds all similar string pairs $<r, s>$, $r \in R, s \in S$ such that $ed(r, s) \leq \tau$.*

An example with two string sets R, S is shown in Table 1. In a row of the example sets, the number before flag '#' is string's ID and the right characters are string's content.

Table 1. Example string set R and S

String set R	String set S
1#TAATGA	1#ATATGA
2#TACTTGTG	2#TAAGTGA

2.2 Related Work

Parallel algorithms run on a computer cluster, but it is difficult to share data among computer nodes. Vernica et al. [10] utilizes the prefix filtering to support set-based similarity functions. They used each token in its prefix as a key and the string as a value to generate the key-value pairs. However, a single token will generate many false positives and thus lead to poor pruning power. V-SMART-Join [11] is a 2-stage algorithm for similarity joins on sets. They also used a single token as a key. Afrati et al. [12] proposed multiple algorithms to perform similarity joins in a single MapReduce stage. However, it is expensive to transfer the strings using a single MapReduce stage for long strings. Lin et al. [6] extended PassJoin algorithm for large-scale data using MapReduce framework, and proposed two algorithms to do similarity joins, i.e. PassJoinKMR and PassJoinKMRS. However, its verification time is a little longer. Deng et al. [7] also extended PassJoin and proposed a new MapReduce based algorithm, called MassJoin, to support both set-based and character-based similarity functions. They devised a merge-based algorithm to significantly reduce the number of key-value pairs without sacrificing the pruning power. Ma et al. [13] proposed a parallel similarity joins on massive high-dimensional data using MapReduce. Rong et al. [14] propose a duplicate-free framework, called FS-Join, to perform set similarity joins. FS-Join employs three powerful filtering methods to prune dissimilar string pairs without computing their similarity scores.

3 Fixed-Sample Partition Scheme

Given a string r and an edit distance threshold τ. We can partition it into $\tau+1$ disjoint segments, also called signatures, and we ensure that the length of each segment is not smaller than one. Consider another string s, if s has no substring that matches a segment of r, r and s cannot be a similar pair because their edit distance must larger than τ based on the pigeonhole principle [15]. For a given string r, there are many strategies to partition the string into $\tau+1$ disjoint segments. Pass-Join [15] and Mass-Join [7] employed an even-partition scheme, and it makes each segment have nearly the same length. But the more segments we partition, the higher pruning power it is. So we can partition string into more than $\tau+1$ segments.

Lemma 1. *Given a string r with $\tau+k$ disjoint segments and a string s. There must exist at least k segments of r are matched by substrings of s if $ed(r,s) \le \tau$.*

Lemma 1 is an inference of lemma 1 in [15], and it can also be proofed using pigeonhole principle. In MapReduce based methods, more different segments means that it will take more time for shuffling and sorting. In this paper, we devise a new partition scheme to improve the performance of similarity joins by generating high-quality signatures in filter stage. There are many strategies to partition the string into $\tau+k$ disjoint segments, here we partition strings with Definition 2.

Definition 2. *Given a string r and an edit distance threshold τ, if $|r| \ge \tau+k, k \ge 1$ we partition r into $\tau+k$ disjoint substrings with fixed length q, called q-samples. The rest of substring is discarded because it is shorter than q.*

In Definition 2, string r cannot be partitioned if $|r| < \tau+1$, otherwise it is divided into $\tau+k$ or $\tau+k+1$ segments. The length of $(\tau+k+1)$-th segment must be shorter than q if it exist. Here, the $(\tau+k+1)$-th segment is discarded for reducing signatures and easy processing.

Lemma 2. *Given a string r and an edit distance threshold τ, r is partitioned with Definition 2. Given another string s. There must exist at least k q-samples of r are matched by substrings of s if $ed(r,s) \leq \tau$.*

Lemma 2 is a special case of Lemma 1, and it can also be proofed with the pigeonhole principle. There are a huge amount of strings in set S, and the vast majority are not similar to r. Another important issue is how to eliminate these strings which are not similar to r quickly. Given two strings r and s, we can transform one into another with edit operations. Let r_i denotes a substring of r and s_j denotes a substring of s. A **true τ match** is a pair $<r_i, s_j>$ which have two apparent features. (a) s_j and r_i have the same content. (b) s_j and r_i are corresponding pairs, i.e., we can align s_j to r_i by using at most τ edit operations on both left and right of s_j, and vice versa.

Lemma 3 (Standard-Match filter). *Given two strings r, s, r is partitioned with Definition 2. Let r_i denotes the i-th q-sample of r with start position p_i^r and s_j denotes a substring of s with start position p_j^s. Suppose $|r|$ is the length of r and $|s|$ is the length of s. If $\left|p_j^s - p_i^r\right| + \left||s| - |r| + p_i^r - p_j^s\right| > \tau$, $<r_i, s_j>$ must not be a true τ match between r and s. In other word, $<r_i, s_j>$ is not a true τ match if $p_j^s \notin [p_i^r + \lceil(-\tau + |s| - |r|)/2\rceil, p_i^r + \lfloor(\tau + |s| - |r|)/2\rfloor]$.*

Proof. Suppose $<r_i, s_j>$ is a match pair between r and s, i.e., $r_i = s_j$ and $|r_i| = |s_j|$. Suppose $p_1^r = 0, p_1^s = 0$. Let r_l denotes the left substring of r_i and r_r denotes the right substring of r_i. Let s_l denotes the left substring of s_j and s_r denotes the right substring of s_j. If we cannot align s_j to r_i by edit on s_l and s_r within τ edit operations, then $<r_i, s_j>$ must not be a true τ match. In other word, $ed(s_l, r_l) + ed(s_r, r_r) > \tau$. Suppose l_1 is the length difference between s_l and r_l, then $l_1 = ||s_l| - |r_l|| = \left|p_j^s - p_i^r\right|$. Based on the principle of edit distance, we have $ed(s_l, r_l) \geq l_1 = \left|p_j^s - p_i^r\right|$, i.e., $ed(s_l, r_l) \geq \left|p_j^s - p_i^r\right|$. Suppose l_2 is the length difference between s_r and r_r, then $l_2 = ||s_r| - |r_r|| = \left|(|s| - (p_j^s + 1) - |s_j|) - (|r| - (p_i^r + 1) - |r_i|)\right|$. Based on the principle of edit distance and $|r_i| = |s_j|$, then we have $ed(s_r, r_r) \geq l_2 = \left||s| - |r| + p_i^r - p_j^s\right|$, i.e., $ed(s_r, r_r) \geq \left||s| - |r| + p_i^r - p_j^s\right|$. If $\left|p_j^s - p_i^r\right| + ||s| - |r| + p_i^r - p_j^s| > \tau$ then we have $ed(s_l, r_l) + ed(s_r, r_r) > \tau$. In a result, if $\left|p_j^s - p_i^r\right| + ||s| - |r| + p_i^r - p_j^s| > \tau$ then $<r_i, s_j>$ must not be a true τ match between r and s. Now, we discuss the range of p_j^s, and we already have $\left|p_j^s - p_i^r\right| + \left||s| - |r| + p_i^r - p_j^s\right| > \tau$. (a) When $p_j^s \geq p_i^r$, then $\left|(|s| - |r|) - (p_j^s - p_i^r)\right| > \tau - (p_j^s - p_i^r) \Rightarrow p_j^s - p_i^r > (|s| - |r| + \tau)/2$ or $|s| - |r| > \tau$. (b) When $p_j^s < p_i^r$, then $|(|s| - |r|) + (p_i^r - p_j^s)| > \tau + (p_j^s - p_i^r) \Rightarrow p_j^s - p_i^r < (|s| - |r| - \tau)/2$ or $|s| - |r| < -\tau$. Based on principle of edit distance, $<r_i, s_j>$ must not be a true τ match if $|s| - |r| > \tau$ or $|s| - |r| < -\tau$. So we only concern the condition $-\tau \leq |s| - |r| \leq \tau$. Since (a) and $-\tau \leq |s| - |r| \leq \tau$, then we have $p_j^s - p_i^r > (|s| - |r| + \tau)/2 \geq 0$. Since (b) and $-\tau \leq |s| - |r| \leq \tau$, then we have $p_j^s - p_i^r < (|s| - |r| - \tau)/2 \leq 0$. We combine $p_j^s - p_i^r > (|s| - |r| + \tau)/2 \geq 0$ with

$p_j^s - p_i^r < (|s| - |r| - \tau)/2 \leq 0$, then we have $p_j^s \notin [p_i^r + \lceil(-\tau + |s| - |r|)/2\rceil, p_i^r + \lfloor(\tau + |s| - |r|)/2\rfloor]$ because $p_j^s - p_i^r$ is an integer.

Lemma 3 shows that some match pairs are invalid because they do not satisfy the position constraint. With Standard-Match filter, match pairs which satisfy $\left|p_j^s - p_i^r\right| + \left||s| - |r| + p_i^r - p_j^s\right| \leq \tau$ are reserved and others are eliminated.

4 Similarity Join with Fixed-Samples

Given two string sets R, S and an edit distant threshold τ. The task of string similarity joins is to find all similar pairs between R and S. To avoid enumerating all string pairs from two given string sets, we adopt the filter-verify framework. Here, a fixed-sample-based similarity joins algorithm, called FSampleJoin, is proposed to perform string similarity joins using MapReduce. In our method, the parameter Q is a given fixed length of q-sample in Definition 2 and Q is inversely proportional to τ. We formalize a function as follow.

$$Q = \begin{cases} \infty & \tau = 0 \\ \max(1, \lfloor \frac{b}{\tau^a} + \frac{1}{2} \rfloor) & \tau > 0 \end{cases} \tag{1}$$

In (1), a and b are two unknown parameters which vary from string sets, and they will be discussed in experiment section. In our algorithm, three MapReduce stages are designed to do similarity joins, i.e. filter stage, verify1 stage and verify2 stage.

4.1 Filter Stage

In filter stage, we generate index signatures for R and match signatures for S. Our filter stage includes three phases, i.e., map, shuffle and reduce. We generate signatures for two string sets in map. Each mapper's input is a key-value pair $< sn, split >$, sn is the split number and $split$ is the content of a row in set R or S. First, the input split's source set is identified, and then we generate index signatures for R or match signatures for S. For example string sets in Table 1, the index signatures and match signatures are shown in filter stage of Fig. 1.

Signature for R: If the input split's source is R, we emit index signatures. First, string ID and content are extracted from *split* by identifying flag '#'. Suppose r is a string of R. Let *rid* denotes r's ID and $|r|$ denotes the length of r. If $\lfloor|r|/(\tau+1)\rfloor \geq Q$ the string r is partitioned using Definition 2 with $q = Q$, and it generate $\tau + k$ q-samples, i.e., $k \geq 1$. If $\lfloor|r|/(\tau+1)\rfloor < Q$, the string r is partitioned using Definition 2 with $q = \lfloor|r|/(\tau+1)\rfloor$, and it generates $\tau + 1$ q-samples. In summary, we partition r using Definition 2 with $q = \min(\lfloor|r|/(\tau+1)\rfloor, Q)$. Let p_i^r denote the start position of i-th q-sample in r, i.e., $1 \leq i \leq \tau + k, p_1^r = 0, p_i^r = (i-1) * q$. $r[p_i^r, q]$ denotes the i-th q-sample. The outputs of each map are key-value pairs. We take each q-sample as an index signature and emit $< r[p_i^r, Q], ('I', rid, |r|, p_i^r) >$, $1 \leq i \leq \tau + k, p_1^r = 0$, $p_i^r = (i-1) * q$. Therein, flag 'I' is a mark which represents an index signature. At last, there at least $\tau + 1$ index signatures are generated for each string r.

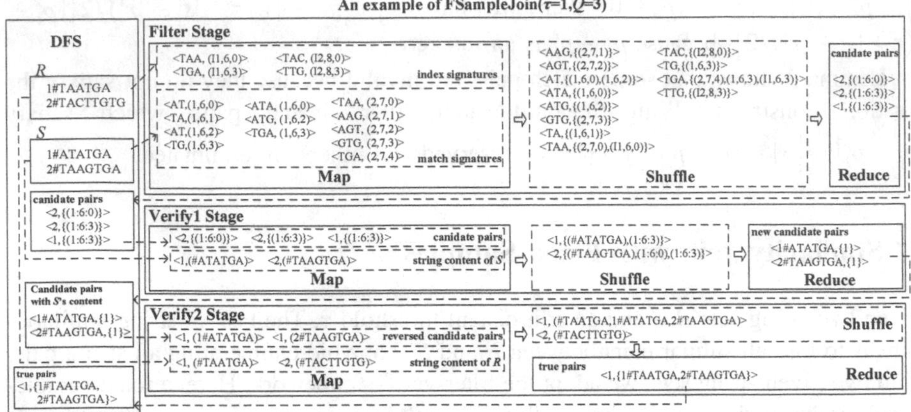

Fig. 1. An example of FSampleJoin

map: $<sn, split> \;-> \;<r[p_i^r, q, ('I', rid, |r|, p_i^r)>$

Signature for S: If the input split's source is S, we emit match signatures. First, string ID and content are extracted from *split*. Suppose s is a string of S. Let *sid* denotes s's ID and $|s|$ denotes the length of s. Because r is partitioned with Definition 2 as above. According to Lemma 2, s must contains at least k index signatures of r if s is similar to r with $ed(r, s) \leq \tau$. There are many substrings in s, but it is unnecessary to generate all substrings as signatures. Based on edit distance, r must not similar to s if r's length satisfies $|r| < |s| - \tau$ or $|r| > |s| + \tau$. So we only need to generate signatures for these string r which length satisfies $|s| - \tau \leq |r| \leq |s| + \tau$. We vary lr from $|s| - \tau$ to $|s| + \tau$ step by one, and s's signatures for matching r with length $|r| = lr$ can be generated in each step. As above, set R's strings with length lr are partitioned into $\tau + k$ q-samples with Definition 2, i.e., $q = \min(\lfloor lr/(\tau + 1) \rfloor, Q)$. So we only generate signatures for these $\tau + k$ q-samples. So only s's substrings with length q are considered and others are ignored. A **q-gram** is a substring with fixed length q, such as $s[p_j^s, q]$ with start position p_j^s. Q-gram is different form q-sample because q-grams can be overlapped. According to Lemma 3, $<r_i, s_j>$ must not be a true τ match if $p_j^s \notin [p_i^r + \lceil (-\tau + |s| - lr)/2 \rceil, p_i^r + \lfloor (\tau + |s| - lr)/2 \rfloor]$. Since $p_i^r = (i - 1) \times q$, we only generate all q-grams in $[(i - 1) \times q + \lceil (-\tau + |s| - lr)/2 \rceil, (i - 1) \times q + \lfloor (\tau + |s| - lr)/2 \rfloor]$ as signatures for q-sample r_i. As lr varies from $|s| - \tau$ to $|s| + \tau$, we discover that there exist many reduplicated q-grams which are generated by different lr. So a non-reduplicated hash set *pqs* is created to eliminate these reduplicated q-grams. The outputs are also key-value pairs, we emit $<s[p_j^s, q], (sid, |s|, p_j^s)>$.

map: $<sn, split> \;-> \;<s[p_j^s, q], (sid, |s|, p_j^s)>$

In shuffle phase, the key-value pairs emitted in maps are shuffled and sorted, and then key-value pairs with same signatures are transferred to the same reduce node.

In reduce phase, each reducer's input is a key-value pair, i.e., $<signature, list(('I', rid, |r|, p_i^r)/(sid, |s|, p_j^s))>$. First, the list is traversed and values are processed one by one. Each value can be identified to be an index value or a match value with flag 'I'. Then all values are added into two lists separately, i.e., index values are added into *Ilist* and match values are added into *Slist*. In this signature, we can confirm that there is no candidate pair if *Ilist* is null or *Slist* is null because there is no match between match signatures and index signatures. Now, we process items in *Slist* one by one, and suppose *Slist*[*j*] is the *j*-th item in *Slist*. For a *Slist*[*j*], we traverse *Ilist* one time to find match pairs. Let *Ilist*[*i*] denotes the *i*-th item in *Ilist*. The pair $<Ilist[i], Slist[j]>$, $Ilist[i] = (rid, |r|, p_i^r), Slist[j] = (sid, |s|, p_j^s)$, is a potential pair. We adopt the Standard-Match filter criterion to judge whether it is a true τ match or not. In other word, if $<Ilist[i], Slist[j]>$ satisfy $\left|p_j^s - p_i^r\right| + \left||s| - |r| + p_i^r - p_j^s\right| \leq \tau$ we add $rid : |r| : p_i^r$ into a list $list(rid : |r| : p_i^r)$. Otherwise *Ilist*[*i*] are ignored. At end of processing *Slist*[*j*], we emit a key-value pair for *Slist*[*j*], i.e., $<sid, list(rid : |r| : p_i^r)>$. For the example above, the other signatures are invalid except "TAA" and "TGA".

reduce: $<signature, list(('I', rid, |r|, p_i^r)/(sid, |s|, p_j^s))>$ –> $<sid, list(rid : |r| : p_i^r)>$

4.2 Verify1 Stage

The main task of verify stage is to find true pairs. At the end of filter stage, a string pair $<r, s>, r \in R, s \in S$ which shares at least one q-sample is added into a candidate set. But there also exist many candidate pairs can be removed further because they must shares more than one q-sample according to Lemma 2. Through the analysis of candidate set, we find two problems to be solved urgently. (a) There exist many reduplicated $rid : |r| : p_i^r$ in a *sid*'s candidate list. (b) We cannot verify the candidate pairs because there are only strings' IDs but contents. We discuss the second problem first. Here the method proposed in MassJoin [7] is adopted to read contents of all candidate pairs, and two verify stages are designed to solve problem (a) and (b), i.e., verify1 stage and verify2 stage.

The main task of verify1 are reading contents of *S* and filtrating with the secondary filter. It also includes three phases. The inputs of map phase are string set *S* and the output of filter stage. In a mapper, the input source is judged first. If it is a string *s* of set *S*, we emit a key-value pair $<sid, \#s>$. Therein '#' is a flag which represents the content of string *sid*. If the input is a key-value pair of filter result, we output the key-value pair directly, i.e., $<sid, list(rid : |r| : p_i^r)>$.

map: $<sn, split>$ –> $<sid, \#s>$ map: $<sid, list(rid : |r| : p_i^r)>$ –> $<sid, list(rid : |r| : p_i^r)>$

In shuffle phase, the pairs with same *sid* are transferred to the same reduce node. In reduce phase, each reducer's input is a key-value pair $<sid, list(list(rid : |r| : p_i^r)/\#s)>$ which contains all candidate pairs between string *s* and set *R*. First, an empty non-reduplicated hash map *rhm* is created and each item *rhm*[*id*] is a list. Then the list $list(list(rid : |r| : p_i^r)/\#s)$ is traversed one by one. For an item, it is the content of *s* if it contains flag '#', otherwise it is a list $list(rid : |r| : p_i^r)$. For $\#s$, we store this content. For $list(rid : |r| : p_i^r)$, we push $|r|$ and p_i^r into *rhm*[*rid*] if *rhm* don't contains this *rid*, otherwise we append p_i^r to *rhm*[*rid*]. We process all items of $list(list(rid : |r| : p_i^r)/\#s)$ like this. To count the number of a *rid*'s distinct q-samples which are matched by *s*, all items in *rhm*[*rid*] are traversed. For *rhm*[*rid*], we get out $|r|$ from the first item of *rhm*[*rid*], and then others p_i^r are added into a non-reduplicated hash set *phs* to eliminate reduplications. At end of processing $rhm[rid]$, the size of phs is the number of distinct q-samples of rid matched by s. Now we perform the secondary filtration. According to Lemma 2, the rid is added into final list $list(rid)$ if $size(phs) \geq \lfloor |r|/\min(\lfloor |r|/(\tau+1) \rfloor, Q) \rfloor - \tau$. Otherwise we discard it. At last, all items in rhm is processed and a candidate list $list(rid)$ is formed. At the end of reduce, we emit a key-value pair, i.e., $< sid\#s, list(rid) >$.

reduce: $< sid, list(list(rid : |r| : p_i^r)/\#s) >$ –> $< sid\#s, list(rid) >$

4.3 Verify2 Stage

At the end of verify1 stage, some false candidate pairs are discarded and the final candidate set is formed. In this candidate set, each candidate pairs' contents of S are extracted. But we still cannot verify the candidate pairs for the absence of the contents of R. The mains task of verify2 are reading contents of R and verifying candidate pairs. The inputs of map phase are string set R and the output of verify1 stage. In a mapper, the input source is judged first. If it is a string r of set R, we emit a key-value pair as verify1, i.e., $< rid, \#r >$. If it is a key-value pair $< sid\#s, list(rid) >$ which is the output of verify1, then we traverse all rid in list. For each rid, we emit a key-value pair which is composed of rid and $sid\#s$, i.e., $< rid, sid\#s >$.

map: $< sn, split >$ –> $< rid, \#r >$ map: $< sid\#s, list(rid) >$ –> $< rid, sid\#s >$

In reduce phase, we verify the candidate pairs and the true pairs are drawn. In a reducer, the input is a key-value pair $< rid, list(sid\#s/\#r) >$. The items of $list(sid\#s/\#r)$ are traversed to get out the content of r. A value is r's content if its first character is '#', otherwise it is $sid\#s$. For $\#r$, we store this content. At the end of process, we can confirm that no candidate pair is found if there is no $\#r$ or $sid\#s$, and we output nothing. Otherwise, we traverse all $sid\#s$ in $list(sid\#s/\#r)$, and then all candidate pairs $< rid\#r, sid\#s >$ are verified with length-aware verification method [15]. A candidate pair is a true pair if $ed(r, s) \leq \tau$, and we emit a result key-value pair, i.e., $< ed(r, s), (rid\#r, sid\#s) >$.

reduce: $< rid, list(sid\#s/\#r) >$ –> $< ed(r, s), (rid\#r, sid\#s) >$

5 Experiment

5.1 Experiment Environment

We implement our algorithm FSampleJoin with Java under Hadoop 1.2.1, and the MassJoin's Merge algorithm (we called MassJoinMerge) [7] is implemented with the same tool. Three real-world datasets are used in our experiments. They are DBLP author + title (http://dblp.uni-trier.de/xml/), GenBank EST (ftp://ftp.ncbi.nlm.nih.gov/genbank/) and PubMed abstract (ftp://ftp.ncbi.nlm.nih.gov/pubmed/baseline/). The information of datasets is shown in Table 2. All experiments were performed on Hadoop and run on a 5-node cluster. Each node has Intel i5 4590 3.7 GHZ processor with 4 cores, 16 GB RAM, and 1 TB disk. Each node is installed 64-bit Ubuntu 17.10, Java 1.7 and Hadoop 1.2.1. In the following experiments, we split each dataset into two datasets with equal number of strings (R and S) to conduct similarity joins.

Table 2. The information of datasets

Datasets	Size (MB)	Number of strings	Average length	Alphabet size
DBLP author + title	327.8	4,000,000	76.2	96
GenBank EST	667.6	2,000,000	340.6	15
PubMed abstract	332.5	400,000	862.9	158

5.2 Performance of FSampleJoin

The most important evaluation criterion for similarity joins is the time consumption of join. We first evaluated our algorithm's performance by varying Q. We run our algorithm on three datasets with different τ and Q. Then we gain the optimal lengths with different datasets and the edit distances, and then the results are shown in Table 3.

Table 3. The optimal fixed length Q

Datasets	The optimal combination of τ and Q				
DBLP author + title	τ=1, $Q = 35$	τ=2, $Q = 20$	τ=4, $Q = 15$	τ=6, $Q = 10$	τ=8, $Q = 8$
GenBank EST	τ=2, $Q = 80$	τ=5, $Q = 44$	τ=10, $Q = 20$	τ=15, $Q = 16$	τ=20, $Q = 12$
PubMed abstract	τ=4, $Q = 78$	τ=12, $Q = 42$	τ=24, $Q = 18$	τ=36, $Q = 16$	τ=48, $Q = 14$

By analyzing the relationship between the optimal lengths and edit distance in each dataset, it proves that Q is inversely proportional to τ. To find out the optimal value of a and b in formula (1), we fit curves using experimental data in Table 3. Then we gain the optimal parameters on each dataset, i.e., {a = 0.6844, b = 34.311} on DBLP author + title, {a = 0.7997, b = 142.9912} on GenBank EST and {a = 0.7101, b = 214.0078} on PubMed abstract. These parameters are adopted in the experiments below.

5.3 Comparison with Existing Methods

We perform MassJoinMerge and FSampleJoin on DBLP author + title, on GenBank EST, and on PubMed abstract. The experimental results are calculated and shown in Figs. 2, 3 and 4.

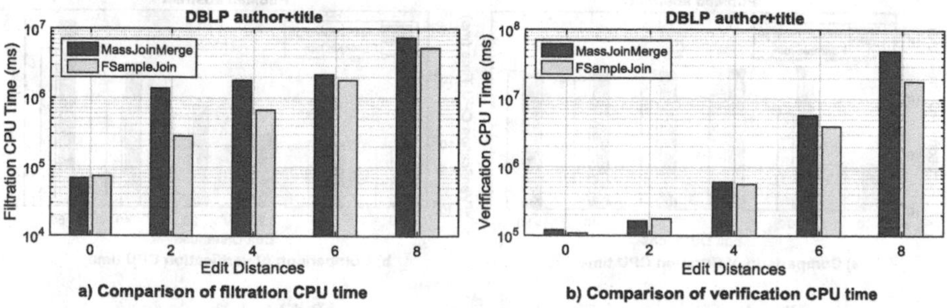

Fig. 2. Filtration time and verification time on DBLP author + title

As shown in Fig. 2, 3 and 4(a), the filtration times of FSampleJoin are shorter than those of MassJoinMerge in condition of most edit distances, and they are similar when the edit distance is zero. As shown in Figs. 2, 3 and 4(b), the verification times of FSampleJoin are shorter than those of MassJoinMerge in condition of big edit distances, and they are similar when the edit distances are small. The reasons are presented as follows.

(1) In FSampleJoin, the rest of substrings except fixed q-samples are discarded in generating index signatures for dataset *R*. In generating match signatures, only fixed q-samples' match signatures are generated, and these signatures are also filtrated by Standard-Match filter. The total number of signatures is incomparable between MassJoinMerge and FSampleJoin because the generating scheme is different. But the total workload of filtration is reduced in condition of most edit distances compared with MassJoinMerge.
(2) In FSampleJoin, fixed q-sample scheme is adopted and the length *Q* is compute with different parameters for different datasets. The total filtration ability of our method is increased because these parameters in formula (1) do a good tradeoff between filtration and verification.

The total CPU time of each algorithm is also calculated, and the performances of algorithms are shown in Fig. 5. The total CPU time of FSampleJoin is always shorter than that of MassJoinMerge except the condition of edit distance 0. And it is similar to that of MassJoinMerge when edit distance is zero. Compare with MassJoinMerge, the join speed is increased by using the fixed-sample scheme in our FSampleJoin.

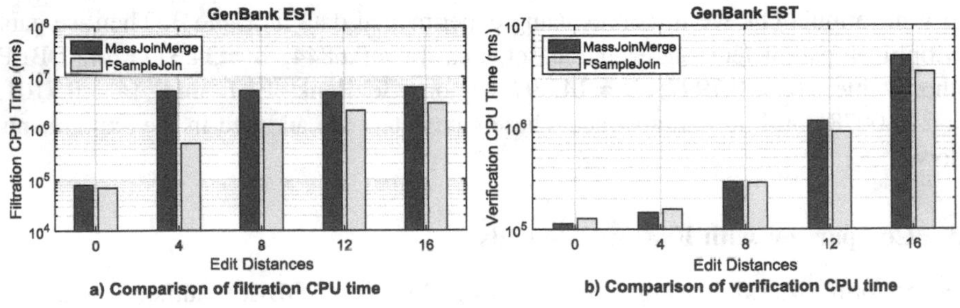

Fig. 3. Filtration time and verification time on GenBank EST

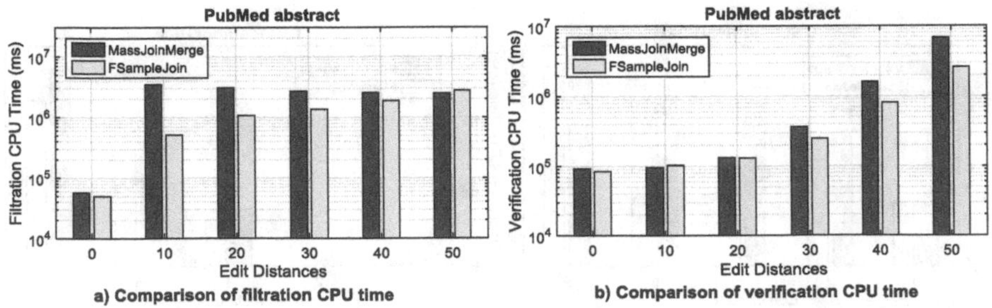

Fig. 4. Filtration time and verification time on PubMed abstract

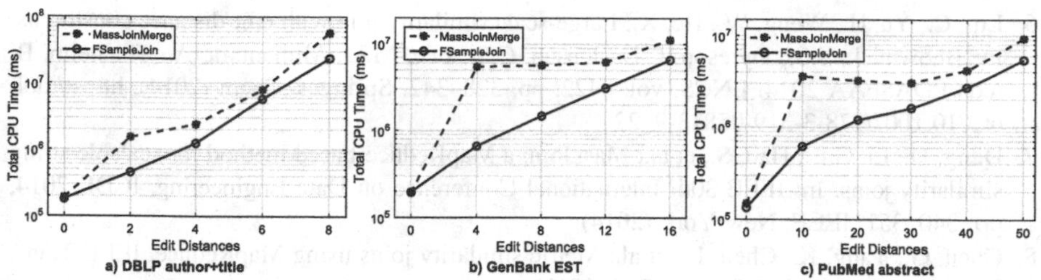

Fig. 5. Total CPU time

6 Conclusion

In this paper, we research on the problem of string similarity joins with edit distance constraints. We propose a MapReduce-based algorithm to do similarity joins in parallel. In our algorithm, the filter-verify framework is employed to eliminate the dissimilar string pairs quickly. In filter stage, a fixed-sample-based scheme is proposed to generate high-quality signatures, and then a large number of dissimilar string pairs are eliminated with Standard-Match filter. In verify stage, the candidate pairs are filtrated with the secondary filter and their contents are extracted. Then the true pairs are extracted by verifying each candidate pair with length-aware verification method. Experimental results on real-world datasets show that our algorithm outperforms state-of-the-art approaches though they are similar in condition of edit distance zero. To improve the versatility of our algorithm, we will research on designing new filtration criterions to decrease the total time consumption.

Acknowledgements. This work was supported in part by the Humanity and Social Science Youth foundation of Ministry of Education of China under Grant 15YJC870021, Scientific Research Foundation of the Education Department of Liaoning Province of China under Grant L2015010, NSFC under Grant 61602056, Natural Science Foundation of Liaoning Province of China under Grant 20170540015, and Social Science Foundation of Liaoning Province of China under Grant L18AXW001.

References

1. Silva, Y.N., Pearson, S.S., Chon, J., et al.: Similarity joins: their implementation and interactions with other database operators. Inf. Syst. **52**(8–9), 149–162 (2015)
2. Yu, M., Li, G., Deng, D., Feng, J.: String similarity search and join: a survey. Front. Comput. Sci. **10**(399–417), 2 (2016)
3. Pagh, R.: Large-scale similarity joins with guarantees. In: 18th International Conference on Database Theory, ICDT 2015, pp. 15–24. Dagstuhl, Brussels Belgium (2015)
4. Wu, C., Zapevalova, E., Chen, Y., Li, F.: Time optimization of multiple knowledge transfers in the big data environment. CMC: Comput. Mater. Continua **54**(3), 269–285 (2018)
5. Levenshtein, V.: Binary codes capable of correcting deletions, insertions, and reversals. Sov. Phys. Dokl. **10**(8), 707–710 (1966)

6. Lin, C., Yu, H., Weng, W., He, X.: Large-scale similarity join with edit-distance constraints. In: Bhowmick, S.S., Dyreson, C.E., Jensen, C.S., Lee, M.L., Muliantara, A., Thalheim, B. (eds.) DASFAA 2014. LNCS, vol. 8422, pp. 328–342. Springer, Cham (2014). https://doi.org/10.1007/978-3-319-05813-9_22
7. Deng, D., Li, G.L., Hao, S., et al.: MassJoin: a MapReduce-based method for scalable string similarity joins. In: IEEE 30th International Conference on Data Engineering, ICDE 2014, pp. 340–351. IEEE, New York (2014)
8. Chen, G., Yang, K., Chen, L., et al.: Metric similarity joins using MapReduce. IEEE Trans. Knowl. Data Eng. **29**(656–69), 7–8 (2017)
9. Xiao, B., Wang, Z., Liu, Q., Liu, X.: SMK-means: an improved mini batch K-means algorithm based on Mapreduce with big data. CMC: Comput. Mater. Continua **56**(3), 365–379 (2018)
10. Vernica, R., Carey, M.J., Li, C.: Efficient parallel set-similarity joins using MapReduce. In: 2010 ACM SIGMOD International Conference on Management of data, pp. 495–506. ACM, Indianapolis (2010)
11. Metwally, A., Faloutsos, C.: V-SMART-Join: a scalable MapReduce framework for all-pair similarity joins of multisets and vectors. Proc. Vldb Endowment **5**(8), 704–715 (2012)
12. Afrati, F.N., Sarma, A.D., Menestrina, D., et al.: Fuzzy joins using MapReduce. In: IEEE 28th International Conference on Data Engineering, pp. 498–509. IEEE, Washington, DC (2012)
13. Ma, Y., Meng, X., Wang, S.: Parallel similarity joins on massive high-dimensional data using MapReduce. Concurrency Comput. Pract. Experience **28**(1), 166–183 (2016)
14. Rong, C. Lin, C., Silva, Y.N., Wang, J., Lu, W., Du, X.: Fast and scalable distributed set similarity joins for big data analytics. In: Proceedings of the IEEE 33rd International Conference on Data Engineering, pp. 1059–1070. IEEE, New York (2017)
15. Li, G., Dong, D., Wang, J., et al.: PASS-JOIN: a partition-based method for similarity joins. Proc. Vldb Endowment **5**(3), 253–264 (2011)

Mass Diffusion Recommendation Algorithm Based on Multi-subnet Composited Complex Network Model

Zhou Shuang, Bin Sheng, and Sun Gengxin(✉)

Qingdao University, Qingdao 266071, China
sungengxin@qdu.edu.cn

Abstract. Social recommendation algorithm that integrates social networks is widely used in big data information recommendation. However, there are many relationships among users of social networks, and the influence of each relationship on recommendation is different. Simply introducing a certain social relationship will inevitably affect the accuracy of recommendation algorithm. Based on multi-subnet composited complex network model, the multi-relationship composite network is constructed by loading multi-relationship social network on the user-commodity bipartite graph, and a mass diffusion recommendation algorithm based on multi-relationship composite network is proposed. The experimental results on real datasets Epioions and FilmTrust show that the proposed recommendation algorithm with two kinds of social relations has a significant improvement in recommendation accuracy and diversity compared with the recommendation algorithm with one kind of social relations and the traditional mass diffusion algorithm.

Keywords: Multi-subnet composited complex network model · Mass diffusion algorithm · Multi-relationship social network · Recommendation algorithm

1 Introduction

With the advent of the era of big data, information on the Internet has exploded. Although people is given more choice, this brings information overload problems [1–5]. It is difficult for traditional information retrieval methods to provide users with personalized information. It has become an urgent need for users to accurately obtain the personalized information they need from the vast amount of information. Recommendation system is produced under this background. It is considered as an effective way to solve the information overload problems. According to the user's historical information, the user interest is modeled. The personalized recommendation system is to recommend the information that the user may be interested in but not browsed to the user [6–8].

At present, personalized recommendation technology is divided into graph-based model recommendation [9], collaborative filtering recommendation [10], hybrid recommendation [11], and content-based recommendation [12]. There are two kinds of collaborative filtering recommendation algorithms, one is user-based collaborative

X. Sun et al. (Eds.): ICAIS 2019, LNCS 11633, pp. 263–274, 2019.
https://doi.org/10.1007/978-3-030-24265-7_23

filtering recommendation algorithm, the other is item-based collaborative filtering recommendation algorithm, such as mass diffusion algorithm [13] and heat conduction algorithm [14]. Traditional mass diffusion algorithm introduces the energy distribution principle of mass diffusion in physical dynamics into the bipartite graph. The similarity between different items is calculated by energy diffusion to recommend to users.

Guo et al. [15] proposed a mass diffusion algorithm that considers the influence of item popularity on user interest preferences by introducing adjustable parameters of item popularity. Hu et al. [16] introduced vocabulary into the bipartite graph. He discussed the recommendation implementation mechanism based on user, item and vocabulary tripartite graph, and proposed a tripartite graph recommendation implementation strategy for energy allocation. Zhou et al. [17] used the bipartite user-item graph to establish an association network. They proposed a mass diffusion algorithm based on network structure by using the association matrix. The above researchers only used the user-item scoring matrix to make recommendations for users. The data source is single. The researchers did not consider the impact of the relationship between users on the recommendation results, the recommendation results are not very accurate. In this paper, by constructing a multi-subnet composited complex network, multiple relationships among users are introduced into the recommendation system, which improves the accuracy of the recommendation algorithm.

2 Multi-subnet Composited Complex Network Model

Many complex systems can be found in the real world, such as recommendation system, biological system, traffic system and so on. By using complex networks [18–20], individuals in complex systems are abstracted into nodes, and relationships between individuals are abstracted into edges. Complex systems are modeled abstractly. For example, in a recommendation system, users and items are abstracted as nodes, and the relationships between users and users and the relationships between users and items are abstracted as edges.

Multi-subnet composited complex network model (referred to as the composite network) [20–23] defines the concept of subnet. Subnets are homogeneous individuals and their relationships. Through the recombination of multiple subnets, multiple relationships between different classes of individuals in a complex system are described. The model can be represented by a four-tuple $G = (V, E, R, F)$:

(1) $V = \{v_1, v_2, \ldots v_m\}$ is the set of nodes, and $m = |V|$ is the number of nodes in the set.
(2) $E = \{v_h, v_l | v_h, v_l \in V, 1 \le h, l \le m\} \subseteq V \times V$, which represents the set of edges between nodes.
(3) $R = R_1 \times \ldots \times R_i \times \ldots \times R_n = \{(r_1, \ldots, r_i \ldots, r_n) | \; r_i \in R_i, 1 \le i \le n\}$. R_i represents a set of interaction relationships between nodes, r_i represents an interaction relationship between nodes, and n is the number of interactions between nodes. If $n = 1$, only an interaction relationship between nodes is described. If > 1, there are multiple relationships between nodes.

(4) Map F: $E \overset{\varphi}{\rightarrow} R$ is the only corresponding mapping found in the set E through the φ function projection in F. It represents the type of relationship that the edges have. Figure 1 is an example of composite network $G = (V, E, R, F)$. Nodes represent different types of individuals, and edges represent the relationship between nodes, where $R = R_1 \times R_2, R_1 = \{r_1\}, R_2 = \{r_2\}$. As can be seen from Fig. 1, the edges $v_1, v_2, v_1, v_3, v_2, v_3$ have only R_1 relationship. The edges $v_2, v_5, v_3, v_5, v_4, v_5$ have only the R_2 relationship, and the edges v_3, v_4 have both the R_1 relationship and the R_2 relationship.

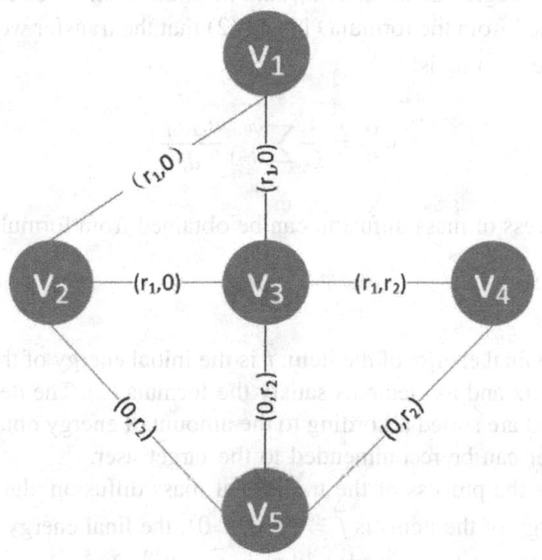

Fig. 1. Example of composite network G = (V, E, R, F)

3 Mass Diffusion Algorithm Based on Composited Network

3.1 Mass Diffusion Algorithm

Zhou et al. [17] proposed the mass diffusion algorithm firstly. The traditional mass diffusion algorithm is based on a user-item bipartite graph network. It recommends items for a specific target user. The item selected by the user is given a unit of energy, and the initial energy of the items unselected is 0, which is regarded as the initial state. The node with energy distributes the energy evenly to the users who have chosen it, so that the energy propagates from the item to the user. After the propagation of items to users, the energy h_i obtained by the user u_i is:

$$h_i = \sum\nolimits_{\beta=1}^{n} \frac{a_{i\beta} f_\beta}{k_\beta} \tag{1}$$

Where, k_β is the degree of o_β. n is the number of items, and f_β is the energy of o_β. If item o_β is selected by user u_i, then $a_{i\beta} = 1$, otherwise $a_{i\beta} = 0$.

Then, the user distributes the energy evenly to the selected item, and the energy is propagated back from the user to the item. After that, the energy f'_α obtained by the item o_α is:

$$f'_\alpha = \sum\nolimits_{i=1}^{m} \frac{a_{i\alpha} h_i}{d_i} \tag{2}$$

Where, d_i is the degree of the user u_i, and m is the number of users.

It can be obtained from the formula (1) and (2) that the transfer weight $w^M_{\alpha\beta}$ between the item o_β and the item o_α is:

$$w^M_{\alpha\beta} = \frac{1}{k_\beta} \sum\nolimits_{i=1}^{m} \frac{a_{i\alpha} a_{i\beta}}{d_i} \tag{3}$$

The whole process of mass diffusion can be obtained from formula (1), (2) and (3):

$$\vec{f}' = W^M \vec{f} \tag{4}$$

Where, $\vec{f}'$ is the final energy of the item. $\vec{f}$ is the initial energy of the item. W^M is the state transition matrix and its elements satisfy the formula (2). The items that the target user has not selected are sorted according to the amount of energy obtained last, and the items ranked higher can be recommended to the target user.

Figure 2 shows the process of the traditional mass diffusion algorithm. Assuming that the initial energy of the items is $\vec{f} = (1, 0, 1, 0)$, the final energy of the items after propagation by the mass diffusion algorithm is $\vec{f}' = (\frac{19}{24}, \frac{5}{24}, \frac{5}{8}, \frac{3}{8})$.

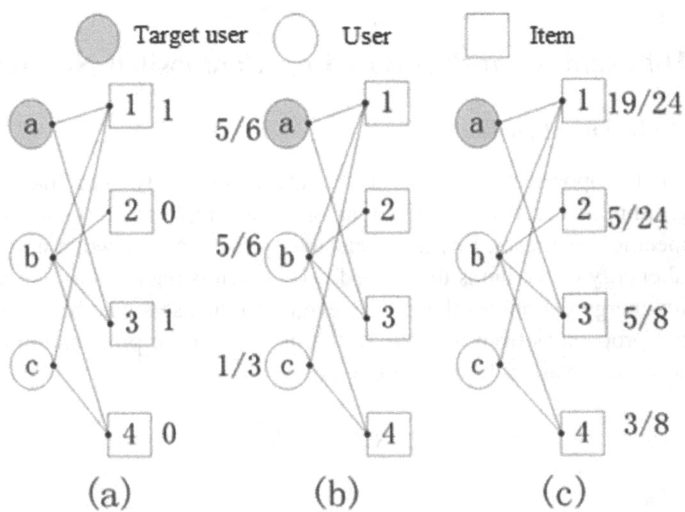

Fig. 2. Mass diffusion process based on user-item bipartite graph

3.2 Mass Diffusion Algorithm Based on Composited Network

The traditional mass diffusion algorithm only recommends items based on users' rating of items, and does not consider the impact of users' social network on recommendations. By building a multi-relationship composite network, the initial energy of item nodes is diffused in the composite network by edges, thus achieving the goal of introducing social network information for recommendation.

Assume that the selection relationship between users and items in the composite network is relationship r_1. If a relationship between users is introduced, the relationship is assumed to be r_2. Assume that the relationship strength of r_1 and r_2 is 1. The relation strength proportion coefficient of r_1 is sf_1. The relation strength proportion coefficient of r_2 is $sf_2.sf_1 + sf_2 = 1$. Assuming that sf_1 is p, then sf_2 is $1 - p$, $p \in (0,1)$. When introducing a relationship between users, the process of mass diffusion algorithm based on composite network is as follows:

(1) The item selected by the target user is given a unit of energy, which is the initial energy of the item.

(2) The energy in the item is transmitted to the user through the edge, and the energy h_i obtained by the user node u_i is:

$$h_i = \sum\nolimits_{\beta=1}^{n} \frac{a_{i\beta}^1 f_\beta}{\hat{k}_{v_\beta}^{r_1}} \tag{5}$$

Where, $a_{i\beta}^1 = 1$ represents that there is an r_1 relationship between the user u_i and the item o_β. $a_{i\beta}^1 = 0$ represents that there is no r_1 relationship between the user u_i and the item o_β. $a_{i\beta}^2$ is the same. $\widehat{k}_{v_\beta}^{r_1}$ represents the degree of the item o_β with respect to the relationship r_1.

(3) The energy in the user is transmitted to the user and the item through the side, and the energy $h_j^{'}$ obtained by the user node u_{j} is:

$$h_j^{'} = \sum\nolimits_{i=1}^{m} \left(\frac{a_{ij}^1 sf_1 h_i}{\hat{k}_{v_i}^{r_1}} + \frac{a_{ij}^2 sf_2 h_i}{\hat{k}_{v_i}^{r_2}} \right) \tag{6}$$

The energy $f_\alpha^{'}$ obtained by the item o_α is:

$$f_\alpha^{'} = \sum\nolimits_{i=1}^{m} \left(\frac{a_{i\alpha}^1 sf_1 h_i}{\hat{k}_{v_i}^{r_1}} + \frac{a_{i\alpha}^2 sf_2 h_i}{\hat{k}_{v_i}^{r_2}} \right) \tag{7}$$

(4) The energy of the users who propagate after the social network is further propagated to the items. The energy $f_{\alpha}^{''}$ obtained by the item o_{α} is:

$$f_{\alpha}^{''} = \sum\nolimits_{j=1}^{m} \frac{a_{j\alpha}^{1} h_{j}^{'}}{\hat{k}_{v_j}^{r_1}} \tag{8}$$

Therefore, the total energy g_{α} obtained by item o_{α} is:

$$g_{\alpha} = f_{\alpha}^{'} + f_{\alpha}^{''} \tag{9}$$

Formula (5) (6) (7) (8) (9) shows that the transfer weight $w_{\alpha\beta}^{SM}$ between item elements o_{α} and o_{β} is:

$$w_{\alpha\beta}^{SM} = \frac{1}{\hat{k}_{v_\beta}^{r_1}} \sum\nolimits_{i=1}^{m} a_{i\beta}^{1} \left(\frac{a_{i\alpha}^{1} sf_1}{\hat{k}_{v_i}^{r_1}} + \frac{a_{i\alpha}^{2} sf_2}{\hat{k}_{v_i}^{r_2}} \right) + \frac{1}{\hat{k}_{v_\beta}^{r_1}} \sum\nolimits_{j=1}^{m} \frac{a_{j\alpha}^{1}}{\hat{k}_{v_j}^{r_1}} \sum\nolimits_{i=1}^{m} a_{i\beta}^{1} \left(\frac{a_{ij}^{1} sf_1}{\hat{k}_{v_i}^{r_1}} + \frac{a_{ij}^{2} sf_2}{\hat{k}_{v_i}^{r_2}} \right) \tag{10}$$

The items that the user has not selected are sorted according to the final energy. And then a recommendation list is formed. When $p = 1$, that is, the relation strength proportion coefficient of relation r_2 is 0, the mass diffusion algorithm based on composite network degenerates to the traditional mass diffusion algorithm. Figure 3 shows mass diffusion process based on composite network introducing one relationship between users. Assume that $p = 0.5$.

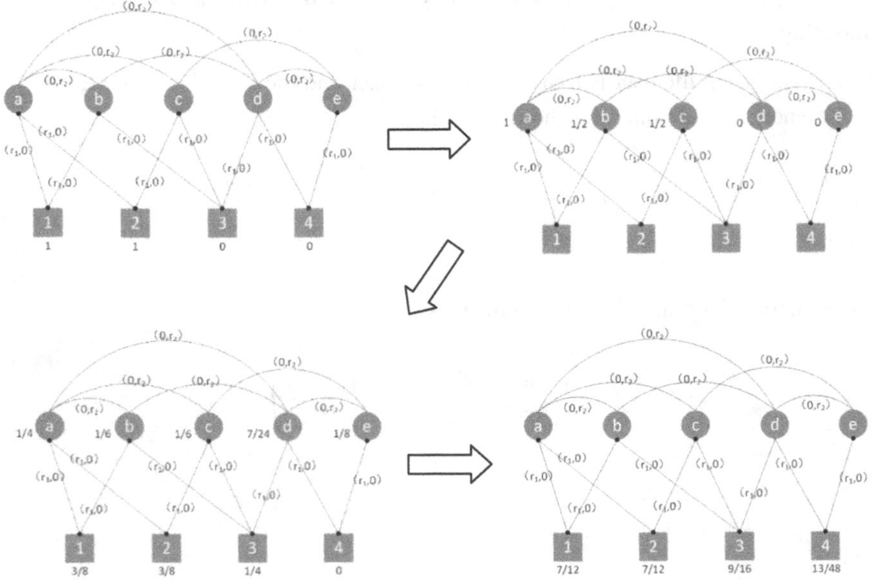

Fig. 3. Mass diffusion process based on composited network introducing one relationship between users

However, there are multiple relationships between users of social networks. The impact of each relationship on the recommendation is different. Multiple relationships between users can be loaded through the composite network's load operation [20]. Assuming that there are two relationships between users, another one can be loaded in the composite network in Fig. 3 using load operations. The relationship between users and items in the new composite network is still r_1, and the relationship between users is changed from r_2 only to r_2 and r_3. Assuming that the relation strength proportion coefficient of r_1 is p, and the r relation strength proportion coefficient of r_2 is $(1-p)q$, the relation strength proportion coefficient of r_3 is $(1-p)(1-q)$. The transfer weight $w_{\alpha\beta}^{SM}$ between the item elements o_α and o_β is:

$$w_{\alpha\beta}^{SM} = \frac{1}{\hat{k}_{v_\beta}^{r_1}} \sum\nolimits_{i=1}^{m} a_{i\beta}^{1} \left(\frac{a_{i\alpha}^{1} sf1}{\hat{k}_{v_i}^{r_1}} + \frac{a_{i\alpha}^{2} sf2}{\hat{k}_{v_i}^{r_2}} + \frac{a_{i\alpha}^{3} sf3}{\hat{k}_{v_i}^{r_3}} \right) + \frac{1}{\hat{k}_{v_\beta}^{r_1}} \sum\nolimits_{j=1}^{m} \frac{a_{j\alpha}^{1}}{\hat{k}_{v_j}^{r_1}} \sum\nolimits_{i=1}^{m} a_{i\beta}^{1} \left(\frac{a_{ij}^{1} sf1}{\hat{k}_{v_i}^{r_1}} + \frac{a_{ij}^{2} sf2}{\hat{k}_{v_i}^{r_2}} + \frac{a_{ij}^{3} sf3}{\hat{k}_{v_i}^{r_3}} \right) \tag{11}$$

Figure 4 shows mass diffusion process based on composite network introducing two relationships between users. Assume that $p = 0.5$ and $q = 0.5$.

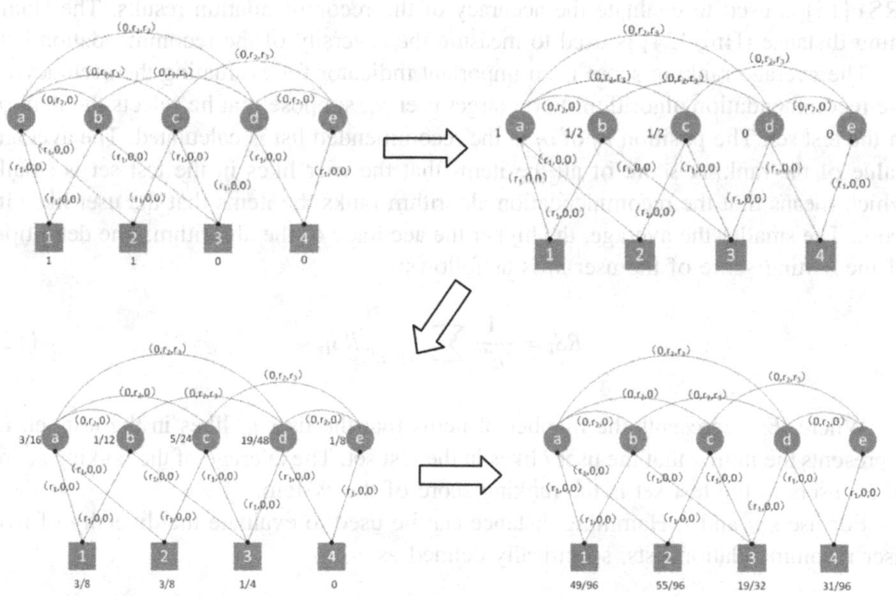

Fig. 4. Mass diffusion process based on composited network introducing two relationships between users

When $q = 0$ or $q = 1$, that is, the relation strength proportion coefficient of r_2 or relation strength proportion coefficient of r_3 is 0, the mass diffusion algorithm based on composite network introducing two relationships between users degenerates into the algorithm introducing one relationship.

4 Experimental Results and Analysis

4.1 Experimental Data

In this paper, the Epinions data set and the FilmTrust data set commonly used in the recommendation system are used to evaluate the proposed recommendation algorithm. The Epinions dataset includes 40,163 users, 139,738 items, 487,182 trust relationships between users and users, and 664,823 user ratings for items. The ratings usually represented by values 1 through 5. The Film Trust dataset includes 1,050 users, 2071 items, 1853 trust relationships between users and users, and 35,497 user ratings for items. When the user's score is more than 2, it means that the user likes the item. An edge is established between the user and the item. In addition, the data in the data set is preprocessed to eliminate the outliers and ensure that each user has at least one choice of items.

4.2 Evaluation Indicators

To verify the performance of the algorithm, the data set was randomly divided into two parts: 90% of the training set and 10% of the test set. The average ranking score (RS) [15] is used to evaluate the accuracy of the recommendation results. The Hamming distance (Hm) [24] is used to measure the diversity of the recommendation list.

The average ranking score is an important indicator for evaluating the accuracy of the recommendation algorithm. For a target user u_i, suppose that he selects the item o_j in the test set. The position r_{ij} of o_j in the recommended list is calculated. The average value of the ranking score of all the items that the user likes in the test set is small, which means that the recommendation algorithm ranks the items that the user likes in front. The smaller the average, the higher the accuracy of the algorithm. The definition of the sorting score of the user u_i is as follows:

$$RS_i = \frac{1}{|E_i^P|} \sum\nolimits_{(i\alpha) \in E_i^P} RS_{i\alpha} \tag{12}$$

Where, E_i^P represents the number of items that the user u_i likes in the test set. $i\alpha$ represents the item α that the user i likes in the test set. The average of the ranking score of all users in the test set is the ranking score of the system.

For users u and t, Hamming distance can be used to evaluate the diversity of two user recommendation lists, specifically defined as:

$$H_{ut}(L) = 1 - \frac{Q_{ut}(L)}{L} \tag{13}$$

Where, $Q_{ut}(L)$ represents the number of identical items in the user u and t recommendation list. L represents the length of the recommended list. The average hamming distance for all users is the hamming distance of the entire recommendation system. The greater the hamming distance, the higher the diversity of recommendations.

4.3 Comparison of Experimental Results

In the experiment, the simulation method was adopted to determine the values of p and q. When $q = 0$ and p take different values, the RS of Epinions data set is shown in Fig. 5.

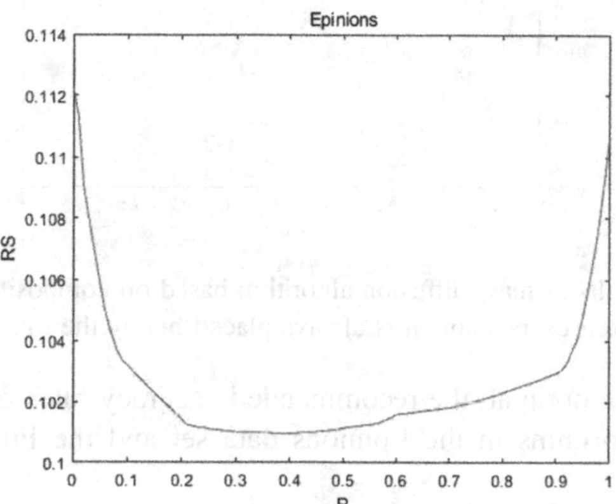

Fig. 5. Simulation results of mass diffusion algorithm based on composite network introducing one relationship between users

It can be seen from Fig. 5 that RS has the minimum value when $p = 0.4$, which represents that in the Epinions data set, the accuracy rate is highest when $p = 0.4$ for mass diffusion algorithm based on composite network introducing one relationship between users.

O_u and O_v respectively represent the collection of items purchased by user u and user v. The more items that users u and v have purchased together, the more likely they will have common interests and influence each other.

$$f_{uv} = \frac{O_u \cap O_v}{O_u \cup O_v} \tag{14}$$

When $f_{uv} > 0.2$, it means that the interests between users are similar, and the relationship between users satisfying this condition is r_3. When $p = 0.4$, the r_3 relationship is loaded by using load operations. When q takes different values, the change of RS is shown in Fig. 6.

It can be seen from Fig. 6 that when $q = 0.13$, the value of RS is the smallest. This represents that in the Epinions data set, the mass diffusion algorithm based on the composite network introducing two relationships between users at p = 0.4 and q = 0.13.

The best values of the Film Trust data sets p and q can be obtained by simulation experiments, which are 0.94 and 0.91, respectively.

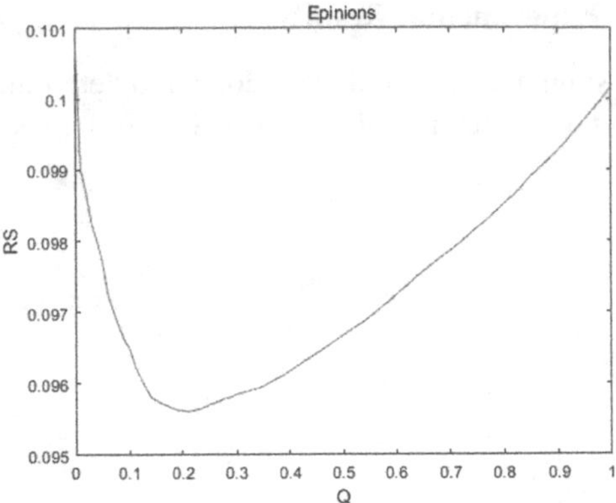

Fig. 6. Simulation results of mass diffusion algorithm based on composite network introducing two relationships between users. caption is always placed below the illustration.

When p and q are optimal, the recommended accuracy rates obtained by different recommendation algorithms in the Epinions data set and the FilmTrust data set are shown in Table 1.

Table 1. Different algorithm experiment results.

Data set	Mass diffusion algorithm based on bipartite graph	Mass diffusion algorithm based on composite network introducing one relationship between users	Mass diffusion algorithm based on composite network introducing two relationship between users
Epinions	0.11078	0.10096	0.09561
Film Trust	0.03507	0.03443	0.03431

It can be seen from Table 1 that on the Epinions data set and the Film Trust data set, the recommendation accuracy rate of the mass diffusion algorithm based on composite network introducing two relationships between users is better than the algorithm introducing one relationship and the algorithm based on bipartite graph.

In addition to accuracy, the diversity of recommendation lists is also an important evaluation indicator for the recommendation system. As can be seen from formula (13), the size of the recommended list length affects the value of the average Hamming distance. Figures 7 and 8 show respectively the changes in the recommended diversity of the Epinions data set and the Film Trust data set for different recommended list lengths.

It can be seen from Figs. 7 and 8 that in the same data set and the same algorithm, when the recommended list length L takes different values, the recommended diversity is different. And the larger the L value, the higher the recommended diversity. On the Epinions dataset and the Film Trust dataset, the recommendation diversity of the recommendation algorithm introducing two social relationships is significantly improved compared to the algorithm introducing one social relationship and the traditional mass diffusion algorithm.

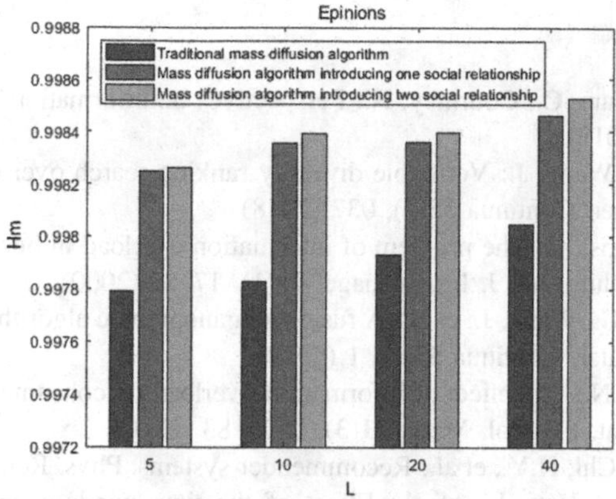

Fig. 7. Experimental results of different algorithm diversity on Epinions

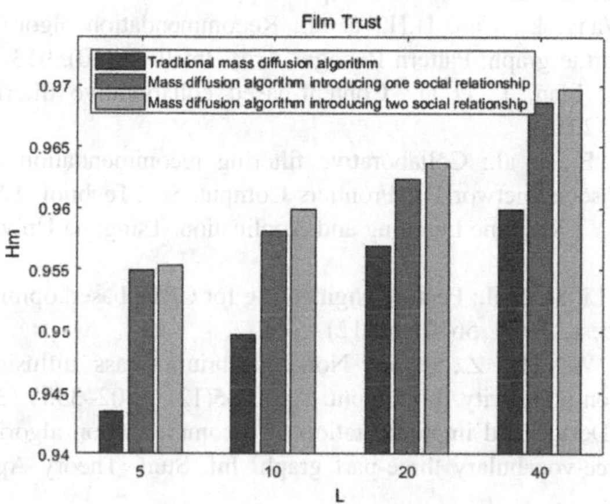

Fig. 8. Experimental results of different algorithm diversity on Film Trust

5 Conclusion

By integrating social network information and constructing multi-relational composite network, the proposed algorithm based on mass diffusion of composite network effectively improves the accuracy of recommendation, which shows that integrating social network information into recommendation system can better identify potential items of interest to users. Introducing two relationships between users is better than introducing one and not introducing. From this, it is better to introduce multiple social relationships. Whether there are other relationships between the user? How they affect the recommendation results? In the future research, we should further explore these problems.

References

1. Bawden, D., Holtham, C., Courtney, N.: Perspectives on information overload. Aslib Proc. **51**(8), 249–255 (2013)
2. Liu, Y., Peng, H., Wang, J.: Verifiable diversity ranking search over encrypted outsourced data. Comput. Mater. Continua **55**(1), 037 (2018)
3. Edmunds, A., Morris, A.: The problem of information overload in business organisations: a review of the literature. Int. J. Inf. Manage. **20**(1), 17–28 (2000)
4. Meng, R., Rice, S.G., Wang, J., et al.: A fusion steganographic algorithm based on Faster R-CNN. Comput. Mater. Continua **55**(1), 1 (2018)
5. Lee, B.K., Lee, W.N.: The effect of information overload on consumer choice quality in an on-line environment. Psychol. Mark. **21**(3), 159–183 (2010)
6. Lü, L., Medo, M., Chi, H.Y., et al.: Recommender systems. Phys. Rep. **519**(1), 1–49 (2012)
7. Guo, Q., Song, W., Hou, L., et al.: Effect of the time window on the heat-conduction information filtering medel. Phys. A **401**(5), 15–21 (2014)
8. Chen, Z., Li, Z.: Collaborative filtering recommendation algorithm based on user characteristics and item attributes. J. Comput. Appl. **31**
9. Zhang, Y.M., Wang, L., Cao, H.H., et al.: Recommendation algorithm based on user-interest-item tripartite graph. Pattern Recogn. Artif. Intell. **28**(10), 913–921 (2015)
11. Lu, Z., Dou, Z., Lian, J., et al.: Content-based collaborative filtering for news topic recommendation (2015)
12. Guo, N., Wang, B., et al.: Collaborative filtering recommendation algorithm based on characteristics of social network. J. Frontiers Comput. Sci. Technol. **12**, 208–217 (2018)
13. Zhou, Z., Wang, Y.: Machine Learning and Application. Tsinghua University Press, Beijing (2007)
14. Wang, R., Ju, J., Li, S., et al.: Feature engineering for CRFs based opinion target extraction. J. Chin. Inf. Process. **26**(2), 56–61 (2012)
15. Guo, Q., Song, W., Hu, Z., et al.: Non-equilibrium mass diffusion recommendation algorithm based on popularity. J. Comput. Appl. **35**(12), 3502–3505 (2015)
16. Hu, J., Lin, X.: Design and implementation of recommendation algorithm based on user-socialized resource-vocabulary three-part graph. Inf. Stud. Theory Appl. **32**(7), 130–134 (2016)
17. Zhou, T., Ren, J., Medo, M., et al.: Bipartite network projection and personal recommendation. Phys. Rev. E **76**(4), 046115 (2007)
18. Watts, D., Strogatz, S.: Collective dynamics of small-world networks. Nature **393**(6684), 440–442 (1998)
19. Barabási, A.L., Bonabeau, E.: Scale-free networks. Sci. Am. **288**(5), 60 (2003)
20. Sui, Y.: Research on multi-subnet composited complex network and its related properties. Qingdao University, Qingdao (2012)
21. Shao, F., Sun, R., Li, S.: Research of multi-subnet composited complex network and its operation. Complex Syst. Complex. Sci. **7**(4), 20–25 (2012)
22. Sui, Y., Shao, F.J., Sun, R.C., et al.: Formalized descriptions of dynamic reorganizations of multi-subnet composited complex network based on vector space. J. Software **26**(8), 2007–2019 (2015)
23. Bin, S., Sun, G.: Important node detection algorithm for multiple relationships online social network based on multi-subnet composited complex network model. J. Nanjing Univ. (Nat. Sci.) **53**(2), 378–385 (2017)
24. Zhu, Y., Lv, L.: Evaluation metrics for recommender systems. J. Univ. Electr. Sci. Technol. China **41**(2), 163–175 (2012)

Optimizing Word Embedding for Fine-Grained Sentiment Analysis

Wei Zhang(✉), Yue Zhang, and Kehua Yang

Key Laboratory for Embedded and Network Computing of Hunan Province, College of Computer Science and Electronic Engineering, Hunan University, Changsha 410082, China
zhangwei@hnu.edu.cn

Abstract. Word embeddings have been extensively used for various Natural Language Processing tasks. However, word vectors trained based on corpus context information fail to distinguish words with the same context but different semantics, which may lead to a similar word vector with opposite semantic terms. This will affect some Natural Language Processing tasks, such as fine-grained sentiment analysis tasks. In this paper, a new word vectors optimization model is proposed. This model can be applied to any pre-trained word vectors. Within a certain range, it can make the opposite semantic words away from each other, and the same semantic words are close to each other. The experimental results show that our model can improve the traditional word embedding in the fine-grained emotional analysis task of Chinese Weibo, and the optimized word vector using our model outperforms the unoptimized word vector.

Keywords: Word embeddings · Word vectors · Fine-grained sentiment analysis

1 Introduction

Deep Learning (DL) is such a powerful tool that we have seen tremendous success in areas such as Computer Vision, Speech Recognition, and Natural Language Processing [21]. And it provided a new direction for the development of these fields. The most exciting contribution of artificial neural network in the field of Natural Language Processing is the breakthrough of word embedding technology. Word embedding technology converts words into dense vectors, which appeared long ago. The early word vector is lengthy and sparse. It takes the size of the whole vocabulary as the dimension of the word vector. For each word appearing in the vocabulary, the corresponding position is marked as 1. This representation is called one-hot. It is common to represent words as indices in a vocabulary. But this fails to capture the rich relational structure of the lexicon, and is prone to dimensional disaster. Later, in 1986, distributional representation was proposed to map words through context information into a k-dimensional real vector [16], which effectively avoids the one-hot dimensional disaster and

X. Sun et al. (Eds.): ICAIS 2019, LNCS 11633, pp. 275–286, 2019.
https://doi.org/10.1007/978-3-030-24265-7_24

makes similar words have similar word vectors. Later, with the combination of word vector technology and artificial neural network, there are many models for generating word vectors through training methods. It includes C&W [3,4], Glove [14], Skip-gram [11,12] (Word2vec) and CBoW [11,12] (Word2vec). With the advent of these models, related tool libraries have also become popular. Among them, Word2vec and Glove have been widely used.

Most of the existing word embedding techniques use context information to train word vectors, and a few use other information to generate word vectors, such as character level subwords [2], semantic knowledge resources [5,6] and WordNet [13]. Ignoring a few parts, similar words have similar contextual structures in corpus, so it is undeniable that similar word vectors can be trained. However, in natural languages, many words with opposite meanings have similar contexts, such as "like" and "hate", and we can replace "I like you" with "I hate you". The context in which people express their likes and hates to someone or something is often similar, that is, context structure is similar. So, "like" and "hate" have similar word vectors, even their meanings are opposite. Such word vectors are difficult to use for some NLP tasks, such as fine-grained emotion analysis, emotion classification, etc.

2 Related Work

In order to distinguish similar word vectors with opposite meanings, some recently published studies have embedded tagged data in a supervised manner (Labutov and Lipson [8]; Ren [15]; Tang [20]; Maas [10]), and some have adjusted word vectors by moving it (Yu [22]). The former usually uses objective function to optimize the word vector based on the emotion polarity label (Positive or Negative) given by training instances; The latter optimizes word vectors by moving it, and needs to consult sentiment lexicons. The former model is to construct a new word vector model from the tag data, which relies on tag data and is not universally used in multiple learning models; The latter, by moving word vectors, in some cases produces a new problem of "different meanings but similar vectors" (For example, there are neutral words or words that are not included in the sentiment lexicons around a word with emotional polarity).

In this paper, we propose another optimization model for optimizing word vectors. By enumerating all the word vectors within a certain similarity range of the words to be optimized and combining with the emotional weights given by the sentiment lexicon, the model calculates the matching degree of all vector positions within the similarity range of the words to be optimized, finds the optimal matching position, and exchanges the word vectors to be optimized and the word vectors at that location. In this way, the word vectors are close to the adjacent word vectors with the same semantics and far away from the adjacent word vectors with different semantics, so that the word vectors in a certain range are sorted from near to far according to the emotional weights. Because we have similar word vectors with constrained swap positions, it does not cause too many changes in context (similar word vectors have the same context). Moreover, by constrained exchange ordering, our mode avoids moving the vector of words to be optimized to make it close to or far from some neutral words or words not included in the sentiment lexicon.

The proposed optimization model is evaluated by examining whether our optimized embeddings can improve conventional word embeddings and outperform previously proposed sentiment embeddings in some cases. To this end, we choose two kinds of common deep neural network classifiers: convolutional neural network (CNN) [7] and Bi-directional long-term memory (Bi-LSTM) [19]. We use traditional word embedding, the moving refined model version which is mentioned above, and our optimized version in these two classifiers respectively. Finally, the performance of the results is compared.

The rest of this paper is organized as follows. Section 3 describes the proposed word vector optimization model. Section 4 presents the evaluation results. Conclusions are drawn in Sect. 5.

3 The Proposed Approach

3.1 Optimization Process

Our word vector optimization requires a set of word vectors pre-trained by Word2vec or Glove and a sentiment lexicon with emotional polarity weights. We calculate all the word vectors of each sentiment word in the sentiment lexicon with its similarity δ (the range allowed to swap), and find the vector that is most suitable for exchanging with the sentiment word, and exchange the position with the constraint, so that the sentiment word is far from the word vector whose emotional polarity value is different from it, and is close to the word vector whose emotional polarity value is similar to it. Finally, after continuous exchange, all the word vectors within a certain range of similarity are reordered according to the emotional orientation value given by the sentiment lexicon, so as to ensure the vectors of similar emotional polarity values are clustered together and the vectors of different emotional orientation values are far away from each other. As shown in Fig. 1, the rank adjustment process is shown in a certain range. In Fig. 1, the closer the word is, the higher the similarity of the word vector. We can see that "喜欢" and "讨厌" are very close, but their emotional polarity values are quite different. By calculation, we find that "讨厌" is more suitable for location of "迷恋", and "迷恋" is also suitable for being exchanged for "讨厌". So we exchange word vectors of "讨厌" and "迷恋". Similarly, when all the word vectors in Fig. 1 are adjusted, we can get a new vector similarity rank in this range. In this rank, word vectors are sorted according to the size of the polarity of emotion.

What is the Constrained Location Exchange? In the process of swapping emotional words, some word vectors may be computed and swapped many times, which will make it farther and farther from the original position (all the positions before the adjustment starts), and lead to the change of the context of the word.

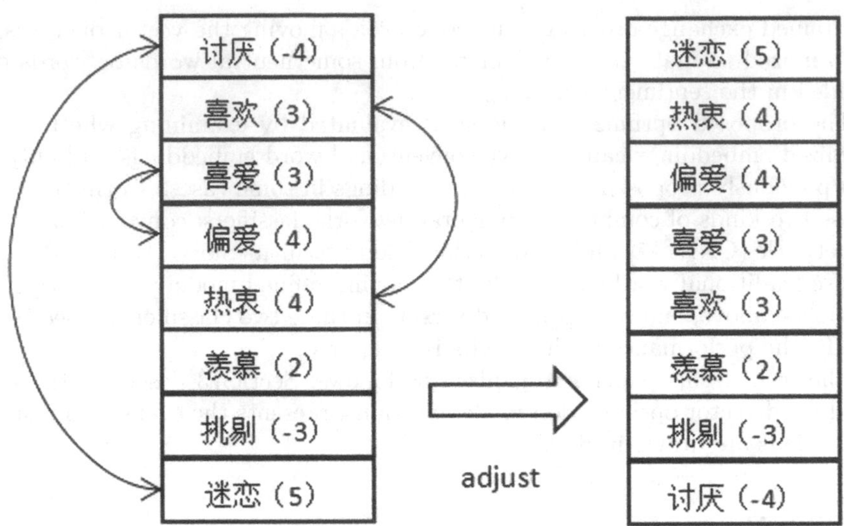

Fig. 1. Examples of word vector adjustment

Therefore, we propose the Constrained Location Exchange. In each exchange, we calculate the similarity between the position to be exchanged and the initial position, and exchange when the similarity is greater than δ.

For the modulus (length) of the word vector, Schakel and Wilson et al. [17] suggested that for the Word2vec vector, the length of the word vector depends on the accumulation in the direction of parameter update during training [17]. The vector modulus has nothing to do with the meaning of the word, so we ignore the change in the word vector modulus caused by the optimization.

What are the Advantages of Constrained Exchange Optimization? The refinement model proposed by Yu et al. [22] adopts the method of movement adjustment, which adjusts the emotional words in the sentiment lexicon, but does not considers some neutral words and emotional words that not included in the sentiment lexicon, which leads to the fact that the optimized word vector is far away from or close to these words. As shown in Fig. 2, "○" and "•" represent positive and negative emotional words respectively (e.g. "喜欢" and "讨厌"), and "⊗" represents emotional words that not included in the sentiment lexicon (e.g. "么么哒"). By moving word vectors, we can see that the model aggregates positive class and negative class respectively, and the emotional word "⊗", which is not included in the sentiment lexicon, is classified into negative class, but it may indicate positive class (e.g. "么么哒"). With the emergence of a large number of buzzwords and new words (such as microblog, Twitter, etc.), such inaccurate categorization will lead to inaccurate emotional analysis using the word embedding model. In addition, moving clustering will lead to accumulation of word vectors, resulting in a large number of word vectors with high similarity. By using our optimization model, the included and uncollected emotional words are compared and exchanged, and the neutral or uncollected emotional words can be well adjusted to the middle of the positive and negative classes (Fig. 3). Furthermore, our model avoids over-moving, does not produces a large number of word vectors with high similarity, and retains the original word vector distribution.

In Fig. 2, we traversed all the emotional words contained in the sentiment lexicon in the current scope. When traversing to the word vector A, we calculate that the most suitable position for A is the location of the word vector X. And when we exchange X to A, we have little influence on X. So, we exchange A and X. Similarly, when we traverse the word vector B, we find that B is suitable for being exchanged to word vector C, and then B and C are exchanged. When we traverse the word vector C, we find that C is suitable for being exchanged to word vector X, and then C and X are exchanged. When the other word vector is traversed, if the original position is the most suitable for it, the word vector remains unchanged. Finally, although we did not traverse the word vector X, we also optimized the X. In contrast to Fig. 3, the word vector X is adjusted to a middle position which is neither near the positive nor near the negative class.

If we improve the moving model and add neutrality to the adjustment, then all word vectors in the corpus will be adjusted. With the increase of emerging Internet vocabulary, the number of words is rapidly increasing. By 2016, the online Xinhua Dictionary had 310000 words, and did not include such common Weibo words as emoticon, mixed words, common English words, names, numbers, etc. Therefore, in the emotional analysis task of micro-blog, the above-mentioned moving model which considers the adjustment of neutral words does not has the advantage of time compared with our model.

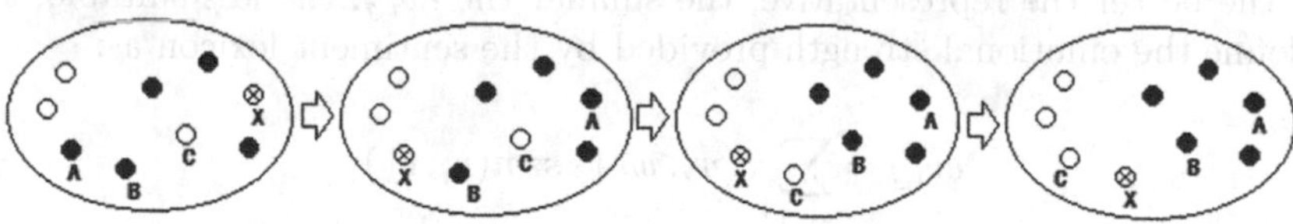

Fig. 2. Exchange model

3.2 The Construction of Sentiment Lexicon

The sentiment lexicon used in this paper is based on "中文情感词典本体库" [1], which is compiled by Professor Lin Hongfei of Dalian University of Technology and his team. In the sentiment lexicon, the emotional intensity of emotional words is taken as an integer between [−5, 5], −5 represents extremely negative emotions, 5 represents extremely positive emotions, 0 represents non-emotional tendencies, and the emotional intensity of words that do not exist in the sentiment lexicon is also regarded as 0.

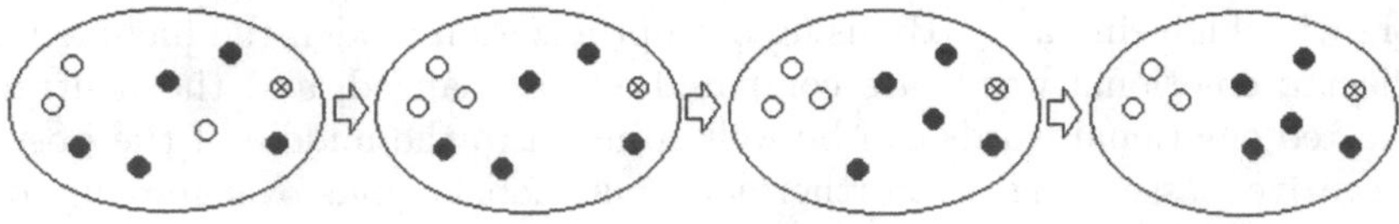

Fig. 3. Moving model

3.3 Our Model

Through the above optimization process, we can conclude that the optimization steps are as follows:

Firstly, for the word vectors v_i to be optimized in the emotional lexicon, we need to find out all the set C of word vectors whose similarity is greater than δ (the range allowed to exchange) and satisfy the constraints. We set word vector $v_j \subseteq C$, v_i' and v_j' as the initial locations of v_i and v_j respectively, and the constraints are defined as:

$$sim(v_j', v_i) \geq \delta, \qquad sim(v_j, v_i') \geq \delta \tag{1}$$

Similarity is calculated by vector cosine similarity:

$$sim(v_i, v_j) = \frac{v_i \cdot v_j}{||v_i|| \cdot ||v_j||} \tag{2}$$

We need to find out the word vector v_j, which is most suitable for exchanging position with v_i. We assume that there are n word vectors with a similarity greater than δ to v_j. We propose an evaluation criterion $ev_{i,j}$, which represents the fitness of word vector v_i at the position of word vector v_j. The bigger the $ev_{i,j}$, the better the representative; the smaller the $ev_{i,j}$, the less suitable it is. We define the emotional strength provided by the sentiment lexicon as:

$$ev_{i,j} = \sum_{k=1}^{n} w(w_i, w_k) \cdot sim(v_j, v_k) \tag{3}$$

where v_k is a word vector with a similarity greater than δ to v_j, it is defined as follows:

$$w(w_i, w_k) = \begin{cases} 0, & w_k = 0 \\ 5 - |w_i - w_k|, & w_i, w_k \in [-5, 5], w_k \neq 0 \end{cases} \tag{4}$$

$w(w_i, w_k)$ represents the difference in the intensity of emotion between word vector v_i and v_k, where w_i and w_k are querying emotional lexicon (If the sentiment lexicon does not contain the word, the value is 0). The value of $w(w_i, w_k)$ is an integer in the range of $[-5, 5]$. When $w > 0$, the polarity of v_i and v_k is the same; when $w < 0$, the polarity of v_i and v_k is opposite; if and only if $k = 0, w = 0$, v_i is a neutral word.

With the above evaluation criteria, we can calculate the fitness of v_i and v_j after exchanging v_i with v_j. We exchange v_i for fitness changes around v_j

as $ev_{i,j} - ev_{i,i}$, and similarly, $ev_{j,i} - ev_{j,j}$ for fitness changes over v_j to v_i. The greatest sum of fitness changes is the most suitable one. We draw the following definitions:

$$V = \arg\max[(ev_{i,j} - ev_{i,i}) + (ev_{j,i} - ev_{j,j})], \qquad (j = 1, 2, 3 \ldots n) \tag{5}$$

Finally, we get the word vector V, which is most suitable for exchanging with v_i, then we exchange the meaning of the word V and v_i.

4 Experiment and Analysis

4.1 The Sentiment Lexicon

The sentiment lexicon used in this paper is based on "中文情感词典本体库" [1], which is compiled by Professor Lin Hongfei of Dalian University of Technology and his team. We divide the original 21 sub categories into two categories: positive and negative. Then, according to the original five emotional intensity levels, we classify emotional intensity into −5, −4, −3, −2, −1, 0, 1, 2, 3, 4, 5 by combining positive and negative classification. We selected 1000 emotional words not included in "中文情感词典本体库" [1] from "知网 Hownet 情感词典", and labeled them emotion according to the above criteria. Finally, our sentiment lexicon contains 28467 emotion words.

4.2 Data Set

Our experimental data were collected from the NLPCC public dataset of the Chinese Weibo sentiment assessment task: NLPCC 2013 and NLPCC 2014 [18]. Its Weibo text comes from Sina Weibo platform. Each Weibo text is labeled as a main tag and multiple secondary tags. We modify and expand it on this basis. We label the non-emotional text "none", the text labeled "happiness" and "like" as "positive", and the text labeled "anger", "sadness", "fear", "disgust" and "scare" as "negative" [18]. We crawled 850996 Weibo data from the network with a crawler script, and selected 2000 positive and 2000 negative emotional texts, and labeled them manually. The final data set is as Table 1.

Table 1. Data set composition.

	Positive	Negative	None
NLPCC2013	3639	3660	6710
NLPCC2014	5146	4658	10194
Expanded	2000	2000	
Total	10785	10318	10194

We use these 850996 Weibo data and NLPCC2013, NLPCC2014 data sets as our corpus. We use Chinese word segmentation tool to segment the corpus.

Before word segmentation, the common expressions of Weibo are used as word segmentation dictionary, which makes it exist as a basic language unit after word segmentation. In addition, we have carried out a series of preprocessing works, such as transforming traditional Chinese characters into simplified ones. In addition, we have carried out a series of preprocessing work, such as transforming traditional Chinese characters into simplified ones. Finally, we choose the 200 dimension to carry out the pre-training of word embedding through the Word2vec.

4.3 Experimental Configuration

We set the parameter δ (Scope of exchange allowed) as a variable to obtain the optimal result of word embedding under different values, observe its influence on the result, and hope to find its optimal range. The value range of this δ is not universal because different vector distributions of primitive words lead to different similarity judgment ranges. We refer to the relevant research and implement the moving adjustment model by ourselves and use it as a comparison. We set the unoptimized word vector, the optimized word vector using the moving optimization model and the optimized word vector using our model as input respectively. We choose CNN model and Bi-LSTM model as the classifier, and 80% of the data set as the training set, the remaining 20% as the test set. We set Fine-grained and Binary Sentiment analysis tasks. Finally, we compare and analyze the accuracy of Fine-grained and Binary of each group.

CNN Model [7] **(Convolution Neural Network).** CNN has achieved great success in the field of digital image processing, which has set off a wave of in-depth learning in the field of natural language processing. The model consists of convolutional layer, pooling layer and fully-connected layer. The convolutional layer extracts features, the pooling layer reduces dimensions, and the fully-connected layer combines all local features into global features to calculate the final score of each category. This model carries out feature learning for word vector representation of Weibo text. In this way, it constructs the semantic representation of Weibo text and completes the task of emotional analysis of Weibo. This is one of the early models for sentiment analysis using the deep learning model.

Bi-LSTM Model [19] **(Bi-Directional Long Short-Term Memory).** Bi-LSTM model is based on one-way LSTM network. The basic idea of Bi-LSTM model is to train two LSTM networks (forward LSTM network and backward LSTM network) according to each training sequence, and the two networks connect the same output layer. The network output layer of Bi-LSTM model can capture the context information about the past and future of each point in the input sequence.

4.4 Comparative Results

It can be seen from Tables 3 and 4 that the experimental results of our model are best at $\delta = 0.83$. So when $\delta = 0.83$, we take the results of the model for comparison (Table 2). Compared with the original word vectors which were not optimized, the accuracy of Fine-grained increased by 2.01% (CNN), 1.58% (Bi-LSTM) respectively, and the accuracy of Binary increased by 1.34% (CNN), 2.00% (Bi-LSTM), respectively. Compared with the moving model, the accuracy of Fine-grained increased by 1.08% (CNN), 0.93% (Bi-LSTM), and the accuracy of Binary increased by 0.69% (CNN), 0.95% (Bi-LSTM), respectively.

Table 2. Accuracy of different classifiers with different word embeddings.

	CNN		Bi-LSTM	
	Fine-grained	Binary	Fine-grained	Binary
Unadjusted	0.4450	0.8616	0.4578	0.8578
Moving adjustment model	0.4543	0.8681	0.4643	0.8683
Our model ($\delta = 0.83$)	0.4651	0.8750	0.4736	0.8778

In Table 3, we compare the results of our model when different δ values are taken. When $\delta \geq 0.9$, the accuracy of our model does not increase significantly, because there are too few word vectors in the range of similarity. When the δ is between 0.85 and 0.75, the accuracy of our model is better. When $\delta = 0.70$, the accuracy decreases, and when $\delta = 0.65$, the accuracy is significantly lower than the unoptimized word vector, because the allowable exchange range is too large, the optimized word vector deviates too much from the original context.

From Table 3, we can see that when the δ is set between 0.85 and 0.75, our model performs better. So we let δ take the value in the range to further find its best value (Table 4). Finally, in $delta = 0.83$, our model performs best. Therefore, we take the group data for comparison.

Table 3. Accuracy of different classifiers with our model.

	CNN		Bi-LSTM	
	Fine-grained	Binary	Fine-grained	Binary
Our model ($\delta = 0.95$)	0.4454	0.8614	0.4576	0.8578
Our model ($\delta = 0.90$)	0.4458	0.8623	0.4580	0.8582
Our model ($\delta = 0.85$)	0.4625	0.8732	0.4698	0.8746
Our model ($\delta = 0.80$)	0.4621	0.8750	0.4716	0.8769
Our model ($\delta = 0.75$)	0.4571	0.8722	0.4627	0.8698
Our model ($\delta = 0.70$)	0.4430	0.8573	0.4540	0.8603
Our model ($\delta = 0.65$)	0.3811	0.7910	0.4159	0.8270

Table 4. Accuracy of different classifiers with our model.

	CNN		Bi-LSTM	
	Fine-grained	Binary	Fine-grained	Binary
Our model ($\delta = 0.85$)	0.4625	0.8732	0.4698	0.8746
Our model ($\delta = 0.84$)	0.4640	0.8742	0.4720	0.8757
Our model ($\delta = 0.83$)	0.4651	0.8750	0.4736	0.8778
Our model ($\delta = 0.82$)	0.4629	0.8741	0.4752	0.8776
Our model ($\delta = 0.81$)	0.4633	0.8745	0.4730	0.8769
Our model ($\delta = 0.80$)	0.4621	0.8750	0.4716	0.8769
Our model ($\delta = 0.79$)	0.4573	0.8722	0.4683	0.8745
Our model ($\delta = 0.78$)	0.4579	0.8728	0.4683	0.8746
Our model ($\delta = 0.77$)	0.4570	0.8719	0.4654	0.8710
Our model ($\delta = 0.76$)	0.4559	0.8718	0.4630	0.8695
Our model ($\delta = 0.75$)	0.4571	0.8722	0.4627	0.8698

5 Conclusion and Future Work

In this paper, we discuss the relationship between word vectors and context, propose an optimization method of word vectors, and apply the word vectors generated by this method to fine-grained emotional analysis of Chinese Weibo. The proposed word embeddings optimization model can be applied to any pre-trained word vectors without labeling corpus. It is neither affected by neutral words and emotional words which is not included in the sentiment lexicon, nor make the word vectors aggregate excessively. Experiments show that the precision of fine-grained sentiment analysis of Chinese Weibo is improved after using our optimization model.

In the future, we will use more classifiers to verify, and further evaluate our optimization model. Further more, we are going to apply this method to the task of emotional multi-classification to explore the case where similar word vectors have multiple meanings. And we will refer to Lingyun Xiang's work [9] and apply the model to a wider range of fields.

Acknowledgement. Our research supported by Innovation Base Project for Graduates (Research of Security Embedded System).

References

1. 徐琳宏, 林鸿飞, 潘宇, 任惠, 陈建美: 情感词汇本体的构造. 情报学报**27**(2), 180–185 (2008)
2. Bojanowski, P., Grave, E., Joulin, A., Mikolov, T.: Enriching word vectors with subword information. Trans. Assoc. Comput. Linguist. **5**, 135–146 (2017)

3. Collobert, R., Weston, J.: A unified architecture for natural language processing: deep neural networks with multitask learning. In: Proceedings of the 25th International Conference on Machine Learning, ICML 2008, pp. 160–167. ACM, New York (2008)
4. Collobert, R., Weston, J., Bottou, L., Karlen, M., Kavukcuoglu, K., Kuksa, P.: Natural language processing (almost) from scratch. J. Mach. Learn. Res. **12**, 2493–2537 (2011)
5. Faruqui, M., Dodge, J., Jauhar, S.K., Dyer, C., Hovy, E., Smith, N.A.: Retrofitting word vectors to semantic lexicons. In: Proceedings of the 2015 Conference of the North American Chapter of the Association for Computational Linguistics: Human Language Technologies, pp. 1606–1615. Association for Computational Linguistics (2015)
6. Kiela, D., Hill, F., Clark, S.: Specializing word embeddings for similarity or relatedness. In: Proceedings of the 2015 Conference on Empirical Methods in Natural Language Processing, pp. 2044–2048. Association for Computational Linguistics (2015)
7. Kim, Y.: Convolutional neural networks for sentence classification. In: Proceedings of the 2014 Conference on Empirical Methods in Natural Language Processing (EMNLP), pp. 1746–1751. Association for Computational Linguistics (2014)
8. Labutov, I., Lipson, H.: Re-embedding words. In: Proceedings of the 51st Annual Meeting of the Association for Computational Linguistics (Volume 2: Short Papers), pp. 489–493. Association for Computational Linguistics (2013)
9. Xiang, L., Li, Y., Hao, W., Yang, P., Shen, X.: Reversible natural language watermarking using synonym substitution and arithmetic coding. CMC: Comput. Mater. Contin. **55**(3), 541–559 (2018)
10. Maas, A.L., Daly, R.E., Pham, P.T., Huang, D., Ng, A.Y., Potts, C.: Learning word vectors for sentiment analysis. In: Meeting of the Association for Computational Linguistics: Human Language Technologies, pp. 142–150 (2011)
11. Mikolov, T., Chen, K., Corrado, G., Dean, J.: Efficient estimation of word representations in vector space. Comput. Sci. (2013)
12. Mikolov, T., Sutskever, I., Chen, K., Corrado, G., Dean, J.: Distributed representations of words and phrases and their compositionality. In: International Conference on Neural Information Processing Systems, pp. 3111–3119 (2013)
13. Miller, G.A.: WordNet: a lexical database for english. Commun. ACM **38**(11), 39–41 (1995)
14. Pennington, J., Socher, R., Manning, C.D.: GloVe: global vectors for word representation. In: Empirical Methods in Natural Language Processing (EMNLP), pp. 1532–1543 (2014)
15. Ren, Y., Zhang, Y., Zhang, M., Ji, D.: Improving Twitter sentiment classification using topic-enriched multi-prototype word embeddings. In: Proceedings of the Thirtieth AAAI Conference on Artificial Intelligence, AAAI 2016, pp. 3038–3044, AAAI Press (2016)
16. Rumelhart, E, D., Hinton, E, G., Williams, J, R.: Learning representations by back-propagating errors. Cogn. Model. 3–5 (1988)
17. Schakel, A.M.J., Wilson, B.J.: Measuring word significance using distributed representations of words. Comput. Sci. (2015)
18. Song, K., Feng, S., Gao, W., Wang, D., Chen, L., Zhang, C.: Build emotion lexicon from microblogs by combining effects of seed words and emoticons in a heterogeneous graph. In: Proceedings of the 26th ACM Conference on Hypertext and & Social Media, HT 2015, pp. 283–292. ACM, New York (2015)

19. Tai, K.S., Socher, R., Manning, C.D.: Improved semantic representations from tree-structured long short-term memory networks. In: Proceedings of the 53rd Annual Meeting of the Association for Computational Linguistics and the 7th International Joint Conference on Natural Language Processing (Volume 1: Long Papers), pp. 1556–1566. Association for Computational Linguistics (2015)
20. Tang, D., Wei, F., Qin, B., Yang, N., Liu, T., Zhou, M.: Sentiment embeddings with applications to sentiment analysis. IEEE Trans. Knowl. Data Eng. **28**(2), 496–509 (2016)
21. Tu, Y., Lin, Y., Wang, J., Kim, J.U.: Semi-supervised learning with generative adversarial networks on digital signal modulation classification. CMC: Comput. Mater. Contin. **55**(2), 243–254 (2018)
22. Yu, L.C., Wang, J., Lai, K.R., Zhang, X.: Refining word embeddings for sentiment analysis. In: Proceedings of the 2017 Conference on Empirical Methods in Natural Language Processing, pp. 534–539. Association for Computational Linguistics (2017)

A Sentiment Classification Model Based on Multiple Multi-classifier Systems

Kehua Yang(✉), Chenglin Liao, and Wei Zhang

College of Computer Science and Electronic Engineering,
Key Laboratory for Embedded and Network Computing of Hunan Province,
Hunan University, Changsha 410082 Hunan,, China
khyang@hnu.edu.cn

Abstract. With the fast development of the Internet, especially the development of the Web technique, more and more people express their views on the Internet. The content of these views involve various aspects of our life, such as books, movies, musics, policies, commodities, technical services, etc. Since these views are usually subjective and possess great potential commercial and social value, the study of sentiment analysis is followed. At the early stage of sentiment analysis, researchers used lexicon based method to solve sentiment analysis problem. With the improvement in machine learning and Natural Language Processing technology, machine learning based method are becoming more and more popular in the field of sentiment analysis. In this study, we propose an ensemble sentiment classification model based on three multi-classifier systems. The proposed model uses majority voting as an ensemble method of multiple multi-classifier systems. The effectiveness of the classification model is verified on five public datasets. Experimental results show that the proposed model is superior to traditional sentiment classification methods and simple multi-classifier systems in the performance of classification accuracy. By using the sentiment classification model proposed in this paper, the accuracy improvement in different domains also show that our proposed model has certain generalization ability.

Keywords: Sentiment analysis · Ensemble learning · Multi-classifier system

1 Introduction

With the rapid development of information technologies, users can easily express their views for a variety of domains. Analyzing and predicting the polarity of the sentiment is very important for understanding social phenomena and overall society trends. For example, the governments can analyze the pros and cons of policy establishment by analyzing the citizens' attitude towards policy [14], strategic adjustment and commercial planning can be adapted to the market

X. Sun et al. (Eds.): ICAIS 2019, LNCS 11633, pp. 287–298, 2019.
https://doi.org/10.1007/978-3-030-24265-7_25

by monitoring product or service reviews [8], e-learning systems can improve teaching resources and teaching methods by capturing students' sentiment [11].

Sentiment analysis aims at determining opinions, emotions and attitudes from different source materials like reviews, blogs, news, etc. There are other terms for sentiment analysis, such as opinion mining, subjectivity analysis, review mining and opinion extraction [9]. Sentiment analysis can be divided into three levels: document, sentence and aspect level. In this study, the sentiment analysis problem is performed at document level. In the research of sentiment classification, we focus our attention on identifying the polarity of text sentiment (either positive or negative) in a given text. Many researchers are committed to using traditional classifiers, such as Naive Bayes (NB), Maximum Entropy (ME) and Support Vector Machine (SVM) to solve sentiment classification problem [15]. In order to enhance the accuracy of sentiment classification, researchers are paying more and more attention to the use of ensemble learning technology, which combine the output of several individual classifiers to form an integrated output [6,20]. In this paper, we use the approach of integrating multiple classifiers for text sentiment classification.

In ensemble learning, there are three popular ensemble ways to integrate multiple classifiers for sentiment classification: Bagging, Boosting and Random Subspace Method (RSM). In Bagging, the base learners are formed by using random independent bootstrap replicates from a training dataset, and Bagging use majority voting as the combination rule of multiple base classifiers for classification problem [2,23]. In Boosting, this ensemble method adjusts the weights of samples according to classification result. Samples which are misclassified will get higher weights, on the contrary, samples which are correctly classified will get relatively lower weights [13]. The process of RSM is similar to the process of Bagging, the difference between them is the base learners of RSM are formed in random subspace of the feature space. In this study, we employ these three ensemble methods in our proposed model due to their excellent ability to improve the performance of a certain classifier.

The datasets involved in our research are reviews from different domains. Therefore, some big challenges in review sentiment classification may be encountered. Firstly, the length of some reviews may be very short, and the sentiment clues it can provide is rather limited. Secondly, the performance of a certain sentiment classification model may be closely related to one field, excellent performance in one field does not mean good performance in other fields. Thirdly, the application of ensemble learning for sentiment analysis may get an increasement in accuracy while at the same time leading to an increasement in consumption time.

Our main contributions can be summarized as follows. Firstly, we propose a novel sentiment classification model based on three multi-classifier systems, which can further improve the performance of review sentiment classification. Secondly, our experimental results on five public datasets show an evidence that the use of integrating multiple multi-classifier systems is promising for identifying sentiment polarities.

The remainder of this paper is organized as follows. Section 2 explains the related works in sentiment classification. Section 3 shows the proposed sentiment classification model. Section 4 describes the experiments on the five public datasets. Section 5 presents the conclusion and future work.

2 Related Work

Document processing in natural language includes retrieval, sentiment analysis, theme extraction, etc. [21]. Research on sentiment analysis is a hot direction in Natural Language Processing. Many researchers have proposed a variety of sentiment classification methods. In general, sentiment classification method can be divided into lexicon based method and machine learning based method. The advantage of lexicon based method in sentiment classification is that it is simple to use and simple to understand. A major problem of lexicon based method in sentiment classification is this kind of method requires pre-configured lexicon and rules. Machine learning based method outperforms lexicon based method in classification accuracy performance and generalization ability, but it requires labeled training data and time to build the classification model. The method used in our proposed model is belong to machine learning based method. There are many studies on sentiment analysis, but the studies based on ensemble learning for review sentiment classification are relatively limited.

Pang et al. [12] proposed a machine learning based method for sentiment classification. In their study, they compared three common machine learning algorithms: NB, ME, SVM, and they found the SVM is superior to other two algorithms based on their experiments. Whitehead et al. [19] considered the problem of automatically classifying human sentiment from natural language written text, the accuracy of different ensemble methods (Bagging, Boosting, RSM) were compared in their experiments, and the experimental results showed that ensemble machine learning models can significantly improve sentiment classification for free-form text. Based on their experiments, they declared that RSM and Bagging ensemble methods typically provide the best performance.

Wang et al. [17] conducted a comparative assessment of the performance of three popular ensemble methods (Bagging, Boosting, RSM) based on five base learners for sentiment classification. The empirical results revealed that the RSM has the better comparative results, although it was seldom discussed in the literature. Fersini et al. [5] proposed an ensemble method based on Bayesian Model Averaging, which addresses classifier selection problem by proposing a greedy approach that evaluates the contribution of each model with respect to the ensemble. Jonior et al. [7] developed a voting ensemble system based on two Linear SVM classifiers and one Logistic Regressor (LR) classifier, in which each base classifier is trained in a different feature space.

Zhang et al. [22] proposed a Piecewise Pooling Convolutional Neural Network (PPCNN) for sentiment classification, which is superior to baseline methods, especially for datasets with transition sentences. Catal et al. [3] developed a sentiment classification model based on vote ensemble classifier utilizes from three individual classifiers: Bagging, NB, and SVM, and the experimental results showed that their model increase the performance of individual classifiers on Turkish sentiment classification. Tripathy et al. [16] tried to use four supervised machine learning algorithms, such as NB, ME, Stochastic Gradient Descent and SVM, to classify movie reviews. These algorithms were further applied using n-gram approach on IMDB dataset, it was observed that unigram and bigram perform better than trigram, four-gram and five-gram. Motivated by the work done by Catal et al. [3] and the experiments conducted by Wang et al. [17], we propose an ensemble sentiment classification model based on three multi-classifier systems, and the experimental results on five public datasets indicate that our proposed model is superior to traditional classification methods and simple multi-classifier systems.

3 Methodology

In this section, the proposed sentiment classification model based on three multi-classifier systems will be introduced. The proposed model includes two commonly-used classification algorithms: NB and SVM. Three ensemble learning methods are used in the proposed model. To simply the description of the proposed model, we use Bagging+SVM to represent the first multi-classifier system which use Bagging with SVM as the base classifier, using RSM+SVM to represent the second multi-classifier system which use RSM with SVM as the base classifier, using Boosting+NB to represent the third multi-classifier system which use Boosting with NB as the base classifier.

3.1 Classification Algorithms

Support Vector Machine. SVM is a supervised learning method for classification problem. With SVM, the nonlinear dataset can be transformed into a higher-dimensional feature space. SVM attempts to find a decision boundary that maximizes the margin between two classes [7]. Although SVM is a time-consuming algorithm for classification problem, SVM is widely used in sentiment classification domain because of its high performance in accuracy.

Naive Bayes. NB originated from classical mathematics and has solid mathematical foundation. It is a simple machine learning algorithm based on a probabilistic theory, it assumes the features of dataset are independent. The probability of a review belonging to a class can be obtained using the following equation:

$$P(c_i|w) = \frac{P(w|c_i) \cdot P(c_i)}{P(w)} \tag{1}$$

Where w represents the features of a review and c_i represents the class of the review (positive or negative).

3.2 Ensemble Methods

Bagging. Bagging (Bootstrap aggregating) is one of the earliest ensemble learning algorithms, this algorithm is very simple in both thought and implementation. In the selection process of each training sub-dataset of Bagging algorithm, extracted training samples will be put back into the original dataset, K training sub-datasets will be obtained after K selections on the original dataset. Subsequently, the K training sub-datasets will be used to train K base classifiers. The combination of different training sub-datasets and relatively unstable algorithm can make the final classification model have different decision boundaries. The prediction approach of Bagging is based on the nature of the problem. Typically, majority voting is used for classification problems, and averaging result is used for regression problems [3].

Random Subspace Method. RSM is a bagging-based method also called attribute bagging or feature bagging. RSM trains the base classifiers on random samples of features instead of the entire feature set, this can reduce the correlation between classifiers in an ensemble approach. When there are many redundant or unrelated features in the dataset, the use of RSM may lead to a better sub-feature space than the original feature space.

Boosting. The Boosting algorithm is an ensemble learning method, which can effectively enhance the predictive performance of base learning algorithms. This ensemble learning method adjusts the weight values of samples in the training dataset, the weight values of misclassified samples will be increased and the weight values of correctly classified samples will be decreased. Boosting contains a serials of methods, one of the most widely used Boosting algorithm is AdaBoost, AdaBoost can obtain a final classifier with a lower classification rate and less variance [10]. Therefore, we use AdaBoost in our experiments.

3.3 Proposed Model

Our proposed model is an ensemble model which contains three multi-classifier systems: Bagging+SVM, RSM+SVM, Boosting+NB. Wang et al. [17] investigated various classification algorithms based on the selected five public datasets (the detail information of five datasets is described in Sect. 4.1), they discovered that NB and SVM achieved better accuracy performance than other algorithms (such as k-Nearest Neighbor (KNN), ME, Decision Tree (DT)). Therefore, in our proposed model, SVM and NB are selected as basic classification algorithms. Three frequently-used ensemble methods in the proposed model are Bagging, RSM and Boosting. Considering the high performance of SVM when used alone and in order to improve the performance of a single classifier, we determined to use SVM as the base classifier of Bagging and RSM. We also tried to use SVM as the base classifier of Boosting, which is another popular ensemble method, but experimental results on the five datasets revealed that Boosting performed worse than Bagging and RSM.

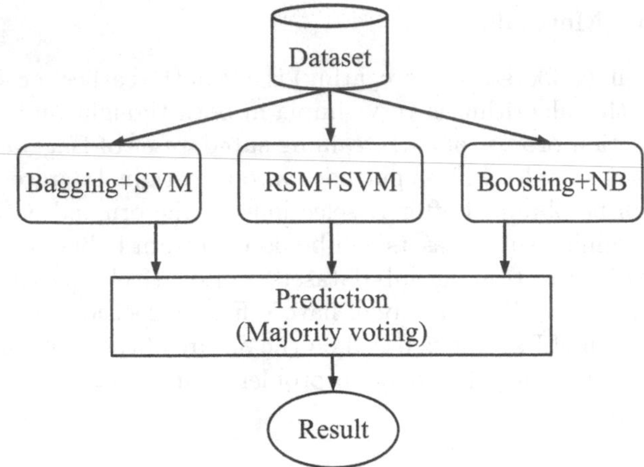

Fig. 1. An overall view of the proposed model.

Figure 1 visualizes our proposed model, the proposed model uses three multi-classifier systems as its components. Since the text sentiment analysis task we focused is belong to classification problem, both Bagging+SVM and RSM+SVM use majority voting method as their combination rules. Figure 2 illustrates the generation process of Bagging+SVM or RSM+SVM. When Fig. 2 represents the

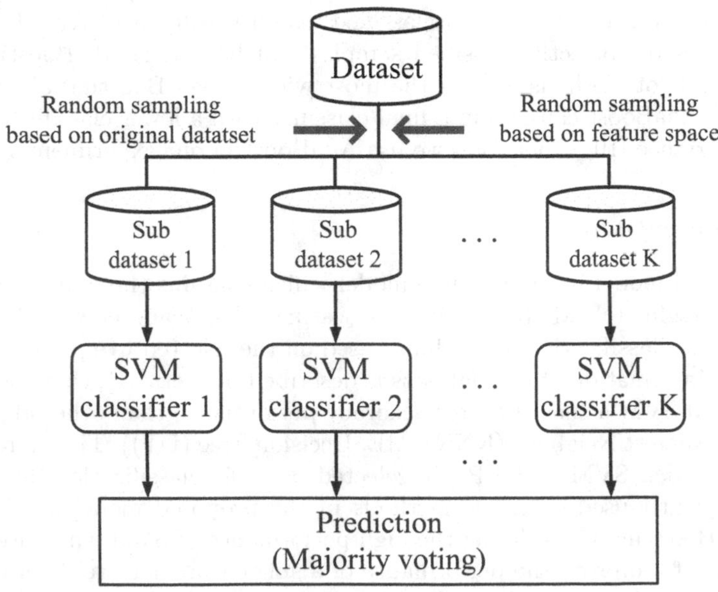

Fig. 2. Generation process of Bagging+SVM or RSM+SVM.

generation process of Bagging+SVM, it uses random sampling based on the original dataset to generate sub-datasets. When Fig. 2 represents the generation process of RSM+SVM, it uses random sampling based on feature space to generate sub-datasets. The base classifier used in Fig. 2 is SVM classifier that trained in different sub-datasets.

After Bagging+SVM and RSM+SVM are determined as two components of the proposed model, we attempted to use NB as the base classifier of aforementioned three ensemble methods, experimental results are recorded in Table 4. As can be seen from Table 4, Boosting achieve the best performance on five datasets except for the Camp review dataset when using NB as its base classifier. Therefore, Boosting is used for NB to construct the third multi-classifier system of the proposed model.

Figure 3 illustrates the generation process of Boosting+NB. Boosting first trains a base classifier from the initial training dataset. The distribution of training samples will be adjusted according to the performance of base classifier. In this process, the training samples which are incorrectly classified by previous base classifier receive more attention, and then next base classifier will

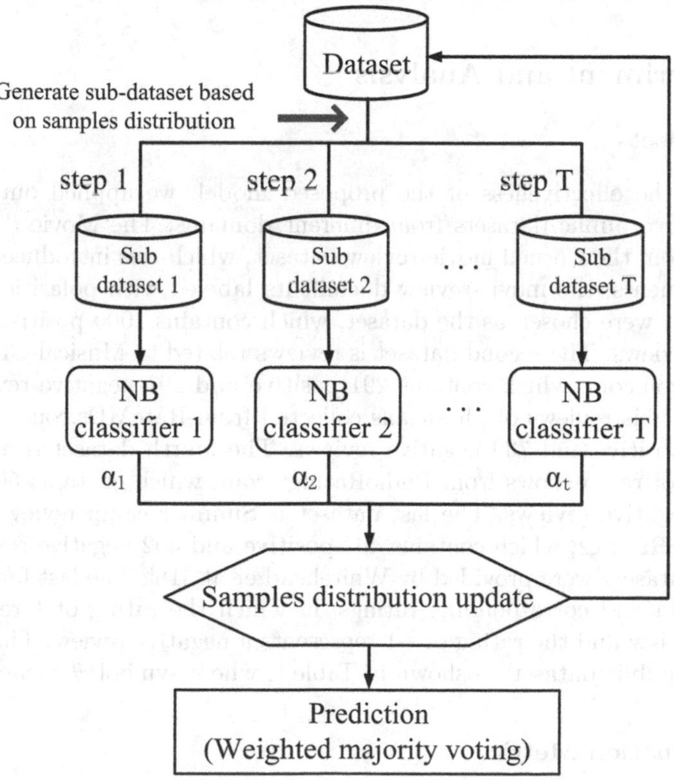

Fig. 3. Generation process of Boosting+NB.

be trained based on the adjusted training samples. This process is repeated until the number of base classifiers reaches a preset value of T. The symbol α_i in Fig. 3 means the weight of i-th base classifier, the base classifier used by the third multi-classifier system is NB classifier. The combination rule of Boosting used in our model is a weighted majority voting.

The classification model we proposed is novel, it is an ensemble model based on three multi-classifier systems, it uses majority voting as its final prediction approach for sentiment polarity classification. In previous studies, researchers usually use some simple classifiers to integrate a better classifier. The use of integrating multiple simple classifiers can improve the classification performance, then our proposed model which includes three multi-classifier systems may further improve the classification performance. In addition, diversity can be reflected in the proposed model, different multi-classifier systems may capture different sentiment parts of a given text. Based on these assumptions, we came up with the this model. The drawback of the proposed model is obvious, the application of using an ensemble model based on three multi-classifier systems means the reduction of time efficiency. However, the training process of different multi-classifier systems can be parallel, and our attention is focused on improving the accuracy of review sentiment classification.

4 Experiment and Analysis

4.1 Datasets

To testify the effectiveness of the proposed model, we applied our proposed model on five public datasets from different domains. The Movie dataset was collected from the Cornell movie-review dataset, which was introduced in [1]. In our experiments, the movie-review documents labeled with polarities (positive or negative) were chosen as the dataset, which contains 1000 positive and 1000 negative reviews. The second dataset is reviews related to Musical CD collected from Amazon.com, which contains 291 positive and 291 negative reviews. The third dataset is reviews of physicians collected from RateMDs.com, which contains 739 positive and 739 negative reviews. The fourth dataset is a collection of reviews of radio shows from RadioRatingz.com, which contains 502 positive and 502 negative reviews. The last dataset is Summer camp reviews collected from CampRatingz, which contains 402 positive and 402 negative reviews. The last four datasets were provided by Whitehead et al. [18]. The last four datasets include data and corresponding ratings, in which the rating of 1 represents a positive review and the rating of -1 represents a negative review. The statistics of the five public datasets is shown in Table 1, where symbol # means number.

4.2 Evaluation Metric

Our experimental results are evaluated based on a confusion matrix, as shown in Table 2. We use an definition of accuracy to evaluate the performance of

Table 1. Statistics of the five review datasets.

Dataset	# of positive reviews	# of negative reviews	Source
Movie	1000	1000	[1]
Music	291	291	[18]
Doctor	739	739	[18]
Radio	502	502	[18]
Camp	402	402	[18]

Table 2. Confusion matrix of review sentiment classification.

	Actual sentiment	
	Positive sentiment	Negative sentiment
Positive sentiment	True positive (TP)	False positive (FP)
Negative sentiment	False negative (FN)	True negative (TN)

each classification method in our experiments, the definition of accuracy can be illustrated as:

$$accuracy = \frac{TP + TN}{TP + TN + FP + FN} \tag{2}$$

4.3 Experimental Settings

In our experiments, our datasets are limited in size. In order to ensure the reliability of the experimental results, we use 10-fold cross-validation method to evaluate the performance of each classification method. This method divides each dataset into ten parts, each time taking nine parts for training, and the remaining one is used to test our model performance. For each classification method on each dataset, we record 10 testing accuracy values and then calculate the average accuracy value.

4.4 Experimental Results Analysis

Five comparative classification methods: NB, SVM, Bagging+SVM, RSM+SVM, Boosting+NB, are compared with our proposed model on five public datasets. The performance of each classification method on five public datasets is shown in Table 3. For the Movie review dataset, the average accuracy value of NB and SVM reach 80.23% and 78.56%. When ensemble learning method Bagging and RSM are used for SVM, the accuracy performance improved, and the average accuracy value reached 80.68% and 81.24% respectively. The average accuracy value of Boosting+NB is 81.46%, the highest average accuracy value 81.76% on the Movie review dataset is achieved by our proposed model.

The data performance of five comparative classification methods and our proposed model on the Music and Doctor datasets is generally consistent with

Table 3. Experimental results on five public datasets.

Datasets	NB	SVM	Bagging+SVM	RSM+SVM	Boosting+NB	Proposed model
Movie	80.23 ± 2.54	78.56 ± 2.65	80.68 ± 2.73	81.24 ± 2.68	81.46 ± 3.87	**81.76** ± 2.45
Music	68.78 ± 5.71	69.32 ± 5.66	69.62 ± 5.42	72.24 ± 5.38	69.46 ± 6.19	**73.18** ± 5.26
Doctor	78.62 ± 3.62	81.23 ± 3.47	82.34 ± 3.31	83.25 ± 3.12	78.97 ± 3.58	**83.87** ± 3.35
Radio	64.12 ± 4.54	67.46 ± 4.58	67.23 ± 3.87	67.63 ± 3.87	65.64 ± 4.12	**67.75** ± 3.24
Camp	81.16 ± 4.36	82.08 ± 3.86	82.52 ± 3.65	81.87 ± 3.78	81.48 ± 4.14	**82.89** ± 3.32

that on Movie review dataset. As we can see from Table 3, the highest average values on Music and Doctor datasets also achieved by our proposed model. When we use SVM as the base classifier of Bagging or RSM, the experimental results on the first four datasets show that RSM is an excellent ensemble method, although it was seldom discussed in the literature.

Table 4. Experimental results on five datasets when Naive Bayes as the base classifier of Bagging, RSM and Boosting.

Datasets	Bagging+NB	RSM+NB	Boosting+NB
Movie	80.52 ± 2.62	80.73 ± 3.16	**81.46** ± 3.87
Music	69.12 ± 6.65	68.55 ± 6.68	**69.34** ± 6.19
Doctor	78.86 ± 3.06	77.52 ± 2.85	**78.97** ± 3.58
Radio	64.28 ± 4.35	64.05 ± 4.35	**65.64** ± 4.12
Camp	**81.64** ± 3.96	80.82 ± 4.17	81.48 ± 4.14

For the Radio review dataset, the average accuracy value of SVM is calculated to be 67.46%, and the average accuracy value of Bagging+SVM is calculated to be 67.23%, which is worse than a simple SVM classifier. This result indicates that the performance of using an ensemble learning method for a base classifier not always better than just using this classifier. Although, the proposed model still perform better than other five classification methods.

For the last Camp review dataset, the average accuracy value of Bagging+SVM and RSM+SVM reach 82.52% and 81.87% respectively, which is better than 82.08% of SVM. The average accuracy value of Boosting+NB reaches 81.48%, which is higher than 81.16% of NB. We can also see that Bagging performs better than RSM on this dataset. Similarly, the average accuracy value of the proposed model reaches 82.89%, the highest among the six classification methods. In summary, the comparison experiments on the five datasets show that the proposed model outperforms traditional sentiment classification methods (NB, SVM) and simple multi-classifier systems. (Bagging+SVM, RSM+SVM, Boosting+NB).

5 Conclusion and Future Work

As the Internet has become an excellent source of consumer reviews, academic interest in sentiment analysis has grown considerably over the past few years [4]. In this study, we consider to use multiple multi-classifier systems as the components of our proposed model, and we compare our proposed model with traditional classification algorithms and simple multi-classifier systems. The effectiveness of our proposed model is verified on five public datasets, the experimental results present that our proposed model can effectively improve the accuracy of review sentiment classification. In addition, our proposed model reaches the highest average accuracy value in five different domains, which states that our model has certain generalization ability.

In the future work, we may expand our dataset to more fields, such as books, hotels, policies, etc. Our experimental datasets are limited in size, so we may attempt to apply our proposed model to larger datasets. The approach of integrating multiple multi-classifier systems in the proposed model may be used for multi-class sentiment classification, since the sentiment in the text are not only positive and negative, neutral and conflicting sentiment are also common.

Acknowledgement. We would like to express our gratitude to Innovation Base Project for Graduates (Research of Security Embedded System) for its support.

References

1. Bo, P., Lee, L.: A sentimental education: sentiment analysis using subjectivity summarization based on minimum cuts. In: Meeting on Association for Computational Linguistics, p. 271 (2004)
2. Breiman, L.: Bagging predictors. Mach. Learn. **24**(2), 123–140 (1996)
3. Catal, C., Nangir, M.: A sentiment classification model based on multiple classifiers. Appl. Soft Comput. **50**, 135–141 (2017)
4. Fang, Y., Tan, H., Zhang, J.: Multi-strategy sentiment analysis of consumer reviews based on semantic fuzziness. IEEE Access **PP**(99), 1 (2018)
5. Fersini, E., Messina, E., Pozzi, F.A.: Sentiment analysis: Bayesian ensemble learning. Decis. Support Syst. **68**, 26–38 (2014)
6. Ho, T.K.: The random subspace method for constructing decision forest. IEEE Trans. Pattern Anal. Mach. Intell. **20**(8), 832–844 (1998)
7. Júnior, E.A.C., Marinho, V.Q., Santos, L.B.D.: NILC-USP at SemEval-2017 task 4: a multi-view ensemble for twitter sentiment analysis, pp. 611–615 (2017)
8. Li, Y.M., Li, T.Y.: Deriving market intelligence from microblogs. Decis. Support Syst. **55**(1), 206–217 (2013)
9. Liu, B.: Sentiment Analysis and Opinion Mining. Morgan & Claypool Publishers, San Rafael (2012)
10. Onan, A., Korukoğlu, S., Bulut, H.: A multiobjective weighted voting ensemble classifier based on differential evolution algorithm for text sentiment classification. Expert Syst. Appl. **62**, 1–16 (2016)
11. Ortigosa, A., Martn, J.M., Carro, R.M.: Sentiment analysis in Facebook and its application to e-learning. Comput. Hum. Behav. **31**(1), 527–541 (2014)

12. Pang, B., Lee, L., Vaithyanathan, S.: Thumbs up? Sentiment classification using machine learning techniques. In: Empirical Methods Natural Language Processing, pp. 79–86 (2002)
13. Priore, P., Ponte, B., Puente, J., Gomez, A.: Learning-based scheduling offlexible manufacturing systems using ensemble methods. Comput. Ind. Eng. **126** (2018)
14. Ramisch, C.: Application 1: lexicography. In: Multiword Expressions Acquisition. TANLP, pp. 159–179. Springer, Cham (2015). https://doi.org/10.1007/978-3-319-09207-2_6
15. Silva, N.F.F.D., Hruschka Jr., E.R., Hruschka, E.R.: Tweet sentiment analysis with classifier ensembles. Decis. Support Syst. **66**, 170–179 (2014)
16. Tripathy, A., Agrawal, A., Rath, S.K.: Classification of sentiment reviews using n-gram machine learning approach. Expert Syst. Appl. **57**(C), 117–126 (2016)
17. Wang, G., Sun, J., Ma, J., Xu, K., Gu, J.: Sentiment classification: the contribution of ensemble learning. Decis. Support Syst. **57**(1), 77–93 (2014)
18. Whitehead, M., Yaeger, L.: Building a general purpose cross-domain sentiment mining model. In: 2009 WRI World Congress on Computer Science and Information Engineering, pp. 472–476 (2009)
19. Whitehead, M., Yaeger, L.: Sentiment mining using ensemble classification models. In: Sobh, T. (ed.) Innovations and Advances in Computer Sciences and Engineering, vol. I, pp. 509–514. Springer, Dordrecht (2010). https://doi.org/10.1007/978-90-481-3658-2_89
20. Xia, R., Zong, C., Li, S.: Ensemble of feature sets and classification algorithms for sentiment classification. Inf. Sci. **181**(6), 1138–1152 (2011)
21. Xiong, Z., Shen, Q., Wang, Y., Zhu, C.: Paragraph vector representation based on word to vector and CNN learning. Comput. Mater. Continua **55**, 213–227 (2018)
22. Zhang, Y., Wang, Q., Li, Y., Wu, X.: Sentiment classification based on piecewise pooling convolutional neural network. Comput. Mater. Continua **56**, 285–297 (2018)
23. Zhou, Z.: Ensemble Methods: Foundations and Algorithms. Taylor & Francis, New York (2012)

Task Scheduling Algorithm Based on Campus Cloud Platform

Zuo-cong Chen(✉)

College of Computer Science and Technology,
Hainan Tropical Ocean University, Sanya 572022, China

Abstract. To further share the resources in the campus to serve the students and teachers more widely, we design a task scheduling algorithm based on genetic algorithm. Our method introduces the structure of the campus cloud platform, the principle of genetic algorithm, niche technique, chromosome coding, the generation of the initial population, the selection of the fitness function, the operation of selection, crossover and mutation and finally the definition of the whole algorithm. To verify the effectiveness of our method, our method is compared with other two methods in simulation environment of campus cloud platform, the result shows that our method not only has the highest fitness function but also has the least user fee.

Keywords: Cloud computing · Task scheduling · Resource allocation

1 Introduction

With the development of the cloud computing, the campus network is combined with cloud computing to provide the students, the teachers and the research members with more reliable and more friendly services. The campus cloud platform serves these users through the virtual machines, where all resources can be dynamically scheduled to manage the resources for the cloud platform efficiently. The main applications in the campus cloud platform mainly refers to two kinds of tasks, the teaching and research [1–3]. The difference of the two kinds of tasks is that research task cannot estimate the using time and the number of the needed virtual machines accurately, at the meantime, the teaching tasks are characteristic of periodical, predictable and cyclable [4–7]. Therefore, how to solve the task scheduling for the two tasks are important and key for the task scheduling.

The task scheduling problem in campus cloud platform is a NP problem [8]. The traditional methods [9–11] to solve this problem are shown the algorithms such as UDA (user directly assigning), MCT (minimum completion time), Min-min and Sufferage. Every task in UDA has to be assigned to the physical resources to implement, and the user doses not have to know the state of the allocated resources, thus this method has the advantages of simple implementing and easy achievement. However, when the number of the tasks are numerous, they are not guaranteed to be implemented for all if the number of the resources are not enough. MCT estimate the execution time need for every task, and assign the task to the resource that is expected to be finished earliest. This method pays attention to the ended time of the resource rather than the

X. Sun et al. (Eds.): ICAIS 2019, LNCS 11633, pp. 299–308, 2019.
https://doi.org/10.1007/978-3-030-24265-7_26

expected execution time. Min-min algorithm as a popular task scheduling method, puts all the tasks required to be scheduled together to construct a task set. The execution time for every task in the task set is computed, the task with the shortest execution time will be scheduled to the corresponding resource to execute, then the task will be removed from the task se1q`azt until the set is null. The algorithm Sufferage assign every task with a value. In every match for resource and task, the earliest time and sub-earliest time for the task are computed.

From the above analysis, we can find that the above works can be divided into as two kinds: scheduling based on the execution time or based on load prediction. If we use the scheduling policy based on execution time, and when the resources are overloaded or they are free, the migration will consume much bandwidth and also takes a long time, that will affect the teaching quality. However, when we take the scheduling method based on load prediction, the load also cannot be predicted for the new applied virtual machines, because there are not any historical data. According to the characteristic of the current campus platform, the traditional task scheduling method can be directly applied to. Therefore, we propose a new task scheduling method based on the prediction of the task scheduling and particle swarm optimization.

2 Problem Definition

The scheduling goal of campus cloud platform is to improve the resource rate and shorten the finished time for all the tasks. Assume there are m atomic tasks $P = \{p_1, p_2, \ldots, p_m\}$ needing to be assigned, the n independent tasks are represented as $T = \{t_1, t_2, \ldots, t_n\}$, so the goal is to search a match policy to map from the tasks to the resources, making the cost for the finished time of the task execution in the solution space m^n.

Definition 1. The atomic tasks are the tasks which are irrespective in the process of the resource scheduling.

Definition 2. The matrix ET_{n*m} represents the prediction execution time for n tasks in m resources, which can be represented as Eq. (1):

$$EF = \begin{bmatrix} et_{11} & et_{12}, \ldots & et_{1m} \\ \vdots & & \vdots \\ et_{n1} & et_{n2}, \ldots & et_{nm} \end{bmatrix} \tag{1}$$

where the symbol et_{ij} is the predicted time for the task t_i executed in resource p_j.

Definition 3. The matrix ETF_{n*m} represents the earliest time for n tasks in m resources, which can be represented as Eq. (2):

$$ETF = \begin{bmatrix} etf_{11} & etf_{12}, \ldots & etf_{1m} \\ \vdots & & \vdots \\ etf_{n1} & etf_{n2}, \ldots & etf_{nm} \end{bmatrix} \tag{2}$$

where the symbol etf_{ij} represents the earliest time of the task t_i executed in resource p_j, which can be computed by Eq. (3):

$$Finish\_Time = etf_{ij} = et_{ij} + s_j \tag{3}$$

where the symbol s_i represents the earliest time of the task t_i executed in resource p_j.

Definition 4. The matrix Q_{n*m} represents the service quality of n tasks allocated in m resources, which can be represented as Eq. (4):

$$Q = \begin{bmatrix} q_{11} & q_{12}, \cdots & q_{1m} \\ \vdots & & \vdots \\ q_{n1} & q_{n2}, \vdots & q_{nm} \end{bmatrix} \tag{4}$$

where the element q_{i*j} in the matrix Q represents the service quality of task t_i allocated in resource p_j, the symbol q_{i*j} is a three-tuple, where q_{i*j}^F is the execution time for the task t_i executed in p_j, q_{i*j}^F represents the operation reliability of the task t_i executed in p_j, q_{i*j}^P represents the cost of the task t_i executed in p_j.

The goal function of task scheduling can be denoted as Eq. (5):

$$sum = \sum_{i=1}^{n} \sum_{j=1}^{m} Sig_{ij} \frac{q_{ij}^R}{q_{ij}^F q_{ij}^P} \tag{5}$$

In Eq. (5), Sig_{ij} is an indication symbol, which can be represented as:

$$Sig_{ij} = \begin{cases} 1 & \textit{the task } t_i \textit{ executed in } p_j \\ 0 & \textit{other cases} \end{cases} \tag{6}$$

From the Eq. (5), we can see the service quality is larger, the value of the goal function will be larger too. Meanwhile, the cost and the execution time are smaller, the value of the goal function are larger.

3 Task Scheduling Based on Improve Gene Algorithm

This section introduces the structure of the campus cloud platform, the principle of genetic algorithm, niche technique, chromosome coding, the generation of the initial population, the selection of the fitness function, the operation of selection, crossover and mutation and finally the definition of the whole algorithm.

3.1 The Principle of Genetic Algorithm

The structure of the campus cloud platform is shown as Fig. 1.

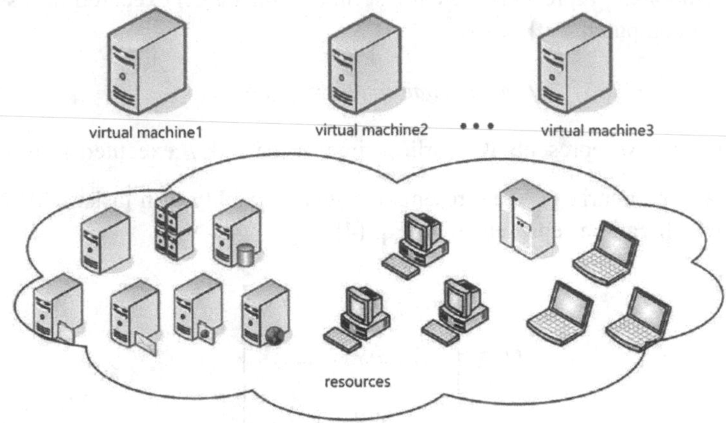

Fig. 1. The structure of campus cloud platform

In Fig. 1, the resources and the virtual machines have to be matched accurately with the goal of maximizing the fitness function.

3.2 The Principle of Genetic Algorithm

Genetic algorithm as an optimal algorithm that simulates the biological evolution, is introduced by J. Holland of the university Michigan in 1975. Genetic algorithm optimizes the solution of the problem through the continuous iteration, and it gradually become a computation model for optimal problem.

Genetic algorithm has the property of strong flexibility and robustness. When the problem and the goal are complex, it also can confront perfectly. Therefore, it is easy to fall into the local optimum, and we will use the niche technique to improve it in the next subsection, so that multiple property of the individual can be kept.

3.3 Niche Technique

Niche originates from a notion of the nature, that is, the biology in a given environment is liven with the same species to propagate the descendants. Niche technique is mainly applied in genetic algorithm, and the goal is increasing the multiple property of the individuals and giving some penalty to the individual with small fitness. The main approaches in Niche technique comprise the preselection mechanism and the crowding mechanism.

Preselection mechanism can divide the population into several subpopulations, the individuals with higher fitness will be selected to comprise a new population. The former population will be evolved to the new generation by the selection, crossover and mutation, and then it will be entered the next evolution of the population to accelerate the obtain of the optimal solution.

Crowding mechanism will select the individuals with higher fitness, the Euclidean distance between the reminder individuals is computed. When the Euclidean distance between individuals is smaller than the predefined the radius of the niche technique, the individual with small value of fitness will be punished, so that the evolution of the individual will be accelerated.

At every new generation of population, the individuals generated by selection, crossover and mutation are combined with the former generation of population. The Euclidean distance between every two individuals is computed as follows:

$$dist(i,j) = \sqrt{\sum_{k=1}^{h} (x_{ih} - x_{ih})} \tag{7}$$

Where the radius of the niche is denoted as d, the symbol h denotes the dimensionality of the individual. If the distance between two individuals are smaller than d, then the individuals with the small fitness will be punished to decrease the fitness. After all the fitness of all the individuals are computed over, the individual with high fitness will be selected.

3.4 Individual Coding

The traditional genetic algorithm usually takes binary coding approach to code the individuals. However, this kind of the coding cannot suit the campus cloud platform due to the scheduling approach not only needing to consider which resource the task will be implement on but also the sort of the task execution.

The individual is coded by natural number approach, for example, if there are 6 resources and 10 tasks, one feasible coding for individual in continuous time steps is as follows:

$$\begin{bmatrix} 7 & 1 & 2 & 9 & 4 & 5 & 6 & 3 & 8 \\ 2 & 3 & 5 & 7 & 1 & 8 & 9 & 4 & 6 \\ 2 & 5 & 7 & 8 & 9 & 4 & 1 & 6 & 3 \end{bmatrix} \tag{8}$$

Where the line index denotes the specific the task and the column represents the resource.

3.5 Fitness Function

Fitness function is used to measure whether the solution is good or not. Therefore, we will design good fitness function to keep the good individual and also keep the multiple property of the population, so that the global optimal solution can be found. Because the goal of the scheduling for campus cloud platform is to find a global solution in the solution space. The fitness is shown as Eq. (5).

3.6 The Selection of the Individuals

The roulette approach is a method which is used to select the individuals, where the fitness functions for every individual in the population are computed. The probability of selecting individual is decided by the proportion of the fitness of the current individual in the sum of the fitness of all the individuals. The probability of the individual is computed as:

$$P_{ros} = \frac{f_i}{\sum_{i=1}^{\gamma} f_i} \tag{9}$$

Where the symbol γ is the number of individuals in the population. We can see from Eq. (4), the larger of the individual fitness will result in a larger selection probability for that individual.

3.7 Crossover and Mutation

The new population is generated by selecting the individuals with higher fitness until the number of the population reaches γ, then the number N of the γ will be selected to the next generation for crossover and mutation, where $N \leq \gamma$.

Crossover and mutation operators are two important operations in the genetic algorithm. Crossover operator simulate the recombination of the genes in nature, while the mutation operator extends the search space. These two operators cooperate together to achieve the multiple property of the solutions, so that the algorithm will not fall into the local optimum.

Crossover operator use the two-point crossover operator. For the two individuals of the parent generation, we choose a crossover point, and then change two points in the left and the right of this point. To keep the feasibility of the solution, the constraints are computed to satisfy the demand of the campus cloud platform.

However, different from the crossover operator, mutation operator then changes the position of the resources, namely, when we selected two resources to mutate, the tasks are allocated in the two resources are changed.

Crossover probability and mutation probability are determined by the following method. Assume $f_{\max}$ represents the global optimal fitness, f_{avg} denotes the average fitness of the population, f_c is the fitness of the mutation, f_m is the fitness of the mutated individual, the crossover probability and the mutation probability are decided by:

$$p_{roc} = \begin{cases} \frac{c_1(f_{\max} - f_c)}{f_{\max} + f_{avg}} & f_c \geq f_{avg} \\ c2 & f_c < f_{avg} \end{cases} \tag{10}$$

$$p_{rom} = \begin{cases} \frac{c_3(f_{\max} - f_m)}{f_{\max} - f_{avg}} & f_m \geq f_{avg} \\ c4 & f_m < f_{avg} \end{cases} \tag{11}$$

Where the constant c1, c2, c3 and c4 can be adjusted according to the demand.

4 Task Scheduling Algorithm for Campus Cloud Platform

The algorithm of task scheduling algorithm based on improve genetic algorithm for campus cloud platform is shown as Algorithm 1.

Algorithm 1 Task scheduling algorithm based on improved genetic algorithm

Input: the number of the tasks is n, the number of the resources is m, the number of the individuals in the population is I. The preselected number of the individuals is N. The initial number of the individuals is k, the radius of the niche is d, the iteration number is denoted as t, the maximum number of iteration is t_{max}, the constants c1, c2, c3 and c4.

Output: the individual with optimal fitness

Step 1: Initialize the coding of every individual at random and generates a initial population.

Step 2: Use the selection method for the individuals described in section 3.5 to select the individuals in the initial population, namely, compute the fitness of the individual according to the equation (5), the probability of the individual is computed as equation (9).

Step 3: Use the crossover and mutation operators defined in section 3.6 to change the individual coding, the probabilities of crossover and mutation are decided by equation (10) and (11), until the number of the population reaches the maximum value I.

Step 4: The new population generated from step 2 and step 3 are combined here. Then according to the niche technique, namely, compute the Euclidean distance between every two individuals by equation (7). The individuals are sorted according to the values of the fitness, and the former I individuals are selected to construct the next population.

Step 5: Compute whether the fitness of the new generated optimal solution is higher than the former optimal solution:

If it is not equal

$$\phi = 0$$

Else

$$\phi = \phi + 1$$

Step 6: Judge if current iteration times reaches the maximum value t_{max}:

If $t_{max} == t$

the algorithm ends and output the optimal solution with the high value of the fitness

Else

$t = t + 1$, and then transfers to the step 2.

5 Simulation Experiment

5.1 Experiment Environment and Parameter Selection

To verify the proposed scheduling method, the task scheduling method is simulated in the campus cloud platform. The simulation experiment environment is shown as: 1 server of ShuGuang 3000 (IBM power3-II 375 MHz, 16 CPU, memory 16 GB, AIX4.3.3, RedHat Linux 9.0), 2 servers of Dell PowerEdge 2600 (Double Intel Xeon 1.8 GHz CPU, memory 2 GB, RedHat Linux 9.0), 20 PC (Intel P4 1.7 GHz, memory 512M, RedHat 9.0).

The parameter selection are as follows: the number of the tasks is $n = 200$, the number of the resources is $m = 5$, the number of the individuals in the population is $I = 100$. The preselected number of the individuals is $N = 20$. The initial number of the individuals is $k = 50$, the radius of the niche is $d = 10$, the iteration number is denoted as $t = 1$, the maximum number of iteration is $t_{max} = 200$, the constants c1, c2, c3 and c4 are all initialized as 0.25.

5.2 Simulation Result

The proposed method is compared with literature [10] and [11], the fitness obtained from the three method is shown as Fig. 2.

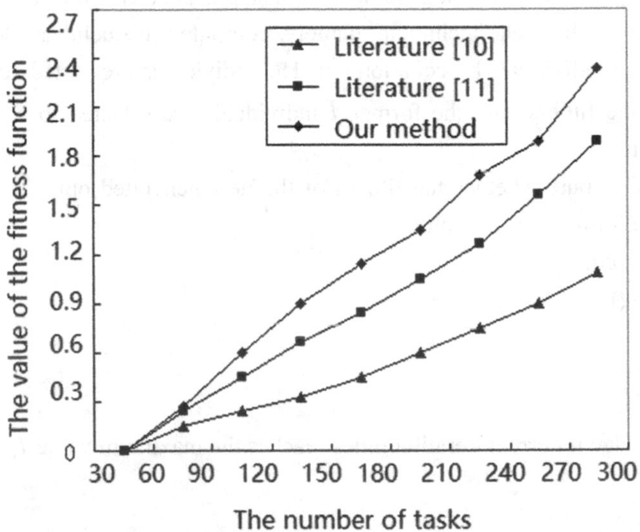

Fig. 2. The comparison of the fitness of three methods

From the Fig. 2, we can see our method has the highest fitness. The fitness obtained in Literature [10] is always smaller than our method and Literature [11]. When the number of the tasks is less than 90, the fitness of Literature [10] and our method are almost the same. However, when the number of the tasks is larger than 90, the fitness of

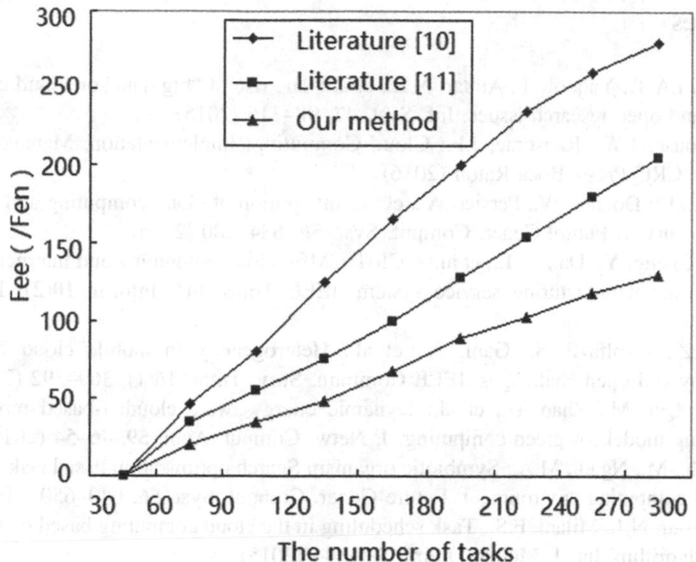

Fig. 3. The comparisons of the user fee

our method is larger than that of the Literature [10]. Therefore, our method has the best value of fitness.

The comparisons of the three methods are shown in Fig. 3. We can see that whether the number of the task is more or less, the user fee of our method is still lower than the other two methods. It proves our method has the best performance in fee.

6 Conclusion

To schedule effectively in the campus cloud platform, we design an improved task scheduling method based on genetic algorithm. Our method introduces the structure of the campus cloud platform, the principle of genetic algorithm, niche technique, chromosome coding, the generation of the initial population, the selection of the fitness function, the operation of selection, crossover and mutation and finally the definition of the whole algorithm. Through the simulation experiment, our method is implemented and compared with the other methods. The result shows that our method has the best fitness function and the least user fee. Therefore, it is a suitable method for the campus cloud platform.

Acknowledgments. This work was financially Project supported by the Education Department of Hainan Province, project number:hnjg2017ZD-17. the Hainan Provincial Department of Science and Technology under Grant No. ZDKJ201602 and the Natural Science Foundation of Hainan Province under Grant No. 20156222.

References

1. Hashem, I.A.T., Yaqoob, I., Anuar, N.B., et al.: The rise of "big data" on cloud computing: review and open research issues. Inf. Syst. **47**, 98–115 (2015)
2. Rittinghouse, J.W., Ransome, J.F.: Cloud Computing: Implementation, Management, and Security. CRC Press, Boca Raton (2016)
3. Botta, A., De Donato, W., Persico, V., et al.: Integration of cloud computing and internet of things: a survey. Future Gener. Comput. Syst. **56**, 684–700 (2016)
4. Tao, F., Cheng, Y., Da Xu, L., et al.: CCIoT-CMfg: cloud computing and internet of things-based cloud manufacturing service system. IEEE Trans. Ind. Inform. **10**(2), 1435–1442 (2014)
5. Sanaei, Z., Abolfazli, S., Gani, A., et al.: Heterogeneity in mobile cloud computing: taxonomy and open challenges. IEEE Commun. Surv. Tutor. **16**(1), 369–392 (2014)
6. Gai, K., Qiu, M., Zhao, H., et al.: Dynamic energy-aware cloudlet-based mobile cloud computing model for green computing. J. Netw. Comput. Appl. **59**, 46–54 (2016)
7. Abdullahi, M., Ngadi, M.A.: Symbiotic organism Search optimization based task scheduling in cloud computing environment. Future Gener. Comput. Syst. **56**, 640–650 (2016)
8. Navimipour, N.J., Milani, F.S.: Task scheduling in the cloud computing based on the cuckoo search algorithm. Int. J. Model. Optim. **5**(1), 44 (2015)
9. Guo, F., Yu, L., Tian, S., et al.: A workflow task scheduling algorithm based on the resources' fuzzy clustering in cloud computing environment. Int. J. Commun. Syst. **28**(6), 1053–1067 (2015)
10. Wang, T., Liu, Z., Chen, Y., et al.: Load balancing task scheduling based on genetic algorithm in cloud computing. In: 2014 IEEE 12th International Conference on Dependable, Autonomic and Secure Computing (DASC), pp. 146–152. IEEE (2014)
11. Li, Y., Chen, M., Dai, W., et al.: Energy optimization with dynamic task scheduling mobile cloud computing. IEEE Syst. J. **11**(1), 96–105 (2017)
12. Li, Z.Y., Yun, Q.S.: On the privacy-preserving outsourcing scheme of reversible data hiding over encrypted image data in cloud computing. Comput. Mater. Continua **55**(3), 523–539 (2018)
13. Jie, R.C., Ruo, M.X., et al.: An abnormal network flow feature sequence prediction approach for DDoS attacks detection in big data environment. Comput. Mater. Continua **55**(1), 95–119 (2018)

Automatic Self-feedback for the Studying Effect of MOOC Based on Support Vector Machine

Zuo-cong Chen(✉)

College of Computer Science and Technology,
Hainan Tropical Ocean University, Sanya 572022, China
twsf2005@163.com

Abstract. Unlike the off-line teaching, the feedback from the student is hard to capture, so that the teaching effect of the course is hard to be improved. In order to solve this problem and achieve a better teaching effect as the same as the offline one, we propose a method for the feedback of MOOC course by combing PCA (principle component analysis) and SVM (support vector machine). The dataset for analysis are collected from the cameras in the courses, KECA (kernel entropy component analysis) is used here to extract the feature vectors for the dataset. The features are feed into the SVM to achieve the recognition of the students studying feedback. The recognition is finally transferred to a classification process. To verify the priority of our method, our method is compared with the other two methods, the result shows that our method not only has the optimal dimensionality for samples, but also has the higher classification rate.

Keywords: Self-feedback · Feature vectors · Decrease the dimensionality · Recognition

1 Introduction

MOOC (Massive Open Online Course) as a new course form developed after the year 2012, receives high attention from the government, the university and the enterprise and serves as an important force to promote the reform of high education [1, 2]. Recent years, it is applied in practical. Therefore, how to provide satisfactory service and effect in such a large-scale environment, is a key problem in the development of MOOC. Moreover, the high dropout degree and low participate degree are still main problems in the current MOOC course learning [3, 4]. As we consider, the prediction of learning result for course learning behavior in the former phase and the middle phase will affect the teaching policy and content in the latter teaching [5]. In this process, we have to obtain as much information about the studying behavior as possible. Moreover, the information has to be extracted further, to get the most key information, so that the studying behaviors for all the individuals can be explored thoroughly. In the traditional courses, the speaker can get the feedback from the face expression and the direct answer and then improve the course through the analysis for it. Unfortunately, the current MOOC course can not achieve it, so we consider collecting the facial expression figures

X. Sun et al. (Eds.): ICAIS 2019, LNCS 11633, pp. 309–320, 2019.
https://doi.org/10.1007/978-3-030-24265-7_27

through the camera, and then use the designed algorithm to analyze the figures to obtain the course effect, so as to improve the teaching quality.

Ekman designed 6 basic facial expressions such as sadness, anger, fear, surprise and disgust in 1971, then coding system for face recognition was developed in 1978. Most of the current facial expression algorithms are extension of the six expression-models. However, the facial expressions of MOOC are different from the traditional 6 expressions, it may have the expressions such as sleep and consider, making many current expression recognition algorithms unsuitable for the MOOC course. The result is that some facial expression will be not recognized.

Therefore, we propose a model specially for the MOOC course. Firstly, we use kernel PCA (principal component analysis) to decrease the dimensionality of the primitive figures and then design the SVM with kernel to distinguish the facial expressions of the course.

2 PCA and KPCA

2.1 PCA

PCA [6–9] proposed by Kirby in 1990, is a common method to decrease the dimensionality. PCA can transfer the primitive random vectors to the new random vectors with independent members. However, the defects of PCA is the large capacity of storage memory and high complexity of computation. The principles of PCA can be described as:

(1) Transfer the primitive facial figure to the vectors with high dimensionality through the line and column.
(2) Construct the training samples of vectors with high dimensionality and obtain the covariance matrix, the features of the covariance vectors are obtained, then compose the transform matrix by feature vectors.
(3) Project the data obtained in Step (1) through the transpose matrix constructed in Step (2) to eliminate the correlation of data and get the principal features.
(4) Reconstruct the figure from the primitive one by using the new members.

For the facial figure $f(x,y)$ with the size $m \times n$, it will be reshaped to the vector $D = m \times n$, the training samples are $X = \{x_1, x_2, \ldots x_M\}$, where x_i is the *i-th* sample with the dimensionality n, $1 \le i \le M$, so the average face can be computed as:

$$\bar{x} = \frac{1}{M}\sum_{i=1}^{M} x_i \tag{1}$$

After minus the average face, the covariance is expressed as:

$$S = \frac{1}{n}\sum_{i=1}^{M} (x_i - \bar{x})(x_i - \bar{x})^{\mathrm{T}} \tag{2}$$

where the dimensionality of the covariance is $D \times D$.

The feature value λ_i and the feature vector z_i can be obtained, and the dimensionality of the main components of is determined by the accumulative contribution rate α as follows:

$$\alpha = \frac{\sum_{i=1}^{K} \lambda_i}{\sum_{i=1}^{D} \lambda_i} \tag{3}$$

When the former several contribution rates α is larger than the threshold th, the feature vectors corresponding to the respecting feature values are used to construct the feature space Σ, the threshold th is usually larger than 0.9.

The training sample set is projected to the feature space Σ, so that the training feature face is obtained for every sample, the feature vector set A after reducing dimensionality is shown as follows:

$$A = \Sigma^{\mathrm{T}} X \tag{4}$$

When the former several contribution rates α is larger than the threshold th, the feature vectors corresponding to the respecting feature values are used to construct the feature space Σ, the threshold th is usually larger than 0.9.

2.2 KECA

KECA (Kernel entropy component analysis) [10] has received perfect effects in many applications. As a non-linear extension of PCA, it can handle many non-linear problems with high efficiency. KECA as a new data transform method, it introduces the entropy on the basis of the KECA so that the data transform can be achieved though the entropy analysis in the feature space. Recently, KECA is applied in the data aggregation and image denoising and it receives perfect effect, but it still has not received comprehensive research in reducing the dimensionality.

Given the sample x with the dimensionality N, $p(x)$ is the probability density function, then the Renyi entropy is as:

$$H(p) = -\lg \int p^2(x)\mathrm{d}x \tag{5}$$

Let $V(p) = \int p^2(x)$ and the Parzen window $\widehat{p}(x) = \frac{1}{N}\sum_{x_t \in D} K_\sigma(x, x_t)$, we estimate $V(p)$ by using the average value, as follows:

$$\begin{aligned}\hat{V}(p) &= \frac{1}{N}\sum_{x_t \in D} \hat{p}(x_t) \\ &= \frac{1}{N}\sum_{x_t \in D} \frac{1}{N}\sum_{x_t \in D} K_\sigma(x, x_t) \\ &= \frac{1}{N}\mathbf{1}^T \boldsymbol{K}\mathbf{1}\end{aligned} \tag{6}$$

Let the vector with the dimensionality $k(k<N)$ is mapped to the subspace U_k. Only if the subspace is related with the Renyi entropy, the feature vector and the feature value will be resorted according to the entropy, the mapping Φ_{eac} of KECA is computed as:

$$\Phi_{eac} = P_{U_k}\Phi = D_k^{\frac{1}{2}} E_k^{\mathrm{T}} \tag{7}$$

Where the diagnose matrix is D, $E = [e_1, e_2, \ldots, e_{\mathrm{N}}]$.

The solution of the feature matrix can be obtained by transforming to the minimum problem, namely:

$$\Phi_{eac} = D_k^{\frac{1}{2}} E_k^T : \min \hat{V}(p) - \hat{V}(p) \tag{8}$$

Combing with the Eq. (6), the Eq. (4) is transferred to:

$$\min \frac{1}{N}\mathbf{1}(\mathbf{K} - \mathbf{K}_{eca})\mathbf{I} \tag{9}$$

where $\mathbf{K}_{eca} = \Phi_{eac}^T \Phi_{eac} = E_k D_k E_k^T$.

KECA uses the operation similar with KPCA to achieve the reduction dimensionality, so as to transform the optimization of minimum value to the data transform. The reducing dimensionality based on KECA is shown as:

(1) Input the data set composed of N-dimension vectors $X = [x_1, x_2, \ldots, x_{\mathrm{N}}]$.
(2) Compute the Euclidean distance of the data set $X = [x_1, x_2, \ldots, x_{\mathrm{N}}]$ and establish the kernel matrix $\mathbf{K}_{eca}$ through Parzen window function.
(3) Compute the feature value and feature vector through the nonlinear mapping in the feature space.
(4) Compute the Renyi entropy for the feature value and the feature vector, and then resort the feature value and the feature vector according to the entropy, so as to generate the KECA mapping Φ_{eac}.
(5) Select the former k-dimension mapping according to the demand of the reducing dimensionality and establish the relation between kernel matrix and the mapping, so as to achieve the data transform from high-dimensionality to low dimensionality.

The process of reducing dimensionality is shown as Fig. 1:

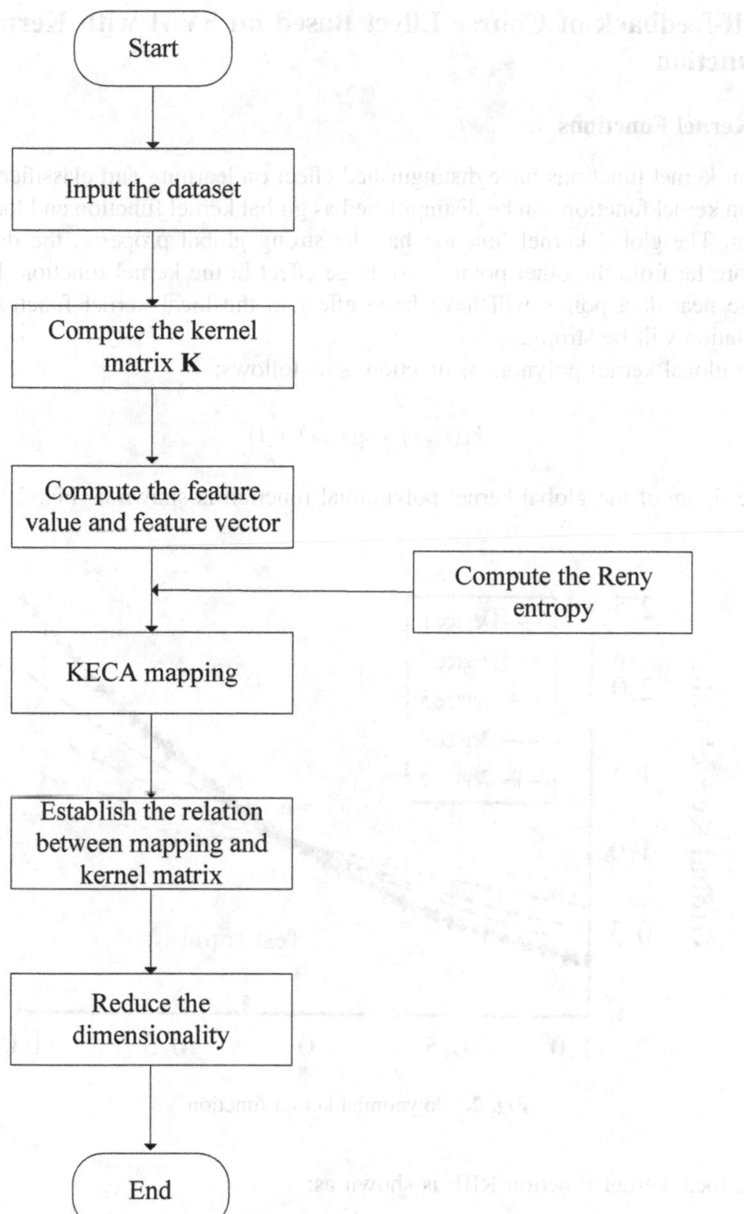

Fig. 1. The process of reducing dimensionality

3 Self-feedback of Course Effect Based on SVM with Kernel Function

3.1 Kernel Functions

Different kernel functions have distinguished effect on learning and classification. The common kernel function can be distinguished as global kernel function and local kernel function. The global kernel function has the strong global property, the data points which are far from the other points have large effect in the kernel function. However, only the near data points will have large effect in the local kernel function, so the interpolation will be stronger.

The global kernel polynomial function is as follows:

$$k_1(x_i, x) = [(x_i, x) + 1]^d \tag{10}$$

The figure of the global kernel polynomial function is shown as Fig. 2.

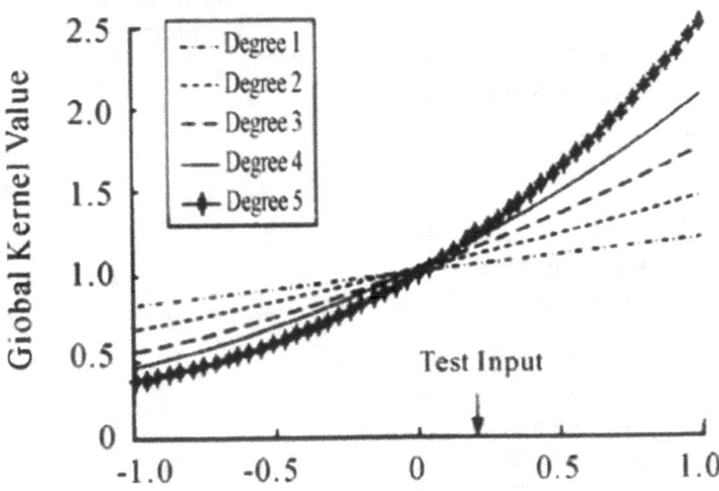

Fig. 2. Polynomial kernel function

The local kernel function RBF is shown as:

$$k_2(x_i, x) = \exp(-||x_i - x||^2/\sigma^2) \tag{11}$$

The figure of the local kernel polynomial function is shown as Fig. 3.

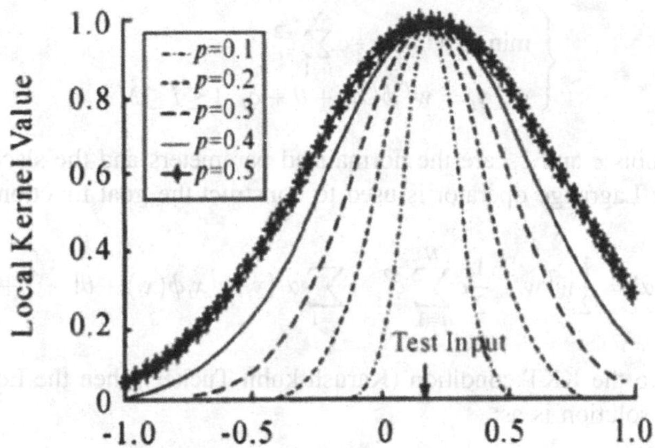

Fig. 3. The curves of the radius radical function

From Figs. 1 and 2, we can establish a learning model with the high interpretation and extrapolation ability, the two kinds of kernel functions can be weighted as:

$$k(x_i, x) = w_1 k_1(x_i, x) + w_2 k_2(x_i, x) \tag{12}$$

Where w_1 and w_2 are weights, with the values larger than 1 and satisfying $w_1 + w_2 = 1$.

3.2 Self-feedback Based on SVM

Least Squares Support Vector Machine (LSSVM) is a machine learning method based on the minimum structure risk of statistical machine learning method. By introducing the kernel function, the linear separable problem in low-dimension is transformed to the inner product of the high dimension space, so that the samples can be separated linearly. LSSVM has the advantages such as small requirement of samples and strong generalization ability.

The basic idea in the classification of LSSVM is as follows: the data in low dimension space R^N is mapped to the high dimension kernel space H, so that the optimal super plane can be established in high dimension goal space.

$$w^T \phi(x) + \theta = 0 \tag{13}$$

where w and θ are the normal vector and bias of the super plane, the classification problem can be transformed as the following goal function:

$$\begin{cases} \min \ \frac{1}{2}w^T w + \frac{1}{2}c\sum_{i=1}^{N}\xi_i^2 \\ s.t. \ y_i = w^T\phi(x_i) + \theta + \xi_i \ \ 1 \le i \le N \end{cases} \quad (14)$$

where the symbols c and ξ_i are the normalized parameters and the slack variables.

Assume the Lagrange operator is used to construct the goal function:

$$L(w, \theta, \xi, \alpha) = \frac{1}{2}w^T w + \frac{1}{2}c\sum_{i=1}^{N}\xi_i^2 - \sum_{i=1}^{N}\alpha_i\{y_i[w^T x_i\phi(x_i) + \theta] - 1 + \xi_i\} \quad (15)$$

According to the KKT condition (Karush-kuhn-Tucker), then the Eq. (15) can be solved and the solution is as:

$$\begin{cases} w = \sum_{i=1}^{N}\alpha_i y_i\psi(x_i) \\ w = c\xi_i \ \ w^T\phi(x_i) + \theta + \xi_i - y_i = 0 \\ \sum_{i=1}^{N}\alpha_i = 0 \end{cases} \quad (16)$$

The recognition goal function of the facial expression is transformed as:

$$f(x) = sign(\sum_{i,j=1}^{m} a_i y_i k(x_i, x_j) + \theta) \quad (17)$$

Where the symbol *sign* is the basic symbol function that can be defined as:

$$sign(x)\begin{cases} 1 & x \ge 0 \\ -1 & x < 0 \end{cases} \quad (18)$$

When the samples are attributed to the first class, the value of $f(x)$ will be 1, or else will be −1.

$k(x_i, x_j)$ as a kernel function determined by the demand, and the selection principle is the Mercer condition, namely, for any nonlinear mapping $\phi(x) \neq 0$ and $\int \phi^2(x)dx < \infty$, the following equation will be hold.

$$\iint k(x, x')\phi(x)\phi(x')dxdx' \ge 0 \quad (19)$$

3.3 Self-feedback Based on Facial Expression Based on Kernel Functions

A LSSVM can solve the classification problem for two kinds. To recognize more kinds, for example, when the number of the classifications are more than n, it needs $n(n-1)/2$ LSSVM to achieve classification. Finally, the classification with most votes will be regarded as the final recognition result.

4 Self-feedback of Course Effect Based on SVM with Kernel Function

In order to verify the efficacy of this paper, LSSVM is used to self-feedback of the course effect. Experiment samples are obtained from the course, where the average duration time for facial expression will be 2 s, the durations of most of the facial expressions are 2 to 9 s. The figure is fetched every 5 frames, so that every expression can be fetched 4–5 frames and no information will be lost.

4.1 Generation of Feature Vectors

The tradition images from the camera are 128 * 128, and then use the KECA to decrease the dimensionality. We divide the dataset to four parts, namely, Group 1, Group 2, Group 3 and Group 4. The effect of the KECA with the basic PCA and KPCA are shown as Table 1:

Table 1. The result of three methods for reducing dimensionality

DataSet	The optimal dimensionality		
	KECA	PCA	KPCA
Group 1	34	38	44
Group 2	23	35	39
Group 3	19	45	23
Group 4	20	20	32

From Table 1, we can see the method KECA needs less dimensions than the other two methods. The methods PCA and KPCA have more redundant information that will have no effect in the final classification. Through the operation of reducing dimensionality, the method has a tighter and more economic characteristic. Moreover, the operation of reducing dimensionality decreases the number of the feature dimensions, resulting in that the computation complexity is decreased and the efficiency is improved.

4.2 The Self-feedback Classification Based on LSSVM

After the feature vectors are obtained via KECA, then it will be feed into the LSSVM to achieve the classification. In order to verify the effect of the classification, it is compared with two classification methods on two datasets collected from the course, the result is shown as Fig. 4.

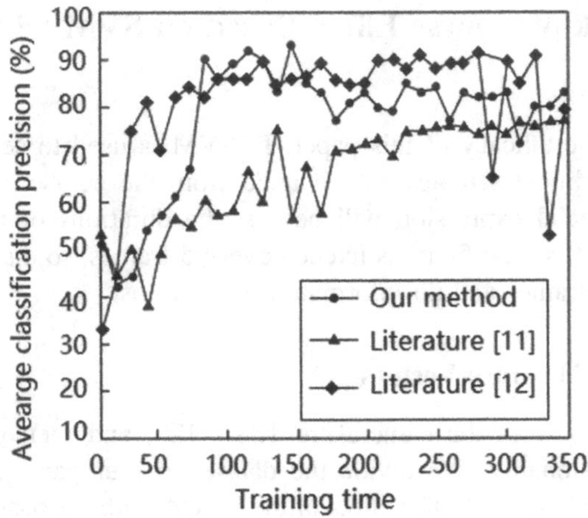

Fig. 4. The compared result of our method with other two methods in dataset 1

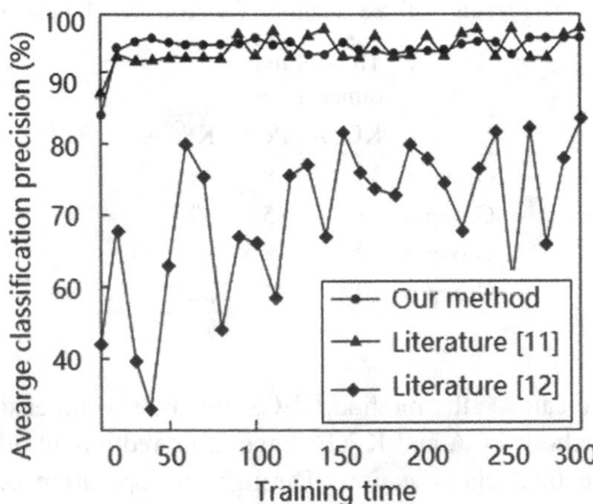

Fig. 5. The compared result of our method with other two methods in dataset 2

From the Figs. 4 and 5, we can find that our method behaves best not only in the dataset 1 but also in dataset 2. In the dataset 1, the method PCA behaves worst. The performance of the literature [11] and the literature [12] are almost the same, but our method does not fluctuate as heavily as the method of KECA. In the dataset 2,

KPCA behaves worst in three of all. KECA learns quickly in the former 50 ms, in the latter training, it behaves as nearly well as that of PCA. In words, our method has the best performance.

5 Conclusion

The feedback from the MOOC course are difficult to be analyzed, so the course quality is hard to be improved. To solve this problem and improve the course teaching effect, we propose a self-feedback method for MOOC course. The dataset for analysis are collected from the cameras, KECA is used here to extract the feature vectors for the dataset. To identify the effect of the course, we propose a method based on LSSVM with two kernel to achieve the classification. Through such a classification, we can identify every expression of the students. Compared with other two methods, the result of our method not only has the optimal dimensionality for samples, but also has the higher classification rate.

Acknowledgments. This work was financially Project supported by the Education Department of Hainan Province, project number:hnjg2017ZD-17. The Hainan Provincial Department of Science and Technology under Grant No. ZDKJ201602 and the Natural Science Foundation of Hainan Province under Grant No. 20156222.

References

1. Guo, P.J., Kim, J., Rubin, R.: How video production affects student engagement: an empirical study of MOOC videos. In: Proceedings of the First ACM Conference on Learning, SCALE 2014, pp. 41–50. ACM (2014)
2. Reich, J.: Rebooting MOOC research. Science **347**(6217), 34–35 (2015)
3. Bruff, D.O., Fisher, D.H., McEwen, K.E., et al.: Wrapping a MOOC: student perceptions of an experiment in blended learning. J. Online Learn. Teach. **9**(2), 187 (2015)
4. Baggaley, J.: MOOC rampant. Distance Educ. **34**(3), 368–378 (2013)
5. Daradoumis, T., Bassi, R., Xhafa, F., et al.: A review on massive e-learning (MOOC) design, delivery and assessment. In: 2013 Eighth International Conference on P2P, Parallel, Grid, Cloud and Internet Computing (3PGCIC), pp. 208–213. IEEE (2013)
6. Maćkiewicz, A., Ratajczak, W.: Principal components analysis (PCA). Comput. Geosci. **19** (3), 303–342 (1993)
7. Holland, S.M.: Principal components analysis (PCA). Department of Geology, University of Georgia, Athens, GA, 30602-2501 (2008)
8. Schölkopf, B., Smola, A., Müller, K.-R.: Kernel principal component analysis. In: Gerstner, W., Germond, A., Hasler, M., Nicoud, J.-D. (eds.) ICANN 1997. LNCS, vol. 1327, pp. 583–588. Springer, Heidelberg (1997). https://doi.org/10.1007/BFb0020217
9. Kim, K.I., Jung, K., Kim, H.J.: Face recognition using kernel principal component analysis. IEEE Signal Process. Lett. **9**(2), 40–42 (2002)
10. Shekar, B.H., Kumari, M.S., Mestetskiy, L.M., et al.: Face recognition using kernel entropy component analysis. Neurocomputing **74**(6), 1053–1057 (2011)

11. Moreno, P.J., Ho, P.P., Vasconcelos, N.: A Kullback-Leibler divergence based kernel for SVM classification in multimedia applications. In: Advances in Neural Information Processing Systems, pp. 1385–1392 (2004)
12. Ebrahimi, M.A., Khoshtaghaza, M.H., Minaei, S., et al.: Vision-based pest detection based on SVM classification method. Comput. Electron. Agric. **137**, 52–58 (2017)
13. Bao, J.W., Ping, Z.L., et al.: Research on hybrid model of garlic short-term price forecasting based on big data. Comput. Mater. Continua **57**(2), 283–296 (2018)
14. Jayaprakash, G., Muthuraj, M.P.: Prediction of compressive strength of various SCC mixes using relevance vector machine. Comput. Mater. Continua **54**(1), 83–102 (2018)

Prediction on Payment Volume from Customer Service Electricity Channel

Gong Lihua[1(✉)], Sheng Yan[1], Liu Kunpeng[1], Zhu Longzhu[1], and Zhang Yi[2]

[1] State Grid Corporation Customer Service Center, Tianjin 300000, China
1623546008@qq.com
[2] Beijing DataOcean Technology Co., Ltd., Beijing 100081, China

Abstract. The paper aims to predict the service channel payment Volume from electricity customer, so as to support the managers of companies in each province to allocate the channel resources scientifically. In terms of methods, by exploring the relevant data of the big data platform, it is found that there were few factors influencing the payment Volume. Therefore, the time series algorithm was adopted to establish the prediction model, and then established the ARIMA model to predict the payment Volume by only taking the impact of time on the business volume of payment from various channels into consideration. Firstly, smooth data processing was carried out. Then, parameters of the model were confirmed through ACF and PACF, fitting model, and the model was evaluated from the perspective of statistical hypothesis. Finally, the prediction was performed, the final mean absolute error of the model (MAE) is 14.81%, and the root mean square error (RMSE) is 14920. The model satisfied the normal hypothesis test, and the predicted results were within the confidence interval between 80% and 95%, so the model had good effect and reached the application level.

Keywords: Payment volume · Time series · ARIMA model · Assumption of normality · Confidence interval

1 Introduction

With the rapid development of the Internet economy, the number of online users participating in the payment of electricity through online methods such as Alipay, WeChat public number, 95598 intelligent interactive website, "handheld power" and "Electronic e-bao" has exploded [1]. Contrary to this, the flow of people in each offline channel has been decreasing. Managers cannot match the resources of each channel through the business volume of each channel, so that scientific channel management cannot be performed [2]. We look for the time variation law of the peak and trough of the business volume of each channel and the related event factors that affect the traffic flow, and construct a forecasting model for the payment Volume of each channel by studying the method of forecasting the business volume of each channel. The model can predict the amount of payment Volume of each channel to provide reasonable reference and support for channel management and resource allocation. What's more,

The original version of this chapter was revised: It included an error in the first author affiliation which has now been corrected. The correction to this chapter is available at https://doi.org/10.1007/978-3-030-24265-7_57

X. Sun et al. (Eds.): ICAIS 2019, LNCS 11633, pp. 321–331, 2019.
https://doi.org/10.1007/978-3-030-24265-7_28

the model implements customizable, executable, manageable, and traceable active boot functions in the application [3].

This paper takes Shanxi State Grid Corporation as an example, and relies on the massive payment data of the National Grid Customer Service Center and the State Grid Shanxi Branch to accumulate the business volume of each channel as the goal and study the characteristics of business volume change with time. Through the mining and analysis of historical data of business volume, the paper explores the law of business volume time series change, and constructs the forecasting model of electricity customer service channel payment Volume.

2 Research Ideas and Methods

Based on the exploration of data related to the big data platform, we find that there are few factors affecting the payment Volume, and it may not be possible to model the regression forecasting of the payment Volume. Therefore, at this stage, we mainly forecast the future based on the existing historical data of Shanxi company payment Volume. In view of the model's objectives and the availability of data indicators, this paper selects a time series algorithm to build a prediction model.

The time series (or dynamic sequence) is a sequence in which the values of the same statistical indicator are arranged in chronological order [4]. The main purpose of time series analysis is to predict the future based on existing historical data [5]. The time series has the following characteristics:

(1) The time series analysis and forecasting is to predict future development based on past trends in things [6]. Its premise is to assume that the past of things will continue into the future. This is because the reality of things is the result of historical development, and the future of things is an extension of reality. So we can consider that the past and future of things are related. This method uses past historical data to speculate further on the future development trend of things through statistical analysis. In the prediction, the past of things will continue into the future, which means that things will not suddenly change in the future, but gradually change.

(2) The time series analysis forecasting method highlights the role of time factors in forecasting, and does not consider the influence of specific factors outside. The time series is at the core of the time series analysis prediction method. In other words, without time series, there is no such method [7]. Although the development of predictive objects is affected by many factors, the use of time series analysis to predict the quantity actually attributes all the influencing factors to the time factor. It can be considered that the method only recognizes the combined effects of all the influencing factors, and still plays a role in predicting objects in the future, and does not analyze the causal relationship between the predicted objects and the influencing factors [8]. Therefore, in order to obtain accurate predictions that reflect the future development of things, we must combine quantitative analysis methods with qualitative analysis methods when we use time series analysis [9]. In other words, we must fully analyze the relationship between various factors and market

changes from the qualitative aspect, and determine the predicted value on this basis. It should be pointed out that the time series prediction method has the defect of prediction error because the prominent time series does not consider the influence of external factors. This kind of error defect is reflected in the fact that when the application scene encounters a large change in the outside world, there is often a large deviation. Time series prediction is better for short-term and medium-term predictions than for long-term predictions [10]. Due to objective things, especially economic phenomena, are more likely to change external factors over a longer period of time, they must have a major impact on market economic phenomena. If this happens, when using time series for forecasting, only the time factor is considered regardless of the influence of external factors on the predicted object, and the predicted result will be seriously inconsistent with the actual situation [11]. If we use time series to predict the above objects, the prediction results will be seriously inconsistent with the actual situation only considering the time factor and not considering the influence of external factors on the predicted objects.

3 Analytical Mining Verification Standard

The forecast of payment Volume for each channel is essentially a numerical prediction of the amount of payment Volume [12]. The evaluation of numerical prediction effect mainly compares the true value with the predicted value, or compares the true numerical column with the predicted numerical value column. The closer the performance is, the better the predictive model is. Conversely, the farther the performance is, the worse the prediction model is [13].

It supposes that $y_i, i \in [1, n]$ represents the true value, and $\widehat{y}_i, i \in [1, n]$ represents the predicted value.

Mean Square Error (MSE): It takes the square of the absolute error value compared to the average error. This increases the effect of the error compared to the absolute value of the error, that is, it is more sensitive to the estimation of the error. In addition, it avoids the problem that the positive and negative cannot be added, and averages the sum of the squares of the difference between all the predicted values and the true values. The MSE is also a representative indicator of the prediction effect. Its definition is as follows:

$$\mathrm{MSE} = \frac{1}{n}\sum\nolimits_{i=1}^{n} E_i^2 = \frac{1}{n}\sum\nolimits_{i=1}^{n} (y_i - \widehat{y}_i)^2 \tag{1}$$

In numerical prediction, the smaller the value of MSE is, the better the representative model effects.

Root mean square error (RMSE): It is the square root of the mean square error and represents the average deviation of the predicted value from the true value. For example, if the mean square error is 5 and the true value is 20, the predicted value is likely to be in the range [15, 25]. MSE is also a widely used numerical predictor evaluation indicator, and the smaller it is, the better. Its definition is as follows:

$$\mathrm{RMSE} = \sqrt{\frac{1}{n}\sum\nolimits_{i=1}^{n} E_i^2} = \sqrt{\frac{1}{n}\sum\nolimits_{i=1}^{n} (y_i - \widehat{y}_i)^2} \tag{2}$$

Mean Absolute Error (MAE): Compared with the absolute error, MAE takes the absolute value and avoids the problem that the positive and negative errors cannot be added. In addition to the error between all predicted and true values, MAE takes the absolute value of all errors and averages them. It is more representative of the assessment of the prediction effect. Its definition is as follows:

$$\mathrm{MAE} = \frac{1}{n}\sum\nolimits_{i=1}^{n} |E_i| = \frac{1}{n}\sum\nolimits_{i=1}^{n} |y_i - \widehat{y}_i| \tag{3}$$

Mean Absolute Percentage Error (MAPE): MAPE is the average of the sum of absolute values of relative errors. Compared with the relative error, it avoids the problem that the positive and negative relative errors cannot be added, and the average value of the calculated error also reflects the average level of the relative error of the prediction. MAPE is a numerical prediction evaluation index that is often used. It is generally believed that MAPE is less than 15%, indicating that the prediction effect is better. Its definition is as follows:

$$\mathrm{MAPE} = \frac{1}{n}\sum\nolimits_{i=1}^{n} |e_i| = \frac{1}{n}\sum\nolimits_{i=1}^{n} \left|\frac{y_i - \widehat{y}_i}{y_i}\right| \tag{4}$$

Among the above four statistics, MAPE gives the ratio of the error to the true value. It has no unit, so it can be used to compare the prediction accuracy between different timings. The RMSE is more comparable than the other three statistics because it measures degree of error. There is no optimal metric in these kinds of prediction accuracy metrics. However, RMSE and MAPE are relatively well-known and commonly used, so we choose the error root mean square and the mean absolute percentage error.

The Akaike Information Criterion (AIC): is a standard for measuring the goodness of statistical model fitting. It was founded and developed by Japanese statistician Akio Hiroshi. The Akaike information criterion is based on the concept of entropy, which can weigh the complexity of the estimated model and the superiority of the model fitting data. AIC is a method of discriminating a variety of models in digital signal processing. In the general case, AIC can be expressed as:

$$\mathrm{AIC} = 2k - 2\ln\square(L) \tag{5}$$

Where k is the number of parameters and L is the likelihood function. The assumption is that the model error obeys an independent normal distribution. Let n be the observation number and SSR (SUM SQAURE OF RESIDUE) be the sum of the residuals, then AIC can be expressed as: AIC = 2k + nln(SSR/n). Increasing the number of free parameters improves the goodness of the fit. AIC encourages the goodness of data fitting but tries to avoid overfitting, so the preferred model should be the one with the lowest AIC value. The Akaike Information Criterion approach is to find models that best explain the data but contain the fewest free parameters.

In terms of forecasting, there are two points to note evaluating the model. One is that the better the model fits within the sample, the better the prediction is not. The other one is that the prediction effect of the small model is often better than that of the large model due to the existence of model parameter estimation errors. Therefore, we should combine the degree of fitting with the prediction effect when evaluating the model.

4 ARIMA Model

This paper builds the ARIMA model and forecasts it based on the monthly payment Volume data of the State Grid Shanxi Company from 2016 to 2017, taking the third party's Alipay payment Volume as an example [14].

The ARIMA model is called the autoregressive integral moving average model. It was proposed by Box and Jenkins in the early 1970s [15]. It is also called the Box-jenkins model and the Boksi-Jenkins method [16]. In a p-order autoregressive model, each value of a sequence can be represented by a linear combination of its previous p values:

$$AR(p): \ Y_t = \mu + \beta_1 Y_{t-1} + \ldots + \beta_p Y_{t-p} + \varepsilon_t \tag{6}$$

Where Y_t is any observation in the time series, μ is the mean of the sequence, β is the weight, and ε_t is the random disturbance. In a q-order moving average model, each value in the time series can be represented by a linear combination of the previous q residuals:

$$MA(q): Y_t = \mu - \theta_1 \varepsilon_{t-1} - \ldots - \theta_q \varepsilon_{t-q} + \varepsilon_t \tag{7}$$

Where ε is the predicted residual and θ is the weight. The mixture of these two methods is ARMA(p, q), whose expression is:

$$Y_t = \mu + \beta_1 Y_{t-1} + \ldots + \beta_p Y_{t-p} - \theta_1 \varepsilon_{t-1} - \ldots - \theta_q \varepsilon_{t-q} + \varepsilon_t \tag{8}$$

At this point, each observation in the sequence is represented by a linear combination of past p observations and q residuals.

The ARIMA(p, d, q) model means that the time series is differentiated by d times, and each observation in the sequence is represented by a linear combination of past p observations and q residuals. The forecast is "error free" or "complete" to achieve the final forecast.

The steps to build an ARIMA model include:

(1) Ensure that the timing is stable;
(2) Find one (or a few) reasonable models (ie, select possible p-values and q-values);
(3) Fit the model;

(4) Evaluate the model from the perspectives of statistical assumptions and prediction accuracy;
(5) Forecast.

This paper will apply these steps in turn to fit the ARIMA model to the payment Volume sequence of the Alipay channel in Shanxi Province.

4.1 Verify the Stability of the Sequence

We need to draw a discounted graph of the sequence df2 (ie, business volume) and determine its stationarity [17]. As can be seen from the figure, the difference in the mode of each observation month is stable, but the sequence has a rising trend, so we need to differently process the data, We use the R language's ndiffs() function for processing.

The original sequence is differently divided twice and stored in ddf2 (see Fig. 1). The lower half of Fig. 1 is a line graph of the differential post-sequence, which is clearly smoother than the original sequence, and the trend of rising raw data after the difference is removed. The ADF test is performed on the difference sequence, and the test result shows that the sequence is stable at this time, and the next step can be performed.

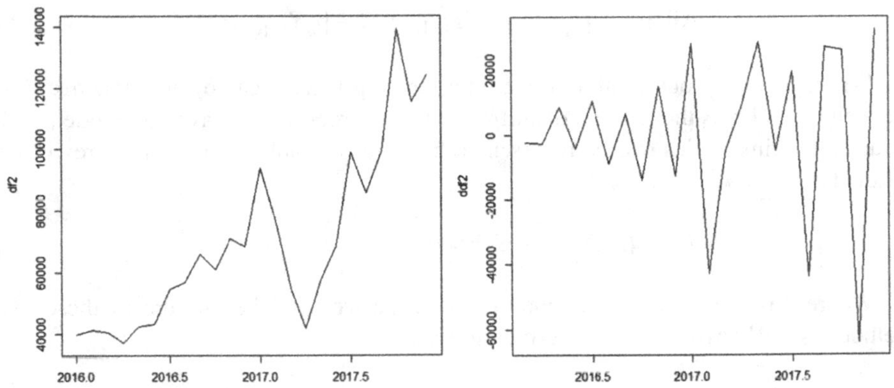

Fig. 1. Alipay payment Volume in 2016–2017 (left) and a line chart after being differentially divided twice (right)

4.2 Model Selection

We can select alternative models through ACF maps and PACF maps (see Fig. 2).

We need to specify the parameters p, d, and q for the ARIMA model, which can be obtained from the previous d = 2. Table 1 shows the method of selecting the parameters p and q in combination with the ACF and PACF maps.

Table 1 gives the theoretical approach to ARIMA model selection. Although the ACF graph and the PACF graph do not necessarily match the conditions in the table, it

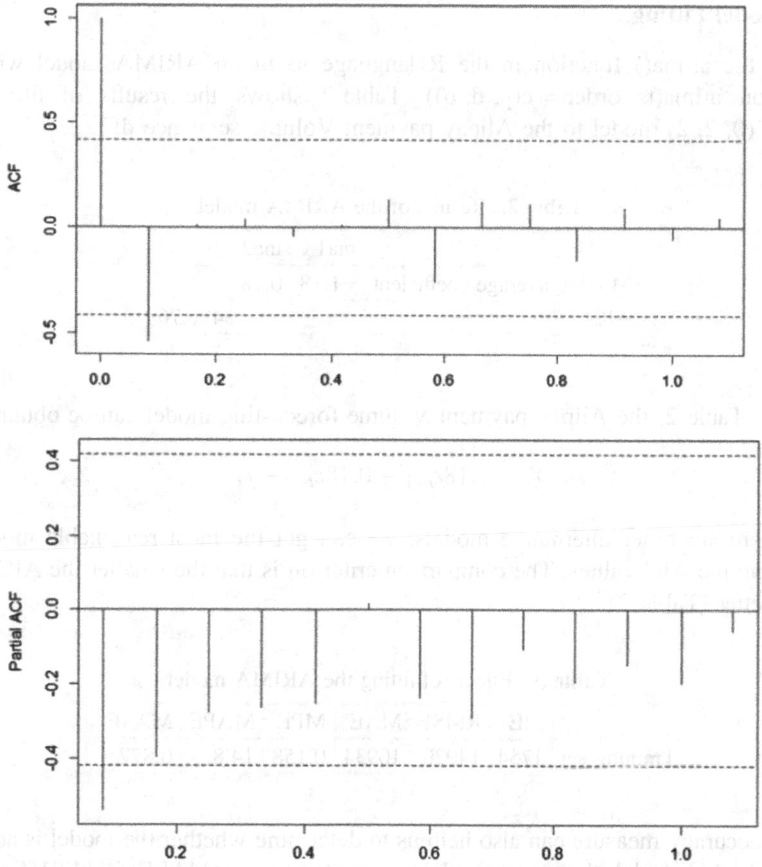

Fig. 2. Autocorrelation and partial autocorrelation of the df2 sequence after two differences

Table 1. Methods for selecting an ARIMA model

Model	ACF	PACF
ARIMA(p, d, 0)	Decreasing to zero gradually	Decreases to zero after p steps
ARIMA(p, d, q)	Gradually decrease to zero	Gradually decrease to zero
ARIMA(0, d, q)	Decrease to zero after qth order	Gradually decrease to zero

still gives us a general idea. For the Alipay business volume sequence in the figure, we can obtain that there is a relatively obvious autocorrelation when the lag term is second order, and the partial autocorrelation gradually decreases to zero when the lag order is gradually increased [18]. Compare the AIC values, so we consider the ARIMA (0, 2, 2) model.

4.3 Model Fitting

We use the arima() function in the R language to fit an ARIMA model with the expression arima(ts, order = c(p, d, q)). Table 2 shows the results of fitting the ARIMA (0, 2, 2) model to the Alipay payment Volume sequence df2.

Table 2. Results of the ARIMA model

	ma1	ma2	
Moving average coefficient	−1.18	0.18	
AIC			496.76

From Table 2, the Alipay payment Volume forecasting model can be obtained as:

$$Y_t = 1.18\varepsilon_{t-1} - 0.18\varepsilon_{t-2} + \varepsilon_t \tag{9}$$

If there are other alternative models, we can get the most reasonable model by comparing the AIC values. The comparison criterion is that the smaller the AIC value is, the better (Table 3).

Table 3. Effects of fitting the ARIMA model

	ME	RMSE	MAE	MPE	MAPE	MASE
Training set	1754	14920	10934	0.158	14.83	0.877

The accuracy measure can also help us to determine whether the model is accurate enough. In this model, the mean absolute percentage error (MAPE) is 14.81% and the root mean square error (RMSE) is 14920.

4.4 Model Evaluation

In general, if a model is appropriate, the residual of the model should satisfy a normal distribution with a mean of 0, and for any lag order, the residual autocorrelation coefficient should be zero [19]. In other words, the residuals of the model should satisfy an independent normal distribution (ie, there is no correlation between the residuals) [20]. The output of the qqnorm() and qqline() functions in the R language is shown (see Fig. 3).

If the data satisfies a normal distribution, the points in the data will fall on the line in the graph. Obviously, the model of this example works well.

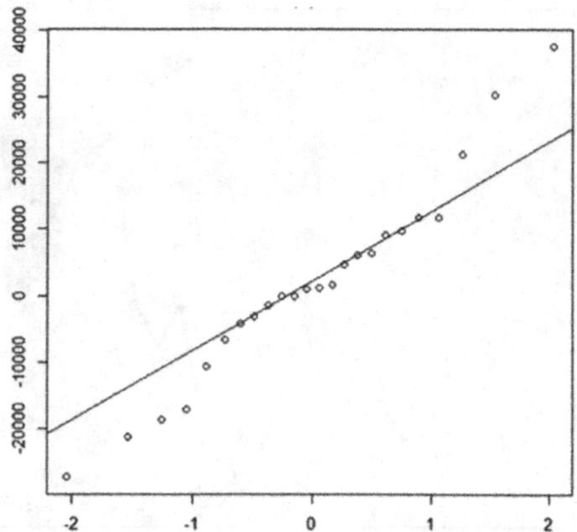

Fig. 3. Normal Q-Q plot to determine if the sequence residual satisfies the normality assumption

The Box.test() function can check if the autocorrelation coefficients of the residuals are all zero. The results are shown in Table 4 below.

Table 4. Box.test() test results

	Box-Ljung test
X-squared	0.688
DF	1
p-value	0.793

It can be seen from Table 4 that the residual of the model does not pass the significance test, that is, we can think that the autocorrelation coefficient of the residual is zero. The ARIMA model can better fit the business volume payment data of Alipay channels.

4.5 Prediction

If the model residual does not satisfy the normality assumption or the zero autocorrelation coefficient hypothesis, then the model needs to be adjusted, the parameters added, or the number of differences changed [21]. Once the model is selected, it can be used to make predictions [22]. We use the forecast() function in the forward package of the R language to implement the prediction for the next three months. The plot() function can draw the prediction graph (see Fig. 4) [23]. The blue point is the point estimate for the predicted point, and the light gray and dark gray areas represent the 80% and 95% confidence intervals, respectively.

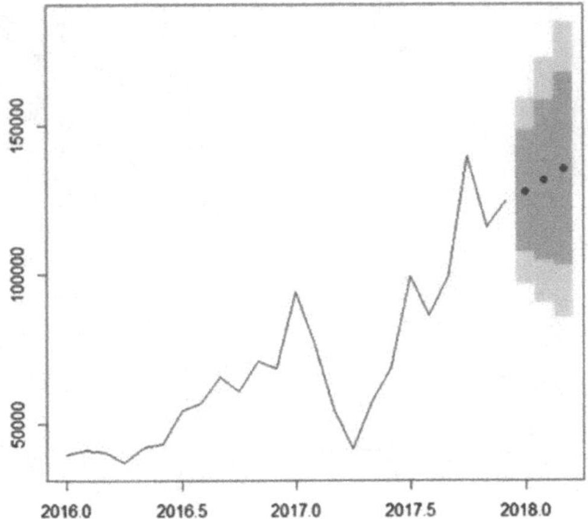

Fig. 4. The predicted values for the ARIM(0, 2, 2) model, and the time is from 2016 to 2017.

5 Conclusion

The model of this paper is based on the forecast of business volume under the premise of the smooth period of the payment service. However, as the business environment changes, business trends are likely to change, such as turning points. Simply using this method for prediction will result in a large error. Therefore, the prediction results based on the time series model need to pay close attention to various marketing policies, market strategies, business logic and other changes affecting the payment Volume, and quantitatively assess the impact of these factors on business volume in advance. At the same time, we should dynamically track changes in traffic trends and update forecast results on a regular basis. Considering the above factors comprehensively and referring to the results predicted by this model, managers can make scientific allocation of resources in various channels more scientifically. It can also help analysts to analyze the reasons for changes in the amount of payment Volume based on business analysis, and help to understand the true demands of customers.

References

1. Geng, R.: Research on nonlinear correction of electrochemical sensors based on PSO-SVM. Xi'an University of Science and Technology (2016)
2. Cheng, W., Yang, J.: "Handheld Power" blooms in Beijing. State Grid **9**, 1673–4726 (2015)
3. Zhai, W., Guo, H., Fan, M., et al.: Discussion on classification methods of unbalanced data sets. Comput. Sci. **39**(b06), 304–308 (2012)
4. Pan, Y.: Application of time series analysis in finance. Econ. Trade Pract. **18**, 1671–3494 (2017)
5. He, H.: Research on passing weight discrimination of bridge overloaded vehicles based on time-varying reliability. Hunan University (2016)

6. Chen, X., Xu, L., Hao, Y., Zhang, J., Jiang, C., Pan, T.: Model fitting of photosynthesis light response curve of Pinus massoniana. J. Jiangxi Agric. Univ. **10**, 1001–8581 (2017)
7. Qin, X.: Combined forecast analysis of China's GDP. Mod. Bus. Ind. **7** (2016)
8. Ma, S.: Prediction of total retail sales of consumer goods in China based on ARIMA model. Mod. Bus. **1**, 1673–5889 (2015)
9. Li, Y.: Fault diagnosis and GUI design of internal combustion engine based on time series analysis. Xidian University (2014)
10. Zhang, W.: Research on time series prediction of foreign exchange rate based on ARIMA model. J. East China Jiaotong Univ. **5**, 1005-0523 (2009)
11. Li, X.: Simple season model and product season model of ARIMA recognition using SAS. Comput. Knowl. Technol. (Acad. Exch.) **2**, 1009–3044 (2007)
12. Song, J.: Mathematical statistical analysis of actual operational data of interconnected power grids. Dalian University of Technology (2006)
13. Zhang, Z.: Research on Key technology of statistical tolerance design and inspection. Zhengzhou University (2014)
14. Xie, C.: Analysis of the total retail sales of social consumer goods in Suzhou. Master. Suzhou University (2015)
15. Li, R.: Research on the Relationship between Retail Business and Population Development in Beijing. Master. Capital University of Economics and Business (2007)
16. Tang, G.: Application of time series analysis in economic forecasting. Stat. Inf. Forum P90–P94 (2005)
17. Chen, Y.: Empirical analysis of factors affecting the total retail sales of social consumer goods in China. New Fin. P29–P29 (2011)
18. Pang, H., et al.: Pathway analysis using random forests classification and regression. Bioinformatics **22**(16), 2028–2036 (2006)
19. Fang, W., Wu, J., Zhu, J., et al.: Review of random forest methods research. J. Stat. Inf. **26** (3), 32–38 (2011)
20. Yao, X., Wang, X., Zhang, Y., et al.: Overview of feature selection methods. Control Decis. **27**(2), 161–166 (2012)
21. Ma, J., Xie, B.: Comparison of random forest and bagging classification trees for classification. J. Stat. Inf. **25**(10), 18–22 (2010)
22. Zhang, J., Xie, N., Zhang, X., Yue, K., Li, W., Kumar, D.: Machine learning based resource allocation of cloud computing in auction. CMC Comput. Mater. Continua **56**(1), 123–135 (2018)
23. Yin, W., Zhang, X., Abulimiti, B., Liu, Y., Yan, Y., Zhou, F., Jin, F.: Electronic structure and physical characteristics of dioxin under external electric field. CMC Comput. Mater. Continua **55**(1), 165–176 (2018)

Delay-Tolerant Rendezvous-Based Data Collection for Target Tracking in Large-Scale Wireless Sensor Networks with UGV

Jian Zhang[1,2](✉), Jiang Xu[2], and Tianbao Wang[3]

[1] College of Computer and Software, Nanjing University of Information Science and Technology, Nanjing 210044, China
jianzhang_neu@163.com
[2] Jiangsu Engineering Center of Network Monitoring, Nanjing 210044, China
[3] School of Electrical and Information Engineering, Jiangsu University, Zhenjiang 212013, China
wtbcn@163.com

Abstract. Energy efficiency receives significant attention in wireless sensor networks. In this paper, a UGV is employed as an energy-efficient solution to prolong the network lifetime in target tracking. Data collection strategies for target tracking are investigated including the amount of data and the transmitted distances. For contributed data, the quantization technology is exploited for energy efficiency. Considering the uncertainty of sensing data, we determine a group from intra-cluster members to gather data. And then, we formulate our design a selection optimization problem, maximizing the utilization of the quality of contributed data using information matrix. As a result, we develop an optimization algorithm named rendezvous-based data collection (RDC). Furthermore, two stages of data collection for target tracking are analyzed with a UGV. Simulations verify that the proposed scheme achieves network energy saving as well as energy balance in the framework of target tracking.

Keywords: Wireless sensor networks · UGV · Rendezvous nodes
Data collection · Fisher information matrix · Target tracking

1 Introduction

Wireless sensor networks (WSNs) have received considerable attention in emerging applications for decades, such as environmental monitoring [1], industrial applications [2] and target tracking [3]. In these applications, data collection as one of the most challenging issues has been extensively researched owing to the energy constraints of battery-powered nodes [4]. Especially in sink-fixed WSNs, nodes closed to the sink run out its battery faster because of heavy traffic from others, on the contrary, those far away from the sink still maintain more than 90% of their initial energy [5], which leads to a critical issue of short network lifetime caused by unbalanced traffic distribution. In fact, energy-efficiency problem meeting in WSNs for data collection applications is still a fundamental problem researched all the time by researchers.

X. Sun et al. (Eds.): ICAIS 2019, LNCS 11633, pp. 332–344, 2019.
https://doi.org/10.1007/978-3-030-24265-7_29

Basically in the process of data collection, it is impossible to replace the batteries of nodes due to the significant effort and cost after WSNs operating with unmanned intervention. To adapt the special situation, approaches of mobile elements have been introduced to address the shortage problem of network resources [6]. In this way, the mobile element takes the responsibility to collect data by decreasing hop counts [7]. Generally by mobility, the long-distance data route is shortened and then energy surely are conserved. In fact, the mobile element meanwhile leads to delay-tolerant networks. In this sense, rendezvous-based data collection approaches are suitable for WSNs, since a optimal tour can be determined according a rendezvous node optimization selection [8]. However, multi-hop routing can still result in unbalanced energy consumption, although rendezvous design algorithms are optimized according to the tour of mobile elements.

Compared to multi-hop rendezvous routing with ME, clustering mechanism develops a promising solution for data collection [9]. Generally, a cluster consists of node numbers whose distance to the CH is in one-hop distance, sensing data by rotating mechanism and being shown to save and balance energy consumption [10]. In applications, the cluster structures are formed according to requirement for energy efficiency and ME-based data collection, and hence the performance of WSNs is improved as far as the energy bottleneck which also occurs in cluster-based data transmission [11]. Naturally, clustering structure takes the advantages of scalability and energy efficiency, however, intra-cluster or/and inter-cluster data transmission should be paid attention to. The challenging issue of energy bottleneck is addressed by a solution named hierarchical routing based on clustering [4], and unmanned ground vehicle (UGV) still plays a significant role [12]. Actually, the cluster-based structure refers to network partitioning and UGV as a type of ME has the double-edged sword attribute. Combining them seems a complementary way to achieve energy efficiency for data collection.

As one of most special applications for data collection in WSNs, target tracking has attracted much attention [13], referring a complicated problem for energy consumption i.e. sensing, communication and moving [3]. For example, collaborative target tracking exploits sensor selection procedures in a cluster to realized target position and data transmission [14]. Although approaches of sensor scheduling in WSNs promote the performance of WSNs as far as energy efficiency, accuracy of target tracking, and other aspects, it is difficult to develop a comprehensive approach to support the WSNs operating smoothly. Many negative factors are still full of the process of target tracking, such as NP-hard problem in sensor scheduling for energy balance, energy bottleneck, sensing uncertainty of nodes, and so on.

2 Related Works

Energy-efficient data collection is a major research challenge in wireless sensor networks and especially combining the ME-based data collection and clustering seems a promising way to achieve a better savings of the energy consumption. After LEACH [15], many clustering algorithms are designed considering different situations. Chen [16] proposed clustering algorithm which constructs a multi-sized to realize the energy efficiency of WSNs. Naturally, clustering structure take the advantages of scalability and energy efficiency for WSNs. However, intra-cluster or/and inter-cluster data transmission should be paid attention to. Xu et al. [17] proposed a joint clustering and routing protocol where a random back off and gradient routing schemes are exploited to carry out CH selection and multi-hop routing simultaneously for data collection. In this process, mobile elements still play an important role for improvement of WSNs' function. And then based on Chen' clustering algorithm, Charalampos Konstantopoulos [18] modify the approach to build clusters by introducing the ME to relieve CHs from heavy traffic coming from the network. Considering the energy balance as far as nodes near the sink, the annular buffer area and its optimization are figured out for data collection using ME in cluster structure networks [11]. [4] dealt with the challenging issue to increase the efficiency by hierarchical routing based on clustering and by mobile elements when more complicated situation arise, i.e. hybrid data collection. In [19], a mathematical model with clusters is constructed to collect data by data mules, presenting analytical approaches to determine the optimization problem of the number of clusters for energy consumption. At present, combining network partitioning and ME data collection is also an interesting topic for future research.

The rendezvous technologies are utilized to develop solutions for time-sensitive applications because they are suitable for reducing latency and energy efficiency with ME. It has been verified in [20] that finding an optimal set of rendezvous points will improve the data gathering process of the sink and also maximize the network lifetime. In [21], rendezvous-based routing protocols, which creates a rendezvous region in the middle of the network and constructs a tree within that region, is proposed. Zhang [22] utilized mobile elements moving along solid trajectories and assigned RNs for intra-cluster data transmission to realize the solution of energy efficiency. In [23], a rendezvous-based data dissemination algorithm based on multi-hop clustering is proposed to achieve energy-efficient and reliable data delivery for supporting MEs. [24] presents rendezvous-based data collection solutions with a multi-hop clustering structure by employing MEs and building energy efficient routes.

WSNs have the capacity of collaboration among sensors for data gathering address energy-efficient target tracking [25]. In [26], a dynamic cluster members scheduling algorithm for target tracking is proposed by a partially observable Markov decision process. As far as energy efficiency, more and more applications are exploited: a novel sensor scheduling scheme for intruder tracking in [27], Coverage Control [28], as well as cooperative networks for multi-UAV [29], and other applications [30, 31].

3 Data Collection Framework

3.1 Rendezvous Nodes in a Cluster

We take into account further reducing energy consumption, rendezvous nodes (RNs) are selected to route data in a cluster or a close proximity with the MS trajectory. To the end, we presents the definition of rendezvous nodes.

Definition 1 (intra-cluster RN, ICRN). Let Ξ is a set including all sensors of a cluster, $E_{\cdot\to\cdot}$ indicates energy consumption between tow nodes, then the definition of intra-cluster rendezvous nodes is given as follows

$$\{i|i \in \Xi \wedge E_{Transmitter \to i} + E_{i \to \mathrm{Receiver}} < E_{Transmitter \to \mathrm{Receiver}}\} \tag{1}$$

For convenience, we show an example of the definition of intra-cluster RN in Fig. 1. Note that the intra-cluster RNs refer to the energy balance for the operating nodes due to the significant difference among radius in a cluster. In this sense, the set of data collection involves the sensing nodes besides intra-cluster RNs only for relaying data without sensing data.

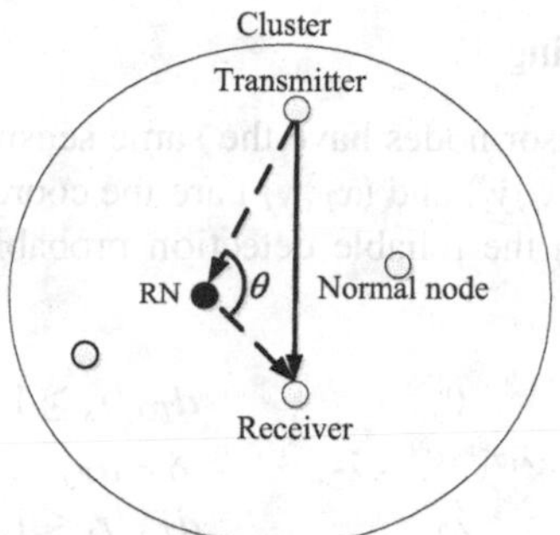

Fig. 1. Clustering rendezvous nodes

3.2 Data Quantization for Energy Efficiency

In order to further reduce and balance the consumption of network energy under some constraints (e.g. accuracy), quantization technology [25] is usually exploited.

We consider the reading $z_{i,t}$ of each node is quantized as follows.

$$D_{i,t} = \begin{cases} 0, & -\infty < z_{i,t} < \eta_1 \\ 1, & \eta_1 < z_{i,t} < \eta_2 \\ \vdots & \vdots \\ L-1, & \eta_{(L-1)} < z_{i,t} < \infty \end{cases} \tag{2}$$

where η_i in the Eq. (2) indicates the quantization thresholds, $L = 2^m$ is the number of quantization levels. The probability that $D_{i,t}$ takes value l is given by

$$p(D_{i,t} = l) = Q\left(\frac{\eta_l - a_{i,t}}{\sigma}\right) - Q\left(\frac{\eta_{l+1} - a_{i,t}}{\sigma}\right) \tag{3}$$

where $Q(g)$ is the complementary distribution of the standard normal distribution. In this sense, we design an optimal mechanism to realize the goal of cluster-based minimum energy consumption under the condition of load balancing and packet allocation.

$$\min \sum_{i=1}^{N} (d_i^a + c_i) g_i^l$$
$$s.t. \sqrt{(E_1 - \bar{E})^2 + (E_2 - \bar{E})^2 + \text{L} + (E_N - \bar{E})^2} \le \Phi \qquad (4)$$
$$p(D_{i,t} = l) = Q\left(\frac{\eta_l - a_{i,t}}{\sigma}\right) - Q\left(\frac{\eta_{l+1} - a_{i,t}}{\sigma}\right)$$

3.3 Uncertainty for Sensing

It is assumed that all the sensor nodes have the same sensing range r_s and uncertainty sensing range $\delta \cdot r_s$ $(\delta < 1)$, (x_i, y_i) and (x_T, y_T) are the coordinates of sensor node i and the target, respectively, then the reliable detection probability of sensor node on the target is defined as

$$R_i = \begin{cases} 0, & d_{T,i}/r_s \ge 1 + \delta \\ e^{-\lambda_1 \alpha_1^{\beta_1} / \alpha_1^{\beta_1}} \cdot \lambda_2, & 1 - \delta < d_{T,i}/r_s < 1 + \delta \\ \lambda_2, & d_{T,i}/r_s \le 1 - \delta \end{cases} \qquad (5)$$

where $d_{T,i}$ is the Euclidean distance between sensor node i and the target; λ_1, λ_2, β_1, and β_2 are constants measuring detection probability. Parameters α_1 and are α_2 defined as

$$\alpha_1 = r_s \cdot (\delta - 1) + d_{T,i} \qquad (6)$$

$$\alpha_2 = r_s \cdot (\delta + 1) - d_{T,i} \qquad (7)$$

Due to the inherent redundancy of WSNs, one target is covered by K sensor nodes at the same instant. If the reliable detection probability of the K sensor node on the target is denoted by R_i, then the joint reliable detection probability for this target is calculated as

$$R = 1 - \prod_{i}^{k} (1 - R_i) \qquad (8)$$

Therefore, a high joint detection reliability can be achieved by (8) even though the detection reliability of individual sensor node is constrained.

4 Target Tracking in WSNs

4.1 Motion Model

Model-based wireless sensor networks consist of motion model of target and observation model of a node. In this paper, the single target tracking is addressed in the region monitored by wireless sensor networks.

In two-dimensional space, the dynamic system is described by

$$x_t = Fx_{t-1} + u_t \tag{9}$$

where $x_t = (x_{1,t}, x_{2,t}, \dot{x}_{1,t}, \dot{x}_{2,t})^T$ is the target state vector at the time step t, $x_{1,t}, x_{2,t}$ indicate the corresponding speeds of coordinates respectively. F is the system state transition matrix, and can be followed by

$$F = \begin{bmatrix} 1 & 0 & T_s & 0 \\ 0 & 1 & 0 & T_s \\ 0 & 0 & 1 & 0 \\ 0 & 0 & 0 & 1 \end{bmatrix} \tag{10}$$

where T_s is the sampling interval. u_t is the process noise which is a Gaussian distribution with mean 0 and variance $Q = Ddiag\{\sigma_x^2, \sigma_y^2\}D^T$, where D is given by

$$D = \begin{bmatrix} T_s^2/2 & 0 \\ 0 & T_s^2/2 \\ T_s & 0 \\ 0 & T_s \end{bmatrix} \tag{11}$$

4.2 Observation Model

At time step t, it is assumed that the measurement model of the system is given by

$$z_{i,t} = h_i(x_t, v_{i,t}), i = 1, 2, \ldots N_t \tag{12}$$

where $z_{i,t}$ is the measurement of sensor s_i, $h_i(\cdot)$ denotes the measurement function of sensor s_i, and $v_{i,t}$ is the measurement noise at time step t. In this paper, the measurement function is specifically described by

$$z_{i,t} = \sqrt{(x_{1,t} - x_{1,s_i})^2 + (x_{2,t} - x_{2,s_i})^2} + v_{i,t}\, , i = 1, 2 \cdots, N_t \tag{13}$$

where (x_{1,s_i}, x_{2,s_i}) indicates the coordinate of sensor s_i. $v_{i,t}$ is the observation noise which is a Gaussian distribution with mean 0 and variance $\sigma_{i,t}^2$.

4.3 Fisher Information Matrix for Data Collection

We assume that $\hat{x}_t$ is the unbiased estimate of the state vector x_t, and P_t is the covariance matrix of x_t. A lower bound about P_t is

$$P_t = E\{(\hat{x}_t - x_t)(\hat{x}_t - x_t)^T\} \geq J_t^{-1} \tag{14}$$

where J_t is the Fisher information matrix at time t, and can be recursively derived in

$$J_{t+1} = D_t^{22} - D_t^{21}(J_t + D_t^{11})^{-1}D_t^{12} \tag{15}$$

where

$$\begin{aligned}
D_t^{11} &= -E\{\nabla_{x_t}[\nabla_{x_t} \log p(x_{t+1}|x_t)]^T\} \quad D_t^{21} = -E\{\nabla_{x_t}[\nabla_{x_{t+1}} \log p(x_{t+1}|x_t)]^T\} \\
D_t^{12} &= [D_t^{21}]^T \\
D_t^{22} &= -E\{\nabla_{x_{t+1}}[\nabla_{x_{t+1}} \log p(x_{t+1}|x_t)]^T\} - E\{\nabla_{x_{t+1}}[\nabla_{x_{t+1}} \log p(z_{t+1}|x_t)]^T\}
\end{aligned}$$

Especially, we supposed that the noise of model is additive Gaussian, then the expressions of D_t^{11}, D_t^{12} and D_t^{22} are simplified as follows:

$$D_t^{21} = F^T Q^{-1} F; D_t^{12} = -F^T Q^{-1}; D_t^{22} = Q^{-1} + E\{H_{t+1}^T R^{-1} H_{t+1}\}$$

where H_{t+1} is the Jacobian matrix of $h(x_{t+1})$: $H_{t+1} = [\nabla_{x_{t+1}} h(x_{t+1})]^T$, According to the measurement model H_{t+1} is given by $H_{t+1} = \left[\frac{2x_{t+1}}{\sqrt{(x_{t+1}-x_i)^2 + (y_{t+1}-y_i)^2}} \frac{2y_{t+1}}{\sqrt{(x_{t+1}-x_i)^2 + (y_{t+1}-y_i)^2}} 0\,0\right]^T$. Consequentially, the recursion in (15) can be simplified by

$$J_{t+1} = Q^{-1} + E\{H_{t+1}^T R_t^{-1} H_{t+1}\} - Q^{-1} F(J_t + F^T Q^{-1} F)^{-1} F^T Q^{-1} \tag{16}$$

4.4 Cluster Determination of Target Tracking

It is assumed that $J^{-1}(i,j)$ is the (i, j) entry of J^{-1}, the corresponding predicted PCRLB for the position is

$$\Omega_t = trace\{diag\{(J_t)^{-1}(1,1), (J_t)^{-1}(2,2)\}\} \tag{17}$$

where the $(J_t)^{-1}(1,1)$ and $(J_t)^{-1}(2,2)$ are the bounds on the MSE corresponding to x_t and y_t, respectively. In this paper, considered the uncertainty of the individual sensor node and the joint reliable detection probability, the optimal combination of sensor nodes is determined,

$$\begin{aligned} S_{opt}^{t} &= \arg\min_{s_i \in S_n^t} (trace(diag\{(J_t)^{-1}(1,1), (J_t)^{-1}(2,2)\})) \\ s.t. R &= 1 - \prod_{i}^{|M_t|} (1 - R_i) \geq \theta_d \end{aligned} \tag{18}$$

Generally speaking, this is a combinatorial optimization problem, so we have the following theorem as far as sensor selection for target tracking to operate network functions.

5 Stages Analysis with UGV

5.1 Sensing Stage

The sensing stage, which refers to selection of sensor nodes for sensory data and RNs for energy efficiency, is constructed for data collection. This stage is prepared for tracking before the target goes though the interesting region. Actually, the ready stage describes a dynamic definition of WSNs as far as functions of this framework, such as clustering, classifying roles of nodes, constructing hierarchical routing, and so on.

In this stage, the tradeoff of energy efficiency only exists the initialization of WSNs for target tracking, and just reviews what maybe happen in next step. The sensing stage occurs when the target enters the region of WSNs' coverage, and it is also a local sensing activity because the target happens to campaign only in a cluster at one moment. In fact, the sensing stage is process of a dynamic clustering after detect the target. Due to operation of a dynamic cluster in a moment for target tracking, the energy efficient is held by avoiding maintaining a clustered WSNs. For sensing data, the sensing stage is responsible for the accuracy of target tracking.

5.2 Transmitting Stage

The transmitting stage is in charge of energy efficiency of WSNs operating for target tracking as a system after the sensing stage, contributing data to UGV. Compared with sensing stage, transmitting stage is a global transmitting activity since the collected data should be routed by cluster head or other nodes through the multi-hop way. The destination end of collected data is UGV which campaigns along with a predetermined trace which maybe a road.

In this stage, contributed data are transmitted in a structured network where specific clusters are formed and cluster heads are also selected on duty to relay data. Contrary to the dynamic cluster, this structured network builds a cluster structure of unequal clusters depending on the distance of the CHs from the UGV's predetermined trace [18], which has been proven to be an effective approach for organizing the network to achieve energy efficiency as far as clustering [16]. In addition, the transmitting stage deals with the bottleneck of energy for CHs near the UGV's trace owing to transfer data to UGV frequently. As a result, proximity RNs defined below are used to transfer data instead of CH in a cluster. In this way, the energy balance of clusters near the UGV's trace can be realized avoiding running out of CH's energy earlier.

Definition 2 (Proximity RN, PRN). Let Ξ is a set including all sensors of a cluster, d' presents a given constant distance, and $d_{i \to \mathrm{UGV}}$ stands for distance between node i and UGV, then the definition of proximity rendezvous nodes is given as follows

$$\{i | i \in \Xi \wedge d_{i \to UGV} \leq d'\} \tag{19}$$

Note that the proximity RNs mainly have the solution of the bottleneck problem for cluster heads near a mobile sink because of heavy traffic occurring on them. As shown in Fig. 2, the proximity RNs actually play the role of the cluster head, then store data and transmit data when the mobile sink approaches them at a time interval.

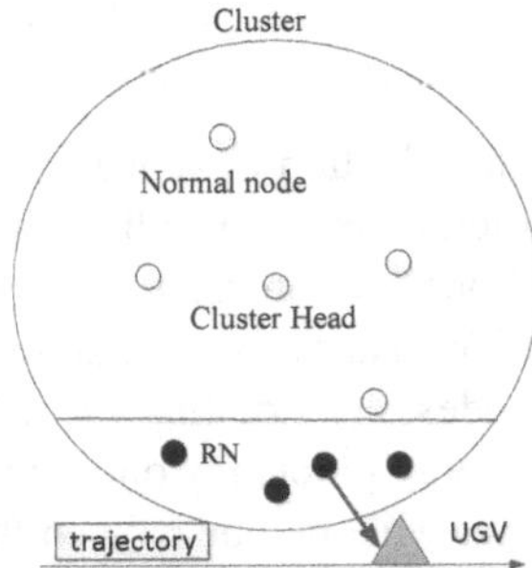

Fig. 2. Proximity rendezvous nodes

In fact, seen from Fig. 3(a), data transmission by CHs when UGV passed by is a centralized pattern since data are delivered to UGV via the CH whose burden maybe heavy resulting in congestion, storage overflow, data loss, and so on. When these shortages give WSNs a feedback, it is fetal for delay-tolerant WSNs. While the definition of PRN is a decentralized pattern of transmission due to traffic from other CHs loaded by sensor balance. As shown in Fig. 3(b), several PRNs distribute the traffic decreasing the risk of failure for target tracking as well as balance the energy consumption of local region.

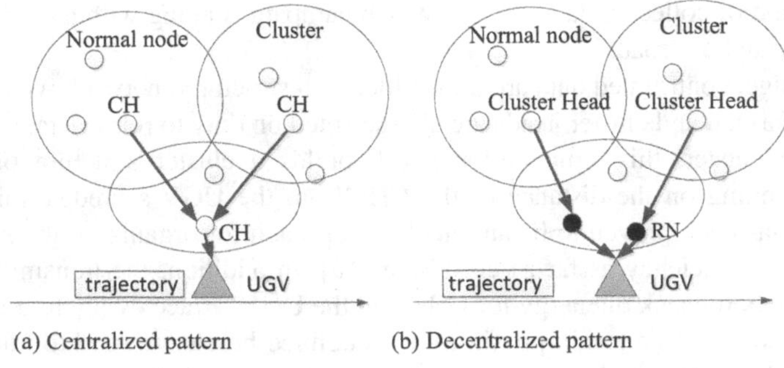

Fig. 3. Data delivery patterns of CH and PRN

6 Simulations

To illustrate advantages of the new method, We firstly simulate a wireless sensor network with N randomly deployed sensors respectively to supervise an area of 300 m * 300 m. Assume that the true process noise variance is *diag*([0.125 0.125 0.5 0.5]), and the measurement noise variance of each sensor node is 0.00005 at every sampling interval $T_s = 1$ s. In particle filter algorithm, the true process noise variance is *diag*([0.025 0.025 0.1 0.1]), and the measurement noise variance of each sensor node is 0.00002. Assume a moving target is detected in the sensor detecting field at time $t = 0$. The initial target state is $x0 = [0033]$. The simulation tracking time is $t = 50$, velocity $v = 3\,\mathrm{m/s}$. We also use other parameters the same as in [22].

For convenience, we compare our algorithms with other strategy for describing the function of WSNs. Our algorithms include Rendezvous Data collection (short for RDC), Quantization-based Rendezvous Data collection (short for Q-RDC). The other strategy is described as ALL sensors sensing the event at a unit time (short for ALL).

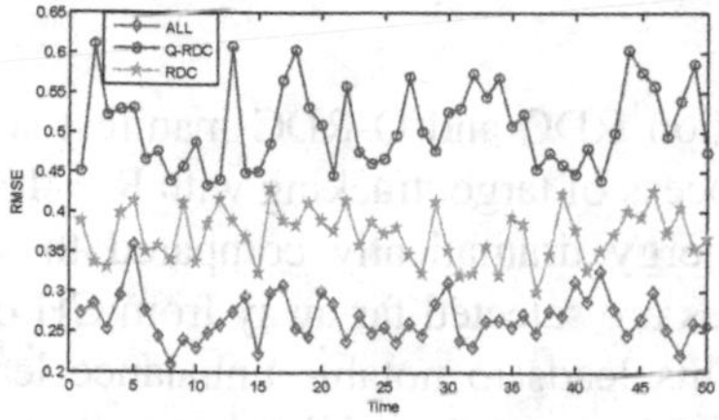

Fig. 4. N = 100 with R = 120 m

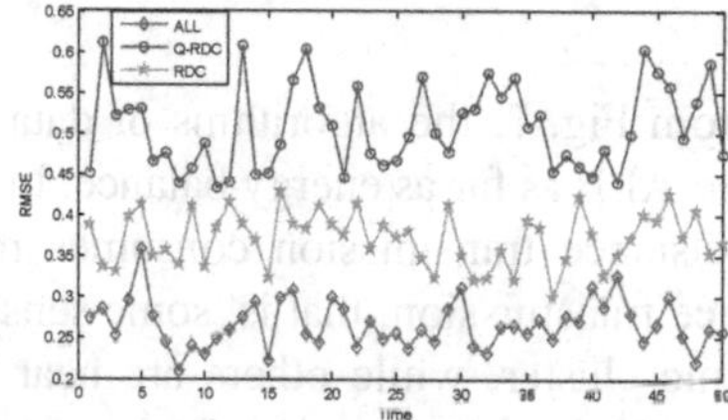

Fig. 5. N = 200 with R = 120 m

From Fig. 4, the RMSE of three algorithm is shown with $R = 120\,\mathrm{m}$ through investigating different sensor nodes. One assumption is that the sensing radius changes when the transmission radius changes. In this situation, the ALL algorithm definitely deserves the best accuracy. The RMSE of ALL in Fig. 4 is almost same just because the accuracy converges when the sensor node increase up to a definite amount. The difference of amplitude of the two ALL algorithms reflects the process of accuracy convergence.

Generally, values of RDC in Fig. 5 gradually approach to the convergent accuracy which guarantees the optimization of combination for target tracking. In the case, Q-RDC is proposed to develop the function of WSNs under the meaning of accuracy guarantee. As a result, the gap between RDC and the QRDC becomes more and more larger with the increase of radius until this gap trends to a fixed value. Although we present only 200 nodes in simulations, the tendency of RMSE in several scenarios for target tracking can be predicted though above numerical instances.

As far as Fig. 6, owing to the introduction of rendezvous, long-distance transmission model is avoided, and the behavior of data collection becomes short-distance transmission model. The function of energy consumption of RDC naturally precedes ALL selecting all sensing nodes. Nevertheless, increase in transmission radius directly leads to the energy expenditure after all. RDC eventually selects relative long-distance transmission due to the energy balancing listed next and this is the essence algorithm of RDC. In the process of sensor selection for target tracking, RDC transfers enough data up to improve the target tracking accuracy. Actually, some combination of sensors can also realize the objective of relevant target tracking accuracy just though quantization. In this way, data volume of Q-RDC is reduced and then the energy is saved rationally.

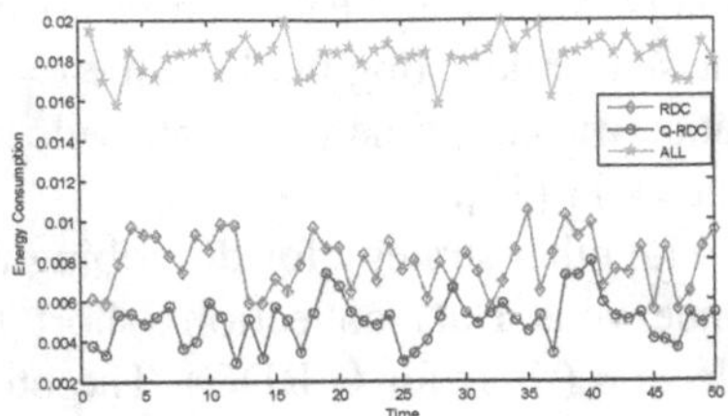

Fig. 6. Energy consumption with R = 120 m

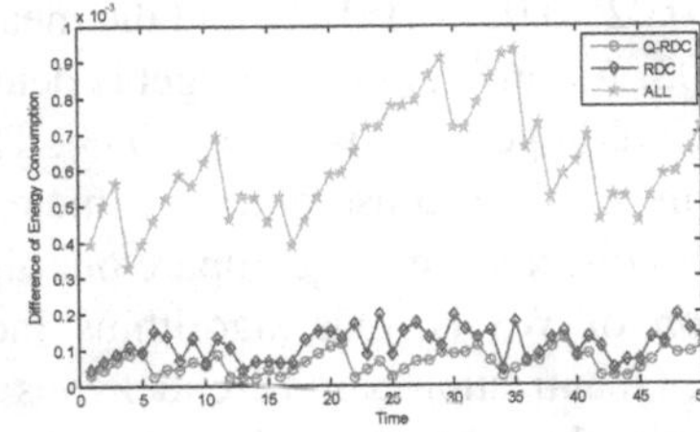

Fig. 7. Difference of energy consumption with R = 120 m.

From Fig. 7, the algorithms of data collection RDC and Q-RDC manifest superiority to ALL as far as energy balance. In the process of target tracking with R = 120 m, long-distance transmission consumes more energy dramatically compared to short-distance transmission, that is, some sensor nodes are selected far away from CH of the dynamic cluster, while others are near CH. This leads to notable unbalance leaving some node dead earlier, therefore, rendezvous nodes are selected for data collection in order to balance local energy. RN strategy is reasonable because more sensor nodes are involved in ALL, which actually owns alternation among sensor nodes under the optimization. The second way to reduce energy expenditure is quantization technology which decreases transmission quantity. AS a result, Q-RDC not only saving energy consumption but also balance energy consumption. In this point, the difference of energy consumption for RDC and Q-RDC have significant dominance to ALL in dealing with energy balance.

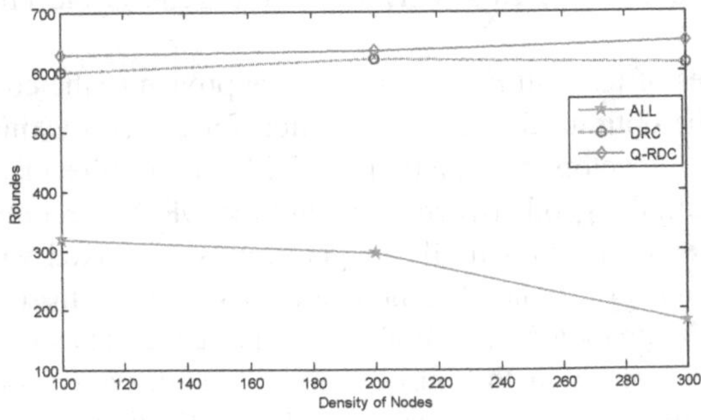

Fig. 8. Rounds of WSNs.

Figure 8 demonstrates the lifetime of WSNs in different scenarios First of all, we suppose that the target keeps moving along with the same trajectory repeatedly considering the contradiction of short moving time of target and relevant longer internet lifetime. With the amount of senor nodes increasing, the lifetime is decreased as far as R = 120 respectively. This is well-understood because the affect factor of inter-clustered WSNs' lifetime lie in hot points when the whole WSNs are used to transfer collected data. Here, more sensor nodes which sense the target produce more data volume. Then all the data are sent to the CHs near the UGV, CHs have to expenditure more energy and then get death earlier than other sensor nodes in WSNs, although the rotated mechanisms are adopted. On the contrary, RDC and Q-RDC provided a solution of the problem of hot points. Through putting forward the concept of PRN instead of CH in the cluster and proposing algorithm 2 to rotate PRN as relay nodes for UGV, we acquire a longer lifetime of WSNs. The principle is that either RDC or Q-RDC is utilized to balance energy consumption and reduce generated data under the condition of WSNs' function. Therefore, the lifetime of either RDC or Q-RDC with different radius maintain stable and even some promotion.

Acknowledgment. This work was supported by the Foundation of Nanjing University of Information Science and Technology (Grant No. 2241101201101), Open Foundation of Education Ministry Demonstration Base of Internet Application Innovation Open Platform (Meteorological Cloud Platform and Application) (Grant No. 2201101401063), PAPD and Jiangsu Government Scholarship for Overseas Studies.

References

1. Aslan, Y.E., Korpeoglu, I., Ulusoy, O.: A framework for use of wireless sensor networks in forest fire detection and monitoring. Comput. Environ. Urban Syst. **36**(6), 614–625 (2012)
2. Harb, H., Makhoul, A.: Energy-efficient sensor data collection approach for industrial process monitoring. IEEE Trans. Industr. Inf. **14**(2), 661–672 (2018)
3. Mahboubi, H., Masoudimansour, W., Aghdam, A.G.: An energy-efficient target-tracking strategy for mobile sensor networks. IEEE Trans. Cybern. **47**(2), 511–523 (2016)
4. Zhang, R., Pan, J., Xie, D.: NDCMC: a hybrid data collection approach for large-scale WSNs using mobile element and hierarchical clustering. IEEE Internet Things J. **3**(4), 533–543 (2016)
5. Chuang, S.C.: Survey on target tracking in wireless sensor networks, Department of Computer Science National Tsing Hua University (2005)
6. Tunca, C., Isik, S., Donmez, M.Y.: Distributed mobile sink routing for wireless sensor networks: a survey. IEEE Commun. Surv. Tutor. **16**(2), 877–897 (2014)
7. Zhao, M., Yang, Y.: Bounded relay Hop mobile data gathering in wireless sensor networks. IEEE Trans. Comput. **61**(2), 265–277 (2011)
8. Salarian, H., Chin, K.W., Naghdy, F.: An energy-efficient mobile-sink path selection strategy for wireless sensor networks. IEEE Trans. Veh. Technol. **63**(5), 2407–2419 (2014)
9. Yang, S., Adeel, U., Tahir, Y.: Practical opportunistic data collection in wireless sensor networks with mobile sinks. IEEE Trans. Mob. Comput. **16**(5), 1420–1433 (2017)
10. Nguyen, M.T., Teague, K.A., Rahnavard, N.: CCS: energy-efficient data collection in clustered wireless sensor networks utilizing block-wise compressive sensing. Comput. Netw. **106**(1), 171–185 (2016)

11. Na, W., Xiao-gang, Q., Li, D., Hua, J.: Clustering-based routing algorithm in wireless sensor networks with mobile sink. J. Netw. **9**(9), 2376–2382 (2014)
12. Rucco, A., Sujit, P.B., Aguiar, A.P.: Optimal rendezvous trajectory for unmanned aerial-ground vehicles. IEEE Trans. Aerosp. Electron. Syst. **PP**(99), 1 (2016)
13. Yu, Y.: Distributed target tracking in wireless sensor networks with data association uncertainty. IEEE Commun. Lett. **21**(6), 1281–1284 (2017)
14. Zhang, J., Wu, C.D., Zhang, Y.Z.: Energy-efficient adaptive dynamic sensor scheduling for target monitoring in wireless sensor networks. ETRI J. **33**(6), 857–863 (2011)
15. Heinzelman, W.B., Chandrakasan, A.P., Balakrishnan, H.: An application-specific protocol architecture for wireless microsensor networks. IEEE Trans. Wirel. Commun. **1**(4), 660–670 (2002)
16. Chen, G., Li, C., Ye, M.: An unequal cluster-based routing protocol in wireless sensor networks. Wirel. Netw. **15**, 193–207 (2007)
17. Xu, Z., Chen, L., Chen, C.: Joint clustering and routing design for reliable and efficient data collection in large-scale wireless sensor networks. IEEE Internet Things J. **3**(4), 520–532 (2016)
18. Konstantopoulos, C., Pantziou, G., Gavalas, D.: A rendezvous-based approach enabling energy-efficient sensory data collection with mobile sinks. IEEE Trans. Parallel Distrib. Syst. **23**(5), 809–817 (2012)
19. Ang, L.M., Seng, J.K.P., Zungeru, A.M.: Optimizing energy consumption for big data collection in large-scale wireless sensor networks with mobile collectors. IEEE Syst. J. **99**, 1–11 (2018)
20. Kumar, D.P., Tarachand, A., Annavarapu, C.S.R.: ACO-based mobile sink path determination for wireless sensor networks under non-uniform data constraints. Appl. Soft Comput. **69**, 528–540 (2018)
21. Sharma, S., Puthal, D., Jena, S.K.: Rendezvous based routing protocol for wireless sensor networks with mobile sink. J. Supercomput. **73**, 1–21 (2017)
22. Zhang, J., Tang, J., Wang, T.: Energy-efficient data-gathering rendezvous algorithms with mobile sinks for wireless sensor networks. Int. J. Sens. Netw. **23**(4), 248–257 (2017)
23. Lee, E., Park, S., Oh, S.: Rendezvous-based data dissemination for supporting mobile sinks in multi-hop clustered wireless sensor networks. Wirel. Netw. **20**(8), 2319–2336 (2014)
24. Konstantopoulos, C., Vathis, N., Pantziou, G.: Employing mobile elements for delay-constrained data gathering in WSNs. Comput. Netw. **135**, 108–131 (2018)
25. Cao, N., Choi, S., Masazade, E.: Sensor selection for target tracking in wireless sensor networks with uncertainty. IEEE Trans. Signal Process. **64**(20), 5191–5204 (2015)
26. Wu, B., Feng, Y.P., Zheng, H.Y.: Dynamic cluster members scheduling for target tracking in sensor networks. IEEE Sens. J. **16**(19), 7242–7249 (2016)
27. Diddigi, R.B., Prabuchandran, K.J., Bhatnagar, S.: Novel sensor scheduling scheme for intruder tracking in energy efficient sensor networks. IEEE Wirel. Commun. Lett. **7**(5), 712–715 (2018)
28. Wang, J., Ju, C.: A PSO based energy efficient coverage control algorithm for wireless sensor networks. CMC Comput. Mater. Continua **56**(3), 433–446 (2018)
29. Gu, J., Su, T., Wang, Q.: Multiple moving targets surveillance based on a cooperative network for multi-UAV. IEEE Commun. Mag. **56**(4), 82–89 (2018)
30. Wenyan, L., Xiangyang, L., Yimin, L.: Localization algorithm of indoor Wi-Fi access points based on signal strength relative relationship and region division. CMC Comput. Mater. Continua **55**(1), 071–093 (2018)
31. Ming, W., Jiangyuan, Y., Yuan, J., Xi, J.: Event-based anomaly detection for non-public industrial communication protocols in SDN-based control systems. CMC Comput. Mater. Continua **55**(3), 447–463 (2018)

Energy-Efficient Data-Collection with Rendezvous-Based Approaches in Large-Scale WSNs with Multi-UGV

Jian Zhang[1,2](✉), Ling Tan[2], and Wei Zhuang[2]

[1] College of Computer and Software, Nanjing University of Information Science and Technology, Nanjing 210044, China
jianzhang_neu@163.com

[2] Jiangsu Engineering Center of Network Monitoring, Nanjing 210044, China

Abstract. Prolonging the lifetime of wireless sensor networks (WSNs) is a crucial issue referring to energy conservation or balancing of data collection. In this paper, we propose an optimal algorithm for data collection using UGVs based on clustering by definition of rendezvous nodes (RNs). Due to the considerable large difference of long-distance transmission, the rendezvous-based clustered model for load balancing with multiple UGVs is proposed. Furthermore, considering different delay-tolerant applications, we design a data transmission mode called Two-Orbit Back-Propagation algorithm (TOBPA). In these process, we utilized utility function on energy to realize the optimal energy consumption in the sense of energy transmission model and take energy balancing into account meanwhile. As a result, we analyze the cluster lifetimes in different situations and achieve balance to save significant.

Keywords: Wireless sensor networks · Energy efficiency · Rendezvous nodes · UGV · Data collection

1 Introduction

Wireless sensor networks play more and more important roles in the real world [1] and actually provide practical solutions for application areas [2]. However, the data collection often meets challenges of energy efficiency [3] due to battery constraint of sensor nodes. Therefore, how to balance the energy consumption becomes a critical issue which prevents this phenomena. Although traditional multi-hop WSNs support real-time data delivery, they may lead to earlier death in large-scale sensing applications [5] because energy expenditure.

Proper data selection schemes of the routing path [6] is seen as one of requirements to achieve the energy efficiency. Cluster heads concentrate on sensing and forwarding data and they deplete energy faster than others. In addition, researchers have proved that clustering can distinctly improve the network lifetime [7, 31] by distributing some more powerful nodes or utilizing a mobile sinks [8]. In other word, clustering is an effective way of organizing the network, achieving energy efficiency. As a matter of fact, the clustering algorithm [32] constructs a specific structure to minimize the overall

X. Sun et al. (Eds.): ICAIS 2019, LNCS 11633, pp. 345–357, 2019.
https://doi.org/10.1007/978-3-030-24265-7_30

network overhead and energy consumption, while ensuring energy balance among sensors to prolong network lifetime.

In order to further reduce energy consumption, nodes located in the periphery of the sensing region can be recognized as rendezvous nodes so that sensory data from neighbor nodes can be collected and delivered to a MS which approaches within sensing range [9]. In the process, RN refers to rendezvous and shortening transmission distance. nevertheless, transmission distances is one of reasons to unbalance energy consumption in a sensing filed.

In addition, the clustering technique is also an efficient approach for supporting mobile sinks [10]. Owning to the energy consumption of multi-hop WSNs is rather high, cluster-based sensing and transferring are required, even though the data delay-tolerant problem exits. Therefore, UGVs or MEs tracing predetermined paths, and collecting data by a set of prearranged locations regularly [33] are used more often. By employing clustering and the mobility of the UGV, the long-distance transmissions are avoided by reducing long-distance transmission among inter-cluster; In fact, not only UGV [34] but also RN [27] are made a combination to shorten long-distance transmission. However, the difference of the transmission distance is considerable large [29], even though one-hop intra-cluster transmission. In this paper, we investigate the utility of UGVs for efficient data collection. Our proposed algorithm aims at minimizing the overall network overhead and energy expenditure associated with the selection of RNs and employment of UGVs, while also considers energy consumption balance with SN and UGVs. This is achieved through building cluster-based structures consisting of sensor nodes that route data to their assigned RNs and UGVs. To this end, we successfully realize the energy efficiency through dealing with complex transmission radius.

2 Related Works

The issue of energy efficiency has been extensively studied in wireless sensor networks [11–13], and one of the main issues focus on utilizing the mobile element to report and carry data as an effective technique, which can enhance efficiency of energy consumption in the networks [15–17]. Generally, to collect data from WSNs, there are mainly two approaches to increase the efficiency: (1) by hierarchical routing based on node clustering and (2) by mobile elements [18].

In many practical applications of wireless sensor networks, mobile sinks tend to move around within the sensor fields and receive data during their movements [19, 20]. And efficient data-forwarding strategies for wireless sensor networks with a mobile sink which visits rendezvous points (RPs) to gather data from sensor nodes come forth. In [23], Xing et al. offered an efficient rendezvous algorithm to determine the trajectory for the MS. They considered a subset of sensor nodes to serve as RPs that buffer and aggregate data that originated from sources, and they transferred them to the MS when it arrived. They determined the trajectory of the MS by considering a routing tree rooted at RPs. [21, 22] also utilize RPs to select an energy-efficient mobile-sink path to address energy challenge problems.

Combining the MS-based data collection and hierarchical clustering seems a promising way to achieve a better tradeoff between the energy consumption and the data latency [18]. Clustering is also wildly use as an effective approach for organizing the network and achieving energy efficiency [28, 29]. In general, LEACH [12] can provide fair distribution of clusters in the network. It rotates the CH roles among the nodes to ensure load balancing and energy consumption equity. It is also scalable, however since the CH election phase is stochastic, it does not guarantee the election of nodes with high energy levels. The clusters may also be concentrated in a restricted geographic region which prevent some nodes to belong to any cluster. This may have negative impact on network performance in terms of energy consumption and data collection. For this reason, many variants have been proposed to overcome these drawbacks [7, 28, 33].

Actually, one bottleneck of such approach is the large data collection latency incurred by the slow-moving mobile collector. In [24], Liu formulated the latency problem as rendezvous-based mobile data collection and performed local data aggregation to shorten it. Different from Liu [25] proposed age-optimal trajectories proposed for age of information characterized by the data uploading time and the time elapsed to deal with the latency problem. However, for real-time data, mobile robots are coordinated to establish a connected path between source node and base station, namely minimizing distance traveled by the robots and minimizing hop count [26]. In [27], by introducing mobile elements and assigned RPs, the problems, latency from mobility, one-hop transmission and energy balance, are referred to meanwhile. Shusen [5] focus on low-delay and high-throughput opportunistic data collection in WSN-MSs with general network topologies and arbitrary numbers of mobile sinks. In [34], UGV and UAV is utilized to realized data collection with rendezvous, then the function of WSNs is dramatically improved. Additionally, other applications [35, 36] are included in this field.

3 Problem Formulation

In this section, we will formally demonstrate the problem exists in this paper. For convenience, we first present several definitions used for data collection with UGVs.

3.1 Definitions

Definition 1 (Gradient). Given a transmission range R_t, the gradient of node i, which is denoted as $g(i)$, is the minimum hop count by forwarding a packet from node i to the sink with R_t.

Definition 2 (Ring). The set of nodes, which have the same gradient k, is defined as Ring k which is denoted by

$$R(k) = \{i|g(i) = k, i \in S\} \tag{1}$$

where S is the set of all sensor nodes.

According to the above definitions [29] and the definition of cluster from [27], the network model could be constructed in Fig. 1 as follows.

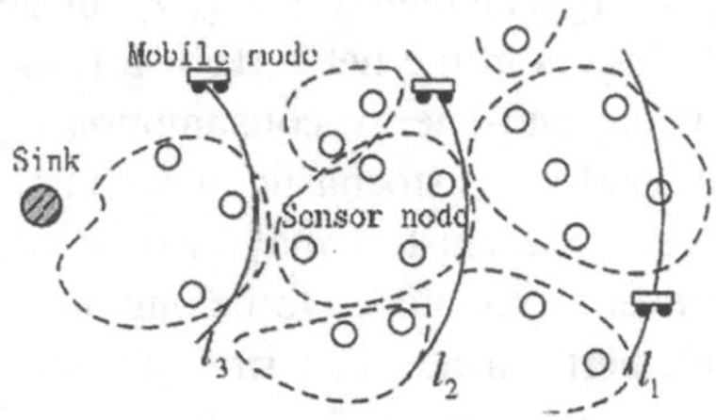

Fig. 1. Example of WSNs.

In Fig. 3 the interval between l_1 and l_2 is called a Ring i.e. $g(3)$ and definition gradient guarantees the distance between two Rings is one-hop. Considering the energy of network, we analyze the roles of all nodes in a cluster, and classify them into two groups as in Fig. 2.

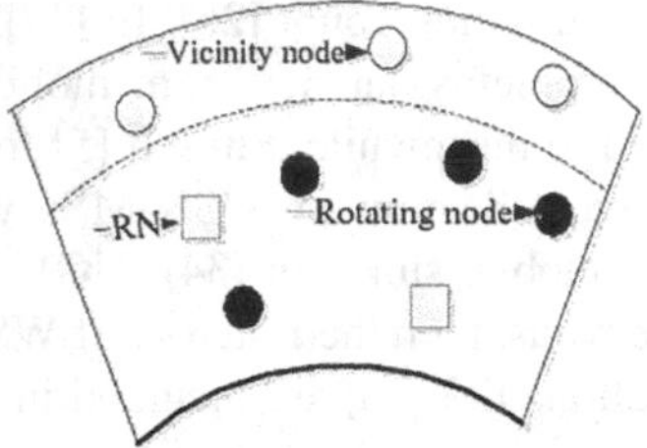

Fig. 2. Definitions of nodes

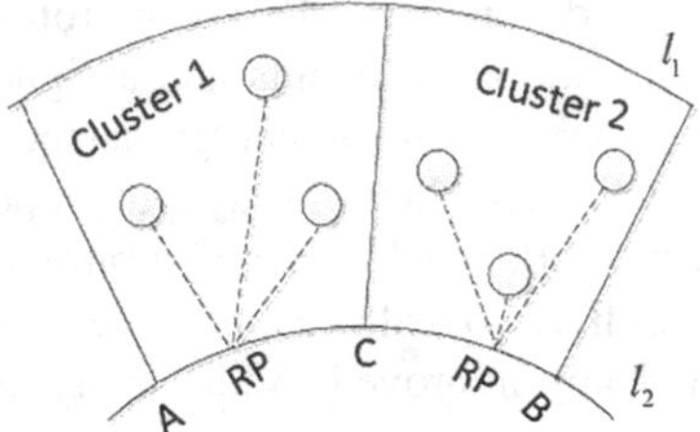

Fig. 3. Clustering scheme

Definition 3 (Vicinity nodes). Given nodes in a cluster, the white circle is called vicinity node, if it satisfies

$$S^V = \{i|E_i \propto d_i^4\} \cup \{i|i \in S_{RN}\} \tag{2}$$

where $S_{RN} = \{RN_1, RN_2, \cdots RN_m\} \subset S$, m is defined as the number of rendezvous nodes in a cluster, S represents the node set of the cluster.

Definition 4 (Rotating nodes). Given node j in a cluster, the white circle is called rotating node, if it satisfies

$$S^R = S - S^V \tag{3}$$

In order to cope with the problem of energy consumption, we introduce UGVs to construct network model. For energy efficiency, We consider two factors: one-hop clustering and data collection with UGVs.

In order to further reduce energy consumption, we utilize RNs as relay nodes so as to increase hops in a cluster. However, how to choose the suit amounts of nodes as RNs is difficult. An optimization algorithm is proposed in the following section.

4 Rendezvous Planning

Definition 5 (directed rendezvous tuple). In a cluster, a triple tuple $<Node, RN, RP>$ denotes the data transmitted route sequence, and element *Node* indicates the source node, element *RN* stands for a relay node, element *RP* is data transmission terminal of the cluster, e.g. a UGV.

Note that the second element *RN* could be set *NULL*, i.e. $<Node, NULL, RP>$. Actually, the triple-tuple $<Node, NULL, RP>$ is equivalent to $<Node, RP>$. This happened in the scenarios of short-distance transmission or low node density without enough relay nodes.

4.1 Rendezvous Transmission Model

When the number of UGVs is not enough or the data is high delay-tolerated, the RN plays roles in rendezvous, relay for rotating nodes and vicinity nodes.

In the process of rendezvous node determination, there are four scenarios as follows. In order to balance energy consumption, we assume that the RN is only for data relay. The reason is that the source nodes have longer transmitted radius and the RN expends energy when it receives and transmits message in the perspective of balancing the energy consumption.

In general, Fig. 4 includes four cases about RNs for transaction model with UGVs.

Case 1: general rendezvous. Seen from Fig. 4(a), the RN is selected to reduce the energy consumption and RN ought to be close to RP on the predetermined trajectory l_2.
Case 2: parallel rendezvous. In Fig. 4(b), sequential rendezvous triple-tuple of $<Node, RN_1, RP>$ in is equivalent to $<Node, RN_2, RP>$. The reason is that the two routes on a parallelogram.
Case 3: Symmetry rendezvous. $<Node, RN_2, RP>$ is coincident with the fact that RN ought to be close to RP. In Fig. 4(c), the energy consumption of $<Node, RN_1, RP>$ is equivalent to $<Node, RN_2, RP>$ because the two triangles are congruent.
Case 4: sharing rendezvous. In Fig. 4(d), either $<Node, RN_1, RP>$ or $<Node, RN_2, RP>$ is chosen as a matter of fact that the energy consumption is minimum and the surplus energy of the cluster is balanced considering energy consumption among the remaining sensor nodes, that is, a RN is avoided using repeatedly.

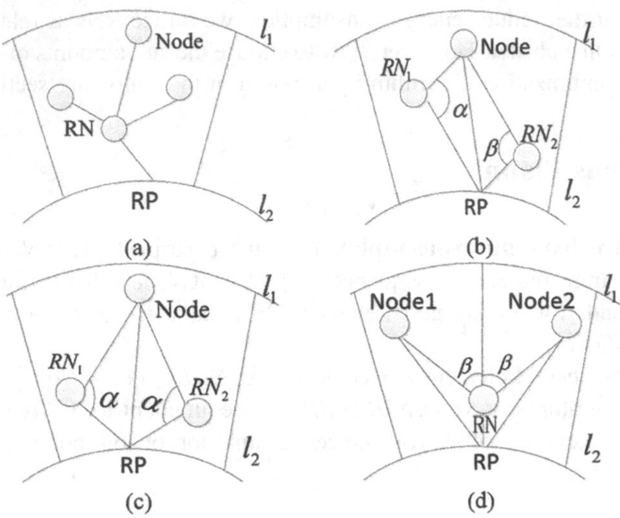

Fig. 4. Scenarios of a RN selection

4.2 Optimization Algorithm

According to energy balance, we modeled optimization of energy consumption as follows.

$$\begin{gathered}\min \sum_{i=1}^{N} (l \cdot \varepsilon_{fs} \cdot d_{i.}^{\alpha} + l \cdot E_{elec} + l \cdot E_{elec}) \\ s.t. \frac{1}{N} \sqrt{(E_1 - \bar{E})^2 + (E_2 - \bar{E})^2 + \cdots + (E_N - \bar{E})^2} \leq \Phi \\ d_{i.} \geq d_0\end{gathered} \tag{4}$$

where N is the amount of the cluster, E_i is the residual energy of node i, $\bar{E}$ denotes average energy of the member of the cluster, d_0 is a constant. Φ indicates a preassigned threshold. Note that the value of Φ is almost empirical value in practice, and it is hard and heavy to operate manually due to complicated situation.

5 UGVs Cooperation

5.1 Number of Mobile UGVs

In order to fully utilize the one-hop cluster, we allocate several mobile sinks in the same layer. We assume that the mobile sink moves with a constant speed v. Meanwhile we suppose that the mobile collectors arrive an RP on at time T and on at time in a cluster, respectively. We also define a deadline that the data chunks must delivered to the BS. Let the deadline be $\Delta t = |T - t|$. In fact, we define the deadline is as follows:

$$\Delta t = \max|T - t| \tag{5}$$

where $\max(\cdot)$ guarantees enough mobile collectors on the trajectory. Then the number of mobile collectors can be gotten:

$$Num_i = \left\lceil \frac{2\pi R_i}{\Delta t \times v} \right\rceil \tag{6}$$

where R_i is the radius of i-th layer. The sign $\lceil \cdot \rceil$ stands for an up-bound value. In the case of equality (6), the $(i + 1)$-th layer's number of mobile collectors is corresponding to

$$Num_{i+1} = Num_i + \left\lceil \frac{2\pi(R_{i+1} - R_i)}{\Delta t \times v} \right\rceil \tag{7}$$

In this way, we could guarantee that the data are collected in a cluster within a delay-tolerant deadline.

5.2 UGV-Enabled Data Collection Algorithm

In some scenarios, the data need to be transmitted under the condition of low time delay. In the network model, we proposed a low delay-tolerated two-orbit reverse transmission algorithm. In this algorithm, two steps are included.

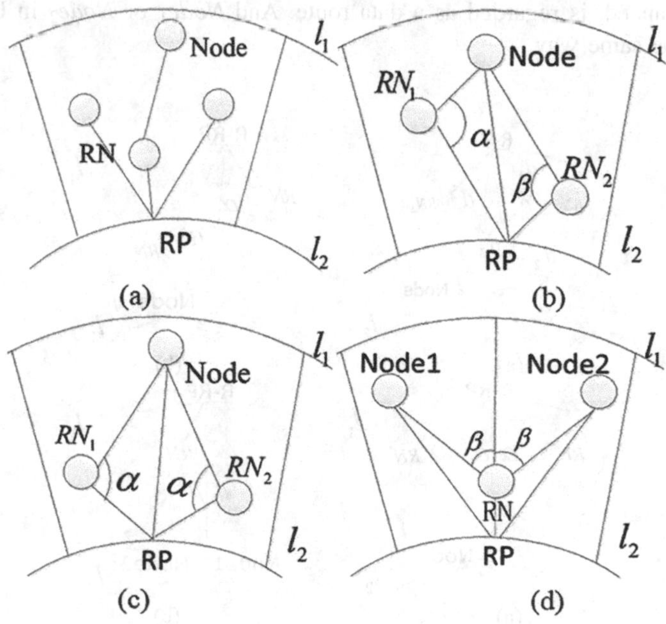

Fig. 5. Assumption of a RN selection in step 1

Step 1 RNs delay. Considering the energy consumption of vicinity nodes and balancing the energy consumption of the cluster, RNs shown in Fig. 5 are selected to relay data from vicinity nodes. The only Difference from high delay-tolerated algorithm, rotating nodes will communicate with the ME.

Step 2 Data Reverse. Due to some sensor nodes are set to rendezvous nodes closed to the RP of the cluster, the count of data is reduced, which maybe result in the problem of precision and accuracy for some application (e.g. target tracking). On the other hand, RNs' roles became singleness and then their functions are solidified, although the energy consumption of cluster reduces. According to these uncertainties, we design a two-orbit reverse transaction scheme for RNs and RPs in a cluster. Vicinity nodes S_2^V adjacent curve l_2 before as the role of RNs become source nodes to sense data, while vicinity nodes S_1^V adjacent curve l_1 before as the role of source nodes become RNs source node to relay data. Rotating nodes S^R only stay sleep state.

In this way, we only concern on the cooperation of the mobile sinks to collect data from WSN and no burden is added for the WSN as a result. In fact, the two-orbit determination scheme is a reverse transmission of rendezvous planning above Fig. 6 (a)–(d), and the corresponding contents are listed as Fig. 6(a)–(d). For scenarios Fig. 5 (a)–(b), we choose the RNs in a cluster according to the distance to the RP, i.e. ones closed to the RP is selected as RNs. In other scenarios like Fig. 6(c)–(d), selections of RNs or sensor nodes is determined to guarantee the balance of energy consumption. For example, in Fig. 6(c), if RN or RN' is selected as a relay node, the energy consumption is equal for tuple $<Node, RN, RP>$ and tuple $<Node, RN', RP>$. However, the tuple, which the energy expenditure is minimum and the surplus energy of the cluster is balanced, is regarded as a data route. And $Node_1$ or $Node_2$ in Fig. 6(d) is selected in the same way.

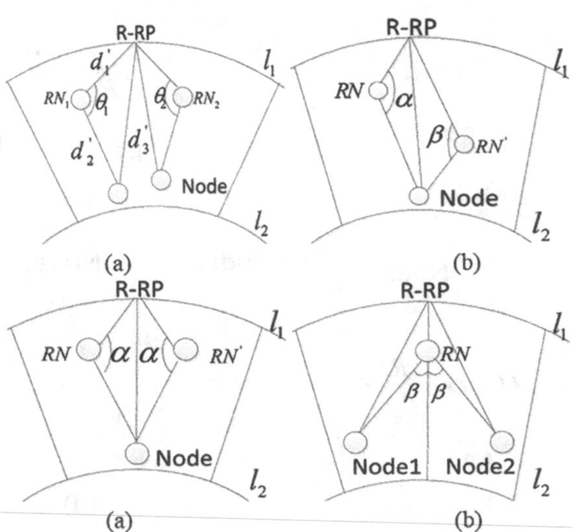

Fig. 6. Assumption of a RN selection in step 2

5.3 Energy Consumption Analysis

We consider the process of energy consumption for RPs. From the two data transmitted model, energy consumption mainly distributes for two stage. Then a challenge, which rotating nodes will be reused when a UGV arrive at the R-RP in step 2, arise currently. Because one UGV maybe stay at more than one RP in a short time interval according to network structure, it is harmful for the rotating nodes to transfer data regardless of UGVs arriving at RP in Fig. 5 or reverse RP in Fig. 6. In order to reduce utilization frequency of rotating nodes, they ought to be used only for once between the interval $[t, t + \Delta t]$.

Seen from Fig. 7, There are no data to be sensed and transmitted by rotating nodes in the time interval $[t_1, t_0 + \Delta t]$ the same as $[t_2, t_0 + 2\Delta t]$. Due less data are transmitted in a loop, the energy expenditure of the cluster naturally descends.

In the end, the data from the same cluster at different time by different mobile collectors in time interval could be fused at the sink without losing data volume.

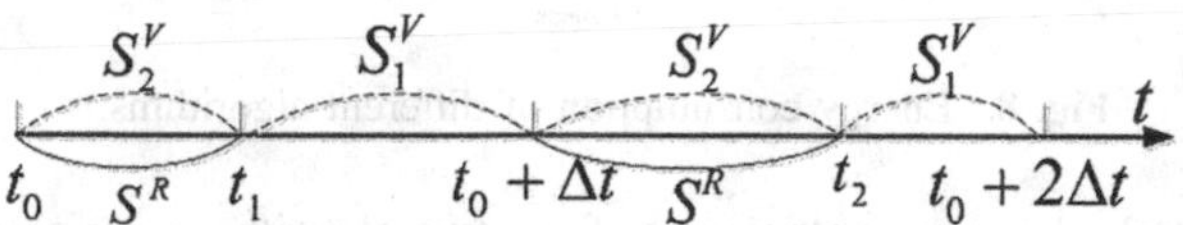

Fig. 7. Working states of rotating nodes and vicinity nodes.

6 Evaluation

In the even distribution, we suppose that nodes are located in a disk of an area with radius in the plane and each node chooses the one hop distance for each communication.

In this section, we evaluate the performance of schemes implemented with MATLAB. To evaluate the performance of the proposed mobile sinks based on the layered structure, extensive simulations have been conducted. As expressed in the above sections, main parameters used in the simulation are listed in Table 1.

Table 1. Simulation parameters

Parameters	Value	Parameters	Value
α	4	ε	10 J/bit /m^2
d	90 m	E_{amp}	0.0013PJ/bit.m^4
E_0	0.5 J	Nodes	100
E_{elec}	50 nJ/bit	Fixed sink	(0, 0)

For convenience, we name our algorithm as TOBPA with UGVs. We compare two metrics (named cluster-based WSNs, TOBPA, respectively) for the death of the first node with different density of WSNs. Seen from Fig. 8, the lifetime of cluster-based WSNs is less than 500 rounds obviously. Because of long-distance transmissions, nodes far away from RP consume much more energy in the data collection framework. As far as data collection density, we utilize the TOBPA to gather data for minimum energy consumption and energy balancing in a cluster. The reason is that TOBPA is a process of network behavior referring to frequency and sensor selection. Although the time interval needs less, the sensors are also less to balance the previous energy consumption.

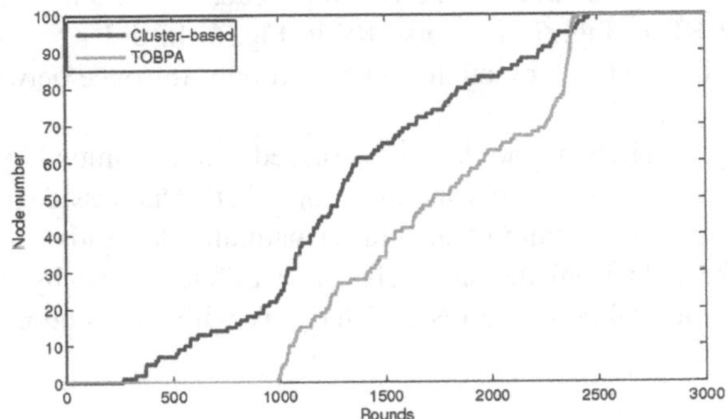

Fig. 8. Energy consumption of different algorithms.

In order to study the energy efficiency of our two algorithms, we consider WSNs in the scale of 100 nodes, 200 nodes and 300 nodes. Simulations are executed to provide energy expenditure of the 100 rounds. The first row of Fig. 9 presents the scenario of cluster-based energy consumption; the second row is TOBPA with UGV. In the first row cluster-based, some nodes always consume more energy than others, as if the tendency, which the phenomenon illuminates the number of nodes consuming more energy, reduces with the increase of nodes in WSNs. For example, node ID 52, node ID 63 for 100, node ID 18, ID 60, ID 65 for 200, and ID 88, ID 107, ID 172, ID 256 for 300. Expending more energy result in the lifetime of cluster shorter than our algorithms.

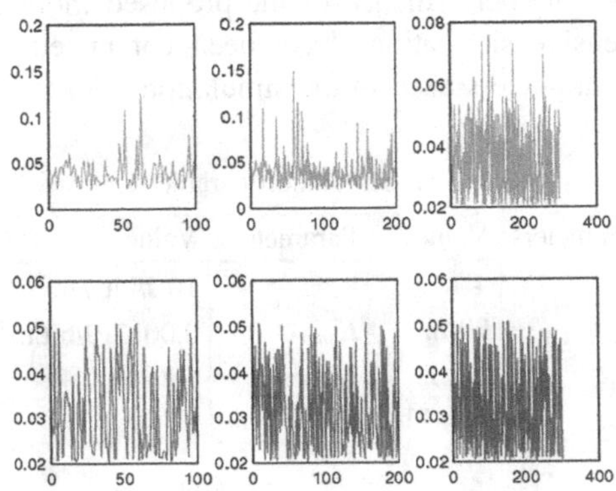

Fig. 9. Node energy of different densities.

On the contrary, TOBPA exploits RNs to relay and aggregate data leading to the decrease of long transmission distance. In this sense, nodes with long transmission distance could save more energy than direct transmission to ME. Seen from the second row, energy consumption of each node fluctuates between 0.02 and 0.05, although the number is changed from 100 to 300. The results prove that TOBPA effectively adjusts the energy consumption among all nodes in WSNs, so the lifetime of WSNs is longer than cluster previously. In order to decrease the impact of delay-tolerant application, TOBPA improves the sample frequency under the condition without increasing energy consumption of each node, even for the cluster. Therefore, TOBPA keeps effect better than cluster-based.

Then we study the network lifetime to evaluate the impact of different distances of data transmission. In this scenario, the radius of cluster are set to 60 to 90, illustrating the impact of critical value of transmission radius caused by RNs and UGVs. As shown in Fig. 10, it proves that the network lifetime of cluster-based mechanism declines sharply when transmission distance grows over critical value transmission radius. For completeness, we also study the network lifetime of cluster-based and TOBPA with the transmission radius R = 90. Due to the optimization algorithm in (4) and RNs' relay, the lifetime of TOBPA is superior to cluster-based. The reason is that TOBPA maintains WSNs balancing just like cluster-based with R = 60.

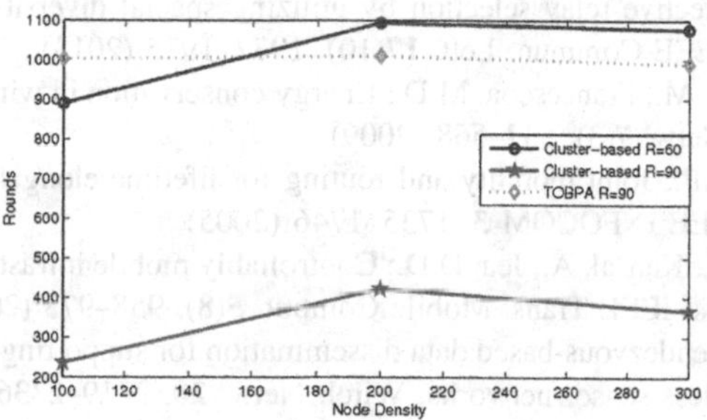

Fig. 10. Impact of radius

In order to exhibit comparability, we also study the accumulated energy consumption of the first 100 rounds with radius R = 90. According to Fig. 11, the cluster-based owns maximum energy expenditure. TOBPA is dramatically less than cluster-based, which is caused by two-orbit back-propagation algorithm and UGV cooperation.

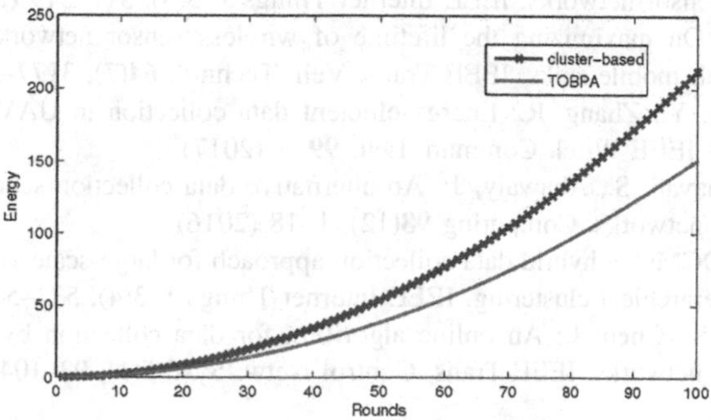

Fig. 11. Accumulated energy consumption.

Acknowledgment. This work was supported by the Foundation of Nanjing University of Information Science and Technology (Grant No. 2241101201101), Open Foundation of Education Ministry Demonstration Base of Internet Application Innovation Open Platform (Meteorological Cloud Platform and Application) (Grant No. 2201101401063), PAPD and Jiangsu Government Scholarship for Overseas Studies.

References

1. Stankovic, J.: Research directions for the Internet of Things. IEEE Internet Things **1**(1), 3–9 (2014)
2. Yick, J., Mukherjee, B., Ghosal, D.: Wireless sensor network survey. Comput. Netw. **52**, 2292–2330 (2008)
3. Liu, X.Y.: CDC: compressive data collection for wireless sensor networks. IEEE Trans. Parallel Distrib. Syst. **26**(8), 2188–2197 (2015)
4. Lian, J., Naik, K., Agnew, G.B.: Data capacity improvement of wireless sensor networks using on-uniform sensor distribution. Int. J. Distrib. Sens. Netw. **2**(2), 121–145 (2006)
5. Shusen, Y.: Practical opportunistic data collection in wireless sensor networks with mobile sinks. IEEE Trans. Mob. Comput. **16**(5), 1420–1433 (2017)
6. Bin, L.: Energy-effective relay selection by utilizing spacial diversity for random wireless sensor networks. IEEE Commun. Lett. **17**(10), 1972–1975 (2013)
7. Anastasi, G., Conti, M., Francescoa, M.D.: Energy conservation in wireless sensor networks. Elsevier Ad Hoc Netw. **7**(3), 537–568 (2009)
8. Jun, L., Hubaux, J.P.: Joint mobility and routing for lifetime elongation in wireless sensor networks. Proc. IEEE INFOCOM **3**, 1735–1746 (2005)
9. Somasundara, A.A., Kansal, A., Jea, D.D.: Controllably mobile infrastructure for low energy embedded networks. IEEE Trans. Mobile Comput. **5**(8), 958–973 (2006)
10. Lee, E., Park, S.: Rendezvous-based data dissemination for supporting mobile sinks in multi-hop clustered wireless sensor networks. Wirel. Netw. **20**, 2319–2336 (2014)
11. Wang, J., Ju, C.: A PSO based energy efficient coverage control algorithm for wireless sensor networks. CMC Comput. Mater. Continua **56**(3), 433–446 (2018)
12. Heinzelman, W.B., Chandrakasan, A.P., Balakrishnan, H.: An application-specific protocol architecture for wireless microsensor networks. IEEE Trans. Wirel. Commun. **1**(4), 660–670 (2002)
13. Tunca, C., Isik, S., Donmez, M.Y.: Distributed mobile sink routing for wireless sensor networks: a survey. IEEE Commun. Surv. Tutor. **16**(2), 877–897 (2014)
14. Dong, M., Ota, K., Liu, A.: RMER: reliable and energy-efficient data collection for large-scale wireless sensor networks. IEEE Internet Things J. **3**(4), 511–519 (2016)
15. Tashtarian, F.: On maximizing the lifetime of wireless sensor networks in event-driven applications with mobile sinks. IEEE Trans. Veh. Technol. **64**(7), 3177–3189 (2015)
16. Zhan, C., Zeng, Y., Zhang, R.: Energy-efficient data collection in UAV enabled wireless sensor network. IEEE Wirel. Commun. Lett. **99**, 1 (2017)
17. Izadi, D., Ghanavati, S., Abawajy, J.: An alternative data collection scheduling scheme in wireless sensor networks. Computing **98**(12), 1–18 (2016)
18. Ruonan, Z.: NDCMC: a hybrid data collection approach for large-scale WSNs using mobile element and hierarchical clustering. IEEE Internet Things J. **3**(4), 533–543 (2016)
19. Deng, R., He, S., Chen, J.: An online algorithm for data collection by multiple sinks in wireless-sensor networks. IEEE Trans. Control Netw. Syst. **5**(1), 93–104 (2018)

20. Ang, K., Seng, J., Zungeru, A.: Optimizing energy consumption for big data collection in large-scale wireless sensor networks with mobile collectors. IEEE Syst. J. **12**(1), 616–626 (2018)
21. Zhao, M., Yang, Y.: Bounded relay hop mobile data gathering in wireless sensor networks. IEEE Trans. Comput. **61**(2), 265–277 (2011)
22. Salarian, H., Chin, K.W., Naghdy, F.: An energy-efficient mobile-sink path selection strategy for wireless sensor networks. IEEE Trans. Veh. Technol. **63**(5), 2407–2419 (2014)
23. Xing, G., Li, M., Wang, T.: Efficient rendezvous algorithms for mobility-enabled wireless sensor networks. IEEE Tran. Mobile Comput. **11**(1), 47–60 (2012)
24. Liu, W., Fan, J.: Efficient rendezvous schemes for mobile collector in wireless sensor networks with relay hop constraint. Ad Hoc Sens. Wirel. Netw. **30**(3/4), 219–240 (2016)
25. Xu, G., Ngai, E.C.H., Liu, J.: Ubiquitous transmission of multimedia sensor data in Internet of Things IEEE. Internet Things J. **5**(1), 403–414 (2018)
26. Wichmann, A., Korkmaz, T., Tosun, A.S.: Robot control strategies for task allocation with connectivity constraints in wireless sensor and robot networks. IEEE Trans. Mob. Comput. **17**(6), 1429–1441 (2018)
27. Zhang, J., Tang, J., Wang, T.: Energy-efficient data-gathering rendezvous algorithms with mobile sinks for wireless sensor networks. Int. J. Sens. Netw. **23**(4), 248–257 (2017)
28. Gharaei, N., Bakar, K.A., Hashim, S.Z.M.: Collaborative mobile sink sojourn time optimization scheme for cluster-based wireless sensor networks. IEEE Sens. J. **18**(16), 6669–6676 (2018)
29. Zhezhuang, X.: Joint clustering and routing design for reliable and efficient data collection in large-scale wireless sensor networks. IEEE Internet Things J. **3**(4), 520–532 (2016)
30. Heinzelman, W.B., Chandrakasan, A.P., Balakrishnan, H.: An application specific protocol architecture for wireless sensor network. IEEE Trans. Wirel. Commun. **4**(1), 660–670 (2002)
31. Mamalis, B., Gavalas, D., Konstantopoulos, C., Pantziou, G.: Clustering in wireless sensor networks. In: RFID and Sensor Networks: Architectures, Protocols, Security and Integrations, pp. 324–353 (2009)
32. Chen, G., Li, C., Ye, M., Wu, J.: An unequal cluster-based routing protocol in wireless sensor networks. Wirel. Netw. **15**, 193–207 (2007)
33. Konstantopoulos, C., Pantziou, G., Gavalas, D.: A rendezvous-based approach enabling energy-efficient sensory data collection with mobile sinks. IEEE Trans. Parallel Distrib. Syst. **23**(5), 809–817 (2012)
34. Rucco, A., Sujit, P.B., Aguiar, A.P.: Optimal rendezvous trajectory for unmanned aerial-ground vehicles. IEEE Trans. Aerosp. Electron. Syst. **99**, 1 (2016)
35. Wenyan, L., Xiangyang, L., Yimin, L.: Localization algorithm of indoor Wi-Fi access points based on signal strength relative relationship and region division. CMC Comput. Mater. Continua **55**(1), 071–093 (2018)
36. Ming, W., Jiangyuan, Y., Yuan, J., Xi, J.: Event-based anomaly detection for non-public industrial communication protocols in SDN-based control systems. CMC Comput. Mater. Continua **55**(3), 447–463 (2018)

Analysis of the Efficiency-Energy with Regression and Classification in Household Using K-NN

Mingxu Sun[1], Xiaodong Liu[2], and Scholas Mbonihankuye[3,4](✉)

[1] School of Electrical Engineering, University of Jinan, Jinan, China
[2] School of Computing, Edinburgh Napier University, 10 Colinton Road, Edinburgh EH10 5DT, UK
[3] Jiangsu Collaborative Innovation Center of Atmospheric Environment and Equipment Technology (CICAEET), Nanjing University of Information Science and Technology, Nanjing 210044, China
scholas.mbonihankuye@yahoo.fr
[4] School of Computer and Software, Nanjing University of Information Science and Technology, Nanjing 210044, China

Abstract. This paper aims to study energy consumption in a house. Home energy management system (HEMS) has become very important, because energy consumption of a residential sector accounts for a significant amount of total energy consumption. However, a conventional HEMS has some architectural limitations among dimensional variables reusability and interoperability. Furthermore, the cost of implementation in HEMS is very expensive, which leads to the disturbance of the spread of a HEMS. Therefore, this study proposes an Internet of Things (IoT) based HEMS with lightweight photovoltaic (PV) system over dynamic home area networks (DHANs), which enables the construction of a HEMS to be scalable reusable and interoperable. The study suggests a technique for decreasing cost of energy that HEMS is using and various perspectives in system. The method that proposed is K-NN (K-Nearest Neighbor) which helps us to analyze the classification and regression datasets. This paper has the result from the data relevant in October 2018 from some buildings of Nanjing University of Information Science and Technology. That dataset allowed us to make analysis of electric energy consumption of each home equipment used and to make a simulation of the energy needed for each apparatus. Finally, we succeeded to find the algorithm which is suitable for efficiency-electric energy.

Keywords: Energy management system · Integrated wireless technology · Home energy storage · Home automation

1 Introduction

In our life, electric energy plays a very important role to make efficient most of our activities. We always need electric energy because with evolution of the technology, most of the needs in daily life require energy and then the problem of energy

X. Sun et al. (Eds.): ICAIS 2019, LNCS 11633, pp. 358–368, 2019.
https://doi.org/10.1007/978-3-030-24265-7_31

management becomes one of the crucial problems that the humanity is facing to especially reducing electricity consumption and its cost. Heating, insulation, consumption, savings are some of the basics to consider while applying electrical devises in one's house. It is important to learn how to reduce your cost bill in order to gain your comfort life with less electric consumption and low electric energy cost. All circumstances or time which we need for accredit energy, we have to use accession of internet on the thing's devices and rising numbering of contrivance acute in the house. The internet of things in energy usage is very significance in the devices convenience on our house [1]. The Home electric energy system has referred to some hardware and/or software, algorithm that can provide feedback about our necessity at home, and/or also enable advanced control energy-using devices at house (Working Group). Durability issues represent the biggest challenges that society is confronted. Least 83% to the world's most, electric energy, renewable energy (untenable) fossil meteorological, solar energy, and biomass is only about 2% sum above total [2]. On one hand a short range is preferred for energy efficient data transmission as a result of the nonlinear path loss ratio. [3]. In KNN, the distance of each test data point to all neighbors is calculated and ranked in rising command. The top 'k' distances are taken, and the most frequent class in that subset used to define the class of that data point. When two element compound and α is picket out correctly, the last score is appointed to minimize a total distance between those two elements, whereas the party of series had done in minimal number possible of bunch [1]. This is repeated for all data points until all have been labelled. Distance is calculated using Euclidean Distance method. For "*n*" objects to be assigned into "*k*" cluster, total of "*nk*",, distance computation will be performed [4].

$$d = \sqrt{(a_1 - b_1)^2 + (a_2 - b_2)^2} \tag{1}$$

$$standardization\,distance\colon X_z = \frac{X - Min}{Max - Min} \tag{2}$$

1.1 Scope

We aim to make a deep analysis of the problem related to home energy management system, and get better understanding of electric energy management based on result of our analysis, relying on efficiency-energy with Regression and Classification in household.

2 Related Work

Different methods or strategies used in electric energy sector in order to decrease energy consumption of household equipment are investigated. Electricity consumption is steadily increasing since the 1990s, lately emerging as the second most used source of energy with a share of 17, 7%, only behind oil with 40, 8%. One of the leading factors for this growth in electricity demand is the change in the habits of energy consumption in domestic environments. In 2010, domestic consumption was responsible for 28% of the total electricity consumption among all sectors with an effective increase of 40% between 1990 and 2010 [5]. It should be accommodated to mention that the potency economies of cooperation in communications have not been exploited in previous works. In the literature of wireless communication base stations (BSs) to sleep through the thin delivery of traffic was the common draw near to save energy [6]. The techniques done by Medasani and Kim shows that eliciting membership function form data are one of the fundamental applications with Fuzzy set theory [7]. In the research done by Jamsandekar and Mudholkar, they proposed an algorithm such as fuzzy inference system (FIS) for classification of electric energy data. In their proposed work, they used a Genetic algorithm (GA) which is an optimal searching technique used for generation rules [6]. The reference energy disaggregation Data Set aeration (REDD) [2], presents a data set containing freely available power information on the use of several houses, which aims to advance search on energy ventilation. These kinds of data are used in testing or implement methods that can be applied to HMES in order to reduce energy consumption. In view of storage problem, stem segmentation technique is used to extract keyword for each document and to build stem set. It has been shown that this method can obtain higher storage efficiency [8]. There are many methods used to process big data. However, there still the problem of detecting which one is the most efficient in big data analysis. Daily the transfer information need network and you must secure your social media as that someone may hacked your information and your secret message must secure which means that your information have not damaged on the process way [9]. Big data play important role on our improving knowledge, must know that we must make our information private and secure as encrypt our system of information using cloud computing knowledge [2, 8, 10].

3 Data and Methodology

In order to efficiently conduct our study, we used data collected from Nanjing University of Information Science and Technology, International students' dormitory number 4, room 322. The data collected concerned energy consumption such as telephone, heat water, heat water dispenser, air conditioner, iron. To achieve the goal on studying energy consumption in household, we used K-Nearest Neighbors (KNN) which is a non-parametric method mainly based on the analysis about big data. It is used for classification and regression to clarify the space among each point which is identified in clustering. The result obtained depends of the value gave by k, where K-NN algorithm used for classification or regression the distance. This method has been used in order to study how to reduce energy consumption in a household. In KNN, the distance of each test data point to all neighbors is calculated and ranked in ascending order. The top 'k' distances are taken, and the most frequent class in that subset are used to define the class of that data point. That step is repeated for all data points until all have been labelled.

Soumadip Ghosh et al. have proposed a genetic algorithm approach for finding frequent item sets which caters to positive and negative association mining [8]. In their result, they showed the rule of mining problem to find frequent item sets using their proposed GA based method, they found that it is a very simple and efficient one. Marmelstein proposed the method in which he tried to explore the different methods of using genetic algorithm with K- nearest neighbor algorithm to improve the classification accuracy and minimize the training error [9]. Soraj et al. proposed a Genetic fuzzy logic methods for the discovery of decision rules of datasets containing categorical and continuous attributes [10]. From the research done by Liu and Zhu, they found that among 2010 to 2030, the save energy increasing should be imprinted to a global energy require twice more than the one known today. According to their analysis and view the rate of the high technology today, their findings are about to be correct. Figure out this challenges, many modifications should be made regarding the existing electrical energy system [11]. Considering the findings from the work done by Liu et al., the alteration of climate had influence on energy electricity. Generally, communication networks and data centers are known to be the largest power consumers and Green House Gases (GHG) emitters among other ICTs, benefit from smart grid driven techniques to enhance energy savings and emission reductions [12] for a sustainable development. In view of storage problem, stem segmentation technique is used to extract keyword for each document and to build stem set. This method can obtain higher storage efficiency [13].

3.1 Appliance Modeling

Regression models are one of the simpler yet powerful analysis methods for understanding relationships in the data and generating predictions from them. This is normally done using the Least Squares Method, which attempts to fit a 'line of best fit' that minimizes the sum of squares of the vertical difference of each point from the line itself [14]. K-Nearest Neighbors (KNN) is the most common algorithm used. It's a supervised learning technique, where given a data point, the algorithm will output a class membership for that point [13–15]. KNN can also be used for identifying outliers in data. The Fig. 1 shows a system which is composed by many devices used to get electric energy. Energy electricity system flows into the lights, appliance from the socket to our devices. We have tried a schematic Fig. 1 with some devices of home energy electricity system. With the many researchers which we had consult their research's, we got that they have focus on important role plays by neural networks to previously their study on the features for analysis and extraction for Distant Supervised Relation. So they had a good reasonless such as that on the electric energy we need network if not the activities is not possible (DSRE) [16, 17].

3.2 KNN Classification and Regression Work

This method is used for processing of classification and regression in a given dataset such as electric energy analysis. The Kernel-Nearest Neighbor (KNN) normally use the classification and regression on their functionality. The output is a category of members. An object is classified by a majority votes by majority adjacent with the object assigned to the most popularly class in the K most related. Its neighbors can also be used for regression. Output value is obtained using production rerun (Fig. 2).

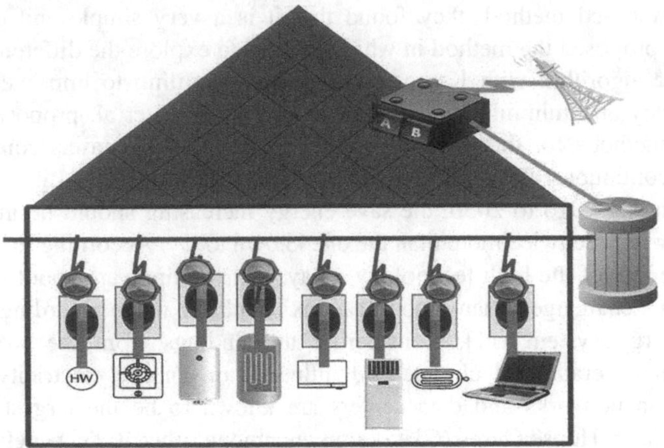

Fig. 1. Formulary system house layout

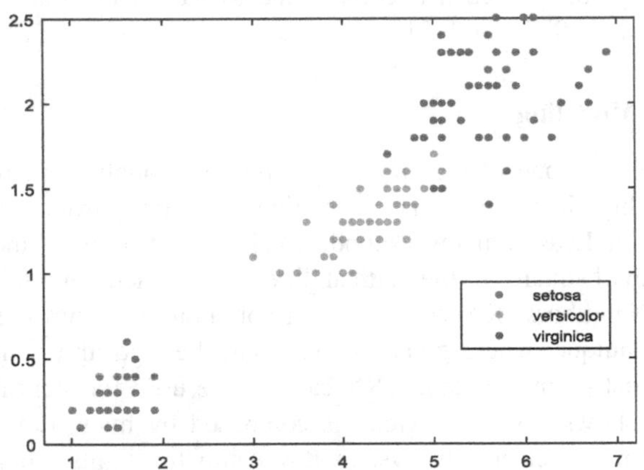

Fig. 2. Classification and regression

Steps by steps to computer KNN algorithm:

- First of all, we determine the parameter k which is the number or proximity of nearest neighbor;
- Computer the distance between patterns;
- Spell outrun and firm the most proximity K-th based on firm minimal;
- Put together patterns by category based on proximity most than nigh;
- Majority sample of the category of nearby most nigh becomes values of prediction of the search. Weigh more similar house more than those less similar in list of K-NN.

3.3 Algorithm Overview

We prefer to use K-Nearest Neighbor algorithm (k-NN) that is one of non-parametric method used for classifying data or regress data because it has been widely used by other authors and is also chosen to be one of the most important techniques in home energy management system analysis [18–21].

$$\hat{Y}q = \frac{C_{qNN1}Y_{qNN1} + C_{qNN2}Y_{qNN2} + C_{qNN3}Y_{qNN3} + \ldots\ldots + C_{qNNK}Y_{qNNK}}{\sum_{J=1}^{K} C_{qNNJ}} \tag{3}$$

For the static modeling regression analysis, it has been set a series of statistical processes in order to estimate the relationship among devices. K-Nearest Neighbor algorithm is a way to classify target with attributes to its nearest neighbor in the Learning set. In K-NN method, the K-Nearest Neighbors are considered [22–24]. Below is formula used to calculate a distance function of the variable:

$$Euclidean = \sqrt{\sum_{i=1}^{k}(x_i - y_i)^2} \tag{4}$$

$$Minkowski = \left(\sum_{i=1}^{k}(|x_i - y_i|)^q\right)^{1_q} \tag{5}$$

$$Distance\,Hamming\colon D_H = \sum_{i=1}^{k}|x_i - y_i| \begin{cases} x = y \Rightarrow D = 0 \\ X \neq Y \Rightarrow D = 1 \end{cases} \tag{6}$$

The problem that we have been resolving in logistic regression, the variable need depends on binary variable (True/False, Yes/No), for example in classification problems. It can be highlighted that logistic regression can be used even if the dependent and independent variables in our model do not have a linear relationship (Fig. 3).

4 Validation with Experimental Data from Room 322, #4 Building of NUIST

The dataset used to validate our experimentation has been personally collected from someone's room, East campus of Nanjing University of Information Science and Technology precisely old dorm room number 322 for a period of 3 days averaging from October 21th to 24th 2018. We tried to analyze different household equipment and studied which devices use high energy consumption.

4.1 Result Found from Experiment

Most of our experimentations have been done using MATLAB software. Thus, all figures used in this study are obtained from the analysis of data electric energy consumption using MATLAB. The electricity was downloaded from different devices and from different sockets (Fig. 4).

The Fig. 5 shows the variation of power consumption within each period of 10 min. Then we found that from 12:08 to 12:10 the power consumption is very high.

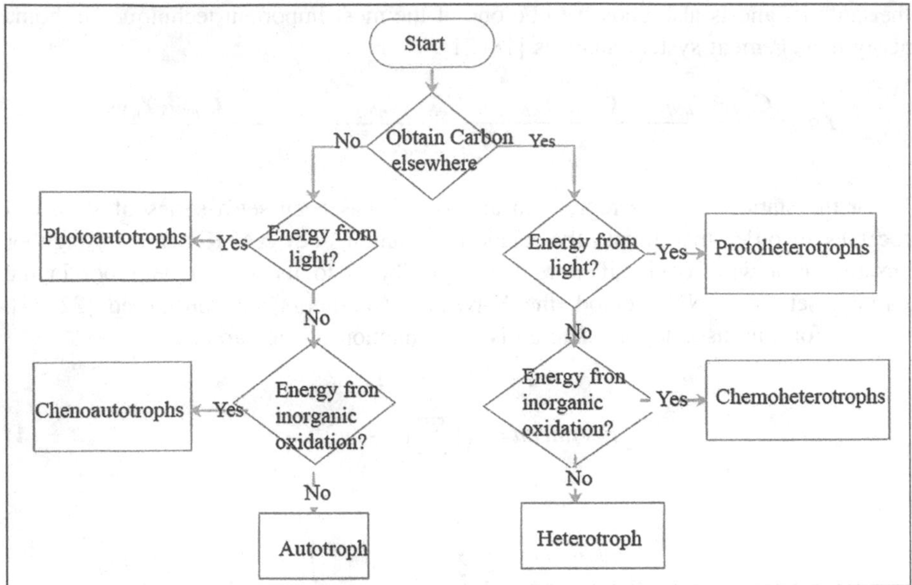

Fig. 3. Classification of problem regression

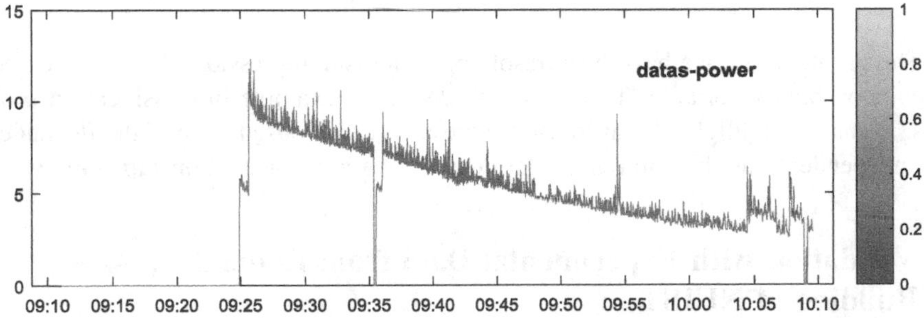

Fig. 4. Curve of data _ power

The question that comes out is why the energy consumption was suddenly getting higher and higher. We noticed that, when someone is heating water or cook something to eat, the energy consumption becomes very high at the time when proceed to finish. During our experimentation after 12:10, it can be seen a sudden decrease like a latent period which resumed around 12:20. During that period, the power consumption became very high. The energy consumption follows a sinusoidal curve. The Fig. 5 shows the result obtained from the data collected on October 24th in 2018 in the room of the East campus in Nanjing University of Information Science and Technology.

In the Fig. 6, we found that the variation starts after 10 min. The data were collected on October 24th, 2018. The result has shown that from the starting time 12:00, the variation starts after 10 min and we observe a sequence of increasing and

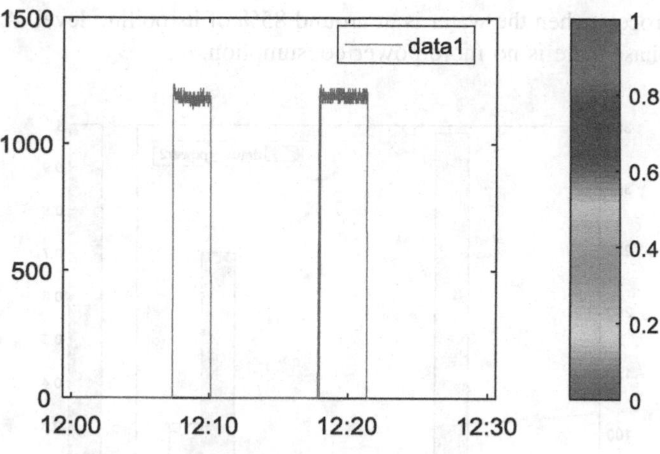

Fig. 5. Curve of data-power2

decreasing phenomena of energy consumption. It can be seen that the heat water energy consumption differs from the previous device. However, at the end of the collecting period, the figure shows us that curve of variation still on the same level of temperature.

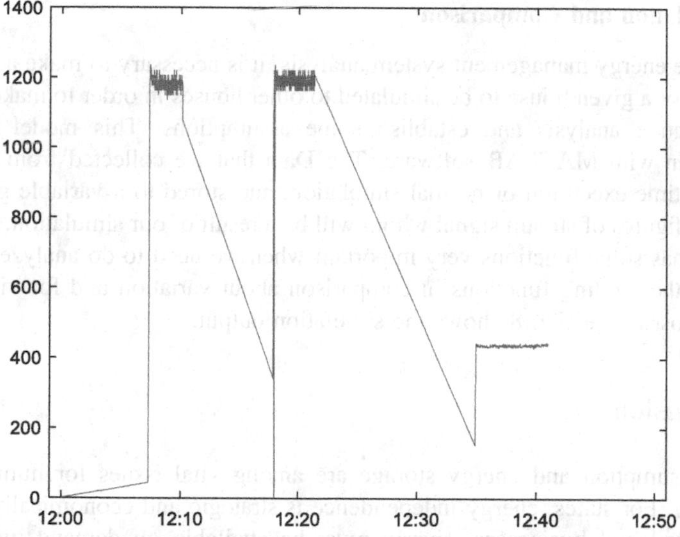

Fig. 6. Curve of data-power3 (heat water)

The Fig. 7 shows a histogram obtained while measuring the heat water energy consumption. Three phases can be identified. At the beginning, the power consumption is low but around 40% of heating, the energy consumption becomes very high then decreases for a certain latent period. The energy consumption increases again at the end of the heat process when the water is at around 85% of its boiling level. At the end of the boiling phase there is no more power consumption.

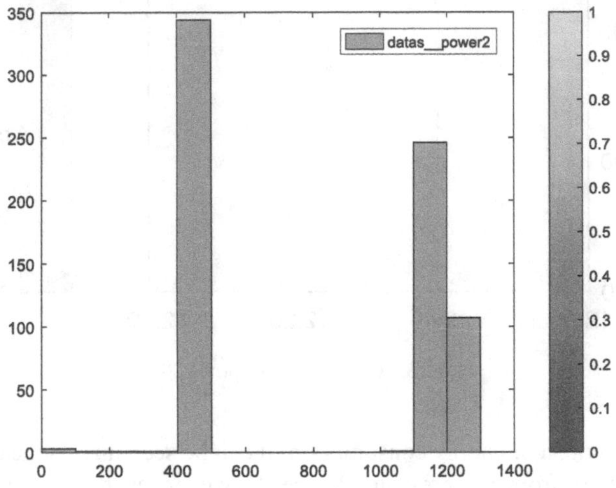

Fig. 7. Histogram of heat water

4.2 Simulation and Comparison

In any home energy management system analysis, it is necessary to make a simulation of the data for a given house to be simulated to other houses in order to make a general and perspective analysis and establish some assumptions. This model simulation has been run with MATLAB software. The Data that we collected from the model during real-time execution or normal simulation, and stored to a variable gave us the schemes or figures of stream signal whom will be a result of our simulation. MATLAB workspace has some functions very important when we need to do analyze of data or if we need the plotting functions in comparison about variation and for visualization of our purposes. The Fig. 8 shows the simulation output.

5 Conclusion

Energy consumption and energy storage are among vital issues for human society and industry. For states, energy independence is strategic and economically essential. For individual and businesses, energy must be available on demand, without any sudden interruption. Any breakdown of energy supply has a high economic and social cost and negative impact in terms of health and safety. The Energy Storage Service will help to uncover the revenue streams and business opportunities most relevant to any project. It provides a foundation in the economics, market landscape and technology advancements that is essential to formulating innovative strategies in the energy storage market. It has been demonstrated that the energy consumption depends on the categories of electric devices, electrical appliance, the allocation and the number of electric

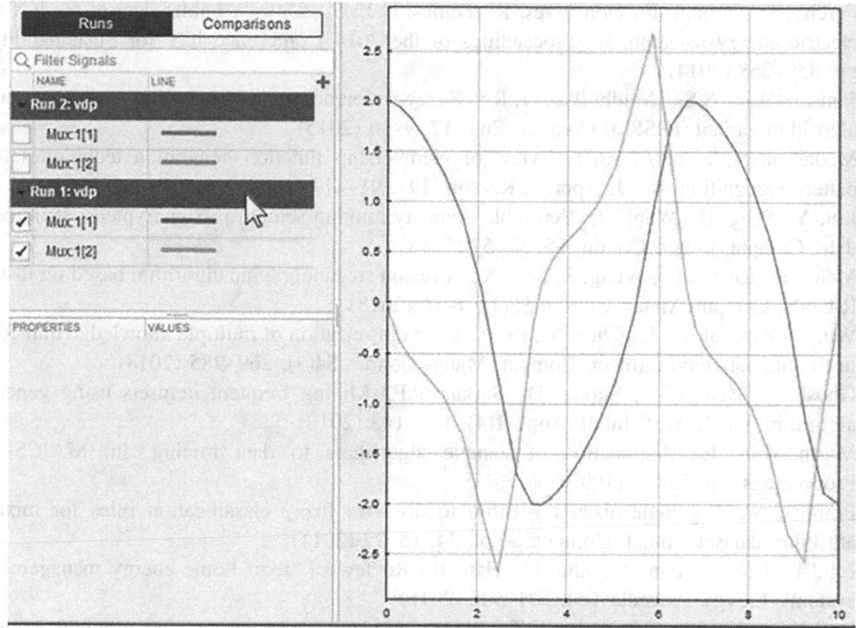

Fig. 8. Stream signal from Simulink

equipment in the house. The energy consumption variation depends also on the way it is used. Some homes used more household electric equipment while others are using few electric equipment. We have shown that for example the telephone and heat water are not consuming the same energy.

Acknowledgement. This work has received funding from the European Union Horizon 2020 research and innovation programme under the Marie Sklodowska-Curie grant agreement no. 701697, Major Program of the National Social Science Fund of China (Grant No. 17ZDA092), Basic Research Programs (Natural Science Foundation) of Jiangsu Province (BK20180794), 333 High-Level Talent Cultivation Project of Jiangsu Province (BRA2018332) and the PAPD fund.

References

1. Kamoto, K.M., Liu, Q., Liu, X.: Unsupervised energy disaggregation of home appliances. In: Sun, X., Chao, H.-C., You, X., Bertino, E. (eds.) ICCCS 2017. LNCS, vol. 10602, pp. 398–409. Springer, Cham (2017). https://doi.org/10.1007/978-3-319-68505-2_34
2. Kolter, J.Z., Johnson, M.J.: REDD : a public data set for energy disaggregation research. In: SustKDD Work, CA, USA, pp. 1–4 (2011)
3. Singh, P., Yadav, R.: Energy efficient and delay based on PSO with LST algorithm for wireless sensor network. In: International Conference on Computational Science and Engineering, vol. 6, pp. 2094–2100 (2016)
4. Paper, C.: Extensive survey on k-means clustering using mapreduce in datamining. In: International Conference on Electronics and Communication Systems, pp. 2–5 (2016)

5. Pereira, L., Quintal, F., Goncalves, R., Nunes, N.J.: SustData: a public dataset for ICT4S electric energy research. In: Proceedings of the 2014 Conference ICT for Sustainability, pp. 359–368 (2014)
6. Jamsandekar, S.S., Mudholkar, R.R.: Fuzzy inference rule generation using genetic algorithm variant. IOSR J. Comput. Eng. **17**, 9–16 (2015)
7. Medasani, S., Kim, J.: An overview of membership function generation techniques for pattern recognition. Int. J. Approx. Reason. **19**, 391–417 (1998)
8. Liu, Y., Peng, H., Wang, J.: Verifiable diversity ranking search over encrypted outsourced data. Comput. Mater. Contin. **55**, 37–57 (2018)
9. Meng, R., Rice, S.G., Wang, J., Sun, X.: A fusion steganographic algorithm based on faster R-CNN. Comput. Mater. Contin. **55**(1), 1–16 (2018)
10. Wu, C., Zapevalova, E., Chen, Y., Li, F.: Time optimization of multiple knowledge transfers in the big data environment. Comput. Mater. Contin. **54**(3), 269–285 (2018)
11. Ghosh, S., Biswas, S., Sarkar, D., Sarkar, P.P.: Mining frequent itemsets using genetic algorithm. Int. J. Artif. Intell. Appl. **1**(4), 133–143 (2010)
12. Marmelstein, E.: Application of genetic algorithms to data mining. In: MAICS-97 Proceedings, pp. 53–57 (1997)
13. Prabhat, N.: A genetic-fuzzy algorithm to discover fuzzy classification rules for mixed attributes datasets. Int. J. Comput. Appl. **34**, 15–22 (2011)
14. Liu, Y., Qiu, B., Fan, X., Zhu, H., Han, B.: Review of smart home energy management systems. Energy Procedia **104**, 504–508 (2016)
15. Erol-Kantarci, M., Mouftah, H.T.: Energy-efficient information and communication infrastructures in the smart grid: a survey on interactions and open issues. IEEE Commun. Surv. Tutor. **17**, 179–197 (2015)
16. Rogozhnikov, A.: Machine Learning in High Energy Physics. University of Landon, Queen Mary (2015)
17. Wang, Z., Ling, C.: On the geometric ergodicity of metropolis-hastings algorithms for lattice Gaussian sampling. IEEE Trans. Inf. Theory **64**, 738–751 (2018)
18. Li, D., Zhang, G., Xu, Z., Lan, Y., Shi, Y.: Modelling the roles of cewebrity trust and platform trust in consumers' propensity of live-streaming: an extended TAM method. Comput. Mater. Contin. **55**, 137–150 (2018)
19. Zeng, D., Dai, Y., Li, F., Sherratt, R.S., Wang, J.: Adversarial learning for distant supervised relation extraction. Comput. Mater. Contin. **55**, 121–136 (2018)
20. Kornaropoulos, E.M., Tsakalides, P.: A novel kNN classifier for acoustic vehicle classification based on alpha-stable statistical modeling. In: IEEE Workshop on Statistical Signal Processing Proceedings, pp. 1–4 (2009)
21. Chen, Q., Li, D., Tang, C.K.: KNN matting. IEEE Trans. Pattern Anal. Mach. Intell. **35**(9), 2175–2188 (2013)
22. Bhatia, N., Vandana: Survey of nearest neighbor techniques. (IJCSIS) Int. J. Comput. Sci. Inf. Secur. **8**(2), 302–305 (2010)
23. García, C., Gómez, I.: Algoritmos de aprendizaje: knn & kmeans. Univ. Carlos III Madrid, pp. 1–8 (2006)
24. Zhang, M.L., Zhou, Z.H.: ML-KNN: a lazy learning approach to multi-label learning. Pattern Recognit. **40**(7), 2038–2048 (2007)
25. Parry, R.M., et al.: k-Nearest neighbor models for microarray gene expression analysis and clinical outcome prediction. Pharmacogenomics J. **10**(4), 292–309 (2010)

Probe Recommendation Algorithm for Link Delay Detection

Liying Tao(✉), DanDan Li, Pei Zhang, and Xiao Liang

Beijing University of Posts and Telecommunications, No.10 Xitucheng Road, Haidian District, Beijing, People's Republic of China
2012213112@bupt.edu.cn

Abstract. Network abnormalities and outages just like hidden bombs that threaten the network healthy. The link abnormal detection can help locate network issue source. In this paper, we propose a probe recommendation algorithm for link delay detection via independent path which to filter duplication and get recommended probes for specified target link. Compared with [1], our algorithm effective draws down the number of probes by 51%–92% under condition of maintaining the accuracy of detection.

Keywords: Probe recommendation · Independent path · Link delay detection

1 Introduction

Detecting outages is an essential work to better monitoring and understanding the network. How to make detecting work more efficient is a valuable task. Network outages can be monitored in two stratums, macroscopic and microscopic. Web detection, DNS resolving [2, 3] and BGP detection [4, 5] are in the first category. Compare with the second category, these detections contain more content, and the detection results are more straightforward for the user, such as Baidu page cannot be accessed an hour ago. Recently research not only pay attention to the Internet, like DDoS attack detection [6], but also in SDN, to do the anomaly detection [7]. The link detection belongs to the microscopic category, compares with other detection measurements, it more focus on path changes and disconnection. Its atomic measurement unit is the link between two adjacent routes. Because of this feature, this detection can help other detection measurements to locate the specific outage source.

Traceroute is one of the most widely used methods for link detection. Though it is easy to use, still there are three challenges when we monitoring network via traceroute: traffic asymmetry [8, 9], RTT variability and packet loss. Researchers try to use several ways to solve the challenges, such as grouping mailing list to signal and share network disruptions knowledge [10], or reverse traceroute techniques based on IP options to expose the return path [11, 12], but the results are not ideal. According to the latest research, Romain and his team using large-scale traceroute measurement to detect pinpointing delay and forwarding anomalies [1]. With its mathematical delay change detection model, we can monitor the links in a network via traceroute data, so that to realize the identification of congested links and report disruptions. Compare with other

X. Sun et al. (Eds.): ICAIS 2019, LNCS 11633, pp. 369–378, 2019.
https://doi.org/10.1007/978-3-030-24265-7_32

link detection measurement, Romain's method can detect pinpointing delay only using traceroute data. They provide a concept of differential RTT, and use this to conquer the traffic asymmetry. Though the latest research has made great progress in traffic poor visibility and abnormal detection, it still cannot be applied in real scenes and applications due to the low efficiency and huge resource consumption. For each time period, Romain's method requires the all probes' scanning data about the whole network links in order to get calculation result.

In this paper, our goal is to propose a probe recommendation algorithm for link disruption detection base on Romain's mathematical method [1]. Reduce the number of probes for a particular routing link by filtering the duplicate paths. We propose a recommend model for probes in Sect. 2. After that, in Sect. 3 we analyze the result. Finally, the conclusion is given in Sect. 4.

2 Probe Recommendation Model

2.1 Review

Our probe recommendation algorithm is based on Romain's link delay detection method [1]. It introduces a concept named Differential RTT, and use it as a key measurement index to solve different return path problem in traceroute, and further to detect anomalous delays. Its differential RTT calculation method is as follows (Fig. 1):

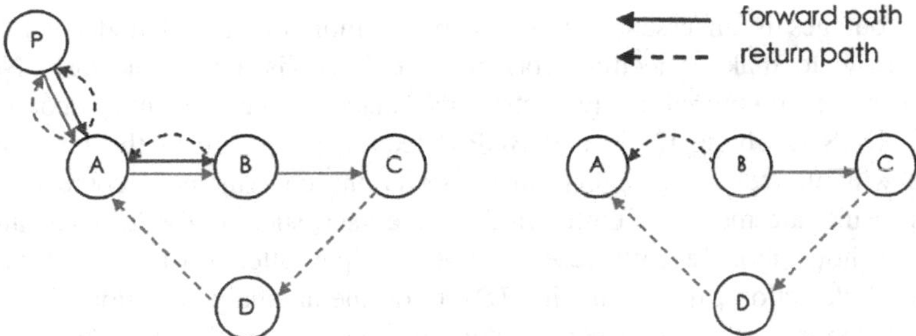

Fig. 1. Example of traceroute return path. P is the probe. A, B, C and D are routers, which D is on the return path unreported by traceroute, and others are reported.

$$\Delta_{PBC} = RTT_{PC} - RTT_{PB} \tag{1}$$

$$= \delta_{BC} + \delta_{CD} + \delta_{DA} - \delta_{BA} \tag{2}$$

$$= \delta_{BC} + \varepsilon_{PBC} \tag{3}$$

where Δ_{PBC} is the difference between the RTT of P to B and the RTT of P to C, i.e. the differential RTT. δ is the delay for a link, and ε is the difference between two return paths.

[1] detects anomalous delay though the deviation between the measurement value and its reference. Once the measurement value not in the reference, then it will be detected as an anomalous delay. It uses median as its measurement index because of the stability. Use Wilson score to define two differential RTT median reference bounders, the lower and the upper. $\bar{\Delta}$ is the median of reference, and Δ is the median of measurement. The anomalous delays detection method is as follows:

$$d(\Delta) = \begin{cases} \frac{\Delta^{(l)} - \bar{\Delta}^{(u)}}{\bar{\Delta}^{(u)} - \bar{\Delta}^{(m)}}, & if \bar{\Delta}^{(u)} < \Delta(l) \\ \frac{\bar{\Delta}^{(l)} - \Delta^{(u)}}{\bar{\Delta}^{(m)} - \bar{\Delta}^{(l)}} & f \bar{\Delta}^{(l)} > \Delta(u) \cdot \\ 0, & \text{otherwise} \end{cases} \tag{4}$$

where the superscript m, l, u means median, lower and upper.

2.2 Problem Description and Model Building

The filtration work of [1] focuses on AS level. It uses entropy *H*(*A*) to ensure the probe diversity, so that the observed link is monitored by more than 3 different ASs. Although in this way we can discard the concentrated probes to ensure the accuracy of result, the raw traceroute data don't contain the AS field, which means if you want to get the AS information, you need to link with another AS database. In addition, it doesn't consider about the inner AS issue. And what's more, this filtration method still can't reduce the usage of probes. In the meanwhile, [1] needs to collect all probes' data in network to do detection work, this way can guarantee the accuracy of the result, however, it will cause more waste of resources. Because probe can concurrence execute multiple tasks simultaneously, usually with different destination. When we have a target link, it may be observed by different probes, and each probe may include this link more than once. And these probes may have repeated paths, these paths will lead to huge network overhead, so we propose a probes recommendation model.

This model aims to maintain the accuracy of detection result with the minimum number of probes for a certain target link. The simple analog topology is as follows in Fig. 2. We only left the data of efficacious probes for each calculation round. And these efficacious probes are the recommended probes to user for its network. The model is as following:

$$P = \{p | \textit{the number of probes to complete the measrement}\} \tag{5}$$

$$R = \{r | \textit{the accuracy of detection result}\} \tag{6}$$

$$\min\{P\} \tag{7}$$

$$s.t. \left| R_{original} - R_{recommendation} \right| \leq 5\% \tag{8}$$

where $R_{original}$ [1] means the accuracy of detection result without probe recommendation. And the $R_{recommendation}$ means the accuracy of detection result with probe recommendation. On the condition of maintaining the accuracy of detection result, we set the deviation value to less than 5% based on the empirical value.

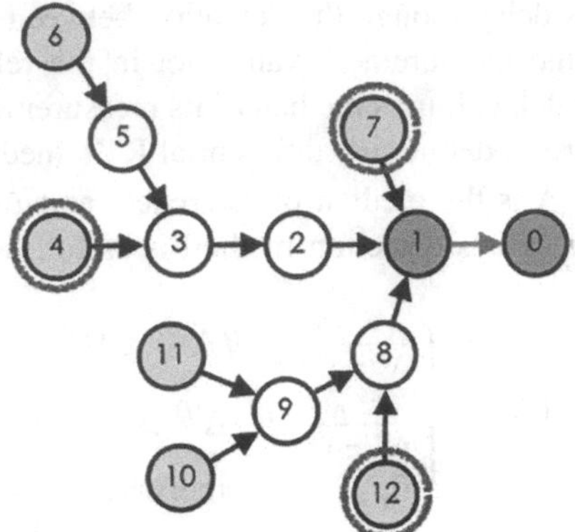

Fig. 2. Simple analog topology of network. The red path is the target link which needed to be observed. The orange nodes are the origin and the end of target link, 1 is the origin, and 0 is the end. The yellow nodes are the observing probes. The nodes which are circled by blue are the recommended probes. (Color figure online)

2.3 Probe Recommendation Algorithm

The primary work for a target link probe recommendation is to calculate the usage of probes amount. These probes must contain the target link. And if the forwarding path not change, for the specified source (the probe) and destination (the target link), the traffic path will not be changed.

Independent Path. Once we get the redundant probe set, the probe recommendation algorithm can be applied. The core idea of this probe recommendation is to reduce the duplication of repeated path, and find out the shortest independent path of each target link to ensure the variety of data and the accuracy of result. The higher the separation, the better the result. The independent path is the path which doesn't have a shared path, i.e. the path has no branches. For a specific link, the number of its independent path is the in-degree of this link, i.e. the in-degree of the origin of target link.

For node p, the recommendation algorithm can be written as:

$$N_t = \{n_t | all\ in\_degree\ nodes\ of\ p\ in\ time\ t\} \tag{9}$$

$$N_{t-1} = \{n_{t-1} | all\ in\_degree\ nodes\ of\ p\ in\ time\ t-1\} \tag{10}$$

$$end\ node = \begin{cases} n_t & N_t = \varnothing \\ N_{t-1} & N_t \neq \varnothing \end{cases} \tag{11}$$

where p in $time\ t-1$ means it at the pervious adjacent hop. For initialization, p is the origin of target link in time 0. The traversal will not stop until the $N_t = \varnothing$, and the node of p is the end node, i.e. the recommended probe. There is a simple example of probe recommendation in Fig. 3. The pseudocode of recommendation algorithm is as follows, where $Q = \{q | the\ object\ in\ queue\}$, and $A = \{a | all\ adjacent\ in\_degree\ nodes\ of\ point\}$.

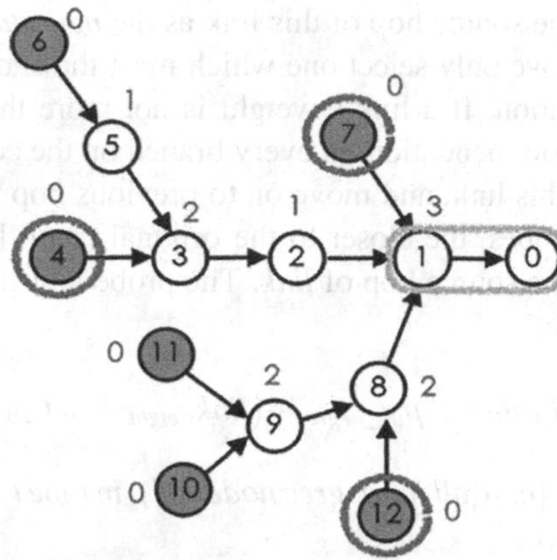

Fig. 3. Example of the shortest independent path of target link 1 to 0. The in–degree of 1 is three. The red number above the node is its in-degree. Three of the shortest independent paths are the path 7 to 1, 4 to 1, and 12 to 1. The recommended probe is 4, 7, 12. (Colour Figure Online).

```
Algorithm 1. Probe Recommendation

Input: queue
while queue is not empty:
    point ← the first object in Q
    Q - point
    if point.in_degree = 0 then
        return point
    else:
        for ∀a ∈ A do
            queue.add(a)
Output: point
```

Adjustment for Accuracy. The condition of probe recommendation is to maintain the accuracy of the detection result. According to the experiment, we find that the accuracy is not stable if only use the probe of the shortest independent path. So we need to dynamically adjust the number of probes. The number of start paths still is the in-degree of the target. We do the shortest independent path first, then compare with the original detection result [1], if the differential accuracy is not more than 5%, then we do the final recommendation with these probes. If the differential accuracy not satisfy the requirement, then we need to do the adjustment to meet the accuracy standard.

The aim of adjustment is to find out the minimum number of probes in the condition of the accuracy standard. We set a variable named *set_weight*, this variable can be changed according to the result differential accuracy. If a link's weight is less than the *set_weight*, we take the source hop of this link as the *new start point*, for all probes after this *new start point*, we only select one which meet the shortest independent path condition as recommendation. If a link's weight is not more than the *set_weight*, we will take one probe as recommendation on every branch on the condition of the shortest independent path before this link, and move on to previous hop to do the link's weight comparison. The more probes, the closer to the original result [1].

For node p, and p is the source hop of *link*. The probe adjustment algorithm can be written as:

$$threshold\,value = p_{in\_degree} - \left(link_{weight} - set\_weight\right) \tag{12}$$

$$C_{t-1} = \{c_{t-1} | all\ in\_degree\ nodes\ of\ p\ in\ time\ t-1\} \tag{13}$$

$$new\,start\,point = \begin{cases} p & if\ threshold\ value \geq 2 \\ C_{t-1} & if\ threshold\ value < 2 \end{cases} \tag{14}$$

where $p_{in_{degree}}$ is the in-degree of node p, $link_{weight}$ is the weight of *link*. For the condition of in-degree is more than 2, we determine whether if the point p is the *new start point* by calculating whether the *threshold value* is less than 2. There is a simple example of probe adjustment in Fig. 4. The pseudocode of recommendation algorithm is as follows, where $Q = \{q | \text{the object in queue}\}$, and $A = \{a | \text{all adjacent in\_degreenodes } ofpoint\}$.

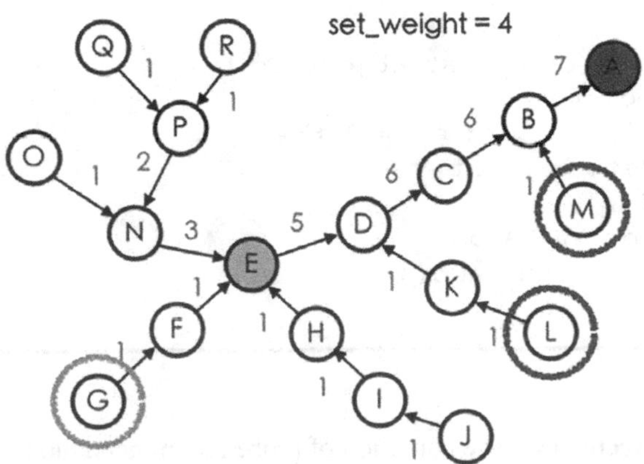

Fig. 4. Example of probe adjustment for the in-degree of *new start point* is more than 2. The *set_weight* is 4, the blue point 'A' is the start point, and the yellow point 'E' is the *new start point*. The probe in circles are the recommended probes which green circle represents the recommendation after the *new start point*, and the orange circle represents the recommendation before the *new start point*. (Colour Figure Online).

Algorithm 2. Probe Adjustment

```
Input: queue
while queue is not empty:
    point ← the first object in Q
    Q - point
    link ← a link with point as the source hop
    threshold = point.in_degree -
                (link.weight - set_weight)
    if threshold >= 2 then
        q1 ← create a new queue
        q1.add(point)
        algorithm1-probe_recommendaation(q1)
    else:
        for ∀a ∈ A do
            queue.add(a)
    if queue is empty:
        return point
Output: point
```

To dynamically adjust *set_weight*, we use Bisection method to fine the most suitable value. For *set_weight*, Δa is the differential accuracy, the Bisection method can be written as:

$$set\_weight = \begin{cases} set\_weight & if\ \Delta a \leq 5\% \\ \frac{set\_weight}{2} & if\ \Delta a > 5\% \end{cases} \tag{15}$$

3 Result and Analysis

We use RIPE Atlas as our data base due to its worldwide Atlas probes deployment [13], and here takes one hour Traceroute data from RIPE Atlas as example. Example 1 is IPv4 data. It is 5.22 GB in total, and holds 1,791,695 data and 10,072 probe points. Example 2 is IPv4 and IPv6. It is 8.88 GB in total, and holds 3, 206,784 data and 14,517 probe points.

Example 1. For a certain target link, after scanning the whole data set, we get 1,139 valid data and 113 probe points as shown below in Fig. 5(a). After probe recommendation only with the shortest independent path without set *set_weight*, the result become to 201 valid data and 9 probe points on the condition of differential accuracy is not more than 5% as shown in Fig. 5(b).

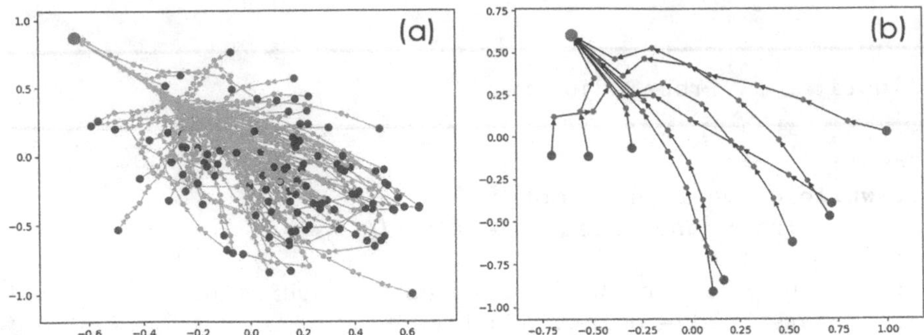

Fig. 5. (a) All observed probes example for a certain target link. The red node is the target, and the blue nodes are the 113 relevant probe points and the yellow line is their trace to the target. (b) Result for probe recommendation. The red node still is the target, the nodes in blue are the recommended probes for this certain target. (Color figure online)

Example 2. For a certain target link, after scanning the whole data set, we get 133,363 valid data and 93 probe points as shown below in Fig. 6(a). The result after probe recommendation as shown in Fig. 6(b), the result become to 61,730 valid data and 48 probe points on the condition of differential accuracy is not more than 5%, and the *set_weight* is 20.

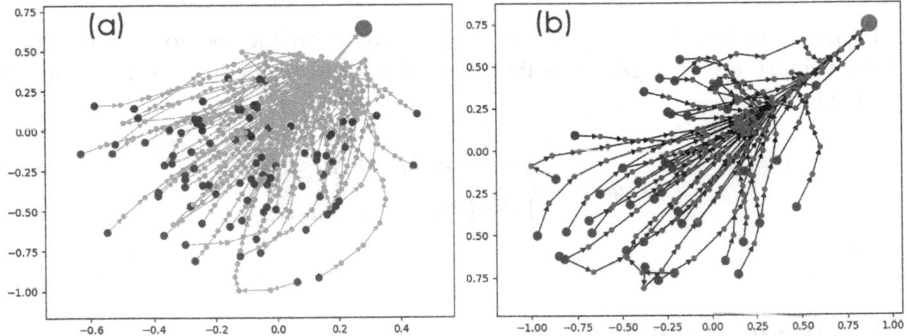

Fig. 6. (a) All observed probes example for a certain target link. The red node is the target, and the blue nodes are the 93 relevant probe points and the yellow line is their trace to the target. (b) Result for probe recommendation. The red node still is the target, the nodes in blue are the recommended probes for this certain target. (Color figure online)

We use the two sets of data to perform link delay detection, though there are some deviations, the recommendation set maintains the accuracy of detection result of original method [1]. The compared result is as follows in Table 1.

The median, lower and upper bounder are the measurement index for [1], to tell whether the link is abnormal or not. As the table shows, probe recommendation reduces the amount of valid data about 51%–92%, and keep the differential accuracy fluctuation not more than 5%.

Table 1. Compared result for a certain target link in one hour IPv4 data.

	Number of valid data	Number of differential RTT	Median value/ms	Lower bounder / ms	Upper bounder / ms
Original [1]	1,139	10,251	0.645	0.640	0.652
Recommendation	201	1,809	0.659	0.646	0.673
Original [1]	133,363	3,186	19.0691	17.308	20.783
Recommendation	61,730	1,800	19.522	17.114	21.043

4 Conclusion

In this paper, we propose a probe recommendation algorithm for link delay detection in order to reduce the network resource consumption. Through independent path, the algorithm can provide user a set of recommended probes for a certain target link, and the paths of these recommended probes always be the shortest. Base on this, we can also increase the possibility of obtaining traceroute data, because the shorter the traceroute path, the higher the probability of success. Validation shows that the recommendation algorithm draws down the number of probes by 50%–92% compared with the original [1] result, and maintain the accuracy of detection result in the same time.

Acknowledgement. This paper is supported by the Project U1603261 supported by Joint Funds of National Natural Science Foundation of China and Xinjiang.

References

1. Fontugne, R., Pelsser, C., Aben, E., Bush, R.: Pinpointing delay and forwarding anomalies using large-scale traceroute measurements. In: IMC 2017 Proceedings of the 2017 Internet Measurement Conference, 1–3 November 2017, London, United Kingdom, pp. 15–28 (2017)
2. Zhang, H.S.: Research of key technology of DNS security protection. Telecommun. Technol. **2015**(09), 99–104 (2015)
3. Yan, B., Fang, B.X., Li, B., Wang, Y.: Detection and defence of DNS spoofing attack. Comput. Eng. **32**(21), 130–132 (2006)
4. Wang, N., Du, X.H., Wang, W.J., Liu, A.D.: A survey of the border gateway protocol security. Chin. J. Comput. **40**(07), 1626–1648 (2017)
5. Li, S., Zhuge, J.W., Li, X.: Study on BGP security. J. Softw. **24**(1), 121–138 (2013)
6. Cheng, J., Xu, R., Tang, X., Sheng, V.S., Cai, C.: An abnormal network flow feature sequence prediction approach for DDoS attacks detection in big data environment. CMC Comput. Mater. Contin. **55**(1), 095–119 (2018)
7. Wan, M., Yao, J., Jing, Y., Jin, X.: Event-based anomaly detection for non-public industrial communication protocols in SDN-based control systems. CMC Comput. Mater. Contin. **55** (3), 447–463 (2018)

8. Teixeira, R., Marzullo, K., Savage, S., Voelker, G.M.: In search of path diversity in ISP networks. In: Proceedings of the 3rd ACM SIGCOMM Conference on Internet Measurement, pp. 313–318. ACM (2003)
9. Zheng, H., Lua, E.K., Pias, M., Griffin, T.G.: Internet Routing Policies and Round-Trip-Times. In: Dovrolis, C. (ed.) PAM 2005. LNCS, vol. 3431, pp. 236–250. Springer, Heidelberg (2005). https://doi.org/10.1007/978-3-540-31966-5_19
10. Banerjee, R., et al.: Internet outages, the eyewitness accounts: analysis of the outages mailing list. In: Mirkovic, J., Liu, Y. (eds.) PAM 2015. LNCS, vol. 8995, pp. 206–219. Springer, Cham (2015). https://doi.org/10.1007/978-3-319-15509-8_16
11. Katz-Bassett, E., et al.: Reverse traceroute. In: NSDI, vol. 10, pp. 219–234 (2010)
12. Marchetta, P., Botta, A., Katz-Bassett, E., Pescapé, A.: dissecting round trip time on the slow path with a single packet. In: Faloutsos, M., Kuzmanovic, A. (eds.) PAM 2014. LNCS, vol. 8362, pp. 88–97. Springer, Cham (2014). https://doi.org/10.1007/978-3-319-04918-2_9
13. RIPE NCC, Atlas. https://atlas.ripe.net. Accessed 2 Nov 2017

Recommendation with Heterogeneous Information Networks Based on Meta-Graph

Ding Zichen, Bin Sheng, and Sun Gengxin(✉)

School of Data Science and Software Engineering, Qingdao University, Qingdao 266071, China
sungengxin@qdu.edu.cn

Abstract. In order to alleviate data sparsity and cold-start problems of traditional collaborative filtering recommendation algorithm, a meta-based fusion heterogeneous information network recommendation algorithm is adopted in this paper. The algorithm integrates the characteristics of multi-relationship social network and user's preference degree and adopts a universal representation for different types of data. A meta-graph-based similarity measurement method makes it possible to better capture the semantic relationships between different types of data and a score matrix decomposition method based on multiple meta-graphs is used. Each project and user generates a variety of potential feature matrices based on different meta-graphs. Effectively integrates multiple feature matrices into a unified, final implicit feature matrix. We use each factor of each line of the implicit feature matrix as a neural network. The input node predicts user ratings by optimizing the scoring neural network. Finally, we used the data set provided by the Yelp website to do user rating prediction experiments, which proved the accuracy of this algorithm is 5% higher than the traditional collaborative filtering recommendation algorithm.

Keywords: Recommendation system · Heterogeneous information network · Collaborative filtering · Matrix factorization · Meta-graph

1 Introduction

With the advent of the era of big data, the problem of information overload has come. As an effective means of filtering information, the recommendation system is one of the effective methods to solve the information overload problem and realize the people-oriented personalized service [1]. In recent years, research on recommendation systems has made a series of advancements [2]. Shopping websites such as Amazon recommend the products that the users are interested in to the corresponding users through the recommendation system, which not only saves the time for the users to find the products, but also improves the shopping experience of the users, and makes the website obtain rich economic benefits [3].

Collaborative filtering recommendation [4–7] is a widely used method, especially the collaborative filtering algorithm based on matrix decomposition (referred to as matrix decomposition recommendation method). The traditional collaborative filtering recommendation method is to represent the user's rating information of the commodity

X. Sun et al. (Eds.): ICAIS 2019, LNCS 11633, pp. 379–390, 2019.
https://doi.org/10.1007/978-3-030-24265-7_33

in a matrix form, and to mine the implicit features in the low-dimensional space by decomposing the matrix, and to re-present the user and the commodity in the low-dimensional space. Thus, the correlation between the user and the product is depicted by the inner product between the user's product vectors. In practical applications, the number of users and projects in the data set is increasing, but the user's rating for the project is limited, resulting in sparse data. At the same time, new users have a cold start problem [8] because it is rare to use the behavior information, it is difficult to give accurate recommendations. These characteristics have led to the recommendation that the traditional matrix decomposition recommendation method is not very satisfactory.

The collaborative filtering method of social network integration [9] considers the impact of social network information on user ratings by introducing social relationships, and solves the problem of data sparseness and cold start to some extent [10–13]. Deng et al. [12] proposed a recommendation algorithm based on the diffusion dynamic process by combining the friend information of the social network with the information of the user's choice of goods. Guo et al. [14] used the friend information to fill the scoring matrix and proposed a collaborative filtering recommendation algorithm that integrates social network information. However, the existing methods only use one of the relationships in the social network and do not make full use of the various relationships that exist in the social network. Therefore, a recommendation system that integrates multiple information is proposed in this paper, which can well overcome the impact of data sparseness, cold start on the recommendation system.

2 Related Work

Current information network analysis has a basic assumption: the type of object or connection is unique. The network is homogeneous. It contains the same types of objects and connections. The author collaboration network and the friend relationship network are such homogeneous information networks (referred to as homogeneous networks), which are usually extracted from real interactive behaviors. The system establishes a relationship connection by ignoring the heterogeneity between objects and objects or by using only one type of relationship. Based on this, the score prediction is performed.

2.1 Heterogeneous Information Network Integrating Multiple Information

Sun et al. [15, 16] firstly proposed a heterogeneous information network. The heterogeneous information network is a directed graph with a relationship model $TG = (A, R)$, which is specifically defined as:

$$G = (V, E) \tag{1}$$

Where V is the node set, E is the edge set, A is the node type set, and R is the edge type set.

Heterogeneous information networks perform score prediction analysis based on modeling different types of objects and connections. Compared with homogeneous information networks, heterogeneous information networks can effectively fuse more information and contain richer semantics in nodes and connections [17], thus forming a new analytical direction.

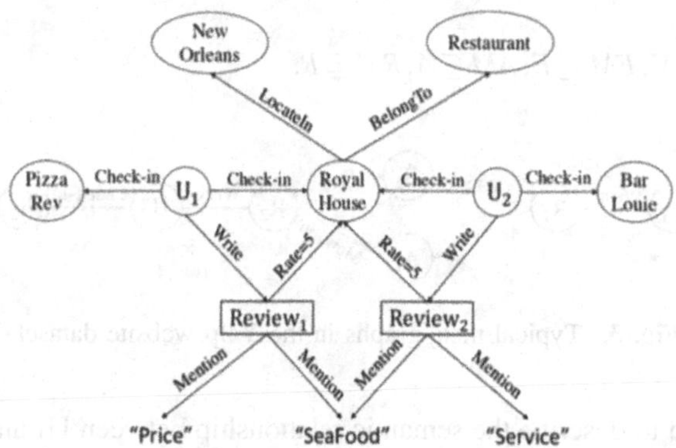

Fig. 1. Heterogeneous network diagram of user information on Yelp website

As can be seen from Fig. 1, the heterogeneous information network includes multiple types of object nodes, such as User, Review, Aspect, City, and Restaurant (Business), and also includes various connection relationships such as Check-in, LocateIn, and Rate, Write, Mention, etc. By abstracting these object node instances and relationships, a relationship schema diagram can be formed.

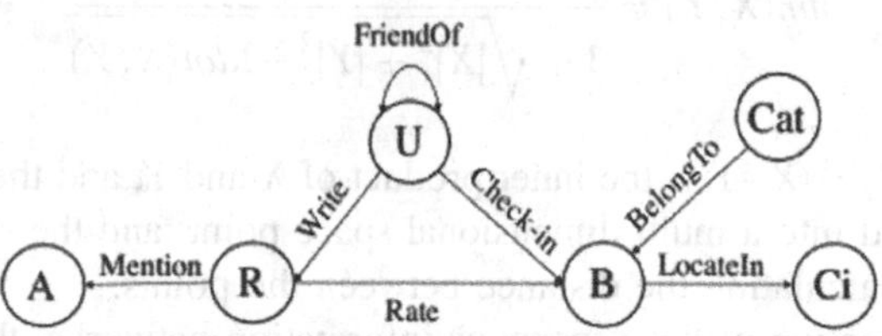

Fig. 2. Relationship pattern diagram in Yelp information network

2.2 Meta-Graph

On the basis of heterogeneous networks, Sun et al. [18] proposed the concept of meta-path, which is a sequence of acyclic relations from the starting node N_s to the target node N_t. For example, *U* and *B* form the simplest meta-path *U-B*. A heterogeneous information network may include a plurality of different meta paths. The network mode shown in Fig. 2 may also have complex meta paths such as *U-B-U-B* and *U-R-A-U-B*. The meta-path representation method is applied in the similarity calculation of the recommendation system because it can easily represent a simple semantic relationship.

However, as the complexity of heterogeneous information networks increases, meta-paths do not intuitively express semantic relationships in complex heterogeneous networks. Zhao et al. [19] proposed a method for calculating node similarity on a meta-graph. In the information network, the meta-pattern M is a directed acyclic graph from a single starting node N_s to a target node N_t, which is defined as follows:

$$M = (VM; EM; AM; RM; ns; nt) \tag{2}$$

Where, $VM \subseteq V, EM \subseteq E, AM \subseteq A, RM \subseteq R$.

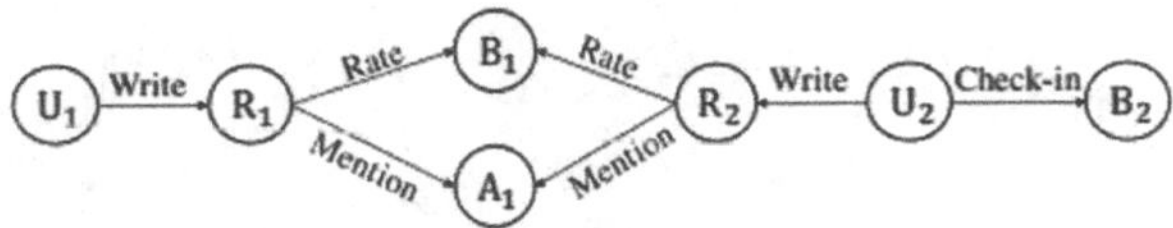

Fig. 3. Typical meta-graphs in the Yelp website dataset

When we need to describe the semantic relationship between U_1 and U_2, Fig. 3 can clearly express that U_1 may be interested in B_2, but the meta-path cannot visually express this relationship.

2.3 Similarity Measure

The traditional similarity measure is mainly calculated by the user's score on the project. The main methods are Euclidean distance similarity, cosine similarity, Pearson similarity, etc. The Euclidean distance similarity calculation formula is as follows:

$$sim(X, Y) = \frac{1}{1 + \sqrt{|X|^2 + |Y|^2 - 2dot(X, Y)}} \tag{3}$$

Where $dot(X, Y) = X \cdot Y$ is the inner product of X and Y, and the object X, Y to be measured is mapped into a multi-dimensional space point, and the similarity of X and Y is measured by calculating the distance between the points.

With the introduction of heterogeneous information networks, the traditional similarity measure method can not calculate the similarity of heterogeneous nodes well, and the similarity calculation method based on meta-path and meta-graph is gradually generated. The similarity calculation methods based on the meta-path mainly include the following:

The *Path count* method determines the similarity based on the number of nodes on the y-element path from the starting node x to the target node. The calculation formula is as follows:

$$s(x, y) = |\{p : p \in P\}| \tag{4}$$

Where $s(x, y)$ is the similarity function of x and y, P is the meta path, $|\cdot|$ is the number of sets, and p is a path instance.

The *Random walk* method determines the similarity based on the probability of random walk from the starting node x to the target node y. The calculation formula is as follows:

$$s(x,y) = \sum\nolimits_{p \in P} Prob(p) \tag{5}$$

Where p is a path instance, P is a meta path, and $Prob(p)$ represents the probability that x will reach y along p.

Given a meta-path P, the similarity between the objects x and y can also be calculated using *PathSim*, which is calculated as:

$$s(x,y) = \frac{2 * \left|\{p_{x \rightsquigarrow y} : p_{x \rightsquigarrow y} \in P\}\right|}{\left|\{p_{x \rightsquigarrow x} : p_{x \rightsquigarrow x} \in P\}\right| + \left|\{p_{y \rightsquigarrow y} : p_{y \rightsquigarrow y} \in P\}\right|} \tag{6}$$

Where $p_{x \rightsquigarrow y}$ is an instance of a path from x to y, $p_{x \rightsquigarrow x}$ is an instance of a path from x to itself, and $p_{y \rightsquigarrow y}$ is an instance of a path from y to itself.

It can be seen from Eq. (6) that the *PathSim* similarity measure consists of two parts. The formula numerator part expresses the connectivity between x and y, and the denominator part expresses the visibility of x and y respectively. The visibility of a node in the network is measured by the number of path instances from the node to the node itself.

3 Recommendation Based on Heterogeneous Information Network

3.1 Extraction of Network Meta-Graphs

There are many heterogeneous information network scenarios in real life, such as Taobao users, commodities, users' communities, etc., which constitute different types of nodes. User product purchase relationships, user relationships, and product relationships constitute different types of relationship connections. In order to illustrate the information network construction process, the information network is constructed in this paper using the data set provided by the Yelp website. First, extract the User, Review, Aspect, City and other entities from the dataset to establish object nodes, and then extract the connection between Check-in, LocateIn, Rate, Write, and Mention to establish the connection between objects. On this basis, the meta-graphs contained in the heterogeneous information network are analyzed.

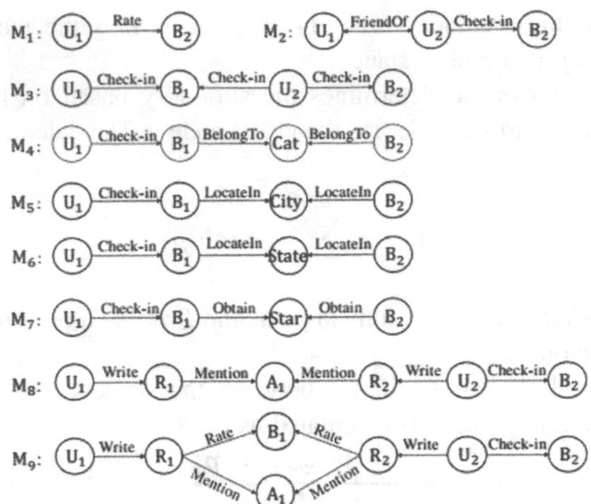

Fig. 4. Network meta-graph on the Yelp website

3.2 Node Similarity Measure

The meta-path based AC matrix representation method is defined as follows

Given a network $G = (V, E)$, its network mode is T_g. A meta-path $P(A_1, A_2 \ldots A_l)$ is selected, and its communication matrix is defined as follows:

$$M = W_{A_1A_2}W_{A_2A_3}\ldots W_{A_{l-1}A_l} \tag{7}$$

Where $W_{A_iA_j}$ is the adjacency matrix of type A_i, A_j. $M(i, j)$ represents the number of paths from one instance object $x_i \in A_1$ to another instance object $y_j \in A_l$ on path P. For the meta path M_8 in Fig. 4, the communication matrix is:

$$C_{M_8} = W_{UR}W_{RA}W_{UR}^TW_{RA}^TW_{UB} \tag{8}$$

3.3 Decomposition of Feature Matrix Based on Meta-Graph

In each communication matrix, it is assumed that the user's preference is determined by K influence factors. Based on this assumption, the implicit decomposition of the user project can be obtained using the matrix decomposition method for the L communication matrices. Decompose the scoring matrix $R_{m\times n}$ into the product of two matrices $U_{m\times k}$ and $B_{k\times n}$:

$$R_{m\times n} \approx U_{m\times k} \times B_{k\times n} = R'_{m\times n} \tag{9}$$

Each element of the matrix $U_{m\times k}$ and $B_{k\times n}$ need to be solved, which can be transformed into a regression problem in machine learning. The square of the error between the original scoring matrix $B_{m\times n}$ and the reconstructed scoring matrix $R'_{m\times n}$ is used as the loss function:

$$e_{i,j}^2 = \left(r_{i,j} - \sum_{k=1}^{K} u_{i,k} b_{k,j} \right)^2 + \frac{\beta}{2} \sum_{k=1}^{K} \left(u_{i,k}^2 + b_{k,j}^2 \right) \tag{10}$$

Finally, solve the minimum of the sum of the losses of all non-empty terms:

$$min\,loss = \sum_{r_{i,j}!=null} e_{i,j}^2 \tag{11}$$

The gradient is used to optimize the above formula. Solve the negative gradient of the loss function:

$$\frac{\partial}{\partial_{u_{i,k}}} e_{i,j}^2 = -2\left(r_{i,j} - \sum_{k=1}^{K} u_{i,k} b_{k,j} \right) b_{k,j} + \beta u_{i,k} = -2e_{i,j} b_{k,j} + \beta u_{i,k} \tag{12}$$

$$\frac{\partial}{\partial_{b_{k,j}}} e_{i,j}^2 = -2\left(r_{i,j} - \sum_{k=1}^{K} u_{i,k} b_{k,j} \right) u_{i,k} + \beta b_{k,j} = -2e_{i,j} u_{i,k} + \beta b_{k,j} \tag{13}$$

Update u and b according to the direction of the negative gradient:

$$u'_{i,k} = u_{i,k} - \alpha \left(\frac{\partial}{\partial_{u_{i,k}}} e_{i,j}^2 + \beta u_{i,k} \right) = u_{i,k} + \alpha (2e_{i,j} b_{k,j} - \beta u_{i,k}) \tag{14}$$

$$b'_{k,j} = b_{k,j} - \alpha \left(\frac{\partial}{\partial_{b_{k,j}}} e_{i,j}^2 + \beta b_{k,j} \right) = b_{k,j} + \alpha (2e_{i,j} b u_{i,k} - \beta b_{k,j}) \tag{15}$$

Update u and b every iteration until the set convergence criteria are reached.

After obtaining the L –group implicit user matrix and the item matrix, all user item matrices are connected into a total implicit feature matrix. For an observed user u_i and project b_j, the score x^n is:

$$x^n = F\left(u_i^{(1)}, \ldots u_i^{(l)}, \ldots u_i^{(L)}, b_j^{(1)}, \ldots b_j^{(l)}, \ldots b_j^{(L)} \right) \tag{16}$$

Where u_i^l, b_j^l is the implicit feature of the user item under the l-th meta-graph, and x^n is composed of $2KL$ items, where K is the dimension describing the implicit features of the user and the project in the matrix decomposition, which varies with the meta-graph. For the convenience of calculation, set K to a constant value shared by different meta-graphs.

Its converted expression is:

$$x^n = F(u_1 b_1, u_2 b_2, \ldots u_l b_l) = F(s_1, s_2, \ldots s_l) \tag{17}$$

Where F is a function that approximates x^n, and u and b are hidden vectors of length L, $s_1 = u_1 b_1$.

In order to consider the mutual influence between different meta-graphs, $s_l \times s_t$ is taken as the quadratic factor of F, where $l < t < L$.

In summary, the final expression of x^n is:

$$x^n = F(s_1, s_2, \ldots, s_l, s_1 s_2, s_1 s_3, \ldots, s_2 s_3, s_2 s_4, \ldots) \tag{18}$$

The parameters of the incoming F have a total of $I = L + C_L^2 = \frac{L^2+L}{2}$ items. Where C_L^2 is the combination number operation.

The neural network is used to train the F function, and its loss function is:

$$Loss = log\left(\sum_{i=1}^{n}(y_i - y_i')^2) + \lambda||W||_2\right) \tag{19}$$

Where y_i is the observed value, y_i' is the predicted value, and $||W||_2$ is the L_2 norm of the parameter matrix W.

4 Experiment and Result Analysis

4.1 Experimental Data Set

The data set provided by the Yelp Challenge is used in this paper. In this paper, based on the data provided by the Yelp website, the effectiveness of the method is proved by experiments, and the advantages and disadvantages of the model are analyzed on the basis of experiments. The experimental selection training set and test set included 37,659 and 9415 scoring data, respectively.

Figure 4, extracted from Yelp, was used as a meta-graph in the experiment; Aspect was obtained from user comment text using Gensim software. For convenience, the number of aspects is defined as 10 and the number of meta-graphs is set to 9.

Table 1. Experimental data set

Data set: Yelp-200K			
Relationship (A-B)	Number of A	Number of B	Number of A-B
User-Business	36105	22496	191506
User-Review	36105	191506	191506
User-User	17065	17065	140344
Business-Category	22496	869	67940
Business-Star	22496	9	22496
Business-State	22496	18	22496
Business-City	22496	215	22496
Review-Business	191506	22496	191506
Review-Aspect	191506	10	191506

4.2 Experimental Evaluation Indicators

There are several indicators for predicting the accuracy of the score, mainly by calculating the difference between the predicted score and the true score. The most classic are mean absolute error (MAE) and root mean squared error (RMSE).

MAE is defined as:

$$MAE = \frac{1}{|E^P|} \sum_{(u,\alpha)\in E^P} \left| r_{u\alpha} - r'_{u\alpha} \right| \tag{20}$$

Where $r_{u\alpha}$ represents the true score of the user u for the commodity α, $r'_{u\alpha}$ represents the predicted score of the user u for the commodity α, and E^P represents the test set.

RSME is defined as:

$$RMSE = \sqrt{\frac{1}{E^P} \sum_{(u,\alpha)\in E^P} \left(r_{u\alpha} - r'_{u\alpha} \right)^2} \tag{21}$$

The smaller the values of MAE and RMSE, the smaller the prediction error, and the better the recommended performance of the model.

4.3 Analysis of Experimental Results

In order to measure the influence of the number of iterations on the algorithm in the matrix decomposition process, experiments are carried out with different iteration times. It can be seen from Fig. 5 that when the number of iterations reaches 300, it gradually becomes stable. In order to eliminate the influence of the number of matrix decomposition iterations on the RMSE value, the number of matrix decomposition iterations is selected 350 times.

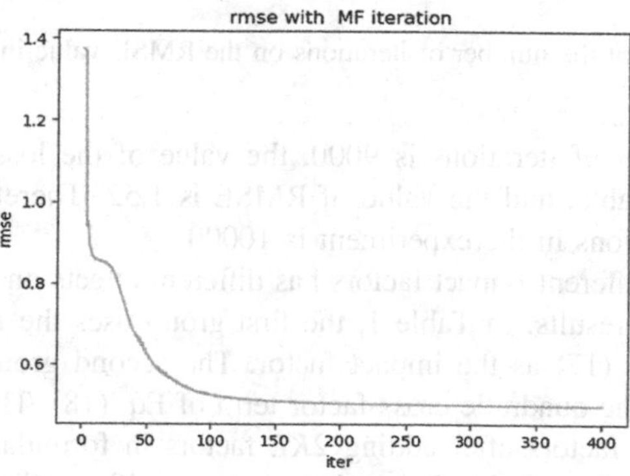

Fig. 5. Influence of the number of iterations on the RMSE value in matrix decomposition

In the process of neural network training, different iteration orders also have different effects on the value of the objective function and the value of RMSE. The more iterations, the closer the predicted scoring matrix is to the true value, and the higher the RMSE value (Figs. 6, 7).

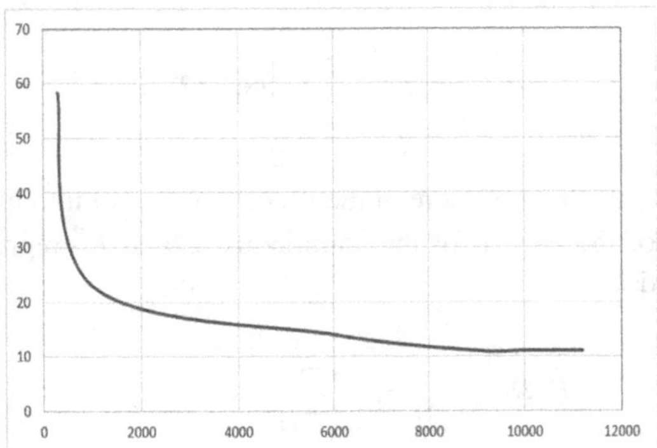

Fig. 6. Influence of the number of iterations on the loss function in neural network training

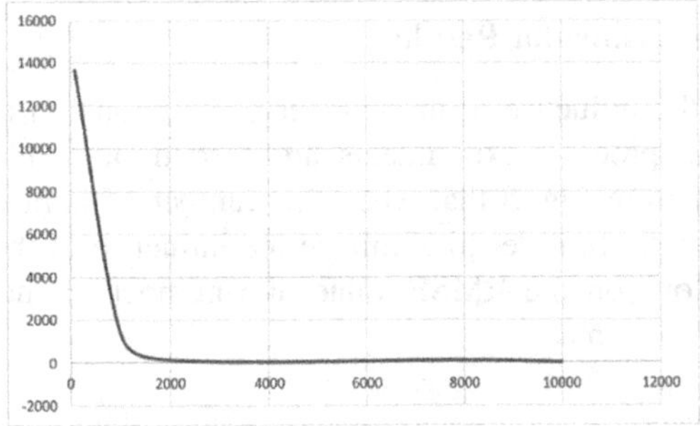

Fig. 7. Influence of the number of iterations on the RMSE value in neural networks

When the number of iterations is 9000, the value of the loss function is 11.02, which tends to be stable, and the value of RMSE is 1.52. Therefore, the number of neural network iterations in the experiment is 10000.

The number of different impact factors has different effects on the RMSE value of the recommendation results. In Table 1, the first group uses the L user item implicit feature matrix in Eq. (17) as the impact factor. The second group is the number of impact factors after the quadratic cross-factor term of Eq. (18). The third group is the number of influence factors after adding $2KL$ factors in formula (16) to the second group. It can be seen from Table 2 that there is no significant difference between the $\frac{L^2+L}{2}$ factors and the $\frac{L^2+L}{2}+2KL$ factors when using the neural network method. However, when linear optimization is used, the predicted effect is better after adding $2KL$ of influence factors after matrix decomposition.

Table 2. The effect of different factor numbers on RMSE values

Optimization method/number of factors	First group (L)	The second group $(\frac{L^2+L}{2})$	The third group $(\frac{L^2+L}{2}+2KL)$
Linear optimization	3.81	3.75	1.81
Neural network- optimization	1.30	1.27	1.28

In order to evaluate the algorithm, the user-item scoring data for training is recommended by the traditional matrix decomposition method (Table 3).

Table 3. Comparison of accuracy of different recommendation algorithms

Evaluation method/Recommendation algorithm	Recommendation for heterogeneous information networks	Traditional matrix decomposition
MAE	0.95	1.05
RMSE	1.28	1.35

As shown in Table 2, the proposed method for heterogeneous information networks based on meta-pattern fusion proposed in this paper is superior to the traditional matrix decomposition algorithm in effect.

5 Summary

The meta-graph-based heterogeneous information network recommendation algorithm is proposed in this paper. By using heterogeneous information in the network, the complex semantic relationship between the user and the project can be established by using the meta-pattern derived from the network model. A plurality of meta-graph-based scoring matrix decomposition methods are used to generate multiple latent feature matrices for each project and user according to different meta-graphs, and various feature matrices are effectively merged into a unified implicit feature matrix. The individual factors of each row of the implicit feature matrix are used as input nodes of the neural network, and the user score is predicted by optimizing the scoring neural network. Compared with the traditional matrix decomposition algorithm, the effectiveness of the algorithm is proved, but there is still room for improvement. In the similarity calculation phase, the similarity measurement method based on the path counting principle is used, and it is not possible to completely include more score value information. How to make more use of more score information is the direction of the next step of this paper.

References

1. Amatriain, X.: Mining large streams of user data for personalized recommendations. ACM SIGKDD Explor. Newsl. **14**(2), 37–48 (2013)
2. Xu, H.-L., Wu, X., Li, X.-D., Yan, B.-P.: Comparison study of Internet recommendation system. J. Softw. **20**(2), 350–362 (2009)
3. Linden, G., Smith, B., York, J.: Amazon.com recommendations item-to-item collaborative filtering. IEEE Internet Comput. **7**(1), 76–80 (2003)
4. Adomavicius, G., Tuzhilin, A.: Toward the next generation of recommender systems: a survey of the state-of-the-art and possible extensions. IEEE Trans. Knowl. Data Eng. **17**(6), 734–749 (2005)
5. Deshpande, M., Karypis, G.: Item-based top-n, recommendation algorithms. ACM Trans. Inf. Syst. **22**(1), 143–177 (2004)
6. Konstan, J.A., Miller, B.N., Maltz, D., Herlocker, J.L., Gordon, L.R., Riedl, J.: GroupLens: applying collaborative filtering to usenet news. Commun. ACM **40**(3), 77–87 (2000)
7. Koren, Y., Bell, R., Volinsky, C.: Matrix factorization techniques for recommender systems. Computer **42**(8), 30–38 (2009)
8. Meng, X.-W., Liu, S.-D., Zhang, Y.-J., Hu, X.: Research on social recommender sysrems. J. Softw. **26**(6), 1356–1372 (2015)
9. Shi, Y., Larson, M., Hanjalic, A.: Collaborative filtering beyond the user-item matrix: a survey of the state of the art and future challenges. ACM Comput. Surv. (CSUR) **47**(1), 1–45 (2014)
10. Meng, R., Rice, S.G., Wang, J., Sun, X.: A fusion steganographic algorithm based on Faster R-CNN. Comput. Mater. Contin. **55**(1), 1 (2018)
11. Zeng, D., Dai, Y., Li, F., Sherratt, R.S., Wang, J.: Adversarial learning for distant supervised relation extraction. Comput. Mater. Contin. **55**(1), 121–136 (2018)
12. Deng, X.-F., Zhong, Y.-S., Lv, L.-Y., et al.: Mass diffusion on coupled social networks. J. Shangdong Univ. (Nat. Sci.) **52**(3), 51–59 (2017)
13. Schein, A.I., Popescul, A., Ungar, L.H., et al.: Methods and metrics for cold-start recommendations. In: 25th Annual International ACM SIGIR Conference on Research and Development in Information Retrieval, pp. 253–260. ACM, New York (2002)
14. Guo, L.-J., Liang, J.-Y., Zhao, X.-W.: Collaborative filtering recommendation algorithm incorporating social network information. Pattern Recognit. Artif. Intell. **29**(3), 281–288 (2016)
15. Sun, Y., Han, J., Zhao, P., et al.: RankClus: integrating clustering with ranking for heterogeneous information network analysis. ACM SIGKDD Explor. Newsl. **14**(2), 20–28 (2009)
16. Yu, X., Ren, X., Sun, Y., et al.: Personalized entity recommendation: a heterogeneous information network approach. In: ACM International Conference on Web Search & Data Mining, pp. 283–292. ACM (2014)
17. Shi, C., Li, Y., Zhang, J., et al.: A survey of heterogeneous information network analysis. IEEE Trans. Knowl. Data Eng. **29**(1), 17–37 (2017)
18. Sun, Y., Han, J., Yan, X., et al.: PathSim: meta path-based top-k similarity search in heterogeneous information networks. VLDB Endow. **4**(11), 992–1003 (2011)
19. Zhao, H., Yao, Q., Li, J., et al.: Meta-graph based recommendation fusion over heterogeneous information networks. In: ACM SIGKDD International Conference on Knowledge Discovery and Data Mining, pp. 635–644. ACM (2017)

A GA-Optimized Weighted Mixed Kernel Function of SVM Based on Information Entropy

Xuejian Zhao[1], Xinhui Zhang[1], Feng Xiang[2], Feng Ye[3], and Zhixin Sun[1](✉)

[1] Key Laboratory of Broadband Wireless Communication and Sensor Network Technology, Nanjing University of Posts and Telecommunications, Nanjing, China
sunzx@njupt.edu.cn

[2] National Engineering Laboratory for Logistics Information Technology, YuanTong Express Co. Ltd., Shanghai, China

[3] Department of Electrical and Computer Engineering, University of Dayton, Dayton, OH, USA

Abstract. The parameters selection and optimization of kernel function is the core of support vector machine (SVM), which is closely related to the distribution of datasets. It can be obtained a series of different group index, either mapped by different kernel functions on the same dataset or did by same kernel function on the different subsets. We analyze the impact of the choice of kernel functions and parameters on the performance of SVM, and propose a GA-optimized weighted mixed kernel function of SVM based on information entropy (GA-IE-RBF-SVM). The algorithm uses the information entropy to improve the contribution of the features that are conducive to classification firstly to mitigate falling into a local optimum, then learn from the idea of multi-core learning to enhance the adaptability of the algorithm. The optimal genetic algorithm (GA) is used to select the type of mixed kernel function, kernel function parameters and error penalty factor. The experimental results show that compared with other similar algorithms, this algorithm has a higher classification accuracy rate and faster convergence speed.

Keywords: Support vector machine (SVM) · Kernel function · Information entropy · Feature weighting · Genetic algorithm (GA)

1 Introduction

Support vector machine (SVM) is a design criterion based on Vapnik-Chervonenkis (VC) dimension and the principle of structural risk minimization proposed for linear classifiers, which is a method for finite sample information to seek the best compromise

This work is supported by the National Natural Science Foundation of China (No. 61373135, No. 61672299, No. 61702281, No. 61602259), by the Natural Science Foundation of Jiangsu Province (No. BK20150866, No. BK20140883, No. BK20160913), and by the Postgraduate Research & Practice Innovation Program of Jiangsu Province (KYCX17_0773).

X. Sun et al. (Eds.): ICAIS 2019, LNCS 11633, pp. 391–405, 2019.
https://doi.org/10.1007/978-3-030-24265-7_34

between the complexity and the learning ability of the model [1, 2]. However, many researches on the application of SVM show that the selection of kernel function, kernel function parameters, and error penalty factor are the key issues affecting the learning and generalization capabilities of SVM, and they are also the core issues when designing SVM classifiers [3].

At present, many scholars have done a lot of research on the optimization of various parameters and the improvement of recognition performance of traditional kernel functions. The authors of [4] attempted towards selection of SVM parameters, kernel and kernel parameter optimization using the Bat algorithm. The results indicate higher classification accuracy when compared to particle swarm optimization (PSO) based selection and optimization. The authors of [5] used k-Cross Validation and Grid Search to find the optimal SVM parameters, and compared the classification performance of different kernel function. The experiment results show that the type of kernel function affects classification rate most and Polynomial performs best. The authors of [6] regarding mixed kernel function as a starting point, respectively introduced the mixed kernel function construction method, its application in the process of different information modeling. The authors of [7] adopted algorithms of principle component analysis (PCA) and information gain (IG) to accomplish images feature optimizing and acquire its weight matrix. Then it proposed a new support vector machine based on dimensionality reduction and feature weighting. The authors of [8] presented a local weighted mixed-kernel partial least squares algorithm for soft-sensing online modeling, to improve the nonlinear processing capacity of the partial least-squares algorithm based on a kernel function, reduce the sensitivity of the soft-sensor model to abnormal data, and improve the generalization ability of this model. The authors of [9] attempts to represent the mapped data in the RBF feature space under non-negativity constraints and develops an RBF kernel based non-negative matrix factorization (KNMF-RBF) algorithm.

The analysis and summarization of the SVM parameter optimization methods above that there are two main categories: (1) Research how to choose the mixed kernel function to optimize the SVM performance. (2) Research how to determine kernel function parameters and error penalty factor after the kernel function is selected. There is no literature research on how to determine the mixed kernel functions of the above three parameters at the same time. In addition, we consider that SVM usually treats all data and the attributes of all dimensions of data in a unified manner in the process of pattern recognition analysis. However, in a specific application, when the task pattern to be solved is complex, the information carried by different characteristic attributes is different for the same data set, and the influence of each feature on the final discrimination result is also not the same. Therefore, we need to assign different weights to different features to distinguish their contribution to classification tasks.

In view of this, we propose a GA-optimized weighted mixed kernel function of SVM based on information entropy (GA-IE-RBF-SVM) in order to achieve the goal of optimizing the kernel function and improving the classifier performance. Finally, the experimental results prove that this algorithm has lower sensitivity to the attribute distribution of data in each dimension than other similar SVM algorithms, with high stability of classification and discrimination, strong pertinence of objects, and wide application scope.

2 Support Vector Machine

2.1 Basic Theory

SVM is a machine learning method established based on statistical learning theory and structural risk minimization principle [10]. It solves practical problems such as small sample, nonlinearity, high dimension and local minimum point, and has strong generalization ability. At the same time, SVM is a powerful tool for data classification and is a statistical classification method designed for binary classification. The principle of the algorithm is to make the researched problem approach the real model, that is, use the kernel function to perform specific transformation on the original data features, map to the high-dimensional space, and improve the feature dimension of the data. Then, the transformed characteristic matrix is decomposed and finally the task to be solved is transformed into a process for solving the convex quadratic programming problem.

The three key ideas that SVM relies on include: (1) Mapping data to high-dimensional space and transforming complex classification problems into a simple problem of finding a linear classifier in this space. (2) Only the training pattern known as the support vector is used, that is, near the decision surface for classification. (3) Find the optimal separating hyperplane (OSH), which separates the data with the largest margin. Such a maximal margin classifier has good generalization characteristics.

The kernel function is a tool that maps data to a high-dimensional feature space to solve linear indivisible problems in the original space. It is any symmetry function that satisfies the Mercer condition [11]. Table 1 summarizes some commonly used kernel functions. (1) Linear kernel functions are mainly used in the case of linear separability. (2) The polynomial kernel function belongs to the global kernel function, which allows data points far away from each other to affect the value of the kernel function. The larger the parameter d, the higher the dimension of the map and the greater the amount of computation. When d is too large, overfitting is prone to occur due to the high learning complexity. (3) The RBF kernel function belongs to the local kernel function. When the data point is far from the center point, the value will be smaller. It has good anti-interference ability for the noise existing in the data. At the same time, due to its extremely strong locality, its parameters determine the scope of the function. (4) Sigmoid kernel functions originate from neural networks and are widely used in deep learning and machine learning. When Sigmoid is used as a kernel function, what SVM achieves is a multilayer perceptron neural network. The theoretical basis of SVM (convex quadratic programming) determines that it ultimately seeks a global optimal solution rather than a local optimal solution, and it also guarantees that it has a good generalization ability for unknown samples.

Table 1. Standard kernel function (r is kernel function parameter).

Kernel function	Type of classifier
$K(x, x_i) = x^T x_i + c$	Linear, dot product
$K(x, x_i) = [r(x^T x_i) + c]^d$	Polynomial of degree d
$K(x, x_i) = e^{-r\|x - x_i\|^2} + c$	RBF
$K(x, x_i) = \tanh[r(x^T x_i) + c]$	Sigmoid

2.2 Influence of Parameters Selection

The kernel function of the SVM transforms nonlinear separable samples into a linearly separable feature space. Different kernel choices make the separating hyperplane generated by the SVM different. Therefore, the change of the kernel function will make the SVM produce a large difference, which has a direct impact on the performance of the SVM [12]. Table 2 shows the predictive accuracy rate of test sample when using the same kernel function parameters and error penalty factors but using different kernel functions. We can see that the influence of different kernel functions on SVM performance is obvious.

Table 2. Influence of kernel function on SVM performance.

Kernel function	Error penalty factor	Parameter	Predictive accuracy rate (%)
$K(x, x_i) = x^T x_i + c$	1	-	86.56
$K(x, x_i) = [r(x^T x_i) + c]^d$	1	1	80.24
$K(x, x_i) = e^{-r\|x-x_i\|^2} + c$	1	1	87.12
$K(x, x_i) = \tanh[r(x^T x_i) + c]$	1	1	83.33

Because the kernel function, the mapping function and the feature space have a one-to-one correspondence, determining the kernel function implicitly determines the mapping function and feature space. However, the change of the kernel function parameter r actually changes the mapping function parameters, changes the function relationship, and thus also changes the complexity of the sample mapping feature space. Therefore, the advantages and disadvantages of SVM performance are also affected by the kernel function parameters r. The error penalty factor C is a trade-off between the proportion of misclassified samples and the complexity of the algorithm. Adjusting the ratio of confidence range and experience risk of learning machines in the determined characteristic subspace has a greater impact on the generalization and promotion capabilities of the SVM.

The authors of [13] uses the spam classification data as an example to test. To verify the influence of the kernel function parameters and the error penalty factor on the SVM performance when using RBF. The test results are shown in Table 3. We can conclude that when using the same kernel function, the reasonable choice of the kernel function parameter and the error penalty factor is the key way to improve the SVM performance.

Table 3. Influence of parameters on predictive accuracy rate.

Error penalty factors c	Parameters r	Predictive accuracy rate (%)
0.01	1	48.54
0.1	1	49.92
1	1	56.32
10	1	60.28
100	1	65.89

(*continued*)

Table 3. (*continued*)

Error penalty factors c	Parameters r	Predictive accuracy rate (%)
1000	1	57.96
10000	1	56.57
1	0.01	50.89
1	0.1	52.92
1	1	53.55
1	10	60.23
1	100	56.67
1	1000	50.02

In summary, the selection of kernel function, kernel function parameters and error penalty factors will greatly affect the performance of SVM. Only by selecting the appropriate model parameters can the superiority of SVM be better achieved. Based on the analysis and discussion above, the current SVM parameter selection technology has the disadvantage that it is difficult to simultaneously determine the three parameter combinations. In this paper, we first use the information entropy feature weights to optimize the RBF kernel function. On this basis, we try to select and optimize the combination of the mixed kernel function type including the optimized RBF, the mixed kernel parameter and the error penalty factor, to improve the speed and efficiency of parameter selection and improve the learning and generalization capabilities of SVM. Because the genetic algorithm (GA) has the ability of global parallel optimization and is widely used to solve the optimization problem, we select GA to optimize the combination of the three parameters above.

3 A Weighted RBF Based on Information Entropy

The RBF kernel function is a strong locally kernel function. When the data point is far from the center point, the value will be smaller. Because it has good anti-interference ability for the noise existing in the data, it is the most widely used kernel function. In addition, RBF has good performance for large-sample or small-sample, and has fewer parameters than polynomial kernel function. Therefore, RBF is generally preferred in most cases.

For the problem that RBF has different predictive recognition effects on different feature subsets of the same dataset, combined with information entropy theory, this section analyzes the sample data and treats each dimension as a feature, which is applied to the process of constructing the reconstructed kernel. Based on the RBF, we construct a spatial feature weighted kernel function, which is radial basis function based on information entropy (IE-RBF). The optimized RBF should be able to improve the classification accuracy of SVM while avoiding the nonlinear optimization problems such as local optimum.

3.1 Kernel Entropy Component Analysis

Information entropy is used as a quantitative evaluation index to describe the uncertainty of an event. The greater the information entropy, the more information the data carries. Assuming that $p(x)$ is the probability density function of the N dimensional sample data $D = x_1, x_2, \ldots, x_N$, then the information entropy of the data can be expressed as,

$$H(p) = -\lg \int p(x)d(x) \tag{1}$$

As the development of information entropy, Renyi entropy is defined as,

$$H(p) = -\lg \int p^2(x)d(x) \tag{2}$$

Since information entropy can be used to measure how much information the data carries, this section uses the value of the information entropy as a criterion to weight the characteristics of the sample. The characteristics of the corresponding data are analyzed using the kernel entropy component analysis (KECA), and Renyi entropy has a large contribution to the discrimination of the sample.

Information entropy has been widely studied and applied as a new data analysis method. For example, KECA is a good feature analysis method that combines kernel learning method with information entropy theory. It projects the original sample set into the high-dimensional feature space, performs feature decomposition in the form of a kernel matrix, selects the eigenvectors that have the largest contribution to the Renyi entropy of the analyzed events, and projects these eigenvector projections into a new feature set. The following is the theoretical analysis process of KECA.

Since the amount of information of the eigenvectors in the Renyi entropy $H(p)$ is generally positive, and (2) can be regarded as,

$$V(p) = \int p^2(x)d(x) \tag{3}$$

Insert Parzen window density estimator,

$$\hat{p}(x) = \frac{1}{N}\sum_{i=1}^{N} K_\sigma(x, x_i) \tag{4}$$

Parzen window density estimation belongs to kernel density estimation method. $W_\sigma(x, x_i)$ is called a Parzen window, also called nuclear density, whose width is controlled by the parameter σ. The average of $V(p)$ can be estimated,

$$\begin{aligned}\hat{V}(p) &= \int p^2(x)d(x) \\ &= \frac{1}{N^2}\sum_{i=1}^{N}\sum_{j=1}^{N}\int K_\sigma(x,x_i)K_\sigma(x,x_j)d(x) \\ &= \frac{1}{N^2}\sum_{i=1}^{N}\sum_{j=1}^{N}K_{\sqrt{2}\sigma}(x_i,x_j) \\ &= \frac{1}{N^2}1^TK1\end{aligned} \tag{5}$$

K is the sample kernel matrix of $N \times N$,

$$K_{i,j} = K_{\sqrt{2}\sigma}(x_i, x_j) \tag{6}$$

1 is an N dimensional vector of 1 for each element, so the Renyi entropy can be estimated by the sample kernel matrix.

The Renyi entropy can be calculated from the eigenvalues and eigenvectors of the kernel matrix. The diagonalization of K can be decomposed into $K = ED_\lambda E^T$, where $D_\lambda = diag(\lambda_1, \lambda_1, \ldots, \lambda_N)$ is the eigenvalue matrix, and $E = diag(e_1, e_1, \ldots, e_N)$ is the unit matrix of the eigenvectors $e_1, e_1, \ldots, e_N$ corresponding to λ. In addition, the kernel matrix is the inner product of the matrices in the feature space. Assuming that φ_x is a matrix of points in the feature space corresponding to D_λ, then we get $\varphi_x = D_\lambda^{1/2}E^T$, and $K = \varphi_x^T\varphi_x = ED_\lambda E^T$. Therefore, by (4) we can calculate,

$$\hat{V}(p) = \frac{1}{N^2}\sum_{i=1}^{N}\left(\sqrt{\lambda}e_i^T 1\right)^2 \tag{7}$$

From (7) we can conclude that the eigenvalues and eigenvectors of the kernel matrix contribute to $\hat{V}(p)$ in the original data space. Since $\hat{V}(p)$ is linearly related to the Renyi entropy and the entropy of each dimension is defined as $V_i(p) = \sum_{i=1}^{N}\left(\sqrt{\lambda}e_i^T 1\right)^2$, each term in (7) contributes to the Renyi entropy as,

$$\hat{V}_i(p) = \left(\sqrt{\lambda}e_i^T 1\right)^2 \tag{8}$$

Then normalize each variance, and the entropy contribution rate C_i of the feature term x_i is,

$$C_i = \frac{\lambda_i}{\sum_{i=1}^{N}\left(\sqrt{\lambda}e_i^T 1\right)^2} \tag{9}$$

3.2 Weighted RBF Based on Information Entropy

There is a dataset $D = \{x_i\}_{i=1}^{N}$ containing N samples, and the m-th dimension of this dataset is combined into eigenvectors $x_m = (x_{1m}, x_{2m}, \ldots, x_{Nm})^T$, and its corresponding kernel matrix is $k_m = \langle \varphi(x_m), \varphi(x_m)^T \rangle$. The contribution rate of the information entropy of the m-th dimension obtained by (9) is $C_m = \frac{\lambda_m}{\sum_{m=1}^{N} (\sqrt{\lambda} e_m^T 1)^2}$, and the linear registration method is calculated to weight the corresponding kernel matrix to obtain,

$$C_m k_m = \langle C_m \varphi(x_m), C_m \varphi(x_m)^T \rangle \tag{10}$$

Using the principle of kernel function construction: Assuming that K_1 is a kernel function on $X \times X$, $X \subseteq R_m$, $a \in R^+$. By the nature of convolution, the following function formed by the basic kernel function is also a kernel function,

(1) $K(x,z) = K_1(x,z) + K_2(x,z) + \ldots + K_m(x,z)$
(2) $K(x,z) = aK_1(x,z)$

Then, the reconstructed kernel function constructed on the basis of (10) is,

$$\begin{aligned} & K(x_i, x_j) = \\ & C_1(\varphi(x_{i1}), \varphi(x_{j1})) + C_2(\varphi(x_{i2}), \varphi(x_{j2})) + \ldots + C_m(\varphi(x_{im}), \varphi(x_{jm})) \end{aligned} \tag{11}$$

where x_{im}, x_{jm} are the m-th dimension of x_i, x_j.

We extend and optimize on the basis of traditional RBF and construct the weighted RBF based on information entropy (IE-RBF). By calculating the information entropy of each dimension of x_i, x_j, and using the entropy value as a criterion to assign corresponding weights to each feature dimension, the purpose of optimizing the traditional RBF kernel function is achieved.

The traditional RBF kernel function is

$$K_{RBF}(x_i, x_j) = e(x_i, x_j) = e^{-\frac{\|x_i - x_j\|^2}{2\sigma^2}} \tag{12}$$

where x_j is the center of kernel function and σ is the width factor of kernel function, which is used to define the radial range of the function. Substituting formula (12) into formula (11) yields IE-RBF,

$$K_{IE-RBF} = \sum_{m=1}^{N} C_m e(x_{im}, x_{jm}) \tag{13}$$

where parameter C_m is the same as (10).

4 Optimization of Mixed Kernel Parameters Based on GA

Although IE-RBF can avoid falling into a local optimum and the classification accuracy is improved, the mixed kernel function has higher classification accuracy for high dimensional linear inseparable vectors than a single kernel function. This section introduces the global polynomial kernel function and the Sigmoid kernel function to form a mixed kernel function.

The determination of the mixed kernel function type, the mixed kernel parameters and the error penalty factor will greatly affect the performance of the SVM. In order to further improve the classification accuracy of SVM and the speed and efficiency of parameter selection, this section uses GA to optimize the combination of the three parameters above.

4.1 Constructing Mixed Kernel Functions

Since the performance of SVM is mainly determined by the kernel function type and the kernel function parameters, the kernel function K_{IE-RBF} in (13) is again optimized in this section. Two different kernel functions are weighted linearly to form a mixed kernel function. Commonly used global kernel functions include,

Polynomial kernel function (Poly):

$$K(x, x_i) = \left[\left(x^T x_i\right) + 1\right]^d + c \tag{14}$$

Sigmoid kernel function (Sigmoid):

$$K(x, x_i) = \tanh\left[\left(x^T x_i\right) + 1\right] \tag{15}$$

The mixed kernel functions that can be formed include,
Poly+IE-RBF:

$$K(x, x_i) = \alpha\left[\left(x^T x_i\right) + 1\right]^d + (1 - \alpha)\sum_{m=1}^{N} C_m e\left(x_{im}, x_{jm}\right) + c \tag{16}$$

Sigmoid+IE-RBF:

$$K(x, x_i) = \alpha \tanh\left[\left(x^T x_i\right) + 1\right] + (1 - \alpha)\sum_{m=1}^{N} C_m e\left(x_{im}, x_{jm}\right) + c \tag{17}$$

The weighting coefficient $\alpha(0 \leq \alpha \leq 1)$ is used to adjust the co-action weights of the two kernel functions.

Through the analysis of the principle of SVM prediction, we can see that when the kernel function is determined, its prediction performance is mainly determined by the kernel function parameters, the error penalty factor C and the weighting factor α. How to choose an optimal parameter is a problem in the current SVM application. In this paper, GA is used to optimize parameters.

4.2 GA-Optimized Mixed Kernel Parameters

GA uses the idea of biogenetics to combine the idea of suitable survival and random information exchange, and to achieve population evolution through natural selection, crossover, and mutation mechanisms [14]. In the optimization process, GA randomly generates multiple starting points in the solution space and starts searching at the same time. By using the fitness function to guide the search direction, a global optimization solution can be quickly found in the complex search space.

Coding Method
The primary problem addressed by GA is individual gene design and coding. When optimizing the three parameters of mixed kernel function, there are two types of mixed kernel functions, and the mixed kernel parameter and error penalty factor are real numbers. We use binary coding to solve this problem. The individual gene string structure is shown in Fig. 1. In the coding design, the mixed kernel function type code $c_0 = 0$ corresponds to Poly+IE-RBF, and $c_0 = 1$ corresponds to Sigmoid+IE-RBF. The mixed kernel parameter and error penalty factor are binary coded in the range of values, which are l_1-bit and l_2-bit binary strings respectively. Combining $(1 + l_1 + l_2)$-bit binary codes yields individual chromosomal strands.

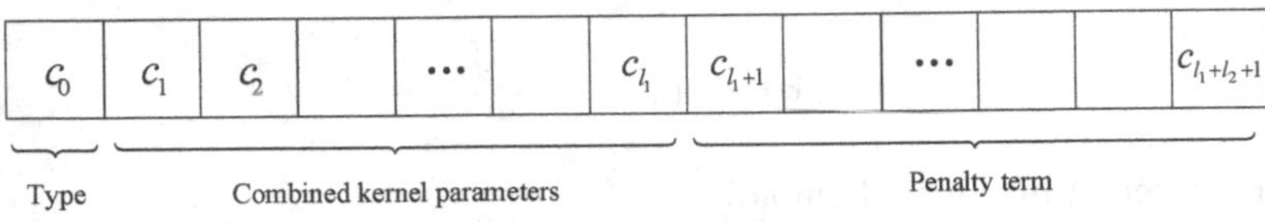

Fig. 1. Gene string structure diagram.

Fitness Function
The goal of genetic operations is to optimize the performance of the SVM, that is, to make the SVM get better generalization ability. The training sample is divided into two parts, one for the training sample and the other for the test sample. The prediction accuracy rate of the test sample is R_{test}, which characterizes the generalization capability of the machine. The predictive accuracy rate R_{test} is used as a fitness evaluation function, as shown in (16). This method can effectively avoid the machine over-learning phenomenon (the phenomenon that the learning accuracy is too high and the generalization ability is poor).

$$Fit = R_{test} \tag{18}$$

Selector Operator
To ensure that evolution proceeds in the direction of optimization, the selector operator uses the principle of optimal preservation and worst substitution. The optimal preservation strategy is to calculate the fitness value of individuals in a certain generation of populations, and save the individuals with the best fitness as the optimal chromosomes of the generation. The specific method is to make the optimal chromosome as the first chromosome of the next-generation population, and not to implement the first

chromosome in subsequent crossover and mutation operations. The worst alternative strategy is to replace the calculated worst chromosome with the optimal chromosome. This algorithm can not only preserve the optimal chromosome to avoid the occurrence of degenerative, but also accelerate the speed of genetic evolution by eliminating the worst chromosomes.

Crossover Operator

Crossover operator swaps the gene at the same position on two different chromosomes in the individual selected by the selector operator to propagate the next generation, thereby producing a new chromosome. It plays a central role in GA. Crossover operator is also known as recombination operator. The recombination of chromosomes is divided into two steps, random pairing is performed first, and then crossover operations are performed. We use the two-point crossover method, which is to set two cross points in the individual code string, and then some of the genes are exchanged. The second code point in the gene string is used as the first cross point, and then a cross point is randomly generated in the rest of the binary coding section, and the corresponding gene segments between the two cross points are exchanged.

The following describes the operation method with a cross instance, as shown in Fig. 2. Suppose that $l_1 + l_2 = 7$, the two individual gene strings of the k generation are $X_A(k) = 10100101$, $X_B(k) = 11110100$, and the two individual gene strings are $X_A(k+1)$, $X_B(k+1)$ after two-point crossover.

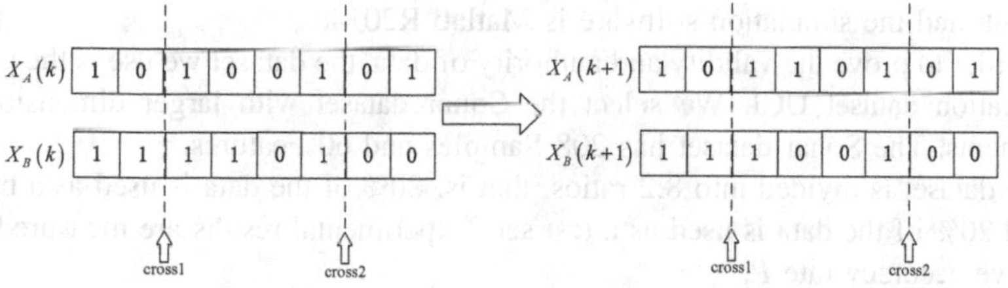

Fig. 2. Two-point crossover operation diagram.

Mutation Operator

The mutation operator increases the ability of GA to find the global optimal solution. The mutation operator randomly changes the value of a position in the string with a certain probability. For the gene string we designed, we randomly changed the position of a binary encoding gene string from 0 to 1 or changed 1 to 0.

The steps to optimize SVM parameters are as follows: (1) Initialize the population and randomly generate initial population individuals. (2) Each individual gene string in the population is decoded into the corresponding mixed kernel function type, the mixed kernel parameter and the error penalty factor. Three parameters are substituted into the SVM to train and test the training data and test data. (3) According to the fitness calculation rule, calculate the fitness value of each individual. (4) Determine if the termination condition is satisfied. If the termination condition is satisfied and the cycle is exited, the genetic optimization ends, and the optimized parameter combination is obtained. Otherwise go to the next step. (5) Perform selector operators and follow the principles of optimal preservation and worst substitution. (6) The crossover operator and the mutation operator are executed. The crossover probability is 0.7 and the mutation probability is 0.1. After forming a new generation of individuals, return to step 2 to continue execution.

5 Simulation and Experiment

First of all, we show that the greater the Renyi entropy, the more contribution it makes to the discrimination of the sample. Introducing the Renyi entropy of feature during the construction of RBF can effectively increase the class intensity of the classification vector. Therefore, SVM can effectively avoid falling into a local optimum during training and testing. Subsequently, we show that the mixed kernel function has higher classification accuracy for high-dimensional linear inseparable vectors than a single kernel function. However, it is very important to determine the mixed function kernel type, the mixed kernel parameter, and the error penalty factor. For the subjectivity of the parameter selection, we introduce GA to optimize the parameters. The finally formed GA-IE-RBF-SVM algorithm is used to classify the samples effectively.

5.1 Basic Environment and Data Indicators

The computer environment used in this experiment was configured as Thinkpad E460 with quad-core Intel I7 processor and 16 GB RAM. The operating system is Windows 10 64-bit, and the simulation software is Matlab R2014a.

In order to prove the validity and authority of data, the dataset we use is the popular classification dataset UCI. We select the Sonar dataset with larger dimensions for experiments. The Sonar dataset has 208 Samples and 60 Features.

The dataset is divided into 8:2 ratios, that is, 80% of the data is used as a training set, and 20% of the data is used as a test set. Experimental results are measured using predictive accuracy rate P,

$$P = \frac{Number\ of\ correctly\ classified\ samples}{Number\ of\ samples} \times 100\% \tag{19}$$

5.2 Validation of Weighted SVM Based on Information Entropy

The main role of Renyi entropy in this paper is to increase the category strength of feature in RBF, and to select feature that can provide higher feature strength. This not only can reduce the feature of SVM to reduce the complexity of algorithm, but also can avoid the algorithm falling into local optimum to improve the classification accuracy. In order to prove that the introduction of Renyi entropy can achieve the above purpose, we first calculate the Renyi entropy of the features of the experimental dataset, and only select features with entropy greater than 10% as the features used in the final classification. Then use the weighted SVM based on information entropy (IE-RBF-SVM) and SVM without entropy (RBF-SVM) to carry out training model and classification prediction. The result of experiment shows that the accuracy rate of RBF-SVM is 93.47% and IE-RBF-SVM is 92.34%. We can see that IE-RBF-SVM can effectively improve accuracy.

Although it is feasible and effective to use information entropy to assign different weights to the features of a vector to distinguish its contribution to classification tasks, this method is only applicable to RBF. In order to deal with different classification environments and absorb the advantages of different kernel functions to improve accuracy, the mixed kernel function becomes the best kernel function choice for SVM. We use Poly kernel function and Sigmoid kernel function to construct mixed kernel function and use GA to select the adaptive parameters to form the final GA-IE-RBF-SVM algorithm.

5.3 GA Optimization Model Parameters

In order to form an optimal mixed kernel function, we construct the GA-based parameter optimization model of SVM mixed kernel function, that is (16) and (17). Coding scheme in experiment: (1) The decoding encoding method of GA is that the first bit is 0 or 1 indicates the selected mixed kernel function type, 0 indicates selection (16), and 1 indicates selection (17). (2) The kernel parameter encoding scheme for mixed kernel functions is to multiply a by 16 times and then round down to $\alpha(0 \leq \alpha \leq 1)$ binary value, $l_1 = 4$. For example, 1 can be converted to 1111. (3) The penalty factor is binary coded, $l_2 = 3$. This encoding method is more efficient than the traditional GA. GA has the maximum number of iterations of 100, the population of 20, and exits after reaching the maximum number of iterations. After obtaining the optimal solution of GA, the optimal mixed kernel function suitable for a certain dataset and the optimal GA-IE-RBF-SVM classification model can be obtained by directly inversely solving the above process.

First of all, GA proposed solves the problem more accurately and efficiently than using the PSO algorithm [15] (Alg. 1) and the traditional GA algorithm (Alg. 2) [16].

From the comparison results in Fig. 3, we can conclude that GA proposed is more efficient and accurate in solving SVM parameters than other two algorithms. In the figure, Alg. 1 uses PSO, which has the fastest convergence speed, but the accuracy is not high, and the problem of local optimization appears. Alg. 2 adopts the traditional GA, the convergence speed and the solution accuracy are generally. The GA proposed

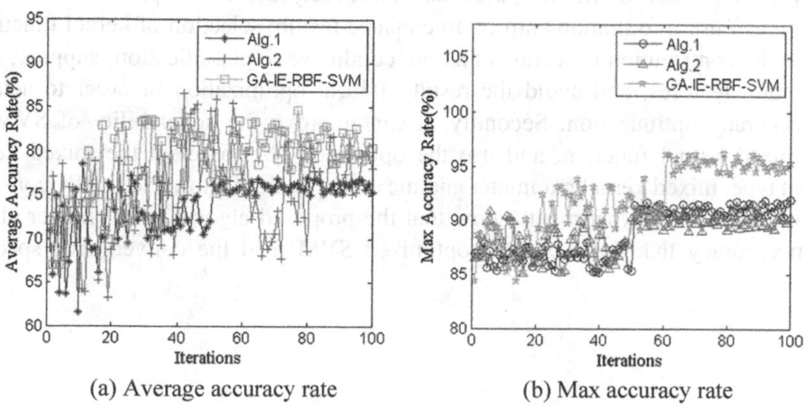

(a) Average accuracy rate (b) Max accuracy rate

Fig. 3. The relationship between iterations and accuracy rate of Sonar.

starts to converge around 60 steps, and the accuracy is as high as 95%. In summary, the GA model constructed can well optimize the mixed kernel parameters. Table 4 shows the results of the solution in detail,

5.4 GA-IE-RBF-SVM Result Analysis

In order to prove the validity of the proposed GA-IE-RBF-SVM, we use the remaining 20% of the test data for experiments and compare the experimental results with Alg. 1 in [17] and Alg. 2 in [18]. The result is shown in Table 5,

Table 5 shows that the accuracy of the proposed GA-IE-RBF-SVM is significantly higher compared with other optimized SVM algorithms. Therefore, it can be proved that the SVM classification model proposed can effectively improve the classification accuracy of high-dimensional data.

Table 4. GA-IE-RBF-SVM results.

Dataset	Parameter α	Type	Penalty factor c	Accuracy rate (%)
Sonar	0.64	Poly+IE-RBF	3	95.63%

Table 5. Comparison of results.

Algorithm	Accuracy rate (%)
Alg. 1	92.5
Alg. 2	94.6
GA-IE-RBF-SVM	97.2

6 Conclusion

The GA-optimized weighted mixed kernel function of SVM based on information entropy (GA-IE-RBF-SVM) proposed can effectively solve two problems of SVM. Firstly, it can use information entropy to enhance feature selection of kernel functions, improve the contribution of features that are conducive to classification, suppress low-contribution features, and avoid the result of local optimization in order to achieve SVM accuracy optimization. Secondly, it can improve the adaptability of SVM by using mixed kernel function, and use the optimized GA to select the mixed kernel function type, mixed kernel parameter and the error penalty factor, and finally construct an optimized SVM. Experiments show that the proposed algorithm has higher classification accuracy than other similar optimized SVM, and the convergence speed is faster.

References

1. Sun, H., McIntosh, S.: Analyzing cross-domain transportation big data of New York city with semi-supervised and active learning. Comput. Mater. Contin. **57**(1), 1–9 (2018)
2. Fang, W., Zhang, F., Sheng, V.S., et al.: A Method for improving CNN-based image recognition using DCGAN. Comput. Mater. Contin. **57**(1), 167–178 (2018)
3. Sharma, A., Dey, S.: A boosted SVM based ensemble classifier for sentiment analysis of online reviews. ACM SIGAPP Appl. Comput. Rev. **13**(4), 43–52 (2013)
4. Sherin, B.M, Supriya, M.H.: Selection and parameter optimization of SVM kernel function for underwater target classification. In: Underwater Technology, pp. 1–5. IEEE (2015)
5. Ren, Y., Hu, F., Miao, H.: The optimization of kernel function and its parameters for SVM in well-logging. In: International Conference on Service Systems and Service Management, pp. 1–5. IEEE (2016)
6. Su, L.I., Lu-Wen, L.I., Zhuang, D.F., et al.: Research on mixed kernel function and its application in the field of data modeling. Comput. Simul. (2015)
7. Wang, H.T., Zhang, Z., Yang, X.Y., et al.: Steganalysis method based on optimized feature weighted SVM. Appl. Res. Comput. **30**(7), 2105–2104 (2013)
8. Sun, M., Yang, H.: Local weighted mixed kernel partial least squares algorithm and its applications to soft-sensing. Inf. Control **44**(4), 481–486 (2015)
9. Chen, W.S., Huang, X.K., Fan, B., et al.: Kernel nonnegative matrix factorization with RBF kernel function for face recognition. In: International Conference on Machine Learning and Cybernetics, pp. 285–289. IEEE (2017)
10. Liao, Z., Couillet, R.: Random matrices meet machine learning: a large dimensional analysis of LS-SVM. In: IEEE International Conference on Acoustics, Speech and Signal Processing. IEEE (2017)
11. Wu, X., Tang, W., Wu, X.: Support vector machine based on hybrid kernel function. J. Chongqing Univ. Technol. **154**, 127–133 (2011)
12. Negri, R.G., Silva, E.A.D., Casaca, W.: Inducing contextual classifications with kernel functions into support vector machines. IEEE Geosci. Remote. Sens. Lett., **PP**(99), 1–5
13. Saidala, R.K, Devarakonda, N.R.: Bubble-net hunting strategy of whales based optimized feature selection for e-mail classification. In: International Conference for Convergence in Technology, pp. 626–631 (2017)
14. Gao, B., Li, X., Woo, W.L., et al.: Physics-based image segmentation using first order statistical properties and genetic algorithm for inductive thermography imaging. IEEE Trans. Image Process. **PP**(99), 1 (2018)
15. Raj, S., Ray, K.C.: ECG signal analysis using DCT-based DOST and PSO optimized SVM. IEEE Trans. Instrum. Meas. **66**(3), 470–478 (2017)
16. Sukawattanavijit, C., Chen, J., Zhang, H.: GA-SVM algorithm for improving land-cover classification using SAR and optical remote sensing data. IEEE Geosci. Remote Sens. Lett. **14**(3), 284–288 (2017)
17. Wu, J., Yang, H.: Linear regression-based efficient SVM learning for large-scale classification. IEEE Trans. Neural Netw. Learn. Syst. **26**(10), 2357–2369 (2017)
18. Xu, J., Tang, Y.Y., Zou, B., et al.: The generalization ability of SVM classification based on Markov sampling. IEEE Trans. Cybern. **45**(6), 1169–1179 (2015)

Modeling and Simulation of Network Public Opinion Propagation Model Based on Interest Matching in Social Network

Zhang Deliang, Bin Sheng(✉), and Sun Gengxin

Qingdao University, Qingdao 266071, China
binsheng@qdu.edu.cn

Abstract. By using a variety of explicit or implicit relationships in social networks, we can reproduce the real propagation process of network public opinion in the social network from the perspective of complex networks. The relation of users and the data of microblog content in Sina microblog was obtained by programming and web crawler, multiple relationships between microblog users were discovered by using big data analysis. On the basis of this, a semi-supervised user interest matching prediction algorithm was proposed in this paper. According to the individual state division method of compartment model, network public opinion propagation model is constructed based on user interest matching through state transition analysis and inference of state transition probability. The results show that the model can well describe the law of public opinion propagation in social networks, and truly reflect the propagation of network public opinion in the Internet.

Keywords: Public opinion propagation · Propagation model · Complex network · Social networks

1 Introduction

In recent years, with the rise of technologies such as Web 2.0, online communities represented by Weibo and virtual communities (such as Facebook, Douban, Twitter, Sina Microblog, etc.) have emerged in large numbers, which has become the main platform for netizens to obtain and propagate information and exchange views. The online community [1] is a group formed by the Internet to communicate with users who share common interests, publish and discuss topics of interest. In the online community, users no longer passively accept information, but actively provide information and propagate information. Through this active and strong interaction, information sharing and propagation are completed.

Internet public opinion refers to a common opinion or remark that has a certain influence on the network and has a certain degree of influence on the "focus" and "hot spot" issues. Due to the large number of participants, frequent contacts, and large dynamic changes in the network community, the propagation and acquisition of resource information is also faster and more convenient, which fundamentally changes the contact range and network behavior of network users. Therefore, on the open

X. Sun et al. (Eds.): ICAIS 2019, LNCS 11633, pp. 406–418, 2019.
https://doi.org/10.1007/978-3-030-24265-7_35

Internet, the online community has become an important platform for online public opinion communication, and these widely propagated public opinion information has an increasing influence on the public opinion caused by the whole society. Internet public opinion has deeply intervened in real life, changed the ecological environment of social public opinion in China, and formed a brand-new network public opinion field. From the Hangzhou drag racing case, hide-and-seek cat incident, to the "7.23" Yongwen line motor vehicle accident, Guo Meimei incident, and the recent "Qingdao sky-high price prawn" incident, we can see that the network community has a significant impact on public opinion. The Internet public sentiment has also changed from the initial intermittent "staged" to the situation of major public emergencies that must be rushing on the Internet.

The origin and propagation of public opinion events on the Internet are mainly embodied in the process of information provision, transmission and interaction among users in the network community. Due to the convenience of information propagation and the concealment of the subject, the original topic that may become a hot spot can be easily spread in the online community, thus arousing the attention of more people with the same interests, making the propagation scope and influence of the topic enlarged instantaneously and emerging network hotspot events. The propagation process of these network hotspots is very rapid, and the scope of influence is also very wide. If these hot topics of network public opinion are properly guided and utilized, huge economic benefits and positive social impacts can be formed. If it is not properly guided, maliciously hyped by people or organizations with ulterior motives, confusing people's audiences and trying to control the guidance of network public opinion, it will have a very bad impact on the government, society and the people. Therefore, for the study of the law of public opinion spread in the online community, establish the relevant public opinion communication model, and then explore the key nodes and key paths in the process of public opinion communication, which will provide theoretical support and Intellectual support for the establishment of an equal, free, democratic and open network world, and has very important theoretical significance and practical application value.

The public opinion information propagation model has always been a hot topic in network communication studies. Over the years, researchers in different fields have accumulated many methods and conclusions on the study of the law of public opinion information propagation. Kermark proposed the SIR (Susceptible-Infected-Recovered) model [2] in 1927, which was originally used to study the spread of epidemics, and later widely used in the study of network information transmission. The network information transmission model based on the classical infectious disease model is too idealized on the assumption of the subject and carrier of transmission, resulting in a large gap between the transmission model and the real situation. With the rise of complex network theory, research on public opinion information propagation model based on complex network topology and dynamic properties has produced many research results. Zanette et al. conducted research on public opinion propagation on small-world networks [3, 4] and scale-free networks [5] respectively, and found that the impact of public opinion information on complex networks is much smaller than that of random networks. Liu found through empirical research that public opinion information is the most easily spread in random networks [6, 7]. Kesten et al. regard the crowd as a multi-particle system and study the spread of public opinion information in the population through probabilistic theory [8]. Domestic scholars use complex network theory to study the network public opinion information propagation work is relatively less, Wang et al. studied the public opinion propagation behavior on the scale-free network and found that the network aggregation coefficient is proportional to the network's suppression of information transmission [9]. Hu used complex network models to study the role and influence of online communities such as forums and blogs on public opinion communication [10, 11].

However, in the existing research on the propagation of public opinion information on social networks, it is often overlooked that the effective goal of information propagation should be the individuals with interest matching and the positive or negative impact on information propagation due to the differences of interest among individuals in the process of propagation, which results in a great difference between the research results and the real situation. Based on the warehouse model, this paper uses the social network and complex network theory to predict the interest matching between the communication subjects according to the various relationships among the information communication subjects, and then constructs the network public opinion propagation model based on interest matching, by setting the parameters in the public opinion propagation model to simulate, the rules of the network public opinion propagation process are discovered, and these rules are summarized, so as to provide some methods and suggestions for controlling the network public opinion communication.

2 Explicit and Implicit Relationship Analysis of Network Community Users

The network community is a typical complex network [12, 13]. It is formed by the interaction between individual members of the online community. It mainly studies the connections and behaviors between individuals. The relationship between users in the online community may come from the real world, or may from the network behavior and communication of network users in the network community, and gradually form the network community structure with the development. Therefore, the network community must be a multi-relationship network, and there must be many relationships among network users as network nodes.

In most online communities, users can become friends, so that users have a more stable relationship, and they can communicate freely in the online community in the future. This relationship may be the embodiment and extension of the friendship relationship in the online community, or it may be formed through communication in the online community. This kind of communication between users is obvious in the online community, called explicit relationship. The behavior of users in the online community will reflect the interests and preferences of users, such as users may comment or share resources of interest. Although users in the online community have different interests, some users will have the same or similar interests. In the online community, there may not be an explicit relationship between these similar users, but because they have similar interests, they may establish a solid relationship in the online community in the future. This kind of latent relationship embodied by users' network behavior or hobbies is called user implicit relationship. For example, in micro-blog system, according to the behavior of micro-blog users, there are at least four explicit relationships among micro-blog users: attention, reply, forwarding and reading. If we further analyze the interaction between micro-blog content and micro-blog users, we can find the similarity of users 'interests, so as to find the various of implicit relations of micro-blog users.

In the process of public opinion propagation in network community, user implicit relationship and user explicit relationship play different roles. Explicit relation is the necessary condition for communication of public opinion among users, that is, it is impossible for users without explicit relation to propagate public opinion directly. Implicit user relationship is implicit in user behavior. Implicit relationship does not exist in the network community like explicit relationship. It is set up virtually to study the influence of interest similarity among users on the propagation of public opinion. Therefore, the side of the implicit relationship in the online community is a "virtual edge", but since the user often only propagates information of interest to him during the public opinion communication, the impact of the implicit relationship on public opinion communication must be taken into account.

2.1 Data Source and Collection

The micro-blog system pushes messages according to user tags, microblog texts, and user lists, and makes full use of the information to discover the interests of the microblog users, to establish a user interest matching model, and to predict the interest matching relationship between users. This article takes Sina Weibo as the research object, and uses experimental and web crawler software to obtain experimental data. Using Sina Weibo API, starting from the seed user, from January 2017 to February 2017, crawling for one month, and finally getting the attribute information of 577467 users, a total of 36271212. The number of users with mutual concern relationship among them is 145,776, which is the number of users with explicit relationships.

2.2 Data Processing

The collected attribute information data of micro-blog users include user ID, region, user name, number of users concerned, label, list of users concerned and other fields. The user microblog text information includes: a microblog published and forwarded by the user. The collected raw data is shown in Table 1.

Table 1. Raw data collected from micro-blog

Micro-blog user attribute information data	User micro-blog text information
2549228714, British things,male,,,British,hereinuk,391,821,765,,, http://weibo.com/hereinuk," British anecdote, things, British things, international students, interesting things, Britain",2011 .11.21 日,,,,,"6128774301,3149183682,6073974932,6034931374,5124266126,3503381065,5693047492,5081752463,2647236162,6124463229,....",0,2279,20231	<comment><content> "Poachers do not ask for sin and shoot! "This wildlife sanctuary, known for its one-horned rhinoceros, is also a bit embarrassing about poachers... </content><time>2017-2-12 19:59</time><repostsCount>758</reposts Count> <comments Count>1022</comments Count></comment>

In order to accurately extract user interest, it is necessary to extract and classify the microblog data information. This article uses the Chinese version of the Chinese Academy of Sciences NLPIR Chinese word segmentation Java version as a data segmentation tool. According to the Chinese corpus and word segmentation model provided by the tool, the results of the word segmentation are shown in Table 2.

Table 2. Segmentation results of micro-blog raw data

Before the word segmentation	British anecdote, things, British things, international students, interesting things, do not ask for sin and shoot! "This wildlife sanctuary, known for its one-horned rhinoceros, is also a bit ruthless about poachers…
After the word segmentation	Britain, anecdotes, things, those, international students, interesting stories, poachers, don't ask, sin, uniformity, shooting, this, one-horn, rhinoceros, famous, wild, animals, protected areas, treatment, poachers, attitude, also, a little bit, ruthless

After word segmentation of microblog data information, some meaningless words in the result of word segmentation are removed, such as "those", "don't ask", "uniform", "yes" and "a little". Key words such as "Britain", "foreign students", "poachers", "animals" and "protected areas" are extracted.

2.3 Data Analysis

Based on the mutual concern information of weibo users obtained from data collection, using the complex network theory to build an explicit relationship network of sina weibo users with weibo users as the node and the concern relationship among weibo users as the edge. The size of the node degree of a weibo user represents the influence of that user. The distribution of the degree of all nodes in the network reflects the distribution of the concern relationship among users in the whole network. According to Gephi tool statistics, 8% of users with 1 degree of nodes and 24% of users with less than 10 degree of nodes are in the network. Its distribution is shown in Fig. 1.

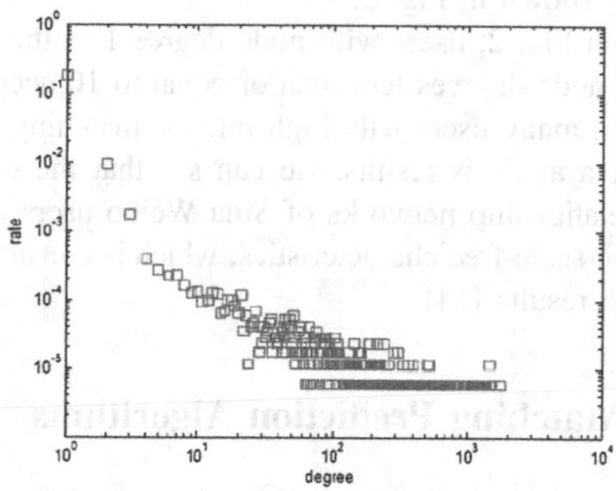

Fig. 1. Degree distribution of Sina micro-blog user explicit relationship network

Referring to the criteria of user interest in mainstream social networks, user interest can be divided into 21 categories (food, education, entertainment, sports, fashion, finance, technology, culture, military, reading, car, music, game, constellation, film and television, shopping, photography, pets, news, funny, life). Through text segmentation, extract keywords, and according to these 21 interest classes, keywords in each user label are corresponded to each interest class, in which each interest class corresponds to multiple keywords. The paper defines user interest vectors as: (food, education, entertainment funny, life, …) Through the keywords corresponding to each interest class, the tag and the text information of microblog can be defined as the interest vector

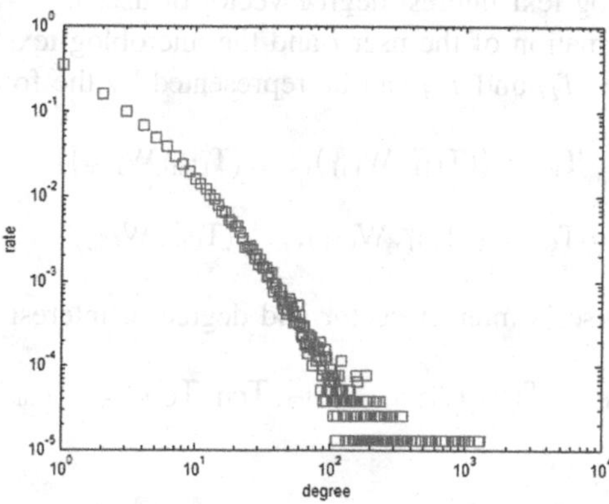

Fig. 2. Degree distribution of Sina micro-blog user implicit

of each user, so as to get the number of common interest tags among users and the corresponding number of interest classes in the text information of microblog. In the paper, if two users have more than five common interest tags, or the number of forwarding/commenting microblogs is more than 10, or the number of similar interest classes in the text information of the microblog is more than 10, then the interest matching relationship between such users is determined. The nodal degree distribution of sina weibo user implicit relational network constructed according to the interest match between users is shown in Fig. 2.

As can be seen from Fig. 2, users with node degree 1 in the network account for 35.1%, and users with node degrees less than or equal to 10 account for 85.7%. This shows that there are not many users with high interest matching in the network.

From the above data analysis results, we can see that the degree distribution of explicit and implicit relationship networks of Sina Weibo users obeys the power distribution, and all exhibit scale-free characteristics, which is consistent with the existing social network research results [14].

3 User Interest Matching Prediction Algorithms

The crawled microblog data contains label information and text information of each user. Through word segmentation and keyword extraction of these data information, interest classes reflecting users' interests can be obtained. Therefore, the interest vector of user i can be described as:

$$T_i = (T_{Li}, T_{Ci}) \tag{1}$$

Where T_{Li} represents the interest vector obtained from the user tag of user i, and T_{Ci} represents the interest vector obtained from the microblog text information of user i. The corresponding weight vector is:

$$W_i = (W_{Li}, W_{Ci}) \tag{2}$$

Among them, W_{Li} represents the user tag interest degree vector of user i, and W_{Ci} represents the microblog text interest degree vector of user i.

Since the tag information of the user i and the microblog text information contain multiple feature values, T_{Li} and T_{Ci} can be represented by the following vector form:

$$\mathrm{T_{Li}} = ((\mathrm{T_{Li1}}, \mathrm{W_{Li1}}), \ldots, (\mathrm{T_{Lim}}, \mathrm{W_{Lim}})) \tag{3}$$

$$\mathrm{T_{Ci}} = ((\mathrm{T_{Ci1}}, \mathrm{W_{Ci1}}), \ldots, (\mathrm{T_{Cin}}, \mathrm{W_{Cin}})) \tag{4}$$

At this point, the user's interest vector and degree of interest vector are:

$$\mathrm{T_i} = (\mathrm{T_{Li1}}, \mathrm{T_{Li2}}, \ldots, \mathrm{T_{Lim}}, \mathrm{T_{Ci1}}, \mathrm{T_{Ci2}}, \ldots, \mathrm{T_{Cin}}) \tag{5}$$

$$W_i = (W_{Li1}, W_{Li2}, \ldots, W_{Lim}, W_{Ci1}, W_{Ci2}, \ldots, W_{Cin}) \tag{6}$$

It can be seen from the above definition that the user's microblog text interest is represented by the feature value corresponding to the interest class in the microblog text information, and the user tag interest is represented by the user tag information. If the user's interest does not include an interest class, the corresponding interest value is set to 0 in the interest degree vector. In this section, the interest similarity between users is calculated according to the user interest vector and the interest degree vector, so that the user interest matching prediction is performed.

3.1 User Interest Matching Prediction Algorithm

Assuming that there are *V* users in user *i*′ s list of concerns, and the tag union set of *v* users is obtained, which is the label set of user *i*′ s list of concerns. For user tag interest, this paper considers that the degree of preference of user *i* for its m interest classes can be characterized by the frequency of occurrence of tags in the tag set *X* of all users in the user's attention list. User *i*′ s interest in interest class *J* in his tag is measured by the frequency of interest class appearing in the attention list, which can be expressed as:

$$W_{Lij} = \frac{\sum c_j}{v} \tag{7}$$

Where $\sum c_j$ represents the number of users in the list of interest that contain the interest class *j*, and *v* represents the number of users in the attention list.

For the user's interest in micro-blog text, the closer the time of the micro-blog is to the current moment, the more it reflects the user's current interest, this phenomenon is similar to the attenuation function [15] of interest in human behavior dynamics. Therefore, the user's microblog text interest can be described by defining an interest attenuation function. The interest attenuation function is defined as follows:

$$x(t) = \frac{1}{(1+kt)}, t \in (0, \infty) \tag{8}$$

Where *k* represents the attenuation rate.

The attenuation function can represent the change of memory capacitance over time in $[t_0, t]$. Assuming that the user's interest degree at time t_0 is $P(t_0)$, according to the interest attenuation function, the user's interest degree will be reduced from t_0 to t:

$$P(t) = \frac{P(t_0)}{(1+k_t(t-t_0))} \tag{9}$$

Where k_t represents the rate of decay of interest over time period t_0 to t. The user's microblog text interest degree vector can be calculated based on the attenuation function.

3.2 User Similarity Calculation

According to the measure of user interest defined by formula (7) and formula (9), user interest vectors T_i and W_i can be obtained for each user, and user similarity can be calculated using these two vectors. The cosine similarity measure is used to calculate the similarity of interest of any two users in the paper. The specific formula is:

$$S_{ij} = \cos\left(T_i W_i, T_j W_j\right) = \frac{T_i W_i * T_j W_j}{\sqrt{(T_i W_i)^2} + \sqrt{(T_j W_j)^2}} \tag{10}$$

The similarity between users is calculated by the above formula. If the similarity value S_{ij} is large, it means that there is a greater possibility that the users have an interest matching relationship; otherwise, the possibility is smaller.

In the paper, the Sina Weibo user data obtained by crawling is divided into 90% training set and 10% test set, and the user's interest is obtained according to the user's label, Weibo text content and attention list. In order to verify the prediction effect of the proposed algorithm, the classic user interest matching prediction algorithms TF-IDF and LDA [16], semantic analysis user interest matching prediction algorithm DPLSA [17] and user interest matching of converged network topology and Weibo content prediction algorithm TFP [18] are selected, and compared with the user interest matching prediction algorithm, these algorithms are evaluated by AUC and Precision evaluation index [19]. By comparing the evaluation values of these algorithms, it can be found that the user interest matching prediction algorithm proposed in this paper has the best prediction effect, can describe the interest matching relationship between users more accurately, and improve the accuracy of interest matching prediction between users.

4 Network Public Opinion Propagation Model Based on Interest Matching

4.1 Model Definition

Please The network public opinion propagation model based on interest matching proposed in this paper is based on the SIR model, considering the interest matching relationship among users, and defining the transfer process and transition probability between states.

In the network public opinion propagation model, all users in the network are divided into the following four states: a susceptible state *S*, a receiving state *E*, a propagation state *I*, and an immune state *R*. The susceptibility state refers to that the user has never received the public opinion information propagated in the network, that is, the public opinion information is in an unknown state; Receiving state means that the user has received the public opinion information propagated in the network, but has not yet propagated the information out of the network. The state of propagation refers to the state in which the user has transmitted the public opinion information transmitted in the network; The immune status refers to the state in which the user no longer receives the public opinion information transmitted in the network and will not propagate it again. According to the relationship of interest matching among users and the distribution of node degree in the network, the state transition process of the four types of nodes is defined as follows:

(1) Let $N(k,t)$ be the number of nodes with k degree in the network at time t, and $S(k,t)$, $E(k,t)$, $I(k,t)$ and $R(k,t)$ represent the proportion of four types of nodes with k degree in the network at time t to the total number of nodes with K degree, that is, the sum of $S(k,t)$, $E(k,t)$, $I(k,t)$, $R(k,t)$ is 1.
(2) When the propagation node I propagated public opinion information to a susceptible node S, the susceptible node will transfer the probability p_{se} from the susceptible state to the receiving state, then p_{se} is called the infection probability.
(3) According to the interest matching relationship between the receiving node E and the propagation node I, the receiving node E transitions from the receiving state to the propagation state with the probability p_{ei}, and the p_{ei} is called the transmitting probability of the receiving node E for the public opinion information;
(4) According to the interest matching relationship between the receiving node E and the propagating node I, the receiving node E transitions from the receiving state to the immune state with the probability p_{er}, then p_{er} is called the direct immunization probability of the receiving node E for the public opinion information;
(5) The propagation node I transitions from the propagation state to the immune state with the probability p_{ir}, and p_{ir} is called the immune probability of the propagation node I for the public opinion information;
(6) The immune state is the final state in the network, that is, when a node in the network is in an immune state, its state will not be transferred again.

According to the above description of the state transition rules for the four types of nodes, the network public opinion propagation model based on interest matching in the social network is as follows:

$$\begin{cases} \frac{dS(k,t)}{dt} = -p_{se}k\theta(t)S(k,t) \\ \frac{dE(k,t)}{dt} = p_{se}k\theta(t)S(k,t) - p_{ei}E(k,t) - p_{er}E(k,t) \\ \frac{dI(k,t)}{dt} = p_{ei}E(k,t) - p_{ir}I(k,t) \\ \frac{dR(k,t)}{dt} = p_{er}E(k,t) + p_{ir}I(k,t) \end{cases} \tag{11}$$

4.2 Model Simulation and Analysis

In this paper, Matlab is used as a tool to simulate the network public opinion propagation model. After 200 iterations in the simulation process, the propagation process of public opinion information in the network is basically stable. By analyzing the simulation results, the following conclusions can be obtained.

$S(T)$, $E(T)$, $I(T)$ and $R(T)$ denote the density of 4 types of nodes in t time network, respectively. Set the model parameters $p_{ei} = 0.2$, $p_{er} = 0.1$, $p_{ir} = 0.3$, $p_{se} = 1$, and select the node with the largest degree in the network as the initial node of public opinion information propagation. At this time, the changing trend of different types of nodes in the network with time is shown in Fig. 3.

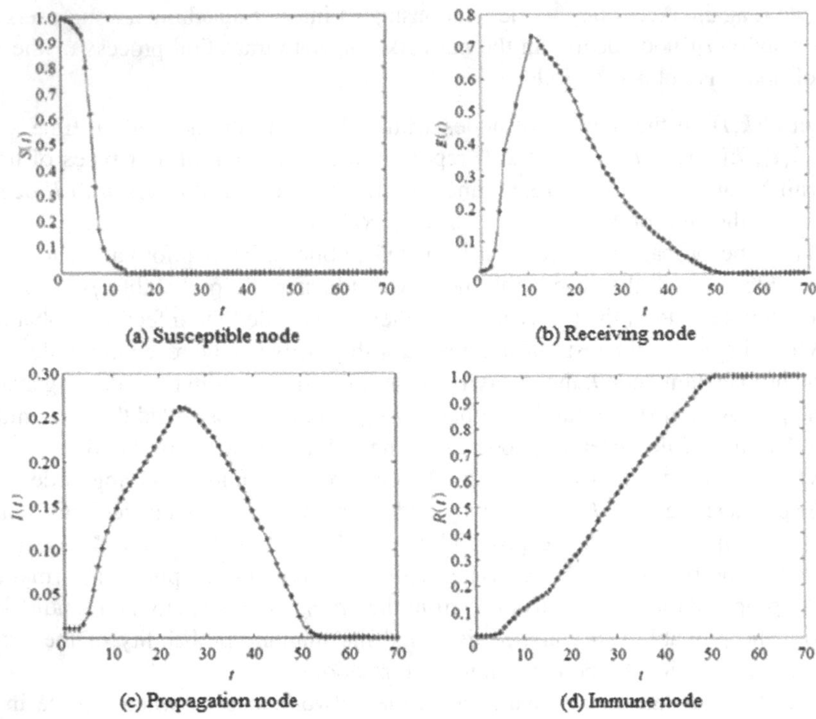

Fig. 3. The relationship between different types of nodes over time

As can be seen from Fig. 3, the number of susceptible nodes in the network decreases rapidly in the initial stage of public opinion propagation. This is because once a node is in the state of propagation, all other nodes in the network that are bounded by the node will be transformed into receiving state, which reflects the "fission" mode of public opinion information propagation in social networks. The number of receiving nodes in the network will increase rapidly in the initial stage of public opinion propagation and reach its maximum in a very short time. Then, with the decrease of the number of susceptible nodes and the transition of receiving nodes to propagating and immune states, the number of receiving nodes will gradually decrease with time, and eventually reach 0. Similar to the change trend of the receiving node, the propagation node in the network increases rapidly at the initial stage of propagation and reaches its maximum value, then decreases gradually and eventually approaches zero, but the time lags behind the receiving node in each stage of change. Immune nodes in the network will gradually increase in the initial stage of transmission, and will eventually approach 1, that is, all nodes in the network will eventually be transformed into immune state, which also reflects that immune state will become the absorption state of the network.

5 Conclusion

The actual network public opinion communication process is often completed by sharing information among network users with similar interests. Therefore, it effectively spreads the communication subject mainly for interest matching. From the perspective of communication, this paper considers the influence of interest differences among the communication subjects on the public opinion communication in the network, and establishes a network public opinion communication model that is more consistent with the actual situation, and reproduces the network process chain of the network public opinion on the whole network.

The paper analyzes the data set captured from Sina Weibo, extract and analyze many kinds of explicit or implicit relationships in social networks, and user interest matching relationship is an implicit relationship widely existing in social networks, which directly affects the process of network public opinion propagation. Based on this, the propagation model of network public opinion based on interest matching is constructed. The influence of the change of parameters in the model on the propagation process is analyzed through experimental simulation, and the law of network public opinion propagation and the main factors affecting the propagation of public opinion are found.

References

1. Ziegler, C.N., Lausen, G.: Propagation models for trust and distrust in social networks. Inf. Syst. Front. **7**(4), 337–358 (2005)
2. Sudbury, A.: The proportion of the population never hearing a rumour. J. Appl. Probab. **22**(2), 443–446 (1985)
3. Zanette, D.H.: Critical behavior of propagation on small-world networks. Phys. Rev. E **64**(1), 901–907 (2001)
4. Zanette, D.H.: Dynamics of rumor propagation on small-world networks. Phys. Rev. E **65**(4), 1–9 (2002)
5. Moreno, Y., Zanette, D.H.: Dynamics of rumor spreading in complex networks. Phys. Rev. E **69**(2), 130–137 (2004)
6. Liu, Z., Lai, Y.C., Ye, N.: Propagation and immunization of infection on general networks with both homogeneous and heterogeneous components. Phys. Rev. E **67**(3), 11–19 (2003)
7. Zhou, J., Liu, Z., Li, B.: Influence of network structure on rumor propagation. Phys. Lett. A **368**(6), 458–463 (2007)
8. Kesten, H., Sidoravicius, V.: The spread of a rumor or infection in a moving population. Ann. Probab. **33**(6), 2402–2462 (2003)
9. Pan, Z.F., Wang, X.F., Li, X.: Simulation investigation on rumor spreading on scale-free network with tunable clustering. J. Syst. Simul. **18**(8), 2346–2348 (2006)
10. Liu, C.Y., Hu, X.F., Si, G.Y.: Public opinion propagation model based on small world networks. J. Syst. Simul. **18**(12), 3608–3610 (2006)
11. Liu, C.Y., Hu, X.F., Luo, P.: Study on consensus emergency model based on asymmetric personal relationship influence. J. Syst. Simul. **20**(4), 990–992 (2008)
12. Liu, Y., Peng, H., Wang, J.: Verifiable diversity ranking search over encrypted outsourced data. Comput. Mater. Contin. **55**(1), 037 (2018)

13. Zeng, D., Dai, Y., Li, F., Sherratt, R.S., Wang, J.: Adversarial learning for distant supervised relation extraction. Comput. Mater. Contin. **55**(1), 121–136 (2018)
14. Fu, F.: Social dilemmas in an online social network: the structure and evolution of cooperation. Phys. Lett. A **371**(1), 58–64 (2007)
15. Zhang, Y.M., Tang, C.S., Li, W.G.: Research on interest attenuation and social reinforcement mechanism for rumor spreading in online social networks. J. China Soc. Sci. Tech. Inf. **34**(8), 833–844 (2015)
16. Liu, N., Lu, Y., Tang, X., et al.: Multi-document summarization algorithm based on significance topic of LDA. Zhongnan Daxue Xuebao **44**(2), 205–209 (2013)
17. Yan, M., Zhang, X., Yang, D., et al.: A component recommender for bug reports using discriminative probability latent semantic analysis. Inf. Softw. Technol. **73**(3), 37–51 (2016)
18. Yu, J., Zhu, T.: Combining long-term and short-term user interest for personalized hash tag recommendation. Front. Comput. Sci. **9**(4), 608–622 (2015)
19. Zhang, J.P., Jiang, Y.L.: A link prediction algorithm based on node similarity. China Sci. Pap. **8**(7), 659–662 (2013)

Power Consumption and Coverage Test of NB-IoT in the Substation Edge Computing Environment

Chunhe Song[1,2(✉)], Huan Li[3], Zhongfeng Wang[1,2], Shuai Ren[3], and Peng Zeng[1,2]

[1] Chinese Academy of Sciences, Shenyang Institute of Automation, Shenyang 110016, People's Republic of China
songchunhe@sia.cn
[2] Chinese Academy of Sciences, Institutes for Robotics and Intelligent Manufacturing, Shenyang 110016, China
[3] Liaoning Electric Power Research Institute, State Grid Liaoning Electric Power Co., Ltd., Shenyang 110000, People's Republic of China

Abstract. With the continuous development of smart grids, the application of Internet of Things technology in the substation edge computing environment is becoming more and more widespread. Traditional communication technologies, such as ZigBee and 4G, have limited transmission distances with low reliability, or high power consumption with inconvenient deployment. Narrowband Internet of Things (NB-IoT) is a new cellular technology introduced in 3GPP with wide coverage, large capacity, low power consumption and low cost. It provides a new kind of IoT communication technique in substation, which has complex electromagnetic interference that can cause interference to wireless transmission. In this paper, the power consumption and coverage performance of NB-IoT devices in substation environment are tested by our testbed-based experimental study. We leverage results from our experiments in providing an analysis on the power consumption and the impact of coverage when there are complex electromagnetic interferences.

Keywords: NB-IoT · Coverage · Substation · Experimental study

1 Introduction

As the Smart Grid continuously developed, IoT technologies are increasingly applied in power systems [1, 2]. Various types of sensors, smart meters and other terminals are widely used in the substation edge computing environment. These terminals are often stationary, and only a small amount of data needs to be usually transferred, while the number of these terminals may be quite big. Traditional communication technologies, such as ZigBee and 4G, have limited transmission distances and low reliability, or high power consumption and inconvenient deployment. Greatly hindered the promotion of IoT technologies in substations.

Narrowband Internet of Things (NB-IoT) is a new cellular technology introduced in 3GPP Release 13 for providing wide-area coverage for the Internet of Things (IoT) [3, 4].

X. Sun et al. (Eds.): ICAIS 2019, LNCS 11633, pp. 419–429, 2019.
https://doi.org/10.1007/978-3-030-24265-7_36

It is currently taking increasing relevance in the development of the IoT and Machine-to-Machine (M2M) communications [5–7]. More and more businesses have been integrated connectivity solutions with sensors, actuators, meters (water, gas, electric, or parking), cars, appliances, etc. by NB-IoT [9, 10]. According to Cisco, the number of M2M connections will grow to 3.3 billion by 2021, with a 34 percent compound annual growth rate [11]. With increased coverage and capacity, long battery life and low User Equipment (UE) device complexity, NB-IoT can be very appropriate used in the substation edge computing environment [8].

In Smart Grid substation, the increasing voltage level brings heavy electromagnetic interference. The electromagnetic environment of the substation is very complicated. Electromagnetic interference generated by power frequency electric field, power frequency magnetic field, corona discharge, partial discharge and switching operation is common in today's power system. These electromagnetic interferences during on-site operation have potential electromagnetic effects on the wireless transmission of the Internet of Things, which may result in abnormal operation, transmission error, packet loss and inability to communicate. Experimental studies show that electromagnetic interference can seriously affect the communication of 2.4 GHz-based wireless sensor networks [12–14]. NB-IoT is mainly operated in band B5 (center frequency 850 MHz) and band B8 (center frequency 900 MHz) in China. The spectral component of electromagnetic interference near the circuit breaker is 200 MHz to 2.75 GHz [12]. Therefore, NB-IoT communication is very likely to be affected by electromagnetic interference.

Low power consumption and high coverage performance are two of the main advantages of NB-IoT. The life of the NB-IoT terminal is claimed to be more than 10 years with a 5000mAh AA battery. On the other side, in the same frequency band, NB-IoT has a gain of 20 dB over the existing network and a 100-fold increase in coverage. In this paper, we present an experiment-based study on the power consumption of a NB-IoT device and the coverage performance in substation environment.

The rest of the paper is organized as follows. In Sect. 2, we provide a brief overview of the coverage of NB-IoT. In Sect. 3, we describe our experimental setup followed by results in Sect. 4. In Sect. 5, we leverage our experimental results to demonstrate the effect of electromagnetic interference on the coverage of NB-IoT. Finally, we conclude our paper in Sect. 6.

2 Preliminaries

NB-IoT features low power consumption, wide coverage, large connectivity and low cost. This article focuses on low power consumption and wide coverage.

2.1 Low Power Consumption

The goal of NB-IoT for terminal power consumption is that it can last for more than 10 years (AA battery, 5000mAh). The key technologies to achieve this goal are PSM and eDRX.

In the PSM state, the radio of the terminal is turned off and cannot receive or send any information, which can be treated as deep sleep state. The terminal will only wake up when the terminal has uplink data waiting to be transmitted, or the sleeping timer ends. When the terminal is in the Idel state, the eDRX can be used to further save power. In this case, the terminal uses the discontinuous reception mode to monitor the downlink-paging message. If no paging is detected, the terminal can enter the sleep state according to the eDRX cycle. In NB-IoT, the eDRX cycle can be set longer than in LTE. The longer the cycle, the less power is consumed, but the downlink flexibility is reduced.

2.2 Wide Coverage

NB-IoT has two options for the uplink transmission bandwidth: 3.75 kHz and 15 kHz. When the power is constant, the smaller the bandwidth, the larger the power spectral density and the larger the coverage gain. With a subcarrier of 3.75 kHz, the NB-IoT can achieve a PSD (Power Spectral Density) gain of 7 dB compared to GSM. On the other hand, NB-IoT supports more retransmissions than other wireless communication standards. The maximum retransmission of the uplink is 128 times, and the maximum retransmission of downlinks is 2048 times. Each time the number of retransmissions is doubled, the transmission rate is halved and a 3 dB coverage gain is achieved.

The NB-IoT system supports coverage levels configuration to reflect current channel conditions. Up to three coverage levels can be configured, which are CEL 0, CEL 1 and CEL 2. The terminal determines which coverage level it is in based on its own RSRP measurement of the cell and the RSRP threshold value sent by the cell. The terminal then needs to adjust the random access parameters according to the current coverage level, including number of retransmissions, cycle, start time, number of subcarriers, frequency domain location, and so on. A coverage level map is shown in Fig. 1.

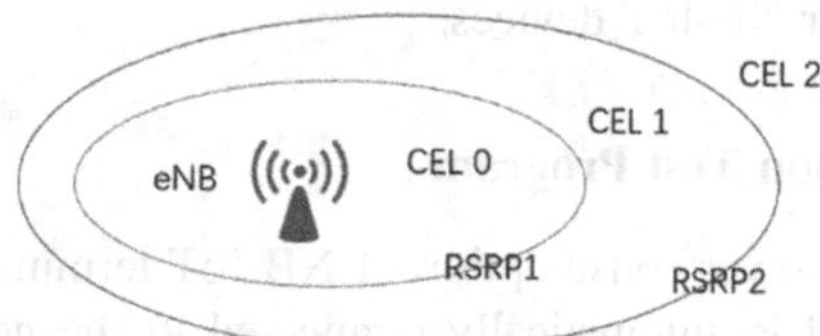

Fig. 1. A sketch map of the coverage level map

3 Testbed Setup

We build our own experimental testbed to test the communication between a server and two NB-IoT terminals. The example graph of the experimental testbed is shown in Fig. 2. We use the Quectel LTE BC95 NB-IoT module as the NB-IoT terminal. The relay server communicates with the test server by binding IP addresses and ports. Through the forwarding of the relay server, our server can receive the UDP uplink packets sent by the NB-IoT terminal.

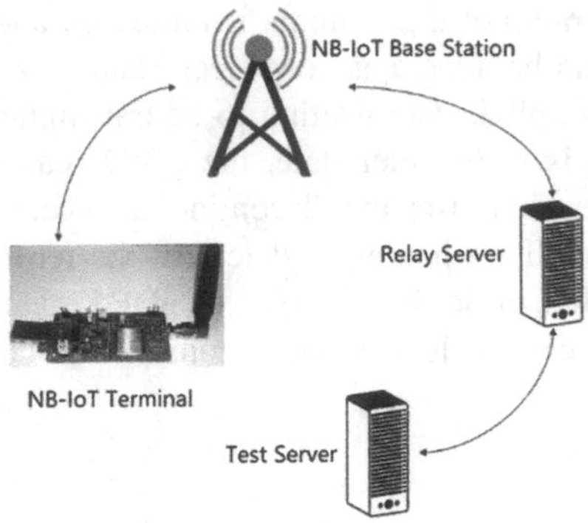

Fig. 2. Example graph of the experimental testbed

We also design and implement a test software that include a basic setting module for the NB-IoT terminal and GPS module, an NB terminal decoder, and a GPS decoder. The basic settings of the NB-IoT terminal and GPS module include settings for serial port, baud rate, and so on. The NB terminal decoder achieves serial communication between the personal computer and the NB-IoT terminal, and the content includes writing the command to the terminal through the serial port, and analyzing the result returned by the terminal from the serial port. The GPS decoder is responsible for reading and parsing the GPS information in the NMEA format returned by the GPS module through the serial port.

4 Test Program

In this section, we introduce our test program for the power consumption and the coverage performance for NB-IoT devices.

4.1 Power Consumption Test Program

We mainly measure the power consumption of NB-IoT terminals in different working states. Since the terminal is automatically connected to the network, the connection speed is fast, which is not conducive to control the working state of the terminal at each moment. Therefore, it is necessary to set the terminal device to prohibit automatic networking after booting, and then manually control the terminal to gradually connect to the base station. During the measurement, the terminal device BC28 selects the external power supply mode. The Power Channel's Main Channel is used to power the BC28 with a voltage of 3.6 V. The connection diagram of the experimental equipment is shown in Fig. 3.

Fig. 3. The connection of the experimental devices for power consumption test

4.2 Coverage Performance Test Program

The NB-IoT base station periodically broadcasts the reference signal. When a certain area is covered by multiple cells, the NB-IoT terminal performs cell selection and determines its own coverage level by receiving the received reference signal quality after being powered on. On the one hand, we measure the coverage level of nodes at different locations in a fixed cell, and also measure the impact of cell selection on node coverage level.

We use two NB-IoT terminals, named UE1, UE2, to collect NB-IoT signals in the substation area. UE1 is set to allow cell reselection, UE2 is set to disable cell reselection, and forced search for a fixed cell signal and access. UE1 can still search for nearby cells after camping on the appropriate cell, perform neighbor cell measurement, and select a better cell to camp. UE2 will camp on the set cell as long as possible, and will not search other cells until it leaves the coverage of the cell.

The two terminal devices and the GPS module are simultaneously connected to the laptop through the USB HUB, the terminal device is moved at a walking speed. We query the information of the cell currently camped on by the terminal device at the sampling frequency of 3 times per second, including physical cell number (PCI), carrier frequency (EARFCN), cell ID (CELL_ID), reference signal acceptance strength (RSRP) and other signal quality measurements, while recording the current location GPS information.

5 Experimental Results

5.1 Power Consumption Test Results

We draw the image of the terminal's current as a function of time from the acquired data. The startup current diagram is shown in Fig. 4. Combined with the state transition mechanism of NB-IoT, the meaning of the current diagram in this section is analyzed against the work current consumption in each state of the BC28 hardware manual.

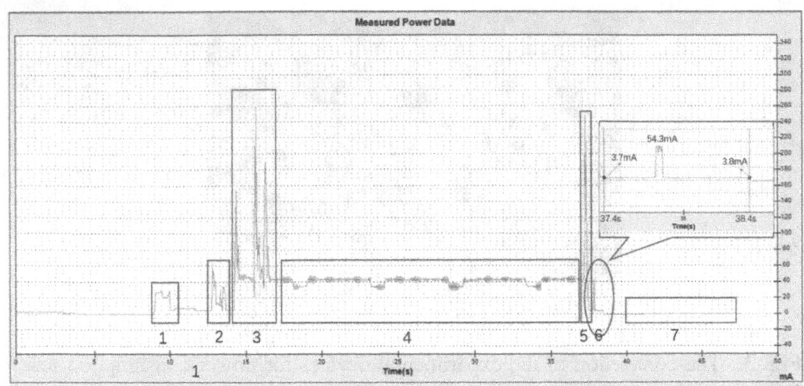

Fig. 4. The startup current diagram of BC28

The first stage: All the functions of the terminal including the transceiver are turned on. Since there is no need to search for a cell at this stage, the current is the current that all the circuit components except the transceiver, and the average value is 4.436 mA.

The second stage: The current is about 60 mA. The terminal turns on the RF transceiver to search for the PLMN and the cell. Some of the small peaks below 50 mA are the terminals to select the appropriate cell by calculation. At this time, because only the RF receiver is working, the transmitter does not work, so the current is not high.

The third stage: The current reaches up to 260 mA. At this stage, the terminal is in the RF transmission state. Here, there are three peaks, which are some signaling interactions between the terminal and the base station. The clock and the retransmitted times are decided through negotiation.

The fourth stage: The terminal is still in the active state, and the radio is in the receiving state. This stage is controlled by a timer. When the terminal does not have uplink or downlink services for 20 s, the terminal automatically ends the state.

The fifth stage: After 20 s of radio frequency monitoring, the terminal has no uplink and downlink services, then the terminal disconnects the network and enters to the IDLE state. When the terminal is about to enter the IDLE state, the terminal will report to the base station that the current peak in this segment reaches 250 mA.

The sixth stage: IDLE state with a duration of 1 s. The current in the IDLE state averages 4.2 mA. As can be seen from the enlarged thumbnail, a peak of 54.3 mA appears in the IDLE state. Since the IDLE state does not completely shut down the transceiver, the terminal is still reachable downstream, so the peak may be a data packet sent by the base station.

The seventh stage: The terminal turns off all functions except the clock and enters the PSM mode. The average current in PSM mode is 8.6 uA.

5.2 Coverage Performance Test Results

Figures 5 and 6 show the distribution of cell IDs when UE1 and UE2 reside at different locations, respectively. The different colors represent different cells in which the terminal resides, the horizontal axis is longitude and the vertical axis is dimension. Comparing Figs. 1 and 2, UE1 allows cell reselection, so it can be seen that there are more different cells in which it resides, while UE2 is more fixed in most cases (Cell No. 5).

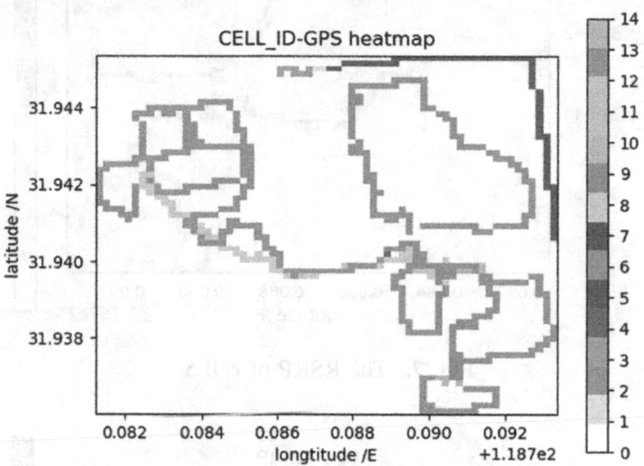

Fig. 5. The distribution of cells from UE1

From the data collected by the UE2, we filter out all the information of the "Cell 5". Then the change of the RSRP (Reference Signal Receiving Power) of the cell with the geographical location is plotted in Fig. 7, where the darker the color, the larger the RSRP and the stronger the signal strength. This figure reflects the coverage performance of cell 5.

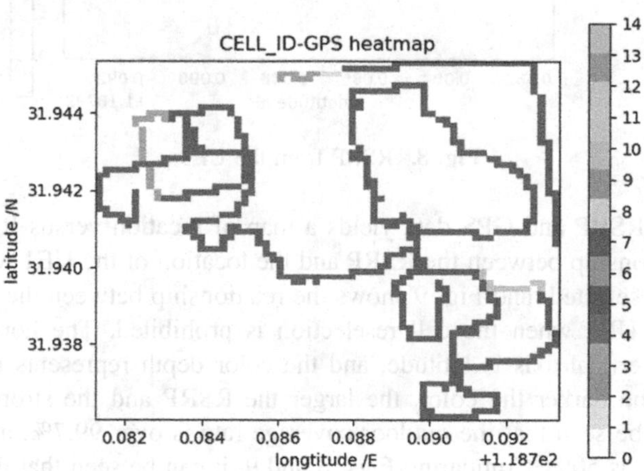

Fig. 6. The distribution of cells from UE2

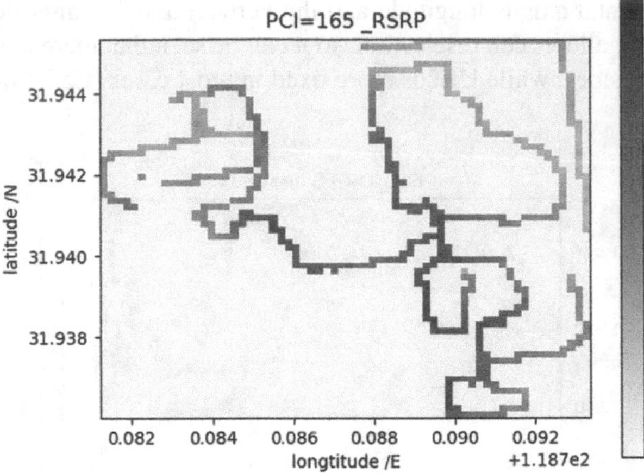

Fig. 7. The RSRP of cell 5

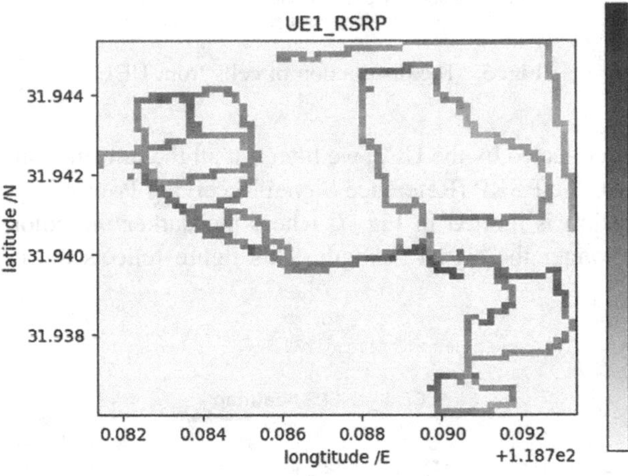

Fig. 8. RSRP from the UE1

Combining RSRP and GPS data yields a map of location versus RSRP. Figure 8 shows the relationship between the RSRP and the location of the UE1 when the cell is allowed to be reselected, and Fig. 9 shows the relationship between the RSRP and the location of the UE2 when the cell reselection is prohibited. The horizontal axis is longitude, the vertical axis is latitude, and the color depth represents the size of the RSRP value. The darker the color, the larger the RSRP and the stronger the signal strength. It can be seen that the outdoor coverage rate is over 99.7%, and the ratio of coverage level 0 is 50%. Comparing Figs. 8 and 9, it can be seen that the color of the UE2 in the marked area is darker than that of the UE1, indicating that the signal strength of the terminal that is prohibited from being reselected by the cell is stronger, and the coverage performance of the terminal when the cell reselection is prohibited is better than the coverage performance of the terminal when the cell is allowed to be reselected. This is contrary to the purpose of the cell reselection mechanism.

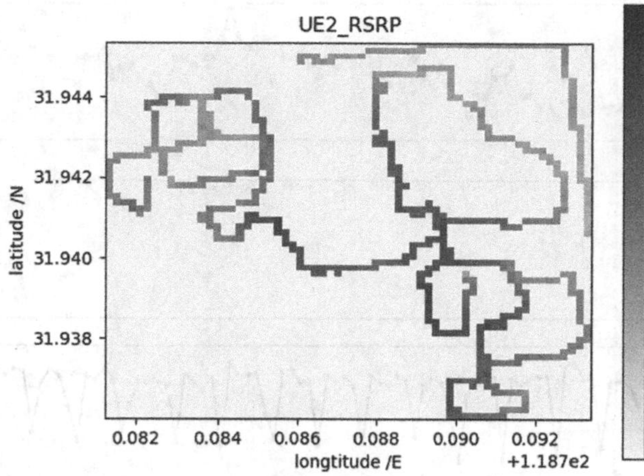

Fig. 9. RSRP from the UE2

6 Analysis and Discussion

It can be seen from the test results that the area is under the coverage of multiple cells. In the cell selection control experiment, allowing cell reselection not only does not allow the UE to camp on a better cell, but the coverage performance is worse than the case of forbidding cell reselection. We analyze the possible causes in this section.

When the base station deployment is relatively dense, the same location can search for several cell signals. When the terminal performs cell selection, it calculates the following formula:

$$\text{Srxlev} = \text{RSRP} - \text{P1}, \ \text{Squal} = \text{RSRQ} - \text{P2},$$

where P1 is a fixed parameter related to the lowest reception level value of the cell, the maximum transmission power of the terminal, and the maximum RF output power of the terminal, and P2 is a fixed parameter related to the lowest received signal quality value of the cell. The terminal can select to camp only when the cell satisfies the discriminant formula Srxlev > 0 and Squal > 0. When Srxlev is less than a certain threshold, the terminal performs neighbor measurement. Let the RSRP of the current cell be R_s, and the RSRP of the neighboring cell be R_n. When R_n > R_s, the terminal will reselect to reside in the neighboring cell.

Complex electromagnetic interference exists in the substation area, resulting in the measurement of RSRP and RSRQ becoming extremely unstable. Figure 10 shows the measured changes of RSRP, RSRQ and SNR over time at a fixed location. It can be seen that all three parameters have different degrees of fluctuation, and RSRQ and SNR show regular fluctuations, which implies there is a regular disturbance. The impact of interference on RSRP and RSRQ results that the terminal is not able to select the optimal cell when performing cell selection.

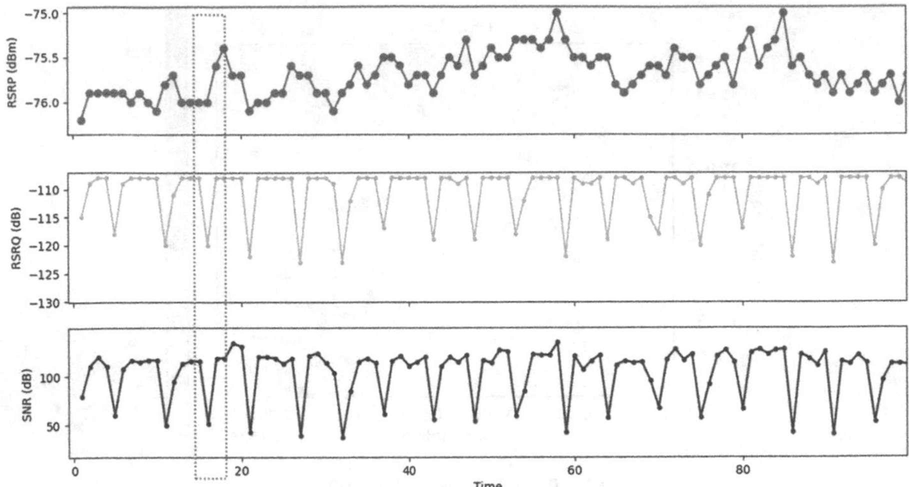

Fig. 10. RSRP, RSRQ and SNR over time at a fixed location

7 Conclusion

In this paper, we study the power consumption of an NB-IoT device and the effect of complex electromagnetic interference on NB-IoT coverage performance based on real experiments. We find that an area is usually covered by multiple cells, and the terminal needs to choose which cell to camp according to the measured RSRP value. However, the measurement of RSRP is often inaccurate due to the effect of the complex electromagnetic environment, which affects the cell selection of the terminal. If the terminal does not select the cell with the best performance to camp, it will affect its coverage performance. In this case, the cell reselection function of the terminal should be forbidden to achieve better coverage performance.

Acknowledgments. This work was supported by the State Grid Corporation Science and Technology Project (Contract No.: SG2NK00DWJS1800123).

References

1. Sarwat, A.I., Sundararajan, A., Parvez, I.: Trends and future directions of research for smart grid IoT sensor networks. In: Rao, N.S.V., Brooks, R.R., Wu, C.Q. (eds.) ISSNSS 2017, pp. 45–61. Springer, Cham (2018). https://doi.org/10.1007/978-3-319-75683-7_4
2. Reka, S.S., Dragicevic, T.: Future effectual role of energy delivery: A comprehensive review of Internet of Things and smart grid. Renew. Sustain. Energy Rev. **91**, 90–108 (2018)
3. Chi, X., Song, C., Zeng, P., Haibin, Y.: Secure resource allocation for energy harvesting cognitive radio sensor networks without and with cooperative jamming. Comput. Netw. **141**, 189–198 (2018)
4. Xu, C., Xia, C., Song, C., Zeng, P., Yu, H.: Multi-hop cognitive wireless powered networks: outage analysis and optimization. IEEE Access **99**, 1–10 (2018)

5. Shang, W., Cui, J., Song, C., Zhao, J., Zeng, P.: Research on industrial control anomaly detection based on fcm and svm. In: 2018 17th IEEE International Conference on Trust, Security and Privacy in Computing and Communications/12th IEEE International Conference on Big Data Science and Engineering (TrustCom/BigDataSE), pp. 218–222 (2018)
6. Ming, W., Jianming, Z., Weiwei, Y., Peng, Z., Junrong, C., Wenli, S.: Intrusion detection of industrial control based on semi-supervised clustering strategy. Inf. Control **46**(4), 462–468 (2017)
7. Song, C., Jing, W., Zeng, P., Haibin, Y., Rosenberg, C.: Energy consumption analysis of residential swimming pools for peak load shaving. Appl. Energy **220**, 176–191 (2018)
8. Song, C., Jing, W., Zeng, P., Rosenberg, C.: An analysis on the energy consumption of circulating pumps of residential swimming pools for peak load management. Appl. Energy **195**, 1–12 (2017)
9. Zhu, H., Pak, C.H., Song, C., Dou, S., Zhao, H., Cao, P., Ye, X.: A novel lung cancer detection algorithm for cads based on ssp and level set. Technol. Health Care **25**(S1), 1–11 (2017)
10. Song, C., Zeng, P., Wang, Z., Zhao, H., Yu, H.: Wearable continuous body temperature measurement using multiple artificial neural networks. IEEE Trans. Ind. Inform. **99**(1), 1–12 (2018)
11. Cisco: Cisco Visual Networking Index: Global Mobile Data Traffic Forecast Update 2016–2021 White Paper. http://www.cisco.com/c/en/us/solutions/collateral/service-provider/visual-networking-index-vni/mobile-white-paper-c11-520862.html. Accessed 4 Oct 2017
12. Bo, A., Weidong, Z., Haijie, M., et al.: A study on electromagnetic disturbance and immunity of wireless sensor unit in substation. General Assembly and Scientific Symposium. pp. 1–4 (2014)
13. Zhiguo, Q., Zhu, T., Wang, J., Wang, X.: A novel quantum steganography based on brown states. Comput., Mater. Continua **56**(1), 47–59 (2018)
14. Liu, W., Chen, Z., Liu, J., Zhaofeng, S., Chi, L.: Full-blind delegating private quantum computation. CMC: Comput., Mater. Continua **56**(2), 211–223 (2018)

Research on the Optimization of Spark Big Table Equal Join

Suzhen Wang(✉), Lu Zhang, and Yanpiao Zhang

Hebei University of Economics and Business, Shijiazhuang 050061
Hebei, China
wsuz@163.com

Abstract. The big table equal join operation is one of the key operations of Spark for processing large-scale data. However, when Spark handles large table equal join problems, the network transmission overhead is relatively expensive and the I/O cost is high, so this paper proposes an optimized Spark large table join method. Firstly, this method proposes a Split Compressed Bloom Filter algorithm which is suitable for filtering data sets with unknown data volume. Then, the Maxdiff histogram is used to statistically analyze the data distribution of the connected data tables, and the skew data in the data set is obtained. According to the statistical results, the RDD is split, and finally the data connection is joined by a suitable join algorithm, and the sub-results are combined to obtain the final result. Experiments show that the Spark large table equal join optimization method proposed in this paper has obvious advantages in shuffle write, shuffle read and task running time compared with Spark original method.

Keywords: Spark · Big table equal join
Split Compressed Bloom Filter (SCBF) · Maxdiff histogram · RDD split

1 Introduction

Spark [1] is an emerging computing framework which is based on memory for calculation, it is more suitable for iterative data processing and interactive data processing, and improves the real-time of data processing in a big data environment. Meanwhile, Spark SQL components include relational processing and the functional programming API of Spark, which can handle SQL statements that cannot be executed in the MapReduce framework and perform real-time data analysis. In the process of data processing analysis and data query, it is necessary to carry out the operation of equal join. Spark has a high efficiency in dealing with the operation of equal join between small data tables or between large data table and small data table, but it takes a lot of time and costs to process the join operation between large data tables. Therefore, it becomes the focus of this paper about how to optimize the operation of equal join between large data tables.

In literature [2], a two-way connection optimization algorithm based on Bit-map and Distributed Cache mechanism is proposed. This method can reduce the network transmission overhead and filter out some data that does not satisfy the connection condition. Literature [3] proposes an improved equal join algorithm, it first uses Bloom

X. Sun et al. (Eds.): ICAIS 2019, LNCS 11633, pp. 430–441, 2019.
https://doi.org/10.1007/978-3-030-24265-7_37

Filter to filter the dataset to be connected, and uses Spark's own pool sampling algorithm and Spark Statistics library to sample and analyze the connection properties. According to the data analysis result and the greedy algorithm, the one-sided table is split, and finally the connected subset is the final result. Literature [4] performs a de-duplication operation on the Fact table to obtain the Fact UK dataset, and records the corresponding position, and then the Fact UK and Dim tables are connected, which creates the Joined UK, finally, assembling Joined UK and Fact according to the location recorded by Joined UK to get the final result. This method is only suitable for equal join between large and small tables. The scalable hash join algorithm proposed in literature [5] can be used to process coarse-grained distributed data, and it can consistently give approximately consistent connection results even in the case of memory overflow, and the scalability of it is very good. The Spatio-Temporal join algorithm proposed in document [6] is mainly used to process a large number of spatial data. The join operation of this algorithm combines space, time and attribute predicates, and can solve the join problem based on space, time and attribute. Aiming at the large network transmission overhead and data skew problem of the equal join operation between big data tables in Spark, this paper proposes an optimized Spark big table equal join strategy. The specific work is as follows:

(1) This paper proposes a Split Compressed Bloom Filter (SCBF) data filtering method to pre-process the data to be connected and reduce the amount of data in the shuffle process.
(2) In this paper, the Maxdiff histogram is used to calculate the data distribution of the join key, in order to find the skew data.
(3) This paper proposes an RDD splitting mechanism to optimize the data skew problem in equal join operations.

2 Related Works

2.1 Spark Operation Mode and Architecture

Spark [8] is a full-stack computing platform written in Scala language to deal with large-scale data, including local, standalone, yarn and other operating modes. This paper is based on the Standalone running mode of Spark for load balancing research. The Spark-Standalone eco-architecture is shown in Fig. 1. It consists of a four-layer structure that includes the resource management layer, the data storage layer, the Spark core layer, and the Spark component layer [7, 9]. The Spark component layer and Spark core layer are the basic frameworks of Spark. Spark core is a core component of Spark and provides the most basic and core functions of Spark data processing. The Spark component layer provides support for SQL queries, streaming calculations, graph calculations, and machine learning. The data storage layer is mainly composed of Tachyon, HDFS and HBase. Spark can invoke data from the data storage layer to relieve the storage pressure of Spark. The resource management layer adopts standalone mode to dynamically manage and schedule Spark resources and achieve reasonable resource allocation.

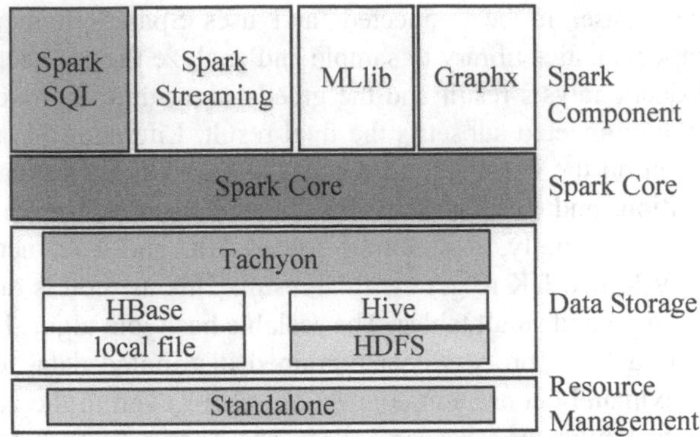

Fig. 1. Spark-standlone architecture.

2.2 Spark Common Join Algorithm Analysis

Spark often uses join operations for data processing analysis. The join operation in Spark includes the connection between two tables and the connection between multiple tables. This paper takes the connection between the two tables as the optimization goal. The join operation essentially connects data with equal key values in two RDD[key, value], where key represents the connection property and value represents the other properties in each tuple. Spar mainly includes three commonly used join algorithms [10, 11]: Broadcast Hash Join, Hash Join and Sort Merge Join. Broadcast Hash Join is only suitable for join operations between small tables or between large tables and small tables. Hash Join and Sort Merge Join are suitable for most join operations, but if the data table is too large, network communication and I/O cost will be very high.

2.3 Bloom Filter

Bloom Filter [12, 22] is a data structure with good spatial and temporal efficiency, which is usually used to detect whether an element belongs to a large number of data sets. The basic idea of Bloom Filter is as follows: Initializing an array of bits with a length of m and set each bit of the array to 0. For the set $S = \{x1, x2, \ldots, xn\}$, each element in the set is mapped to a bit array by k independent hash functions, and the mapping position is set to 1. Assuming that x is a element in the set S, and the mapping function of x is shown in formula 1.

$$h_i(x) = y(1 \leq i \leq k, 1 \leq y \leq m) \tag{1}$$

The formula (1) indicates that the element x is mapped to the position y through the i hash function, and the position y is set from 0 to 1. All elements in the set S are mapped by k hash functions, and the w bits ($w < m$) in the bit array are set to 1, and then the set S completes the set representation of the bit array.

Bloom Filter contains three important parameters: error rate f, number of hash functions k, and bit array size m. The calculation formulas for the three parameters are as follows.

$$f = (1 - (1 - \frac{1}{m})^{kn})^k \approx (1 - e^{-kn/m})^k \tag{2}$$

$$k_{best} = (m/n)\ln 2 \tag{3}$$

$$m = -(n \ln p)/(\ln 2)^2 \tag{4}$$

2.4 Histogram Method

The histogram [13, 14] is a two-dimensional statistical graph that approximates represents the distribution of data, such as the center, spread, and shape of the data, by using binning technology. The histogram generally has three basic attributes: segmentation constraint, sorting parameter and source parameter. These attributes respectively define the segmentation mode of the histogram bucket, the data sorting mode and the bucket boundary, which have great significance for the construction of the histogram. Based on the bucket and attribute values, the histogram can be divided into the following types: equal-width histogram, isometric histogram, V-Optimal histogram [15, 16], and Maxdiff histogram. Among them, Maxdiff and V-Optimal are the two most accurate histograms for evaluating the data distribution. The Maxdiff histogram is superior to the V-Optimal histogram in both time complexity and space complexity [17], so this paper uses Maxdiff histogram to statistic data distribution.

3 Optimization Method of Spark Big Table Equal Join

The Spark large table equal join optimization method proposed in this paper is mainly divided into five stages: (1) connection attribute filtering and statistics, (2) analysis of skew data distribution, (3) RDD segmentation, (4) join operation, and (5) result combination. The symbol names involved in this section are shown in Table 1.

3.1 Data Filtering Based on Split Compressed Bloom Filter

Split Compressed Bloom Filter. This paper proposes a Split Compressed Bloom Filter (SCBF) algorithm based on the split idea of Split Bloom Filter (SBF) [19] and the compression mechanism of Compressed Bloom Filter (CBF) [18], which can be applied to data processing with unknown data set and the space occupancy rate will not be too high.

The main idea of the algorithm is as follows: Assuming that the initial bit array size is m, the total number of hash functions is k, and the compressed array size is z. The CBF is used to process the elements contained in the data set S. When the limitation of the CBF bit array is reached, a new CBF bit array of the same size as the

Table 1. Symbol name table.

Symbol name	Description
RDDA/B	RDD which is corresponding to Table A/B
JoinKeyA/B	Connection attributes of Table A/B
SCBF_A/B	SCBF bit array of Table A/B
$SCBF_{final}$	Filtered bit array
RDDA/B_new	New RDD obtained after filtering in Table A/B
JoinKeyA/B_new	Filtered connection properties of Table A/B
SkewA/B	Skew key set obtained after filtering in Table A/B
SkewAB	All skew key set obtained after filtering in Table A/B
Result	The RDD corresponding to the join result obtained after filtering in Table A and Table B
RDDA/B_original	The RDD corresponding to the un-skewed part data obtained after filtering in Table A/B
RDDA/B_Skew1-m	The RDD corresponding to the skewed part data obtained after filtering in Table A/B

initial CBF bit array is generated until the elements in the data set S all complete the set representation of the bit array. When querying whether an element exists in the SCBF bit array, as long as the value of the element mapped to one or more sub-CBF bit arrays in the SCBF is 1, the element exists in the SCBF array.

The size of the bit array after compression is as shown in Eq. (5).

$$z = mH(p) \tag{5}$$

$$H(p) = -p\log_2^p - (1-p)\log_2^{(1-p)} \tag{6}$$

$$p \approx e^{-kn/m} \tag{7}$$

SCBF Data Filtering Operation. In this paper, SCBF is used to compress and filter two tables to be connected, and remove the invalid data in the two tables, which reduces the amount of data in the shuffle process during table connection. The specific process is as follows:

(1) Extracting the connection attributes of the two tables to be connected respectively, and performing deduplication operations on them, so that every key value in every group of connection attributes has one and only one;
(2) Using SCBF to compress the connection properties of two tables to be joined to obtain two bit arrays;
(3) Two newly generated bit arrays do logical AND to obtain the final bit array SCBFfinal;
(4) Using SCBFfinal to filter two data tables to be connected, so as to get two new data tables.

The processing flow at this stage is shown in Fig. 2.

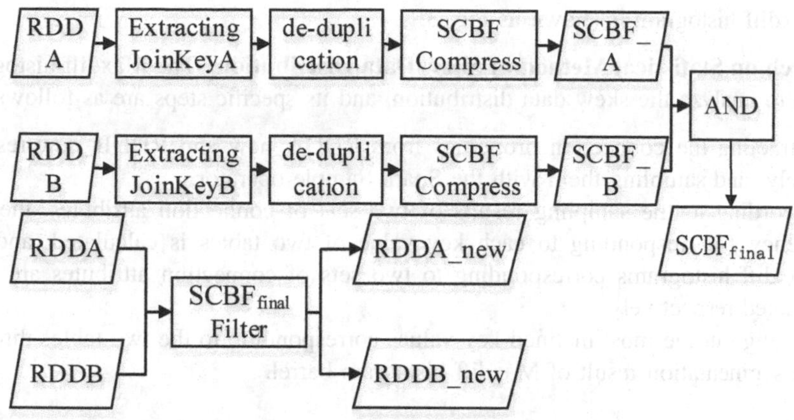

Fig. 2. SCBF filter flow.

3.2 Skew Data Distribution Statistics Based on Maxdiff Histogram

Maxdiff Histogram. Maxdiff histogram [20, 21] takes the key value extracted from the filtered data table as the sorting parameter and the frequency difference *fd* of the adjacent key value as the source parameter to represent the data distribution. The data with large frequency difference of the adjacent key value are divided into different buckets, and the frequency of the key value in the same bucket remains small difference. By dividing the Maxdiff histogram into bucket operation, we can get the tilted data in the two data tables.

Among them, the frequency difference *fd* is calculated as formula (8).

$$fd_{ij} = f_i - f_j \tag{8}$$

f_i and f_j represent the frequencies of key_i and key_j respectively.

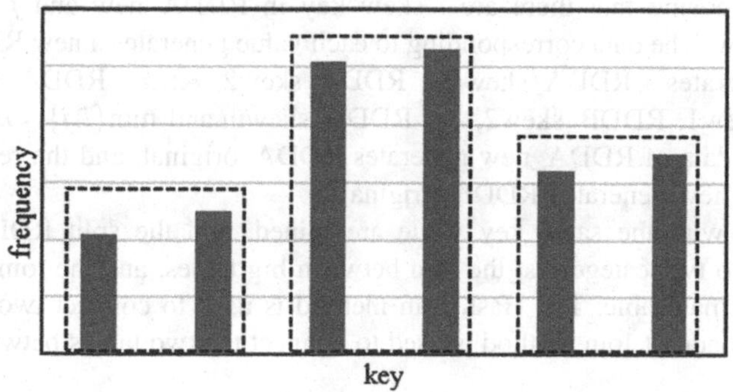

Fig. 3. Maxdiff histogram.

Maxdiff histogram is shown as Fig. 3.

Research on Statistical Method of Skew Data Distribution. The Maxdiff histogram is used to analyze the skew data distribution, and its specific steps are as follows:

(1) Extracting the connection properties from RDDA_new and RDDB_new respectively, and sampling them with the Spark Sample operator.
(2) According to the sampling results of two sets of connection attributes, the frequency f corresponding to each key value of two tables is calculated, and the Maxdiff histograms corresponding to two sets of connection attributes are constructed respectively.
(3) Finding out the most inclined key values corresponding to the two tables through the segmentation result of Maxdiff histogram barrel.

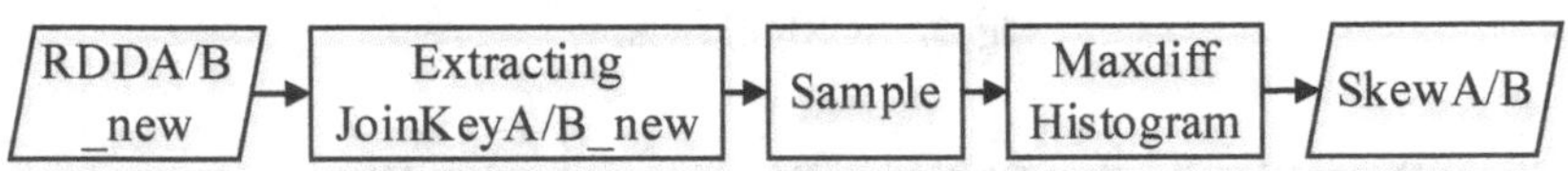

Fig. 4. The flow of counting data distribution.

The process of count data distribution based on Maxdiff histogram is shown in Fig. 4.

3.3 RDD Split and Result Combination

RDD splitting connection and result combination are mainly completed in three steps, and its specific steps are as follows:

(1) Splitting RDD to RDDA_new and RDDB_new according to the skew distribution of the two data tables. First, the skew key in the two RDD do logical AND to obtain the full skew key SkewAB of the two RDD, and then the tuples corresponding to SkewAB in the two RDDs are separately split to generate new RDD, and finally the remaining tuples corresponding to the ordinary key generate a new RDD. Supposing that there are i skew key in RDDA_new and j skew key in RDDB_new. The data corresponding to each value generates a new RDD, which in turn generates RDDA_skew1, RDDA_skew2, …, RDDA_skewm and RDDB_skew1, RDDB_skew2, …, RDDB_skewm,and $\min\{i,j\} \leq m \leq i+j$. The remaining data of RDDA_new generates RDDA_original, and the remaining data of RDDB_new generates RDDB_original.
(2) The RDD with the same key value are joined, and the split RDD are mainly divided into two categories: the join between big tables, and the join between big table and small table. The Hash Join method is used to connect two large tables, and the Broadcast Join method is used to connect the two tables between large and small.
(3) All the join results are combined by the union operator, and the result is the join result of the two data tables.

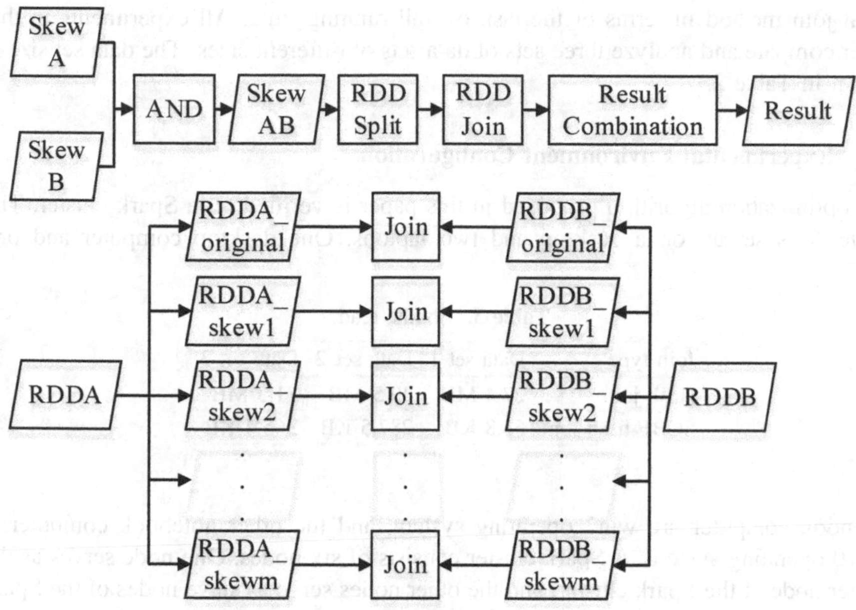

Fig. 5. The flow of RDD split and result combination.

The flow of RDD split, RDD join and result combination are shown in Fig. 5.

4 Experimental Result and Analysis

The Spark big table equal join method proposed in this paper is experimentally verified in the Spark cluster environment, including three aspects: (1) verifying the effectiveness of the SCBD algorithm in data filtering; (2) verifying the effectiveness of RDD splitting mechanism on tilting data process; (3) verifying the effectiveness of the Spark big table

Table 2. Experimental data set.

Data set	1	2	3
Data table 1	326 M	765 M	1.14G
Data table 2	283 M	781 M	1.35G

equal join method in terms of the task overall running time. All experiments in this paper compare and analyze three sets of data sets of different sizes. The data set size is shown in Table 2.

4.1 Experimental Environment Configuration

The optimization algorithm proposed in this paper is verified on a Spark cluster. The cluster was set up on a desktop and two laptops. One desktop computer and one

Table 3. Shuffle read.

Join type	Data set 1	Data set 2	Data set 3
Hash join	27.4 MB	40.5 MB	71.3 MB
SCBF-hash join	53.8 KB	287.5 KB	365.4 KB

notebook computer are win7 operating system, and the other notebook computer is win10 operating system. A Spark cluster consists of six nodes. One node serves as the master node of the Spark cluster, and the other nodes serve as slave nodes of the Spark cluster.

4.2 Data Filtering Comparison Experiment

The two data tables to be connected are filtered by the SCBF method, and then the hash join are performed respectively on the original data tables and the filtered tables. The shuffle read and shuffle write results of the shuffle phase are as shown in Tables 3 and 4 shows.

It can be seen from Tables 3 and 4 that compared with performing Hash Join on the data set directly, the method this paper proposed that using SCBF to filter data of two tables, and then performing Hash Join, is relatively low in shuffle read and shuffle write and has obvious advantages.

4.3 Data Skew Degree Comparison Experiment

Comparing the data skew degree of the two data sets before and after RDD split, and the experimental results are shown in Fig. 6. The data skew degree is defined in definition 1.

Definition 1. Data skew degree DS. This paper uses the standard deviation calculation formula to measure the skew degree of the data partition. The smaller the degree, the more balanced the data partition is. The calculation formula is as follows.

$$DS = \frac{\sum_{i=1}^{m} DS_i}{m} \tag{9}$$

Table 4. Shuffle write.

Join type	Data set 1	Data set 2	Data set 3
Hash join	21.6 MB	28.7 MB	49.6 MB
SCBF-hash join	45.3 KB	227.3 KB	298.7 KB

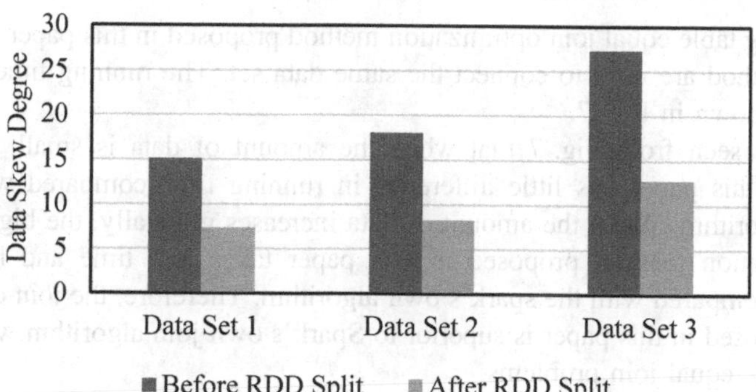

Fig. 6. Data skew comparision.

$$DS_i = \sqrt{\frac{\sum_{j=1}^{n} (x_j - \bar{x})^2}{n}} \tag{10}$$

Where m represents the number of RDD, DS_i represents the data skew of the i-th RDD, n represents the partitions number of the i-th RDD, and x_j represents the amount of data of the partition j.

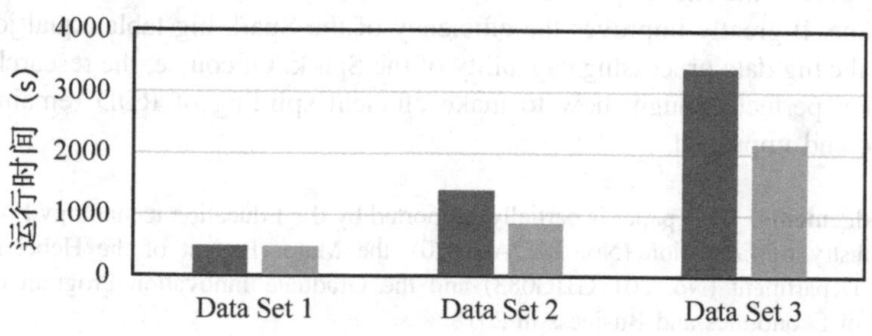

Fig. 7. Running time comparison.

It can be seen from Fig. 6 that the split data set has a lower data skew degree and a more balanced data distribution than the un-split data set. Therefore, the RDD split method proposed in this paper can solve the data skew problem encountered in the Spark data join process.

4.4 Task Running Time Comparison Experiment

The Spark big table equal join optimization method proposed in this paper and Spark's own join method are used to connect the same data set. The running time of the two methods is shown in Fig. 7.

It can be seen from Fig. 7 that when the amount of data is small, the method proposed in this paper has little difference in running time compared with Spark's own join algorithm. When the amount of data increases gradually, the big table equal join optimization method proposed in this paper takes less time and has obvious advantages compared with the spark's own algorithm. Therefore, the join optimization method proposed in this paper is superior to Spark's own join algorithm when dealing with big table equal join problems.

5 Conclusions

Spark is one of the mainstream frameworks for big data processing, and it is of great significance for the processing and analysis of large-scale data. However, Spark itself has some shortcomings, such as when it handles the join operation between two large tables, the efficiency is not high and the cost is too large. Aiming at this problem, this paper proposes a big table equal join method based on filtering and splitting. Firstly, the Split Compressed Bloom Filter algorithm is used to filter the data set to be connected, then the Maxdiff histogram is used to obtain the skew data distribution, and then split them, finally join the split data and merge the result. The method not only reduces the amount of data in the shuffle process of the join operation, but also reduces the overall running time. It greatly improves the efficiency of the Spark big table equal join, and improves the big data processing capability of the Spark. Of course, the research in this paper is not perfect enough, how to make efficient splitting of RDD remains to be researched and improved.

Acknowledgements. This paper is partially supported by the Education technology Foundation of the Ministry of Education (No. 2017A01020), the Major Project of the Hebei Province Education Department (No. 2017GJJG083) and the Graduate Innovation Program of Hebei University of Economics and Business in 2018.

References

1. Apache Spark. http://spark.apache.org. Accessed 28 Apr 2018
2. Sun, H.: Join processing and optimization on large datasets based on hadoop framework. Nanjing University of Posts and Telecommunications (2013)

3. Zhang, Z.D., Zheng, Y.B.: Optimizaiton of two-table equivalent connection process based on spark. Appl. Res. Comput. **02**, 1–2 (2019)
4. Bian, H.Q., Chen, Y.G., Du, X.Y.: Equi-join optimization on spark. J. East China Normal Univ. (Nat. Sci.) **2014**(5), 263–270 (2014)
5. Liu, H., Xiao, J., Peng, F.: Scalable hash ripple join on spark. In: 23rd International Conference on Parallel and Distributed Systems, pp. 419–428. IEEE, Shenzhen (2014)
6. Hoel, E., Whitman, R.T., Park, M.B.: Spatio-temporal join on apache spark. In: 25th ACM SIGSPATIAL International Conference on Advances in Geographic Information Systems, ACM, California (2017)
7. Wang, S.Z., Zhang, Y.P., Zhang, L., et al.: An improved memory cache management study based on spark. Comput., Mater. Continua **56**(3), 415–431 (2018)
8. Lin, D.G.: Hadoop + spark big data massive analysis and machine learning integration development, 1st edn. Tsinghua University Press, Beijing (2017)
9. Zhang, X.: An Intermediate Data Placement Algorithm for Load Balancing in Spark Computing Environment. Hunan University (2016)
10. Zhang, WH.: Implementation and optimization for join operation in spark, National University of Defense Technology (2016)
11. Pi, X.J.: Optimization and Application of the Equi-join Problem based on Grid Big Data in Spark. Chongqing University (2016)
12. Bloom, B.H.: Space/time trade-offs in hash coding with allowable errors. Commun. ACM (CACM) **13**(7), 422–426 (1970)
13. Ioannidis, Y.: The history of histograms (abridged). In: 29th International Conference on Very Large Data Bases, pp. 19–30. VLDB Endowment, Berlin (2003)
14. Chaudhuri, S., Das, G., Srivastava, U.: Effective use of block-level sampling in statistics estimation. In: 2004 ACM SIGMOD International Conference on Management of Data, pp. 287–298. ACM, Paris (2004)
15. Jagadish, H.V., Poosala, V., Koudas, N.: Optimal histograms with quality guarantees. In: 24th International Conference on Very Large Data Bases, pp. 275–286. Morgan Kaufmann Publishers Inc (1998)
16. Tang, M.W.: Efficient and scalable monitoring and summarization of large probalistic data. In: SIGMOD 2013 PhD Symposium, pp. 61–66. New York (2013)
17. Zhang, C.C.: Design and optimize big-data join algorithms using MapReduce. University of Science and Technology of China (2014)
18. Mitzenmacher, M.: Compressed bloom filters. IEEE/ACM Trans. Networking **10**(5), 604–612 (2001)
19. Xiao, M.Z.H., Dai, Y.F., Li, X.M.: Split Bloom filter. Acta Electronica Sinica **32**(2), 241–245 (2004)
20. Poosala, V., Haas, P.J., Ioannidis, Y.E.: Improved histograms for selectivity estimation of range predicates. ACM SIGMOD Rec. **25**(2), 294–305 (1996)
21. Zhang, D.D.: Load balancing in MapReduce based on Maxdiff histogram. Zhengzhou University, (2015)
22. Wang, S.Z., Zhang, L., Zhang, Y.P., et al.: Natural language semantic construction based on cloud database. Comput., Mater. Continua **57**(3), 603–619 (2018)

Towards Effective Gait Recognition Based on Comprehensive Temporal Information Combination

Hefei Ling(✉), Jia Wu, and Ping Li

HuaZhong University of Science and Technology, Wuhan, China
{lhefei,wujia,lpshome}@hust.edu.cn

Abstract. In this paper, we propose a novel deep learning based framework to effectively combine CNN (Convolutional Neural Network) and LSTM (Long Short-Term Memory) to facilitate accurate gait identification. Distinguished from traditional methods based on spatial information, our framework can take both spatial information and temporal cures into account. Meanwhile, its architecture applies novel hybrid layering structure, whose first layer is based CNN and aims at extracting gait's spatial information. In the second layer, LSTM is used to obtain dynamic dependency among the gaits and thus achieve optimal modeling of sequential and spatial information of gait. Moreover, our architecture leads to (1) optimal contrastive loss and (2) maximized difference between inter-classes and minimized gap between intra-classes. Consequently, the recognition accuracy has been improved tremendously. Using the gait dataset CASIA-B test collection containing 124 subjects in different conditions and various views, our comprehensive experimental study demonstrates a variety of advantages over the state of the art approaches.

Keywords: LSTM · Gait recognition · Spatial-temporal information · CNN · Contrastive loss

1 Introduction

In recent years, biometric traits play a significant role in human identification. Most of static traits such as fingerprint [25] and iris have been used in reality. But these traits are limited by distance and the interaction with subjects [1]. However, there are still many challenges for applying gait recognition in the real world. Robust and discriminative features are important for the task of human identification for the co-factors (e.g. carrying condition, camera viewpoint, clothing, the variation of walking speed, walking surface and so on). The biggest challenge of gait recognition is viewpoint. The appearance of human changes drastically with the change of viewpoint. To solve the problem, many methods [2,4,24] are proposed. View-invariant features [2] have been proposed for viewpoint. It is a handcrafted feature which is always applied in ideal conditions. so it is impractical and rarely used in real life. Despite the view-invariant

X. Sun et al. (Eds.): ICAIS 2019, LNCS 11633, pp. 442–451, 2019.
https://doi.org/10.1007/978-3-030-24265-7_38

features, the 3D [4] gait information is another method proposed for the problem of viewpoint, because the sufficient information for 2D of any viewpoint can be extracted from 3D gait information. The problem of viewpoint will be easy to solve if we can get 3D information which includes all Angels of 2D-information. But the collecting of 3D information is not easy to finish for high expense for 3D cameras and complicated processing of images calibration. Cross-view is a practical way to solve the problem, it can be used in non-cooperation environment. Convolutional neural network (CNN) has been applied in lots of fields such as road traffic sign recognition [26]. The recent paper [24], a new CNN-based method analyses the features gotten from different views and captured the final decision. If the difference between two viewpoints is larger than 18°, the similarity between two features will decrease sharply.

Another challenge of gait recognition is the variation of the walking conditions. In previous paragraph, many methods have been proposed to solve the problem of viewpoint. But when the walking conditions is changed, the accuracy for these methods vary widely. the change of walking conditions becomes a challenge for gait recognition. There are many methods are compared with the method in the paper [5], results from these methods showed that the results under the condition with bags and coats are poor. The main reason is that these methods are lack of temporal information, which means that temporal information is not made full use of. And there are many other reasons such as the features are not robust and the dependent on appearance and so on. A large part of methods mentioned in the previous paragraph are dependent on GEIs [19–21]. GEIs are the average of a cycle of images about gait, so it's inevitable to lose a part of temporal information. It is urgent for a new way of extracting temporal information.

LSTM has high reputation in processing arbitrary length sequences, it has solved the problem of vanishing gradient [6] and successfully gotten the dependency from long-term sequence. Long-term dependency is also a significant part of gait. It has been applied extensively in nature language processing [22,23], human action recognition, handwriting generation and machine translation [23]. So, LSTM is available for extracting temporal information for gait recognition.

Contrastive loss is used in face verification [8], it shows that the contrastive loss is capable for adjusting the intra-classes and inter-classes. From what has been discussed above, it is also capable for solving the problem of gait recognition. We propose a new method of temporal information extraction for gait recognition and use LSTM in gait recognition to reserve the temporal information of gait and get an excellent accuracy. The combination of soft-max loss and contrastive loss helps for adjusting the distance between intra-class and inter-class which is useful for tackling the problem of viewpoints. The CNN method within LSTM balances the spatial information and temporal information and gets a better result, and LSTM leads to realize a end-to-end method for gait recognition.

The rest of paper is organized as follow: related work about LSTM and gait recognition is introduced in Sect. 2. After Sect. 2, our method is described in

Sect. 3. Then, experimental results are shown in Sect. 4. Finally, conclusion is drawn in Sect. 5.

2 Related Work

Much gait recognition work published in the literature can be divided into two categories including model-based [9–18] work and appearance-based [19–25] work. Model-based methods are focus on the physical traits about human such as limb length and body structure, the motion trail and walk speed also plays an important role in the method. But it is difficult to model precisely and the resolution in many videos are always low, the structure of body and face are not clear in most of time. Appearance-based methods are more liable to extract the gait temporal information and almost ignore the information about human body. The former pays much attention to the physical structure can't be used in common for which distinguish the structure of human body is hard. With the appearance-based methods and cross views mentioned in Sect. 1, we can get a better result compared to previous ones. But there are many methods concerning GEIs [19–21] to express the temporal information about gait. However, GEIs are the average of a cycle of images. Although GEIs can eliminate the effect of background and the color of clothes, it still ignores some sequential information. So, we consider to maintain the original temporal information from videos. And the LSTM is known for handing the temporal information.

The LSTM network is excellent for sequences task and it has been applied extensively in nature language processing [22–24], human action recognition, handwriting generation and machine translation [23,25]. There are three types of LSTM:

The input of this type of LSTM is a sequence and the output is also a sequence.

The input is a sequence but the output of the LSTM is the label of the sample.

Input is a simple sample, the output is a sequence.

In machine translation, two LSTM are combined, the first is to represent the semantic vector, the second is to generate an output semantic sequence. Here we joint LSTM and CNNs which learn the projections with different viewpoints, it is a practical way to solve the problem of viewpoints and represent the specific spatial and temporal information.

3 Method

The overall process is illustrated in Fig. 1. Spatial information of gait is a basic feature for gait recognition, it is gained from pre-trained CNN. The architecture of CNN method is combined with five convolutional and two fully connected layers. Spatial information is the feature of an image which can be thought as a problem of classification. The feature from pre-trained CNN is a vector with

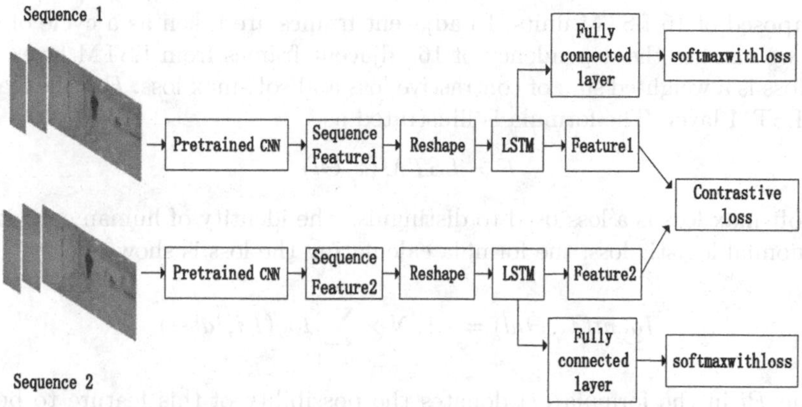

Fig. 1. The overall process of our method. The pretrained CNN in the figure is that the CNN trained to extract spatial features for gait, the architecture of it is described in detail latter in the paper. The sequence feature is a sequence of features that extracting from a sequence of raw frames by pretrained CNN. Reshape is used to reshape the sequence features. Then LSTM takes a sequence of features as input and computes the dependency for a sequence. The feature 1 and feature 2 is the long-time dependency from two sequences, then the features are connected by contrastive loss, their Euclidean distance is computed as a part of cost. At the same time the features enter fully connected layer and get high-dimensional feature then go to the soft-max layer and get the other part of cost.

4096 dimensions. We take the a sequence of vectors from a cycle of images about gait as an input of LSTM layer (Fig. 2).

The process is divided into two stage. The first stage is to train the CNN we used to extract the spatial information. And the second stage is to train the overall network. Spatial features sent to LSTM layer are extracted from the first fully connected layer of pre-trained CNN. The features are from a cycle of raw frames which include 16 adjacent frames from one video. They are reshaped to $16 \times 1 \times 4096$, because they are all tackled by LSTM layer and the LSTM layer

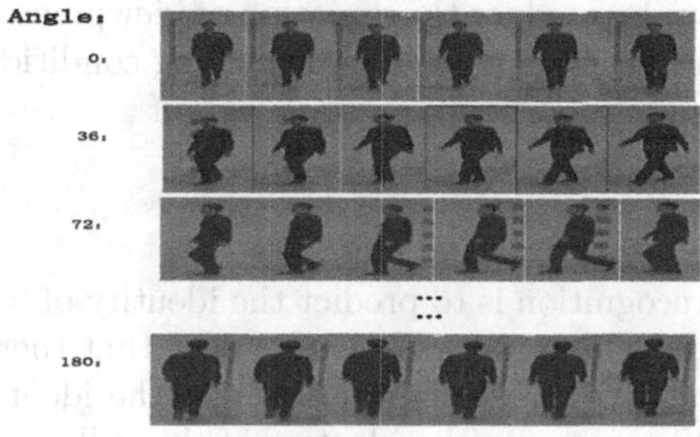

Fig. 2. The raw frames we used in the paper.

is composed of 16 LSTM units, 16 adjacent frames are taken as a cycle of gait. Then we can get the dependency of 16 adjacent frames from LSTM layer. The joint-loss is a weighted sum of contrastive loss and soft-max loss. F is the feature from LSTM layer. The formula is illustrated as:

$$F = LSTM(x, \Theta l) \tag{1}$$

The soft-max loss is a loss used to distinguish the identity of human gait, it is a multinomial logistic loss, the formula calculating the loss is shown below:

$$Ident(fi, \Theta id) = -1/N \times \sum_{n=1}^{N} log(Pi, label) \tag{2}$$

The Pi in the formula (7) donates the possibility of this feature to be the $i-th$ kind of class in the label. N denotes the number of classes. And another loss, Θid is the parameter of network and is updated by stochastic gradient descent. The formula of contrastive loss is shown as following:

In the formula, yij = 1 means that the sample i and j is from the same class. Otherwise, if the value is Yij −1, then they are not from the same class. our goal is to reduce the absolute value of distance between i and j from the same class. And when i and j are from different classes. Then the distance is be maximized. $Theta$ is the parameters from contrastive loss layer. It is effective in the verification of gait, and improves the accuracy in some extent. The final loss is illustrated as the formula:

$$Loss = \sigma \times Ident(f, \Theta id) + (1 - \sigma) \times Verif(fi, fj, Yij, \Theta ve) \tag{3}$$

In the formula, we can see two losses work together in the final loss. We should choose a proper value of σ. Then the final loss cam work excellently. If the parameter is not proper the effect may be worse than soft-max loss only. The contrastive loss in the network assist the soft-max loss which can only classify different classes in small difference, it is clear that soft-max is not sensitive to slight difference. We can conclude the second stage of our algorithm as following: Our method joints the CNN, LSTM and two kinds of loss. Firstly, the jointing of CNN and LSTM balances the spatial and temporal information. Secondly, soft-max loss is combined with contractive loss, and they are jointed with LSTM. The combination of the two loss reduce the variation of viewpoints. The participation of LSTM improves the accuracy of changing walking conditions, and contrastive loss solves the problem of viewpoints in some extent.

4 Experiments

The purpose of gait recognition is to predict the identity of human gait from the gallery which is composed of gait samples. Suppose that there is a probe X and N identities in the gallery. The formulation to get the identity is (X, Yi (i = 1, 2, 3, 4, ... N) = P), Yi represents the identity of the gallery, P is the possibility of X = Yi. Find the most similar one in the probe set to get the identity. It is illustrated in Fig. 3.

Algorithm. the second stage training algorithm
procedure Working mechanism of LSTM
and two kinds of loss
Input $\eta(t)$ the learning rate
$S_{x1}, S_{x2} .... S_{xN}$ the features from CNN
of a sequence of raw frames
of another sequence of raw frames
F_1, F_2 the feature extracted from LSTM
W_l is a vector of LSTM parameters
C_i the value of cell of LSTM
H_i the output of hidden layer of LSTM
Output L loss of the network
calculate the temporal feature from LSTM
for (i =1 to N) do
    (C_{1i}, H_{1i})=LSTM$(C_{1i-1}, H_{1i-1}, S_{1i}, W_l)$
    (C_{2i}, H_{2i})=LSTM$(C_{2i-1}, H_{2i-1}, S_{2i}, W_l)$
F1=H_{1i}
F2=H_{2i}
calculate the loss, S is the soft-max loss
C is the contrastive loss
L= $\sigma\times$ S(F,Θid)+$(1-\sigma)\times$ C(F1,F2,Θve)
% back-propagation and update W_l
$\nabla F1 = \frac{\partial L1}{\partial F_1} \quad \nabla F2 = \frac{\partial L2}{\partial F_2};$
$V_1 = \nabla F1 \cdot \frac{\partial LSTM(C_{1i-1}, H_{1i-1}, S_{1i}, W_l)}{\partial w_1}$
$V_2 = \nabla F2 \cdot \nabla \frac{\partial LSTM(C_{2i-1}, H_{2i-1}, S_{2i}, W_l)}{\partial w_l}$
Calculate the derivative $\nabla W_l = V_1 + V_2$
Update $W_l = W_l - \eta(t) \cdot \nabla W_l$

4.1 Data Preparation

In our experiment, our proposed method is evaluated on the CASIA-B. CASIA-B is a gait datasets which contains 124 objects with various views in different conditions. There are 11(0, 18, 36, 54, 72, 90, ... 180) views and 10 sequences per object. Six of the 10 sequences is under normal working conditions (NM), and 2 of 10 are with coats, the rest are with bags. Here 2 of 6 NM, 1 of 2 in coats and 1 of 2 with bags are used in the phrase of test. And the rest are used in the phrase of train. Its a reasonable way to arrange the images for testing and training. CASIA-B is a collection of videos, silhouettes and GEI. But what we used here are videos for raw frames directly.

4.2 Evaluation on CASIA-B

There are three experiments done on CSIA-B. The dataset is divided into two parts here. There are 124 subjects in total. We take 50 subjects as training set, 24 as the validating set the rest as evaluation set.

The first experiment compares the performances of two networks. One of them is our method mentioned in Sect. 2. The overall process is shown in Fig. 1.

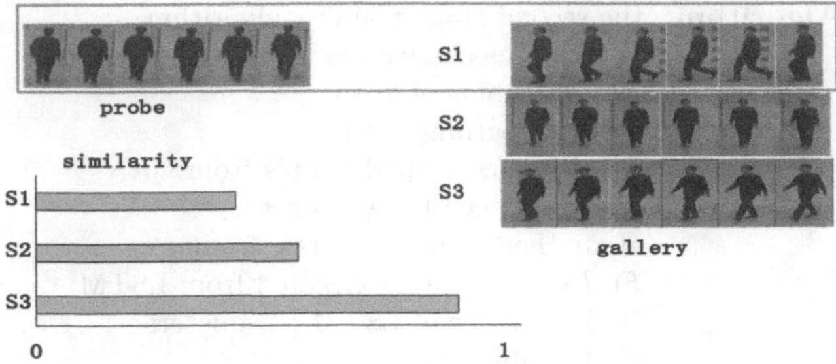

Fig. 3. The pipeline of gait recognition. The probe sample is seen as S3, they have the highest similarity.

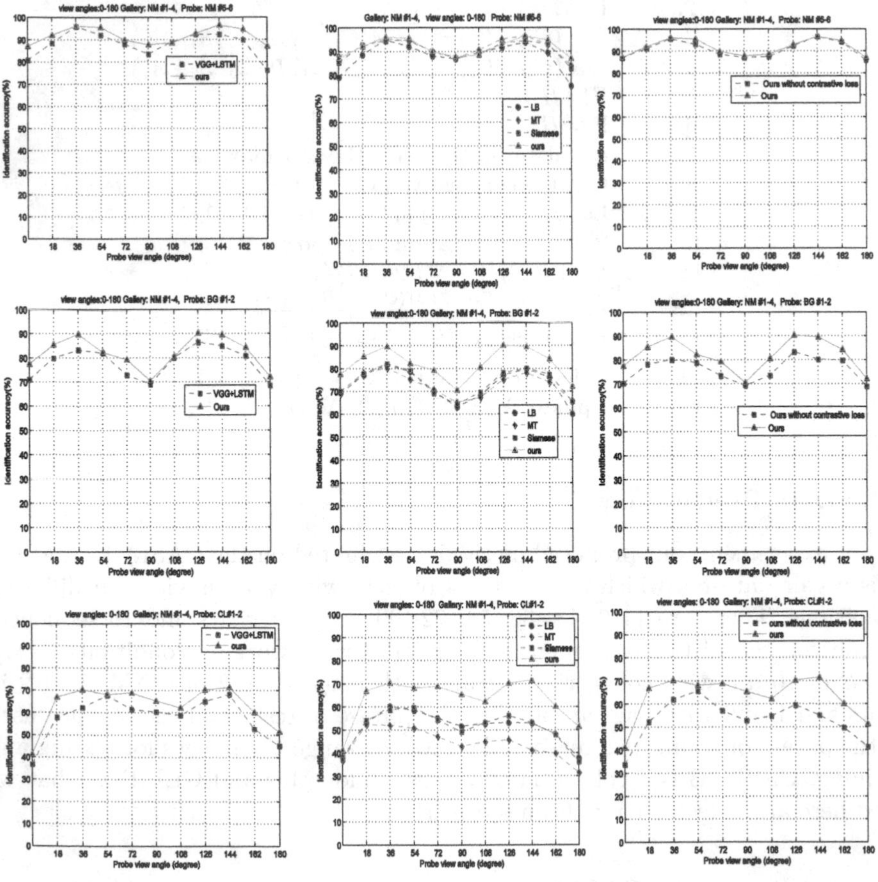

Fig. 4. The left column is the comparison of our method and VGG+LSTM. VGG+LSTM is a method. The middle column is the comparison of our method and many other methods. LB, MT and Siamese are three great methods in gait recognition. the right column is the comparison of our method and our method without contrastive loss. In these experiment, gallery set is NM1-4, probe sets are NM5-6, CL1-2 and BG1-2 respectively. NM: normal working, CL: with coats, BG: with bags

They are all the same except the CNN used for spatial information extraction. The CNN here we choose for spatial information extraction is a deep convolutional neural network. But nowadays which network is excellent in classification. We choose VGG here for its great achievement in classification. The overall process of this network is illustrated in Fig. 1.

Using our method and the network combining with VGG we can get the result shown in the left column of Fig. 4.

The result in left column of Fig. 4 shows that the network used for spatial information extraction is not the deeper the better. The spatial information of gait is not complex, and the main information we would like to obtain is the temporal information. It is not reasonable to choose deeper convolutional network.

The second experiment is a comparison of our method and other three experiments, the result is illustrated in the middle of Fig. 4. It is obvious from the result that our method has an obvious advantage under the condition of walking with coats and bags. Our method with LSTM improves the accuracy for the condition with coats and bags obviously.

In order to demonstrate the effect of contrastive loss, our method and our method without contrastive loss are compared in the last experiment. The result is shown in the right of Fig. 4. The result of our method outperforms the method without contrastive loss.

5 Conclusions

In this paper, we have investigated on a jointing network with LSTM and contrastive loss to extract robust and discriminative features. Firstly, the LSTM which uses raw frames is applied for gait identification, which makes the process end-to-end, and the LSTM in our method play the most important role for the dependency it obtains. After the effect of LSTM, contrastive loss which is excellent for obtaining discriminative features is employed to adjusting the distance of intra-class and inter-class. The results of experiments on CASIA-B show that our method is better than any other classical methods under the condition with bags and coats.

References

1. Bouchrika, I., Carter, J.N., Nixon, M.S.: Towards automated visual surveillance using gait for identity recognition and tracking across multiple non-intersecting cameras. Multimedia Tools Appl. **75**(2), 1201–1221 (2016)
2. Liu, N., Lu, J., Tan, Y.P.: Joint subspace learning for view-invariant gait recognition. IEEE Signal Process. Lett. **18**(7), 431–434 (2011)
3. Bashir, K., Xiang, T., Cross, G.S.: Correlation, view gait recognition using, strength. In: Proceedings of the DBLP British Machine Vision Conference, BMVC: Aberystwyth, UK, August 31 - September 3, 2010, pp. 1–11 (2010)

4. Zhao, G., Liu, G., Li, H., et al.: 3D gait recognition using multiple cameras. In: International Conference on Automatic Face and Gesture Recognition, pp. 529–534. IEEE Computer Society (2006)
5. Wu, Z., Huang, Y., Wang, L., et al.: A comprehensive study on cross-view gait based human identification with deep CNNs. IEEE Trans. Pattern Anal. Mach. Intell. **39**(2), 209–226 (2016)
6. Hochreiter, S., Schmidhuber, J.: Long short-term memory. Neural Comput. **9**(8), 1735–1780 (1997)
7. Zhang, C., Liu, W., Ma, H., et al.: Siamese neural network based gait recognition for human identification. In: IEEE International Conference on Acoustics, Speech and Signal Processing, pp. 2832–2836. IEEE (2016)
8. Sun, Y., Wang, X., Tang, X.: Deep learning face representation by joint identification-verification. Adv. Neural. Inf. Process. **27**, 1988–1996 (2014)
9. Lee, C.S., Elgammal, A.: Gait tracking and recognition using person-dependent dynamic shape model (2006)
10. Cunado, D., Nixon, M.S., Carter, J.N.: Using gait as a biometric, via phase-weighted magnitude spectra. In: Bigün, J., Chollet, G., Borgefors, G. (eds.) AVBPA 1997. LNCS, vol. 1206, pp. 93–102. Springer, Heidelberg (1997). https://doi.org/10.1007/BFb0015984
11. Bobick, A.F., Johnson, A.Y.: Gait recognition using static, activity-specific parameters. In: Proceedings of the 2001 IEEE Computer Society Conference on Computer Vision and Pattern Recognition. CVPR 2001, vol. 1, pp. I-423-I-430. IEEE (2001)
12. Bouchrika, I., Nixon, M.S.: Model-based feature extraction for gait analysis and recognition. In: Gagalowicz, A., Philips, W. (eds.) MIRAGE 2007. LNCS, vol. 4418, pp. 150–160. Springer, Heidelberg (2007). https://doi.org/10.1007/978-3-540-71457-6_14
13. Wang, L., Ning, H., Tan, T., et al.: Fusion of static and dynamic body biometrics for gait recognition. In: IEEE International Conference on Computer Vision, p. 1449. IEEE Computer Society (2003)
14. Yam, C., Nixon, M.: Model-based gait recognition. In: Li, S.Z., Jain, A. (eds.) Enclycopedia of Biometrics, pp. 633–639. Springer, Boston (2009)
15. Abdelkader, C.B., Davis, L., Cutler, R.: Stride and cadence as a biometric in automatic person identification and verification. In: Proceedings of the IEEE International Conference on Automatic Face and Gesture Recognition, pp. 372–377. IEEE (2002)
16. Ning, H., Tan, T., Wang, L., et al.: Kinematics-based tracking of human walking in monocular video sequences. Image Vis. Comput. **22**(5), 429–441 (2004)
17. Johnson, A.Y., Bobick, A.F.: A multi-view method for gait recognition using static body parameters. In: Bigun, J., Smeraldi, F. (eds.) AVBPA 2001. LNCS, vol. 2091, pp. 301–311. Springer, Heidelberg (2001). https://doi.org/10.1007/3-540-45344-X_44
18. Yam, C.Y.: Gait recognition by walking and running: a model-based approach 1–6 (2002)
19. Man, J., Bhanu, B.: Individual recognition using gait energy image. IEEE Trans. Pattern Anal. Mach. Intell. **28**(2), 316–322 (2005)
20. Ajayi, R.: Gait recognition using pose kinematics and pose energy image. Sig. Process. **92**(3), 780–792 (2012)
21. Chen, C., Liang, J., et al.: Frame difference energy image for gait recognition with incomplete silhouettes. Pattern Recogn. Lett. **30**(11), 977–984 (2009)
22. Graves, A.: Generating sequences with recurrent neural networks. Comput. Sci. (2013)

23. Sutskever, I., Vinyals, O., Le, Q.V.: Sequence to sequence learning with neural networks, vol. 4, pp. 3104–3112 (2014)
24. Chao, H., He, Y., Zhang, J., et al.: GaitSet: regarding gait as a set for cross-view gait recognition (2018)
25. Liu, J., Sun, N., Li, X., Han, G., Yang, H., Sun, Q.: Rare bird sparse recognition via part-based gist feature fusion and regularized intraclass dictionary learning. Comput. Mater. Continua **55**(3), 435–446 (2018)
26. Zhou, S., Liang, W., Li, J., Kim, J.-U.: Improved VGG model for road traffic sign recognition. Comput. Mater. Continua **57**(1), 11–24 (2018)

Research on Load Balancing Algorithm Optimization Based on Spark Platform

Suzhen Wang(✉), Zhanfeng Zhang, and Shanshan Geng

Hebei University of Economics and Business,
Shijiazhuang 050061, Hebei, China
wsuz@163.com

Abstract. Spark is an efficient big data processing platform based on memory computing. However, the default task scheduling algorithm in Spark does not take into account the difference in capability and resource usage of nodes under the Spark cluster. Therefore, an uneven load on the nodes might be resulted with the high-capability node in idle state and the low-capability node in high-load state which will affect the work efficiency. To this end, we propose an adaptive task execution node allocation algorithm based on the ant colony-simulated annealing algorithm. The proposed algorithm optimizes the Spark cluster task execution node allocation method based on the resource usage of the node, which is used to achieve the purpose of load balancing. Experiments show that in comparison with the task scheduling algorithm of the Spark cluster, the task scheduling algorithm proposed in this paper has a significant improvement in cluster load balancing and task completion time.

Keywords: Spark cluster · Task scheduling · Load balancing
Ant colony algorithm · Simulated annealing algorithm

1 Introduction

With the rapid development of Internet technology, the era of big data has come, and the amount of data generated by various industries has increased dramatically. Therefore, the convenient, practical, efficient and fast big data processing platform has become the goal pursued by people. As one of the important indicators to evaluate the performance of big data platform, load balancing plays a vital role in optimizing the performance of big data platform. So, there are many kinds of research on load balancing of big data processing platforms. The research on Hadoop load balancing mainly includes partition [1], data placement [2], task scheduling [3], etc. The research on load balancing of Storm mainly includes using multi-tenant load balancing scheduling strategy [4] and the use of resources aware scheduling algorithm [5], and so on. In recent years, Spark has become one of the mainstream big data processing platforms due to its application for real-time processing and iterative processing. So, how to improve the processing efficiency of the Spark platform and optimize the data processing performance of the Spark platform has become one of the focuses of people's research. Paper [6] proposes a scheduling strategy based on the heterogeneity of nodes, and the paper [7] used the filtering method to reduce the computational cost.

X. Sun et al. (Eds.): ICAIS 2019, LNCS 11633, pp. 452–465, 2019.
https://doi.org/10.1007/978-3-030-24265-7_39

However, the research on load balancing of Spark is relatively rare. This paper according to the usage of nodes and takes Spark load balancing as the main goal to do an in-depth study on the load imbalance which caused by the task scheduling on the Spark platform and give a solution.

2 Related Research

2.1 Spark Platform Ecosystem

Spark is a generic parallel framework for Hadoop MapReduce [8] and developed by the AMP Lab at the University of California, Berkeley. However, unlike MapReduce, the intermediate output of Spark is stored in memory, eliminating the need to read and write HDFS [9], so Spark can better adapt to the rapid processing of large-scale data.

The Spark platform ecosystem is very large, with Spark Core as the core, supports for reading data from multiple data sources and has a variety of resource scheduling managers including Standalone, YARN, Mesos, etc., as shown in Fig. 1:

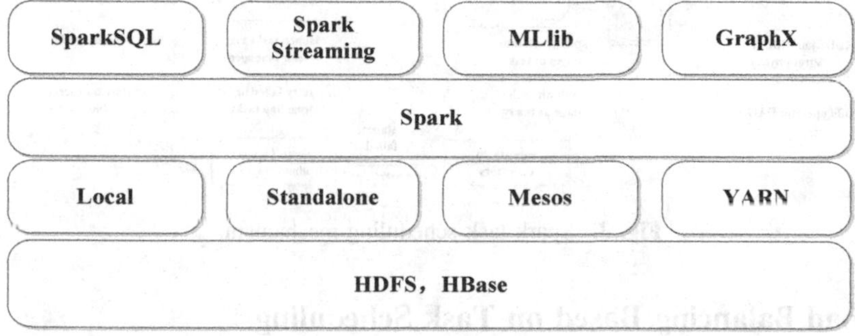

Fig. 1. Spark ecosystem.

2.2 Spark Overall Architecture

Spark uses the master-slave architecture. A cluster consists of a master node and multiple slave nodes. At the same time, Spark contains many components [10], as shown in Fig. 2:

2.3 Spark Task Scheduling Mechanism

As shown in Fig. 3, in the Spark platform, there are dependencies between the RDDs. These dependencies form a DAG [11]. The DAGScheduler performs Stage partitioning on the DAG formed by these dependencies, and generates a TaskSet based on each stage, then submits the TaskSet to the TaskScheduler. TaskScheduler is responsible for specific task scheduling. In this process, the task scheduling mechanism of Spark is as follows:

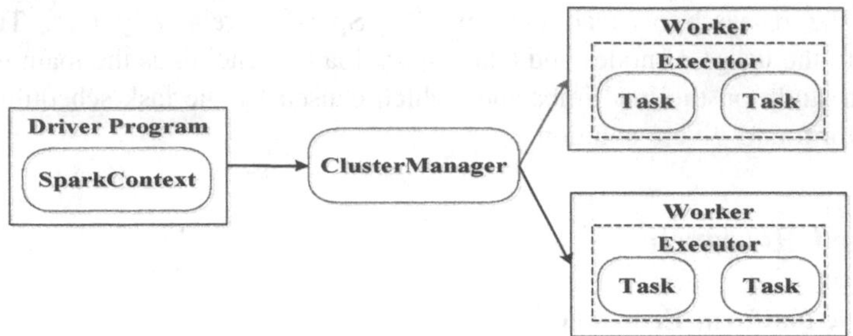

Fig. 2. Spark overall architecture.

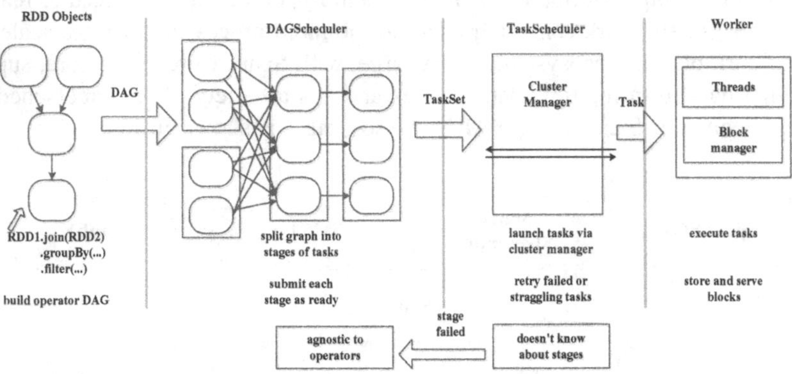

Fig. 3. Spark task scheduling mechanism.

3 Load Balancing Based on Task Scheduling

3.1 Problem Description

When performing task deployment on the Spark platform, the default way is to use the data locality-based task assignment method [12]. That is, the task is assigned to an execution node which follows the principle that the node with the highest data locality performs the task. However, the default way does not take into account the difference in capability and resource usage of nodes. In actual process however, due to dynamic changes of node resource caused by different task execution conditions of each node, there may be in circumstances that the computing power of each node and the load are both different. Therefore, when the task assignment is subsequently performed and the default scheduling mode is still used, the following scenario may occur: when the scheduler performs the task assignment, it is easy to ignore the dynamic changes of resources and load of each node because of the default allocation mode, which is prone to imbalance of node task assignment. In other words, current node resources are richer and the computing power is higher, but the task allocation is less with a low load, the other node has fewer remaining resources and weaker computing power, but the task allocation is more with a high load, which causes the load imbalance. Therefore, to solve the load imbalance problem caused by task scheduling of the Spark platform, this paper uses an ant colony-simulated annealing algorithm based on ant colony algorithm. In the algorithm, a reasonable task allocation strategy is used to find a relatively optimized task allocation mode, and the tasks to be executed are allocated to the computing nodes of the Spark cluster to achieve load balancing.

The Spark task assignment problem is described as follows: Assigning n independent tasks to m compute nodes by the task assignment scheme, and $n \gg m$. It means the total number of compute nodes in the Spark cluster is m, and the number of tasks to be executed is n, and the tasks are independent of each other, and each individual task can only be executed on one node. The goal of Spark task allocation is to distribute n relatively independent tasks to m compute nodes for execution so that each node in the calculation process is load balanced.

3.2 Building the Model

For the load balancing optimization problem to be solved, this paper uses the CPU usage and task volume of the node to represent the node load situation:

Definition 1: Establish the ratio relationship between the total task amount of node j and the total amount of all assigned tasks:

$$Tpoint_j = \frac{taskpoint_j}{\sum_{j=1}^{m} taskpoint_j} \tag{1}$$

In Eq. (1), $taskpoint_j$ represents the number of tasks of the node j.

Definition 2: The load condition of node is represented by *Load*, and Cm_j indicates the CPU usage of node j. The load condition of node is expressed as:

$$Load_j = \mu_1 \cdot Cm_j + \mu_2 \cdot Tpoint_j \tag{2}$$

In Eq. (2), μ_1, $\mu_2 \in (0,1)$ and $\mu_1 + \mu_2 = 1$.

Definition 3: The expected value of load balancing of node after all task scheduling is completed as *Ehope*:

$$Ehope = \frac{\sum_{j=1}^{m} Load_j}{m} \tag{3}$$

Definition 4: Establish the value of load deviation as *Loaderror*:

$$Loaderror = \sqrt{\frac{\sum_{j=1}^{m} (Load_j - Ehope)^2}{m}} \tag{4}$$

In Eq. (4), *Loaderror* indicates the degree of deviation between the current task allocation mode and the load balancing expectation value. That is, the smaller the *Loaderror* value is, the lower the load deviation degree of the allocation mode is, which indicates that the load balancing degree of the cluster is higher.

Definition 5: Define the task calculation speed of node as Vp_j, and the size of the task i as $tasklength_i$, then the processing time of the task on this node is:

$$Time_{i,j} = \frac{tasklength_i}{Vp_j} \tag{5}$$

4 Ant Colony-Simulated Annealing Algorithm Based on Load Balancing

4.1 Coding of Algorithmic

In the ant colony-simulated annealing algorithm, the algorithm coding method and decoding method required to be solved first:

According to the requirements of this paper, each ant represents a feasible solution of task scheduling. Suppose the number of tasks to be executed is set to $taskNum$ = 10, and the number of nodes that can perform the task is $nodeNum$ = 5, and the solution of an ant in the algorithm is as follows:

$$\begin{bmatrix} 1 & 0 & 0 & 0 & 0 \\ 0 & 0 & 1 & 0 & 0 \\ 0 & 1 & 0 & 0 & 0 \\ 0 & 0 & 0 & 1 & 0 \\ 0 & 0 & 0 & 0 & 1 \\ 0 & 1 & 0 & 0 & 0 \\ 0 & 0 & 1 & 0 & 0 \\ 0 & 0 & 0 & 1 & 0 \\ 1 & 0 & 0 & 0 & 0 \\ 0 & 0 & 0 & 0 & 0 \end{bmatrix}$$

In this matrix, the row subscript is labeled as the task number, the column subscript is labeled as the node number, and the matrix element as 1 indicates that the task is assigned to the node. The decoded code is shown in the following figure:

This paper employs the matrix to represent the load used by each task after executed on the node. The matrix is described as follows (Fig. 4):

$$\begin{bmatrix} Load_{1,1} & Load_{1,2} & Load_{1,3} & \cdots & Load_{1,m} \\ Load_{2,1} & Load_{2,2} & Load_{2,3} & \cdots & Load_{2,m} \\ Load_{3,1} & Load_{3,2} & Load_{3,3} & \cdots & Load_{3,m} \\ \cdots & \cdots & \cdots & \cdots & \cdots \\ Load_{n,1} & Load_{n,2} & Load_{n,3} & \cdots & Load_{n,m} \end{bmatrix}$$

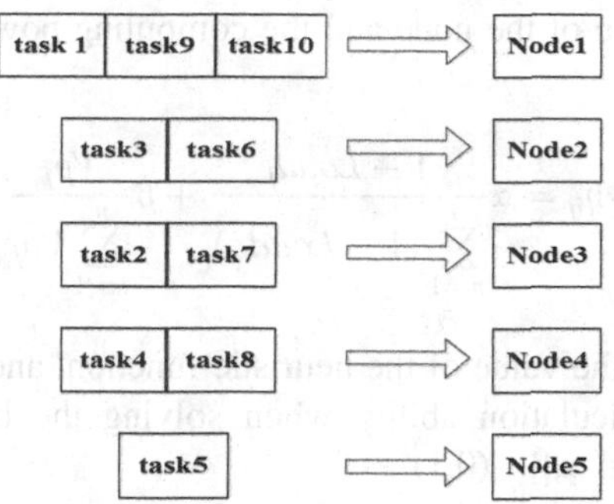

Fig. 4. Decoding.

In the matrix, $Load_{i,j}$ indicates the load condition of node j after task i is assigned to node j.

The execution time of each task on the node is represented by a matrix which is shown below:

$$\begin{bmatrix} Time_{1,1} & Time_{1,2} & Time_{1,3} & \cdots & Time_{1,m} \\ Time_{2,1} & Time_{2,2} & Time_{2,3} & \cdots & Time_{2,m} \\ Time_{3,1} & Time_{3,2} & Time_{3,3} & \cdots & Time_{3,m} \\ \cdots & \cdots & \cdots & \cdots & \cdots \\ Time_{n,1} & Time_{n,2} & Time_{n,3} & \cdots & Time_{n,m} \end{bmatrix}$$

In this matrix, $Time_{i,j}$ indicates the execution time of task i on node j.

4.2 Algorithm Parameter Setting

Initial Pheromone Setting. In the traditional ant colony algorithm, the initial pheromone is often a fixed value. Papers [13, 14] have improved the initial pheromone setting. In this paper, based on the load balancing problem to be solved, the node pheromone is characterized using the current load situation and computing power, as defined below:

$$\tau_{ij} = \omega_1 \cdot (1 - Load_j) + \omega_2 \cdot Vp_j \tag{6}$$

In the above equation, τ_{ij} represents the pheromone for node j, ω_1 and ω_2 are the weights of the node's current load and node computing power in the pheromone calculation. Moreover, $\omega_1, \omega_2 \in (0,1)$ and $\omega_1 + \omega_2 = 1$.

Heuristic Function Setting. When the traditional ant colony algorithm is utilized to solve the TSP problem, the heuristic function indicates the degree of expectation that the ant will move from the current city to the next one. In this paper, to solve the load balancing problem based on task scheduling, the heuristic function is represented by the current load condition of the node and the computing power of the node, which is defined as follows:

$$\eta_{ij} = \alpha \frac{1 - Load_j}{\sum_{m=1}^{n} (1 - Load_m)} + \beta \frac{Vp_j}{\sum_{m=1}^{n} Vp_j} \tag{7}$$

In the Eq. (7), η_{ij} is the value of the heuristic function, and α, β are the weights of load case and node calculation ability when solving the heuristic function value, moreover, α + β = 1 and α,β ∈(0,1).

4.3 Node Selection Probability

For load balancing based on task scheduling, the node selection probability is determined by both the node pheromone and heuristic function, so the node selection probability is defined as follows:

$$P_{choose} = \xi_1 \cdot \frac{\tau_{ij}}{\sum_{j=1}^{m} \tau_{ij}} + \xi_2 \cdot \frac{\eta_{ij}}{\sum_{j=1}^{m} \eta_{ij}} \tag{8}$$

In the above equation, ζ_1, ζ_2 are the weights of the pheromone and the heuristic function.

4.4 The Fitness Function of Algorithm

In terms of the algorithm fitness function, the paper [15] uses time as the algorithm fitness function. For the load balancing based on task scheduling problem to be solved in this paper, a multi-objective function using load deviation and task execution time is proposed to deal with the problem.

$$\begin{cases} target = \lambda_1 \cdot Loaderror + \lambda_2 \cdot Time_{max} \\ Time_j = \sum_{i=1}^{n} Time_{i,j} \\ Time_{max} = max\{Time_1, Time_2, Time_3, \ldots, Time_j\} \end{cases} \tag{9}$$

In fact, the actual overall completion time of a task is determined by the node with the longest task completion time, which is the completion time of all tasks assigned to that node. In Eq. (9), $Time_j$ represents the task completion time of node j, and $Time_{max}$ represents the maximum of the task completion time of each node, that is the task completion time. Target is the value of the fitness function, λ_1, λ_2 are the weight values, and $\lambda_1, \lambda_2 \in (0, 1)$, $\lambda_1 + \lambda_2 = 1$.

4.5 Feasible Solution Optimization

After obtaining the local optimal solution by ant colony algorithm, the current local optimal solution is updated in order to avoid falling into the local optimal solution and improve the load balancing degree of the feasible solution. Firstly, the genetic algorithm [16] is employed to perform random node exchange on the current local optimal solution. Then the simulated annealing algorithm is used to determine whether to accept the new solution [17]. If the fitness function value of the new solution is lower than the original one, accept the new solution, otherwise judge whether to accept the new solution according to the Metropolis criteria: analyze whether new solution probability is greater than a threshold. If so, accept the new solution, otherwise reject [18]. When the new solution is accepted, the pheromone is updated according to the new solution.

The probability is calculated as follows:

$$\begin{cases} \Delta T = target_{new} - target_{old} \\ p_{allow} = \begin{cases} e^{-\frac{\Delta T}{T}}, \Delta T > 0 \\ 1, \Delta T < 0 \end{cases} \end{cases} \tag{10}$$

$target_{new}$ represents the value of fitness function of the new generated solution obtained, P_{allow} indicates the probability of the new solution will be accepted, that is, when the new solution fitness function is lower than the original solution, then the new solution will be accept, otherwise the new solution will be accept according to the probability.

4.6 Update the Pheromone

In the term of updating the pheromones, different improvements are used in papers [19–21] to update the pheromones. In this paper, the pheromone of each node is updated by combining local update and global update. The local pheromone update is performed first, then the global pheromone update is performed according to the specific situation of the feasible solution.

For the load balancing problem based on task scheduling, the larger the *target* value is, the smaller the impact of task allocation strategy on updating pheromone. So the pheromone increment can be expressed as:

$$\Delta\tau_{ij}^{k} = \frac{Q}{target_k} \tag{11}$$

After all the ants have completed a single optimization, the pheromone intensity of each node is gradually reduced by volatilization, at the same time the ants release the pheromone, moreover, in order to improve the convergence speed of the algorithm, a load balancing factor which named as φ is used to strengthen the pheromone improvement effect of the current optimal solution. So the pheromone is updated as follows:

$$\begin{cases} \tau_{ij}(t+1) = (1-\rho)\cdot\tau_{ij}(t) + \Delta\tau_{ij} + \Delta\tau', 0<\rho<1 \\ \Delta\tau_{ij} = \sum_{k=1}^{o} \Delta\tau_{ij}^{k} \\ \varphi = \frac{\Delta Load_j}{\sum_{j=1}^{m} (\Delta Load_j)} \\ \Delta\tau' = \begin{cases} \varphi\cdot\Delta\tau_{ij}, (\textit{the optimal solution}) \\ 0, \textit{otherwise} \end{cases} \end{cases} \quad (12)$$

In the above equation, $\Delta Load_j$ is the load variation of the each node of the current optimal solution, o is the total number of ants.

4.7 Algorithm Flow

The algorithm flow is shown in Fig. 5:

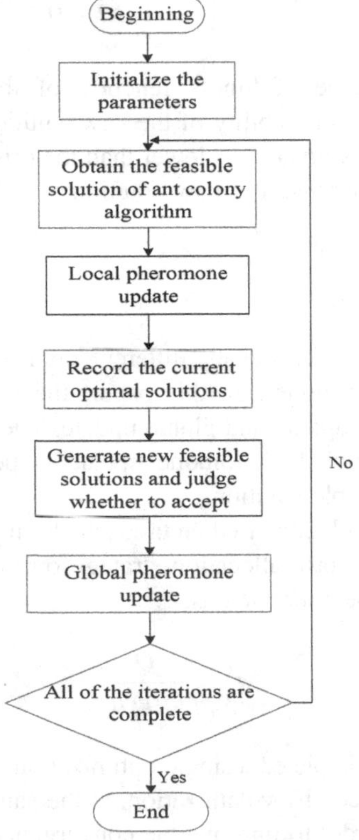

Fig. 5. Algorithm flow chart.

Step 1. Initialize the algorithm related parameters.
Step 2. Assigning the tasks to nodes to obtain the feasible solution of ant colony algorithm,then the local pheromone update is performed and the local optimal solution of current iteration is obtained according to the fitness function.
Step 3. Generate a new solution based on the replacement rules, decide whether to accept the new solution according to the Metropolis guidelines.
Step 4. Update the global pheromone.
Step 5. Determine whether the maximum number of iterations is reached or not. If the condition is met, the algorithm ends, otherwise the iteration continues.

5 Experimental Verification and Analysis

The experiment in this paper is divided into two parts:

1. Verify the performance of the algorithm in a simulated environment.
2. Validate the proposed algorithm in the cluster environment.

5.1 Simulation Verification Experiment

In this paper, the performance of the ant colony-simulated annealing algorithm and the ant colony algorithm is compared in a simulated environment. Experimental results are shown in the following figures:

As can be seen from Fig. 6, the fitness function value obtained by the ant colony-simulated annealing algorithm is smaller than the one obtained by the ant colony algorithm. At the same time, it can be seen from Fig. 7 that the optimal solution completion time obtained by the ant colony-simulated annealing algorithm is shorter than the optimal solution completion time obtained by the ant colony algorithm. Therefore, the ant colony-simulated annealing algorithm has a better effect on solving the load balancing problem based on task scheduling.

5.2 Cluster Verification

The experimental verification of the load balancing optimization algorithm proposed in this paper is carried out in a cluster environment, which mainly includes effectiveness verification of the load balancing strategy in terms of two aspects of load deviation and overall task completion time.

Experimental Environment Configuration. A Spark cluster consists of six nodes, one of which serves as the master node and the others as slave nodes of the Spark cluster and use the Spark 2.0.1 as the computing framework.

Comparison of Experimental Results. This article uses different sized product evaluation data-sets for performance comparison. Results are shown in the following figures:

It can be seen from Fig. 8 that when the workload is small, the load balancing degree of the proposed algorithm is not much different from that of the algorithm of Spark. When the data volume exceeds 1G, the load deviation degree of the proposed

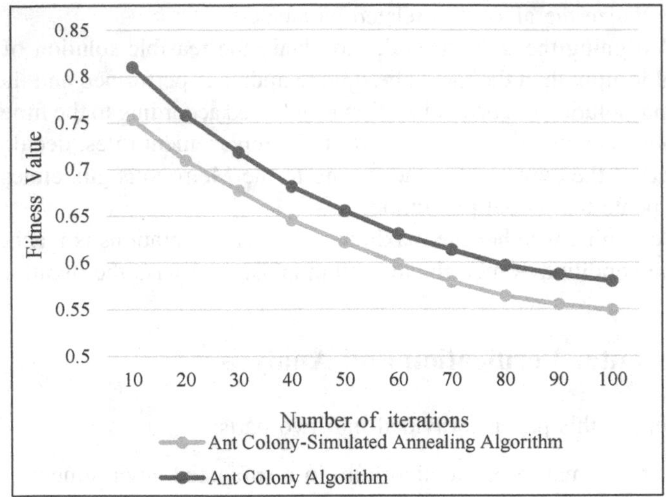

Fig. 6. The comparison of fitness function values.

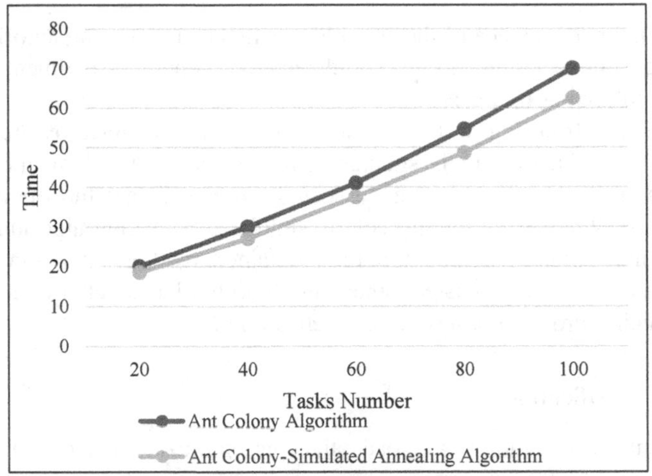

Fig. 7. The comparison of task completion time.

algorithm increases slowly. Compared with the load balancing algorithm that comes with Spark, it has obvious advantages.

As can be seen from Fig. 9 that when the task volume is small, the proposed algorithm has a small difference in the running time of the task compared with the algorithm of Spark. When the amount of data exceeds 1G, the proposed algorithm algorithm is more effective in terms of task running time than Spark's own algorithm.

From Figs. 8 and 9, it can be seen that in comparison with Spark's own algorithm, the algorithm proposed in this paper has more obvious advantages in terms of load deviation and the task running time.

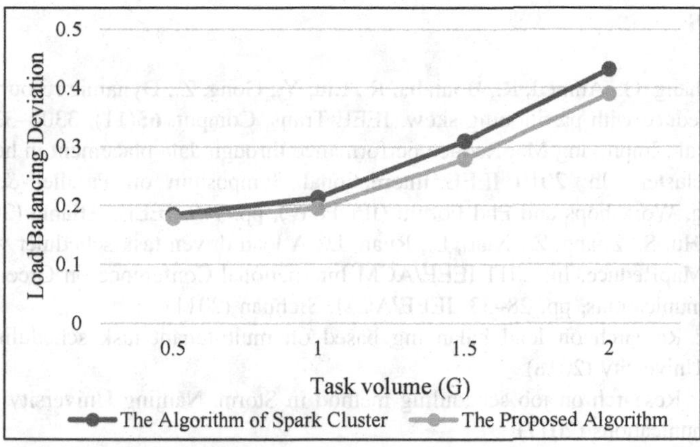

Fig. 8. Load deviation comparison.

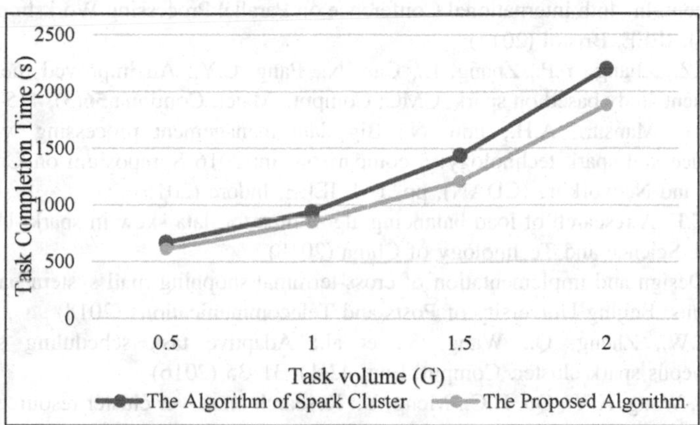

Fig. 9. Task running time comparison.

6 Conclusion

Spark is one of the most mainstream distributed computing frameworks. The performance of Spark computing affects the efficiency of big data processing and analysis. Aiming at the load imbalance problem on Spark clusters, this paper proposes an optimized Spark load balancing algorithm to optimize it. Experiments show that the algorithm not only ensures the load balance of the Spark cluster, but also reduces the overall running time of the task. The next step of this paper will continue to optimize the calculation of Spark cluster load balance, making task assignment more efficient.

Acknowledgements. This paper is partially supported by the Education technology Foundation of the Ministry of Education (No. 2017A01020), and the Major Project of the Hebei Province Education Department (No. 2017GJJG083)

References

1. Liu, Z., Zhang, Q., Ahmed, R., Boutaba, R., Liu, Y., Gong, Z.: Dynamic resource allocation for MapReduce with partitioning skew. IEEE Trans. Comput. **65**(11), 3304–3317 (2016)
2. Xie, J., et al.: Improving MapReduce performance through data placement in heterogeneous Hadoop clusters. In: 2010 IEEE International Symposium on Parallel & Distributed Processing, Workshops and Phd Forum (IPDPSW), pp. 1–9. IEEE, Atlanta (2010)
3. Mao, H., Hu, S., Zhang, Z., Xiao, L., Ruan, L.: A load-driven task scheduler with adaptive DSC for MapReduce. In: 2011 IEEE/ACM International Conference on Green Computing and Communications, pp. 28–33. IEEE/ACM, Sichuan (2011)
4. Shi, K.L.: Research on load balancing based on multi-tenant task scheduling in storm. Xinjiang University (2018)
5. Liu, M.Q.: Research on job scheduling method in Storm. Nanjing University of Posts and Telecommunications (2017)
6. Zhang, X.W., Li, Z.H., Liu, G.S., Xu, J.J., Xie, T.K., Nees, J.P.: A spark scheduling strategy for heterogeneous cluster. CMC: Comput., Mater. Continua **55**(3), 405–417 (2018)
7. Liu, W., Li, Z., Zhou, Y.: An efficient filter strategy for theta-join query in distributed environment. In: 46th International Conference on Parallel Processing Workshops (ICPPW), pp. 77–84. IEEE, Bristol (2017)
8. Wang, S.Z., Zhang, Y.P., Zhang, L., Cao, N., Pang, C.Y.: An improved memory cache management study based on spark. CMC: Comput., Mater. Continua **56**(3), 415–431 (2018)
9. Verma, A., Mansuri, A.H., Jain, N.: Big data management processing with Hadoop MapReduce and spark technology: a comparison. In: 2016 Symposium on Colossal Data Analysis and Networking (CDAN), pp. 1–4. IEEE, Indore (2016)
10. Huang, C.J.: A research of load balancing algorithms for data skew in spark. University of Electronic Science and Technology of China (2018)
11. Ma, S.: Design and implementation of cross-terminal shopping mall system based on web components. Beijing University of Posts and Telecommunications (2018)
12. Yang, Z.W., Zheng, Q., Wang, S., et al.: Adaptive task scheduling strategy for heterogeneous spark cluster. Comput. Eng. **42**(1), 31–35 (2016)
13. Liu, W.J., Wang, X.Y., Qu, H.C., Meng, Y.: Research on server cluster resource scheduling based on improved ant colony algorithm. Microelectron. Comput. **33**(03), 98–101 (2016)
14. Song, X.Q., Gao, L., Wang, J.P.: Job scheduling based on ant colony optimization in cloud computing. In: 2011 International Conference on Computer Science and Service System (CSSS), pp. 3309–3312. IEEE, Nanjing (2011)
15. Tawfeek, M.A., El-Sisi, A., Keshk, A.E., Torkey, F.A.: Cloud task scheduling based on ant colony optimization. In: 2013 8th International Conference on Computer Engineering & Systems (ICCES), pp. 64–69. IEEE, Cairo (2013)
16. Cao, Y., Liu, Y.J., Yu, Y.: Task scheduling and optimization of cloud computing based on genetic algorithm and ant colony algorithm. J. Jilin Univ. (Science Edition) **54**(05), 1077–1081 (2016)
17. Qin, J., Dong, Q.Q., Hao, T.S.: Improvement of algorithm for cloud task scheduling based on ant colony optimization and simulated annealing. Comput. Technol. Dev. **27**(03), 117–121 (2017)
18. Zhang, H.R., Chen, P.H., Xiong, J.B.: Task scheduling algorithm based on simulated annealing ant colony algorithm in cloud computing environment. J. Guangdong Univ. Technol. **31**(03), 77–82 (2014)

19. Sun, W., Zhang, N., Wang, H., Yin, W., Qiu, T.: PACO: a period ACO based scheduling algorithm in cloud computing. In: 2013 International Conference on Cloud Computing and Big Data, pp. 482–486. IEEE, Fuzhou (2013)
20. Gupta, A., Garg, R.: Load balancing based task scheduling with ACO in cloud computing. In: 2017 International Conference on Computer and Applications (ICCA), pp. 174–179. IEEE, Doha (2017)
21. Jia, R.X.: Research on hybrid task scheduling algorithm simulation of ant colony algorithm and simulated annealing algorithm in virtual environment. In: 2015 10th International Conference on Computer Science & Education (ICCSE), pp. 562–565. IEEE, Cambridge (2015)

A System for Calculating the Amount of Motion Based on 3D Pose Estimation

Yu Huo[1], Liming Zou[1], Min Gao[1], Jun Wang[1], Xin Guo[2], and Jiande Sun[1(✉)]

[1] School of Information Science and Engineering, Shandong Normal University, Jinan, China
jiandesun@hotmail.com

[2] Shandong Hai Yi Digital Technology Co., Ltd., Jinan, China

Abstract. We designed a human motion statistics system, which is used to count users' physical activity. The system is based on the recognition of human action, which depends on 3D human pose estimation. We combine the probability model of 3D human pose with the multi-layer CNN architecture to obtain the 3D human pose estimation. Then, different actions are defined by the proportion of distance between each joint, and the amount of action is counted. The total calories burned during exercise are obtained by calculating the calories consumed in each action. Our system is simple and convenient, and can be used in many situations. The experimental results show that our system achieved the desired results.

Keywords: Deep learning · Action recognition · Motion statistics

1 Introduction

Computer vision has been working on human action recognition for many years. Analyzing and recognizing different actions from video data is very important in many visual applications. For example, in the field of security monitoring, human action recognition is used in the video monitoring system, which can provide automatic warning for emergencies. It has important significance in urban security, fire protection and traffic dispatch. In the field of intelligent monitoring, it can provide an alarm for timely rescue when the elderly or children fall or make dangerous behavior. To a certain extent, it can solve the problem that some contemporary people have no time to take care of the elderly and children. In the field of healthcare, the degree of injury to the patient's leg can be analyzed by studying the performance of human gait, to make a best treatment plan. In the field of virtual reality technology, the popular somatosensory games and virtual dressing rooms among young people are all the applications of human action recognition technology.

However, in the field of calculation the amount of exercise, the research is relatively simple. For example, recently popular sports bracelet, the movement recognition is not accurate, resulting in the step results are not accurate. We have designed an application system to count users' amount of exercise by recognizing and counting actions. Ordinary cameras are used as data acquisition equipment, and a combined

X. Sun et al. (Eds.): ICAIS 2019, LNCS 11633, pp. 466–476, 2019.
https://doi.org/10.1007/978-3-030-24265-7_40

method based on the 2D coordinate detection and 3D pose estimation of a single RGB image is used. The two tasks mentioned above are processed through the combined reasoning of the 2D and 3D coordinate position estimation. The probabilistic model of 3D human posture is combined with the multi-layer CNN architecture to obtain the 3D human posture estimation. And then, different actions are defined by using the distance proportional relation between each joint when the human do the actions. This part of the content will be introduced in Sect. 3.

In this paper, the application of action recognition is based on action recognition, and action recognition is based on 3D pose estimation of human body. Estimating a person's 3D pose from an RGB image is a challenging problem in computer vision. It involves dealing with two issues. Firstly, the position coordinates of each joint of the human body need to be obtained from the image. However, different cameras have different perspectives, and there are occlusion problems in the external and itself, or the changes in clothing, body shape and lighting lead to unpredictable changes in visual appearance, which makes this problem full of ambiguity. Secondly, the conversion of 2D coordinates of human joint positions into 3D from image is still an unknown problem. In order to find the correct 3D pose that matches the image, it is often necessary to inject other information in the form of a 3D geometric pose priors and temporal or structural constraint [1].

In Sect. 3, we introduce the network architecture and the model of the system, and introduce the process of count users' physical activity. In Sect. 4, the good experimental results of the system are demonstrated.

2 Related Work

The method of action recognition based on 3D pose estimation first needs to get the 3D pose estimation as accurately as possible, namely the coordinate position information of each joints of human body. Because the human body movement itself is non-rigid and has the characteristics of high degree of freedom, and the body parts are likely to produce their own cover during the movement, so the accurate extraction of human body structure characteristics is a key issue in research. A lot of early studies on human post estimation are based on trained models, which map directly to 3D human posture through recognition of image features (such as silhouette, HOG, or SIFT) rather than 2D coordinate estimation [2–6].

Recent direct methods take advantage of deep learning. Kanazawa et al. [7]. described human grid recovery (HMR), an end-to-end framework for recreating a complete 3D grid of the human body from a single RGB image. Unlike most current methods for calculating the position of 2D or 3D joints, a richer and more useful grid representation is proposed, which is parameterized by shape and 3D joint Angle. Minimizes the heavy projection loss of critical points [16].

Zhou et al. [8]. proposed a new method combining the sparse drive 3D geometric priors smoothing with time smoothing. A deep full convolution network is trained to predict the uncertainty of joint position in 2D. For the unknown situation of 2D joint, input image sequence. The position range of 2D joint was detected based on the heat map of CNN [17]. In combination with the 3D pose dictionary, the 3D posture sequence was recovered through the EM algorithm to achieve the 3D pose estimation.

Pavlakos et al. [9]. proposed an efficient direct prediction method based on convolutional network, and solved the problem of estimating the body posture and shape of 3D human body from a single color image by iterative optimization combined with the parametric statistical body model (SMPL) in the end-to-end framework. In this way, we can obtain very detailed 3D grid results, while only a few parameters need to be estimated, which is conducive to direct network prediction.

Howard et al. [10]. provided an efficient model called Mobilenets for mobile and embedded vision applications. Mobilenets is based on a streamlined architecture that uses deep separable convolution to build a lightweight deep neural network. We introduce two simple global hyperparameters to effectively balance the delay and accuracy. These two hyperparameters allow the model builder to select an appropriate size model for its application based on the constraints of the problem, and shows good performance in terms of resource and accuracy tradeoffs.

Junhui et al. [14] proposed that pyroelectric infrared (PIR) detectors can sense changes in infrared radiation caused by human movement. A low cost and low power consumption human motion counter is designed. The human motion signal generated by the PIR detector is amplified and then converted into analog-to-digital signal, and the signal generated by the PIR detector is analyzed by the single chip microcomputer. This paper designs a low-computation algorithm of the number peak, and carries on the real-time number peak. The test results show that the system can operate stably, accurately and assist indoor movement.

Zhichao et al. [15] proposed a pull-up counting method based on machine vision. Ada Boost algorithm was used to construct the Haar-like feature human face classifier, and the area and centroid coordinates of human face were obtained by calculating the image invariant moment. The motion foreground was extracted by using the mixed Gaussian background model, the gray level of ROI region was statistically changed in the image sequence, then the elliptic skin color was detected, and the image invariant moment was calculated to obtain the centroid coordinates of the face in the image sequence. The gray value and centroid coordinate changes of each frame are analyzed. The number of pull-up is obtained by comparing with the set threshold.

Wei et al. [11] used CNN to estimate human posture, and use sequential convolution architecture to express spatial information and texture information. Sequential convolution architecture is represented by the fact that the network is divided into multiple stages, each of stages has a part of supervised training to avoid the problem of too deep network optimization. In addition, multiple scales are used to process the input characteristics and responses of the same convolutional architecture at the same time, which can not only guarantee the accuracy, but also take into account the distance relationship between the parts.

3 System Overview

In this paper, we designed a human motion statistics system, which is used to count users' physical activity. We use a multi-stage CNN architecture that can be trained end-to-end to obtain human 3D pose estimation. The action is defined by the proportional relation between the coordinate information of each joint of the human body. Counting the actions and the energy consumed by the action is calculated by the formula of gravitational potential energy and the distance between the moving joints.

3.1 Network Architecture

Figure 1 shows the network framework of human posture estimation of the system. It is a multi-stage CNN architecture that can be trained end-to-end to estimate 3D joint information of the human body.

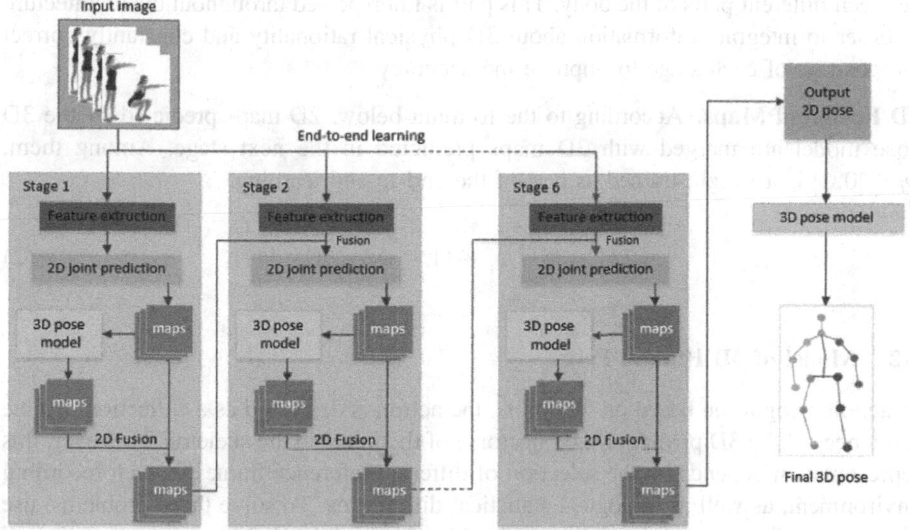

Fig. 1. The network framework of multi-stage human posture estimation.

As shown in Fig. 1, the 3D pose learned from 2D pose at each stage is injected with 3D posture information and then a new set of 2D maps is generated. The maps generated at the end of each stage are added as input to the next stage. From this, the accuracy of the maps increases progressively through the stages. The network architecture consists of 6 stages. Each stage consists of four parts. After the maps generated in the last stage are converted to 3D, the final 3D pose estimation is obtained.

2D Maps Prediction. We use a set of convolutional and pooling layers, similar to the original CPM architecture [11]. At each stage t and each position p, a map $m_t^p[u, v]$ for each $pixel(u, v)$ is returned, representing the joint center or position at any pixel [12]. For stage $t \geq 2$, the maps also includes information calculated in the previous stage. The collection of each input and output layer of the architecture grows larger and larger. After training, the CPMS returned the pixel estimates for the 2D position. To translate these maps into location information, make the following choices.

$$Y_{\mathrm{p}} = \underset{(u,v)}{\arg\max}\, m_p[u, v] \tag{1}$$

2D Maps Convert to 3D. Use the output of the previous section of 2D maps as input for this section 2D maps convert to 3D using the pre-training probability 3D model of human pose.

Convert to 2D Maps. The 3D pose estimation obtained in the previous part is projected back to the plane image to generate a new set of 2D maps. However, the 2D maps are different from the previous 2D maps, which encapsulate the 3D dependence between different parts of the body. This part is interspersed throughout the architecture in order to integrate information about 3D physical rationality and constantly correct the position of each stage to improve the accuracy.

2D Fusion of Maps. According to the formula below, 2D maps predicted by the 3D pose model are merged with 2D maps predicted in the next stage. Among them, $w_t \in [0, 1]$ is a weight trained as part of the end-to-end learning.

$$f_t^p = w_t * m_t^p + (1 - w_t) * \hat{m}_t^p \tag{2}$$

3.2 Model of 3D Human Pose

In action recognition based on 3D joints, the action is described as a collection of time sequences of the 3D position (3D trajectory) of the joints in the skeleton. However, this representation depends on the selection of different reference frames in each recording environment, as well as biological statistical differences. To solve these problems, use various coordinate system variations. Consider the joint Angle between any two joined limbs and represent the motion as a time series joint Angle. Next, the other coordinates in the skeleton are normalized by the head length. Each coordinate of the normalized pose vector is smoothed using a gaussian filter (mesh = 1). Pose is normalized to compensate for the biometric differences. By standardizing the data, the square of the length of the limb on the human skeleton is 1, solving the size difference [13].

3.3 Action Recognition

According to the anthropometry, skeleton of different people is different in length, position of joints, height ratio, etc., which results in different pose of each person during exercise. For the unknown action, the position information of each joint obtained from the previous 3D pose estimation of the human body is calculated to calculate the relative distance between the joints related to the action and whether the proportion is within the specified range and return the corresponding action. Such as

$$t = (ty\_8 - ty\_1)/(ty\_9 - ty\_8) > 1.73 \tag{3}$$

return to deep squats. *ty_8* is the distance of hip joint on the Y-axis, *ty_1* is the distance of neck joint on the Y-axis, and *ty_9* is the distance of knee joint on the Y-axis. The distribution of human joints is shown in Fig. 2.

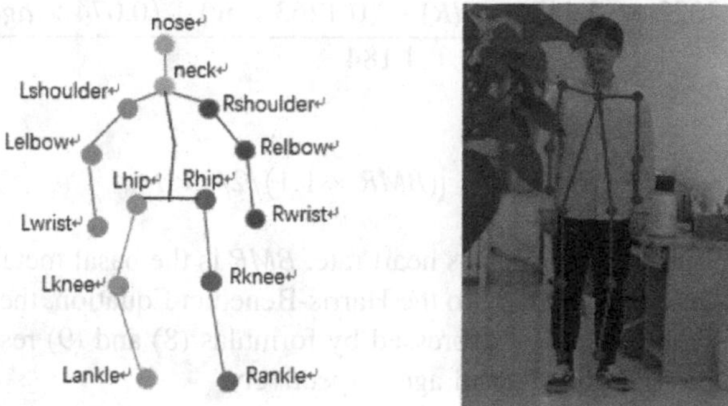

Fig. 2. The distribution of human joints. Left: Human joint histogram. Right: Real-time 3D pose estimation results of the system.

Since the proportion of each part of the body is different, the initial value after the user walks into the range of the lens is first taken, and the proportion range between the part with change and the part without change is taken.

3.4 Motion Statistics and Application

We design this system for people whose exercise time, ways and venues are limited. For example, office workers can do some simple exercises when watching TV at home after work. The elderly or patients recovering from injuries can exercise at home. Therefore, this system designed several simple actions, including deep squat, clap, chest movement, high-knee, and so on.

In our daily life, calorie consumption (*TCB*) includes both exercise and non-exercise consumption. Non-exercise burn refers to the amount of calories used to support resting metabolic rate (*BMR*), which is consumed in people all the time. It does not affect fat reduction, so the calculation of calories should be based on the net calories. As the name implies, Net calories burn (*NCB*) are simply exercise consumption, as in formula (4). Among them, *TCB* is the total calorie consumption. The *TCB* of males and females is different, which is associated with a person's weight, age and heart rate after exercise. *RMRCB* is the calorie consumption of resting metabolic rate. Resting metabolic rate (*RMRCB*) can be calculated by the Harris-Benedict Equation, as in formulas (7), (8) and (9).

$$NCB = TCB - RMRCB \tag{4}$$

$$TCB_m = \left[\frac{(-55.0969 + (0.6309 \times HR) + (0.1988 \times w) + (0.2017 \times age))}{4.184}\right] \times 60 \times t \tag{5}$$

$$TCB_f = \left[\frac{(-20.4022 + (0.4472 \times HR) - (0.1263 \times w) + (0.074 \times age))}{4.184}\right] \times 60 \times t \tag{6}$$

$$RMRCB = [(BMR \times 1.1)/24] \times t \tag{7}$$

In formulas (5) and (6), *HR* means heart rate. *BMR* is the basal metabolic rate and *t* is the time of movement. According to the Harris-Benedict Equation, the *BMR* of males and females is different, which is expressed by formulas (8) and (9) respectively. *w*, *h* and *age* represent weight, height and age respectively.

$$BMR_m = 13.75 \times w + 5 \times h - 6.76 \times age + 66 \tag{8}$$

$$BMR_f = 9.56 \times w + 1.85 \times h - 4.68 \times age + 665 \tag{9}$$

We asked seven males and seven females to calculate how many actions they could make in three minutes (0.05 h), and also recorded their heart rates (*HR*) after exercise. The 14 people are in different height, weight and age. Then, Using the above formula to calculate the *NCB* in each person's three minutes of exercise. Combine the *NCB* values of 14 people and obtain the *NCB* of each action by taking the average value. Table 1 shows the weight, height and age of the participants and the final data.

According to the *NCB* data of the weight, height, age and four actions of 7 males and 7 females in Table 1, The calorie consumption formulas of these four actions were obtained by multiple linear regression.

$$NCB_1 = -0.1134 - 0.0002w + 0.0007h + 0.0009age \tag{10}$$

$$NCB_2 = -0.1134 - 0.0002w + 0.0007h + 0.0009age \tag{11}$$

$$NCB_3 = 0.0373 + 0.001w - 0.0002h + 0.001age \tag{12}$$

$$NCB_4 = -0.2465 + 0.0005w + 0.0019h + 0.0008age \tag{13}$$

We used the existing data to do the residual analysis of the above four formulas (Fig. 3), and found that the results were basically within the confidence interval.

Therefore, we can approximately get the total number of calories by the number of each action and the number of calories (NCB_{final}) consumed by each action.

$$NCB_{final} = \sum count_i \times NCB_i \tag{14}$$

Table 1. The information of the participants and the value of calories each person consumed per action. NCB_1, NCB_2, NCB_3 and NCB_4 represent deep squat, clap, chest movement and high-knee respectively.

Male	w(kg)	h(cm)	Age	NCB_1	NCB_2	NCB_3	NCB_4
1	75	180	25	0.27	0.03	0.11	0.14
2	80	175	28	0.29	0.04	0.13	0.16
3	68	175	23	0.23	0.02	0.09	0.16
4	65	170	22	0.27	0.01	0.09	0.16
5	80	183	48	0.27	0.05	0.14	0.18
6	60	173	24	0.25	0.02	0.10	0.16
7	72	180	23	0.27	0.01	0.09	0.14
Female	w(kg)	h(cm)	Age	NCB_1	NCB_2	NCB_3	NCB_4
1	56	165	24	0.18	0.02	0.09	0.11
2	50	165	23	0.17	0.03	0.09	0.10
3	67	174	24	0.19	0.01	0.07	0.10
4	60	160	25	0.19	0.01	0.10	0.09
5	48	163	22	0.21	0.02	0.09	0.11
6	58	162	35	0.23	0.01	0.08	0.13
7	62	170	28	0.22	0.03	0.09	0.12

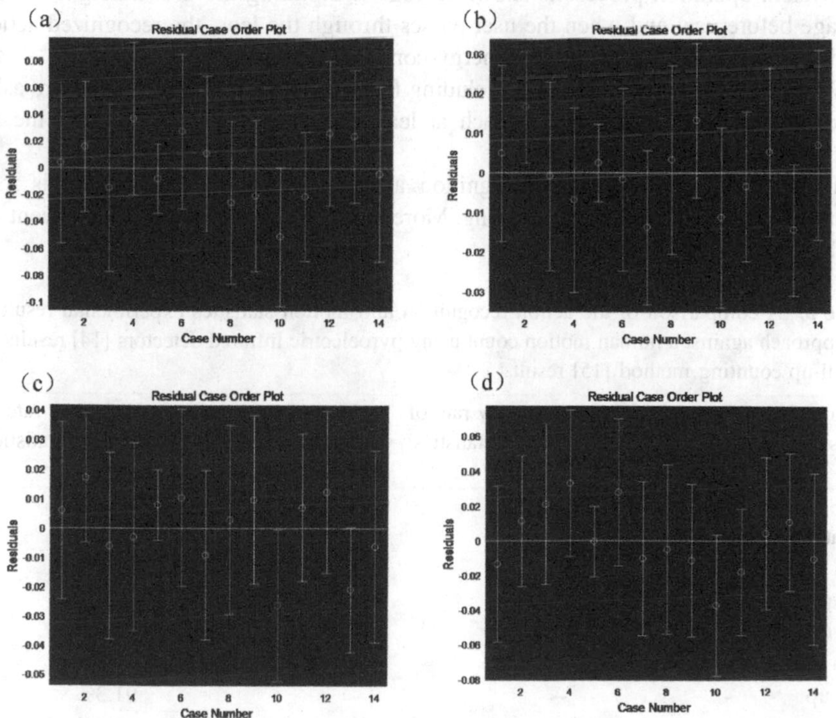

Fig. 3. Residual analysis chart. (a) deep squat (b) clap (c) chest movement (d) high-knee.

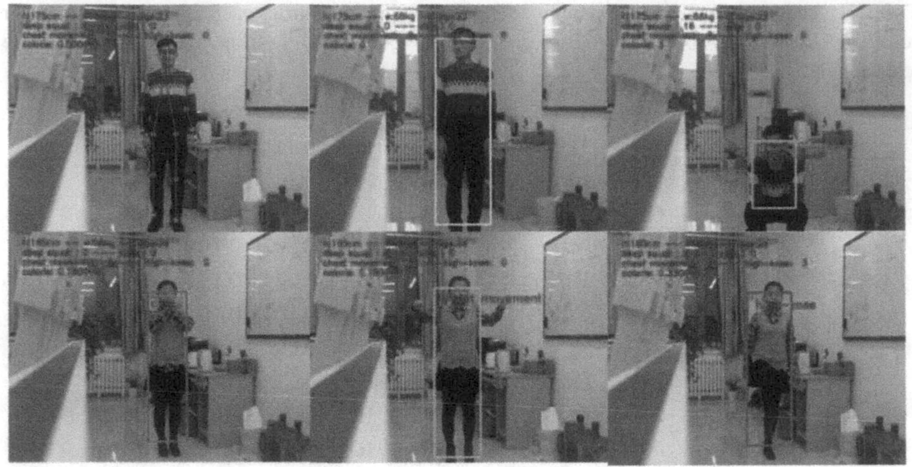

Fig. 4. The system operation process. We can identify the above actions and count each one. We can also count the amount of exercise.

4 Experiments

The system operation process is shown in Fig. 4. Inputting the user's height, weight, and age before use, and when the user passes through the lens, the recognized actions are displayed in real time, and the energy consumed are displayed.

We randomly tested 10 people, including five boys and five girls. They were asked to do the movements at random, each at least three times. Table 2 shows the test results.

Test results show that the recognition action is accurate. Our system is more accurate than other methods of counting. Moreover, our system is more convenient and flexible in our daily life.

Table 2. A comparison of the action recognition and motion statistics experimental results of our approach against a human motion count using pyroelectric infrared detectors [14] results and A pull-up counting method [15] results.

Action class	Recognition accuracy rate (ours)	Accuracy rate of motion statistics (ours)	Accuracy rate of motion statistics (PIR detectors)	Accuracy rate of motion statistics (pull-up)
deep squat	99%	100%	–	–
clap	98%	100%	–	–
chest movement	98%	100%	–	–
high-knee	98%	100%	–	–
pull-up	–	–	–	91.3%
average value	**98.25%**	**100%**	**98%**	**91.3%**

5 Conclusion

The human motion statistics system we designed can be used to count users' amount of exercise. Action recognition is based on 3D human pose estimation. The probabilistic model of 3D human pose is combined with the multi-layer CNN architecture. We treat 3D pose estimation as an iterative optimization problem, and the addition of 3D information is beneficial to the accuracy of 2D estimation. Then, use the ratio of distance between each joint to define the different actions. Calculate the number of calories burned during exercise by calculating the amount of energy consumed per action. In our daily life, it is convenient and practical. Due to limited conditions, the number of samples is small. So there will be some errors in the final result. In future work, we will try to increase the number of samples to get more accurate results. And we can add more actions as needed, as well as reduce the delay problem of action recognition by changing the method of action recognition.

References

1. Tome, D., Russell, C., Agapito, L.: Lifting from the deep: convolutional 3D pose estimation from a single image. In: CVPR 2017 Proceedings, pp. 2500–2509 (2017)
2. Agarwal, A., Triggs, B.: Recovering 3D human pose from monocular images. IEEE Trans. Pattern Anal. Mach. Intell. **28**(1), 44–58 (2006)
3. Elgammal, A., Lee, C.: Inferring 3D body pose from silhouettes using activity manifold learning[C]. In: CVPR 2004 Proceedings of the 2004 IEEE Computer Society Conference, p. 2, II-II. IEEE (2004)
4. Ek, C.H., Torr, P.H.S., Lawrence, N.D.: Gaussian process latent variable models for human pose estimation. In: Popescu-Belis, A., Renals, S., Bourlard, H. (eds.) MLMI 2007. LNCS, vol. 4892, pp. 132–143. Springer, Heidelberg (2008). https://doi.org/10.1007/978-3-540-78155-4_12
5. Mori, G., Malik, J.: Recovering 3D human body configurations using shape contexts. IEEE Trans. Pattern Anal. Mach. Intell. **28**(7), 1052–1062 (2006)
6. Sigal, L., Memisevic, R., Fleet, D.J.: Shared kernel information embedding for discriminative inference [C]. In: CVPR 2009. pp. 2852–2859. IEEE (2009)
7. Kanazawa, A., Black, M.J., Jacobs, D.W., et al.: End-to-end recovery of human shape and pose [C]. In: The IEEE Conference on Computer Vision and Pattern Recognition (CVPR) (2018)
8. Zhou, X., Zhu, M., Leonardos, S., et al.: Sparseness meets deepness: 3D human pose estimation from monocular video [C]. In: Proceedings of the IEEE Conference on Computer Vision and Pattern Recognition, pp. 4966–4975 (2016)
9. Pavlakos, G., Zhu, L., Zhou, X., et al.: Learning to estimate 3D human pose and shape from a single color image. In: The IEEE Conference on Computer Vision and Pattern Recognition (CVPR) (2018)
10. Howard, A.G., Zhu, M., Chen, B.: Mobilenets: efficient convolutional neural networks for mobile vision applications. arXiv preprint. arXiv:1704.04861 (2017)
11. Wei, S.E., Ramakrishna, V., Kanade, T., et al.: Convolutional pose machines [C]. In: Proceedings of the IEEE Conference on Computer Vision and Pattern Recognition, pp. 4724–4732 (2016)

12. Ramakrishna, V., Munoz, D., Hebert, M., et al.: Pose machines: articulated pose estimation via inference machines [C]. In: European Conference on Computer Vision, pp. 33–47 (2014)
13. Pitelis, N., Russell, C., Agapito, L.: Learning a manifold as an atlas [C]. In: Proceedings of the IEEE Conference on Computer Vision and Pattern Recognition, pp. 1642–1649 (2013)
14. Junhui, Y., Yonggui, D.: Human movement counter using pyroelectric infrared detectors. In: Chinese Journal of Scientific Instrument, pp. 33–38 (2012)
15. Zhichao, H., Wenming, Z.: A pull-up counting method based on machine vision. Sens. Actuators, A **53**(2), 113–125 (2018)
16. Daojian, Z., Yuan, D., Feng, L.: Adversarial learning for distant supervised relation extraction. Comput., Mater. Continua **55**(1), 121–136 (2018)
17. Zeyu, X., Qiangqiang, S., Yijie, W., Chenyang, Z.: Paragraph vector representation based on word to vector and cnn learning. CMC: Comput., Mater. Continua **055**(2), 213–227 (2018)

Design of Security Portrait Big Data Application System

Yin Hui(✉)

Shandong Judicial Police Vocational College, Jinan, China
183304836@qq.com

Abstract. A security portrait big data application system is introduced in this paper. Including its design requirements, business database, overall architecture, logical integration architecture and key technologies. The security portrait data application system has been used in the police industry. The application results show that the system can dynamically monitor and track the suspects. The system can effectively predict the crime situation, and has played a role in practice. It provides effective data support and assistant decision-making services for social security, crime search and prediction. And the system effectively improves the actual combat ability of police departments.

Keywords: Face recognition · Big data · Application system

1 Introduction

The public security system has mastered a large amount of video image resources in the process of peace city construction and discerning project construction. And the public security system has gradually changed from "passive investigation after the event" to "active early warning before the event "through" face recognition" technology. However, with the large increase of face data, the efficiency of face data retrieval is low and the ability of actual combat application mining needs to be improved. Portrait big data application system is designed to gather resources to serve actual combat applications.

2 System Requirements Analysis

2.1 Portrait Application

Structured processing of image data, such as ID card database, former research database, key database and fugitive database, is applied to portrait database through graph search technology and massive data retrieval technology.

2.2 Portrait Data Aggregation

The real-time data of the city are gathered to realize the intercommunication and information sharing of portrait resources and provide support for emergency treatment.

X. Sun et al. (Eds.): ICAIS 2019, LNCS 11633, pp. 477–486, 2019.
https://doi.org/10.1007/978-3-030-24265-7_41

2.3 Dynamic Portrait Construction

The key personnel portrait is put into storage. The typical concerned personnel trajectory is depicted subsequently. Early warning and judgment of high-risk behaviors are conducted. Such as theft, juvenile delinquency, terrorism, involvement in cases, drug-related and other security-related personnel, high-risk personnel, sensitive personnel, etc.

2.4 Static Portrait Construction

To realize portrait inquiry, identity information confirmation, identity information duplicate checking, identity confirmation of white washing personnel, etc.

3 System Business Database

The system database includes three kinds of service databases: face capture database, face registration database and blacklist database.

3.1 Face Capture Database

It contains information such as historical snapshot scene pictures, small face im-ages, structured face feature data, snapshot location and snapshot time, etc. The main business application scenario of this class library is image retrieval, image comparison and inquiring about the location, time and track of the portrait of the target personnel, etc.

3.2 Face Registration Database

It mainly import some large-scale portrait images, structured facial feature data and identity information, such as local social security portrait information base, local resident population information base and local mobile population information base in prefecture-level cities. After import, the main application scenarios are image retrieval, image comparison and identity information query to determine the identity of personnel.

3.3 Blacklist Database

The blacklist database contains face pictures of high-risk personnel, special personnel, structured face feature data and personnel identity information. The main application scenario is real-time human face comparison and early warning at each face bayonet.

Usually, the face capture database and the face registration database are used as static databases, suitable for later query and retrieval targets. The blacklist database is used as dynamic databases for real-time comparison and alarm. One or more blacklists can also be checked and controlled to form a targeted human face control database, which can be compared with front-end real-time videos or pictures for alarming.

4 Face Recognition Process

The system data stream includes face real-time comparison and face historical inquiry. The real-time comparison takes place in advance or in the process, and when the system finds that there are personnel in charge, the personnel on duty can react quickly. Historical inquiry is aimed at the investigation of key personnel after the event, and personnel information recorded by the system can be queried through suspicious personnel pictures.

4.1 Real-Time Video Face Comparison

The real-time video stream of the ordinary high-definition network camera or the face picture stream of the face capture unit will be extracted from the face feature data by the dynamic portrait algorithm under the face recognition server and compared with the face feature database in the blacklist database in real time, and the result of each comparison will be fed back to the platform.

4.2 Image Retrieval Face Comparison

After submitting face images and videos to be retrieved through the platform client. The face recognition server automatically extracts face image feature data and compares it with the face feature data in the face snapshot database or the face registration database. Finally, the comparison results are displayed on the platform.

5 System Overall Architecture

The system adopts a unified cloud architecture. The server nodes can expand linearly according to the actual needs, which easily meeting the explosive growth of business requirements. At the same time, the system supports hundreds of millions of face registration databases, face snapshot databases, and millions of blacklist databases, which greatly satisfying the needs for pre-warning and post-tracking of key personnel.

The core idea of the whole networking design is to elaborate the dynamic portrait application networking mode, static portrait application networking mode and multi-level platform cascading networking mode.

A portrait recognition system is deployed in the security video private network. Front-end cameras are installed at entrances and exits, key roads and other locations. Portrait collection equipment is deployed at stations, hotels, checkpoints and other locations. And unified access management of equipment is realized through the shared cloud platform. The shared cloud platform stores the full amount of video and pictures (big picture and small picture) in the video private network into the storage system, and sends the portrait pictures or real-time video streams collected by the front end to the dynamic portrait recognition service cluster to realize the face picture matting (video stream) and feature extraction, and then performs collision comparison with the blacklist database controlled by the government. The generated warning information is pushed to the portrait big data platform, and the portrait big data platform service in the private network can synchronize the corresponding information to the portrait big data platform under the public security network. After the warning information is obtained in real time, the portrait big data platform issues warning instructions and arranges police deployment according to the target haunting time and location. The shared cloud platform in the video private network can push people's records and pictures into the network in the whole city. Through the deployment of static portrait comparison server clusters, people's data mining, data cleaning, data analysis and collision with the public security information database data can finally realize the portrait big data service function.

6 System Logic Architecture

The overall logical architecture of the system is shown in Fig. 1, from bottom to top, it is the acquisition equipment layer, intelligent device layer, PAAS layer, SAAS layer and application layer.

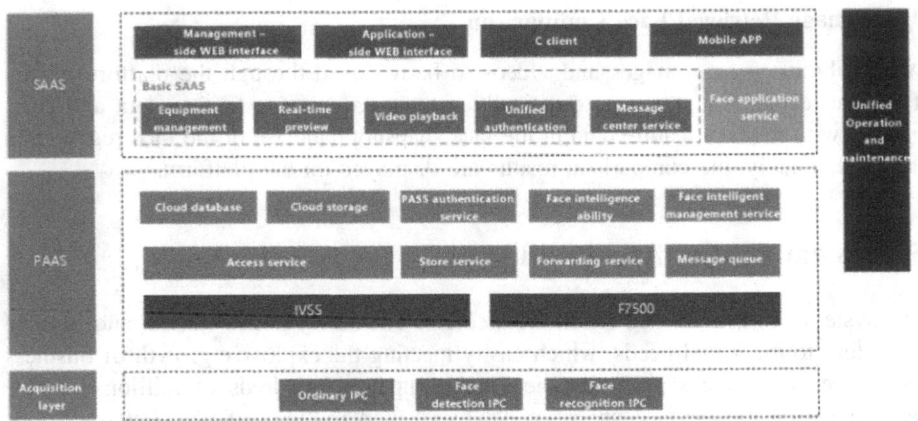

Fig. 1. Portrait system logic architecture diagram

The acquisition equipment layer includes all front-end perception equipment, and there are common IPC, face detection IPC and face recognition IPC related to face business.

PAAS layer realizes the management and access of front-end equipment (including acquisition equipment layer and intelligent equipment layer equipment), shields the protocol differences of various front-end equipment, and provides a unified interaction protocol internally. Completing the storage of structured data (such as car passing records) and unstructured data (such as pictures, videos, etc.) generated by the front-end equipment and providing a unified query interface. After the relevant intelligent analysis services for video and images are performed, a unified pool of human face intelligence capabilities is formed to provide a unified human face interaction protocol for the SAAS layer.

SAAS layer includes basic SAAS, face application service and service display terminal, and relies on SAAS layer's basic capabilities to realize functions such as equipment management, user and authority management, unified authentication, message center, etc. The human face application service provides the functions of human face database management, human face analysis management, distribution management, snapshot and alarm information query and retrieval (to search for images) by encapsulating the capabilities provided by the human face intelligent management service and the cloud database. It also provides a unified display interface to display and apply business data, and supports the management side web page, the application side web page, the C client and the mobile APP.

7 System Data Process

The data process chart of the portrait big data system is shown in Fig. 2.

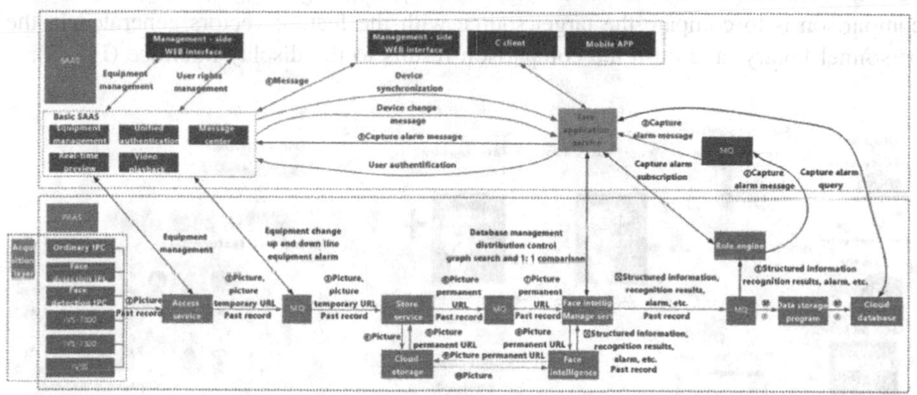

Fig. 2. Portrait system data process chart

The front-end acquisition layer writes the collected face image into MQ through the access service and generates a temporary URL of the image. MQ writes it to cloud storage through the storage service and generates a permanent URL for the picture, and then writes this URL to MQ a second time. The face intelligent management service uses the URL of the picture obtained from MQ to retrieve the picture from the cloud storage and perform structured analysis and processing, and writes the corresponding information into MQ for the third time through the unified interface of the face intelligent management service. These structured information, comparison results, alarms and other data are finally written into the cloud database through data warehousing procedures. At the same time, MQ will send such information to the SAAS layer face application service, which will push the corresponding snapshot alarm information to the message center through the message queue so as to push the message to the service presentation end.

The face application service implements face-related services by invoking the capabilities provided by basic SAAS and PAAS, and the face application service provides a unified interface for applications. By invoking the face intelligent service management service, we can realize database management, distribution control, graph search and 1: 1 comparison. Call the PAAS layer rule engine to subscribe to alarms and call the cloud database to query and retrieve snapshot alarms.

8 System Key Technologies

8.1 Face Recognition Technology

Face recognition is a biometric recognition technology based on human face feature information. A camera is used to collect images or video streams containing human faces, automatically detect and track human faces in the images, send the selected face pictures to the recognition module for feature modeling, extract corresponding feature vectors from the detected faces through the deep learning recognition model, feature comparison is to compare the target source with the feature vectors generated in the personnel library, and push the comparison results to the display interface (Fig. 3).

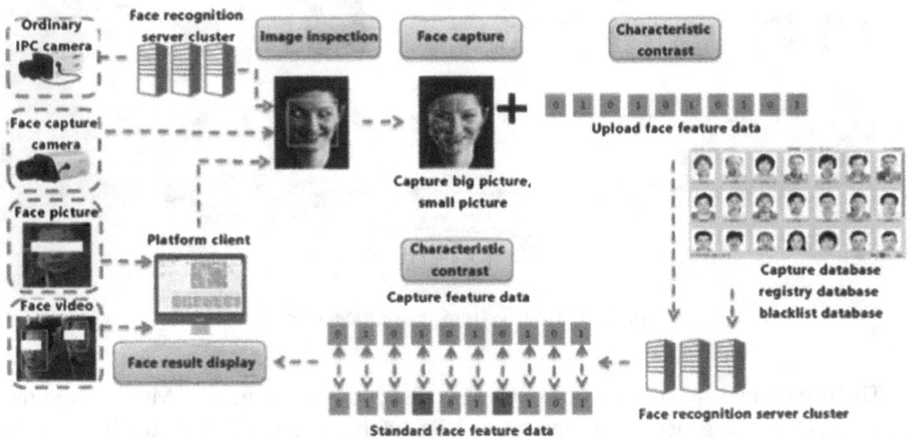

Fig. 3. Face recognition technology

Face Recognition Process. The system data stream includes real-time face comparison and face history query. Real-time comparison occurs in advance or in the event, when the system finds out that there are deployment controllers, the attendants can react quickly; historical inquiry is for key personnel after the event, and the personnel information recorded by the system can be inquired through suspicious personnel pictures.

Real-Time Video Face Comparison. Real-time video stream of ordinary high-definition network camera or face image stream of face capturing unit will extract face feature data by dynamic portrait algorithm under the face recognition server, and real-time traversal comparison with the face feature database in the blacklist database, and feedback the results of each comparison platform.

Face Image Retrieval Comparison. Face image feature data is automatically extracted from the face recognition server by submitting face images/videos to be retrieved by the client of the platform, and is traversed and compared with the face feature data in the face capture database or the face registration database. Finally, the result of the comparison is displayed by the platform.

Several Key Technologies of Face Recognition. Feature-based face detection technology - through the use of color, contour, texture, structure or histogram features for face detection.

Face detection technology based on template matching - extracting face template from database, and then adopting a certain template matching strategy to match the captured face image with the extracted image from template database. The face size and location information are determined by the correlation and the matched template size.

Statistical-based face detection technology - By collecting a large number of positive and negative face samples from “face” and “non-face” images, the system is strengthened by statistical methods, so as to realize the detection and classification of face and non-face patterns.

8.2 Fine Face Recognition Algorithm Based on Deep Convolution Neural Network

Using Dahua face recognition system, it uses face detection algorithm, face tracking algorithm, face capture algorithm, face quality scoring algorithm and face recognition algorithm with fully independent intellectual property rights, and combines the matching front-end camera equipment and back-end platform business system to realize the functions of dynamic blacklist comparison alarm and static face image retrieval.

Basic Structure of Convolutional Neural Network. The basic structure of convolution neural network can be divided into four parts: input layer, convolution layer, full connection layer and output layer.

Input layer: The convolution input layer can directly act on the original input data. For the input image, the input data is the pixel value of the image.

Convolution layer: Convolution layer of convolution neural network, also known as feature extraction layer, consists of two parts. The first part is the real convolution layer, whose main function is to extract input data features. Each convolution core extracts different features of input data. The more convolution core data in convolution layer, the more features of input data can be extracted. The second part is the pooling layer, also known as the subsamping layer. The main purpose is to reduce the amount of data processing and speed up the training network on the basis of retaining useful information.

Full connection layer: It can contain multiple Full Connection Layers, which is actually the hidden layer part of the Multilayer Perceptron. Generally, the ganglion points in the posterior layer are connected with each ganglion point in the preceding layer, and there is no connection between the neuron nodes in the same layer. Each layer of neuron nodes propagates forward through the weights on the connecting line, and the weights are combined to get the input of the next layer of neuron nodes.

Output layer: The number of ganglion points in the output layer is determined according to specific application tasks. If it is a classification task, the output layer of convolutional neural network is usually a classifier, usually a softmax classifier.

Convolution. Generally, convolution kernels are used to extract image features. The design of convolution kernels generally involves the size of convolution kernels, the number of convolution kernels and the step size of convolution kernels. In theory, the number of convolution kernels represents the number of feature maps obtained from the upper layer through convolution filtering. The more feature maps extracted, the larger the feature space of network representation, the stronger the learning ability, and the more accurate the final recognition result. But there are too many convolution cores, which increase the complexity of the network, the number of parameters, the complexity of calculation, and the over-fitting phenomenon. The number of convolution cores should be determined according to the size of specific data set images.

Pooling. The feature map of the input image is obtained by convoluting the neighborhood of the input image, and then the new features are obtained by downsampling in the small neighborhood through the sub-sampling layer using pooling technology. By pooling the upper layer, the feature result can reduce the parameters (reduce the feature dimension), and enhance the feature so that the final feature expression keeps some invariance (rotation, translation, expansion, etc.). The essence of pooling is a process of latitude reduction.

8.3 New Cloud Architecture, Micro-service Design

The standard video library architecture is adopted to shield protocol differences between front-end devices and realize standard access to multi-party front-end devices. The access service cluster manages a large number of front-end equipment. In order to ensure the high performance of the system, the access service adopts a distributed architecture with management nodes and sub - nodes, which can increase the capacity of the front-end access equipment through the lateral expansion of the sub - nodes, thus completing the stable access of mass front-end equipment. At the same time, the front-end equipment accesses are different from sub-nodes in a load-balanced manner, ensuring the high reliability of the system in the event of a single node failure. The platform provides unified management services for equipment, shields equipment differences, and provides a standard interface for managing logical equipment to realize decoupling between business logic and equipment protocols.

8.4 Human Face Intelligent Capability Resource Pool

The platform access service realizes mass access management of rich front-end intelligent devices such as face detection cameras, face recognition cameras, picture extraction equipment and face recognition analysis servers. And the platform access service provides a unified interface to the outside world.

The intelligent service acquires the intelligent capability of the equipment by calling the interface of the access service to form an intelligent capability pool, which realizes the relevant intelligent capabilities such as face detection capability, feature extraction capability, face recognition capability (control capability), query capability (query based on structured values), search capability (search for images by diagrams), etc. Business systems do not need to perceive the intelligent capabilities of specific devices, they only need to invoke the unified interface provided by intelligent services to use the intelligent capabilities. Business system can realize the management of personnel database and personnel information. Business system can realize the management functions of adding video channel, picture channel, distribution control, over-the-person database retrieval and static database retrieval.

8.5 Multi-algorithm Engine Fusion, Operator and Business Layer Decoupling

Through the cascade mode, cities upload feature data to the database of corresponding algorithm manufacturers. The unified combat platform has multi-party data standard access management capabilities. Security Portrait Big Data Application System implements unified scheduling and management of data while realizing overall construction and global retrieval at the business application level. In the aspect of data collision between Intranet and External Network, the layout control pictures of Intranet are extracted by the algorithm manufacturer, then ferry to the video private network, and send to the corresponding lower algorithm pool to realize the dynamic layout control of key personnel. At the same time, ensure intranet information does not leak.

9 Conclusion

The security portrait data application system has been used in the police industry. The application results show that the system can dynamically monitor and track the suspects. Once a crime is committed, the police can carry out accurate arrest with the fastest speed. Since the launch of the "big data portrait" system, more than 10000 suspects have been captured, including more than 100 nationwide fugitives wanted by the Ministry of Public Security. The "big data of portraits" system establishes a feature library for the faces of many special groups of people. It can provide early warning and intervention for potential case risks by setting up tens of thousands of video capture points in crowded places such as stations and airports. If there are pickpockets in the station area, the system will automatically warn, the police will quickly find these people to interrogate and focus on monitoring, forcing them to abandon the crime. The system can effectively predict the crime situation, and has played a role in practice. It provides effective data support and assistant decision-making services for the security and prevention of social security, crime search and prediction, and effectively improves the actual combat ability of police departments.

References

1. Lane, J.: Building an infrastructure to support the use of government administrative data for program performance and social science research. Ann. Am. Acad. Polit. Soc. Sci. **675**(1), 240–252 (2018)
2. Lin, L.: Application of data mining in library-based personalized learning. Int. J. Emerg. Technol. Learn. **12**(12), 127–133 (2017)
3. Hong, Y., Ruiqi, Z.: Data analysis framework of user information search behavior and its key technologies. Libr. Sci. Res., 39–46 (2016)
4. Ramesh, B.: Big data architecture. In: Mohanty, H., Bhuyan, P., Chenthati, D. (eds.) Big Data. SBD, vol. 11, pp. 29–59. Springer, New Delhi (2015). https://doi.org/10.1007/978-81-322-2494-5_2
5. Park, E., Kim, K.: An integrated adoption model of mobile cloud services. Telematics Inform. **31**(3), 376–385 (2014)
6. Turel, O., Connelly, E.: Too busy to help: antecedents and outcomes of interactional justice in web-based service encounters. Int. J. Inf. Manag. **33**(4), 674–683 (2013)
7. Dong, X., Chang, Y., Wang, Y.: Understanding usage of Internet of Things (IOT) systems in China: cognitive experience and affect experience as moderator. Inf. Technol. People **30**(1), 117–138 (2017)
8. Shin, H.: Effect of the customer experience on satisfaction with smartphones: assessing smart satisfaction index with partial least squares. Telecommun. Policy **39**(8), 627–641 (2015)
9. Bae, S.J., Lee, H., Suh, E.K.: Shared experience in pretrip and experience sharing in posttrip: a survey of Airbnb users. Inf. Manag. **54**(6), 714–727 (2017)
10. Lowry, P.B., Wilson, D.: Creating agile organizations through IT: the influence of internal IT service perceptions on IT service quality and IT agility. J. Strateg. Inf. Syst. **25**(3), 211–226 (2016)
11. Park, M.: Human multiple information task behavior on the web. Aslib J. Inf. Manag. **67**(2), 118–135 (2015)
12. Wenjia, X., Shijun, X., Vasily, S.: A cryptograph domain image retrieval method based on Paillier homomorphic block encryption. CMC Comput. Mater. Continua **055**(2), 285–295 (2018)
13. Zhenjun, T., et al.: Robust image hashing via random Gabor filtering and DWT. CMC Comput. Mater. Continua **55**(2), 331–344 (2018)
14. Xiang, W., Chen, X., Qingqi, P., Youyang, Q.: Expression preserved face privacy protection based on multi-mode discriminant analysis. CMC Comput. Mater. Continua **57**(1), 107–121 (2018)
15. Guoyuan, L., Bowen, L., Pengcheng, X., Min, L., Wei, B.: Phishing detection with image retrieval based on improved text on correlation descriptor. CMC Comput. Mater. Continua **57**(3), 533–547 (2018)

Urban Traffic Flow Forecast Based on ST-SEResNet

Yan Kang, Hao Li(✉), Ruicheng Niu, Yaoyao Yuan, and Xudong Liu

YunNan University, Kunming 650500, China
1585572177@qq.com

Abstract. Traffic flow forecasting is important for urban planning and road network recommendation. Traffic flow is affected by time and space which makes the traffic forecasting difficult, so traffic forecasting model should have the characteristics of real-time, accuracy and reliability. In recent years, deep learning has achieved great success in image classification, feature extraction and computer vision which makes the predict of traffic flow based on historical trajectory data possible. In this paper, we introduce ST-SEResNet, we converts the collected traffic data into 2-channel in and out images, and input it into the ST-SEResNet network after a convolutional operation, and use the net to obtain the inflow and outflow channels of the traffic image. The SENet model is used to extract the importance factor of traffic region, and the ResNet model is used to extract the spatial correlation of traffic flow. Compared with the traditional traffic prediction model, The experimental results show that the model not only improves the efficiency of the network but also raise the prediction accuracy of the network.

Keywords: Traffic flow prediction · SENet network · ResNet network · ST-SEResNet model

1 Introduction

In recent years, with the development of shared economy and smart city, a series of new urban data has gradually emerged, such as taxi trajectory data, shared bicycle trajectory data, crowd traffic behavior data, etc. [1]. Compared with traditional data, new data has the features of wide spatial distribution, small time interval and large latitude [2, 3], which become the basis and key of intelligent transportation, so how to obtain valuable information from them to realize the management and utilization of intelligent transportation, urban planning, has become significant issues. With the advancement of urbanization and economic development, the population of urban residents has increased rapidly. Accidents often occur due to excessive traffic [4, 5]. For example, on December 31, 2014, Shanghai Bund tourists gathered to welcome the New Year, there was an unbalanced in the bottom of the ladder, which causes crowded stampede events, resulting in 36 people died and 49 people were injured [4]. In July 2016, hundreds of "Pokemon" players ran through the Central Park in New York City to hold events, resulting in crowded tread events [5]. Forecasting the traffic volume in

X. Sun et al. (Eds.): ICAIS 2019, LNCS 11633, pp. 487–498, 2019.
https://doi.org/10.1007/978-3-030-24265-7_42

hotspots can help timely traffic accident handling, road network monitoring, urban planning, route guidance and personalized route recommendations for visitors.

The taxi trajectory data is collected in real time from the current vehicle based on the vehicle GPS, including the latitude, longitude, time, speed, direction and passenger status of the current vehicle [6]. These data not only records the traffic conditions of the road, but also reflects the traffic flow of the city. The characteristics of the study found that calculating and processing the taxi trajectory data can help obtain the driving time of the vehicle, the average speed of the road section and the congestion of the road [7], besides the travel rules of the residents and the urban hotspot area can be analyzed.

In this paper, our contributions are as follows:

ST-SEResNet uses SENet to extract the importance factor of traffic prediction in the near and far regions, which can better find the area that has a greater impact on traffic in the next time period.

Consolidating ResNet and SENet, on the basis of SENet, using ResNet to capture the spatial dependencies between the near and far regions, which can better predict traffic flow.

Dividing the flow time of the crowd into recent, periodic and long-term, then using ST-SEResNet to build three models, the output of them is integrated by fusion mechanism dynamically and assigned different weights, in addition to this, external factors (such as weather, etc.) are further aggregated.

2 Related Work

Traffic flow forecasting is an important task. In recent years, with the continuous research and discussion of data and models by scholars at home and abroad, the theories and methods of traffic forecasting have become increasingly mature. The forecasting models for short-term traffic flow are mainly divided into three categories.

Based on statistical theory model: the statistical theory model mainly includes time series prediction model, adaptive weight prediction method and Kalman filter prediction method. The literature [8] used the time series method to predict short-term traffic flow. Literature [9] proposed an adaptive parameter estimation method for univariate traffic condition prediction. Literature [10, 11] proposed an adaptive Kalman filter model that can update the process variance based on the traditional Kalman filter model (AKFM) to predict short-term traffic flow through time window. Literature [12] proposed an improved ARIMA-based method to predict passenger flow trends, determine urban hotspots, and help drivers find the next passenger. Literature [13] proposed a short-term average speed prediction and adjustment (ASFA) method, which can predict the average speed of the corresponding sections.

Based on knowledge discovery model: this type of model mainly includes neural network, support vector machine (SVM) and non-parametric model. In recent years, neural network are becoming more and more popular in traffic flow prediction and road traffic sign recognition [14]. The literature [15, 16] proposed a real-time prediction model of taxi demand based on recurrent neural network. Through the model of recurrent neural network long-short memory (LSTM), the taxi history trajectory data is stored and predicted. Literature [17] studied the feasibility of deep learning for urban taxi demand forecasting. Literature [18] proposed a short-term urban traffic predictor based on artificial intelligence and advanced counting. The literature [19] proposed BP neural network optimization algorithm based on artificial ant colony algorithm and particle swarm optimization. Compared with the intelligent models based on knowledge discovery, support vector machine regression prediction can better solve problems such as "local minimum points" and "small samples". While non-parametric models are as a method of traffic flow prediction, it has the characteristics of portability, high prediction accuracy, real-time and so on, which can better simulate the uncertainty and nonlinearity of traffic flow [20]. Literature [21] used nonparametric regression (NPR) and Gaussian model maximum likelihood (GML) to analyze Hong Kong daily vehicle statistics and predict short-term traffic flow at a certain moment.

Based on combined model: Combining the advantages of multiple models with a single model compared to a single model, the literature [22] adapted to the model through three different methods to prove that the SARIMA time series model is very suitable for short-term forecasting of freeway traffic flow. The literature [23] proposed a local linear wavelet neural network based on K nearest neighbor (KNN-LLWNN), the experimental results show that the prediction method has better prediction accuracy than KNN, LLWNN and support vector machine (SVM). In [24], a neural network-based hybrid index traffic flow prediction smoothing and Levenbreg-Marquardt algorithm was proposed to improve the generalization ability of neural network (NN) for short-term traffic flow prediction.

3 ST-SEResNet Network Structure

In this part, we introduced SENet and ResNet respectively, then in Sect. 3.3 we specifically introduced ST-SEResNet Network framework, and how the network can be used in short-term traffic forecasting.

3.1 SENet

With the development of neural networks, scholars consider the dependence of picture channels, in addition to deepening the number of layers in the network and changing the number of layers in the network [25]. The SENet is produced in this context, mainly consisting of two parts, squeeze and excitation. SENet module can construct arithmetic unit for arbitrary input information: $D_{tr} : X \rightarrow A, A \in R^{H' \times M' \times N'}$, D_{tr} is a convolution operation, $T = [t_1, t_2, \ldots, t_n]$ represents the convolution kernel set of learning [26]. The calculation of the first convolution of the SENet network and structure are as follows (Fig. 1):

$$A_N = T_N \times X = \sum\nolimits_{S=1}^{N'} T_N^S \times X^S \tag{1}$$

Squeeze Module: When the input image is convoluted, the convolutional neural network extracts the local features of the image with a convolutional kernel. When the local receptive field is too small, the extracted image range is too small to make the

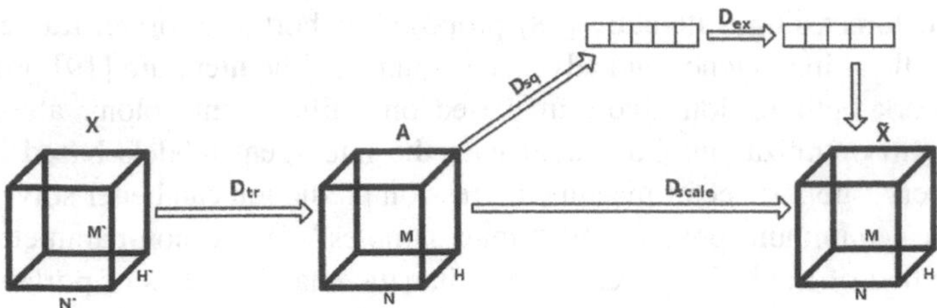

Fig. 1. SENet structure

image feature. Hu and other authors input X to compress global spatial information into a channel descriptor. Squeeze transforms the two-dimensional feature channel into a real number by characterizing the spatial dimension. The real number is from a certain number. To a certain extent, there is a global experience field [27]. The calculation process of this process is as follows:

$$Z_N = D_{sq}(A_N) = \frac{1}{H \times M}\sum_{i=1}^{H}\sum_{j}^{M} A_N(i,j) \tag{2}$$

In the formula, $Z \in R^N$ is obtained by scaling the size of A, D_{sq} changes the $M \times H \times N$ of input size to $1 \times 1 \times N$ of the output size, thereby obtaining global information of N feature maps.

Excutation Module: Excutation module is a mechanism similar to the gate in a recurrent neural network. The weight of A is generated for each feature channel by the parameter w, where the parameter w is learned to explicitly model the correlation between the feature channels. The result of the squeeze is fully connected and activated, $W_1 \times Z$ is a fully connected operation, then multiplying by W_2 after the RELU activation function [28], finally the dimension of Y is $1 \times 1 \times N$, N means that there are N weight of feature map in the tensor A.

$$Y = D_{ex}(Z, W) = \sigma(\delta(Z, W)) = \sigma(W_2\beta(W_1Z)) \tag{3}$$

Where σ represents the activation function operation, $W_1 \in R^{\frac{N}{r}\times N}$, $W_2 \in R^{N\times\frac{N}{r}}$, the dimensions of Z and $W_1 \times Z$ are $1 \times 1 \times N$ and $1 \times 1 \times \frac{N}{r}$, in order to reduce the number of channels, setting r is the scaling parameter. After getting Y, we can operate on the original tensor A, the formula is as follows:

$$\tilde{X}_N = D_{scale}(A_N, Y_N) = A_N \times Y_N \tag{4}$$

Where A_N is a two-dimensional matrix and Y_N is a number that represents the weight relationship dependence.

3.2 ResNet Network

As the depth of the network continues to increase, the accuracy of the network on the training set and test set decreases. The study found that adding a y = x congruent mapping to a shallower network reduces the error of the network, so whether the congruence can be added as the network deepens to improve the accuracy of the network. Resnet's idea comes from this, its calculation formula is as follows:

$$y = H(x, \{W_i\}) + x \tag{5}$$

In this formula, x and y are the input and output of the function, Since x is known, only $H(x, \{W_i\})$ is required through out the online learning process. Compared with the traditional convolutional neural network, as the number of network layers increases, information is more or less lost in the process of transmission. ResNet directly transmits the input information to the output, which reduced the problem of disappearance in the process of information transfer.

3.3 ST-SEResNet Network Architecture

Our ST-SEResNet is divided into three major components: the human traffic grid data information component, additional information components, and fusion information components, as shown in Fig. 2.

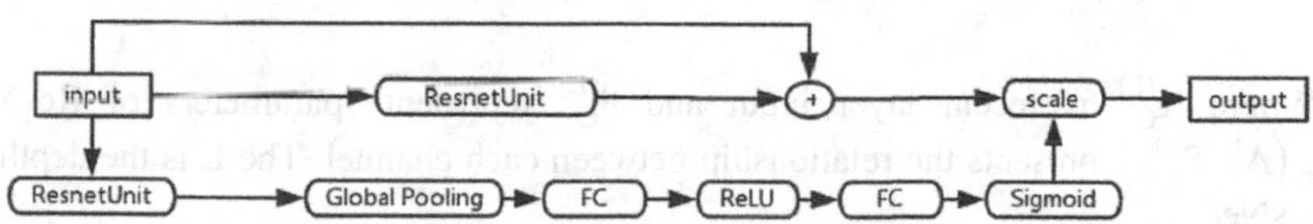

Fig. 2. ST-SeResnet structure

Human Traffic Grid Data Information Component. This component consists of two small parts: convolution and SeResnet Unit, as shown in Fig. 3.

For traditional convolution operations, the input size is larger than the output size. For example, the input size is 5 * 5, the convolution kernel is 3 * 3, and the step size is 1. The size of the output is 3 * 3. But in our task, we need to keep the output and input has the same size, so we need to use the same convolution, this filter can slide to exceed the input boundary, and use zero to fill each boundary side.

It is well known that convolutional neural networks makes it difficult to train deep networks by using existing activation functions and regular techniques. When predicting traffic, we need to use deep networks to extract long-distance dependencies, and need to consider the extent to the region affects traffic. So we use ResNet to train deep neural networks and extract spatial dependencies between distant regions. SENet was added to ResNet to extract the impact factor of each region on traffic prediction.

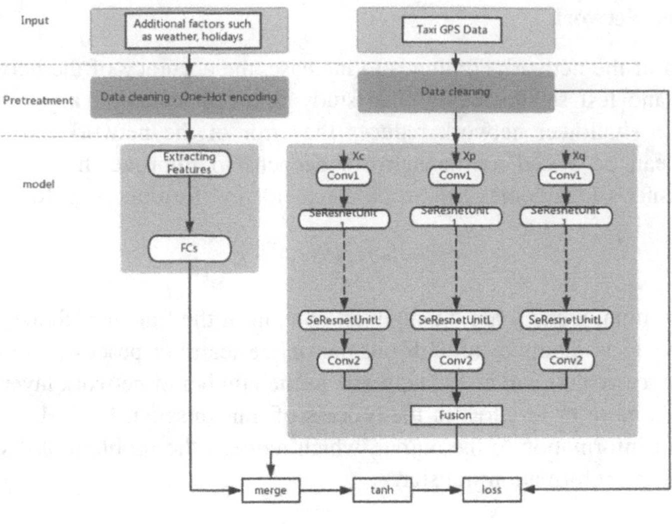

Fig. 3. SEResnet Unit

In our ST-SEResNet, SEResNet unit is as follows:

$$X_C^{(L+1)} = \left(X_C^L + \left(X_C^{(L)}; \theta_C^{(L)}\right)\right) * D_{scale}\left(A_C^L, S_C^L\right), L = 1, \ldots, L \tag{6}$$

Where $X_C^{(L)}$ is recent layer input and $\theta_C^{(L)}$ represents parameters of ResNet, $D_{scale}\left(A_C^L, S_C^L\right)$ represents the relationship between each channel. The L is the depth of SEResNet.

Additional Information Processing Component. Traffic flow is likely to be affected by many external factors such as weather and holidays. For example, in the holiday season, the traffic volume of the work area greatly will reduce compared with the normal day. So in order to predict the flow of people in the time interval, we map the extra data through the fully connected layer to the same dimension as the traffic matrix.

Fusion Information Component. When we process traffic information, we use three kinds of time data, the same day, the most recent, and one month ago, show in Fig. 4. There three polylines are drawn as the mean of each time interval. We can see from the picture that the similarity between the same day and the most recent is very high. Although there is a similar trend in the same day and one month ago, there are differences in some time intervals, which may be affected by additional factors such as weather. So in the final output, we need to merge the final results of the three different data processing and reassign weights to data for each time type. Converged into a traffic matrix.

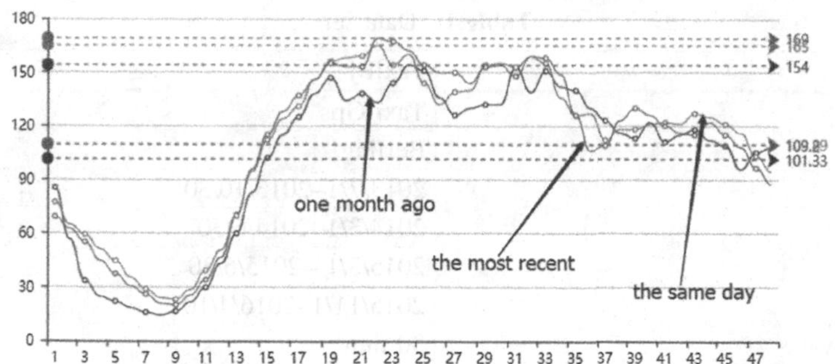

Fig. 4. Three kinds of time data

The specific method is as follows:

$$X_{SERes} = W_c * X_c + W_p * X_p + W_q * X_q \tag{7}$$

We finally add the extra factors directly to the final output, defining Xt as:

$$\mathrm{X_t} = \tanh(\mathrm{X_{SERes}} + \mathrm{X_{Ext}}) \tag{8}$$

4 Experiment

4.1 Setting

Dataset: Our data comes from the TaxiBJ open source dataset. The dataset we use is shown in Table 1. The dataset contains: trajectory and weather, as follows:

TaxiBJ: The trajectory data is the taxi GPS data and weather data includes four different time periods in Beijing, from July 1, 2013 to October 30, 2013, from March 1, 2014 to June 30, 2014, from March 1, 2015 to June 30, 2015, from November 1, 2015 to April 10, 2016, our data includes outflows and inflows. We selected the last four weeks of data as test data, and all other data was used for training.

There are six common traffic flow comparison models:

ARIMA: Fully called Autoregressive Integrated Moving Average Model (ARIMA) [29, 30], a famous time-series approach was proposed by Box and Jenkins in the early 1970s.

SARIMA: Seasonal differential autoregressive moving average model, one of the methods of time series prediction analysis.

RNN; Recurrent Neural Network (RNN) is a deep learning model in which dynamic temporal behavior can be demonstrated and effectively captures time dependence [31]. In our experiments, we fixed the input sequence length to {3, 12, 24, 48}. Taking 3 as an example, the time interval is 30 min, then the slave input sequence is only 3 time periods. So our RNN is divided into four types.

Table 1. Data set

Data set	TaxiBj
Data type	Taxi Gps
Place	BeiJing
Time slot	2013/7/1–2013/10/30
	2014/3/1–2014/6/30
	2015/3/1– 2015/6/30
	2015/11/1–2016/4/10
Time interval	30 min
Network size	(32, 32)
Trajectory data	
Taxi count	34000+
Available time interval	22459
Additional information (Weather and holidays)	
Weather type	The 16 type (e.g. Rainy days, thunderstorm days)
Temperature range (°C)	[−24.6, 41.0]

LSTM: The long- and short-term memory network is a time recurrent neural network suitable for processing and predicting the problem of relatively long intervals and delays in time series. Like RNN, we experimented with four variants of LSTM.

ST-ResNet: This is the best model for predicting traffic in the past. The model uses ResNet to simulate the connections between the near and far regions, so that it can accurately predict regional traffic.

ST-SEResNet: This is the model proposed in this paper. There are 12 residual units, and SENet is added to each residual unit to extract the relationship between inflow and outflow, and extract the multi-flow influence factor in the near and far regions to accurately predict.

We tested our model by Root Mean Square Error (RMSE).

$$\mathrm{RMSE} = \sqrt{\frac{1}{z}(x_i - \widehat{x}_i)^2} \tag{9}$$

Where x represents the actual grid flow graph, $\widehat{x}$ indicates the corresponding predicted value, and z refers to the total number of data for the current batch.

4.2 Verification

We use historical data to evaluate our model. As shown in Table 2, our model has achieved significant improvements in the TaxiBJ dataset, surpassing all models. The results show that the RMSE mean of our model is 26% higher than ARIMA, 37.5% more than SARIMA, 41% to 68% higher than RNN model, and 36% to 43% more than

LSTM, 2.15% more than ST-ResNet. From the experimental results, we can see that the average result of LSTM should exceed the RNN. Many of them are shown in Fig. 5. This is because LSTM can capture long-term time dependence and can better utilize data between three different time periods. The relationship is predicted.

Table 2. Verification results RMSE mean

Model	RMSE
ARIMA	22.78
SARIMA	26.88
RNN3	30.41
RNN12	47.25
RNN24	52.53
RNN48	43.81
LSTM3	28.81
LSTM12	29.69
LSTM24	26.25
LSTM48	28.87
ST-ResNet	17.17
ST-SEResNet	16.80

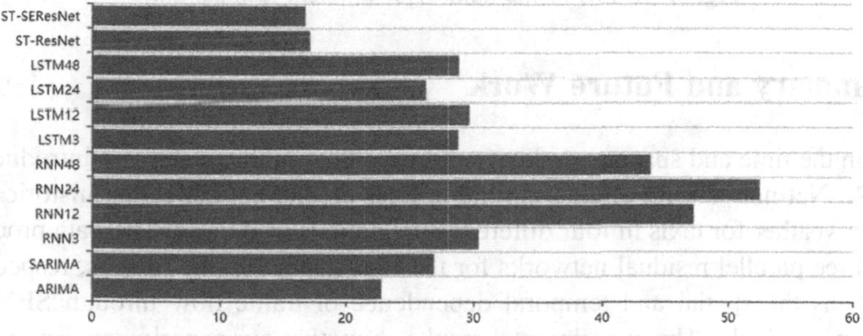

Fig. 5. Model RMSE

In SENet, for the value of r, there will be different effects on the results. In this experiment, we conclude the experiment with r equal to 2, 4, 8, and 16 respectively. The results are shown in Table 3. The fluctuation of the RMSE of our model fluctuations is not large. This effectively demonstrates that the robustness of ST-SEResNet is good.

Table 3. RMSE of ST-SEResNet with different r

r	RMSE
2	16.835037
4	16.924950
8	16.940733
16	16.806225

Throughout the experiment, the number of residual units has a crucial impact on the experimental results, because each residual unit represents the connection between the near and far regions, The number of values is 2, 4, 6, 8, 10, 12 and 14 respectively, and the results are shown in Fig. 6.

The experiment mainly requires the GPU server to calculate. The specific configuration of the server is shown in Table 3. The Python environment dependency library, including TensorFlow and Keras, is the primary responsibility for building our model.

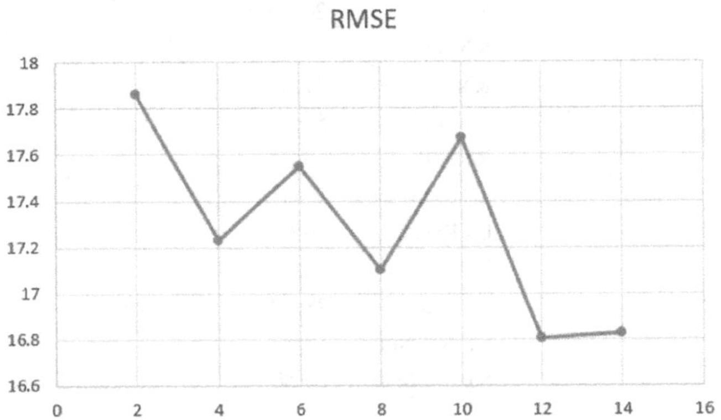

Fig. 6. RMSE of the number of different residual units

5 Summary and Future Work

Based on the time and space complexity of traffic flow in this paper, we introduced the ST-SEResNet network for short-term traffic flow prediction, collecting historical GPS data and weather for taxis in four different time periods in Beijing. The data processing inputs three parallel residual networks for the two-channel traffic images, respectively, and obtains the spatial and temporal dependence of traffic flow through SENet and ResNet respectively. The experimental results show that our experiments can be better compared with other networks. Traffic flow is also affected by regional types and major events, For example, when the residential area is at the peak of work, the traffic will increase significantly, when the star concerts, the surrounding traffic will rise sharply. So, in the future work, we expect to be able to add event factors to the model during traffic prediction to improve the accuracy of the prediction.

Acknowledgement. This work has been supported by the National Science Foundation of China Grant No. 61762092, “Dynamic multi-objective requirement optimization based on transfer learning,” and the Open Foundation of the Key Laboratory in Software Engineering of Yunnan Province, Grant No. 2017SE204, “Research on extracting software feature models using transfer learning,” and the National Science Foundation of China Grant No. 61762089, “The key research of high order tensor decomposition in distributed environment”.

References

1. Zhang, N., Chen, H., Chen, X., et al.: Forecasting public transit use by crowdsensing and semantic trajectory mining: case studies. ISPRS Int. J. Geo-Inf. **5**(10), 180 (2016)
2. Rasmussen, T.K., Ingvardson, J.B., Nielsen, O.A.: Improved methods to deduct trip legs and mode from travel surveys using wearable GPS devices: a case study from the Greater Copenhagen area. Comput. Environ. Urban Syst. **54**, 301–313 (2015)
3. Sun, H., McIntosh, S.: Analyzing crossdomain transportation big data of New York city with semisupervised and active learning. CMC Comput. Mater. Continua. **57**(1), 1–9 (2018)
4. Zhang, J., Zheng, Y., Qi, D.: Deep spatio-temporal residual networks for citywide crowd flows prediction (2016)
5. Fan, Z., Song, X., Shibasaki, R., et al.: CityMomentum: an online approach for crowd behavior prediction at a citywide level. In: ACM International Joint Conference on Pervasive and Ubiquitous Computing, pp. 559–569. ACM (2015)
6. Ashbrook, D., Starner, T.: Using GPS to learn significant locations and predict movement across multiple users. Pers. Ubiquitous Comput. **7**(5), 275–286 (2003)
7. Wen, H., Zhongwei, H.U., Guo, J., et al.: Operational analysis on beijing road network during the olympic games. J. Transp. Syst. Eng. Inf. Technol. **8**(6), 32–37 (2008)
8. Moorthy, C.K., Ratcliffe, B.G.: Short term traffic forecasting using time series methods. In: Transportation Planning Technology, pp. 45–56 (1988)
9. Shekhar, S., Williams, B.M.: Adaptive seasonal time series models for forecasting short-term traffic flow. Transp. Res. Rec. **2024**, 116–125 (2007)
10. Guo, J., Huang, W., Williams, B.M.: Adaptive Kalman filter approach for stochastic short-term traffic flow rate prediction and uncertainty quantification. Transp. Res. Part C **43**, 50–64 (2014)
11. Zhang, L., Ma, J., Zhu, C.: Theory modeling and application of an adaptive Kalman filter for short-term traffic flow prediction. J. Inf. Comput. Sci. **9**(16), 5101–5109 (2012)
12. Li, X., Pan, G., Wu, Z., et al.: Prediction of urban human mobility using large-scale taxi traces and its applications. Front. Comput. Sci. **6**(1), 111–121 (2012)
13. Yang, J.Y., Chou, L.D., Tung, C.F., et al.: Average-speed forecast and adjustment via VANETs. IEEE Trans. Veh. Technol. **62**(9), 4318–4327 (2013)
14. Zhou, S., Liang, W., Li, J., Kim, J.-U.: Improved VGG model for road traffic sign recognition. CMC Comput. Mater. Continua **57**(1), 11–24 (2018)
15. Xu, J., Rahmatizadeh, R., Bölöni, L., et al.: Real-time prediction of taxi demand using recurrent neural networks. IEEE Trans. Intell. Transp. Syst. **PP**(99), 1–10 (2017)
16. Xu, J., Rahmatizadeh, R., Boloni, L., et al.: A sequence learning model with recurrent neural networks for taxi demand prediction. In: IEEE, Conference on Local Computer Networks, pp. 261–268. IEEE Computer Society (2017)
17. Liao, S., Zhou, L., Di, X., et al.: Large-scale short-term urban taxi demand forecasting using deep learning. In: Design Automation Conference. IEEE (2018)
18. Vlahogianni, E., Karlaftis, M., Golias, J., et al.: Pattern-based short-term urban traffic predictor. In: IEEE Intelligent Transportation Systems Conference, pp. 389–393. IEEE (2006)
19. Zhu, Y., Zhang, G., Qiu, J.: Network traffic prediction based on particle swarm BP neural network. J. Netw. **8**(11), 2685–2691 (2013)
20. Castro-Neto, M., Jeong, Y.S., Jeong, M.K., et al.: Online-SVR for short-term traffic flow prediction under typical and atypical traffic conditions. Expert Syst. Appl. **36**(3), 6164–6173 (2009)

21. Lam, W.H.K., Tang, Y.F., Tam, M.L.: Comparison of two non-parametric models for daily traffic forecasting in Hong Kong. J. Forecast. **25**(3), 173–192 (2010)
22. Shekhar, S.: Recursive methods for forecasting short-term traffic flow using seasonal ARIMA time series model (2004)
23. Lin, L., Li, Y., Sadek, A.: A k nearest neighbor based local linear wavelet neural network model for on-line short-term traffic volume prediction. Procedia Soc. Behav. Sci. **96**, 2066–2077 (2013)
24. Chan, K.Y., Dillon, T.S., Singh, J., et al.: Neural-network-based models for short-term traffic flow forecasting using a hybrid exponential smoothing and Levenberg-Marquardt algorithm. IEEE Trans. Intell. Transp. Syst. **13**(2), 644–654 (2012)
25. Zeng, D., Xu, J., Gu, J., et al.: Short term traffic flow prediction using hybrid ARIMA and ANN models. In: The Workshop on Power Electronics and Intelligent Transportation System, pp. 621–625. IEEE Computer Society (2008)
26. He, K., Zhang, X., Ren, S., et al.: Deep residual learning for image recognition, pp. 770–778 (2015)
27. Hu, J., Shen, L., Sun, G.: Squeeze-and-excitation networks (2017)
28. Nair, V., Hinton, G.E.: Rectified linear units improve restricted boltzmann machines. In: International Conference on International Conference on Machine Learning, pp. 807–814. Omnipress (2010)
29. Tseng, F.M., Yu, H.C., Tzeng, G.H.: Combining neural network model with seasonal time series ARIMA model. Technol. Forecast. Soc. Change **69**(1), 71–87 (2002)
30. Liang, Y.H.: Combining seasonal time series ARIMA method and neural networks with genetic algorithms for predicting the production value of the mechanical industry in Taiwan. Neural Comput. Appl. **18**(7), 833–841 (2009)
31. Ji, S., Vishwanathan, S.V.N., Satish, N., et al.: BlackOut: speeding up recurrent neural network language models with very large vocabularies. Comput. Sci. **115**(8), 2159–2168 (2015)

A Novel Power System Anomaly Data Identification Method Based on Neural Network and Affine Propagation

Li Shen[1], Yang Shen[1], Chunhe Song[2,3](✉), Zhao Li[1], Ran Ran[1], and Peng Zeng[2,3]

[1] State Grid Liaoning Electric Power Co., Ltd., Shenyang 110000, People's Republic of China
[2] Shenyang Institute of automation, Chinese Academy of Sciences, Shenyang 110016, People's Republic of China
songchunhe@sia.cn
[3] Institutes for Robotics and Intelligent Manufacturing, Chinese Academy of Sciences, Shenyang 110016, China

Abstract. Identification of anomaly data is very important for power system state estimation. In this paper, a method of power system anomaly data identification based on neural network and affine propagation is proposed. In this first step, a 3-layer neural network is trained as a predictor using normal data. In the second step, data to be detected is preprocessed using the trained neural network, and predicted residuals are obtained. In the third step, these predicted residuals are clustered using the affine propagation clustering algorithm, and in the final step, anomaly data is identified based on the clustering results. As the neural network training process is easy to fall into local minimum, which reduces the prediction accuracy of the neural network, in this paper a novel chaotic particle swarm optimization algorithm is proposed to train the neural network. From the experimental results it can be seen that, compared with previous anomaly data identification method using the BP neural network and the gap statistic algorithm or the K-mean clustering algorithm, the proposed method can effectively improve the accuracy of anomaly data identification.

1 Introduction

Detection and identification of abnormal data in power system is one of the important functions of power system state estimation. Complex power network contains a large amount of real-time data. The accuracy of these data determines the security and reliability of power system operation. Anomaly data in power system may affect dispatchers to make wrong decisions, thus affecting the normal operation of power system, and may even threaten the security of the whole power system [1]. Therefore, in order to ensure the stable and safe operation of the power system, it is of great significance to detect these bad data and extract

X. Sun et al. (Eds.): ICAIS 2019, LNCS 11633, pp. 499–508, 2019.
https://doi.org/10.1007/978-3-030-24265-7_43

them from the original data to correct them. How to reliably detect and correct bad data becomes a difficult problem in the application of state estimation [2].

The identification method of abnormal data in power system generally includes several steps of data preprocessing, clustering and judging of abnormal data. As an important means of data mining and an unsupervised learning method, cluster analysis has been widely used in various engineering and scientific fields, including fault diagnosis, data analysis and image processing. However, with the increasing complexity of data structures, no data mining algorithm can be widely used to effectively reveal the various structures presented by various data sets. In view of the characteristics of data sets, as well as the differences in the presentation structure of these data in clustering, the representation rules and the application methods of these rules, many clustering algorithms are proposed: k-means algorithm, k-center point algorithm and AP clustering algorithm, etc. Although AP algorithm and k-center algorithm have the same clustering objective, AP algorithm does not require symmetry of similarity matrix. Compared with k-means, AP algorithm has the following advantages: (1) this algorithm takes all data points as candidate class center points to avoid the impact of the selected initial class center on the clustering results; (2) optimize the objective function based on the alternating propagation of similarity information to achieve simple and efficient calculation; (3) similarity matrix symmetry is not required. Based on these advantages of AP algorithm, AP algorithm has been applied in many fields.

At present, the BP neural network commonly used in data preprocessing methods is easy to fall into local extremum, which reduces the accuracy of data preprocessing [3,4]. Clustering algorithm often uses K mean method and middle clearance statistics [5–7]. However, K-means method needs to pre-set the number of clusters, and improper setting will seriously affect the accuracy of the algorithm. Although the gap statistical algorithm can automatically calculate the number of clusters, it relies on the sampling distribution of data and requires a large number of sampling to obtain stable results, which results in the disadvantage of complex calculation and large amount of calculation of the algorithm, and is not suitable for the processing of massive data [8,9].

In order to solve the above problems, a method of power system anomaly data identification based on chaotic particle swarm optimization neural network and affine propagation clustering algorithm is proposed in this paper. To effectively improve the accuracy of power system anomaly data identification, the core idea of the proposed method is to use chaotic particle swarm optimization to train neural network, and use the affine propagation clustering algorithm to realize data clustering. From the experimental results it can be seen that, compared with previous anomaly data identification method using the BP neural network and the gap statistic algorithm or the K-mean clustering algorithm, the proposed method can effectively improve the accuracy of anomaly data identification.

2 Related Work

The detection and identification of abnormal data in power system is one of the important functions of power system state estimation. The complex power network contains a large amount of real-time data, the accuracy of which determines the safety and reliability of power system operation. Bad data in the power system may affect the dispatcher to make wrong decisions, thus affecting the normal operation of the power system, and may even threaten the safety of the entire power system. Therefore, in order to ensure the stable and safe operation of power system, it is of great significance to detect these bad data and extract them from the original data for correction.

Modern power grid presents the characteristics of large scale, high dimension and strong complexity, which will produce a large amount of data in the operation process. Many scholars have used data mining technology to explore and reveal the operation rules of related equipment in power grid [10–12]. Among them, the method of identifying abnormal data in power system by data mining theory has become an important one. An important branch of application. According to the difference of technology, the identification method of data bundle theory mainly includes three kinds [13,14].

2.1 Identification Method Based on Fuzzy Clustering Analysis

Cluster analysis originated from taxonomy. In ancient taxonomy, people mainly rely on experience and professional knowledge to achieve classification, and seldom use mathematical tools for quantitative classification. With the development of human science and technology, more and more high to the requirement of classification, so that sometimes only by experience and professional knowledge is difficult to exactly, so people gradually to math tool in reference to the taxonomy, formed the numerical taxonomy, and then to multivariate analysis technology is introduced into the numerical taxonomy to form the cluster analysis. The content of clustering analysis is very rich, including systematic clustering method, orderly sample clustering method, dynamic clustering method, fuzzy clustering method, graph theory clustering method, clustering prediction method and so on. The identification method based on fuzzy clustering analysis is a method of identifying bad data in power system by using the theory of fuzzy clustering. It effectively combines the method of fuzzy mathematics with the method of clustering analysis. Abnormal data in the system, first of all, the difference between adjacent measurements and standardized residuals of data are taken as characteristic variables, and the identification of abnormal data is realized through analysis. In this method, the correct data will not be identified as bad data, but the size of the initial clustering matrix and membership degree need to be determined artificially [1,15].

2.2 Identification Method Based on Neural Network Algorithm

Artificial Neural Network (ANN) has been a research hotspot emerging in the field of Artificial intelligence since the 1980s. It abstracts the neural network of human brain from the perspective of information processing, establishes some simple model, and forms different networks according to different connection modes. In engineering and academia, it is often referred to as neural network or quasi-neural network. A neural network is an operational model consisting of a large number of nodes (or neurons) connected to each other. Each node represents a specific output function called activation function. Each connection between two nodes represents a weighted value of the signal passing through the connection, called the weight, which is equivalent to the memory of the artificial neural network. The output of the network depends on the connection mode, weight value and excitation function of the network. However, the network itself is usually an approximation to some algorithm or function in nature, or an expression of a logical strategy. The basic principle of using neural network algorithm to identify bad data is to train the network with training samples. At present, the widely used neural networks mainly include BP neural network, Kohonen neural network and RBF neural network [16]. Although the method of identifying bad data by using neural network algorithm can explain the complex relationship between input vectors and output vectors of neural network, the training process of the network has a great influence on the identification effect of the algorithm [2].

2.3 Identification Method Based on Gap Statistical Algorithm

The basic principle of gap statistics algorithm is to select a distribution which is correlated with the data to be detected, and use this distribution to generate the corresponding reference data set; then to cluster the detection data and reference data, and calculate the gap between the two data based on the clustering results; finally, according to the gap value of large [5]. It is a new identification method for the shortcomings of neural network algorithm. Bad data identification method based on gap statistics has the advantage of automatically selecting the optimal number of clustering, but the algorithm itself is complex, need to consider the reference distribution, the calculation is large, and the quality of training data in the neural network will have an impact on the identification effect of the algorithm [6].

3 The Proposed Algorithm

The proposed method consists of four steps. In this first step, a 3-layer neural network is trained as a predictor using normal data. In the second step, data to be detected is preprocessed using the trained neural network, and predicted residuals are obtained. In the third step, these predicted residuals are clustered using the affine propagation clustering algorithm [17], and in the final step, anomaly data is identified based on the clustering results.

3.1 Training the Neural Network Using Normal Data

Get normal electrical operation process state measurement data set X:

$$X_{M \times N} = \begin{bmatrix} x_{11} & x_{12} & \cdots & x_{1N} \\ x_{21} & x_{22} & \cdots & x_{2N} \\ \vdots & \vdots & \ddots & \vdots \\ x_{M1} & x_{M2} & \cdots & x_{MN} \end{bmatrix} \tag{1}$$

Each line in X is a state measurement value of an electrical apparatus during operation, such as voltage value, current value, active power and reactive power. In X, there are totally M types of measurement values, and each measurement has N sampled data.

Standardizing X:

$$x_{ij}^{*} = \frac{2\left(x_{ij} - x_{j\min}\right)}{\left(x_{j\max} - x_{j\min}\right)} - 1 \tag{2}$$

where $x_{j\min}$ and $x_{j\max}$ are the maximum and minimum values of $j - th$ measurements.

The data sets are randomly divided into training sets $X_{M \times L}$ and test sets $X_{M \times (N-L)}$, where $L : N - L \approx 0.8 : 0.2$.

Set the $i - th$ measurement value as the target value, and the other kinds of measurement value as the input value to train the neural network.

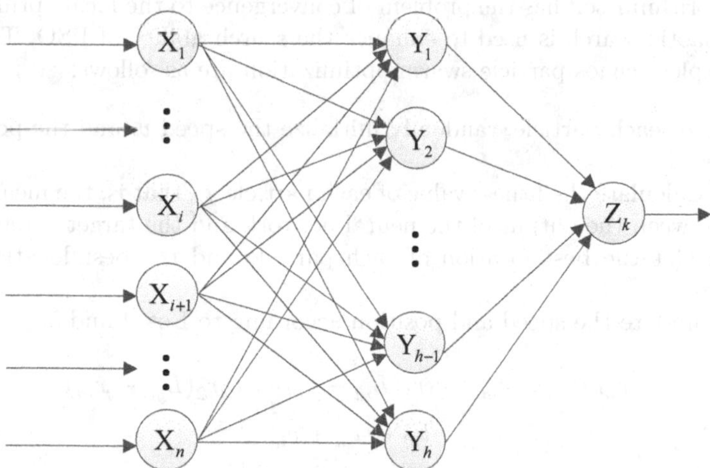

Fig. 1. The structure of the neural network

The neural network consists of three layers, including an input layer, a hidden layer and an output layer, as shown in Fig. 1. The numbers of neurons in the input layer and the hidden layer are set to $M - 1$, and the number of neurons in the output layer is set to 1. The relationship between input and output of the neural network is as follows:

$$Y = g\left(\sum_{j=1}^{h} \beta_j f\left(\sum_{i=1}^{n} \alpha_{ij} x_{ij} + A_j\right) + B\right) \tag{3}$$

Among them, f and g are activation functions, x_i is the $i-th$ input of neurons in the first input layer, α_{ij} is the weight between the $i-th$ neuron in the input layer and the $j-th$ neuron in the hidden layer, and β_j the weight between the $j-th$ neuron in the hidden layer and the output node. A_j and B are bias coefficients, which are initialized by Nguyen-Widrow algorithm. The mean square error is used for the error between the output of neural network and the target value.

This network usually uses gradient back propagation algorithm or particle swarm algorithm and other intelligent algorithms to train. But there will be convergence to local minimum. In order to solve this problem, a particle swarm optimization algorithm based on chaotic search is used to train the neural network.

The core idea of particle swarm optimization (PSO) is to regard the parameter vector to be optimized as the particle position, and the objective function to be optimized as the fitness of the particle. The fitness is optimized by dynamically adjusting the position between the group historical optimal position and the individual historical optimal position. The basic particle swarm optimization (PSO) algorithm itself has the problem of convergence to the local optimal solution, so chaotic search is used to enhance the search ability of PSO. The steps of the complete chaos particle swarm optimization are as follows:

Step 1: for each particle, randomly initialize the speed v_i and the position l_i of it;
Step 2: Calculate the fitness value of each particle f_i, that is, the mean square error between the output of the neural network and the target value.
Step 3: Get the best location of each particle and the best location of all particles.
Step 4: update the speed and position according to Eqs. 4 and 5:

$$v_{id} \leftarrow w * v_{id} + c_1 r_1 (L_{id} - x_{id}) + c_2 r_2 (L_{gd} - x_{id}) \tag{4}$$

$$l_{id} \leftarrow l_{id} + v_{id} \tag{5}$$

where i is the particle index; d is the data dimension index, c_1 and c_2 are constants, r_1 and r_2 are random numbers on the closed interval $[0, 1]$; L_i and L_g are the historical optimal position of the $i-th$ particle and the optimal position of all particles; w is the inertial weight.
Step 5: If the maximum number of iterations is not reached, step 2 is returned; if the maximum number of iterations is reached, the following steps are continued.

Step 6: Chaotic local search is carried out according to Eqs. 6, 7 and 8; if the search result is better, the historical optimal position is updated.

$$\omega_i = \frac{[l_i - a_i]}{d_i} \tag{6}$$

$$\omega_i \leftarrow \mu\omega_i(1-\omega_i) \tag{7}$$

$$l_i \leftarrow a_i + d_i \times \omega_i \tag{8}$$

where a_i and d_i are constants, μ is the attractor.

The chaotic particle swarm optimization (CPSO) algorithm is used to train the weights and bias coefficients of the neural network in the training set, and the training set is tested until the mean square error between the output of the neural network and the target value on the test set is not reduced.

3.2 Date Preprocessing Using Neural Network

Gets the data set to be tested T:

$$Y_{M\times Q} = \begin{bmatrix} y_{11} & y_{12} & \cdots & y_{1Q} \\ y_{21} & y_{22} & \cdots & y_{2Q} \\ \vdots & \vdots & \ddots & \vdots \\ y_{M1} & y_{M2} & \cdots & y_{MQ} \end{bmatrix} \tag{9}$$

Y and the normal dataset X have the same data type for each row, but each measurement has Q sampling data. Standardizing Y:

$$y_{ij}^* = \frac{2\,(y_{ij} - x_{j\,\min})}{(x_{j\,\max} - x_{j\,\min})} - 1 \tag{10}$$

Then the mean square error sequence $E = [e_1, e_2, ..., e_Q]$ is obtained by using the trained neural network.

3.3 Residuals Clustering

Clustering elements in E based on affine propagation clustering algorithm [17]:

Step 1: The attraction matrix R, the attribution matrix A and the damping factor λ are randomly initialized between 0 and 1.

Step 2: Update the attraction matrix R and the attribution degree matrix A:

$$R\,(i,k) \leftarrow (1-\lambda)\times\left(s\,(i,k) - \max_{k\neq k'}\left\{A\,(i,k') + s\,(i,k')\right\}\right) + \lambda\times R\,(i,k) \tag{11}$$

$$A\,(i,k) \leftarrow (1-\lambda)\times\min\left\{0, R\,(k,k) + \sum_{i'\in\{i,k\}} \max\left\{0, R\,(i',k)\right\}\right\} + \lambda\times A\,(i,k) \tag{12}$$

$$A(k,k) \leftarrow (1-\lambda) \times \sum_{i' \notin \{i,k\}} \max\{0, R(i',k)\} + \lambda \times A(k,k) \tag{13}$$

$$D = R + A \tag{14}$$

where $s(i,k) = -\|x_i - x_k\|^2$ is similarity, and D is the decision matrix.
Step 3: in the decision matrix D, set the point in diagonal line greater than 0 as cluster center. The sample points are classified according to the distance between the sample points and the clustering points.
Step 4: if the number of iterations is greater than the maximum number of iterations initialized, stop clustering. Otherwise, step back to Step 2.

3.4 Anomaly Data Identification

For a category whose element number is less than or equal to 3, all elements in this category are considered abnormal data. For categories with more than 3 elements, for the $i-th$ input, the mean square error is e_i, and the corresponding clustering center is $\bar{e}$. If:

$$\left|\frac{e_i - \bar{e}}{\bar{e}}\right| \geq 0.25 \tag{15}$$

Then outliers exist in some dimensions of the measured data vector of the $i-th$ input.

4 Experiments

In this section, the proposed method is compared with some state-of-the-art methods [1,2,5,6]. Data is derived from the sampled data of a transformer in a substation. The collected data include current value (3 phases), voltage value (3 phases), active power and reactive power during the normal operation of the voltage, which form eight-tuples. To carry out anomaly data identification, 10% data are selected randomly, and one item of the selected eight-tuples pluses 10% of its original values. The total number of sample is 10000. In the proposed method, for the chaotic particle swarm optimization algorithm, the total number of particle is 200, c_1 and c_2 are set to 1, w is set to 0.5. The parameters of the affine propagation clustering algorithm is set according to [17]. The parameters of four compared algorithms are set according to [1,2,5,6]. Results are shown in Table 1.

In Table 1, 1 phase means that the results are from 1 phase current and its corresponding voltage. A and B mean the active power and the reactive power, and 3 phase+A+R means that the results are from all three phases current and their corresponding voltage, as well as the active power and the reactive power. From Table 1 it can be seen that, following with the increase of the number of data dimension in the test, the accuracies of all five methods improve. This is because there is a coupling relationship among these dimensional data, and more accurate results can be obtained by using higher dimensional data. Furthermore, it can be seen that the proposed method has the best accuracy among these methods.

Table 1. Anomaly data identification accuracy

Data dimension	1 phase	2 phase	3 phase	3 phase+A	3 phase+A+R
Method in [1]	90.20%	91.40%	93.10%	93.60%	94.20%
Method in [2]	91.20%	91.60%	92.00%	93.60%	94.10%
Method in [5]	90.70%	92.10%	92.60%	93.10%	93.90%
Method in [6]	92.10%	92.90%	93.40%	93.90%	94.80%
The proposed method	94.80%	95.20%	96.60%	97.20%	98.50%

5 Conclusions

The quality of power system measurement data is an important factor affecting the efficiency and results of power system state estimation, and there are a few anomaly data in measurement data objectively. Detection and identification of these anomaly data is an important part of power system state estimation. The existence of anomaly data in power system may reduce the convergence performance of state estimation and even cause less failure of state estimation. How to detect and correct the anomaly data reliably becomes a difficult problem in the application of state estimation.

This paper proposed a novel power system anomaly data identification method based on neural network and affine propagation is proposed. To effectively improve the accuracy of power system anomaly data identification, the core idea of the proposed method is to use chaotic particle swarm optimization to train neural network, and use the affine propagation clustering algorithm to realize data clustering. Compared with previous anomaly data identification method using the BP neural network and the gap statistic algorithm or the K-mean clustering algorithm, the proposed method can effectively improve the accuracy of anomaly data identification.

Acknowledgments. This work was supported by the State Grid Corporation Science and Technology Project (Contract No.: SGLNXT00YJJS1800110).

References

1. Alamin, A., Peng, J.C.: A detailed tuning evaluation of sensitivity threshold using LNRT for bad data detection in state estimation. In 2015 IEEE 8th GCC Conference Exhibition, pp. 1–4 (2015)
2. Wu, Y., Xiao, Y., Hohn, F., Nordström, L., Wang, J., Zhao, W.: Bad data detection using linear wls and sampled values in digital substations. IEEE Trans. Power Delivery **33**(1), 150–157 (2018)
3. Wang, J., Meng, R., Rice, S.G., Sun, X.: A fusion steganographic algorithm based on faster R-CNN. CMC: Comput. Mater. Contin. **55**(1), 001–016 (2018)
4. Li, F., Sherratt, R.S., Zeng, D., Dai, Y., Wang, J.: Adversarial learning for distant supervised relation extraction. CMC: Comput. Mater. Contin. **55**(1), 121–136 (2018)

5. Wang, S., Su, A., Ji, C., Ge, W., Xia, Y., Yan, C.: A fast method for identifying bad data of massive power network data. In: 2017 IEEE Conference on Energy Internet and Energy System Integration (EI2), pp. 1–5 (2017)
6. Wu, Z., et al.: Power system bad load data detection based on an improved fuzzy c-means clustering algorithm. In: 2017 IEEE Power Energy Society General Meeting, pp. 1–5 (2017)
7. Pau, M., Ponci, F., Monti, A.: Analysis of bad data detection capabilities through smart meter based state estimation. In: 2018 IEEE International Conference on Environment and Electrical Engineering and 2018 IEEE Industrial and Commercial Power Systems Europe (EEEIC/I CPS Europe), pp. 1–6 (2018)
8. Song, C., Jing, W., Zeng, P., Rosenberg, C.: An analysis on the energy consumption of circulating pumps of residential swimming pools for peak load management. Appl. Energy **195**, 1–12 (2017)
9. Song, C., Wei, J., Peng, Z., Haibin, Y., Rosenberg, C.: Energy consumption analysis of residential swimming pools for peak load shaving. Appl. Energy **220**, 176–191 (2018)
10. Xu, C., Song, C., Zeng, P., Yu, H.: Secure resource allocation for energy harvesting cognitive radio sensor networks without and with cooperative jamming. Comput. Netw. **141**, 189–198 (2018)
11. Wan, M., Zhao, J., Yuan, W., Zeng, P., Cui, J., Shang, W.: Intrusion detection of industrial control based on semi-supervised clustering strategy. Inform. Control **46**(4), 462–468 (2017)
12. Shang, W., Cui, J., Song, C., Zhao, J., Zeng, P.: Research on industrial control anomaly detection based on FCM and SVM. In: 2018 17th IEEE International Conference on Trust, Security and Privacy in Computing And Communications/12th IEEE International Conference on Big Data Science and Engineering (TrustCom/BigDataSE), pp. 218–222 (2018)
13. Chang, X., Wang, J., Wang, J., Lu, K., Yi, Z.: On the optimal design of secure network coding against wiretapping attack. Comput. Netw. **99**(C), 82–98 (2016)
14. Chang, X., et al.: Accuracy-aware interference modeling and measurement in wireless sensor networks. IEEE Trans. Mob. Comput. **15**(2), 278–291 (2016)
15. Zhu, H., et al.: A novel lung cancer detection algorithm for CADs based on SSP and level set. Technol. Health Care **25**(S1), 1–11 (2017)
16. Song, C., Zeng, P., Wang, Z., Zhao, H., Yu, H.: Wearable continuous body temperature measurement using multiple artificial neural networks. IEEE Trans. Ind. Inform. **14**(10), 4395–4406 (2018)
17. Frey, B.J., Dueck, D.: Clustering by passing messages between data points. Science **315**(5814), 972–976 (2007)

Input-Output Analysis of Chinese National Agricultural Science and Technology Park

Anqi Huang[1], Chao Zhang[1(✉)], Pingzeng Liu[1], Junmei Wang[1], Wanming Ren[2], and Yong Zheng[2]

[1] Shandong Agricultural University, Tai'an 271018, China
zhangchao1478@163.com

[2] Shandong Provincial Agricultural Information Center, Ji'nan 250013, China

Abstract. To explore the conducive to China's agricultural science and technology park of input and output of the related strategy and promote agricultural supply side structural reform in China, we use cobb-douglas production function model, combined with stepwise regression and principal component regression method, the analysis of 2015–2017 China national agricultural science and technology park enterprise data. We summarized the relationship between the input and output by cobb-douglas production function. The investment of labor force and capital investment and the annual output value were positive correlation, but the elasticity coefficient of labor input three years to show the trend of increasing year by year. Elasticity coefficient of capital in three years presents a decreasing trend year by year. By stepwise regression and principal component regression method, you can see that is not the total amount of investment. The greater the output, the more technology innovation factors will become the future main factors influencing the development of the national agricultural science and technology park. Therefore, China should strengthen agricultural science and technology innovation, cultivate agricultural science and technology talents. Develop agricultural science and technology innovation projects, so as to promote China's agricultural supply-side structural reform.

Keywords: Input-output analysis · Cobb-douglas production function · Regression fitting · Stepwise regression · Principal component analysis

1 Introduction

Our country is in a critical period to speed up the realization of agricultural modernization, our country economy also has the high quality development stage of high-speed growth stage the wide application of agricultural technology innovation is the necessary way to realize agricultural modernization work [1] national agricultural science and technology park is an important task of the CPC central committee put forward by the state council, February 2, 2018, six ministries of national agricultural science and technology park development plan (2018–2025) to further accelerate the development of national agricultural science and technology park innovation, environment conducive to innovation and technology diffusion source of power, has important effect on agriculture economic development.

X. Sun et al. (Eds.): ICAIS 2019, LNCS 11633, pp. 509–523, 2019.
https://doi.org/10.1007/978-3-030-24265-7_44

Agricultural science and technology park as the development of the agricultural innovation technology, as well as China's agricultural technological innovation in the new period and the spread of the new model [2], since started construction, the various departments at all levels of government support, has become an important carrier to integrate into modern agriculture, and in establishing agricultural industrialization in our country large-scale standardized production base and modern agriculture industry system plays an important role in [3]. Nowadays, our country gradually open seven batches of national agricultural science and technology park, among them, the fifth group of national agricultural science and technology park, the most open in 45 different areas and open at least for the fourth batch of open area is located in eight areas, at the same time, the seventh group of national agricultural science and technology park enterprises open all located in the western region, so our open state science and technology park enterprises will focus on the Midwest in the future, in order to drive the agricultural development in the Midwest.

At present, the academic study of agricultural science and technology park is mainly focused on the characteristics of agricultural science and technology park and type [4] present situation and the development mode of dynamic mechanism [5, 6, 8, 9] development level comprehensive evaluation promoting innovation and development capacity [10, 11] technology innovation diffusion [2, 12, 13] and its relationship with regional social and economic development [3, 9], etc., and the research about agricultural science and technology park of input and output is less, only a few results are mainly based on DEA method for the research of agricultural science and technology park in Beijing, systematically studies the national agriculture science and technology park enterprise less input and output results. As an important carrier for the transformation of agricultural scientific and technological achievements.

Based on green GDP in the context of the quality measure of economic growth in China, the author Xiao HuanMing to natural resources and environment, as a kind of inputs into ke sermons glass production function, measures and analyzes the quality of economic growth in 2001–2011, that the improvement of growth quality should reflect the resource allocation efficiency, and the efficiency of resource allocation should not only consider the input and output efficiency of labor and capital, the economic system should also be considered for the consumption of natural resources and damage to the environment.

Paul H. Douglas in the paper of 《The Cobb-Douglas Production Function Once Again: Its History, Its Testing, and Some New Empirical Values》 using 7 years of observations on Australian manufacturing industries during the 1950s and 1960s. He found that, in all seven cases, constant returns to scale are very closely approximated, and the coefficient for labor hovers near 0.6.

In the paper of 《Cobb-Douglas Production Function: The Case of a Converging Economy》, Dana Hájková and Jaromír Hurník test whether this fact renders the application of the Cobb-Douglas production function unreliable for the Czech economy. For the period 1995–2005, they do not find significant difference between the calculation of the supply side of the Czech economy by the Cobb-Douglas production function and a more general production function.

2 Materials and Methods

2.1 Data Collection and Pretreatment

Firstly, the distribution of enterprises in China's national agricultural science and technology park is analyzed, which can be obtained through ArcMap software. The current open national agricultural science and technology park enterprises are located in the provinces, autonomous regions and municipalities directly under the central government, as shown in the figure below (Fig. 1).

Fig. 1. Distribution of enterprises in agricultural science and technology parks in China (different colors indicate different batches of enterprises in national agricultural science and technology parks)

Data of enterprises in 92 national agricultural science and technology parks were used in this paper. From 2015 to 2017, a total of 276 original data were obtained from China statistical yearbook of related years.

In terms of data preprocessing, because involves the quantitative calculation of explanation variables so that the fitting model, need to have some qualitative variables into quantitative variables, such as whether in the construction site management system, is to use Numbers 1, said no use Numbers 0 means in addition, data is incomplete, exist in the process of data collection in order to avoid data loss caused the result deviation, according to the common sense, after three years of data for mathematical calculations to fill corresponding data the imperfect items.

2.2 Research Ideas and Methods

In this paper, the cobb-douglas production function is used as the research model. First, the processing results of the model are fitted and analyzed to analyze the influence of different factors on the annual total output value in the same year and the variation trend of different factors in three years. Secondly, by using statistical stepwise regression of the sub sets and principal component regression method, through the R software data for further processing, according to the years to get the corresponding regression model, analysis the relationship between input and output per year, discuss the influence of main factors on the input-output, conducive to national agricultural science and technology park development strategy.

Douglas Production Function

Cobb Douglas production function was originally American mathematician Cobb c. w. Cobb) and economist Paul Douglas (Paul h. Douglas) together to investigate the relationship between the input and output in the production function of creation is to make improvements in the production function, the general form, introduced the technical resources the factors used to predict the national and regional industrial system or large production and analysis of the development way of a economic mathematical model, referred to as "production function. As one of the most widely used forms of production function in economics, it plays an important role in the study and application of mathematical economics and econometrics

$$Y = A(t) \cdot L^{\alpha} \cdot K^{\beta} \cdot \mu$$

Y said gross value of industrial output, A comprehensive technical level (t), L said in the number of Labour (unit is ten thousand people, or people), capital K said, generally refers to the fixed assets net, alpha is the elasticity coefficient of labor, beta is the capital output elastic coefficient, mu said see from this model, the influence of random disturbance, decided to main factors of the development level of industrial system is put into labor for fixed assets and integrated technology based on the combination of alpha.

Gradual Regression

Is one of the basic idea of stepwise regression will be introduced to the investigation of index model, to explain the introduction of every variable F inspection at the same time, has been elected to the interpretation of the variables by t test, excluding new explanatory variables are introduced to become old explanatory variables was not significant, to ensure that the introduction of explanatory variables when the regression equation only contains significant variables, until there is no significant variables can be introduced into the model, and no significant variables in the model, thus obtains the optimal variable set.

Principal Component Regression

Principal component analysis, it is to investigate a method of multivariate statistical correlation between multiple variables, study how to use a few principal components to reveal the internal structure of between multiple variables, namely a few principal components was derived from the original variables, to make them as much as possible to retain the information of the original variables, and related to each other between each other, mathematical processing is usually the original P index as a linear combination, as a new composite indicator.

3 Empirical Analysis

3.1 Fitting and Analysis of Cobb-Douglas Production Function

Model Fitting and Analysis of Data in 2015

According to the data of 2015, the total investment of the number of science and technology personnel in the enterprise in the year of annual output value was selected as the input factor, and the missing data related items were eliminated. Secondly, three variables should be taken as the logarithm when fitting. Since the value of three variables is required to be greater than zero, the data that does not meet the requirements should be deleted. Finally, the linear fitting of data is carried out to obtain the following results (Fig. 2).

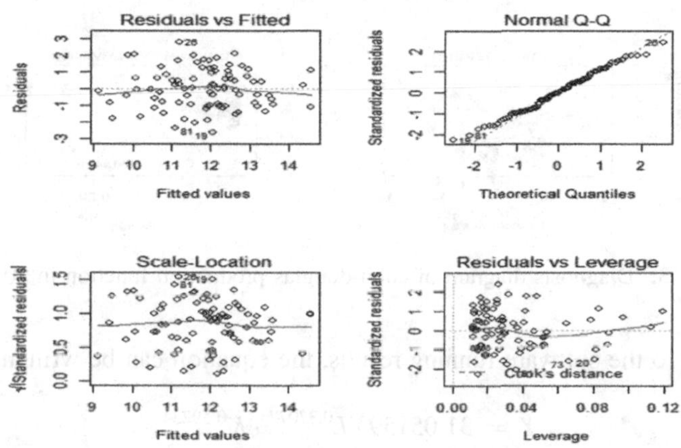

Fig. 2. 2015 cobb-douglas production function diagnosis diagram

According to the software running result 0 s, the equation can be written as

$$Y = 3.52722 \cdot L^{0.22397} \cdot K^{0.80476}$$

The regression equation and the regression coefficient both pass the significance test, so the obtained equation has practical significance.

First, the two elastic coefficients obtained by the model fitting are positive, indicating that the input labor and input capital are positively correlated with the annual gross output value. If the input labor and input capital increase, the annual gross output value will increase accordingly. The elasticity coefficient of labor force is about 0.22, that is, every 1% increase of labor input, the corresponding increase of annual output value is 0.22%. The elasticity coefficient of capital is about 0.80. If the input capital increases by 1%, the annual output value will increase by 0.80% accordingly.

Secondly, the two elastic coefficients are about 1.03/1, which is consistent with the hypothesis proposed by cobb-douglas production function. Correspondingly, this year's agricultural science and technology park is equal to scale return.

Model Fitting and Analysis of Data in 2016

The following results can be obtained after corresponding processing of data in 2016 (Fig. 3).

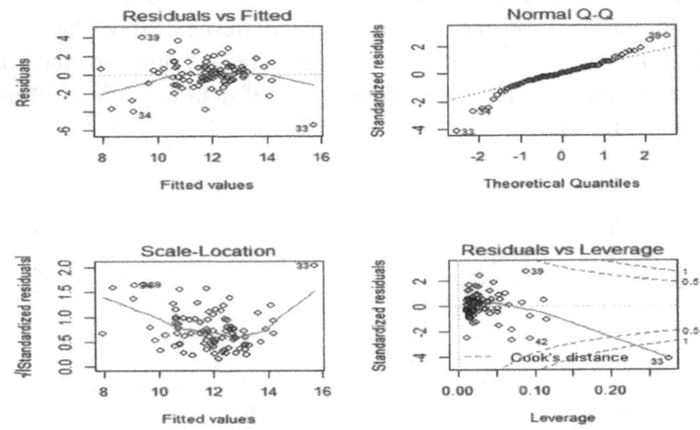

Fig. 3. Diagnosis diagram of cobb-douglas production function in 2016

According to the software running results, the equation can be written as

$$Y = 31.05159 \cdot L^{0.37077} \cdot K^{0.59234}$$

Both the regression equation and the regression coefficient have passed the significance test, and the obtained equation has practical significance.

First of all, the obtained two elastic coefficients are positive, and the input labor and capital are still positively correlated with the annual total output value. The elasticity coefficient of labor input was increased to about 0.37, so every 1% increase in labor input and annual output value was increased by 0.37%. The elasticity coefficient of input capital decreases correspondingly, which is about 0.59. For every 1% increase of capital input, the annual total output value will increase by 0.59%.

Secondly, the two elastic coefficients obtained are about 0.96, and this year's agricultural science and technology park is still the one with constant return on scale.

Model Fitting and Analysis of Data in 2017

The data of 2017 were processed accordingly and obtained (Fig. 4):

The equation can be written as follows:

$$Y = 48.81365 \cdot L^{0.55044} \cdot K^{0.46011}$$

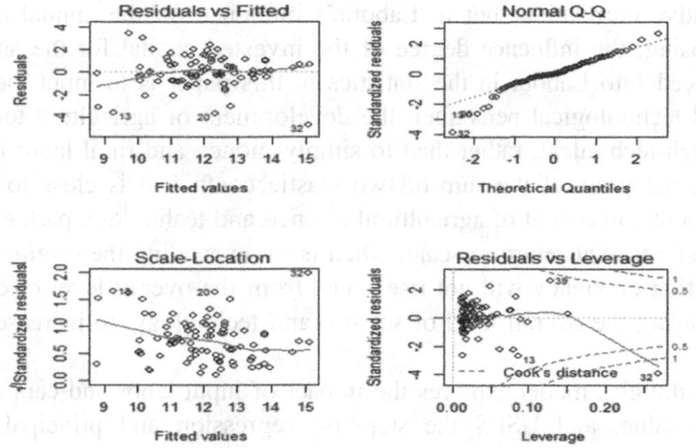

Fig. 4. 2017 cobb-douglas production function diagnosis diagram

The two elastic coefficients are positive, and the annual output value of labor and capital is still positive. The elasticity coefficient of input labor is about 0.55, which is higher than that of 2016. While the elasticity coefficient of input capital is about 0.46, which still shows a decreasing trend, the sum of the two elasticity coefficients is close to 1. This year, the agricultural science and technology park is still the same with the scale return.

Three-Year Model Comparison and Analysis

Although the annual labor elasticity coefficient and the investment clasticity coefficient are both positive, and the labor and capital are both positively correlated with the annual total output value, their influences on the annual total output value are different. The variation trend of the three-year relevant elastic coefficient is shown in the figure below (Fig. 5).

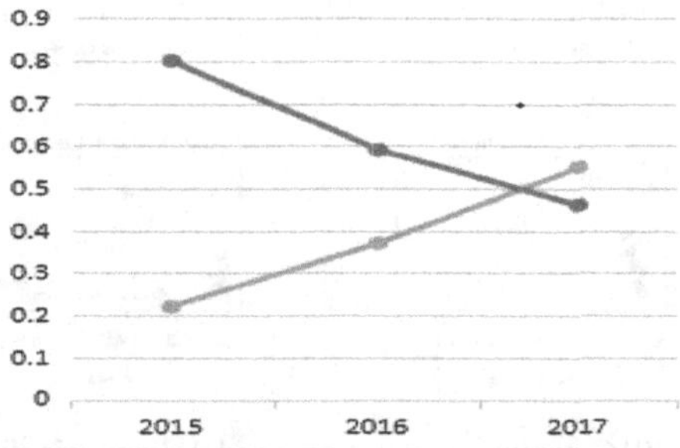

Fig. 5. Labor elasticity coefficient and capital elasticity coefficient in 2015–2017

By above knowable, three years of the elasticity coefficient of labor input presents the increasing trend year by year, the elasticity coefficient of capital presents a decreasing trend year by year, although both elastic coefficient and the annual output value is positive correlation, but in Labour's influence on the annual output value degree increasing, the influence degree of the invested capital for the annual output value is reduced Into Labour in the statistics in this paper is to input the number of scientific and technological personnel, the development of agriculture today increasingly need high-tech talent, rather than to simply money and rural labor input.

Second, three years of the sum of two elastic coefficient is close to 1, from the overall, the input and output of agricultural science and technology park enterprises in China are paid constant return to scale, when is by expanding the original production scale, production efficiency will not rise, must from the overall level of current technology, by raising the overall level of science and technology, to increase production efficiency.

The cobb-douglas model explores the impact of input labor and capital on annual gross output value, and USES the stepwise regression and principal component regression methods to explore other influencing factors on annual gross output value.

3.2 Stepwise Regression Analysis

Model Fitting and Analysis of Data in 2016

Stepwise regression using R software, by using step method of stepwise regression, there is still not significant explanatory variables in the equation, the use of drop1 function, according to the AIC criterion and residual sum of squares of two standards, eliminate variables X22 X12, in front of the variables in the equation regression coefficients are significant, the equation is obtained as the research object, the results are as follows (Fig. 6).

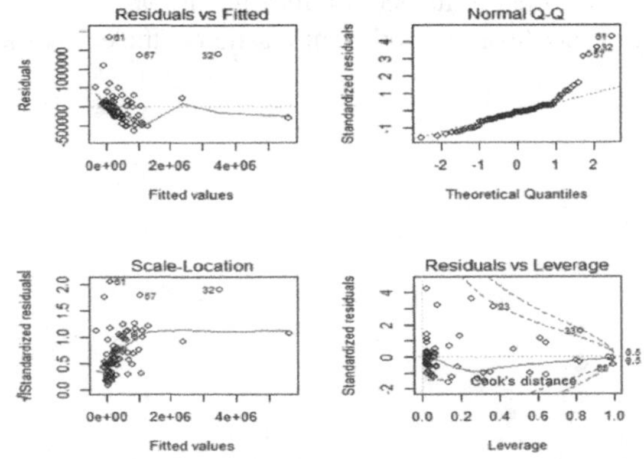

Fig. 6. 2016 stepwise regression model diagnosis diagram

The model can be obtained by stepwise regression of the data in 2016 from the above results:

$$Y = 36412.4 - 6009.5X_5 + 297.7X_9 - 1.2X_{13} - 6480.8X_{21} + 8367.6X_{25} + 3.7X_{27} - 6.7X_{28} - 535.2X_{30} + 1404.1X_{32} + 1825.4X_{33} - 3206.1X_{34} - 18.7X_{35}$$

Among them, the said electric Shang Ping pounced just says the park management committee information into the original value of the said enterprise large scientific instrument total said the introduction of new technology for the enterprise when the enterprise to promote new technology says the total amount of investment says the government said the total amount of investment enterprises technical personnel number said the staff number of science and technology college number said the number of science and technology correspondent said implementation of the development of science and technology project item number said the implementation of science and technology development projects in the total investment'll add X (into English).

Because both the regression equation and the regression coefficient have passed the significance test, the obtained equation has practical significance, and the obtained equation is analyzed.

Model Fitting and Analysis of Data in 2017

According to 2017 data, stepwise regression using R software, by using step after step by step regression equation is still not significant explanatory variables, using drop1 function, according to the AIC criterion sum of squared residuals two standard, in order to variable [8], in order to eliminate the variable X5 X12 X2 X24 X6, in front of the variables in the equation regression coefficients are significant, at this point, the equation of will now serve as the research object, and the results are as follows (Fig. 7).

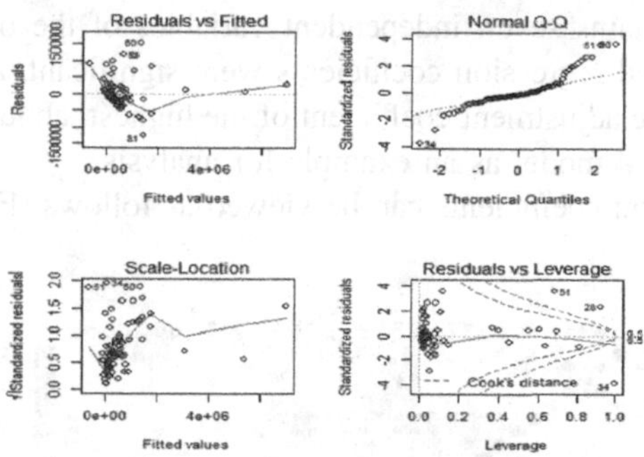

Fig. 7. Diagnostic chart of stepwise regression model in 2017

It can be seen from above that the model can be obtained through progressive regression for the data of 2017:

$$Y = 24090 + 12.6X_1 + 52660X_7 - 2.7X_{15} + 12640X_{16} - 1046X_{20} - 0.1X_{27} + 0.8X_{29} + 293.6X_{30} + 987.7X_{32}$$

Among them, the X1 “park investment management company’s registered capital,” said X7 “high-tech companies,” said X15 said “among them: provincial-level research and development center,” said X16 “the enterprise introduces the construction of production number,” said X20 “when enterprise introduction of livestock and poultry aquaculture varieties (matching) number nine”, X27 said “when the total amount of investment,” said X29 “enterprise funds,” said X30 “enterprise technical personnel number,” said X32 “enterprise technical personnel number the number of college”.

3.3 Principal Component Regression Analysis

Model Fitting and Analysis of Data in 2015

First, because of the serious data loss in 2015, only 32 national agricultural science and technology parks have complete information when all the incomplete data are removed. At this time, the number of available park groups is less than the total number of explanatory variables, so it is not suitable for the gradual regression of data in this year.

Then, another method should be selected for model fitting for 2015 data.

Using the function of regsubsets contained in the R software leaps program package, select the optimal model in case of different number of independent variables, and the following results can be obtained.

First number of the independent variable of fitting with different optimal model respectively, then analyze the optimal model of independent variable number of different, because it contains seven independent variables of the optimal model of the regression equation and regression coefficients were significant, and the equation can be determined after the adjustment coefficient of the highest, about 0.9, so in the seven variables of the optimal model as an example for analysis.

First, the correlation coefficients can be viewed as follows (Fig. 8).

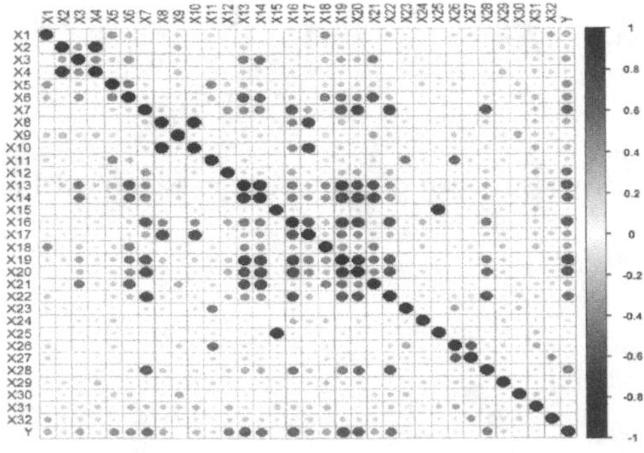

Fig. 8. Correlation coefficient for 2015 can be viewed

From the above figure, there is a correlation between the selected explanatory variables. In order to further confirm whether there is multicollinearity between explanatory variables, the kappa value is obtained by using R software, which indicates that there is serious multicollinearity between explanatory variables. In order to eliminate the influence of multicollinearity, principal component regression was carried out on the model, and R software was used to obtain (Fig. 9).

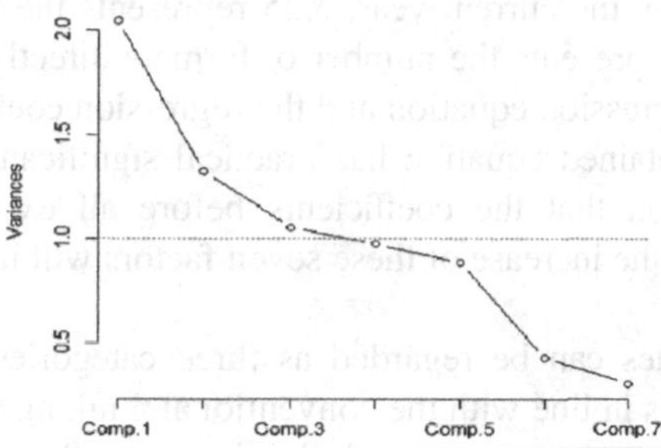

Fig. 9. Gravel map of principal component analysis in 2015

Considering the accumulative contribution rate and lithotripsy, the cumulative contribution rate of the first five principal components is up to 89%. Therefore, we select the first five principal components and conduct principal component regression, and the results are as follows (Fig. 10).

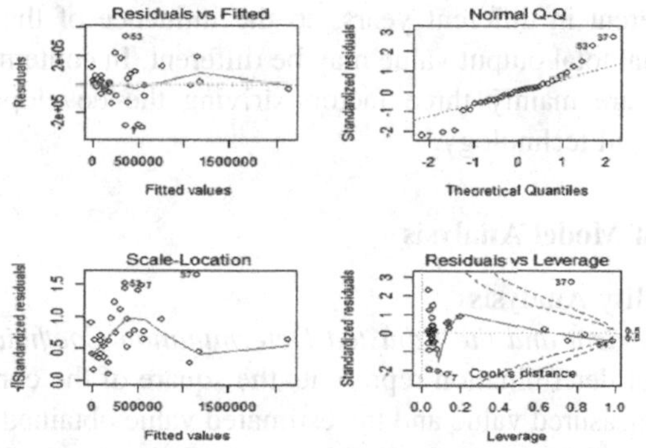

Fig. 10. Diagnosis diagram of 2015 principal component regression model

Because the above equation represents the relationship between the explained variable and the principal component, it will bring great inconvenience in the process of calculation and application. The original coordinates can be obtained by coordinate transformation. Therefore, the above equation can be further modified into the relationship between the explained variable and the explained variable, which is obtained by R software.

The linear equation is

$$Y = -95979.7 + 597.3X_1 + 36.8X_3 + 46711.9X_5 + 6.7X_{12} + 15676.3X_{19} + 2.5X_{25} + 31.4X_{28}$$

Where X1 represents the number of product brands, X3 represents the area of the completed core area of the park, X5 represents the number of investment institutions, X12 represents the annual total investment in R&D, X19 represents the number of new technologies promoted in the current year, X25 represents the total investment in the current year, and X28 represents the number of farmers directly involved.

Because both the regression equation and the regression coefficient have passed the significance test, the obtained equation has practical significance, and it can be seen from the above equation that the coefficients before all explanatory variables are positive, indicating that the increase of these seven factors will increase the annual total output value.

These seven variables can be regarded as three categories of labor, capital and technology, this model is in line with the conventional thinking, namely the increase of these three related investment, output will also increase, this is because most of the points of agricultural science and technology park is in the primary stage of development, in the three years of construction stage, the development is not perfect to promote overall development of the park need inputs, so the three factors on the development of agricultural science and technology park has played a role in promoting.

By fitting and analyzing the data of different years, it can be clearly found that the fitting models are different in different years. This is because the current development status of the scientific and technological level and the agricultural science and technology park is different in different years, so the influence of the same explanatory variable on the annual total output value may be different. In contemporary agricultural development, there are mainly three factors driving the development: labor force, capital and science and technology.

3.4 Two Kinds of Model Analysis

Model Fitting Quality Analysis

Determination Coefficient and the Adjusted Determination Coefficient

The coefficient of determination represents the square of the correlation coefficient between the actual measured value and the estimated value obtained by the model. The higher the coefficient of determination of the model indicates the higher the interpretation degree of the explanatory variable to the explained variable, that is, the better the fitting model is.

$$R^2 = \frac{SSR}{SST} = 1 - \frac{SSE}{SST}$$

Therefore, in the comparative analysis of the models with different number of explanatory variables, the factor of the number of explanatory variables must be taken into account, and the determination coefficient should be adjusted to remove the number of explanatory variables, which will cause different effects. A new measurement index, namely the adjusted determination coefficient, can be obtained.

$$\bar{R}^2 = 1 - \frac{\frac{SSE}{n-k}}{\frac{SST}{n-1}} = 1 - (1 - R^2) \cdot \frac{n-1}{n-k}$$

Where, the SSR in the above formula represents the sum of regression squared, SST represents the total sum of deviation squared, SSE represents the sum of residual squared, n is the observed sample number, and k is the number of parameters.

First, for the two models in 2015, the adjusted determination coefficient of the production function is about 0.47. After principal component regression of the optimal model with different number of explanatory variables, the adjusted determination coefficient of the model with seven variables is the highest, which is about 0.90. Secondly, for the two models in 2016, the adjusted determination coefficient of the production function is about 0.41. The adjusted determination coefficient of the model obtained by stepwise regression is about 0.75. Finally, for the two models in 2017, the adjusted determination coefficient of the production function is about 0.46. The adjusted determination coefficient of the model obtained by stepwise regression is about 0.84.

In conclusion, the explanatory power of the variables to be explained, is obtained by regression fitting model is superior to the original cobb-douglas production function, this is because, through the regression fitting function, is pointing to the park this year, is analyzed, and the cobb-douglas production function is the applicable scope is big, but based on the analysis of the specific circumstances, the explanation of the model is poor.

Comparative Analysis of the Actual Meaning of the Model

Since the cobb-douglas production function only contains two variables, a comparative analysis is made from these two aspects, namely, capital investment and labor input.

First, from the perspective of labor input, the labor elasticity coefficient of cobb-douglas production function is positive in the three years, and the labor elasticity coefficient of labor input shows a trend of increasing year by year. By analyzing the model obtained through regression fitting, the factor of the number of college students in enterprise science and technology personnel in 2016 and the factor of the number of college students in enterprise science and technology personnel in 2017 were positively correlated with the annual total output value in that year.

This shows that, when the infrastructure of the park is improved with the increase of time, the simple increase of capital investment will not cause the increase of annual total output value, and at the same time, it is likely to be counterproductive.

From the two aspects, the influence of labor input on the annual gross output value and the influence of capital input on the annual gross output value are similar in the two models when the park construction is at different degrees with the passage of time.

4 Summary

In three years of cobb-douglas production function, of labor and capital invested and the annual output value were positive correlation, but the elasticity coefficient of labor input three years to show the trend of increasing year by year, three years of elasticity coefficient of capital presents a decreasing trend year by year, in this article the statistical data of labor is the input of science and technology personnel quantity, so today's agricultural development is more and more need to high-tech talent, rather than to simply money and rural labor input, from the overall, the input and output of agricultural science and technology park enterprises in China are paid constant return to scale, when is by expanding the original production rules. Therefore, it is necessary to start with the overall level of current science and technology and increase the production efficiency by improving the overall level of science and technology.

In the regression fitting model, there were 7 explanatory variables in the model in 2015, all of which were positively correlated with the annual gross output value. There were 12 explanatory variables in the model in 2016, among which 7 were negatively correlated with the annual total output value, and 5 were positively correlated with the annual total output value. There are 9 explanatory variables in the model in 2017, 3 of which are negatively correlated with the annual total output value, and 6 of which are positively correlated with the annual total output value. Therefore, over time, more and more scientific and technical personnel are needed to participate in the development and construction of agriculture.

References

1. Dezhi, Q., Huimin, S.: Analysis of the reason for China's agricultural industrial structure adjustment based on the extended cobbe Douglas production function. Rural. Econ. 59–63 (2016)
2. Huanming, X.: Quality measurement of China's economic growth based on green GDP. Stat. Decis. Mak. **09**, 27–29 (2014)
3. Xiaojing, Z.: Analysis of factors influencing China's economic growth based on cobbe Douglas production function. China Mark. **41**, 117–118+133 (2013)
4. Pengpeng, W., Haijun, H.: Empirical study on Chongqing economic growth based on C-D production function. Market BBS **07**, 20+14 (2011)
5. Jie, L., Yinlao, K., Yao, L.: A study of the pan-cobbe Douglas model on the relationship between investment and consumption and GDP growth. Contemp. Econ. **06**, 120–121 (2007)
6. Xiaojie, Z., Guanglin, Y., Fulin, W.: Calculation of agricultural mechanization contribution rate by cobb Douglas production function method. Agric. Mech. Res. **03**, 37–39 (2000)
7. Paulo, D., Diogenes, L.: Cobb-Douglas, translog stochastic production function and data envelopment analysis in total factor productivity in Brazilian agribusiness. J. Oper. Supply Chain. Manag., 20–33 (2009)
8. Humphrey, T.M.: Algebraic production functions and their uses before Cobb-DouglasX. FRB Richmond Econ. Q. **83**(1), 51–83 (2016)
9. Dana, H., Jaromír, H.: Cobb-douglas production function: the case of a converging economy. Czech J. Econ. Financ. **57**(9–10), 465–476 (2007)

10. Antràs, P.: Is the U.S. Aggregate production function Cobb-Douglas? New estimates of the elasticity of substitution. Contrib. Macroecon. **4**(1), 10 (2018)
11. Douglas, P.H.: The Cobb-Douglas production function once again: its history, its testing, and some new empirical values. J. Polit. Econ. **84**(5), 903–916 (1976)
12. Jichang, Z., Xun, Z.: Agricultural modernization was first realized in the construction of agricultural science and technology demonstration park. China Agric. Sci. Technol. Guid. **3**, 10–13 (2001)
13. Tongsheng, L., Yali, L.: Technological diffusion in agricultural science and technology parks. Geogr. Res. **35**(3), 419–430 (2016)
14. Xuexin, Z., Yujun, Z.: Study on interaction between agricultural science and technology park and regional economic and social development in Jiangsu province. Agric. Econ. **9**, 72–76 (2013)
15. Heping, J.: Analysis of characteristics and types of agricultural science and technology parks in China. Chin. Rural. Econ. **10**, 23–29 (2000)
16. Jianzhong, Z., Tongsheng, L., Huidong, L.: Development status and dynamic mechanism of China's agricultural science and technology parks. Rural. Econ. **12**, 56–59 (2006)
17. Heping, J., Kai, C.: Agricultural science and technology park: focus on effective model and demonstration. Agric. Econ. **1**, 9–14 (2009)
18. Hongyong, S., Xiaojing, L., Zhaoqiang, J.: Discussion on development model of Cangzhou national agricultural science and technology park. J. Chin. Ecol. Agric. **8**, 1145–1150 (2016)
19. Donghe, L., Zhilin, S., Yuanyuan, Z.: Study on evaluation index system of Heilongjiang agricultural science and technology park. China Agric. Resour. Reg. **2**, 79–83 (2016)
20. Ou, W., Wenliang, W.: Research on evaluation index system of China agricultural science and technology park. Agric. Tech. Econ. **4**, 25–28 (2003)
21. Wang, B., Liu, P., Chao, Z., et al.: Research on hybrid model of garlic short-term price forecasting based on big data. CMC **57**(2), 283–296 (2018)
22. Chen, W., Feng, G., Zhang, C., et al.: Development and application of big data platform for garlic industry chain. CMC **58**(1), 229–248 (2019)

A Power Grid Operations Monitoring Platform Based on Big Data Technology

Shanting Su[1(✉)], Xiangmao Chang[1], Jing Li[1], Yuan Qiu[1], Sai Liu[2], Lin Qiao[3], and Shuo Chen[3]

[1] Nanjing University of Aeronautics and Astronautics, Nanjing 211106, People's Republic of China
1174583031@qq.com

[2] NARI Group Corporations/State Grid Electric Power Research Institute, Nanjing 211000, People's Republic of China

[3] State Grid Liaoning Electric Power Co., Ltd., Shenyang 110000, People's Republic of China

Abstract. At present, the evaluation of power grid operations is still in the qualitative stage, which is lack of quantitative evaluation and analysis methods, and cannot meet the requirements of modern power grid development and the needs of the lean management of Power Grid Corp. Based on the characteristics of the power grid operations, constructing the power distribution network operation monitoring platform based on big data technology is an effective way to achieve quantitative evaluation of operational efficiency, power supply capacity, and region monitoring. This paper introduces the construction and application of big data based power grid network operation monitoring platform, including the system architecture of the power distribution network operation monitoring platform, the evaluation model of power supply capacity and operation efficiency of distribution network, functions of data access and quality control, power grid operation online visual monitoring analysis, and operation monitoring and control cooperation. Actual operation of the system shows that the power grid network operation monitoring platform provides a quantitative evaluation and decision basis for power grid planning, construction and production operations, makes full use of the existing data value, provides decision support for the business sector, and further enhances the strategic decision-making and operation monitoring center operation control and risk prevention ability. At the same time, the power operation monitoring platform has also played a good reference role for the construction of other power operation monitoring platform.

Keywords: Smart grid · Big data · Operations monitoring

1 Introduction

Power grid operations monitoring plays an important role in improving the efficiency and power supply capability of distribution network. Intelligent distribution network operation monitoring can more timely and accurately find problems in the process of distribution network operation, help enterprises avoid operational risks, realize the

X. Sun et al. (Eds.): ICAIS 2019, LNCS 11633, pp. 524–533, 2019.
https://doi.org/10.1007/978-3-030-24265-7_45

simulation analysis of power supply capacity coordination, load shedding, and on-line evaluation of enterprise power supply capacity, so as to effectively improve the monitoring and management level of business departments and promote enterprises. The management level of battalion allocation and adjustment is [1]. At the same time, by mining daily grid operation data, intelligent distribution network operation monitoring can provide decision-making basis, thereby further optimizing the production, operation and management of power grid [2].

At present, the operation monitoring of distribution network has been extensively studied both at home and abroad. [3] studied the operation mode adjustment and service recovery of distributed generation based on digraph. [4] studied the voltage and reactive power optimization of distribution network based on real-time collaborative simulation monitoring platform. [5] studied the influence of soft open point on distribution network operation. [6] studied the effect of soft open point on distribution network operation. Based on the real-time database, a comprehensive monitoring platform for distribution network switching stations, [7] gave a monitoring system for rural distribution network operation, [8] presented a design method for distribution network online monitoring system, [9] discussed the optimal location of power quality monitoring points in distribution network, [10] studied it the distribution network operation efficiency.

Nevertheless, the actual operation of power grid is still in the stage of qualitative evaluation, lacking of quantitative evaluation and analysis means, unable to meet the requirements of modern power grid development and the needs of lean management of companies, unable to provide quantitative evaluation and auxiliary decision-making basis for power grid planning, construction and production operation, and difficult to fully develop [11–13]. Give full play to the value of existing data to provide decision-making support for business departments, affecting the operational monitoring center's strategic decision-making, operational control, risk prevention and other capabilities.

This paper introduces in detail the construction and application of operation monitoring platform for power grid network based on large data, describes the architecture of operation monitoring platform, discusses in detail the functions of data access and quality control, on-line visual monitoring and analysis of power grid operation, and coordination with operation monitoring and control, and gives the operation of power grid. Monitoring platform's actual operation statistics shows that the power grid network operation monitoring platform provides quantitative evaluation and auxiliary decision-making basis for network planning, construction and production operation, gives full play to the existing data value, provides decision-making support basis for business departments, and further improves the strategic decision-making, operation management and control, risk prevention and other capabilities of the operation monitoring center. At the same time, the power operation monitoring platform has also played a good reference role for the construction of other power operation monitoring platforms.

2 System Functional Framework

In this system, SG-UAP platform is used as the foundation development platform, multi-tier B/S application development mode is adopted, relying on full-service unified data center, and large data and distributed technology are used to construct power network operation monitoring system. Fusion of equipment, assets and operation data across multiple business systems is realized, which lays a solid foundation for on-line monitoring and comprehensive utilization of distribution network data assets. To realize the systematic and quantitative evaluation model of distribution network operation efficiency, and to realize the transformation from equipment layer to efficiency calculation of distribution network system layer, the system can more accurately and comprehensively reflect the operation efficiency of distribution network assets, and support the company's distribution network lean management level to continuously improve. To realize on-line monitoring and on-line evaluation of operation efficiency and coordination degree of power grid at all levels, the system can find the weaknesses and risks of distribution network operation more timely and accurately. To realize the comprehensive mining and analysis of the distribution network full information, change the traditional way of relying on report statistics or partial spot checking, realize the monitoring application based on the distribution network full data, bottom data and massive detailed data across the system, and bring into play the value of "supporting decision-making and service specialty". The specific system functional framework is shown in Fig. 1.

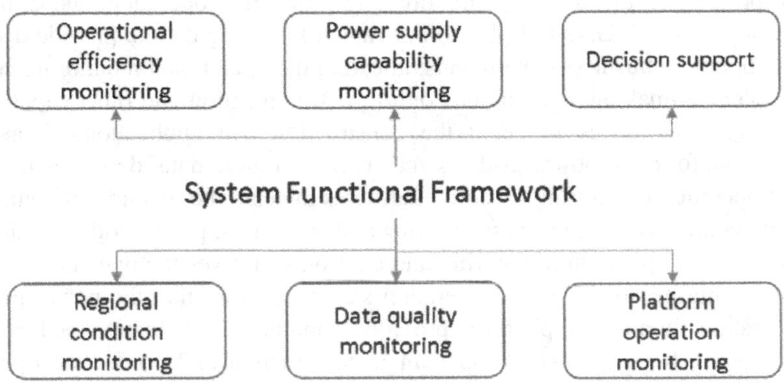

Fig. 1. System functional framework

As shown in Fig. 2, the construction and application project of the operation-related monitoring platform for distribution network based on big data technology achieves the full access of distribution network equipment archives and operation-type detailed data through the full-service unified data center, utilizing the results of operation and distribution, relying on SG-UAP platform, and designs and realizes the operation efficiency monitoring and power supply capability. The functions of monitoring and station area monitoring, such as on-line evaluation of power grid operation efficiency and power supply capacity from three levels of single equipment, same-level equipment to system, promotion of data sharing and effective integration of services between systems, realization of quasi-real-time calculation and monitoring of power grid equipment, system operation efficiency and power supply capacity, are put forward for power grid management. For quantitative analysis support, effective service for major planning, construction, overhaul, operation, marketing and other professional management. Combining with the previous demand investigation work, the provincial power grid operation monitoring system structure, function, model and interface design are carried out to realize the system design of the four main functions of 66 kV power grid operation efficiency monitoring, power supply capacity monitoring, station monitoring and data quality. The system design includes function design, safety protection design, disaster preparedness design, visualization design and database design. Combining with the overall structure design of power grid operation monitoring system, the monitoring of power grid operation efficiency (including 8 secondary modules), power supply capability (including 13 secondary modules), and station area monitoring (including 18 secondary modules) are completed.

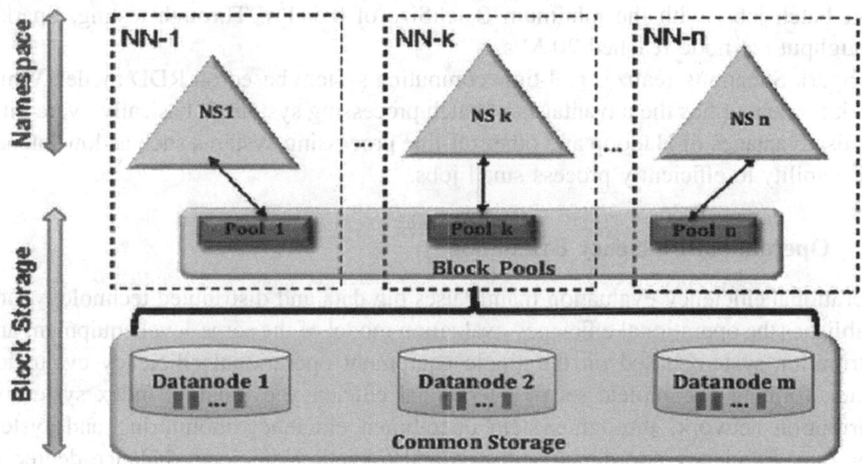

Fig. 2. Namenode management

3 Monitoring Scenario Application

The grid operation related monitoring platform builds the application scenario analysis model, promotes the application of four main monitoring scenarios, including operation efficiency, power supply capacity, station monitoring and data quality, and displays the quasi-real-time calculation and application of the company's distribution network full-scale equipment and system operation efficiency and power supply capacity in the form of maps, charts and curves. Monitoring promotes data sharing and business integration between systems, and achieves good application results. It provides quantitative evaluation and auxiliary decision-making basis for company power grid planning, construction and operation.

3.1 High Availability

Distributed storage HDFS guarantees high reliability of HDFS through a highly reliable Namenode HA scheme. There is always a Namenode as a hot standby to prevent single point failure. HA is implemented by QJM, and file system metadata is stored in a highly reliable cluster composed of Journal Node.

The single failure problem of NameNode is solved by high availability of NameNode HA, but the single performance bottleneck problem of NameNode cannot be solved. The single point performance bottleneck problem in HDFS is solved by managing different namespaces of multiple Namespaces in HDFS Federation. Two NameNodes in each Namespace are highly available for HA, and the namespaces are equivalent to directories mounted under the root partition of HDFS.

3.2 Flow Computing Engine

Spark streaming is a streaming computing engine developed based on Spark streaming. Combined with Kafka, it can be used in almost all streaming quasi-real-time computing scenarios. Its calculation mode is to decompose the flow calculation into a series of short batch jobs, with the minimum BatchSize of 0.5–1 s. Through testing, Spark's throughput per node reached 20 M/s.

Spark Streaming realizes real-time computing system based on RDD model. While Spark Streaming has the advantages of batch processing system, it basically overcomes the disadvantages of Hadoop and other off-line processing systems such as low latency and inability to efficiently process small jobs.

3.3 Operational Efficiency Evaluation

Operational efficiency evaluation mainly uses big data and distributed technology, and establishes the operational efficiency evaluation model of the same-level equipment and distribution system based on the single equipment operational efficiency evaluation model, forming a complete set of operational efficiency evaluation index system of distribution network, through system operational efficiency monitoring and system operation. Efficiency coordination degree and operation efficiency balance degree of main equipment support the evaluation index system of operation efficiency, realize the comprehensive evaluation of operation efficiency of main equipment, same-level equipment and system, visually and stereoscopically display the overall operation efficiency of distribution network, effectively support Liaoning company's penetration monitoring of operation efficiency of power grid from face to point. Measurement and analysis. Operational efficiency evaluation mainly includes system operation efficiency monitoring, system operation efficiency coordination, and main equipment operation efficiency balance monitoring.

3.4 Power Supply Capability Monitoring

Power supply capability is mainly realized by establishing an evaluation model of power supply capability of distribution network considering basic safety rules and operation constraints. The online evaluation of three-level power supply capability of single equipment, same-level equipment and distribution system is realized from the dimensions of maximum available power, power supply capacity reserve and power supply capacity margin. The company's distribution network planning and construction and production operations provide auxiliary decision-making support. Power supply capacity monitoring mainly includes system power supply capacity coordination monitoring, main equipment power supply capacity monitoring, and system load monitoring.

3.5 Platform Monitoring

Power supply capability is mainly realized by establishing an evaluation model of power supply capability of distribution network considering basic safety rules and operation constraints. The online evaluation of three-level power supply capability of single equipment, same-level equipment and distribution system is realized from the dimensions of maximum available power, power supply capacity reserve and power supply capacity margin. The company's distribution network planning and construction and production operations provide auxiliary decision-making support. The monitoring of the area mainly includes the overall monitoring of load monitoring and the overall detection of voltage monitoring.

3.6 Data Quality Detection

Data quality mainly supports the monitoring and analysis of each module of the system, realizes the functions of archives data access, calculation analysis, operation data matching and various archives details of power grid access, so as to ensure the quality of monitoring data of power grid operation of the power supply company. Data quality detection mainly includes file data access detection and operation data matching detection.

4 System Operation Performances

The main interface of the specific monitoring scenario of the distribution network operation monitoring platform is shown in Fig. 3. There are 258 124 power network equipments under 66 kV in this system, including 1063 high-voltage lines, 1982 main transformers, 7371 medium-voltage lines and 247 708 distribution transformers. There are five types of A+, A, B, C and D in the distribution network of 14 prefectural and municipal companies of Liaoning Company. A total of 1581 power supply zones have been included in the operation monitoring of power grid. Among them, 23, 43, 364, 620 and 531 power supply zones are A+, A, B, C and D. Figures 4 and 5 give the system running performance monitoring interface and the system operation efficiency coordination degree monitoring interface.

Combining with the actual business situation, the power grid operation monitoring system is based on the full-service unified data center. It realizes the interface development and debugging of four business systems, namely, production management

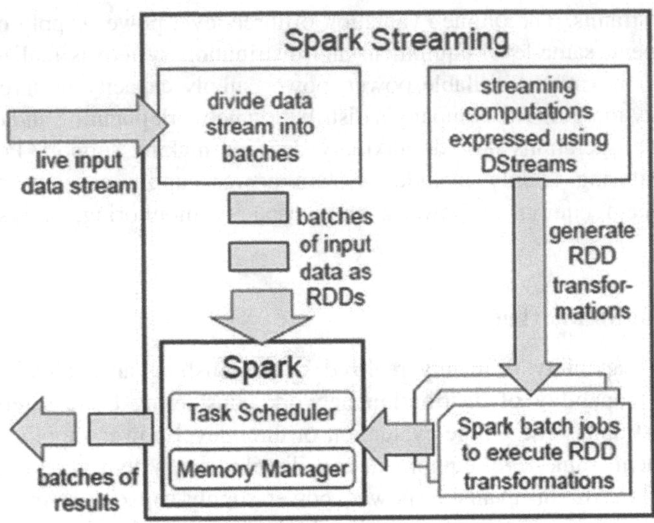

Fig. 3. Flow computing engine framework

system, marketing business application system, power information collection system and power dispatching system. It is connected to production, marketing, dispatching and utilization since January 2016. There are 1.91 billion business data, 800 million calculation data of power grid operation monitoring system, generating 2.71 billion data, occupying 19 T of storage, which provides effective support for the popularization and application of provincial power grid operation monitoring scenarios. Specific data are shown in Table 1:

According to the construction needs of the power grid operation monitoring module project and based on the results of operation and distribution, the data extraction methods of the power grid operation monitoring system and the massive platform 1029 are adjusted and improved. The dispatching operation data are fully accessed through the full-service unified data center, and the matching workers of PMS file data and dispatching operation data are organized and carried out. Do. The file data of main transformer, high voltage line and medium voltage line in PMS 2.0 system are acquired by PMS project group, and the dispatch E file is acquired by dispatching project group. By communicating with dispatching and mass platforms to standardize naming rules, the matching relationship between dispatching data and PMS file data is sorted out and analyzed, and efficient and fast data matching parties are studied. Type.

Up to now, the total number of accessing devices in power network operation monitoring system is 361,000, matched 326,000, and the matching rate of operation data is 90.23%. Among them, the matching rate of main transformer, high voltage line, medium voltage line and distribution transformer is 94.98%, 89.33%, 88.66% and 90.25%, respectively. The popularization and application of provincial power grid operation monitoring module provides data guarantee, and effectively supports the improvement and promotion of operation, distribution and coordination.

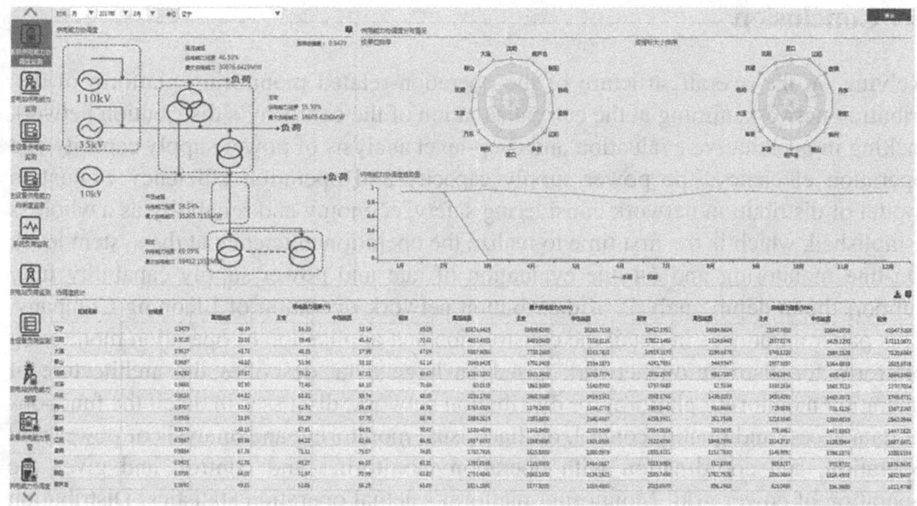

Fig. 4. System running performance monitoring interface

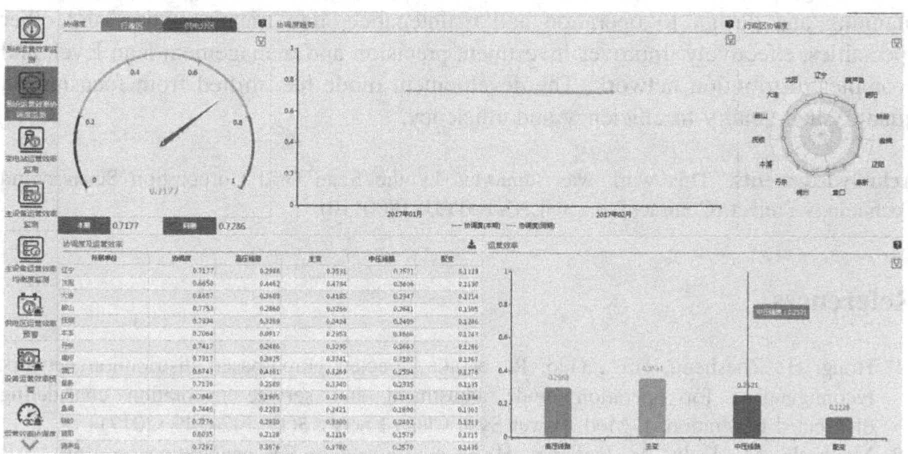

Fig. 5. System operation efficiency coordination degree monitoring interface

Table 1. System performance

No.	Name	Data volume (million)	Storage volume (T)
1	Marketing	8.31	0.068
2	Production management	4.86	0.31
3	Electrical information	3980	0.48
4	Power dispatching	16234	5.11
5	Operation monitoring	9403	0.90

5 Conclusion

Relying on the overall structure of the operation-related monitoring platform of distribution network, aiming at the current situation of the company's distribution network lacking in quantitative evaluation and deep-level analysis of power supply capacity and operation efficiency, the power supply capacity and operation efficiency evaluation model of distribution network considering safety, economy and reliability as a whole is established, which is the first time to realize the operation efficiency at the system level. On-line monitoring and on-line evaluation of rate and power supply capability fully support the in-depth analysis of distribution network operation of Liaoning Company. This paper introduces in detail the construction and application of operation monitoring platform for distribution network based on large data, describes the architecture of operation monitoring platform for distribution network, discusses in detail the functions of data access and quality control, on-line visual monitoring and analysis of power grid operation, and coordination with operation monitoring and control, and gives the operation of power grid. Monitoring platform's actual operation statistics. Distribution network operation monitoring platform based on big data realizes quantitative evaluation of distribution network operation efficiency, power supply capacity and station monitoring, provides quantitative analysis support for distribution network from planning and design to operation and maintenance, line transformation and other specialties, effectively improves investment precision and management lean level, and promotes distribution network. The development mode has shifted from focusing on quantity and quality to efficiency and efficiency.

Acknowledgments. This work was supported by the State Grid Corporation Science and Technology Project (Contract No.: SGLNXT00YJJS1800110).

References

1. Hong, H., Zhesheng, H.U., Guo, R., et al.: Directed graph-based distribution network reconfiguration for operation mode adjustment and service restoration considering distributed generation. J. Mod. Power Syst. Clean Energy **5**(1), 142–149 (2017)
2. Manbachi, M., Sadu, A., Farhangi, H., et al.: Impact of EV penetration on Volt–VAR optimization of distribution networks using real-time co-simulation monitoring platform. Appl. Energy **169**, 28–39 (2016)
3. Cao, W., Wu, J., Jenkins, N., et al.: Benefits analysis of Soft Open Points for electrical distribution network operation. Appl. Energy **165**, 36–47 (2016)
4. Zeng, P., Li, H., He, H., et al.: Dynamic energy management of a microgrid using approximate dynamic programming and deep recurrent neural network learning. IEEE Trans. Smart Grid (2018)
5. Jin, X., Guan, N., Xia, Z.Q., et al.: Packet aggregation real-time scheduling for large-scale WIA-PA industrial wireless sensor networks. ACM Trans. Embed. Comput. Syst. **17**(5), 1–19 (2018)
6. Song, C., Jing, W., Zeng, P., Yu, H., Rosenberg, C.: Energy consumption analysis of residential swimming pools for peak load shaving. Appl. Energy **2018**(220), 176–191 (2018)

7. Jin, X., Kong, F.X., Kong, L.H., et al.: A Hierarchical data transmission framework for industrial wireless sensor and actuator networks. IEEE Trans. Ind. Inform. **13**(4), 2019–2029 (2017)
8. Song, C., Jing, W., Zeng, P., Rosenberg, C.: An analysis on the energy consumption of circulating pumps of residential swimming pools for peak load management. Appl. Energy **195**, 1–12 (2017)
9. Jin, X., Kong, F.X., Kong, L.H., et al.: Reliability and temporality optimization for multiple coexisting wireless HART networks in industrial environments. IEEE Trans. Ind. Electron. **64**(8), 6591–6602 (2017)
10. Song, C., Zeng, P., Wang, Z., Zhao, H., Yu, H.: Wearable continuous body temperature measurement using multiple artificial neural networks. IEEE Trans. Industr. Inf. **14**(10), 4395–4406 (2018)
11. Chi, X., Song, C., Zeng, P., Yu, H.: Secure resource allocation for energy harvesting cognitive radio sensor networks without and with cooperative jamming. Comput. Netw. **141** (4), 189–198 (2018)
12. Cheng, J., Xu, R., Tang, X., Sheng, V.S., Cai, C.: An abnormal network flow feature sequence prediction approach for DDoS attacks detection in big data environment. CMC Comput. Mater. Continua **55**(1), 095–119 (2018)
13. Liu, Y., Peng, H., Wang, J.: Verifiable diversity ranking search over encrypted outsourced data. CMC Comput. Materials Continua **55**(1), 037–057 (2018)

An Efficient Social-Aware Routing Strategy in Mobile Social Networks

Meihua Liu[1], Xinchen Zhang[2(✉)], Shuangkui Xia[3], Jianbin Wu[2], Xiaoli Chen[1], and Mao Tian[1]

[1] School of Electronic Information, Wuhan University, Wuhan, China
[2] School of Physical Science and Technology, Huazhong Normal University, Wuhan, China
zxc9501@hotmail.com
[3] Beijing Institute of Electronic Technology and Application, Beijing, China

Abstract. As a solution to extend the cellular networks' coverage and support more consumers at a lower cost, mobile social networks (MSNs) are used for delay-tolerant data transmission in an opportunistic fashion: messages are transmitted through opportunistic encounters between mobile nodes without the infrastructure. It is common to employ DTN routing algorithm in MSNs, among which Bubble Rap routing is suitable for MSNs since it involves two social characteristics of MSN: community and heterogeneous activity of node. However, there are two important issues that have not been well examined when exploiting Bubble Rap for data transmission in MSN. That is, inaccurate community detection which results from the fact that Bubble Rap neglected transient social groups will leads to a lot of meaningless forwarding of message; and because of the greedy forwarding mode, stuck messages are overlooked by Bubble Rap and will fail to deliver. In this paper, an efficient routing algorithm based on Bubble Rap is proposed. First, the cyclical and time-evolving characteristics in MSN are investigated by analysing the real-world mobility trace and the two social characteristics are utilized to develop a time evolving community detection method. Second, we present a timer-based relay selection mechanism. A timer is designed to discover stuck messages, and an alternative relay is scheduled to deliver those messages. Simulation results show that the proposed routing outperform the original Bubble Rap and other mainstream routing algorithms.

Keywords: MSN · Routing algorithm · Social characteristics · Dynamic community detection · Alternative relay selection

1 Introduction

With ubiquitous of mobile phones and the increasing need for people to share amounts of files, high traffic load has been imposed on the traditional cellular systems, resulting in the high communication costs for both consumers and operators. As a solution, mobile social networks (MSNs) are used to provide some services for delay-tolerant data transmission, such as announcement spreading, or daily audio and video sharing [1, 2]. Generally, mobile social network is a typical social network where individuals of

X. Sun et al. (Eds.): ICAIS 2019, LNCS 11633, pp. 534–545, 2019.
https://doi.org/10.1007/978-3-030-24265-7_46

similar interests or commonalities, converse and connect with one another using the intelligent mobile devices [3]. The users in MSN can share their data in an opportunistic fashion: messages are transmitted through opportunistic encounters between mobile nodes (via short-range communication interfaces such as Bluetooth and WiFi). There are some benefits from exploiting such opportunistic exchanges in MSN. The exchanges can be used to extend the cellular networks' coverage. And more importantly, such exchanges can support more users at a lower cost.

Since mobile nodes with short-range communication capability in MSN cannot provide continuous end-to-end path, it is rational to employ DTN routing algorithm in MSNs [4]. Several DTN routing algorithms can be utilized in MSNs. Note that there are two very distinct features of nodes that need to be considered when applying DTN routing in MSNs. One is community, which indicates the similarity and affinity among people [5, 6]. The other is heterogeneous activity [7, 8]. Based on that, social-based DTN routing algorithms are preferred in the data transmission in MSN [5–12]. Among the existing routing algorithms, Bubble Rap routing considered the two social characteristics of MSN and significantly improved the transmission efficiency [9]. Therefore, it has been deemed as one of the most appropriate and promising routing in MSN. Specifically, it divided nodes into different communities through a proposed community detection method [10], then it estimated the activity level for each node by computing node's centrality in global and local perspective. Global centrality reflects the activity level of node in overall network, while local centrality reflects that in the community which node belongs to. Message is forwarded to the node with higher global centrality they encounters before it is relayed to the node which belongs to the same community as the destination node. And then the message is forwarded to the node with higher local centrality in the community until it is delivered to the destination node.

However, despite the Bubble Rap can improve transmission performance to some extent, there are two important issues that have not been well examined when exploiting Bubble Rap for data transmission in MSN. The first one is community detection. Recall that most nodes have very regular movement patterns in MSN, their contact tend to show cyclical and time-varying characteristics [4, 5, 11]. That means a node may belong to different communities during different time periods. But the community detection method in Bubble Rap makes use of the cumulative contact duration as the basis of community detection, which neglects the transient social groups. This inaccurate community detection leads to a lot of meaningless forwarding of message. The second issue emerges as carrier nodes failed to encounter an appropriate relay node. If an alternative next hop is not scheduled for it, it is quite possible that messages would expire after waiting for a long time. However, Bubble Rap overlooked this disadvantage and still followed greedy forwarding mode, so stuck message will be failed to deliver. These two issues obstruct further improvement of transmission efficiency in MSN.

To address above issues, we propose a routing algorithm based on Bubble Rap algorithm to improve the data transmission efficiency in MSN. First, the cyclical and time-evolving characteristics of mode's mobility in MSN are investigated by analysing the real-world mobility trace. We leverage the two social characteristics in MSN to develop a time evolving community detection method. Then we present a timer-based relay node selection mechanism, where a timer is designed to discover stuck messages, and an alternative relay is found to deliver stuck messages as much as possible. Finally, in order to evaluate the performance of the routing strategy, several performance metrics are calculated from simulations. The results show that the proposed routing outperform the original Bubble Rap and other classic routing algorithms.

2 Distributed Community Detection Method

Intuitively, activities of individuals in MSN often show regularities, so do the social feature of mobile devices carried by humans. In this section, the cyclical and time-evolving characteristics of mode's mobility in MSN are investigated by analysing the real-world mobility trace. And then the social features are exploited in the community detection to improve the efficiency of message forwarding.

2.1 Cyclical and Time-Evolving Characteristics of Contact Time of Node Pair

The real-world data we used is extracted from *Cambridge* [13], which is gathered by the Haggle Project. The trace record contacts among students carrying mobile Bluetooth-enabled iMotes in University of Cambridge. 54 Devices periodically detect each other, and a contact is recorded when two devices come into the communication range of each other. This dataset covers 11 days. Obviously, the students with iMotes formed a typical MSN. In this paper, in order to investigate the time evolving feature of contacts between nodes, we take every 6 h as a time period. Meanwhile, the contact time of node pairs in each time period is calculated. We found that some nodes in *Cambridge* were so inactive that it is hard to observe their regularity. Fortunately, since they have little impact on the forwarding process, we concentrate on those active nodes. Therefore, analysis upon 4 randomly chosen active node pairs is conducted.

Figure 1 shows the variation of contact time of these node pairs in time slots of 7 days. To better represent the periodicity of nodes, we normalized the contact time of node pair in each day. It is shown that there exists an obvious daily periodicity for normalized contact time of each node pair. For each node pair, contact time in different periods of one cycle shows great difference, while contact time in same periods of different cycles have similar proportions.

2.2 Dynamic Community Detection

As discussed in Sect. 2, the distributed contact time-based *k*-clique method of Bubble Rap suffers from the huge communities that is inconsistent with the actual relationships of nodes. Members who have lost contact with others for a long time should be removed from community. According to previous analysis, the social groups change over time with a cycle of one day. Based on that, the proposed method is conducted as follows: firstly, considering the time-varying node relationship, *k*-clique community detection is carried out in individual time periods. For each period, to avoid inaccuracy

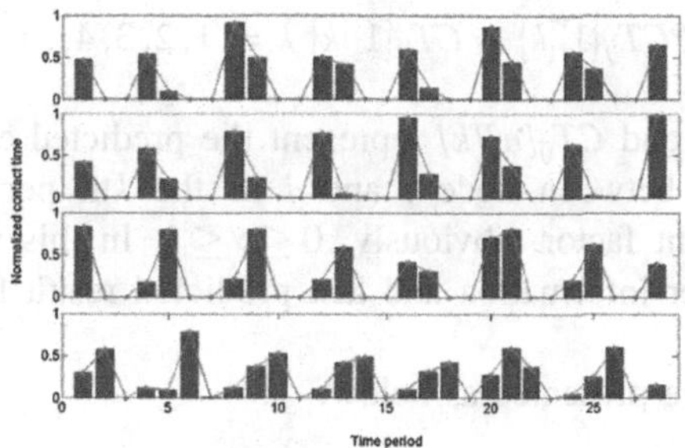

Fig. 1. Cyclical variation of contact time of 4 randomly selected active node pairs

in the early stage, the initial community structure of each time period is estimated on the basis of the cyclicity, then it is updated in real-time.

Cyclicity-Based Community Prediction in Individual Time Period. We make use of historical contact time of node pair to forecast contact time in same periods of current cycle, thus, the initial community structure in time period is acquired. Then it is updated by real-time contact time of nodes. The prediction process is shown in Fig. 2.

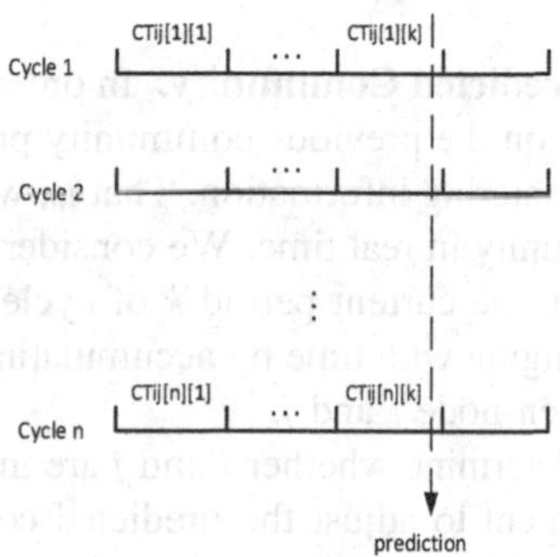

Fig. 2. General view of prediction based community detection

As indicated by the dotted vertical line in this figure, based on the cyclicity, we can predict the contact time of each node pair in periods of the next cycle (cycle n) according to contact time in the same period of multiple cycles (cycle 1 to cycle $n-1$). When implement prediction, contact time between node i and j in period k of nth cycle is calculated as the accumulation of two type of contact times, which is defined as:

$$PCT_{ij}[n][k] = \alpha \times PCT_{ij}[n-1][k] + (1-\alpha) \times CT_{ij}[n-1][k]$$

$$n > 1, n \in N^{+} \quad k = 1, 2, 3, 4, \ldots \tag{1}$$

$$PCT_{ij}[1][k] = CT_{ij}[1][k] \; k = 1, 2, 3, 4, \ldots \tag{2}$$

Where $PCT_{ij}[n][k]$ and $CT_{ij}[n][k]$ represent the predicted encounter time and the actual encounter time between node i and j in the kth period of the nth cycle, respectively. α is weight factor, obviously, $0 \leq \alpha \leq 1$. In this way, every node only needs to save encounter information and last predicted result for each period of last cycle.

The pseudo code are presented as below.

Algorithm 1. Time-based community prediction procedures on node pair i and j

if $PCT_{ij}[n][k] > T_{threshold}$ **then**
in period k of cycle n, i and j belong to the same community;
i add j to the community list of i, the members in community list of i add j to the community list of themselves;
j add i to the community list of j, the members in community list of j add i to the community list of themselves;
end if
if $communitySetOf\ i) \cap (communitySetOf\ j \geq K\ 1$ then
Merge the two community sets;
end if

Real-Time Update of the Predicted Community. In order to improve the accuracy of community detection, based on the previous community prediction, we also considers the impact of real-time encountering information. That is, we use prediction + real-time method to update the community in real time. We consider the real cumulative contact time between node i and j in the current period k of cycle n, denoted as $RCT_{ij}[n][k]$. Note that $RCT_{ij}[n][k]$ is changing with time by accumulating the contact time in period k (the current period) between node i and j.

We use $RCT_{ij}[n][k]$ to determine whether i and j are in the same community. This process serves as a complement to adjust the predicted community. By this way, we can make the detected dynamic communities more accurate than Bubble Rap.

3 Routing Strategy

While the community detection method have been presented in previous section, community and activity of nodes are exploited to design routing strategy. Activity reflects the social popularity of node, it's defined as the number of nodes that this node has encountered. In this section, to further optimize the performance of the proposed routing, a timer is designed to discover stuck messages, and then alternative relays are found to send them out as soon as possible. At the end of this section, the proposed routing algorithm is presented.

3.1 Timer-Based Relay Node Selection Mechanism

To increase the efficiency of our strategy, we additionally consider an overlooked case where the social connection strength between the source and destination is very weak. In message forwarding process, we take 2 critical steps: 1. set a timer to detect stuck messages; 2. select an alternative relay to send the trapped message out as much as possible. More detail are shown as follows.

Design of the Timer. If the message was not relayed during the time period (T_{time}) of the timer, we define it as "stuck". When a message is stuck, the carrier has to send it to the alternate node as soon as possible in case of expiration. Besides, the setting of the T_{timer} is critical, if it is too big, the stuck message is very likely to expire before it find the next hop; otherwise, a too small T_{timer} means overuse of alternate forwarding, which will increase meaningless forwarding. In this section, the value of the timer T_{timer} is determined according to the state of the communication link. For a given message *m*, its time period of the timer is calculated as follows.

$$T_{timer\_m} = \min\left\{\frac{RTTL_m}{2}, 2 * T_{encounter}\right\} \tag{3}$$

Where the $RTTL_m$ represents the remaining time to live of message *m*; and the $T_{encounter}$ represents the average time of the message carrier encountering a node, it is easy to obtain:

$$T_{encounter} = \frac{T_{pass}}{N} \tag{4}$$

Where T_{pass} represents the elapsed time. *N* represents the number of nodes encountered by the message carrier in T_{pass}.

It is worth noting that different messages have different timer values, since the T_{timer} is associated with the remaining lifetime of message *m* and the link state among the carrier and other nodes. Moreover, within a short time after message *m* is generated, the $RTTL_m$ is relatively large, the value of T_{timer} tend to be 2* $T_{encounter}$. As time goes by, the $RTTL_m/2$ will be smaller than 2* $T_{encounter}$, in this case, it is more likely to assign T_{timer} as $RTTL_m/2$. Thus, the T_{timer} is dynamically assigned to send *m* out before expiration with extra reliable paths.

Selection of Alternative Relay for Stuck Message. For a given message *m*, running out of the timer indicates that it is stuck in its carrier's local buffer. Under this condition, it is more urgent to send the message out than continue waiting for the destination or a relay node with higher global/local activity. In this paper, we consider the high cluster coefficient feature of human society, which describes the phenomenon that people tends to contact with friends and their friends' friends more frequently than strangers, to provide more forwarding opportunities. Specifically, if a neighbour node has lower activity than the message carrier, whereas there exists a certain node which has higher activity than the carrier in this neighbour's community, this neighbour can be the alternative relay node for stuck message.

In summary, a universal and efficient social-aware routing strategy (UESAR) in MSN is proposed. The details of the algorithm are described below:

When node *i* carrying message *m* encounters node *j*, then they exchange information with each other, our routing strategy considers four cases provided that *j* is not the destination node *d* of message *m*:

Case 1: Node *i*, node *j* and destination node *d* belong to the same community. In this case, node *i* compares its own local activity value *local_activityof (i)* with that of *j (local_activityof (j))*. If *local_activityof (j)* is larger, *i* forwards *m* to *j* directly; otherwise if *m*'s timer runs out, then *i* will check the community member list of *j*, if there exists a certain node *k* which belongs to the same community as the destination node *d*, and the local activity value *local_activityof(k)* is greater than that of *i*, the node *i* will forward the message *m* to *j* as well.

Case 2: Node *i* and destination node *d* are not in the same community, and node *j* and *d* belong to the same community. Undoubtedly, node *i* forwards message *m* to *j*.

Case 3: Both node *i* and node *j* do not belong to the same community as destination node *d*. In this case, node *i* compares its own global activity value *global_activityof(i)* with the global activity value *global_activityof(j)* of *j*. If *global_activityof(j)* is larger, *i* will forward the message *m* directly to *j*; otherwise, if *m*'s timer runs out, node *i* will check the community member list of *j*, if there exists a certain node *k* which belongs to the same community as the destination node *d*, or the global activity *global_activityof (k)* is greater than that of *i*, node *i* will also forward the message *m* to *j*.

Case 4: Node *i* and destination node *d* belong to the same community, while nodes *j* and *d* are not in the same community. In this case, node *i* will not forward the message no matter if the timer of *m* runs out.

4 Simulation and Evaluation

In this section, a series of simulations is conducted to evaluate the performance of the proposed routing UESAR on the widely-used simulator: the ONE (Opportunistic Network Environment). The real trace data from the "Cambridge [13]" and "Reality [14]" are used in the simulator. The performance of UESAR is compared with two social-aware mainstream routing: Bubble Rap, Simbet, and an encounter utility-based non-social aware routing: PROPHET [11]. Then we validate the effectiveness of critical elements considered in our algorithm: community detection, timer of message. In the simulations, various message TTL values are set to evaluate the performance. We set the buffer size of each node as 10 MB, and message is generated every 100 to 600 s, message size is set as 100 K to 500 K, the transmit bandwidth is set as 250 Kbps, the simulation time is set as 987529 s (about 11 days) for Cambridge, and 7.776E6 s (3 months) for Reality. For the proposed UESAR, time threshold $T_{threshold}$ in Algorithm 1 is set as 300 s, and the community integration threshold K is set as 4, and weight factor α is set to 0.5. For the three routing protocols that used for comparison, we use the default values as recommended in these papers, and multi-copy is implemented in all the simulations. We mainly focus on two performance indicators: message delivery ratio and network overhead ratio.

4.1 Performance of the Proposed Routing UESAR

In this section, we compare the performance of UESAR with Bubble Rap, Simbet and PROPHET. It can be seen from Figs. 3 and 4, the delivery ratio of our proposed UESAR routing outperforms Simbet and PROPHET in terms of delivery ratio and overhead. Compared with Bubble Rap, UESAR achieves significantly improvement in terms of delivery ratio, while keeping a little advantage in overhead. In addition, PROPHET has the highest overhead, while other three social-aware routing algorithm have obvious lower overhead due to the utilization of social features. The advantages of the proposed UESAR are more pronounced in the dataset Reality than in the Cambridge. The efficiency of our routing is validated, and the reasons are illustrated as follows.

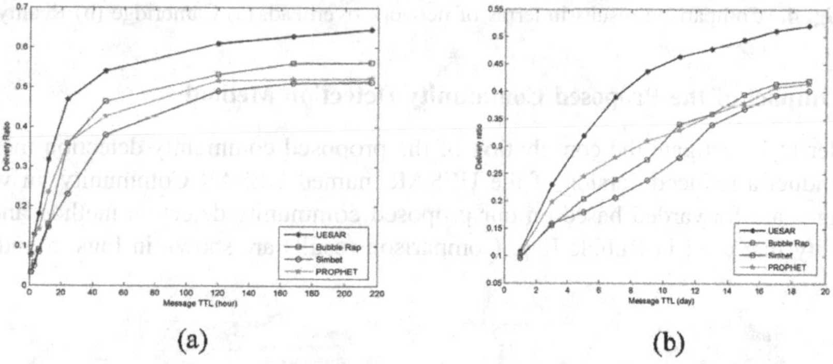

Fig. 3. Comparison results in terms of delivery ratio. (a) Cambridge (b) Reality

1. Community-based routing has obvious advantages in the selection of relay node. It avoids a lot of unnecessary forwarding that happen outside the community where the destination node belongs. Both Simbet and PROPHET overlook the significance of community. Therefore, the proposed UESAR and the Bubble Rap have better performance than Simbet and PROPHET.
2. Although the community detection method of the proposed routing and that of the Bubble Rap are both time-based, our approach can extract transient communities and make use of history encountering information to predict their appearance in next period. Therefore, in our routing, message can be forwarded and delivered more accurately and experiences few forwarding times before it reaches to the community where the destination node is located. Thus we can get more efficient message delivery and lower overhead than Bubble Rap and other protocols.
3. The optimization of message forwarding aims to detect stuck messages that cannot be sent out for a relatively long time, and then forward them as much as possible. In this way, message delivery rate can be improved, at a little cost of overhead.

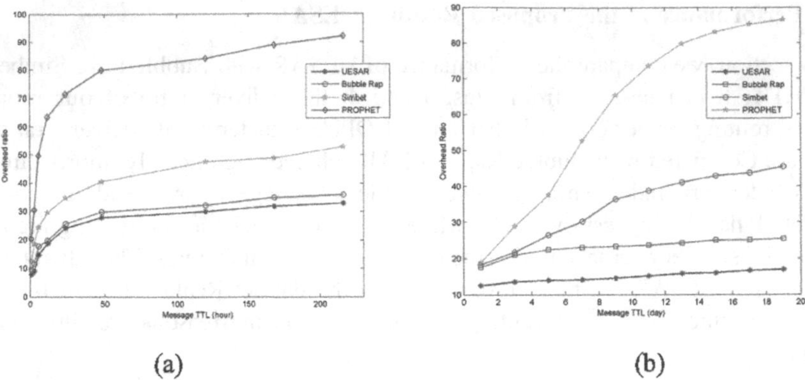

Fig. 4. Comparison results in terms of network overhead. (a) Cambridge (b) Reality

4.2 Impact of the Proposed Community Detection Method

In order to investigate the contribution of the proposed community detection method, we conduct a reduced version of the UESAR, named UESAR-Community, in which messages are forwarded based on our proposed community detection method and the centrality that used in Bubble Rap. Comparison results are shown in Figs. 5 and 6.

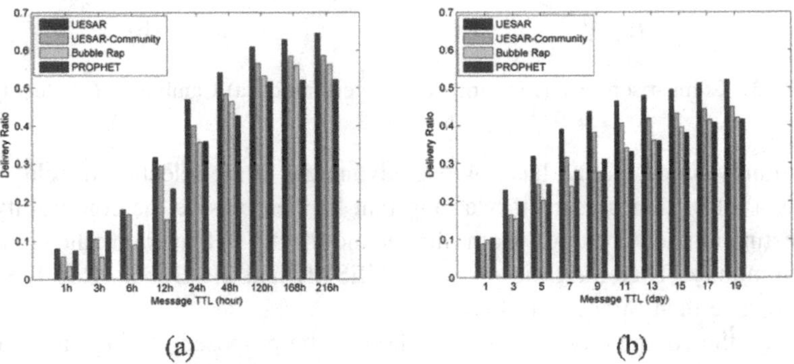

Fig. 5. Impact of the proposed community detection method in terms of delivery ratio. (a) Cambridge (b) Reality

It is reflected that the UESAR-Community performs better than Bubble Rap, and PROPHRT in terms of delivery ratio and network overhead. Compared with the original UESAR, both delivery ratio and network overhead are lower. These results shows that the proposed community method can excavate the social relationships more accurate, and can further reduce the number of forwarding. Hence the message delivery probability can be improved, and we can get a higher performance of routing protocol in MSNs. Meanwhile, it can be seen that, as the message TTL increases, the raise of overhead ratio for all routings on dataset Reality is more gentle than on the dataset Cambridge, we attribute the phenomenon to low contact rate in Reality.

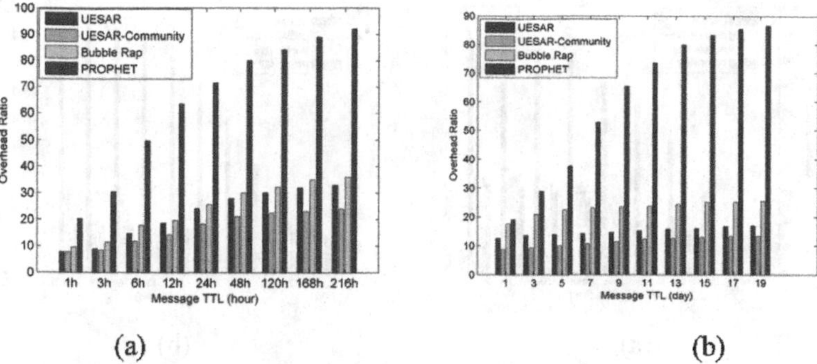

Fig. 6. Impact of the proposed community detection method in terms of network overhead. (a) Cambridge (b) Reality

4.3 Impact of the Proposed Timer-Based Relay Node Selection Mechanism

Similarly, In order to investigate the contribution of the proposed timer-based relay node selection mechanism, we conduct a reduced version of the UESAR, named UESAR-Timer, in which messages are forwarded based on the community detection method that used in Bubble Rap and our proposed timer-based relay node selection mechanism. The comparison result is shown in Figs. 7 and 8. It is shown that the UESAR-Timer performs better in terms of delivery ratio than the Bubble Rap, and PROPHRT. Obviously, the proposed timer-based relay node selection can improve the efficiency of message forwarding. When compared with the original UESAR, the delivery ratio is lower while the network overhead higher, which, we think, results from the inaccurate community detection method. Thus the advantage of proposed UESAR can be further verified by the comparison.

Since UESAR-Timer attempt to forward stuck message out with alternative relay, delivery probability can be improved at the cost of more forwarding times compared with the greedy forwarding mode based Bubble Rap. Thus, the overhead ratio of

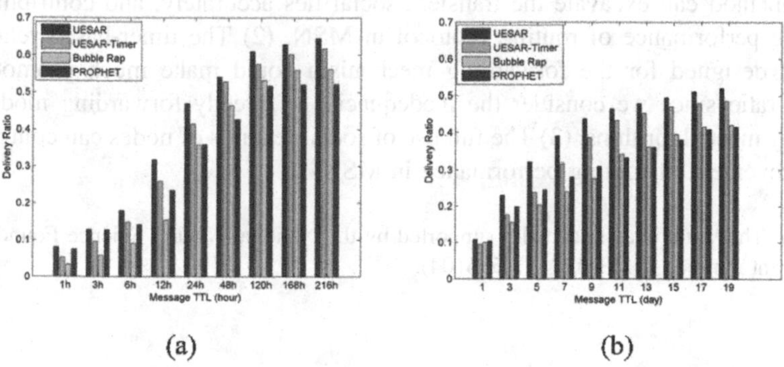

Fig. 7. Impact of the proposed timer-based relay node selection in terms of delivery ratio. (a) Cambridge (b) Reality

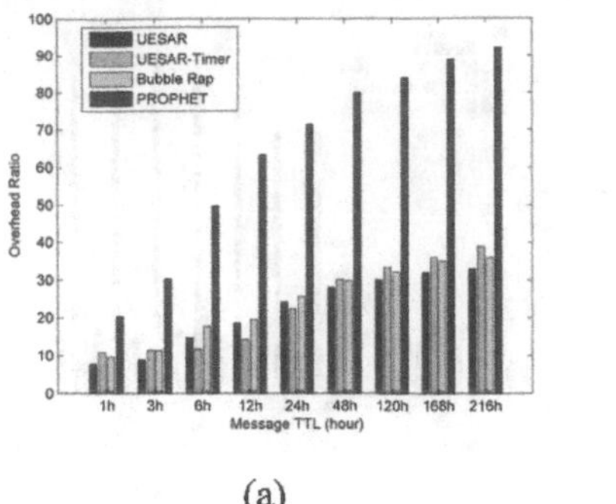

(a)

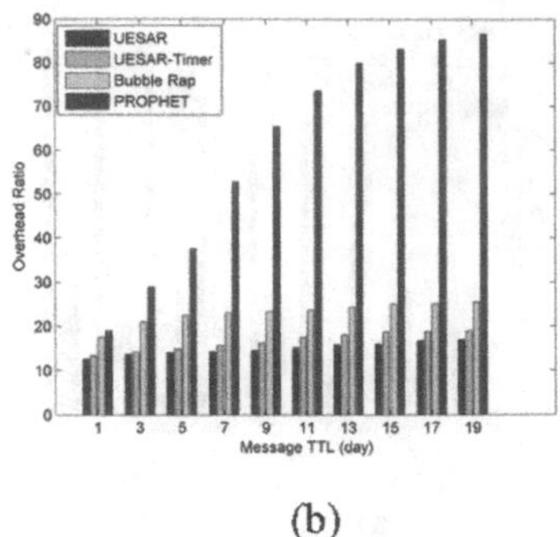

(b)

Fig. 8. Impact of the proposed timer-based relay node selection in terms of network overhead. (a) Cambridge (b) Reality

UESAR-Timer is higher than that of Bubble Rap. It should be noted that no matter which data set is used, UESAR shows the best results in terms of delivery ratio and overhead, which indicates that UESAR has achieved significant improvement.

5 Conclusion

In this paper, an efficient social-aware routing algorithm for MSN are proposed. By making full use of social characteristics of nodes in MSN, the routing performance is improved. We investigate the time-varying and cyclical features of social behaviours of nodes by analysing the real-world mobility traces. Then these social features are exploited to develop a dynamic distributed community detection method, which could predict transient communities in time periods and update them in real time. In addition, to optimize the forwarding process, we set a timer to discover stuck messages and then seek an alternative to send the trapped message out as much as possible.

Various simulations and evaluations based on real world MSN datasets were implemented. According to the results, we can conclude that, (1) the proposed community method can excavate the transient social ties accurately, and contributes to a satisfying performance of routing protocol in MSN. (2) The timer-based relay node selection designed for the forwarding mechanism could make much promotion on delivery ratio since we consider the inadequacies of greedy forwarding mode overlooked by most algorithms. (3) The full use of social features of nodes can contribute to the improvement of routing performance in MSN.

Funding. This study was financially supported by the National Natural Science Foundation of China (grant number: U1736121, U1536104).

References

1. Pietilänen, A.-K., Diot, C.: Dissemination in opportunistic social networks: the role of temporal communities. In: Thirteenth ACM International Symposium on Mobile Ad Hoc Networking & Computing, pp. 165–174. ACM, South Carolina (2012)
2. Cui, J., Zhang, Y., Cai, Z., Liu, A., Li, Y.: Securing display path for security-sensitive applications on mobile devices. CMC Comput. Mater. Continua **55**(1), 017–035 (2018)
3. Huang, Y., Dong, Y., Zhang, S., Wu, G.: TTL sensitive social-aware routing in mobile opportunistic networks. In: 11th Consumer Communications & Networking Conference, pp. 810–814. IEEE, Las Vegas (2014)
4. Li, Z., Wang, C., Yang, S., Jiang, C., Li, X.: LASS: local-activity and social-similarity based data forwarding in mobile social networks. IEEE Trans. Parallel Distrib. Syst. **26**(1), 174–184 (2015)
5. Zhang, X., Cao, G., Zhang, X., Cao, G.: Transient community detection and its application to data forwarding in delay tolerant networks. IEEE-ACM Trans. Netw. **25**(5), 2829–2843 (2017)
6. Li, Y., Li, J., Chen, J., Lu, M., Li, C.: Seed selection for data offloading based on social and interest graphs. CMC Comput. Mater. Continua **57**(3), 571–587 (2018)
7. Daly, E., Haahr, M.: Social network analysis for routing in disconnected delay-tolerant MANETs. In: ACM International Symposium on Mobile Ad Hoc Networking & Computing, pp. 32–40. ACM, Montreal (2007)
8. Wei, K., Liang, X., Xu, K.: A survey of social-aware routing protocols in delay tolerant networks: applications, taxonomy and design-related issues. IEEE Commun. Surv. Tutorials **16**(1), 556–578 (2014)
9. Pan, H., Crowcroft, J., Yoneki, E.: BUBBLE rap: social-based forwarding in delay-tolerant networks. IEEE Trans. Mob. Comput. **10**(11), 1576–1589 (2011)
10. Hui, P., Yoneki, E., Chan, S.Y., Crowcroft, J.: Distributed community detection in delay tolerant networks. In: Proceedings of First ACM/IEEE International Workshop on Mobility in the Evolving Internet Architecture, pp. 7:1–7:8. ACM, Kyoto (2007)
11. Massri, A.K., Vernata, A., Vitaletti, A.: Routing protocols for delay tolerant networks: a quantitative evaluation. In: Proceedings of the 7th ACM Workshop on Performance Monitoring and Measurement of Heterogeneous Wireless and Wired Networks, pp. 107–114. ACM, New York (2012)
12. Guan, J., Chu, Q., You, I.: The social relationship based adaptive multi-spray-and-wait routing algorithm for disruption tolerant network. Mobile Inf. Syst. **2017**(3), 1–13 (2017)
13. Scott, J., Hui, P., Crowcroft, J., Diot, C.: Haggle: a networking architecture designed around mobile users. In: Proceedings of the Third IFIP Wireless on Demand Network Systems Conference, pp. 78–86. HAL, Les Ménuires (2006)
14. Eagle, N., Pentland, A.: Reality mining: sensing complex social systems. J. Pers. Ubiquitous Comput. **10**(4), 255–268 (2006)

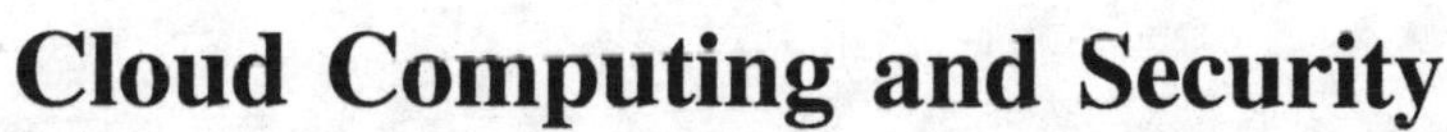

Cloud Computing and Security

Improvement of Differential Fault Attack Based on Lightweight Ciphers with GFN Structure

Yang Gao, Yongjuan Wang(✉), Qingjun Yuan, Tao Wang, and Xiangbin Wang

State Key Laboratory of Mathematical Engineering and Advanced Computing, Zhengzhou 450001, China
gaoyang_1279@126.com, pinkywyj@163.com, gcxyuan@outlook.com, wt107263@163.com, wang_moony@163.com

Abstract. In this paper, we focus on differential fault attack on lightweight block ciphers with GFN (Generalized Feistel Networks) structure. With regard to fault injection model and differential equations solving, two improved DFA (Differential Fault Analysis) methods are proposed. Based on this, we present the improved attack process which aims at applying lightweight block ciphers with GFN structure. We conduct 10000 DFA experiments on TWINE and LBlock. Result shows that it only takes 9.18 and 8.42 faults on average to recover the main key K respectively. Moreover, time and space complexity are both negligible.

Keywords: Generalized Feistel Networks · Differential fault attack · S-box · LBlock · TWINE

1 Introduction

With the advancement of network technology, the demand for people to communicate on the Internet is increasing, and cryptology has also been greatly developed. Considering the encryption environment and computing resources in real life, in order to achieve the standard of efficiency and security of the encryption algorithm, lightweight ciphers have attracted a lot of attention in recent years. For example, LBlock [1], Piccolo [2], LED [3], PRESENT [4] and so on.

On the other hand, in 1996, fault attack was proposed by Boneh et al. [5] to analyze RSA signature algorithms implemented in CRT mode. In the following years, after the improvement of Biham in [6], the well-known DFA method came into being. DFA is a cryptanalysis technique that exploits the results of faults injection and they successfully attacked the block cipher DES algorithm in this method. After nearly two decades of development, researchers constantly put forward new methods of differential fault attack, successfully analyzing SMS4 [7], PRESENT [8], Keeloq [9], Camellia [10] and other lightweight ciphers. In recent years, researchers constantly improve the differential fault attack method.

X. Sun et al. (Eds.): ICAIS 2019, LNCS 11633, pp. 549–560, 2019.
https://doi.org/10.1007/978-3-030-24265-7_47

Since faults injection in encryption circuits may irreversibly damage the device [11], limiting the number of fault injection is usually a key point of DFA.

The remainder of the article is structured as follows. In Sect. 2, we briefly introduce lightweight block ciphers with GFN structure. Our main approach is described in Sect. 3, which proposes the improvement of DFA on two components of lightweight block cipher with GFN, and we give the DFA process of these kinds of algorithms. Section 4 presents our results on some examples of known lightweight block cipher, such as TWINE and LBlock algorithms. Finally, the conclusion is drawn in Sect. 5.

2 GFN Structure and Its Components

2.1 Feistel Structure and GFN Structure

The Feistel network was invented at IBM by Horst Feistel in the 1970's, during the development of the Lucifer cipher, later known as the Data Encryption Standard (DES) [12]. A Feistel network divides the input into two blocks of equal size. One of these two blocks goes into a subkey-dependent function $\mathcal{F}$, called the Feistel function, and the result is xored to the other block. This construction is then repeated several times, switching the roles of the two blocks each time. The main characteristics of this construction [13] are listed below:

- Only half of the state is modified, using the Feistel function.
- Even if the Feistel function itself is not invertible, the construction is invertible.
- The inverse bijection follows the same construction up to reversing the subkeys order.

The GFN structure divides the internal state into more than two blocks, which is a broader class of schemes taking the main ideas of the Feistel network. This innovation was first introduced at CRYPTO'89 by Zheng et al. [14]. One round of a GFN is divided into two successive transformations: the nonlinear layer and the permutation layer. The non-linear layer is also made of one or more key-dependent Feistel functions $\mathcal{F}$. They have some of the blocks of the GFN internal state as input and their output is xored to some other blocks. The permutation layer consists in rearranging the different blocks of the internal state.

In both Feistel and GFN structure, the Feistel function $\mathcal{F}$ is the essential component. We suppose that $\mathcal{F}$ is also made of three kinds of component, which are *Xored with the subkey*, *S-boxes* and *the "mixing" functions.* Among them, the S-boxes are the most important nonlinear component that could affect the complexity of the algorithm.

2.2 S-Boxes in Lightweight Block Ciphers

An $n \times m$ S-box (n-bit input, m-bit output) can be viewed as a mapping of n-bits to m-bits, which can be also viewed as an n-ary vector boolean function

$S(X) = (f_1(X), f_2(X), \ldots, f_m(X))$. In lightweight block ciphers, S-boxes are all bijective and satisfy $m = n = 4$.

In process of designing algorithm, the S-box must be set up delicately so that they can resist all kinds of existing attack methods. For example, well-designed S-boxes should have high algebraic degrees, good avalanche effect, and are also balanced. We focus on the differential analysis of lightweight block ciphers, so the differential uniformity is the key indicator of our research.

Definition 1 [15–17]. *Let $S(X)$ be an S-box, for any fixed input difference $\alpha \in F_2^4$ and output difference $\beta \in F_2^4$, note that*

$$\langle\alpha|\beta\rangle = \{X \in F_2^4 : S(X \oplus \alpha) \oplus S(X) = \beta\},$$
$$ND_S(\alpha, \beta) = \#\langle\alpha|\beta\rangle.$$

The definition of the differential uniformity of $S(X)$ is

$$\mathit{Diff}(S) = \max_{0 \neq \alpha \in F_2^4} \max_{\beta \in F_2^4} ND_S(\alpha, \beta).$$

We also call $S(X)$ differentially uniform.

The minimum of $\mathit{Diff}(S)$ is 2, and $S(X)$ that reaches the lower bound 2 is called Almost Perfect Nonlinear (APN) function. In a lightweight S-box, there exists $\mathit{Diff}(S) \geq 4$. On the other hand, the smaller the differential uniformity of $S(X)$ is, the better S-box can resist the differential analysis. When $ND_S(\alpha, \beta) > 4$, the differential characteristic of S-box is so obvious as to be easily attacked. So we need to guarantee $\mathit{Diff}(S) \leq 4$. In addition, according to properties of XOR operations, when the input-output differential pairs of S-boxes are fixed, the input values X must appear in pairs. Therefore, all X are even numbers, that is, one of 0, 2, and 4.

In fact, the probability of the output difference β which is aroused by any fixed non-zero input difference α is $p(\alpha \to \beta) = ND_S(\alpha, \beta)/2^n \leq \mathit{Diff}(S)/2^n$. Thus we give the Definition 2.

Definition 2. *Let $N_d(S)$ be the number of input-output difference pairs with the largest difference probability, that is,*

$$N_d(S) = \#\{(\alpha, \beta) \in F_2^4 \times F_2^4 : ND_S(\alpha, \beta) = \mathit{Diff}(S)\}.$$

This index can characterize the ability of S-box to resist multi-difference analysis, and it can also be used as an important symbol to distinguish S-box affine equivalence class.

3 Improvement of DFA on Lightweight Block Ciphers with GFN

Since the basic unit of data processing in lightweight block ciphers with GFN structure is nibble, we consider the general description of DFA method under the same attack assumptions. Firstly, we give the attack conditions and specific assumptions. Then we consider improving the attack process by two means. For the permutation layer of GFN, the number of differential equations in a single round is increased by appropriately selecting the inject positions. Then the total number of fault injections is reduced. For the nonlinear layer of GFN, we improve the method of solving differential equations by looking up S-box differential table, which improves the efficiency to a certain extent.

3.1 Attack Conditions and Specific Assumptions

Because the data processing basic units of lightweight block ciphers with GFN structure is nibble, the differential fault analysis methods in this paper are based on models of random nibble faults induction. Here we list the attack conditions and specific assumptions:

- The intruder fully understands the cryptographic devices. Anytime and anywhere he can inject random nibble faults in the encryption process, but the exact value of the fault is unknown.
- The intruder can repeatedly inject random faults multiple times in the same place.
- The intruder can repeatedly restart the cryptographic device, and encrypt the same plaintext with the same main key.

3.2 The Improvement of Fault Injection Model

In differential fault attack, M, the number of differential equations solved per round is a crucial intermediate parameter. It directly determines the number of fault injections when recovering the round key. First of all, it's clear that we can obtain nibbles of round key by solving corresponding differential equations. When the effect of faults injection in previous round have no intersection on the error output, more than one differential equation can be resolved simultaneously. Thus improvement of DFA method is proposed based on properly selecting the fault injection location by fault diffusion properties of algorithm, so as to solve differential equations as many as possible in single round. And thereby the number of faults injection is reduced. The fault diffusion properties are often determined by the permutation layer in GFN structure and *the "mixing" functions* in the Feistel function $\mathcal{F}$.

Here we take TWINE algorithm as an example to illustrate this kind of improvement method.

TWINE is a lightweight block cipher algorithm with typical GFN structure. It adopts 64-bit block size, which supports 80-bit key length and the length of round key is 32-bit. The number of iteration round is 36. All iterative operations and the differential diffusion properties in TWINE are based on mixing of nibbles. Suppose nibble inputs of the r-th round are $x_0^r, x_1^r, x_2^r, \ldots, x_{15}^r$. Then we find the fault induced at position x_{2k}^r will spread to three distinct positions in the next round, which are $x_{2k}^{r+1}, x_{2k+1}^{r+1}$ and $x_{\pi(2k)}^{r+1}$, where π is a transposition function.

And the fault injected at position x^r_{2k+1} will spread to two distinct positions in the next round, which are x^{r+1}_{2k} and x^{r+1}_{2k+1}. The fault diffusion properties are depicted in Fig. 1:

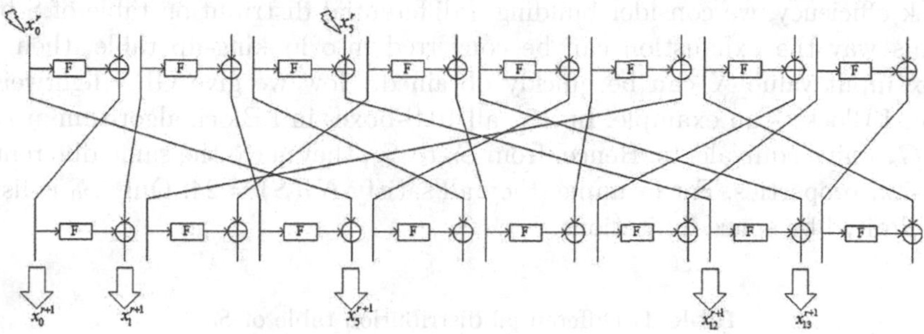

Fig. 1. Fault diffusion properties in TWINE.

In [18], researchers make use of the fault diffusion properties of TWINE. In order to avoid the repeated influence of fault injection on the error ciphertext C, thereby causing differential equations unsolvable, they divide 8 nibble positions with the form of x^{35}_{2k} into 4 groups: $T_1 = \{x^{35}_0, x^{35}_2\}, T_2 = \{x^{35}_4, x^{35}_8\}, T_3 = \{x^{35}_6, x^{35}_{10}\}, T_4 = \{x^{35}_{12}, x^{35}_{14}\}$. Next, arbitrarily select one position from each group and inject 4 nibble faults at the same time. Then 4 nibbles of the 36th round key, Rk^{36}, can be recovered. Finally, inject 4 nibble faults at the rest positions in each group and then the rest nibbles of Rk^{36} can be recovered. Here, the number of differential equations can be solved per round is $M = 4$.

In the above method, fault positions in form of x^{35}_{2k} are selected because these nibble positions can spread the fault to 3 nibbles in ciphertext C. Although the diffusion effect gets optimal, there is a strong restriction because some nibble error ciphertexts are repeated in differential equations. Therefore, we at most inject 4 nibbles of faults in the 35th round at a time. Furthermore, we have to repeat the operation at least 4 times so that Rk^{36} could be completely recovered. Moreover, those error nibbles constitute a complete 16 nibble grouping of the ciphertext C. In this method, 8 differential equations can be solved at a time. Thus, we could inject 8 nibble faults at position x^{35}_{2k+1}, and Rk^{36} can be obtained by at least two groups of fault injection. By decrypting the ciphertext C with Rk^{36}, the intermediate output state of the 35th round can be obtained. Reuse the above method, we can obtain Rk^{35} and Rk^{34}. Combined with key expansion scheme, the main key K can be recovered by Rk^{34}, Rk^{35} and Rk^{36}. With the improved fault injection method, the number of fault injections of recovering round key Rk is reduced from 4 to 2. And theoretically the total number of fault injections required to recover the main key K is reduced from 12 to 6.

3.3 The Improvement of Solving Differential Equations

One of the core steps of DFA is solving differential equations, like $S(X \oplus \alpha) \oplus S(X) = \beta$. The common method adopted by researchers is to traverse the S-box input value X. In order to reduce the amount of exhaustion and improve the attack efficiency, we consider building a differential distribution table of S-box. In this way the exhaustion can be converted into looking-up table, then the S-box input value X can be quickly obtained. Now we give GFN lightweight cipher LBlock as an example. In [19], all 10 S-boxes in LBlock algorithm are fall into G_8 affine equivalents. Hence, from S_0 to S_9, they have the same differential diffusion properties. For example, they all satisfy $N_d(S) = 24$. Only S_0 is listed here limited by space limitations.

Table 1. Differential distribution table of S_0.

α	Relationship between β and X when α is fixed								
1	β	1	3	7	9	B	F		
	X	6,7,C,D	8,9	0,1	4,5,E,F	A,B	2,3		
2	β	1	3	7	9	B	F		
	X	0,2,9,B	D,F	4,6	1,3,8,A	C,E	5,7		
3	β	2	6	A	E				
	X	8,B,C,F	1,2,4,7	9,A,D,E	0,3,5,6				
4	β	3	4	5	6	B	D		
	X	0,4	9,A,D,E	2,6	8,B,C,F	3,7	1,5		
5	β	4	5	7	A	D	F		
	X	1,2,4,7	9,C	8,D	0,3,5,6	A,F	B,E		
6	β	2	4	5	7	D	F		
	X	1,2,4,7	0,3,5,6	B,D	9,F	8,E	A,C		
7	β	3	4	5	B	D	E		
	X	1,6	8,B,C,F	0,7	2,5	3,4	9,A,D,E		
8	β	2	3	6	7	A	B	E	F
	X	5,D	3,B	6,E	2,A	4,C	1,9	7,F	0,8
9	β	3	7	8	B	C	F		
	X	5,C	7,E	1,3,8,A	4,D	0,2,9,B	6,F		
A	β	1	2	6	A	D	E		
	X	4,5,E,F	3,9	0,A	1,B	6,7,C,D	2,8		
B	β	1	B	C	D				
	X	1,3,8,A	4,5,E,F	6,7,C,D	0,2,9,B				
C	β	2	3	5	6	8	9	C	F
	X	6,A	2,E	3,F	5,9	7,B	0,C	4,8	1,D
D	β	3	5	8	9	A	C	E	F
	X	7,A	5,8	0,D	6,B	2,F	3,E	1,C	4,9
E	β	2	5	6	7	8	9	B	C
	X	0,E	4,A	3,D	5,B	2,C	7,9	6,8	1,F
F	β	5	7	8	9	A	B	C	E
	X	1,E	3,C	6,9	2,D	7,8	0,F	5,A	4,B

From Table 1 above, we know that $\langle\alpha|\beta\rangle$ has the following properties:

Property 1. Given S-box fault injection value α, for the distinct differential output β_1, β_2, the probable inputs of S-box have no intersection, that is, $\langle\alpha|\beta_1\rangle \cap \langle\alpha|\beta_2\rangle = \varnothing$.

Property 2. In the case of a certain S-box input X, for two distinct input differences α_1, α_2, there must exist β_1, β_2 which satisfy $X \in \langle\alpha|\beta_1\rangle \cap \langle\alpha|\beta_2\rangle$.

The above two properties follow immediately from the differential distribution of S-box.

Property 3. Given an S-box input X, for arbitrary two distinct differential pairs (α_1, β_1) and (α_2, β_2), then we have either $\langle\alpha_1|\beta_1\rangle = \langle\alpha_2|\beta_2\rangle$ or $\langle\alpha_1|\beta_1\rangle \cap \langle\alpha_2|\beta_2\rangle = X$.

Proof. According to *Property 2*, there exists $X \in \langle\alpha|\beta_1\rangle \cap \langle\alpha|\beta_2\rangle$. Assuming $\langle\alpha_1|\beta_1\rangle \cap \langle\alpha_2|\beta_2\rangle = \{X, X'\}$, then X and X' satisfy the following equations:

$$S(X \oplus \alpha_1) \oplus S(X) = \beta_1 \tag{1}$$
$$S(X \oplus \alpha_2) \oplus S(X) = \beta_2 \tag{2}$$
$$S(X' \oplus \alpha_1) \oplus S(X') = \beta_1 \tag{3}$$
$$S(X' \oplus \alpha_2) \oplus S(X') = \beta_2 \tag{4}$$

Comparing Eqs. (1) and (3), X and X' should satisfy

$$\begin{cases} X \oplus \alpha_1 = X' \\ X' \oplus \alpha_1 = X \end{cases} \tag{i}$$

or

$$\begin{cases} X \oplus \alpha_1 = X' \oplus \alpha_1 \\ X' = X \end{cases} \tag{ii}$$

`Condition 1.` First consider the first case (i). Obviously we have $X' = X$, thus we get $\langle\alpha_1|\beta_1\rangle \cap \langle\alpha_2|\beta_2\rangle = X$.
`Condition 2.` Then we consider the case (ii). Comparing Eqs. (2) and (4), we also have

$$\begin{cases} X \oplus \alpha_2 = X' \\ X' \oplus \alpha_2 = X \end{cases}$$

So there is

$$\langle\alpha_1|\beta_1\rangle \cap \langle\alpha_2|\beta_2\rangle = \{X, X'\} = \{X, X \oplus \alpha_1, X \oplus \alpha_2\}.$$

According to the lightweight S-box differential properties, we have $ND_S(\alpha, \beta) = 2k\,(k = 0, 1, 2)$. Thus, $ND_S(\alpha_1, \beta_1) = ND_S(\alpha_2, \beta_2) = 4$. Therefore, we can suppose

$$\langle\alpha_1|\beta_1\rangle \cap \langle\alpha_2|\beta_2\rangle = \{X, X'\} = \{X, X \oplus \alpha_1, X \oplus \alpha_2, m\}.$$

By putting $X' \oplus \alpha_1 = X$ into this equation we can get $\{X' \oplus \alpha_1, X', X' \oplus \alpha_1 \oplus \alpha_2, m\}$. Similarly, we have $\{X' \oplus \alpha_2, X' \oplus \alpha_2 \oplus \alpha_1, X', m\}$ by putting $X' \oplus \alpha_2 = X$ into the same equation. After comparison we can get

$$\begin{aligned}\langle \alpha_1 | \beta_1 \rangle \cap \langle \alpha_2 | \beta_2 \rangle &= \{X, X \oplus \alpha_1, X \oplus \alpha_2, X \oplus \alpha_1 \oplus \alpha_2\} \\ &= \{X', X' \oplus \alpha_1, X' \oplus \alpha_2, X' \oplus \alpha_1 \oplus \alpha_2\},\end{aligned}$$

hence $\langle \alpha_1 | \beta_1 \rangle = \langle \alpha_2 | \beta_2 \rangle$.

Example 1. From Table 1, we know $\langle 1|1 \rangle = \langle B|C \rangle = \{6, 7, C, D\}$. Note that

$$\{6, 7, C, D\} = \{C \oplus 1 \oplus B, C \oplus B, C, C \oplus 1\} = \{6, 6 \oplus 1, 6 \oplus 1 \oplus B, 6 \oplus B\},$$

we have

$$\alpha_1 = 1, \alpha_2 = B, X = C, X' = 6.$$

We know from Property 3 that given two sets of input and output differential pairs, the S-box input value is determined unless the two sets of S-box input are equal. Then the problem of solving differential equations can be transformed into filtering the intersection of S-box input values in differential distribution table. Although this transformation improves the efficiency, there exist cases where more than two faults are injected to solve one equation. The actual number of fault injections required is often slightly more than the theoretical one.

3.4 Improved Attack Process

The improved attack process proposed in this section is based on the attack conditions listed in Sect. 3.1 and the improvement of two major components of GFN structure introduced in the previous two sections.

(1) Inject random nibble faults

(a) Select plaintext P arbitrarily, then encrypt it with the main key K. After that we correctly obtain the correct ciphertext C. Also we need to determine the number of rounds of the algorithm, r.
(b) Use the same key to encrypt the same plaintext. Combined with the fault diffusion properties, we respectively inject some faults in the output of the $r-1$ th round, x^{r-1}. Next, the incorrect ciphertext C^* is recorded.

(2) List the differential equations

Then subtly select the position of fault injection. By means of inverse row shifting and column mixing together with C and C^*, we can formulate M differential equations. Next step we simplify those equations into the form of $S(X \oplus \alpha) \oplus S(X) = \beta$ according to the specific structure of algorithm, where X represents certain nibbles of round key.

(3) Filter the correct key

(a) For each differential equation we obtained in step (2), look up possible S-box input value in differential distribution table. Then include the nibble values which satisfy the equations into the candidate set N_i $(i = 1, 2, \ldots, M)$.

(b) Repeat step (b) in (1), then we formulate the equations and filter keys into the set $Q_i (i = 1, 2, \ldots, M)$. The intersections of Q_i and N_i are the correct nibbles value of Rk^r.

(4) Restore Rk^r and the rest of the round key

(a) Decrypt the ciphertext with Rk^r we have obtained. Then we can get the correct intermediate-state output of the $r-1$ th round. When the algorithm runs to the $r-2$ th round, we induct several random nibble faults simultaneously. Then repeat those steps until all or part of Rk^{r-1} are recovered.

(b) Repeat those steps above until all or part of $Rk_i^t\,(r' \leq t \leq r)$ are recovered, where r' can be determined by key expansion scheme of cipher.

(5) Recover the main key K according to the key expansion scheme

It is easily seen from the key expansion algorithm that K can be completely expressed by those $Rk_i^t\,(r' \leq t \leq r)$, which are all known.

The attack process is shown in Fig. 2.

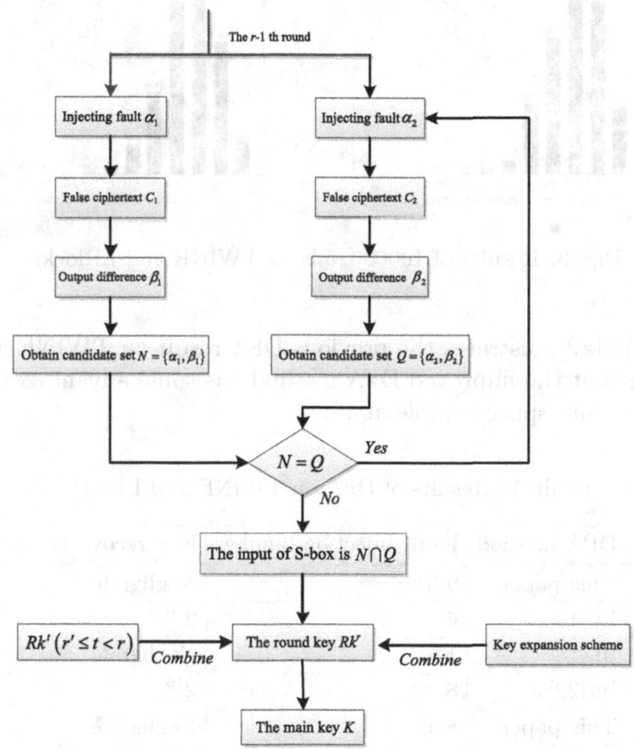

Fig. 2. The improved DFA process.

4 Experimental Results and Analysis

In this section, we use the improved fault attack process in Sect. 3.1 to perform simulated DFA experiments on TWINE and LBlock algorithm. First, We select 1, 2, 3, 4, 5, 6, 7, 8, 9, A, B, C, D, E, F, 0 as plaintext, and 80 bit main key is randomly selected. In order to eliminate the artificial intervention in the process of experiment, we use lightweight stream cipher Trivium to generate 3000 bits pseudo-random data stream. Then we randomly truncate 32 bits as fault values in each round. We conduct 10000 trials on each cipher, and the results are shown in Fig. 3. In [20], we know the expectation of fault injection number required to recover K in TWINE is 8.94. In our experiments, the average number is 9.01, which is close to the theoretical one. For LBlock algorithm, the theoretical expected fault injection number is 8.35 [21], and the practical average number is 8.42.

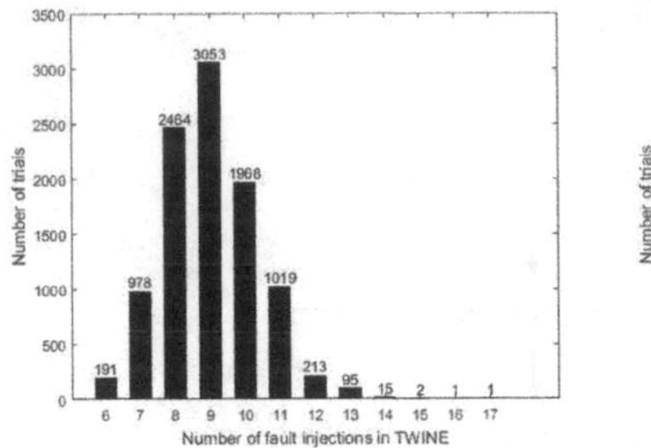

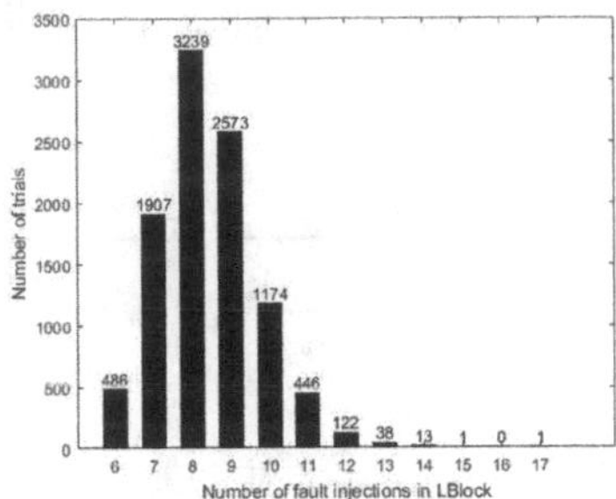

Fig. 3. Results of 10000 trials on TWINE and LBlock.

Besides, Table 2 illustrates the previous DFA result on TWINE and LBlock. It can be seen that the improved DFA method has some advantages in terms of decreasing time and space complexity.

Table 2. Results of DFA on TWINE and LBlock.

Algorithm	DPA method	Fault injection number	Key recovering complexity
TWINE	This paper	9.01	Negligible
	In [18]	4	2^{20}
	In [18]	12	Negligible
	In [22]	8	2^{16}
LBlock	This paper	8.42	Negligible
	In [23]	5	2^{25}
	In [23]	7	2^{30}
	In [24]	10	2^{19}
	In [25]	13.3	Negligible

5 Conclusion

In this paper, we introduce the differential fault attack on GFN structure, then conduct research on two key components of those ciphers. For the permutation layer, the fault diffusion properties can be considered to optimize the fault injection model, and more differential equations are solved in single round. On the other hand, for the S-box, we convert the operation of exhausting nibble input values into looking up S-box differential distribution tables. Thanks to the improvement in this aspect, not only the attack efficiency get improved, but also the expect number of fault injections required to recover the main key K can be calculated. On this basis, we propose the DFA improvement process for the lightweight ciphers with GFN structure. Finally, we respectively perform simulation attack experiments on TWINE and LBlock algorithm. With the improved process above, the efficiency of attack gets enhanced to a certain extent.

The core of improved DFA method is that the basic unit of data processing in GFN structure is nibble. Next step, we will carry out similar discussions and researches on lightweight block ciphers with SPN structure. On the other hand, we continue to study means of reducing the width of the fault, and consider other method so as to improve the efficiency and feasibility of attack. At last, researchers should also pay attention to DFA resilience of Lightweight ciphers.

References

1. Wu, W., Zhang, L.: LBlock: a lightweight block cipher. In: Lopez, J., Tsudik, G. (eds.) ACNS 2011. LNCS, vol. 6715, pp. 327–344. Springer, Heidelberg (2011). https://doi.org/10.1007/978-3-642-21554-4_19
2. Shibutani, K., Isobe, T., Hiwatari, H., Mitsuda, A., Akishita, T., Shirai, T.: *Piccolo*: an ultra-lightweight blockcipher. In: Preneel, B., Takagi, T. (eds.) CHES 2011. LNCS, vol. 6917, pp. 342–357. Springer, Heidelberg (2011). https://doi.org/10.1007/978-3-642-23951-9_23
3. Guo, J., Peyrin, T., Poschmann, A., Robshaw, M.: The LED block cipher. In: Preneel, B., Takagi, T. (eds.) CHES 2011. LNCS, vol. 6917, pp. 326–341. Springer, Heidelberg (2011). https://doi.org/10.1007/978-3-642-23951-9_22
4. Bogdanov, A., et al.: PRESENT: an ultra-lightweight block cipher. In: Paillier, P., Verbauwhede, I. (eds.) CHES 2007. LNCS, vol. 4727, pp. 450–466. Springer, Heidelberg (2007). https://doi.org/10.1007/978-3-540-74735-2_31
5. Boneh, D., DeMillo, R.A., Lipton, R.J.: On the importance of checking cryptographic protocols for faults. In: Fumy, W. (ed.) EUROCRYPT 1997. LNCS, vol. 1233, pp. 37–51. Springer, Heidelberg (1997). https://doi.org/10.1007/3-540-69053-0_4
6. Biham, E., Shamir, A.: Differential fault analysis of secret key cryptosystems. In: Kaliski, B.S. (ed.) CRYPTO 1997. LNCS, vol. 1294, pp. 513–525. Springer, Heidelberg (1997). https://doi.org/10.1007/BFb0052259
7. Zhang, L., Wu, W.: Differential fault analysis on SMS4. Chin. J. Comput. **29**(9), 1596–1602 (2006)
8. Liu, P., Wang, X., Chaudhry, S.R., Javeed, K., Ma, Y., Collier, M.: Secure video streaming with lightweight cipher PRESENT in an SDN testbed. CMC: Comput. Mater. Continua **57**(3), 353–363 (2018)

9. Paar, C., Eisenbarth, T., Kasper, M., Kasper, T., Moradi, A.: KeeLoq and side-channel analysis-evolution of an attack. In: Fault Diagnosis and Tolerance in Cryptography, pp. 65–69. IEEE (2009)
10. Li, W., Gu, D., Li, J., Liu, Z., Liu, Y.: Differential fault analysis on Camellia. J. Syst. Softw. **83**(5), 844–851 (2010)
11. Zhang, S., Yang, X., Zhong, W., Sun, Y.: A highly effective DPA attack method based on genetic algorithm. CMC: Comput. Mater. Continua **56**(2), 325–338 (2018)
12. FIPS PUB: Data Encryption Standard (DES). FIPS PUB 46-3 (1999)
13. Le Bouder, H., Thomas, G., Linge, Y., Tria, A.: On fault injections in generalized Feistel networks. In: Fault Diagnosis and Tolerance in Cryptography, pp. 83–93. IEEE (2014)
14. Zheng, Y., Matsumoto, T., Imai, H.: On the construction of block ciphers provably secure and not relying on any unproved hypotheses. In: Brassard, G. (ed.) CRYPTO 1989. LNCS, vol. 435, pp. 461–480. Springer, New York (1990). https://doi.org/10.1007/0-387-34805-0_42
15. Schneier, B., Kelsey, J.: Unbalanced Feistel networks and block cipher design. In: Gollmann, D. (ed.) FSE 1996. LNCS, vol. 1039, pp. 121–144. Springer, Heidelberg (1996). https://doi.org/10.1007/3-540-60865-6_49
16. Carlet, C.: Vectorial Boolean functions for cryptography. Boolean Models Methods Math. Comput. Sci. Eng. **134**, 398–469 (2010)
17. Chabaud, F., Vaudenay, S.: Links between differential and linear cryptanalysis. In: De Santis, A. (ed.) EUROCRYPT 1994. LNCS, vol. 950, pp. 356–365. Springer, Heidelberg (1995). https://doi.org/10.1007/BFb0053450
18. Xu, P., Wei, Y., Pan, X.: Differential fault attack on TWINE. Appl. Res. Comput. **32**(6), 1796–1800 (2015)
19. Jia, P., Xu, H., Qi, W.: Research on cryptographic properties of lightweight S-boxes. J. Cryptol. Res. **2**(6), 497–504 (2015)
20. Gao, Y., Wang, Y., Wang, L., Wang, T.: Improvement differential fault attack on TWINE. J. Commun. **38**(Z2), 178–184 (2017)
21. Gao, Y., Wang, Y., Yuan, Q., Wang, T., Wang, X., Guo, L.: Methods of differential fault attack on LBlock with analysis of probability. In: Advanced Information Technology, Electronic and Automation Control Conference. IEEE (2018)
22. Li, W., Zhang, W., Gu, D.: Security analysis of the lightweight cryptosystem TWINE in the Internet of Things. KSII Trans. Internet Inf. Syst. **9**(2), 793–810 (2015)
23. Jeong, K., Lee, C., Lim, J.: Improved differential fault analysis on lightweight block cipher LBlock for wireless sensor networks. EURASIP J. Wirel. Commun. Network. **2013**(1), 151 (2013)
24. Gao, S., Chen, H., Fan, L., Wu, W.: Improved fault attack on LBlock: earlier injection with no extra faults. Chin. J. Electron. **26**(4), 754–759 (2017)
25. Wei, Y., Rong, Y., Wang, X.: New differential fault attack on lightweight cipher LBlock. In: International Conference on Intelligent Networking and Collaborative Systems, pp. 285–288. IEEE (2016)

Cloud Management Systems - Load Balancing Algorithms and VDI Implementation Techniques

Micheal Ernest Taylor[1](✉), David Aboagye-Darko[2], and Jian Shen[1]

[1] School of Computer and Software, Nanjing University of Information Science and Technology, Nanjing 210044, Jiangsu, People's Republic of China
delen007@live.com, s_shenjian@126.com

[2] Department of Information Technology, University of Professional Studies, Accra, Greater Accra, Ghana
aboagye.david@upsamail.edu.gh

Abstract. Internet technologies have upsurge the shift from earlier organizational computing processes which were characterized by main frames, client-server models and personal computers (PCs) and have restructured the concept of computing into a phenomenon that uses infrastructure across the globe. This has given rise to IT's reliance on heterogeneous network services and corresponding protocols. Internet technologies and virtualization are key features of cloud management systems. Cloud management system, considered as an evolutionary development, has made the provision of cloud services possible. This is premised on knowledge advancement in technological innovation regarding virtualization, automation of data-centers and network connectivity. A cloud-based VDI solution is a computing model where an end user's system can access all the essential files and data virtually in spite of being alienated from the physical IT infrastructure. However, issues of load balancing and VDI implementation undermine the Quality of Experience (QoE) users obtain from cloud management systems. This study adopts qualitative metrical analysis and comparative metrics on load balancing algorithms to determine algorithms that ensure workload balance. This paper focuses on load balancing algorithms in cloud management systems and virtual desktop infrastructure. The paper further presents rules for implementing a load balancer in cloud management systems, techniques for VDI implementation and a corresponding matrix table.

Keywords: Load balancing · Virtualization · Algorithms · Cloud management systems

1 Introduction

Cloud management system, which is considered as an evolutionary development, has made the provision of cloud services possible [2]. This is premised on knowledge advancement in technological innovation regarding virtualization, automation of data-centers and network connectivity [6]. Cloud management systems are considered as a

X. Sun et al. (Eds.): ICAIS 2019, LNCS 11633, pp. 561–570, 2019.
https://doi.org/10.1007/978-3-030-24265-7_48

relatively new IT-service innovation which has received attention in research and practice. This is in response to the emergence and steady dominance of the service economy; there is a high demand for services in various forms which has led to the addition of service dimensions to most products, including technology [1]. Internet technologies and virtualization are key features of cloud management systems. According to [4], internet technologies have given rise to a shift from earlier organizational computing processes which were characterized by main frames, client-server models and personal computers (PCs) and have restructured the concept of computing into a phenomenon that uses infrastructure across the globe. This has given rise to IT's reliance on heterogeneous network services and corresponding protocols. A cloud-based virtual desktop infrastructure (VDI) solution is a computing model where end users' system can access all the essential files and data virtually in spite of being alienated from the physical IT infrastructure. The VDI layer acts as an intermediary between the backend and the end-user application. Organizations use VDI technologies, from vendors like Citrix and VMware, to manage virtual desktops across their enterprises [8]. A load balancer is a networking tool designed to distribute workload. An end user connects to the port side of the load balancer, while the modules of the application being scaled connect to the trunk side. When an end user's demand arrives, the load balancer directs it to a component based on a fair scheduling algorithm. Public cloud providers, such as AWS, Google and Microsoft Azure, offer load balancing tools on their platforms. In this paper, a discussion on Load balancing algorithms, strategies for implementation in Cloud Systems and Virtual Desktop Infrastructure are presented. The rest of the paper is organized as follows; (1) the second section presents related works, (2) the subsequent section describes in detail the architecture of Cloud Management System and Virtual Desktop Infrastructure (VDI), (3) a load balancing algorithms comparison table, techniques for VDI implementation and a corresponding matrix table are also presented. This paper concludes with remarks on the state of Cloud management systems and virtual desktop infrastructure and its modules (Figs. 1 and 2).

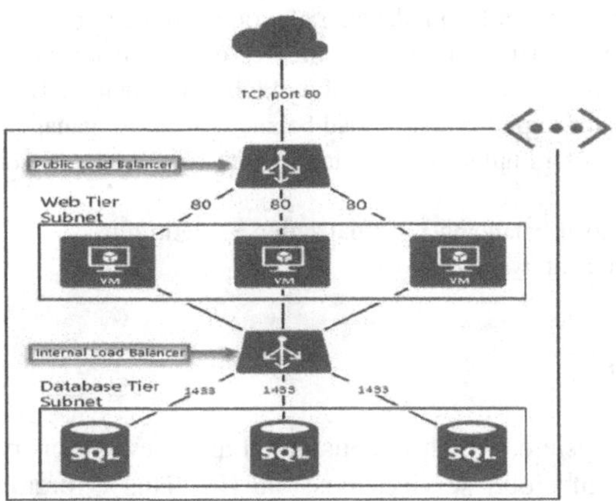

Fig. 1. Load balancing multi-tier applications by using both public and internal load balancer. Source: https://docs.microsoft.com.

2 Problem Statement

Load arrives randomly in a cloud computing systems and can clog the server's bandwidth, overloading some nodes while others are idle. This problem persists and propagates with the cumulative customer base in the cloud system. The solution to this problem is to ensure equal distribution of work load amongst all the nodes in the cloud by efficient planning and resource distribution, refining the overall performance of the system, reducing the response time and total cost of the system. A necessary qualitative metrical analysis and the comparison of various load balancing algorithms is required to achieve Quality of Experience (QoE).

3 Related Works

A number of studies have been conducted to understand Cloud Computing systems, load balancing and virtualization, it's favorable as well as adverse effects on both the CSPs and consumers. Kohler [3] suggests that virtualization emerged as a result of progress made regarding network interconnectivity, bandwidth and three (3) dimensional graphics. Virtualization involves technology generated platforms, physical locations or situations that are generated graphically [3]. Virtualization facilitates real-time, rich media content and great collaboration between individuals and organizations. Internet technologies and virtualization are essential features of cloud services that enhances its value proposition to customers. However, one of the major lapses that undermines the quality of service and performance in cloud computing is load balancing. Load balancing is a technique that facilitates the provision of effective resource time and utilization by decentralizing the overall load to several cloud nodes [5]. Load balancing in cloud management systems engenders optimum performance and effective utilization of resources. Authors in [7] suggest that vendors of cloud management systems consistently engage in proliferation in the provision of services to organizations, hence the load imbalance that characterizes dynamic distribution of services to clients or subscribers. The writers suggest that the issue of load imbalance can be addressed by adopting load balancing algorithms that ensures a balance in workload. This study represents an attempt to address the issue of load balancing in cloud management systems by combining load balancing algorithms that ensure workload balance.

4 Contribution

4.1 Load Balancing Challenges, Strategies and Rules of Implementation

Load balancing in cloud systems is major challenge. As such, we suggest these strategies and rules for successful implementation.

- An effective load balancer must connect to end users and to its scaled application modules: This can be achieved by adding or removing application modules, similarly adding and withdrawing the load balancer's trunk ports. If a module fails and is replaced, an update of the trunk port address of that module is needed. This is problematic for many enterprises, as load balancers are often part of network middleware.

- Performance Management and Quality of Experience: It is doubtful to have same network connections and performance in using public cloud environments as in your data center and most often they are not even similar. Various enterprises including those that use the open internet, have relatively slow connections to CSPs. Network latency and performance can vary, which means that new component instances will perform differently depending on whether they are in the cloud or data center. This variability can be a problem and also confound capacity planning.
- Management of State Control: Most industry applications are transactional, meaning they encompass various messages within a given dialog amid a user and an application. With load balancing, messages related to a particular transaction could be sent to different modules. If those modules are stateful, that is they expect to process transactions as a whole, the result can be a software failure or a corrupted database.

4.2 Rules of Implementation

In order to address load balancing challenges associated with using cloud systems in an organization, the IT teams need in-depth knowledge and critical planning. The following strategies can be implemented:

1. Front-end processing in the cloud is necessary when designing applications: Many enterprises use this method, nonetheless it is not widespread. When implementing front-end processing in the cloud, it is important to use the cloud scalability and load balancing services in the sections where they mostly required, such as the point of end-user connection. Also, this model enables multi-message transactions to trust into a single message which eradicates the issue of state control.
2. Design Load balancer for accessibility and availability: In a hybrid cloud system with a cloud frontend, the load balancer must be placed in the cloud, load balance data center modules and place the load balancer in the data center. This allows an easy update of load balancers to maintain a connection with all the components it supports. Load balancer availability is critical and often overlooked. Most CSPs design their own load balancers for high availability. In a situation where an organization implements its own load balancers, connection to a new instance of the load balancer must be supplied incase the old instance fails. Virtualization, in any form, stimulates scalability. As container orchestrators, such as Kubernetes and other hosting tools progress, we expect to see more load balancing options as well as more risk that they will all work properly in a hybrid cloud architecture.
3. An implementation of a policy-based scalability in the organizations hybrid cloud architecture: A given module should generally scale within its inherent hosting setting whenever possible and scale between the cloud and the data center in case of failure or lack of resources. Furthermore, plan the capacity of connection to public cloud services carefully to handle any workflows that have to cross between the

cloud and data center by limiting the number of cases where the public cloud and data center back each other up. This helps to assess the connectivity requirements between the cloud systems and ensures that the data center recovery strategy does not just create a cloud connection problem. Also, scale modules within restricted resource pools (such as a single data center) and closely connected data centers or a single cloud provider. This method will possibly progress performance steadiness and make it easier to update the load balancer with the addresses of new modules.

5 Load Balancing Algorithms Comparison

Load Balancing algorithms are used to improve the overall performance of the cloud systems. Cost, scalability, flexibility and its executing flow are some major factors that decide the effectiveness and efficiency of an algorithm. In cloud computing, different load balancing algorithm have been proposed which the main tenacity is to realize high throughput and least response time. Basically, load-balancing algorithms are categorized into two: Static load balancing algorithm and Dynamic load balancing algorithm. The successive load balancing parameters are presently dominant in clouds.

- Throughput – It is the amount of work all nodes can process in a specific time period.
- Response time – The elapsed time between the demand placed and the beginning of a response after completion of the job.
- Scalability – Ability of a computer application (hardware/software/service) to continue its function effectively even when its size and topography changes.
- Priority: Preference of tasks based on factors like cost, time and size [9]
- Fault tolerance: A system designed such that it can tolerate and continue functioning amidst any failure.
- Overhead: Refers to the processing time required by the system for installation, operation or any transaction.
- Power Consumption – Information technology consumes tremendous power and involves high energy costs. Efficient power management is vital for the success of IT environment such as cloud computing systems.
- Complexity – Making the entire system difficult. With increasing users associating with the cloud and its properties, the complexity of the system increases.
- Fairness – Indicates that each user has the equal response time and all get their jobs completed within approximately the same time.
- Performance – It is the speed and accuracy at which the jobs are completed and is measured against the preset standards. In simple terms, it is the total efficiency of the system. This can be improved by reducing the task response time and waiting time maintaining a reasonable cost of the system (Table 1).

Table 1. Load balancing algorithms metric table

Algorithms/parameters	ESCE	Round robin	Throttled	Ant colony	Task scheduling
Dynamic/Static	Dynamic	Static	Dynamic	Dynamic	Dynamic
Throughput	Average	Low	Average	High	Good
Response Time	Average	Low	Average	Good	Good
Scalability	Average	Low	High	High	High
Priority	High	Low	High	High	High
Fault tolerance	Low	Low	Average	High	High
Overhead	Average	High	Average	Low	Low
Power consumption	High	High	High	Average	Average
Complexity	Low	Low	Low	Average	High
Fairness	Average	Low	Average	High	Average
Performance	Average	Low	Average	Average	High

Percentage Metrics: Low = 0–39%: Average = 40–69%: High = 70–99%.

Load Balancing affects cloud systems and improves its performance by redistributing the load among the processors with jobs transferred from one node to another through the network involving some delay (queuing delay + processing delay) as it has to determine the destination node through remote processing. In [10], a distributed system model has n no. of users and m no. of computing resources. Nash Equilibrium can be defined for a distributed system model as a strategy "s" for every user "u" as

$$\text{Su} = \text{ArgMin Dj } (\text{S1},\ \text{S2}\ldots.\text{Su}\ldots.\text{Sn}) \tag{1}$$

The Nash equilibrium is realized when no user can decrease its average expected response time by individually changing its strategy. A cloud system which has a normal rate should dispatch jobs instantaneously when it receives from the nodes that would process them. These processors maintain a waiting queue, given the following equations

$$\text{TRT} = \text{Pt} + \text{Wt} + \text{Tt} \tag{2}$$

Where TRT = Total Response Time
Pt = Processing time, Wt = Waiting time, Tt = Transfer time.

$$\text{RPR} = \text{JPR} \ / \ \text{LPR in cluster} \tag{3}$$

Where RPR = Response Processing Rate, JPR = Jobs processing Rate, LPR = Lowest Processing Rate.

$$\text{JGR} = \text{UJGR/TJGR of all users} \tag{4}$$

Where JGR = Job Generation Rate, UJGR = Users Job Generation Rate,
TJGR = Total Job Generation Rate

6 Virtualization and Virtual Desktop Infrastructure

[11] Defines virtualization as "a means of abstracting a computer's physical resources into virtual ones with the help of specialized software. Abstraction layers allow for the creation of multiple VMs [virtual machines] on a single physical machine (ES. 5)".

Virtualization affords encapsulation of processing capabilities of IT resources into virtual platforms and executes these virtual platforms on a host machine in an isolated arena. Many organizations are exploiting a variety of virtual platforms in response to the challenges organizations are experiencing with regards to computing [12].

Presents two categories of virtualization namely hardware and operation system (OS) virtualization. It is important to note that the writers' taxonomy is premised on two fundamental principles. Firstly, the provision of a virtual hardware by the hypervisor which is identified as the system hardware. Secondly, the creation of containers that employ the host hardware through the host OS and the hypervisor. Application virtualization has been identified as a dominant emerging trend in virtual technologies. Thus, it may be considered as the third type of virtualization [12]. However, the focus of this study is on the infrastructure that undergirds desktop virtualization.

6.1 Virtual Desktop Infrastructure

VDI provides a framework for hosting a desktop operating system within a virtual machine (VM) on a server. A user at an endpoint workstation accesses the VM over the network via a remote display protocol that allows the virtualized desktop to be rendered locally. Desktop virtualization is the concept of isolating a logical operating system (OS) instance from the client that is used to access it. There are several different conceptual models of desktop virtualization, which can broadly be divided into two categories based on whether or not the operating system instance is executed locally or remotely. It is important to note that not all forms of desktop virtualization involve the use of virtual machines (VMs). Virtual desktop infrastructure (VDI) is the practice of hosting a desktop operating system within a virtual machine (VM) running on a centralized server [11]. VDI is a variation on the client/server computing model, sometimes referred to as server-based computing. The term was coined by VMware Inc. Many organizations are turning to VDI as an alternative to the server-based computing model used by Citrix and Microsoft Terminal Services.

7 Techniques for Implementing a VDI in Cloud Systems

Successful implementation is necessary in order to exploit the potential benefits (such as centralized IT management) of VDI in cloud systems. The implementation of VDI in cloud systems is dependent not only on the technical reality of IT [13], but also on the complex dynamics that characterize the process by focusing on the needs of users. Therefore, it is imperative that in understanding the techniques for VDI implementation in cloud systems, we also examine the effect of VDI deployment.

User location: When implementing VDI in cloud systems, it is important to consider the location of users. A lot of bandwidth is required for the workstation to work effectively when the distance between the user and data center is greater. IT can address the desktop needs of remote and mobile users by delivering desktops to specific off-site locations. This can be accomplished by upgrading network hardware components (e.g. WAN link controllers to mitigate issues of bottlenecking). When the distance between the user and the data center is great, the cost involved in delivering remote desktops to users will be high.

User Behavior: The behavior of system users such as the kind of applications they use, when they start their day and when they boot their devices influence the VDI needs of an organization. The addition of input output operation per second (IOPS) improves the performance of VDI during peak usage times.

The virtual desktop decision matrix

VDI IS A GOOD FIT AREAS THAT WARRANT DISCUSSION VDI IS NOT A GOOD FIT

ROLE	LOCAL	REMOTE*	MOBILE*	ROAMING
Task workers Single task, minimal applications	Call center operatives	Call center operatives	Meter readers	
Knowledge workers More complex tasks, document creation	HR officers, sales managers, directors	Remote office workers, marketing executives	Sales representatives, mobile service engineers	Sales representatives, mobile service engineers
Power workers Content creators	On-site IT workers, developers, CAD workers, graphic artists	On-site IT workers, CAD workers	IT consultants	Professional services operatives
Kiosk workers Single task, minimal input	Information gatherers/givers	Information gatherers/distributors	Survey takers	Survey takers

Fig. 2. VDI decision matrix Source: www.techtarget.com

Knowledge, task and kiosk workers can use non-persistent desktops and more memory. Power workers require persistent desktops and high memory requirements in view of the fact that they use a variety of applications that consume a lot of resources.

7.1 Effects of VDI on Other Systems

Issues of bandwidth consumption and IP address confront systems after VDI implementation. On the one hand, one IP address is required for the desktop and device in organizations that deploy physical desktops with thick clients. On the other hand, organizations that deploy thin clients require two IP addresses, one for the thin client itself and the other for the virtual desktop. In view of the aforementioned, it is imperative that organizations adopt IP address management tools to address issues of bandwidth consumption and anticipation of required IP addresses per number of users.

8 Conclusion

In this paper, the rules for implementing a load balancer in cloud management systems as well as the techniques for the implementation of VDI were presented. The potential benefits cloud management systems present have resulted in its implementation in several organizations across the globe. Unfortunately, the issue of load balancing and VDI implementation are some of the major lapses that undermine the QoE users obtain while using cloud management systems [14]. To this end, the qualitative metrical analysis and comparative metrics were conducted on load balancing algorithms in VDI and cloud management systems to determine algorithms that ensure workload balance. It was argued that in order to implement load balancers in cloud management systems, rules such as front-end processing in the cloud when designing applications, designing the load balancer for accessibility and availability, and the implementation of a policy based scalability in hybrid cloud architecture are necessary for optimum performance of cloud management systems. Also, user location, user behavior as well as the effect of VDI on other systems should be considered during VDI implementation in cloud systems. Further studies can be conducted to identify combinations of specific load balancing algorithms that completely addresses issues such as load balancing ports and trunks, as well as state control, in cloud management systems.

References

1. Fang, E., Palmatier, R.W., Steenkamp, J.: Effect of service transition strategies on firm value. J. Mark. **72**(5), 1–14 (2008)
2. Iyer, B., Henderson, J.C.: Preparing for the future by understanding the seven capabilities cloud computing. MIS Q. **9**(2), 117–131 (2010)
3. Kohler, T.: Co-creation in virtual worlds: the design of the user experience. MIS Q. **9**(2), 773–788 (2003)
4. Lyytinen, K., Rose, G.M.: The disruptive nature of information technology innovations: the case of internet computing in systems development organizations. MIS Q. **27**(4), 557–596 (2003)
5. Nakai, A.M., Madeira, E., Buzato, L.E..: Improving the QOS of web services via client-based load distribution. In: 29th Proceedings of Brazilian Symposium on Computer Networks and Distributed Systems, pp. 617–629. Unicamp (2011)
6. Venters, W., Whitley, E.A.: A critical review of cloud computing: researching desires and realities. J. Inf. Technol. **27**(1), 179–197 (2012)
7. Taylor, M.E., Shen, J.: Cloud management systems and virtual desktop infrastructure load balancing algorithms - a survey. In: Sun, X., Chao, H.-C., You, X., Bertino, E. (eds.) ICCCS 2017. LNCS, vol. 10602, pp. 300–309. Springer, Cham (2017). https://doi.org/10.1007/978-3-319-68505-2_26

8. Liu, J., Lai, W.: Security analysis of VLAN-based virtual desktop infrastructure. In: International Conference on Educational and Network Technology, pp. 301–304 (2010)
9. Gouda, K.C., Radhika, T.V., Akshatha, M.: Priority based resource allocation model for cloud computing. Int. J. Sci., Eng. Technol. Res. **2**(1), 215–219 (2013)
10. Taylor, M.E., Shen, J.: Cloud management systems and virtual desktop infrastructure load balancing algorithms - a survey. In: Sun, X., Chao, H.C., You, X., Bertino, E. (eds.) Cloud Computing and Security. ICCCS 2017, LNCS, vol. 10602, pp. 1–13. Springer, Cham (2017)
11. Chronopoulos, A.T.: Game Theory Based Load Balanced Job Allocation. http://graal.enslyon.fr/~lmarchal/aussois/slides/chronopoulos.pdf. Accessed 04 Dec 2018
12. Lunsford, D.L.: Virtualization technologies in information systems education. J. Inf. Syst. Educ. **20**(3), 339–348 (2017)
13. Xie, X., Yuan, T., Zhou, X., Cheng, X.: Research on trust model in container-based cloud service. CMC **56**(2), 273–283 (2018)
14. Cheang, C.F., Wang, Y., Cai, Z., Xu, G.: Multi-Vms intrusion detection for cloud security using dempster-shafer theory. CMC **57**(2), 297–306 (2018)

When Side Channel Becomes Good: Kernel Malware Attack Investigation

Libo Yin[1], Chonghua Wang[1(✉)], Jun Li[1], Rongchao Yin[1], Yang Jiao[2], and Hao Jiang[1]

[1] China Industrial Control Systems Cyber Security Emergency Response Team, Beijing, China
chonghuaw@live.com
[2] Institute of Information Engineering, Chinese Academy of Sciences, Beijing, China

Abstract. Security and privacy issues have been a concern and have become one of the main factors hindering the promotion and popularization of cloud computing. In recent years, cache side channel attack are presented by many researchers to crack cryptographic algorithms (e.g., AES, RSA), bypass ASLR and etc. Cache side channel had been considered as a hacking tool to conduct harmful activities on victim systems. However, from a defender's perspective, cache side channel can also be employed to explore valuable information. Our paper employs cache side channel to obtain a deep insight on what kind of behaviors kernel malware may conduct. In specific, we propose a novel approach to conduct kernel malware attack investigation with *Flush+Reload* cache side channel. We have built a proof-of-concept prototype and designed some case studies to conduct extensive experiments. The evaluation results show that our system is capable of understanding what kind of behaviors kernel malware may conduct correctly.

Keywords: Cache side channel · Attack investigation · Cloud security

1 Introduction

With the prevalence of cloud computing in the last decade, lots of platforms are developed by large companies (e.g., Amazon, IBM, Microsoft, and Google) due to the convenience, cost savings, and real-time scalability of the cloud. These cloud platforms provide isolation, reduce cost, and maintain utilization to support different users by virtual machines (VMs). With the increasing amount of secret and sensitive data in the cloud, security and privacy issues [4] have been a concern and have become one of the main factors hindering the promotion and popularization of cloud computing Based on the logical isolation provided by the virtualized environment, access control, intrusion detection and other methods can enhance the security of the cloud computing environment. However, the privacy leakage problem still exists since the underlying shared hardware resources are easy to be exploited by side channel attack.

X. Sun et al. (Eds.): ICAIS 2019, LNCS 11633, pp. 571–583, 2019.
https://doi.org/10.1007/978-3-030-24265-7_49

Cryptographic schemes are used to prevent unanticipated information leakage. For a long time, breaking cryptographic schemes means mathematically cracking the encryption algorithm and inferring the original text from the ciphertext. On the other hand, side-channel attacks are able to extract the secret key without learning the direct relation between plaintext and ciphertext. Once secret key is obtained, deciphering the encrypted information is trivial. When the cryptographic algorithm is specifically executed, various physical state information closely related to the internal operation may be leaked during execution, such as acousto-optic information, power consumption, electromagnetic radiation, and running time. These physical state information leaked through indirect transmission is called the Side Channel Information (SCI). The side channel information generated during the execution, combined with the specific implementation of the cryptographic algorithm, can be used to analyze and crack the key. This attack method using the side channel information for cryptanalysis is called side channel attack [13]. An active area of side-channel attack researches is related to the cache and memory over the last decade with the advantage of high resolution and stability.

The cache between the CPU and main memory (RAM) is used to break the performance gap between them. By buffering the most recently used data, overall memory access time is greatly reduced. Although caching greatly improves average performance, the time difference between cache hits and cache misses has led to many side channel attack studies over the past decade. The basic principle of these attacks is that accessing higher levels of cached data is an order of magnitude faster than low-level data, and an attacker can infer some or all of the victim's memory access information by measuring the access time while sharing the cache.

In recent years, cache side channel attack are presented by many researchers to crack cryptographic algorithms (e.g., AES, RSA) [11,26], bypass ASLR [6] and etc. Cache side channel has been considered as a hacking tool to conduct harmful activities on victim systems. In the scenario of a cache side channel attack, the attacker uses a spy process to steal information from a victim program. However, what if we employ cache side channel to do good things? From a defender's perspective, cache side channel can also be employed to explore valuable information. In this situation, the defender employs a spy process to analyze the activities conducted by an attacker and the attacker is considered as the victim. Kernel malware is considered as one of the most stealthy threats in computer security field and becomes a major challenge for security research communities. We consider a scenario that a user wants to install a kernel driver and downloads a kernel malware without being aware. Our paper employs cache side channel to obtain a deep insight on what kind of behaviors kernel malware may conduct.

In summary, we make the following contributions:

- We show how cache side channel can also be good to explore valuable information and analyze the activities conducted by an attacker.

- We propose a novel approach to conduct kernel malware attack investigation with *Flush+Reload* cache side channel.
- We have built a proof-of-concept prototype and designed some case studies to conduct extensive experiments. The evaluation results show that our system is capable of understanding what kind of behaviors kernel malware may conduct correctly.

2 Background

Kocher [13] and Kelsey et al. [12] first employ cache side channel to access sensitive information. With these theoretical researches, a lot of side-channel attacks are designed to extract key, and broader applicability from single computer to commercial VM servers such as Amazon EC2 [9].

Cache side-channel attacks can be categorized as time-driven and access-driven. The timing-driven attacks need to collect the overall time of encryption/decryption of the cryptographic algorithm, and use the statistical analysis method to infer the key. Access-driven attacks need to collect the set of cache group addresses accessed during the encryption/decryption process through the spy process, and then use the direct analysis or exclusion analysis method to guess the key. In timing-driven attacks, the attacker has to measure the victim process' execution time, while in the access-driven attacks, the attacker measures the execution time of an operation of its own.

2.1 *Prime+Probe*

The attacker first fills a specific cache group with its own data in the *Prime* phase, and then waits for the target virtual machine to use the filled cache group address in the *Trigger* phase. Some data will be evicted from the cache, and the data will be re-read during the probe phase. The evicted cache requires a longer read time. Therefore, based on the cache reload time detected by the *Probe* stage, the cache address used by the target VM in response to the service can be determined. The specific steps of the method are as follows:

- *Prime*: The attacker populates a specific number of cache groups with pre-prepared data.
- *Trigger*: Wait for the target VM to respond to the service request and update the cache data.
- *Probe*: Re-read the data filled in the Prime phase, measure and record the read time of each cache group.

2.2 *Flush+Reload*

The *Flush+Reload* method is a variant of the Prime+Probe method. Based on the shared memory implementation, it is a cache detection method that spans the kernel and crosses the virtual machine. In the *Flush* phase, the attacker evicts the monitored memory block from the cache and then waits for the target user to access shared memory during the *Trigger* phase. During the *Reload* phase, the attacker reloads the monitored shared memory block. If the memory block accessed by the target virtual machine needs to be reloaded while waiting, the time will be shorter because the data has already been cached in the cache. According to the length of the loading time, the data accessed by the target virtual machine can be determined. The specific steps of *Flush+Reload* are as follows:

- *Flush*: Expel the cache data mapped to a specific location in the shared memory.
- *Trigger*: Wait for the target VM to respond to the service request, update the Cache.
- *Reload*: Reload the memory block expelled during the Flush phase, measure and record the reload time of the cache group.

There are two differences between *Prime+Probe* and *Flush+Reload.* First, *Flush+reload* requires the attacker and the the victim processes to share memory, while *Prime+Probe* does not. Second, *Prime+probe* puts the data prepared by the attacker into the cache first, and passively waits for the target virtual machine to fill the cache. However, in *Flush+Reload*, the attack flushes data in the cache actively, and then wait for the target virtual machine to access the shared memory.

3 Related Work

3.1 Cache Side Channel

Gullasch et al. [11] presented the original idea of *Flush+Reload* cache side channel to extract the key of AES algorithm. The technique uses the processor's *clflush* instruction to evict the monitored memory locations from the cache, and then tests whether the data in these locations is back in the cache after allowing the victim program to execute a small number of instructions.

Ristenpart et al. [23] first present that cache side channel attacks can be conducted across the virtual machine in the cloud computing environment. Unlike traditional cache side channel attacks, the sharing and contention for cache and memory between different virtual machines in the same physical machine provides convenient conditions to implement side channel attack. It also greatly enhances the feasibility of cross vm cache side channel in the real environment.

Yarom et al. [26] extended his method to adapt to L3 cache for cross-core attacks and cross-VM scenarios such as VMware ESXi 5.1 and CentOS 6.5 with KVM. They show how to use the *Flush+Reload* technique to extract the components of the private key from the GnuPG implementation of RSA. Their method flushes and measures the time to reload the same instructions in the *Square*, *Multiply*, and *Reduce* functions. The timing variation of reloading reveals the exact execution path of the victim process. The attack is able to recover 96.7% of the bits of the secret key by observing a single signature or decryption round.

Irazoqui et al. [3] demonstrate cross-VM *Flush+Reload* cache attacks in VMware VMs to recover the keys of an AES implementation of OpenSSL 1.0.1 running inside the victim VM. Irazoqui et al. [2] introduce a novel cross-core and crossVM cache-based side-channel attack that exploits the shared L3 cache. The attack a variation of *Prime+Probe* and takes advantage of the additional physical address knowledge gained by the usage of huge size pages. Zhang et al. [28] is the first to demonstrate cache side channel attack can be used on a symmetric multiprocessing system virtualized using a modern VMM (Xen). The attack establishes a side-channel of sufficient fidelity that an attacker VM can extract a private ElGamal decryption key from a co-resident victim VM running Gnu Privacy Guard (GnuPG) , a popular software package that implements the OpenPGP e-mail encryption standard. Zhang et al. [29] present a framework to use the *Flush+Reload* attack of Gullasch et al. [11] as a primitive, and extends this work by leveraging it within an automaton-driven strategy for tracing a victim's execution. The framework first confirms co-location of tenants and then to extract secrets across tenant boundaries in PaaS environments.

Gruss et al. [10] came up with *Flush+Flush* which exploits the same hardware and software properties as *Flush+Reload*: it works on read-only shared memory, cross-core attack and in virtualized environments. In contrast to *Flush+Reload*, *Flush+Flush* does not make any memory accesses and thus does not cause any cache misses at all and only a minimal number of cache hits. Liu et al. [17] present an implementation of the *Prime+Probe* side-channel attack against the last level cache. The attack creates and demonstrate a cross-core, cross-VM attack on multiple versions of GnuPG.

Zhang et al. [27] proposed a return-oriented *Flush+Reload* attack on last-level caches of ARM processors to detect hardware events and trace software execution paths. Lipp et al. [16] showed that Prime+Probe and Evict+Reload attacks can be applied to Android smart- phones without root privileges to recover keys. Zhang et al. [27] demonstrate a novel construction of *Flush+Reload* side channels on last-level caches of ARM processors, which, particularly, exploits return-oriented programming techniques to reload instructions. Lipp et al. [16] demonstrate how to solve key challenges to perform the most powerful cross-core cache attacks *Prime+Probe*, *Flush+Reload*, and *Flush+Flush* on non-rooted ARM-based devices without any privileges.

3.2 Attack Investigation

Attack investigation provides the ability to describe the history of a data object, including the conditions that led to its creation and the actions that delivers it to its present state. Hi-Fi [21] leverages Linux Security Module to collect a complete provenance record from early kernel initialization through system shutdown. It maintains the fidelity of provenance collection under any user space compromise. BEEP [14] instruments an application binary at the instructions and use the Linux audit system to capture the system calls triggered by the application for investigating which application brings the malware into the system for attack Investigation. LogGC [15] employs the garbage collection method to prune some system objects such as temporary files that have a short life-span and have little impact on the dependency analysis to save space. ProTracer [19] proposes to combine both logging and unit level tainting techniques, aiming at reducing log volume to achieve cost-effective attack Investigation. Bate et al. [7] proposes Linux Provenance Module, a generalized framework for the development of automated, whole-system provenance collection on the Linux. However, these systems rely on the safety of provenance collector (e.g., Linux audit system, Linux Security Module). In the events of kernel malware, the adversary is able to compromise the provenance collector or even the kernel, which makes the provenance results untrusted.

4 Design and Implementation

4.1 Threat Model and Assumptions

We have the following assumptions when designing our system:

Assume that we can obtain the system call table information with *System.map* file of the tested VM. In cloud environment, the operating system of VMs is configurable and the *System.map* file is easy to read. This assumption is reasonable.

Regarding the scope of different categories of kernel malware and to focus on the attack investigation problem itself for kernel malware, the kind of system call hooking kernel malware is our initial implementation decision for a prototype.

4.2 *Flush+Reload* Technique

The *Flush+Reload* technique is a variant of *Prime+Probe* that relies on sharing pages between the spy and the victim processes. With shared pages, the spy can ensure that a specific memory line is evicted from the whole cache hierarchy. The spy uses this to monitor access to the memory line.

Figure 1 shows the pseudo code of *Flush+Reload* technique.

- The *mfence* and *lfence* instructions serialise the instruction stream to avoid the instructions surrounding the measured code segment executed within that segment (Line 4,5,7,10).
- The *rdtsc* instruction reads the 64-bit counter, returning the low 32 bits of the counter in *%eax* and the high 32 bits in *%edx* (Line 6).
- *movl %eax, %esi* copies the counter to *%esi* (Line 8).
- movl (%1), %eax reads 4 bytes from the memory address in *%ecx*, i.e. the address pointed by addrs (Line 9).
- After reading the memory, the time stamp counter is read again (Line 11).
- Then it subtracts the value of the counter before the memory read from the value after the read, leaving the result in the output register *%eax* (Line 12).
- It returns the time to read this address in the register *%eax* which is stored in the variable time (Line 14).

- The assembly code takes one input, the address, which is stored in register *%ecx* (Line 15).
- *return time* < *threshold* compares the time difference between the two *rdtsc* instructions against a predetermined threshold (Line 17).

```
1 int probe(char *adrs) {
2 volatile unsigned long time;
3 asm __volatile__ (
4 " mfence \n"
5 " lfence \n"
6 " rdtsc \n"
7 " lfence \n"
8 " movl %%eax, %%esi \n"
9 " movl (%1), %%eax \n"
10 " lfence \n"
11 " rdtsc \n"
12 " subl %%esi, %%eax \n"
13 " clflush 0(%1) \n"
14 : "=a" (time)
15 : "c" (adrs)
16 : "%esi", "%edx");
17 return time < threshold;
18 }
```

Fig. 1. *Flush + Reload* technique.

Loads shorter than the threshold are presumed to be served from the cache, indicating that another process has accessed the memory line since it was last flushed from the cache. Loads longer than the threshold are presumed to be served from the memory, indicating no access to the memory line.

4.3 Kernel Malware Attack Investigation

Detecting attacks is an urgent matter in enterprise environments, but is far from enough. In addition to detecting the existence of the attacks, deep investigation should be performed to find out where the attacks are, how the attacks are derived, and when they are introduced. For instance, a kernel mode attack can modify kernel objects or entities, which is potentially more dangerous. Acquiring such details about how the kernel objects and entities are manipulated is crucial to understand the attack for forensic investigations [7,14,18–21,25].

A kernel malware is typically used by loading a malicious kernel module into the kernel and then interacting with the kernel data to hide itself without being detected. To achieve an malicious goal, the kernel-mode components of malware typically employ hooking or DKOM (Direct Kernel Object Manipulation) strategies [1]. For hooking, the malware hijacks the key functionalities of the operating system such as the system call table, VFS (Virtual File System) functions, or IDT (Interrupt Descriptor Table) and then points to malicious functions. For DKOM, adversaries directly tamper with pointers fields or data values of sensitive kernel objects to hide or manipulate the OS semantics. DKOM adversaries are loaded through the kernel memory devices such as */dev/kmem*. Such devices give access to the memory region occupied by the running kernel. It is possible to overwrite kernel at the runtime and thus perform arbitrary modifications. We collect a variety of kernel malware samples and manually analyzed them. In summary, there are several categories that kernel malware falls into: system service hijacking (e.g., hooking *system call table* entries and replacing *system call table*), dynamic kernel object hooking (KOH, e.g., VFS hooking) and DKOM [22,24].

Kernel malware is considered as one of the most stealthy threats in computer security field and becomes a major challenge for security research communities [5,8,24] since it has the equal privilege as the kernel and often higher privileges than most security tools.

Suppose a user wants to install a kernel driver and downloads a LKM without being aware that it is malicious. The malicious LKM subverts important kernel objects to hide itself and transfers confidential information. The system investigator inspects the victim system and starts scanning and monitoring work as usual. But nothing has been detected for some days which may raise questions to the administrator. Also the user may download more than one malicious LKM which manipulates multiple kinds of kernel objects. What the system investigator needs to know is which LKM tampered with what kind of kernel objects. He has to design some investigation techniques to detect dependences among LKMs, files, kernel objects and memory accesses or even instructions and build causality dependencies through causal analysis of the historical events.

4.4 Enabling Schemes and Techniques

Using the cache side channel, the malware changes the system call table by calling the function entry in each system call of interest. Specifically, there are three key steps involved during the attack investigation using *Flush+Reload*:

- *Step 1:* Flush out all of the cache lines that need to be checked from the cache.
- *Step 2:* The spy process waits for kernel malware to modify the system call table entry.
- *Step 3:* The spy process reloads the cache line to be checked, measures the loading time to understand the hooking behavior to the system call table of kernel malware.

```
1 _NR_NUM ← 0
2 _NR_TOTAL ←311
3 count ← 0
4 while _NR_NUM  < _NR_TOTAL
5   o_sys_entry ← sys_call_table[_NR_NUM]
6   real_sys_NR_NUM ← System.map[NR_NUM]
7   while count < 100
8     flush(o_sys_entry )
9     t0 ← probe(real_sys_entry )
10    t1 ←time_access_noflush(real_sys_entry )
11    if t0 << t1
12    print o_sys_entry
13  end while
14 end while
```

Fig. 2. *Flush+Reload* Technique for kernel malware attack investigation

Figure 2 shows the pseudo code of our method.

_NR_NUM denotes the number of the system call entry in the system call table. For example, if *_NR_NUM* equals 2, then *sys_NR_NUM* denotes *sys_open*. *_NR_TOTAL* denotes the total number of system call entries. The spy program save the entry address of *sys_NR_NUM* function in the current system call table to *flush(o_sys_entry)*, and save the original address of *sys_NR_NUM* found in the System.map file to *real_sys_NR_NUM* (Line 5, 6).

- *Step 1: flush(o_sys_entry).* It clears the cache line where the entry address of the *sys_NR_NUM* function in the current system call table is located (Line 8).
- *Step 2: probe (real_sys_entry).* It accesses the address of the *real_sys_entry* function, loads it into the cache, and measures the access time. Then it evicts the memory line from the cache, and finally returns the access time t0 (Line 9).
- *Step 3: time_access_no_flush(real_sys_entry).* It accesses the address where the *real_sys_NR_NUM* function is located, measures the access time, and returns the time *t1*. Compared with the result of *probe (real_sys_entry)*, *time_access_no_flush(real_sys_entry)* loads the *real_sys_entry* after it had been loaded into the cache line, and no memory lines were evicted from the cache. We repeat this process 100 times or more times to eliminate occasionality. (Line 10, 11).

If the system call table has not been manipulated, then *o_sys_entry* = *real_sys_entry*. *time_access_no_flush* and *flush(o_sys_entry)* is a complete flush+reload process, that is, once the memory line of *real_sys_entry* is accessed, the spy program will evict it from the cache, then $t1 = t0$;

If the system call table has been manipulated, then *o_sys_entry* is not equal to *real_sys_entry*. After *time_access_no_flush(real_sys_entry)* to access *real_sys_entry*, the *flush(o_sys_entry)* does not evict the memory line where *real_sys_entry* is located in the cache. And when measuring the time, since *real_sys_entry* is in the cache, the value of *t0* must be significantly smaller than *t1*. It can be judged that the *sys_entry* function entry in the system call table has been manipulated.

5 Evaluation

We have evaluated the effectiveness of our prototype to demonstrate the kernel malware attack investigation capability enabled by our system. In our experiments, the host machine is an Intel Core i5 desktop running Ubuntu 16.04 and 8GB of RAM. We use Linux kernels as the guest VM, which is configured with 2GB of RAM. To validate our experiments results with the ground truth, we have collected 10 system services hijacking malware samples(e.g., *kbeast*, *xinqyiquan*, etc.) that contain a mix of malicious capabilities found in the wild.

We conduct several experiments to evaluate the effectiveness of our system. We insert one malware sample into the kernel at a time and start *spy* program.

Table 1. Manipulated system call entries. '√' denotes that the entry has been manipulated.

System call entry	Kbeast	Xing-yiquan	Sute-rusu	Knark	Enye-lkm	Syna-psys	Rial	Kis	Kbdv3	Adore-0.42
_NR_open	√	√				√	√	√		√
_NR_read	√		√	√			√			
_NR_write	√		√			√				√
_NR_rmdir	√	√						√		
_NR_mkdir								√		
_NR_unlink	√	√						√		
_NR_chdir		√						√		
_NR_kill	√	√		√	√	√				√
_NR_fork				√		√		√		√
_NR_ioctl				√						
_NR_close										√
_NR_clone				√		√	√	√		√
_NR_exit								√		
_NR_execve				√						
_NR_rename	√	√						√		
_NR_utime									√	
_NR_unlinkat	√									
_NR_socketcall								√		
_NR_getdents				√		√	√	√		
_NR_gentdents64	√			√	√					
_NR_getuid						√				
_NR_getuid32									√	
_NR_gettimeofday										
_NR_quiry_module						√	√			
_NR_init_module								√		
_NR_delete_module	√									
_NR_stat								√		
_NR_lstat								√		

The *spy* program is able to identify which kind of kernel objects are manipulated by the malware sample. Table 1 shows the system call entries that are manipulated by kernel malware samples of system services hijacking we collect. For instance, *Kbeast* tampered with *_NR_open*, *_NR_read*, *_NR_write*, *_NR_rmdir*, *_NR_unlink*, etc.

We also analyze the source code of all the malware samples for the validation purposes, and it turned out that the entries discovered by our attack investigation method correctly matched the malware behaviors in the source code.

6 Discussion

Our paper takes the first step to employ cache side channel for attack investigation from a defender's perspective. Our prototype did not consider the cross-VM scenario yet. In the cross-VM scenario, the spy and malware execute in separate, co-located virtual machines.

Since the cache side channel attack is implemented by flushing and reloading the system call to be detected with *Flush+Reload* technique, the page where the system call table located and the page where the system call entry to be detected located (e.g., *real_sys_entry*) should be acted as the shared page. In the cross-VM scenario, the spy runs in one VM and the kernel malware runs in another VM. However, once the kernel malware manipulate the system call table, the *CoW* mechanism will be triggered, and the page where the system call table located will not be shared. The *o_sys_entry* address accessed by the spy will not be as same as the function address after being tampered with, and it is the address of *real_sys_entry* before manipulation. That is, *t0* is always equal to *t1*. Then our prototype fails in the cross-VM scenario.

7 Conclusion

In this paper, we describe how to employ *Flush+Reload* cache side channel technique to conduct kernel malware attack investigation. While cache side channel had been exploited to compromise systems for intended attackers (e.g., cryptographic algorithms cracking, information leakage, etc.), we present a positive scenario that employs cache side channel to analyze the malicious behaviors of kernel malware. Our system is capable of identifying which kind of kernel objects are manipulated by kernel malware. This kind of capability is useful to help system investigator to reveal the causality dependencies among kernel malware behaviors and impacts on the victim system.

Acknowledgement. We would like to thank the anonymous reviewers for their insightful comments that greatly helped to improve this paper. Any opinions, findings, and conclusions expressed in this material are those of the authors and do not necessarily reflect the views of these agencies.

References

1. Dkom(direct kernel objectmanipulation). https://www.blackhat.com/presentations/win-usa-04/bh-win-04-butler.pdf
2. Irazoqui Apecechea, G., Eisenbarth, T., Sunar, B.: S$ a: a shared cache attack that works across cores and defies VM sandboxing - and its application to AES. In: 2015 IEEE Symposium on Security and Privacy (S&P), pp. 591–604, San Jose, CA, USA, 17–21 May 2015
3. Irazoqui, G., Inci, M.S., Eisenbarth, T., Sunar, B.: Wait a minute! a fast, cross-VM attack on AES. In: Stavrou, A., Bos, H., Portokalidis, G. (eds.) RAID 2014. LNCS, vol. 8688, pp. 299–319. Springer, Cham (2014). https://doi.org/10.1007/978-3-319-11379-1_15
4. Ardagna, C.A., Asal, R., Damiani, E., Vu, Q.H.: From security to assurance in the cloud: a survey. ACM Comput. Surv. **48**(1), 2:1–2:50 (2015)
5. Bahram,S., et al.: Dksm: subverting virtual machine introspection for fun and profit. In: Proceedings of IEEE Symposium on Reliable Distributed Systems (SRDS), pp. 82–91 (2010)
6. Barresi, A., Razavi, K., Payer, M., Gross, T.R.: CAIN: silently breaking ASLR in the cloud. In: 9th USENIX Workshop on Offensive Technologies (WOOT), Washington, DC, USA, 10–11 August 2015
7. Bates, A., Tian, D., Butler, K., Moyer, T.: Trustworthy whole-system provenance for the linux kernel. In: USENIX Security, pp. 319–334 (2015)
8. Carbone, M., Cui, W., Lu, L., Lee, W., Peinado, M., Jiang, X.: Mapping kernel objects to enable systematic integrity checking. In: Proceedings of ACM Conference on Computer and Communications Security (CCS), pp. 555–565 (2009)
9. Cock, D., Ge, Q., Murray, T.C., Heiser, G.: The last mile: an empirical study of timing channels on seL4. In: Proceedings of the ACM SIGSAC Conference on Computer and Communications Security (CCS), pp. 570–581, Scottsdale, AZ, USA, 3–7 November 2014
10. Gruss, D., Maurice, C., Wagner, K., Mangard, S.: Flush+Flush: a fast and stealthy cache attack. In: Caballero, J., Zurutuza, U., Rodríguez, R.J. (eds.) DIMVA 2016. LNCS, vol. 9721, pp. 279–299. Springer, Cham (2016). https://doi.org/10.1007/978-3-319-40667-1_14
11. Gullasch, D., Bangerter, E., Krenn, S.: Cache games - bringing access-based cache attacks on AES to practice. In: 32nd IEEE Symposium on Security and Privacy (S&P), pp. 490–505, Berkeley, California, USA, 22–25 May 2011
12. Kelsey, J., Schneier, B., Wagner, D.A., Hall, C.: Side channel cryptanalysis of product ciphers. J. Comput. Secur. **8**(2/3), 141–158 (2000)
13. Kocher, P.C.: Timing attacks on implementations of Diffie-Hellman, RSA, DSS, and Other Systems. In: Koblitz, N. (ed.) CRYPTO 1996. LNCS, vol. 1109, pp. 104–113. Springer, Heidelberg (1996). https://doi.org/10.1007/3-540-68697-5_9
14. Lee, K., Zhang, X., Xu, D.: High accuracy attack provenance via binary-based execution partition. In: Proceedings of Network and Distributed System Security Symposium (NDSS) (2013)
15. Lee, K., Zhang, X., Xu, D.: LogGC: garbage collecting audit log. In: Proceedings of ACM Conference on Computer and Communications Security (CCS), pp. 1005–1016 (2013)
16. Lipp, M., Gruss, D., Spreitzer, R., Maurice, C., Mangard, S.: Armageddon: cache attacks on mobile devices. In: 25th USENIX Security Symposium (Security), pp. 549–564, Austin, TX, USA, 10–12 August 2016

17. Liu, F., Yarom, Y., Ge, Q., Heiser, G., Lee, R.B.: Last-level cache side-channel attacks are practical. In: 2015 IEEE Symposium on Security and Privacy (S&P), pp. 605–622, San Jose, CA, USA, 17–21 May 2015
18. Ma, S., Lee, K., Kim, C., Rhee, J., Zhang, X., Xu, D.: Accurate, low cost and instrumentation-free security audit logging for windows. In: Proceedings of Annual Computer Security Applications Conference (ACSAC), pp. 401–410 (2011)
19. Ma, S., Zhang, X., Xu, D.: Protracer: towards practical provenance tracing by alternating between logging and tainting. In: Proceedings of Network and Distributed System Security Symposium (NDSS) (2016)
20. Pei, K., et al.: HERCULE: attack story reconstruction via community discovery on correlated log graph. In: Proceedings of Annual Computer Security Applications Conference (ACSAC), pp. 583–595 (2016)
21. Pohly, D., McLaughlin, S., McDaniel, P., Butler, K.: Hi-Fi: collecting high-fidelity whole-system provenance. In: Proceedings of Annual Computer Security Applications Conference (ACSAC), pp. 259–268 (2012)
22. Rhee, J., Riley, R., Xu, D., Jiang, X.: Defeating dynamic data kernel rootkit attacks via VMM-based guest-transparent monitoring. In: 2009 International Conference on Availability, Reliability and Security, pp. 74–81 (2009)
23. Ristenpart, T., Tromer, E., Shacham, H., Savage, S.: Hey, you, get off of my cloud: exploring information leakage in third-party compute clouds. In: Proceedings of the ACM Conference on Computer and Communications Security (CCS), pp. 199–212, Chicago, Illinois, USA, 9–13 November 2009
24. Rudd, E., Rozsa, A., Gunther, M., Boult, T.: A survey of stealth malware: attacks, mitigation measures, and steps toward autonomous open world solutions. IEEE Commun. Surv. Tutor. **99**, 1–28 (2016)
25. Xu, Z., et al.: High fidelity data reduction for big data security dependency analyses. In: Proceedings of ACM Conference on Computer and Communications Security (CCS), pp. 504–516 (2016)
26. Yarom, Y., Falkner, K.: FLUSH+RELOAD: a high resolution, low noise, L3 cache side-channel attack. In: Proceedings of the 23rd USENIX Security Symposium (Security), pp. 719–732, San Diego, CA, USA, 20–22 August 2014
27. Zhang, X., Xiao, Y., Zhang, Y.: Return-oriented flush-reload side channels on ARM and their implications for android devices. In: Proceedings of the ACM SIGSAC Conference on Computer and Communications Security (CCS), pp. 858–870, Vienna, Austria, 24–28 October 2016
28. Zhang, Y., Juels, A., Reiter, M.K., Ristenpart, T.: Cross-VM side channels and their use to extract private keys. In: The ACM Conference on Computer and Communications Security (CCS), pp. 305–316, Raleigh, NC, USA, 16–18 October 2012
29. Zhang, Y., Juels, A., Reiter, M.K., Ristenpart, T.: Cross-tenant side-channel attacks in PaaS clouds. In Proceedings of the ACM SIGSAC Conference on Computer and Communications Security (CCS), pp. 990–1003, Scottsdale, AZ, USA, 3–7 November 2014

Robust Encrypted Watermarking for Medical Images Based on DWT-DCT and Tent Mapping in Encrypted Domain

Yanlin Liu[1], Jingbing Li[1,2](✉), Jing Liu[1], Jieren Cheng[1], Jialing Liu[1], Lingren Wang[1], and Xiaobo Bai[3]

[1] College of Information Science and Technology, Hainan University, Haikou 570228, China
yanlinliu567@163.com, Jingbingli2008@hotmail.com, jingliuhnu2016@hotmail.com, cjr22@163.com, jialing_hainu@163.com, lingren_good@163.com

[2] State Key Laboratory of Marine Resource Utilization in the South China Sea, Hainan University, Haikou 570228, China

[3] Hainan College of Software Technology, Qionghai 57400, Hainan, China
baixiaobols@163.com

Abstract. Medical images are a special kind of image, since the information contained within must be kept strictly confidential. With a view to protecting personal information, a plethora of research has been carried out in the field of digital watermarking. However, in previous studies, watermarkings were encrypted and the processing of original medical images was unencrypted. Original medical images also contain a large amount of patient information that needs to be kept confidential; therefore, the present paper proposes a robust watermarking algorithm for medical images based on DWT-DCT and a tent map in an encrypted domain. Discrete Cosine Transform (DCT) is a form of Fourier transform, and only uses the actual numbers. Discrete Wavelet Transform (DWT) is a type of signal processing tool that is used to discretize the scale and displacement of basic wavele. In the present paper, DWT and DCT are combined to increase robustness. Firstly, the original medical image and the watermarking were encrypted by chaotic tent mapping. The feature vector of the encrypted medical image was extracted by DWT-DCT, and the watermarking was subsequently embedded and extracted. Finally, the normalized correlation coefficient (NC value) between the embedded and extracted watermarking was calculated to observe its robustness. The experimental results show that this algorithm is robust against conventional and geometric attacks.

Keywords: Encrypted domain · DWT-DCT · Tent map · Robustness

1 Introduction

In recent years, the rapid development of computer science and multimedia communication technology has promoted the development of the digital healthcare system. Digital medical imaging is an important modern tool formed by the integration of

X. Sun et al. (Eds.): ICAIS 2019, LNCS 11633, pp. 584–596, 2019.
https://doi.org/10.1007/978-3-030-24265-7_50

multiple technologies, and is widely used in the diagnosis, treatment, and prognosis prediction of diseases [1]. Medical information is a special type of information that must be strictly protected [4]; however, when such information is stored on and transmitted via the internet, it is subject to malicious attack and poor security [5]. Therefore, it is of paramount importance to improve the security of medical information [3].

Digital watermarking technology is an effective means of multimedia copyright protection. Since its inception, it has received great attention from researchers [6, 7]; however, in previous studies, watermarkings were embedded in the plain text domain. Specifically, the patient ID number, name, gender, and other personal information were embedded into unencrypted medical images as watermarkings to ensure the security of personal privacy information [1], but the fact that the medical images themselves contain patient information that is easily leaked was overlooked. Therefore, the original medical images need to be encrypted [11] and the watermarking embedded in it, which is a feasible solution [8, 9]. With respect to image encryption algorithms, our predecessors have made a lot of headway [10, 19]. At present, image encryption technology is mainly divided into: traditional image encryption technology, image encryption based on chaos [12] and image encryption technology based on frequency domain [13]. Bianchi et al., discussed the application of discrete Fourier transform (DFT) and fast Fourier transform (FFT) in the encrypted domain [14], and Zheng et al. [17] applied transformation in the encryption domain and proposed an algorithm to reduce data expansion following encryption [18].

In the present paper, chaotic tent mapping [3, 19, 20] was used to encrypt the original medical image and the watermarking. The feature vector of the encrypted medical image was extracted by DWT-DCT, and the watermarking was subsequently embedded and extracted. We proved that this algorithm is robust against conventional and geometric attacks.

2 Basic Theories

2.1 Discrete Cosine Transform

DCT [2, 15] is a form of Fourier Transform that is similar to Discrete Fourier Transform, but only uses the actual numbers. The formula for two-dimensional DCT is as follows:

$$F(u,v) = c(u)\,c(v)\sum_{x=0}^{M-1}\sum_{y=0}^{N-1}\cos\frac{\pi(2x+1)u}{2M}\cos\frac{\pi(2y+1)v}{2N} \tag{1}$$

$$u = 0, 1, \ldots, M-1;\ v = 0, 1, \ldots, N-1$$

$$c(u) = \begin{cases}\sqrt{\frac{1}{M}}, u = 0\\ \sqrt{\frac{2}{M}}, u \neq 0\end{cases} \qquad c(v) = \begin{cases}\sqrt{\frac{1}{N}}, v = 0\\ \sqrt{\frac{2}{N}}, v \neq 0\end{cases}$$

In the formula:

Where, x and y are spatial domain sampling values, and u and v are sampling values in the frequency domain. In digital image processing, digital images are typically represented by the square pixel matrix, that is, M = N.

2.2 Discrete Wavelet Transform

Discrete Wavelet Transform (DWT) [16] is a type of signal processing tool that is used to discretize the scale and displacement of basic wavelet; a discrete interval sampling of wavelet. It has the advantages of reflecting both spatial and frequency information of the image. The following formulas are used:

Mallat decomposition formula:

$$\begin{aligned} c_{j+1,k} &= \sum_{n \in Z} c_{j,n}\, \bar{h}_{n-2k},\ k \in Z \\ d_{j+1,k} &= \sum_{n \in Z} c_{j,n}\, \bar{g}_{n-2k},\ k \in Z \end{aligned} \tag{2}$$

Mallat reconstruction formula:

$$c_{j+k} = \sum_{n \in Z} c_{j+1,n}\, h_{k-2n} + \sum_{n \in Z} d_{j+1,n}\, g_{k-2n},\ k \in Z \tag{3}$$

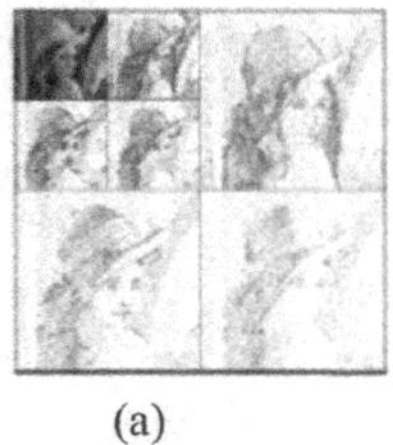

(a)

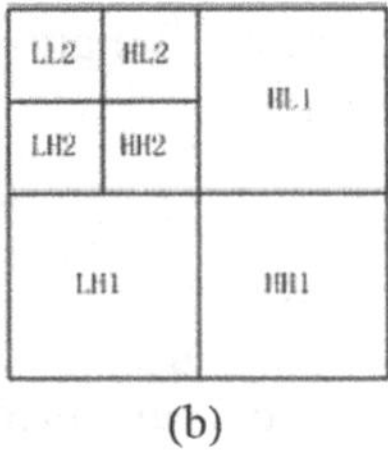

(b)

Fig. 1. Discrete wavelet transform: (a) schematic diagram of the two-layer wavelet decomposition of Lena; (b) corresponding wavelet decomposition sub-band model.

Figure 1(a) is a schematic diagram of the two-layer wavelet decomposition of Lena, and Fig. 1(b) is the corresponding wavelet decomposition sub-band model. In the present study, we use the db2 wavelet.

2.3 Chaotic Tent Mapping

A chaotic tent map is a linear mapping formula in mathematics, with its functional image being similar to a tent. Logistic mapping is one of the most famous chaotic mapping formulas, which is a simple dynamic nonlinear regression with chaotic behavior. Even if the initial value changes slightly, it will still lead to a significant difference in the output sequence, and it has a statistical characteristic similar to white noise. Due to these characteristics, a chaotic logistic sequence is an ideal key sequence, and previous studies [19] have pointed out that tent mapping has a faster iteration speed and better traversal uniformity than logistic mapping; therefore, chaotic tent mapping was adopted in the present paper. When α is equal to 1/2 for tent mapping and μ is equal to 4 topological conjugates. Tent mapping is a segmented function with higher complexity than logistics mapping. And the formula is:

$$x_{n+1} = \begin{cases} \frac{x_n}{\alpha}, 0 \leq x_n < \alpha \\ \frac{1-x_n}{1-\alpha}, \alpha \leq x_n \leq 1 \end{cases} \tag{4}$$

When α∈(0, 1), the mapping is in a state of chaos. It has a uniform distribution function on [0,1], and the chaotic sequence generated by this mapping has good statistical characteristics. When the initial value of ×0 is 0.01, an iterative operation is performed in the computer. Figure 2 is a schematic diagram of the tent map.

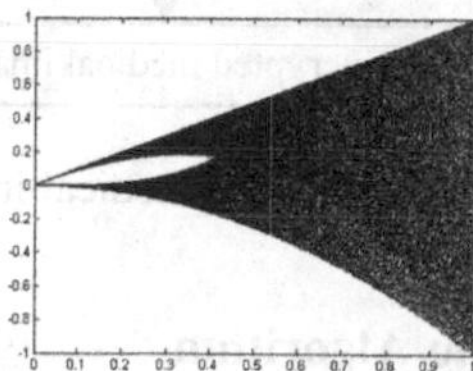

Fig. 2. Schematic diagram of the tent map.

3 The Proposed Method

3.1 Encryption of Original Medical Images

Due to the fact that medical images contain personal information about patients, encryption is a necessity. Figure 3 shows the medical image encryption process. The following steps are:

Step 1: Acquire cA, cH, cV, and cD, which are the wavelet coefficients of the sub-band, by transforming the original medical images I(i,j). Subsequently acquire the DCT coefficients D(i,j) using DCT to each wavelet sub-band coefficient.

Step 2: Use the tent map to achieve sequence X(j); and following operation by the symbol function sgn(x) and reshape(X(i,j)), obtain binary encryption matrix C(i,j).

Step 3: Use the dot multiplication algorithm to process D(i,j) and C(i,j), to acquire the encrypted coefficient matrix $\text{ED}'(\text{i},\text{j})$.

Step 4: Use inverse DCT for $\text{ED}'(\text{i},\text{j})$ to obtain the reconstructed encryption sub-band wavelet coefficient matrix $\text{ED}(\text{i},\text{j})$.

Step 5: Use inverse DWT for the matrix $\text{ED}(\text{i},\text{j})$ to obtain the encrypted medical image $\text{E}(\text{i},\text{j})$.

$$ED'(i,j) = D(i,j) \bullet C(i,j) \tag{5}$$

$$ED(i,j) = IDCT2(ED'(i,j)) \tag{6}$$

$$E(i,j) = IDWT2(ED(i,j)) \tag{7}$$

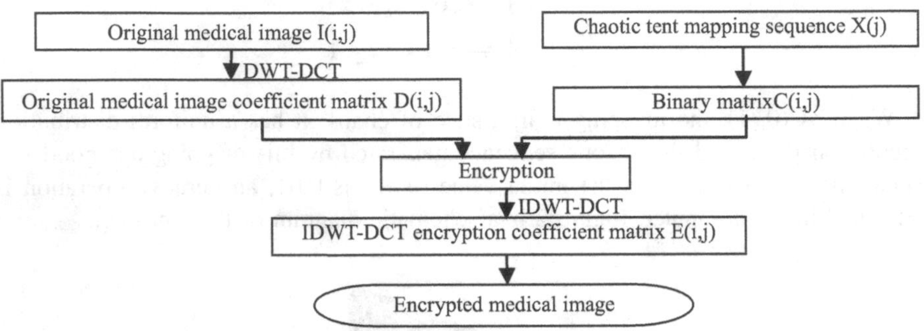

Fig. 3. The process of original medical image encryption.

3.2 Watermarking Embedding Algorithm

In the paper, we used zero-watermarking technology to complete watermarking embedding, since medical images have high requirements for information integrity.

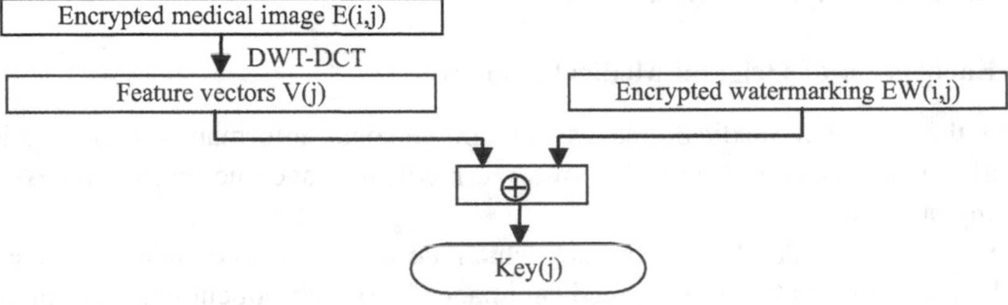

Fig. 4. Watermarking embedding algorithm.

As shown in Fig. 4, we extracted the feature vectors V(j) from the encrypted medical image E(i,j) by using DWT-DCT, and we applied the algorithm to process V(j) and EW(j) to acquire the key sequence Key(j).

$$Key(j) = V(j) \oplus EW(j) \tag{8}$$

3.3 Watermarking Extraction Algorithm

As shown in Fig. 5, it had to be extracted, after the watermarking was embedded.

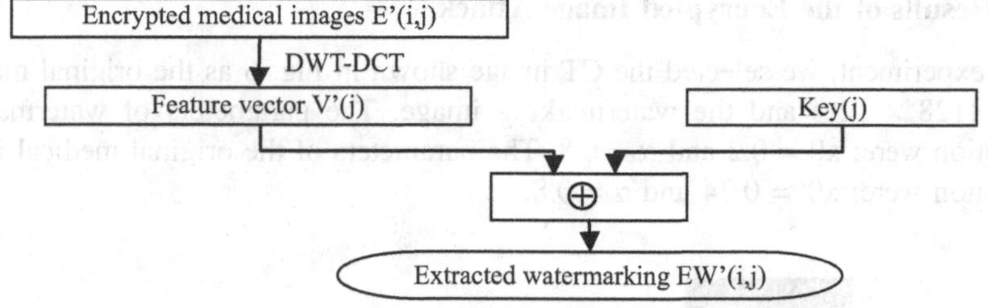

Fig. 5. Watermarking extraction algorithm.

Firstly, we extracted the feature vector $V'(j)$ from the encrypted medical image $E'(i,j)$ by using DWT-DCT, then we applied the hash algorithm to process $V'(j)$ and $Key(j)$, to acquire the encryption watermarking sequence $EW'(j)$. Finally, we decrypted the watermarking.

$$EW'(j) = V'(j) \oplus Key(j) \tag{9}$$

4 Experimental Results and Performance Analysis

4.1 Feature Vector Extraction from Encrypted Medical Images

We conducted different attack experiments on the encrypted image. We took "1" when the value was greater than or equal to zero, and "0" when the value was less than zero, so as to construct the sequence of coefficient signs. From Table 1 it can be seen that the changes in the coefficient sign were small, which were greater than 0.5. Therefore, we could use the coefficient signs as the feature vector of the encrypted medical images.

Table 1. Change in the DWT-DCT coefficients under different attacks of encrypted image

Image processing	Sequence of coefficient signs	NC
Encrypted original image	10000101110110100001001011110101	1.0000
Gaussian noise (10%)	10000101100100000101001011110001	0.9344
JPEG compression (10%)	10000101110110000001001011010101	0.9364
Median filter [7 × 7] (10 times)	10000101100100000001001001010001	0.8667
Scaling (×0.5)	11000101100110100010101101010000	0.8667
Translation (10%, down)	10000101100110000001001111110101	0.9344
Cropping (5%, Y direction)	10000101100110000001001111110101	0.9344
Rotation (clockwise, 3°)	11000101010100000000000001010000	0.6736

*DWT-DCT transformation factor unit: 1.0E + 004

4.2 Results of the Encrypted Image Attack

In the experiment, we selected the CT image shown in Fig. 6 as the original medical image (128 × 128) and the watermarking image. The parameters of watermarking encryption were: x0 = 0.2 and α = 0.8. The parameters of the original medical image encryption were: x0′ = 0.34 and α = 0.8.

Fig. 6. Orginal image: (a) Original medical image. (b) Original watermarking.

Conventional Attacks. Table 2 shows the PSNR and the NC value under different conventional attacks. It can be seen that when different conventional attacks were conducted, the NC values were high; and thus, the algorithm was robust against common attacks.

Table 2. PSNR and NC values under different conventional attacks

Conventional attack	Gaussian noise (%)				JPEG compression (%)				Median filter		
	5	10	20	25	3	5	10	20	3 × 3	5 × 5	7 × 7
PSNR (dB)	13.39	11.09	9.41	8.98	25.27	27.36	30.31	33.04	33.18	28.64	26.78
NC	0.89	0.81	0.79	0.73	0.89	1.00	0.88	0.89	1.00	1.00	0.79

Geometric Attacks

Rotational and Translational Attacks. We attacked the encrypted medical image by rotating it clockwise by 3°. As shown in Fig. 7(a), it can be clearly seen that the encrypted image rotated. Figure 7(b) shows the extracted watermarking, NC = 0.58. When the image was moved down by 15%, as shown in Fig. 8(a), the encrypted image moved down significantly. As shown in Fig. 8(b), the NC value of the extracted watermarking was 0.89.

Fig. 7. Image under rotation: (a) Encrypted image. (b) Extracted watermarking.

(a) (b)

Fig. 8. Image under translation: (a) Encrypted image. (b) Extracted watermarking.

Table 3 shows the PSNR and the NC values under different rotational and translational attacks. It can be seen that when the rotational angle was less than 5° and the translational ratio was 30%, the NC value was lower, but was still greater than 0.5. Moreover, the signal-to-noise ratio was small, as shown in Table 4, indicating that the noise of the original image was large following the encryption and rotational/translational attacks. Although the noise was large, complete watermarking could be extracted, and the NC value was relatively large. It can be seen that this algorithm is robust against rotational and translational attacks.

Table 3. PSNR and NC values under rotational and translational attacks

Geometric attack	Rotational attack (°)				Translational attack (%)			
	1	3	5	8	10	15	25	35
PSNR (dB)	24.02	19.83	18.36	17.20	19.22	17.87	16.31	15.31
NC	0.58	0.58	0.58	0.53	0.89	0.89	0.81	0.68

Scaling and Cropping Attacks. The encrypted image embedded in the watermarking was scaled with a factor of 0.2. Figure 9(b) shows the image of the extracted watermarking, with an NC value of 0.79. Figure 10(a) shows the encrypted image when the cut ratio was 8%. Figure 10(b) shows that the NC value was 0.81.

(a) (b)

Fig. 9. Image under scaling (0.2 times): (a) Encrypted image. (b) Extracted watermarking.

(a) (b)

Fig. 10. Image under cropping: (a) Encrypted image. (b) Extracted watermarking.

Table 4 shows the NC values under different scaling and cropping attacks. It can be clearly seen that the NC values are high; thus, this algorithm is robust against scaling and cropping attacks.

Table 4. PSNR and NC values under scaling and cropping attacks

Geometric attack	Scaling					Cropping ratio (%) (from Y direction)				
	0.2	0.5	0.8	2.0	6.0	2	4	6	8	10
NC	0.79	1.00	1.00	0.79	0.79	1.00	0.89	0.89	0.81	0.73

4.3 Comparison with Other Methods

Comparison of the Robustness of Encrypted Algorithms (DCT and DWT-DCT). In this experiment, we compared the robustness of the encryption algorithms DCT and DWT-DCT. Figure 11 shows the contrast curves of Gaussian noise attack; the performance curves for the two algorithms against Gaussian noise attack in the range of 1–20% are shown. It was found that the anti-Gaussian noise attack performance of the two algorithms was strong, and the difference between the two was relatively small.

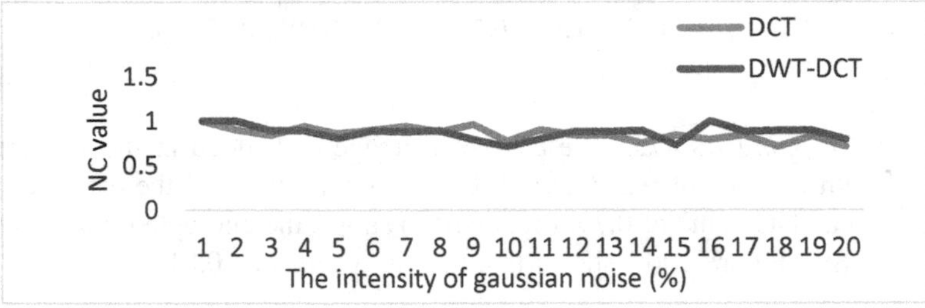

Fig. 11. Gaussian noise attack contrast curve.

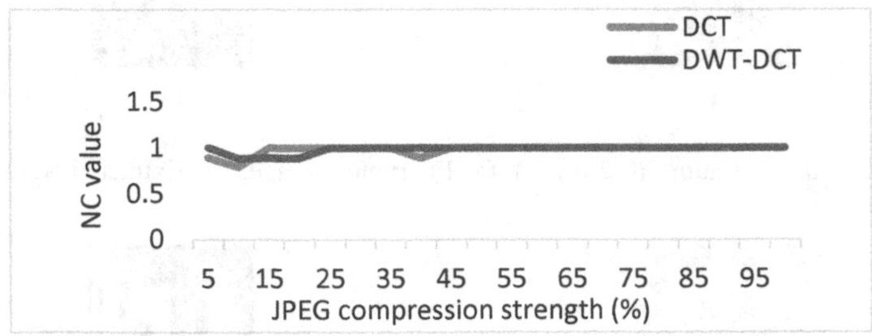

Fig. 12. JPEG compression attack contrast curve.

Figure 12 shows the contrast curves of JPEG compression attack; the performance curves of the two algorithms against JPEG compression attack in the range of 5–100% are shown. It was found that when the Q value was 25 and above, the NC value was 1. The NC values of DCT from 15 to 25 were all 1, and the NC values of DWT-DCT were lower than 1, but above 0.88, which was very large. And from 5 to 15, the NC values of DWT-DCT were higher than DCT. The difference between the two was relatively small.

Figure 13 shows the contrast curves of median filter attack; the performance curves of the two algorithms against median filtering attacks in the range of 5–40 are shown. It was found that the NC values of DCT were larger than those of DWT-DCT from 5 to 25. And from 25 to 40, the NC values of DCT and DWT-DCT were equal. The difference between the two was relatively small.

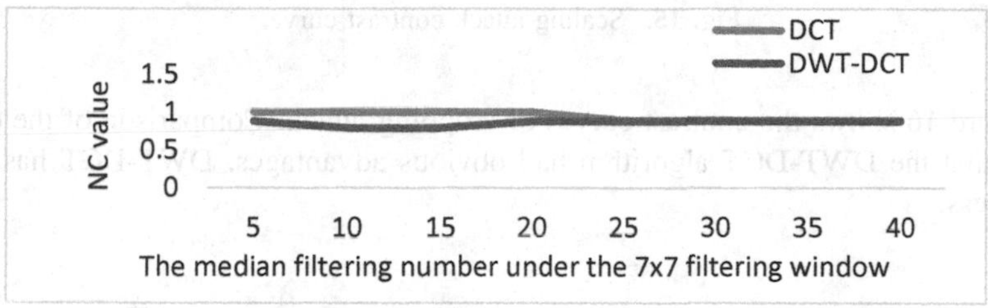

Fig. 13. Median filter attack contrast curve.

Figure 14 shows the contrast curves of translation attack; the performance curves of the two algorithms against translation attacks in the range of 5–35% vertical downward movement are shown. Comparison of the curves shows that the two algorithms had obvious differences in anti-translational attack performance; DWT-DCT had better performance than DCT.

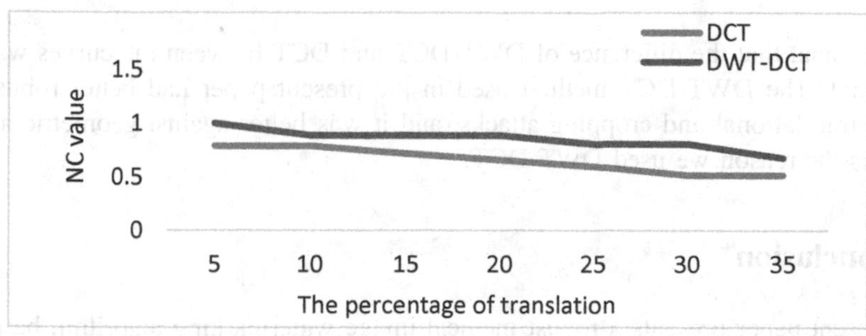

Fig. 14. Translational attack contrast curve.

Figure 15 shows the contrast curves of scaling attack. It was found that although DWT-DCT had a lower anti-scaling attack performance than DCT, its NC value was not low.

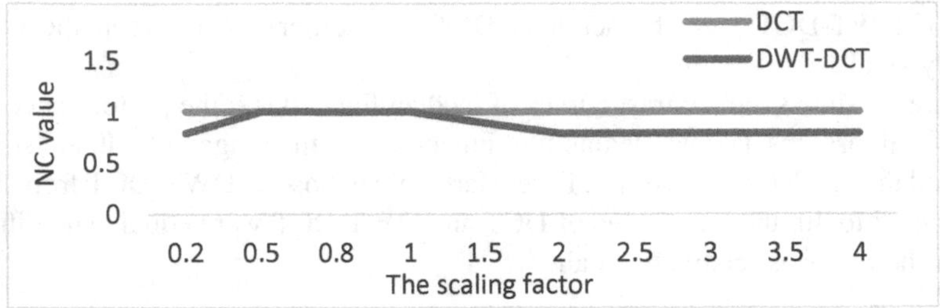

Fig. 15. Scaling attack contrast curve.

Figure 16 shows the contrast curves of cropping attack. Comparison of the curves shows that the DWT-DCT algorithm had obvious advantages. DWT-DCT has better robustness.

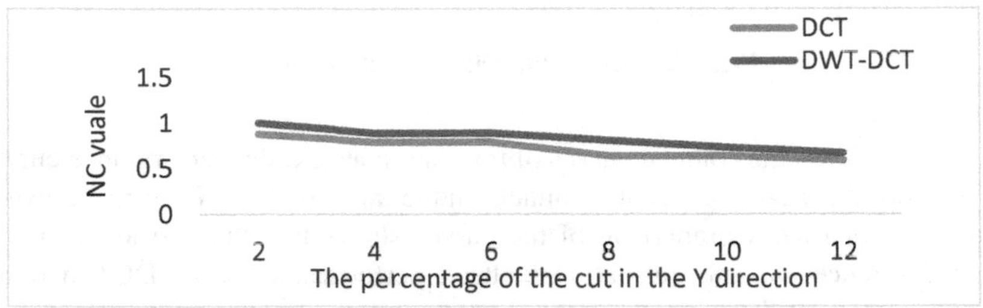

Fig. 16. Cropping attack contrast curve.

We found that the difference of DWT-DCT and DCT between the curves was not significant. The DWT-DCT method used in the present paper had better robustness against translational and cropping attacks, and it was better against geometric attack, which is the reason we used DWT-DCT.

5 Conclusion

The present paper presents a robust medical image watermarking algorithm based on DWT-DCT and tent mapping in the encrypted domain. Firstly, we used tent mapping to encrypt the original medical image in order to carry out different attacks to observe its robustness. The original watermarking was encrypted in the same manner. We embedded the watermarking in the encrypted image and conducted different attacks, using DWT-DCT to extract its feature vectors and subsequently the watermarking.The present paper encrypted the original medical images and watermarking to improve the security of patient information. At the same time, due to the use of zero-watermarking technology, the algorithm has strong robustness against both conventional and geometric attacks.

Acknowledgements. This work is supported by the Key Research Project of Hainan Province [ZDYF2018129], and by the National Natural Science Foundation of China [61762033] and the Natural Science Foundation of Hainan [20166227,617048, 2018CXTD333] and the Key Innovation and Entrepreneurship Project of Hainan University [Hdcxcyxm201711].

References

1. Zhang, J.H.: Research on digital watermarking algorithm for medical image. Nanjing University of Posts and Telecommunications (2016)
2. Wu, X.Q., Li, J.B., Tu, R., Cheng, J.R., Bhatti, U.A., Ma, J.: Contourlet-DCT based multiple robust watermarkings for medical images. Multimed. Tools Appl. **78**, 8463–8480 (2018). https://doi.org/10.1007/s11042-018-6877-5
3. Tang, Z.J., Ling, M., Yao, H., Qian, Z.: Robust image hashing via random gabor filtering and DWT. CMC Comput. Mater. Continua **55**(2), 331–344 (2018)
4. Kaur, S., Farooq, O., Singhal, R.: Digital watermarking of ECG data for secure wireless communication. In: Proceedings of the 2010 IEEE International Conference on Recent Trends in Information, Telecommunication and Computing, pp. 140–144 (2010)
5. Navas, K.A., Sasikumar, M.: Survey of medical image watermarking algorithms. In: Proceedings of the 4th Science of Electronic Technologies of Information and Telecommunications International Conference, pp. 5–29 (2007)
6. Nematollahi, M.A., Vorakulpipat, C., Rosales, H.G.: Digital Watermarking. STSP, vol. 11. Springer, Singapore (2017). https://doi.org/10.1007/978-981-10-2095-7
7. Giri, K.J., Bashir, R.: Digital watermarking: a potential solution for multimedia authentication. In: Dey, N., Santhi, V. (eds.) Intelligent Techniques in Signal Processing for Multimedia Security. SCI, vol. 660, pp. 93–112. Springer, Cham (2017). https://doi.org/10.1007/978-3-319-44790-2_5
8. Shortell, T., Shokoufandeh, A.: Secure signal processing using fully homomorphic encryption. In: Battiato, S., Blanc-Talon, J., Gallo, G., Philips, W., Popescu, D., Scheunders, P. (eds.) ACIVS 2015. LNCS, vol. 9386, pp. 93–104. Springer, Cham (2015). https://doi.org/10.1007/978-3-319-25903-1_9
9. Guo, J., Zheng, P., Huang, J.: Secure watermarking scheme against watermarking attacks in the encrypted domain. J. Vis. Commun. Image Represent. **30**, 125–135 (2015)
10. Saikia, M., Baruah, B.: Chaotic map-based image encryption in spatial domain: a brief survey. In: Mandal, J., Satapathy, S., Sanyal, M., Bhateja, V. (eds.) Proceedings of the First International Conference on Intelligent Computing and Communication. LNCS, vol. 458, pp. 569–579. Springer, Singapore (2017). https://doi.org/10.1007/978-981-10-2035-3_58
11. Huang, X., Ye, G.: An image encryption algorithm based on irregular wave representation. Multimed. Tools Appl. **77**, 2611–2628 (2017)
12. Wang, H.: Overview of image encryption technology based on chaos. Shanghai University, pp. 80–82 (2016)
13. Yu, H.Y.: Arnold scrambling and ridgelet transform based digital watermarking algorithm. Xi'an University of Posts and Telecommunications, pp. 175–177 (2015)

14. Bianchi, T., Piva, A., Barni, M.: On the implementation of the discrete fourier transform in the encrypted domain. IEEE Trans. Inf. Forensics Secur. **4**, 86–97 (2009)
15. Bianchi, T., Piva, A., Barni, M.: Encrypted domain DCT based on homomorphic cryptosystems. EURASIP J. Inf. Secur. **2009**, 716357 (2009)
16. Zheng, P., Huang, J.: Discrete wavelet transform and data expansion reduction in homomorphic encrypted domain. IEEE Trans. Image Process. **22**, 2455–2468 (2013)
17. Zheng, P., Huang, J.: Walsh-Hadamard transform in the homomorphic encrypted domain and its application in image watermarking. In: Kirchner, M., Ghosal, D. (eds.) IH 2012. LNCS, vol. 7692, pp. 240–254. Springer, Heidelberg (2013). https://doi.org/10.1007/978-3-642-36373-3_16
18. Deng, S.J., Xiao, D., Tu, F.H.: Design and implementation of logistic mapping chaotic encryption algorithm. J. Chongqing Univ. **27**, 61–63 (2004)
19. Fan, J.L., Zhang, X.F.: Piecewise logistic chaotic mapping and its performance analysis. Electron. J. **37**, 720–725 (2009)
20. Zhu, K., Yang, D.G., Chen, S.G.: A chaotic encryption method based on oblique tent mapping. J. Chongqing Normal Univ. **26**, 99–102 (2009)

An Analysis of a Three-Factor Authentication Scheme and Its Improved Fix

Songsong Zhang, Xiang Li, and Yong Xie(✉)

Department of Computer Technology and Application,
Qinghai University, Xining 810016, China
mark.y.xie@qq.com

Abstract. With the development of Internet technology, a single authentication method for username and passwords can't satisfy the basic requirements of system security. A multi-server authentication scheme is a useful authentication mechanism in which a remote user can access the services of multiple servers after registering with the registration center (RC). Biometric information is difficult to simulate, therefore biometrics is used for multi-factor authentication. Recently Reedy *et al.'s* proposed a three-factor authentication scheme. They claimed their schemes can resist all types of attacks. But unfortunately, after analyzing the scheme, we demonstrate their scheme cannot defend against impersonation attack and offline guessing attack. At last, we propose improved fix to overcome its deficiency.

Keywords: Multi-factor authentication · Password authentication scheme · Impersonation attack · Offline guessing attack

1 Introduction

After the emergence of Internet technology, the network-based information industry has developed rapidly and developed into multi-server ubiquitous network that starting as single point-to-point wired network. The network-based severs in our daily life, production and even military field show a broad application prospect [2]. Data has been the main part of people's production and life. Now, the mobile terminal is pushing the application of network to another climax. However, more and more incidents of information leakage and virus spreading have also reached another climax [3]. It is for the reason that data security becomes indispensable. It's why we need cryptography and effective encryption architecture to protect our data security.

When attacking a target, an attacker often interprets the user's password as the beginning of the attack. As long as an attacker can guess or determine the user's password, he can gain access to the machine or network and access any resources that the user can access. This is extremely dangerous if the user has domain administrator or root user privileges [12].

Password attack is the hacker's favorite method of intruding into the network. Hackers obtain the passwords of system administrators or other special users, obtain the management rights of the system, steal system information, files on disk and even destroy the system.

X. Sun et al. (Eds.): ICAIS 2019, LNCS 11633, pp. 597–605, 2019.
https://doi.org/10.1007/978-3-030-24265-7_51

Authentication is a process of providing access authorization verification for the person who want to access or a process of giving user the identification [13]. That is applied to mutual authentication between server and user to assure each other exclusively. Apart from traditional username - password authentication method, by means of biometric authentication to establish a key also began to blossom. This process of participating in certification through biometrics is called as mutually authenticated key agreement [1].

Multi-server authentication schemes ca be divided into two main parts: password-based multi-server authentication and smartcard-based multi-server authentication schemes [19]. We can store a large secret parameters for in smartcard-based authentication [20, 21]. Smartcard-based multi-server authentication schemes prevent an adversary from successfully implementing the password-guessing attack. However, it is very inconvenient for users to carry smart cards and smart cards must participate in every process in login authentication [8]. On the contrary, password-based multi-server authentication schemes are easy to use and convenient for practical applications because they do not require a smartcard and card reader [22, 23]. However, the emergence of biometric authentication has made up for the shortcomings of the above two authentication methods and so the biometric authentication began to flourish.

Since Lamport [15] first proposed a password-based authentication in 1981, a series of single-server password-based authentication schemes are proposed. But these schemes are greatly increased burden on users because of one-on-one authentication method [15]. In 2001, Tsaur [16] proposed the smartcard-based password authentication which initiated remote user identity authentication for multi-server environment. Yoon *et al.* [5] demonstrated an anonymous authenticated key agreement scheme for multi-server environment by using elliptic curve cryptography [5]. Soon afterwards, he and Kim [17] pointed out that Yoon *et al.*'s scheme cannot resist masquerade attack, inside attack, stolen smartcards attack and offline password guessing attack and then he proposed the improved scheme. Afterwards, Chuang and Chen [18] proposed scheme that recommended using hash to meet practical application. But Mishra *et al.* [4] proved several weaknesses.

In 2015, Jiang et al. [23] and Odelu et al. [24] proposed biometric key agreement protocol for multi-Server applications. But in the three schemes, RC participates in the authentication stage, the registry load is too high, which is easy to cause a node failure, which not applicable to the actual situation [27, 28]. In addition, they put forward in the password update phase which has security problems and is vulnerable to masquerade attack, inside attack. There are clock synchronization problems in the protocol. As a result, they have put forward improvement plans. In 2016, Wan et al. [25] pointed out Chuang et al. 's [18] schemes can't resist the masquerade attack and proposed a improvement plans. At the same time, Amin et al. [26] also pointed out that the previous schemes have various shortcomings and gave an improved authentication protocol for remote users in multi-server environment [29].

Recently, to resistant to impersonation attack, Reedy *et al.* [1] proposed a design of mutually authenticated key agreement scheme resistant for multi-server environment. They claimed their scheme withstand all types of known attacks. Unfortunately, we find that their scheme cannot resist offline password guessing attack, user impersonation attack and lacks user anonymity protection. We present an improved fix to overcome these deficiencies at last.

We are organized this paper as follows: (i) Firstly, our preparations introduce the attack model and elliptic curve knowledge. (ii) Next, we review Reedy *et al.*'s scheme and point out the drawbacks of the scheme Reedy *et al.*'s. That is, cryptographic analysis. (iii) We present an improved fix to overcome these deficiencies at last.

2 Preliminaries

2.1 Discrete Logarithm Problem of Elliptic Curve

The security of the entire scheme is guaranteed based on the discrete logarithm of the elliptic curve. The discrete logarithm problem is also the basis of the Reedy's scheme. We need briefly talk about the elliptic curve involved in the scheme.

Addition definition of elliptic curve: If we delimit an elliptic curve: $E_p : y^2 = x^3 + ax + b$ and $4a^3 + 27b \neq 0$. Assuming P and Q are the point on the elliptic curve. We define $P + Q = R$ where R satisfies the point R is the negative point of the only intersection where the line passing through the two points P and Q intersects the elliptic curve. Additionally, $P = Q$, the tangent to the point P is crossed to the negative point where the elliptic curve is R, $R = 2P$. However $3P = P + P + P = 2P + P$, we can compute the by this way. Consequently, when a point P is known, the "the number N operate the point $NP(\mathrm{N} \in \mathrm{Z})$" is not difficult, because of the nature of the addition, the operation can be faster [10]. But in turn, "the problem of knowing the point $NP(\mathrm{N} \in \mathrm{Z})$ for N" is very difficult, because only each N can be traversed. This is thc "discrete logarithm problem on elliptic curves" used in elliptic curve cryptography [30].

- Which is the following parameters are known:
  - an elliptic curve: $E_p : y^2 = x^3 + ax + b$
  - a point P on the elliptic curve (base point)
  - $NP(\mathrm{N} \in \mathrm{Z})$ on the elliptic curve $E_p : y^2 = x^3 + ax + b$

  We need solve:
- N

  Because of the difficulty, the security of the elliptic curve cipher is guaranteed.

2.2 Security Model

In recent years, the adversaries model of the remote password authentication scheme has always used the classic Dolev-Yao's model [6], that is the adversaries can arbitrarily monitor, capture, insert and delete the information on the public channel [7]. In recent years, with the development of Internet technology, the ability of adversaries are increased. Adversaries can analyze the message on the smartcards and enhance ability to attack. This paper introduce Wang et al. [7] and Huang's [9] adversaries model.

In this mode, there are enumerated six kinds adversaries model and increments them according to their capabilities [11]. But for Three-factor Mutually Authenticated

Key Agreement schemes, an adversary $\mathcal{A}$ have capabilities which could obtain two of the authentication factors but have no affects to another. The details are shown as following.

(1) $\mathcal{A}$ captures the smartcards and the password, but A can't threaten the biological factors of user.
(2) $\mathcal{A}$ have abilities to obtain password and biological factors, but have inability to get smart card parameters.
(3) $\mathcal{A}$ get the smartcards and the biological factors, but the password is security.

In Huang et al.'s [9] schemes, the probability of success is rare in case 1 or 2. Because the biological factors are fuzzy and extremely difficult to recover. Security parameters of high information entropy are often stored in smart cards [14]. In summary, Scenario three poses a great threat because of the development of the low information entropy and dictionary attack technique.

3 Review of Reedy et al.'s Scheme

In this subsection, we will briefly review Reedy *et al.'s* scheme. Their scheme include six compositions: Registration Server Initialization phase, Application Server Registration phase, User Registration phase, Login phase, Mutually Authenticated Key Agreement phase, Password And Biometrics Change phase, Dynamic Addition Of Application Server phase, User Revocation/Re-Registration phase. In order to save time and space, we simply recall the central few parts.

Registration Server Initialization phase, we will not elaborate on this. This phase are ready for initialization which the registration server RS generates following parameters. RC (RC is registration server) generates an elliptic curve $E_p : y^2 = x^3 + ax + b(\bmod \mathrm{p})$, where P is a larger prime number, private key USK, ASK and finally publishes the parameters $\{E_p, \mathrm{p}, h(\cdot)\}$.

3.1 Application Server Registration Phase

(1) S_j sends SID_j to RC securely.
(2) RC computers $K_j = h(\mathrm{SID_j} \parallel \mathrm{ASK})$ and stores them in its database.
(3) RC responds to S_j the parameters and stores $\{K_j, h(\mathrm{ASK}), \mathrm{P}\}$.

3.2 User Registration Phase

A user must register with RC to become a legitimate user. $\mathrm{U_i}$ need do the according following steps to register with RC via a private channels.

(1) U_i chooses ID_i and PW_i Meanwhile, users need generate a random number $r_i \in Z_p^*$ and compute $PID_i = h(\mathrm{ID_i} \parallel \mathrm{r_i}), \mathrm{PWD_i} = h(\mathrm{PW_i} \parallel \mathrm{r_i})$ and send a request messages $\{PID_i, \mathrm{PWD_i}\}$

(2) RC verifies the whether a registered user and computes $Q_j = h(PID_i \parallel K_j)$, $R_j = Q_j \oplus PWD_i$.
Finally, RC reserves $\{SID_i, R_j\}$ in T_i table and $\{PID_i, C_i, T_R = 1\}$ in T_c table where $T_R = 1$ means U_i registered initially and is in active state. RC computes $W_j = h(PID_i \parallel USK)$ and personalizes $\{W_j, T_i, h(ASK)\}$ into the smartcards to be delivered to U_i.
(3) U_i scans his/her BIO_i at the provided sensor with card reading machine, and computes $X_j = W_j \oplus PWD_i$, $C_i = h(ID_i \parallel W_j)$, $(\sigma_i, \theta_i) = Gen(BIO_i)$, $V_i = r_i \oplus h(\sigma_i)$ U_i replaces W_j with X_j and stores $\{C_i, V_i, \theta_i\}$ on smartcards. Therefore, the smartcards finally contains $\{X_j, V_i, C_i, T_i, \theta_i, P, h(\cdot), h(ASK)\}$.

3.3 Login Phase

User can transmit the login request by inserting smartcards and enter ID_i, PW_i and BIO_i' to get login privileges.

Smartcards compute $\sigma_i' = Rep(BIO_i', \theta_i)$, $r_i = V_i \oplus h(\sigma_i')$, $PID_i = h(ID_i \parallel r_i)$, $PWD_i = h(PW_i \parallel r_i)$, $W_j = X_j \oplus PWD_i$. Finally, smartcards need verify whether the parameter $C_i \stackrel{?}{=} h(ID_i \parallel W_j)$ are correct. If the value doesn't correspond, the login request is terminated.

User choose the server S_j by assessing the list T_i and extract R_j at the same time. User compute $Q_j = R_j \oplus PWD_i$. Smartcards generate random number $N_1 \in Z_p^*$ and compute $B_{ij} = PID_i \oplus h(SID_i \parallel \alpha \parallel h(ASK))$, $D_{ij} = h(PID_i \parallel Q_i \parallel \alpha)$, $\alpha = N_1 P$. Smartcard send out the login request include $\{B_{ij}, D_{ij}, \alpha\}$ by public channel.

3.4 Mutually Authenticated Key Agreement Phase

This phase mainly introduce the process which U_i and S_j authenticate each other and establish a secure long-term channel for further communication over public channel.

(1) S_j computes $PID_i = B_{ij} \oplus h(SID_i \parallel \alpha \parallel h(ASK))$ and $Q_j = h(PID_i \parallel K_j)$ when receive the login request. Afterwards, S_j authenticates U_i only if $D_{ij} \stackrel{?}{=} h(PID_i \parallel Q_i \parallel \alpha)$ matching the condition. Otherwise, the process terminates.
(2) S_j generates a random number $N_2 \in Z_p^*$ and computes $\beta = N_2 P$, $K_{ij} = N_2\,\alpha$, $SK = h(Q_j \parallel K_{ij} \parallel PID_i)$, $E_{ij} = h(SK \parallel SID_j \parallel \beta \parallel \alpha \parallel Q_j)$. And then S_j send $\{E_{ij}, \beta\}$ to smartcards by a public channel.
(3) U_i computes $K_{ij} = N_1\,\beta$, $SK = h(Q_j \parallel K_{ij} \parallel PID_i)$ and verifies $E_{ij} \stackrel{?}{=} h(SK \parallel SID_j \parallel \beta \parallel \alpha \parallel Q_j)$. If the condition holds, U_i authenticates S_j and U_i computer $F_{ij} = h(SK \parallel SID_j \parallel \beta \parallel \alpha \parallel Q_j)$ Otherwise, the process terminates. Smartcards launches F_{ij} to S_j via a public channel.
(4) S_j verifies condition $F_{ij} \stackrel{?}{=} h(SK \parallel SID_j \parallel \beta \parallel \alpha \parallel Q_j)$ and reconfirms the authenticity of U_i. They complete each other certification and rebuild communication channel.

4 Cryptanalysis of Reedy et al.'s Proposed Scheme

After we analyzed the Reedy *et al.*'s scheme and established the basic attack model, we begin to analyze the security of the scheme. We show that the scheme is not resistant to offline password guessing attack and impersonation attack. The following is a description of the Reedy *et al.*'s scheme.

(1) We have established an adversary model in the previous section, that is, two factors are known to determine whether it can threaten the third factor. The proof of the impersonation attack is given in the scheme including user and application. In the proof a, assume $\mathcal{A}$ wants to impersonate a legitimate user, he/she can performs guessing the username and the password. Apart from this, $\mathcal{A}$ need build the message $\{\mathrm{B_{ij}}, \mathrm{D_{ij}}, \alpha\}$. And then $\mathcal{A}$ compute the parameters $\sigma_i^{'}$, $\mathrm{r_i}$ $\mathrm{PID_i}$, $\mathrm{PWD_i}$, W_j and test C_i. Reedy deems the adversaries can't correct credentials. In the proof b, Reedy consider that $\mathrm{Q_j}$ is unique for each S_j. Therefore, $\mathcal{A}$ can't have the session key. The scheme is considered security.

But in the scheme, store the long-term private key h(ASK) of the RC in every user's smartcard. If A can obtain h(ASK), he/she will initiating an impersonation attack.

Firstly, $\mathcal{A}$ can capture $\{\mathrm{B_{ij}}, \mathrm{D_{ij}}, \alpha\}$ and $PID_i = B_{ij} \oplus h(\mathrm{SID_i} \parallel \alpha \parallel \mathrm{h(ASK)})$. Then he/she computes $Q_j = R_j \oplus PWD_k$ which the R_j is extracted from T_k and compute $\alpha^* = N_1^* P$, $B_{ij}^* = PID_i \oplus h(\mathrm{SID_j} \parallel \alpha^* \parallel \mathrm{h(ASK)})$, $\mathrm{D}_{ij}^* = h(\mathrm{PID_i} \parallel \mathrm{Q_j} \parallel \alpha^*)$ to S_j, D_{ij}^* is successful verification.

(2) Guessing attack means that as long as the adversaries can guess or determine the user's password, he can gain access to the machine or network and access any resources that the user can access. The key point is the vulnerability of the user's choice of password. If $\mathcal{A}$ can obtain the message on the smartcards like $\{X_j, \mathrm{V_i}, C_i, \mathrm{T_i}, \theta_i, P, h(\cdot), h(\mathrm{ASK})\}$, then he/she get the biological factors $\mathrm{BIO_{i'}}$ of user. $\mathcal{A}$ can initiate a password guessing attack:
Firstly, $\mathcal{A}$ can compute $\sigma_{i'} = \mathrm{Re}p(\mathrm{BIO_{i'}}, \theta_i)$, $\mathrm{r_i} = \mathrm{V_i} \oplus \mathrm{h}(\sigma_{i'})$. And then $\mathcal{A}$ can guessing the ID, PW. Follow the steps to continue calculating the formula $PWD^* = h(\mathrm{PW} \parallel \mathrm{r_i})$, $\mathrm{W}_j^* = X_j \oplus PWD^*$. We can verify the $\mathrm{C}_i^* = h(\mathrm{ID}$ $rallel \mathrm{W}_j^*) \stackrel{?}{=} C_i$.

Since the actual identity and password space is very limited space ($|D_{id}| \leq |D_{pw}| \leq 10^6$), attacks can be completed within a limited time. Through the establishment of the attack model and the analysis of the above scheme, we show that C_i is the key for adversaries. The C_i parameter is the correctness parameter for the login verification in the smartcard. If adversaries gets the password, they can choose a random number and calculate the $\mathrm{B_{ij}}, \mathrm{D_{ij}}$ for login the S_j. The scheme does not involve the complexity of the time space for offline guessing attack. So the solution is not safe for offline guessing attack.

The user is completely unaware of the circumstances which adversaries get messages from the channel. $\mathcal{A}$ only need derive Q_j with $\mathrm{h(ASK)}$. It is not difficult to find that the above attack is caused by the same security parameters from RC and S_j stored in the user's smartcards. It can be seen that the analysis of this agreement proves to be incomplete.

The user is completely unaware of the circumstances which adversary gets messages from the channel. $\mathcal{A}$ only need derive Q_j with h(ASK). It is not difficult to find that the above attack is caused by the same security parameters from RC and S_j stored in the user's smartcards. It can be seen that the analysis of this agreement proved to be incomplete.

5 Possible Fix

We put forward a solution that may figure out this problem in the light of the problems above. The critical points that the basis of the analysis above is whether the third factor of the first two factors is known to be reliability. Three factors synthesize into parameter to ensure the security of verification. We mainly modify the registration phase and the login phase. The login phase can be executed as following.

U_i chooses ID_i and PW_i. Meanwhile, users need generate random number $r_i \in Z_p^*$ and compute $PID_i = h(\mathrm{ID_i} \parallel \mathrm{r_i}), \mathrm{PWD_i} = h(\mathrm{PW_i} \parallel \mathrm{r_i})$ and send a request messages $\{PID_i, \mathrm{PWD_i}\}$

RC verifies the whether a registered user and computes $\mathrm{Q_j} = h(\mathrm{PID_i} \parallel \mathrm{K_j})$, $\mathrm{R_j} = \mathrm{Q_j} \oplus \mathrm{PWD_i}$.

Finally, RC compute a random number IDR_i reserves $\{\mathrm{SID_i}, \mathrm{R_j}, IDR_\mathrm{i}\}$ in $\mathrm{T_i}$ table and $\{PID_i, \mathrm{C_i}, \mathrm{T_R}{=}\ 1\}$ in T_c table where $\mathrm{T_R} = 1$ means U_i registered initially and is in active state. RC computes $W_j = h(\mathrm{PID_i} \parallel \mathrm{USK})$ and personalizes $\{W_j, \mathrm{T_i}, \mathrm{h(ASK)} \oplus IDR_\mathrm{i}\}$ into the smartcards to be delivered to U_i.

U_i scans his/her BIO_i at the provided sensor with card reading machine, and computes, $(\sigma_\mathrm{i}, \theta_\mathrm{i}) = \mathrm{Gen(BIO_i)}$, $\mathrm{V_i} = \mathrm{r_i} \oplus \mathrm{h}(\sigma_\mathrm{i})$, $C_i = \mathrm{h}(\mathrm{PID_i} \parallel PWD_i \parallel \sigma_i \parallel \theta_i)$, U_i stores $\{C_i, \mathrm{V_i}, \theta_\mathrm{i}\}$ on smartcards. Therefore, the smartcards finally contains $\{W_j, \mathrm{V_i}, C_i, \mathrm{T_i}, \theta_\mathrm{i}, P, h(\cdot), h(\mathrm{ASK})\}$.

Next, login phase is executing as following.

Smartcards compute $\sigma_i' = \mathrm{Re}p(\mathrm{BIO}_i', \theta_i), \mathrm{r_i} = \mathrm{V_i} \oplus \mathrm{h}(\sigma_i'), \mathrm{PID_i} = \mathrm{h}(\mathrm{ID_i} \parallel \mathrm{r_i})$, $\mathrm{PWD_i} = h(\mathrm{PW_i} \parallel \mathrm{r_i})$. In particularity, we need proving the parameters $C_i \stackrel{?}{=} \mathrm{h}(\mathrm{PID_i} \parallel PWD_i \parallel \sigma_i \parallel \theta_i)$. Finally, smartcards need verify whether the parameter are correct. If the value doesn't correspond, the login request is terminated.

User chooses the server S_j by assessing the list $\mathrm{T_i}$ and extract $\mathrm{R_j}$ and IDR_i at the same time. User compute $\mathrm{Q_j} = \mathrm{R_j} \oplus \mathrm{PWD_i}$. Smartcards generate random number $\mathrm{N_1} \in Z_p^*$ and compute $B_{ij} = PID_i \parallel IDR_\mathrm{i} \oplus h(\mathrm{SID_i} \parallel \alpha \parallel (\mathrm{h(ASK)} \oplus IDR_\mathrm{i}))$, $\mathrm{D_{ij}} = \mathrm{h}(\mathrm{PID_i} \parallel Q_i \parallel \alpha)$, $\alpha = N_1 P$. Smartcard send out the login request include $\{B_{ij}, \mathrm{D_{ij}}, \alpha\}$ by public channel.

In Mutually Authenticated Key Agreement phase, S_j inquiry the number IDR_i, and then compute $PID_i \parallel IDR_\mathrm{i} = B_{ij} \oplus h(\mathrm{SID_i} \parallel \alpha \parallel \mathrm{h(ASK)} \oplus IDR_\mathrm{i})$ and compute the parameter PID_i, $\mathrm{Q_j} = h(\mathrm{PID_i} \parallel \mathrm{K_j})$ when receive the login request. Afterwards, S_j authenticates U_i only if $\mathrm{D_{ij}} \stackrel{?}{=} \mathrm{h}(\mathrm{PID_i} \parallel Q_i \parallel \alpha)$ matching the condition. Otherwise the process terminates.

6 Conclusions

In this paper, we demonstrate that Reedy *et al.'s* scheme can't withstand some common attacks. More concretely, we analysis the Reedy's proof on the basis of the Wang *et al.* and Huang *et al.*'s [9] rigorous security model. Unfortunately, we find that Reedy *et al.'s* scheme can't be secure against guessing attack and impersonation attack with limited domain offline passwords. Next, we propose the improved scheme to overcome their scheme's flaws. The proposed improved scheme can overcome the flaws of the Reedy *et al.'s* schemes and be more practically and secure.

Acknowledgments. The work was supported in part by the National Natural Science Foundation of China under Grants 61862052 and the Science and Technology Foundation of Qinghai under Grants 2019-ZJ-7065.

References

1. Reddy, A.G., Yoon, E.J., Das, A.K., et al.: Design of mutually authenticated key agreement scheme resistant to impersonation attacks for multi-server environment. IEEE Access **PP**(99), 1 (2017)
2. Wang, D., Wang, P.: Two birds with one stone: two-factor authentication with security beyond conventional bound. IEEE Trans. Dependable Secur. Comput. **15**(4), 708–722 (2018)
3. He, D., Tian, M., Chen, J.: Insecurity of an efficient certificateless aggregate signature with constant pairing computations. Inf. Sci. **268**(2), 458–462 (2014)
4. Mishra, D., Das, A.K., Mukhopadhyay, S.: A secure user anonymity-preserving biometric-based multi-server authenticated key agreement scheme using smart cards. Expert Syst. Appl. **41**(18), 8129–8143 (2014)
5. Yoon, E.J.: Robust biometrics-based multi-server authentication with key agreement scheme for smart cards on elliptic curve cryptosystem. J. Supercomput. **63**(1), 235–255 (2013)
6. Dolev, D., Yao, A.C.: On the security of public key schemes. IEEE Trans. Inf. Theory **29**(2), 198–208 (1981)
7. Wang, D., Wang, P.: On the anonymity of two-factor authentication schemes for wireless sensor networks. Comput. Netw. **73**(C), 41–57 (2014)
8. Wang, D., He, D., Wang, P., et al.: Anonymous two-factor authentication in distributed systems: certain goals are beyond attainment. IEEE Trans. Dependable Secur. Comput. **12** (4), 428–442 (2015)
9. Huang, X., Xiang, Y., Chonka, A., et al.: A generic framework for three-factor authentication: preserving security and privacy in distributed systems. IEEE Trans. Parallel Distrib. Syst. **22**(8), 1390–1397 (2011)
10. Veyrat-Charvillon, N., Standaert, F.-X.: Generic side-channel distinguishers: improvements and limitations. In: Rogaway, P. (ed.) CRYPTO 2011. LNCS, vol. 6841, pp. 354–372. Springer, Heidelberg (2011). https://doi.org/10.1007/978-3-642-22792-9_20
11. Wang, D., Zhang, Z., Wang, P., et al.: Targeted online password guessing: an underestimated threat. In: ACM SIGSAC Conference on Computer and Communications Security, pp. 1242–1254. ACM (2016)

12. Wang, D., Wang, P.: On the implications of Zipf's law in passwords. In: Askoxylakis, I., Ioannidis, S., Katsikas, S., Meadows, C. (eds.) ESORICS 2016. LNCS, vol. 9878, pp. 111–131. Springer, Cham (2016). https://doi.org/10.1007/978-3-319-45744-4_6
13. Boyd, C., Mathuria, A.: Schemes for authentication and key establishment. In: Schemes for Authentication and Key Establishment, pp. 3215–3230. Springer (2003)
14. He, D., Wang, D.: Robust biometrics-based authentication scheme for multiserver environment. IEEE Syst. J. **9**(3), 816–823 (2015)
15. Lamport, L.: Password authentication with insecure communication. Commun. ACM **24**(24), 770–772 (1981)
16. Tsaur, W.-J.: A flexible user authentication scheme for multi-server internet services. In: Lorenz, P. (ed.) ICN 2001. LNCS, vol. 2093, pp. 174–183. Springer, Heidelberg (2001). https://doi.org/10.1007/3-540-47728-4_18
17. Kim, H., Jeon, W., Lee, K., Lee, Y., Won, D.: Cryptanalysis and improvement of a biometrics-based multi-server authentication with key agreement scheme. In: Murgante, B., Gervasi, O., Misra, S., Nedjah, N., Rocha, Ana Maria A.C., Taniar, D., Apduhan, Bernady O. (eds.) ICCSA 2012. LNCS, vol. 7335, pp. 391–406. Springer, Heidelberg (2012). https://doi.org/10.1007/978-3-642-31137-6_30
18. Chuang, M.C., Chen, M.C.: An anonymous multi-server authenticated key agreement scheme based on trust computing using smart cards and biometrics. Int. J. Netw. Secur. **18**(5), 997–1000 (2014)
19. Tsai, J.L., Lo, N.W.: A new password-based multi-server authentication scheme robust to password guessing attacks. Wirel. Pers. Commun. **71**(3), 1977–1988 (2013)
20. Chang, C.C., Lee, J.S.: An efficient and secure multi-server password authentication scheme using smart cards. In: International Conference on Cyberworlds (2004)
21. He, D.: Security flaws in a smart card based authentication scheme for multi-server environment. Wirel. Pers. Commun. **70**(1), 323–329 (2013)
22. Juang, W.S.: Efficient multi-server password authenticated key agreement using smart cards. IEEE Trans. Consum. Electron. **50**(1), 251–255 (2004)
23. Jiang, P., Wen, Q., et al.: An anonymous and efficient remote biometrics user authentication scheme in a multi server environment. Front. Comput. Sci. **9**(1), 142–156 (2015)
24. Odelu, V., Das, A.K., Goswami, A.: A secure biometrics-based multi-server authentication protocol using smart cards. IEEE Trans. Inf. Forensics Secur. **10**(9), 1953–1966 (2015)
25. Wan, T., Liu, Z.X., Ma, J.F.: Authentication and key agreement protocol for multi-server architecture. J. Comput. Res. Dev. **53**(11), 2446–2453 (2016)
26. Khan, M.K., Kim, S.K., Alghathbar, K.: Cryptanalysis and security enhancement of a 'more efficient & secure dynamic ID-based remote user authentication scheme'. Comput. Commun. **34**(3), 305–309 (2011)
27. Shivraj, V.L., Rajan, M.A., Singh, M., et al.: One time password authentication scheme based on elliptic curves for Internet of Things (IoT) (2015)
28. Qi, X., Na, D., Wong, D.S., et al.: Cryptanalysis and security enhancement of a robust two-factor authentication and key agreement protocol. Int. J. Commun. Syst. **29**(3), 478–487 (2016)
29. Zhong, J., Liu, Z., Xu, J.: Analysis and improvement of an efficient controlled quantum secure direct communication and authentication protocol. Comput. Mater. Contin. **57**(3), 621–633 (2018)
30. Fong Cheang, C., Wang, Y., Cai, Z., Xu, G.: Multi-VMs intrusion detection for cloud security using Dempster-Shafer theory. Comput. Mater. Contin. **57**(2), 297–306 (2018)

A Novel Content Based Image Retrieval Scheme in Cloud Computing

Zhuohua Liu[1], Caijuan Huang[1(✉)], Hui Suo[1], and Bin Yang[2]

[1] School of Computer and Design, Guangdong Jidian Polytechnic, Guangzhou, China
yi_juany@hotmail.com

[2] School of Internet of Things, Jiangnan University, Wuxi, China

Abstract. Image and multimedia data produced by individuals and enterprises is increasing in recent years. The need of outsourcing such intensive image feature detection tasks to cloud computing continues to grow. However, the concerns over the effective protection of private image and multimedia data when outsourcing it to cloud platform become the major barrier that impedes the further implementation of cloud computing techniques over massive amount of image and multimedia data. To address this challenge, a new scheme that supports Content Based Image Retrieval (CBIR) over the encrypted images without revealing the sensitive information to the cloud server is proposed. The novel scheme is based on complex networks theory and Speeded Up Robust Features (SURF) technique. SURF is one of the important local feature detection algorithms and has been broadly employed in different areas, including object recognition, image matching, robotic mapping, and so on. A high-performance privacy-preserving SURF feature detection system is analyzed and modeled for the secure computation purpose. The coordinates of the key-points (features) obtained from SURF detector are used to generate the complex network work. The security analysis and experiments show the security and efficiency of the proposed scheme.

Keywords: Cloud computing · CBIR · Complex networks · SURF · Searchable encryption

1 Introduction

The current rapid improvement in the digital storage media, image capturing devices like scanners, web cameras, digital cameras and rapid development in internet provide a huge collection of images. This leads to the retrieval of these images for visual information efficiently and effectively in different fields of life like medical, medicine, art, architecture, education, crime preventions. Progresses have been made in both the derivation of new features and the construction of signatures based on these features. The richness in the mathematical formulation of signatures grows alongside the invention of new methods for measuring similarity. Meanwhile, cloud services specifically designed for image storage and sharing, such as Instagram, are among the largest growing internet services today. It offers a great opportunity for the on-demand

X. Sun et al. (Eds.): ICAIS 2019, LNCS 11633, pp. 606–616, 2019.
https://doi.org/10.1007/978-3-030-24265-7_52

access to the ample computation and storage resources, which makes it an attractive choice for the image storage and CBIR outsourcing [1].

Nevertheless, the broad use of CBIR may leads to privacy concerns. The image data usually contain private information from data owners. For example, a picture or video may capture private information like personal identity, location, and even financial profiles. Moreover, even features extracted from the image may leak important private information. The attacker can deduce the content of image via feature comparisons in a benchmark image database or even recover part of the image-based on these features [2]. Therefore, exploring privacy-preserving image feature detection over encrypted cloud data becomes of paramount importance. This paper discusses the problems of privacy-preserving CBIR outsourcing with an honest-but-curious cloud server.

The rest of this paper is organized as follows. Section 2 introduces the related reaches about SURF and complex network. The proposed scheme is described in Sect. 3. The experimental results and discussion are presented in Sect. 4. Section 5 gives the conclusions.

2 Related Works

2.1 Searchable Encryption in CBIR

The development of image retrieval has gone through two stages: text-based image retrieval (TBIR) and CBIR. The studies about TBIR begin in 1970s. They focused on converting image contents into keywords or short-text. Some early basic schemes explore the Boolean search to identify whether or not a query term is present in an encrypted text document [3, 4]. Considering the subjectivity and extensive manual annotation while images have a massive increase in number, Hirata et al. [5] proposed a content-based image retrieval scheme in 1992. A filter mechanism was proposed in [6] to reduce false matches for copying detection, which can be applied to some image retrieval. The weakness of their scheme is that it mainly dealt with the problem brought by plain text images but reckoned without the image privacy. A popular solution is to encrypt images with searchable encryption. Lu et al. [7] construct the privacy-preserving CBIR scheme over the encrypted images. The visual words were firstly extracted to represent images, and then the Jaccard similarity between two sets of visual words was calculated. The similarity between the two corresponding images was obtained. Finally, they proposed an order-preserving encryption scheme and a min-hash algorithm to protect the information of visual words. Later, they proposed three image feature protection techniques, i.e. the bitplane randomization, random projection and randomized unary encoding in [8]. They encrypted the features with bitplane randomization and randomized unary encoding. Finally, the encrypted features were used to calculate the Hamming distance in the encryption domain. A novel efficient search scheme for encrypted image by was proposed in [9]. K-means technique together with secure modular hashing was used in their proposed scheme, which can simultaneously achieve privacy-preserving of image search and comparable search accuracy to plaintext image. They also provided comprehensively security analysis on the proposed solution and detailed efficiency evaluation over some real-world datasets. However, the linear search is inefficient and computationally impracticable for a large database.

The proposed scheme is developed to increase the efficiency in image content searching through the use of SURF and complex networks. In the meanwhile, the plaintext data regarding the image content, image features and trapdoors should be transparent to the cloud server.

2.2 Preliminary to SURF and Complex Network

Scale invariant feature transform (SIFT) technique [10], which invariant to various geometrical transformations, has be wildly used to extract the features in computer vision applications. The key-points would be insufficient to meet the forensic need in the area where the textures are almost uniform. We modified the key-point distribution part to increase the efficiency in cloud environment. Details modification is presented in Sect. 3.

The SURF algorithm is composed by two parts: first, key-points detection; second, descriptor vector generation. In the key-points detection step, an integral image $I_{\sum(x)}$ at a location $x = (x, y)^T$ is generated at the beginning of the process. Then, the algorithm detects the key-points based on the Hessian matrix approximation. Given a point $x = (x, y)$ in an image I, the Hessian matrix $H(x, \sigma)$ in x at scale σ is defined as follows

$$H(x, \sigma) = \begin{bmatrix} L_{xx}(x, \sigma), & L_{xy}(x, \sigma) \\ L_{xy}(x, \sigma), & L_{yy}(x, \sigma) \end{bmatrix} \tag{1}$$

where $L_{xx}(x, \delta)$ is the convolution of the Gaussian second order derivative $\frac{\delta^2}{\delta x^2} g(\delta)$ with the image I in point x, and similarly for $L_{xy}(x, \delta)$ and $L_{yy}(x, \delta)$. The approximation of the second order derivatives is denoted as D_{xx}, D_{xy}, and D_{yy}. The Hessian's determinant approximation with the adequately relative weight can be found:

$$\det(H_{approx}) = D_{xx} D_{yy} - (0.9 D_{xy}) \tag{2}$$

In the key-points description step, the SURF algorithm identifies a reproducible orientation for the key-points. After the wavelet responses are computed and weighted via Gaussian centered at the key-points, the responses are represented as points in a space with the horizontal and vertical response strength along the abscissa and ordinate respectively. Then, the dominant orientation is estimated by summing all responses within a sliding orientation window of size π/3. The SURF descriptor is a 64-dimention vector v:

$$v = \left(\sum d_x, \sum d_y, \sum |d_x|, \sum |d_y|\right) \tag{3}$$

where dx and dy are the summed-up wavelet responses in horizontal vertical and direction, respectively.

It has been successfully used in a plethora of multidisciplinary applications such as Image Analysis, system security and biological systems. Regarding the network analysis, a common problem is the network size. When networks become very large, could be difficult to analyze, visualize and extract information and patterns from its topology and dynamics [3]. Figure 1 is an example of the mapping from a complex network into a feature vector. Generic mappings can be used in order to obtain the characterization of the network in terms of a suitable set of measurements [11]. In case the mapping is invertible, we have a complete representation of the original structure.

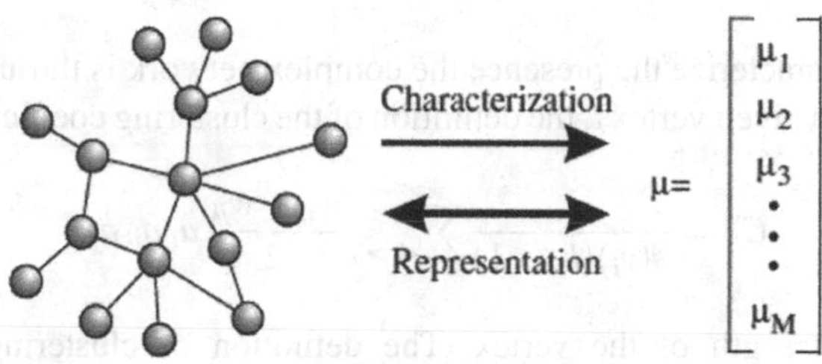

Fig. 1. The mapping from a complex network into a feature vector. Adapted from [11].

Moreover, the network can be represented by measures so that its topological structure is analyzed from them, including representation, characterization and classification. Complex networks can be roughly divided into four main types: weighted digraphs (directed graphs), unweighted digraphs, weighted graphs and unweighted graphs. In this paper, we only focus on the weighted digraphs which is adapted to the feature-extraction application in CBIR. A weighted directed graph *g*, is defined by a set $V(g)$ of *N* vertexes, a set $\Phi(g)$ of *M* edges, and a mapping $\Phi(g) \rightarrow \mathbb{R}$. Each vertex is defined as an integer value $i = 1, 2, \ldots, N$; and each edge is defined as a pair *(i, j)* which represents a connection from vertex *i* to vertex *j*. And *W(i, j)* is the associate weight of the edge *(i, j)*. Any weighted digraph can be transformed into a graph by using the symmetry operation $\delta(W) = W + W^T$, where W^T is the transpose of *W*, s_i is defined as the number of edges connected to vertex *i*. In the case of directed networks, there are two kinds of degrees: the out-degree, $s^{out}i$, equal to the number of outgoing edges, and the in-degree, $s^{in}i$, corresponding to the number of incoming edges. For weighted networks, the quantity *i*, s_i is more generally used, which are defined as the sum of the weights of the corresponding edges:

$$s(v_i)^{out} = \sum\nolimits_{v_i, v_j \in \varnothing(g)} w_{ij} \tag{4}$$

$$s(v_i)^{out} = \sum\nolimits_{v_i, v_j \in \varnothing(g)} w_{ji} \tag{5}$$

where w_{ij} is the element of the adjacency matrix. The degree of a vertex vi is the number of its connections:

$$s(v_i) = s(v_i)^{out} + s(v_i)^{in} \tag{6}$$

If a network has too few edges, i.e. the average connectivity of its vertexes is too small, there will be many isolated area and clusters with a small number of vertexes. Globally, it is possible to characterize the behavior of the vertices of the network using the mean degree:

$$u_s = \frac{1}{|V|} \sum\nolimits_{v_i \in V} s(v_i) \tag{7}$$

One way to characterize the presence the complex network is through the clustering coefficient. Given a given vertex i, the definition of the clustering coefficient is defined as:

$$C_i^w = \frac{1}{s(v_i)(k_i - 1)} \sum\nolimits_{k>j} \frac{w_{ij} + w_{jk}}{2} a_{ij} a_{ik} a_{jk} \tag{8}$$

where s_i is the strength of the vertex. The definition of clustering coefficient for weighted networks is:

$$C^w = \frac{1}{N} \sum\nolimits_i C_i^w \tag{9}$$

The coordinates of the key-points (features) obtained from SURF detector are then used to generate the complex network.

3 Proposed Scheme

3.1 System Architecture

The proposed system architecture is illustrated in Fig. 2. There are three entities involved in this model: the image owner, the cloud server who stores encrypted images and performs image retrieval, and the image users who want to retrieval images.

Image owner going to upload and outsource his local images to the cloud server. The images are encrypted before reaching the cloud server. The image owner has the right of searching over the encrypted images. The image owner only needs to save features as search index.

Cloud server stores the encrypted image with its index uploaded from the image owner. The server needs to respond to the query requests from other users. The specific features are extracted and compared with search index sent by users. The images with smallest distance will be returned to users.

Image users are the authorized to retrieve images from the cloud server. The image user firstly generates a trapdoor for the query image, and then send the trapdoor to the cloud server. The user can decrypt the crypted image downloaded from the cloud server by using the secret key shared by image owner.

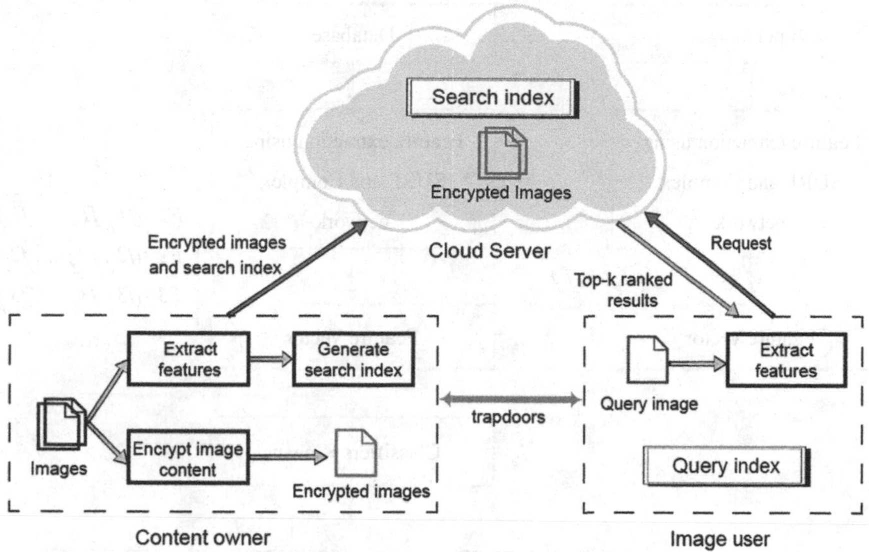

Fig. 2. The proposed system architecture

3.2 Proposed Framework

SURF algorithm and complex network are used for feature extraction providing single feature vector for input image and number of feature vector for database images. Then classifier is used at the feature vector of database providing two types of images.

(1) Relevant images
(2) Non-Relevant images

We select Euclidean distance function as the matching functions due to its simplicity and efficiency. An array of the images is obtained, and image sorting is then performed to retrieve the images. Figure 3 demonstrates the flowchart of proposed framework.

3.3 Features Extraction Algorithm

The key-points would be insufficient to meet the forensic need in the area where the textures are almost uniform. We developed a strategy to adapt the forensic scenario. The details of the algorithm are presented below. In the algorithm, the input is an ordered list Ls, which saves all the key-points extracted from the image. And the output is a list Lo, which saves the suppressed key-points. f_{HM} is the value of the strength of detected feature. Let m and r denote the desired number of key-points and the radius of the testing circle, respectively.

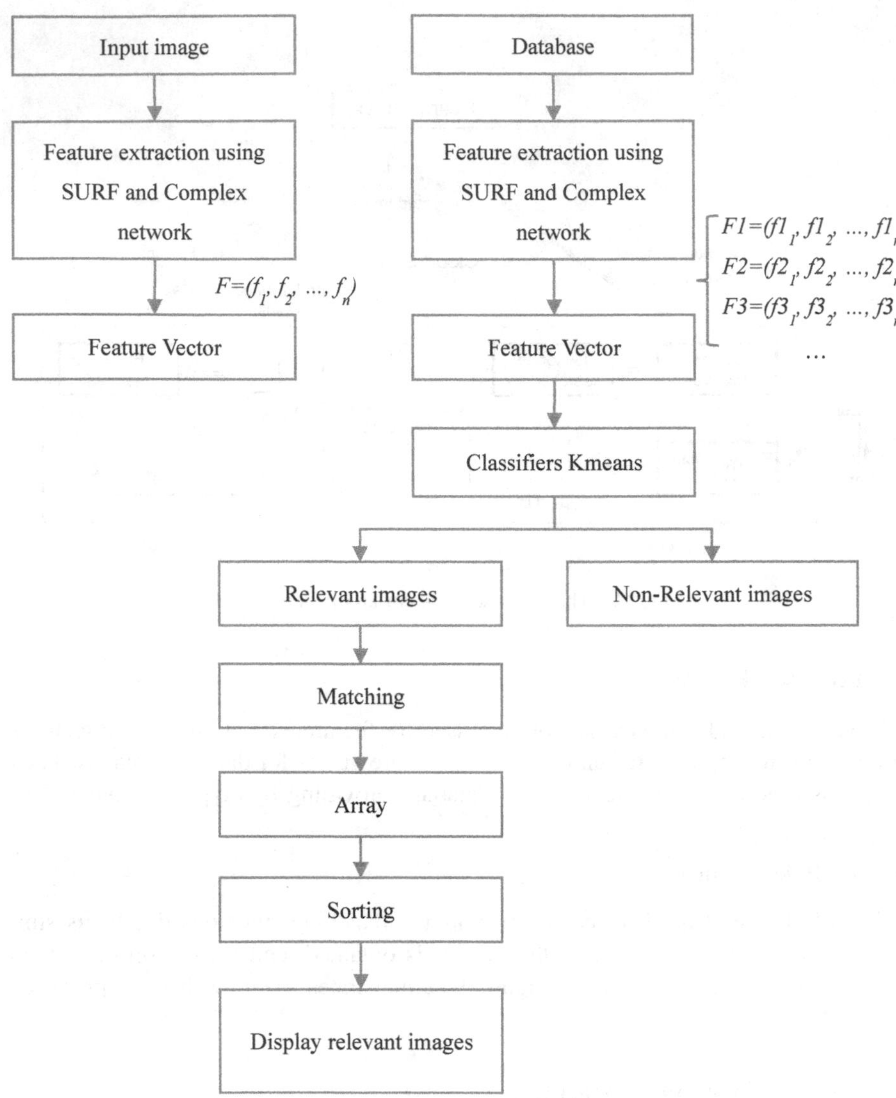

Fig. 3. Flowchart of the proposed framework

Algorithm.

Input: $L_s = \{p_1, p_2, \ldots, p_n\}$, *m (m<=n), r=10 (default)*

Output: $L_o = \{p_1, p_2, \ldots, p_m\}$

Begin:

```
// Initialize
q = ⌊n/m⌋        // q is the number of eliminating key-points in every literation
// Begin of the literation
for i=1,2,...,m do
    select the minimum key-point p_k of f_HM        // 1 ≤ k ≤ n
    select the maximum key-point p_l of f_HM in the area which centered by p_k with radius r
        // 1 ≤ l ≤ n
    insert p_max into L_o
    remove the smallest q key-points and the p_l in L_s
// End of the literation
output the result L_o
```

In the literation, the first selection is the global minimum pk, and then we find the local maximum point pl around pk. Thus, the relatively few key-point in area where the textures are almost uniform could be retained. After inserting the local maximum point into the output list Lo, we eliminate the smallest q points to enlarge the retaining chance of the relatively large key-points.

4 Experimental Results

A thorough experimental evaluation of the proposed system is performed on a real image database, Caltech256, which contains 30,607 images with a total size 1.2 GB. The entire secure search scheme is implemented using C++ language on a Windows 7 operation system with two Intel Core (TM) Xeon E5-2650 2.20 GHz, with 32 GB RAM and a 7200 RPM disk drive. The cloud side process is conducted on Azure with a large standard instance type. The authorized user runs trapdoor-generation process to generate a query trapdoor to retrieve the similar images. Retrieval performance is evaluated by precision and recall rates which are widely used to measure image retrieval performance. In this work, mean average precision (mAP) is selected to present the retrieval performance for a group of queries. It is defined as the means of average precision for a group of queries:

$$mAP = \frac{\sum_{q=1}^{Q} AP(q)}{Q} \tag{12}$$

where Q is the number of queries, *AP()* is the average of all the precisions measured each time a new relevant image is retrieved.

Search and retrieval experiments were performed on Corel dataset [12] which containing 1000 color images. We perform retrieval performance experiment on the same dataset and compare experimental results with the methods proposed in [13] and [14]. The mAP value of each method is shown in Table 1, and several retrieval results are presented in Fig. 4. The overall performance of [14] is lower than others.

Table 1. The mAP value of different method

Image category	Xu et al. [13]	Qin et al. [14]	Proposed
African	73.5	70.2	73.1
Beach	76.8	72.6	78.4
Food	72.6	71.1	73.1
Mountain	69.8	68.7	72.2
Dinosaurs	76.1	70.3	77.2
Elephants	73.3	70.3	79.1
Horses	74.7	66.8	76.3
Flowers	72.1	67.5	74.6
Buses	71.6	70.2	72.1
Architecture	77.6	71.1	79.7

Fig. 4. Retrieval results in Corel dataset.

5 Conclusion

In this paper, a novel scheme that supports CBIR over the encrypted images without revealing the sensitive information to the cloud server is proposed. Features are extracted by SURF algorithm, and then the coordinates of the features obtained from SURF detector are used to generate the complex network. Through this scheme, the cloud server is able to retrieve image from encrypted image database more precise and efficiently. The experimental results show that the proposed system is correct and effective for different image categories in Corel dataset. In the future, we will dedicate to expose the problem in privacy-preserving image detection algorithms, and will continue to improve the efficiency while retrieving the encrypted images.

Acknowledgments. This paper is one of the results of the 2016 Guangdong Provincial Higher Vocational Education Leading Talent Project (Hui Suo). This work is partly supported by the National Natural Science Foundation of China (NO. 51505191) and the Chinese Postdoctoral Science Foundation (NO. 2018M632229).

References

1. Yin, J., Lu, X., Chen, H., Zhao, X., Xiong, N.N.: System resource utilization analysis and prediction for cloud based applications under bursty workloads. Inf. Sci. **279**, 338–357 (2014)
2. Duncan, G., Mukherjee, S.: Optimal disclosure limitation strategy in statistical databases: deterring tracker attacks through additive noise. Publ. Am. Stat. Assoc. **95**, 720–729 (2000)
3. Cui, Q., Mcintosh, S., Sun, H.: Identifying materials of photographic images and photorealistic computer generated graphics based on deep CNNs. Comput. Mater. Contin. **55**, 229–241 (2018)
4. Zhou, S., Liang, W., Li, J., Kim, J.-U.: Improved VGG model for road traffic sign recognition. Comput. Mater. Contin. **57**, 11–24 (2018)
5. Hirata, K., Kato, T.: Query by visual example - content based image retrieval. In: Pirotte, A., Delobel, C., Gottlob, G. (eds.) Advances in Database Technology - EDBT 1992. LNCS, vol. 580, pp. 56–71. Springer, Heidelberg (1992). https://doi.org/10.1007/BFb0032418
6. Zhou, Z., Wang, Y., Wu, Q.M.J., Yang, C.N., Sun, X.: Effective and efficient global context verification for image copy detection. IEEE Trans. Inf. Forensics Secur. **12**, 48–63 (2017)
7. Lu, W., Swaminathan, A., Varna, A.L., Wu, M.: Enabling search over encrypted multimedia databases. In: Media Forensics and Security I, p. 725418 (2009)
8. Lu, W., Varna, A.L., Swaminathan, A., Wu, M.: Secure image retrieval through feature protection. In: IEEE International Conference on Acoustics, Speech and Signal Processing, pp. 1533–1536 (2009)
9. Wang, Y., Miao, M., Shen, J., Wang, J.: Towards efficient privacy-preserving encrypted image search in cloud computing. Soft Comput. 1–12 (2017)
10. Lowe, D.: Distinctive image features from scale-invariant keypoints. Int. J. Comput. Vis. **60**, 91–110 (2004)
11. Costa, L.d.F., Rodrigues, F.A., Travieso, G., Boas, P.R.V.: Characterization of complex networks: a survey of measurements. Adv. Phys. **56**, 167–242 (2007)

12. Li, J., Wang, J.Z.: Real-time computerized annotation of pictures. IEEE Trans. Pattern Anal. Mach. Intell. **30**, 985 (2008)
13. Xu, Y., Gong, J., Xiong, L., Xu, Z., Wang, J., Shi, Y.Q.: A privacy-preserving content-based image retrieval method in cloud environment. J. Vis. Commun. Image Represent. **43**, 164–172 (2017)
14. Qin, Z., Yan, J., Ren, K., Chen, C.W., Wang, C.: SecSIFT: secure image SIFT feature extraction in cloud computing. ACM Trans. Multimed. Comput. Commun. Appl. **12**, 65 (2016)

Mobile Image Retrieval System for Cloud Service Based on Convolutional Neural Network and Hadoop

Caijuan Huang[1], Zhuohua Liu[1(✉)], Hui Suo[1], and Bin Yang[2]

[1] School of Computer and Design, Guangdong Jidian Polytechnic, Guangzhou, China
liuzhuohua@foxmail.com

[2] School of Internet of Things, Jiangnan University, Wuxi, China

Abstract. These years, global digital images are increasing at an unprecedented speed. Using smart mobile is a convenient way to share what users experienced anytime and anywhere through social networks. Retrieving these distributed images has become an important research issue. In order to speed up the image retrieval in mobile cloud service, an efficient content-based image retrieval (CBIR) system based on Hadoop is designed and proposed. Firstly, the features of image are extracted by a convolutional neural network, and the features of the image library are divided into several sub feature databases. Secondly, image retrieval results are obtained according to the matching results by Hadoop distributed platform. The simulation experiments verify the efficiency of the proposed system.

Keywords: Cloud service · CBIR · Mobile service · CNN · Hadoop

1 Introduction

With the spring up of mobile devices as well as the spread of the Internet have produced a large amount of multimedia images in our society. The development of image retrieval can be divided into two classes: text-based image retrieval (TBIR) and content-based image retrieval (CBIR). Considering the subjectivity and extensive manual annotation while images have a massive increase in number, Kato Hirata et al. [1] proposed a CBIR scheme. Data owner, cloud service providers (CSP) and data user can be taken by different parties in cloud environment. Meanwhile, cloud services specifically designed for image storage and sharing, such as Instagram, are among the largest growing internet services today. It offers a great opportunity for the on-demand access to the ample computation and storage resources, which makes it an attractive choice for the image storage and CBIR outsourcing [2]. For mobile image retrieval, the poor wireless channel is mostly a crucial challenge. The limitation of bandwidth and the instability of channel are both problems.

Existing retrieval systems usually need a single query image for the searching application [3–5]. In this case, the system rarely achieves good performance if the object in the query cannot be seen clearly. In [6], Arandjelović and Zisserman

X. Sun et al. (Eds.): ICAIS 2019, LNCS 11633, pp. 617–626, 2019.
https://doi.org/10.1007/978-3-030-24265-7_53

developed the discriminative query expansion (DQE) method by using SVM to obtain a weighted vector. They calculated the distance from the decision boundary to renew the initial ranking list.

The Hadoop Distributed File System (HDFS) is designed to store very large data sets reliably, and to stream those data sets at high bandwidth to user applications. In a large cluster, thousands of servers both host directly attached storage and execute user application tasks [7]. The proposed system is consisted with remote and server parts. Its architecture is depicted in Fig. 1.

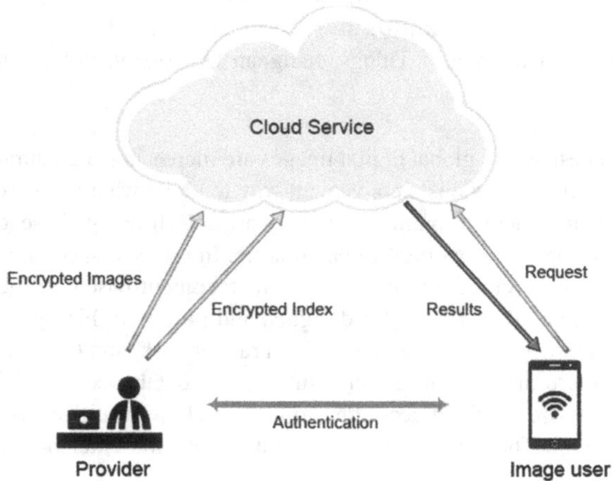

Fig. 1. Traditional encrypted search system over cloud

The rest of this paper is organized as follows. Section 2 introduces the related reaches about image retrieval. In Sect. 3, the proposed method is presented. Section 4 presents the experimental results and discussions. Finally, the concluding remarks are given in Sect. 5.

2 Related Works

2.1 Learning Global Representations for Image Search

Recent years, a number of image retrieval schemes [8] were proposed based on deep learning technique. However, most of them were only using a pre-trained network to perform local feature extraction. Very recently, inspired by impressive results in the closely related fields of machine learning, deep neural networks (DNN) had been used in passive image forensics researches. In [9], a comparison of SIFT and was performed, which conformed that deep features are expected to be much more powerful than SIFT features. This is because that deep features are able to learned more from massive amount of data in a supervised manner. Two experiments had been performed by Babenko et al. which are presented below.

- **Experiment 1.** Three types of descriptors (deep convolutional, original SIFT, embedded SIFT) were tested based on Oxford Buildings dataset. They computed the cosine similarity between features of query-image and the features of all other images in the dataset. Figure 2 (adapted from [9].) demonstrates that SIFT-based matches are significantly worse and many of them correspond to unrelated image patches.

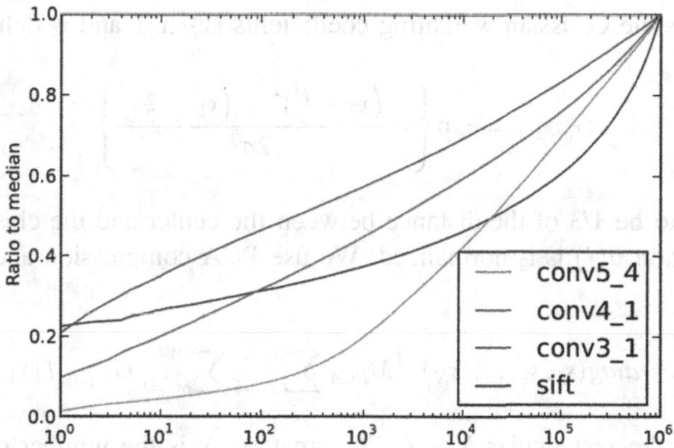

Fig. 2. The average ratio between the distances to the kth neighbour and the median distance to all features for dense SIFT and deep convolutional features with the highest norm from three convolutional layers.

- **Experiment 2.** The statistics of high-dimensional distributions for deep convolutional features and dense SIFTs were analysed. They performed retrieval by sum pooling descriptor. The mAP score for the Oxford Buildings dataset for (1) was only 0.09, which was much smaller than mAP for (2), 0.34. This verifies that features with large norms are much more discriminative than random features.

Results of both experiments demonstrate that the individual similarities of deep features from the last convolutional layer are significantly more discriminative. Inspired by experiments taken above, *SPoC* descriptor is developed based on the aggregation of raw deep convolutional features without embedding. Each deep convolutional feature *f* is calculated from image *I* with a spatial coordinate (x_1, x_2). The spatial position (x_1, x_2) associates to the feature in map stack which is generated by the last convolutional layer. Sum pooling layer in the deep learning structure is defined as:

$$\vartheta(I) = \sum\nolimits_{x_2=1}^{H} \sum\nolimits_{x_1=1}^{W} f(x_1, x_2) \tag{1}$$

where H and W is the height and width of image I, respectively. The scalar product of resulting descriptors corresponds to the simplest match kernel between a pair of images is:

$$\mathrm{Sim}(I_a, I_b) = \langle \vartheta(I_a), \vartheta(I_b) \rangle = \sum\nolimits_{f_x \in I_a} \sum\nolimits_{f_x \in I_b} \langle f_x, f_y \rangle \tag{2}$$

In most case, the interest area would close to the geometrical center of an image. The simple weighting heuristic can modify the centering prior of a SPoC descriptor. This heuristic assign larger weights to the features from the center of the feature map stack, and (1) can be represented as:

$$\vartheta(I) = \sum\nolimits_{x_2=1}^{H} \sum\nolimits_{x_1=1}^{W} G_{(x_1,x_2)} f(x_1,x_2) \tag{3}$$

where $G_{(x_1,x_2)}$ is the Gaussian weighting coefficients (x_1, x_2), and is defined as:

$$G_{(x_1,x_2)} = \exp\left\{-\frac{\left(x_2 - \frac{H}{2}\right)^2 + \left(x_1 - \frac{W}{2}\right)^2}{2\sigma^2}\right\} \tag{4}$$

where σ is set to be 1/3 of the distance between the center and the closest boundary. The representation $\vartheta(I)$ is l_2-normalized. We use PCA compression and whitening to $\vartheta(I)$:

$$\vartheta(I) = diag(s_1, s_2, \ldots, s_N)^{-1} M_{PCA} \sum\nolimits_{x_2=1}^{H} \sum\nolimits_{x_1=1}^{W} G_{(x_1,x_2)} f(x_1,x_2) \tag{5}$$

where M_{PCA} is the rectangular $N \times C$ PCA-matrix, N is the number of the retained dimensions, and s_i are the associated singular values. The l_2-normalized whitened vector of $\vartheta(I)$ is:

$$\vartheta_{spoc}(I) = \frac{\vartheta(I)}{\|\vartheta(I)\|_2} \tag{6}$$

2.2 Hadoop

Hadoop consists of two components of HDFS and MapReduce. HDFS is a distributed file system for big data storage with outstanding scalability and fault tolerance. MapReduce is a distributed framework for data processing, and is especially popular in big-data field. MapReduce consists of two steps, Map and Reduce. Splits of data are inputted into the Map process which will output intermediate key-value pairs. And then lists of these key-value pairs each of which has a common key are inputted into the Reduce process to output final key-value pairs.

MapReduce program should be designed by user first. Subsequently, the program is submitted to the Hadoop cluster as a job. HBase is a kind of NoSQL database software based on Hadoop. A record of a HBase table consists of a sole row key and some column families. Every column family has one or more columns defined by qualifiers. A programmer can access a table easily by APIs provided by HBase.

Recently, fixed numbers of map slots were used in Hadoop framework. The slots on each node were reduced throughout the lifetime of a cluster. However, the fixed slots may lead to poor efficiency in some cases. If a k nodes cluster has received a set of n jobs. Let $J = \{j_1, j_2, \ldots, j_n\}$ represents the set of jobs. Each j_i is configured with $n_m(i)$ map tasks and $n_r(i)$ reduce tasks. Let $b\ (i)$ and $e\ (i)$ record the begin time and the end time of job j_i. The total slots number in the Hadoop cluster is S, and let s_m and s_r be the number of map slots and reduce slots, respectively. The constraint would be $S = s_m + s_r$. Based on the study of [10], we proposed an algorithm to obtain the optimal value of s_m, and s_r can be calculated by $S - s_m$.

Algorithm: The generation of the optimal s_m

```
Osm= 999999    //initial the Osm with an absolute big value
for sm = 1 to S do
  sr = S - sm
  for i = 1 to n do
    qm(i) = nm(i) * tm(i) / sm   // tm(i) is the average time for a map task
    qr(i) = nr(i) * tr(i) / sm   // tr(i) is the average time for a reduce task
  end
  for i = 1 to n do
    b(i) = b(i - 1) + qm(i-1) / sm
    e(i) = (b(i) + qm(i) / sm) / (e(i - 1) + qr(i) / sr )
    if e(n) < Osm then
      Osm = e(n)
    end
  end
end
return Osm    // output the optimal values of sm
```

Thus, the slots to map and reduce tasks can be allocated dynamically while executing of jobs. The architecture design is detailed in Sect. 3.

3 Method

This work presents a mobile image retrieval system based on Hadoop in cloud environment.

3.1 System Architecture

There are three entities involved in this model: the image owner, the cloud server who stores encrypted images and performs image retrieval, and the image users who want to retrieval images.

Image owner going to upload and outsource his local images to the cloud server. The images are encrypted before reaching the cloud server. The image owner has the right of searching over the encrypted images. The image owner only needs to save features as search index.

Cloud server stores the encrypted image with its index uploaded from the image owner. The server needs to respond to the query requests from other users. The specific features are extracted and compared with search index sent by users. The images with smallest distance will be returned to users.

Image users are the authorized to retrieve images from the cloud server. The image user firstly generates a trapdoor for the query image, and then send the trapdoor to the cloud server. The user can decrypt the crypted image downloaded from the cloud server by using the secret key shared by image owner.

In this paper, the cloud server is assumed as "honest-but-curious". That means, the cloud server will honestly follow the designated protocol to execute the search ability properly and return correct results in real time.

3.2 The Architecture

A typical architecture of CBIR systems consists of four components of image collection, image feature extraction, indexing and searching. The proposed architecture of CBIR system is presented in Fig. 3 which is designed based on CNN and Hadoop.

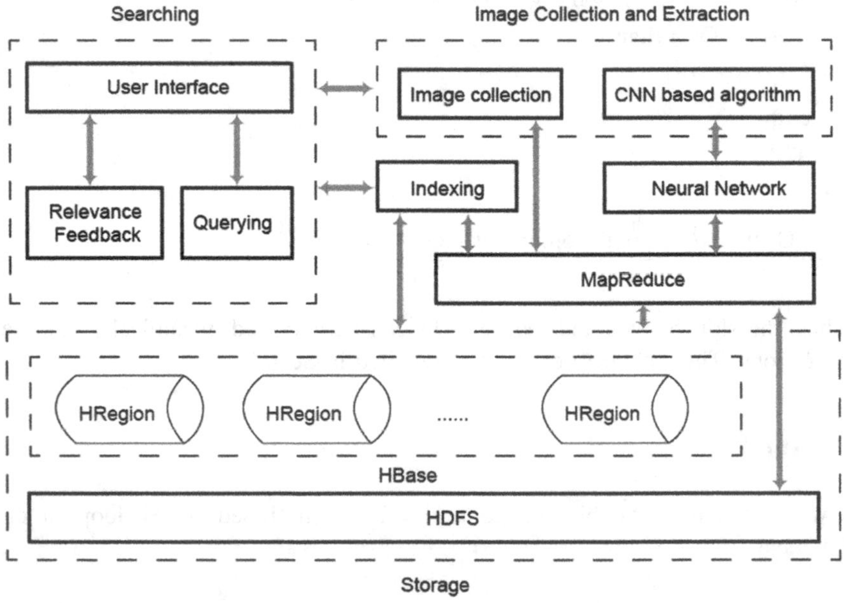

Fig. 3. The architecture of our proposed method

The storage component is the data center in our system. It is not only necessary for a MapReduce Job to run but also includes system's databases which are the image database. The image database is defined as a directory on the HDFS.

The classifier is used at the feature vector of database providing two types of images, i.e. relevant images and non-relevant images. After that Matching function is used for relevant images and Query image. We select Euclidean distance function as the matching functions due to its simplicity and efficiency. An array of the images is obtained, and image sorting is then performed to retrieve the images.

3.3 CNN-Based Representation

Recent years, deep Convolutional Neural Networks have achieved a lot of success in various problems including image classification, object detection, etc. In these years, CNN features were used as off-the-shelf features for image retrieval in many image retrieval applications. However, most of CNN based image retrieval schemes were focused in extracting local deep convolutional features. The discriminability for hand-crafted features is increased but still can be improved further. In this work, we make use to the SPoC descriptor [9], which can significantly enhance the discriminability. The flowchart of proposed CNN-based image retrieval scheme is presented in Fig. 4.

In training step, three groups of images are enhanced and the features are extracted through the proposed network. And then the neutral network learns which image

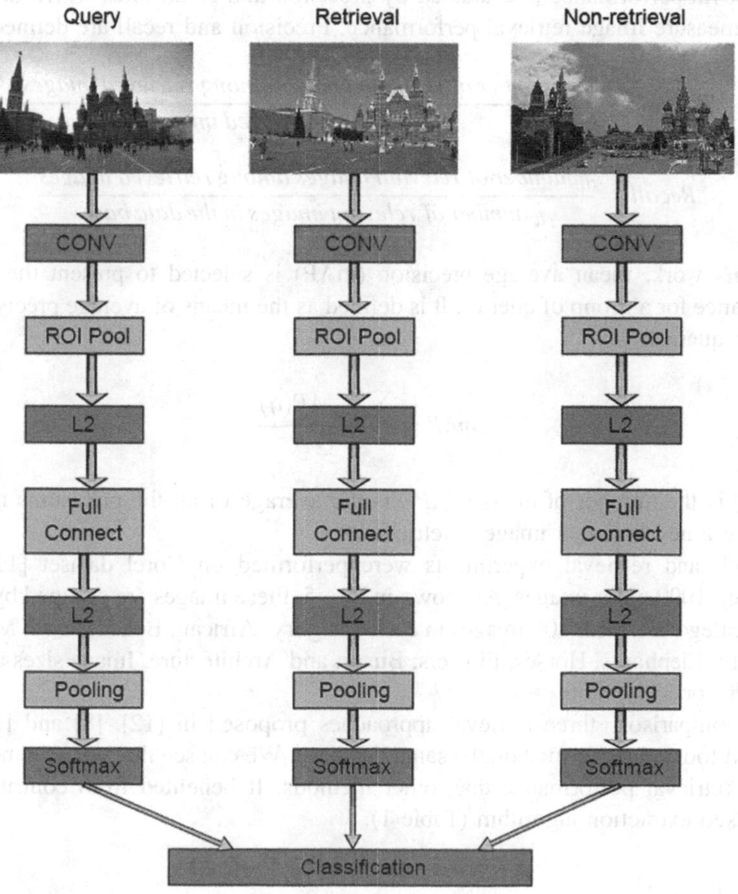

Fig. 4. The flowchart of proposed CNN-based image retrieval scheme.

should be considered as retrieval one. In test step, the query image is fed to the well-trained network to efficiently determine the group of this image. The feature vectors are finally protected by the k-nearest neighbor (kNN) algorithm.

4 Experimental Results

The design of the searching module is based on B/S architecture and JSP/Servlet technique as shown in Fig. 5. Different experiments are performed on an image database, named as Caltech256. Caltech256 contains 30,607 images with a total size 1.2 GB. The entire secure search scheme is implemented using C++ language on a Windows 7 operation system with two Intel Core (TM) Xeon E5-2650 2.20 GHz, with 32 GB RAM and a 7200RPM disk drive. Next, we randomly selected 70% images as the training set, while the complement 30% was the testing set. The trapdoor and his user identity are then sent to the cloud server. The cloud server performs the searching process to get a temporary result set including the top-k most similar images.

Retrieval performance is evaluated by precision and recall rates which are widely used to measure image retrieval performance. Precision and recall are defined as:

$$Precision = \frac{\#number\ of\ relevant\ images\ among\ retrieved\ images}{\#number\ of\ retrieved\ images} \tag{7}$$

$$Recall = \frac{\#number\ of\ relevant\ images\ among\ retrieved\ images}{\#number\ of\ relevant\ images\ in\ the\ data\ base} \tag{8}$$

In this work, mean average precision (mAP) is selected to present the retrieval performance for a group of queries. It is defined as the means of average precision for a group of queries:

$$mAP = \frac{\sum_{q=1}^{Q} AP(q)}{Q} \tag{9}$$

where Q is the number of queries, $AP()$ is the average of all the precisions measured each time a new relevant image is retrieved.

Search and retrieval experiments were performed on Corel dataset [11] which containing 1000 color images. As shown in Fig. 5, these images are grouped by content into 10 categories, with 100 images in each category: African, Beach, Food, Mountain, Dinosaurs, Elephants, Horses, Flowers, Buses, and Architecture. Image sizes are either 256 * 384 or 384 * 256.

For comparison, three retrieval approaches proposed in [12], [8] and [13] were evaluated too and performed on the same database. We can see that our scheme obtains a better retrieval performance than other methods. It benefited from contribution of CNN-based extraction algorithm (Table 1).

Fig. 5. Examples of Corel dataset in ten categories.

Table 1. The mAP value of different method

Image category	Approach [12]	Approach [8]	Approach [13]	Proposed
African	76.1	75.4	78.2	78.6
Beach	73.4	71.3	79.3	82.6
Food	71.3	65.2	72.5	78.5
Mountain	74.8	69.5	71.3	76.6
Dinosaurs	72.1	72.0	75.6	81.6
Elephants	74.2	77.5	78.9	82.9
Horses	71.3	72.2	80.6	81.4
Flowers	74.3	77.1	78.9	75.2
Buses	72.6	74.3	72.6	76.3
Architecture	74.2	75.2	76.6	77.9

5 Conclusion

In this paper, we presented a novel scheme that supports CBIR over the encrypted images without revealing the sensitive information to the cloud server is proposed. An efficient content-based image retrieval (CBIR) system based on Hadoop is designed and proposed. We make most computation tasks perform on Cloud due to the limit ability of mobile. Through this scheme, the cloud server is able to retrieve image from encrypted image database more precise and efficiently. The experimental results show that the proposed system is correct and effective for different image categories in Corel dataset. In the future, we will continue to improve the efficiency and the accuracy on retrieving images by mobile-user.

Acknowledgments. This paper is one of the results of the 2016 Guangdong Provincial Higher Vocational Education Leading Talent Project (Hui Suo). This work is partly supported by the National Natural Science Foundation of China (NO. 51505191) and the Chinese Postdoctoral Science Foundation (NO. 2018M632229).

References

1. Hirata, K., Kato, T.: Query by visual example - content based image retrieval. In: Pirotte, A., Delobel, C., Gottlob, G. (eds.) Advances in Database Technology - EDBT 1992. LNCS, vol. 580, pp. 56–71. Springer, Heidelberg (1992). https://doi.org/10.1007/BFb0032418
2. Yin, J., Lu, X., Chen, H., Zhao, X., Xiong, N.N.: System resource utilization analysis and prediction for cloud based applications under bursty workloads. Inf. Sci. **279**, 338–357 (2014)
3. Lin, J., Duan, L.Y., Chen, J., Ji, R., Luo, S., Gao, W.: Learning multiple codebooks for low bit rate mobile visual search. In: IEEE International Conference on Acoustics, Speech and Signal Processing, pp. 933–936 (2012)
4. Ji, R., et al.: Location discriminative vocabulary coding for mobile landmark search. Int. J. Comput. Vision **96**, 290–314 (2012)
5. Cui, Q., Mcintosh, S., Sun, H.: Identifying materials of photographic images and photorealistic computer generated graphics based on deep CNNs. Comput. Mater. Continua **55**, 229–241 (2018)
6. Arandjelovic, R., Zisserman, A.: Three things everyone should know to improve object retrieval. In: IEEE Conference on Computer Vision and Pattern Recognition, pp. 2911–2918 (2012)
7. Zhang, Y., Wang, Q., Li, Y., Wu, X.: Sentiment classification based on piecewise pooling convolutional neural network. Comput. Mater. Continua **56**, 285–297 (2018)
8. Paulin, M., Mairal, J., Douze, M., Harchaoui, Z., Perronnin, F., Schmid, C.: Convolutional patch representations for image retrieval: an unsupervised approach. Int. J. Comput. Vision **121**, 1–20 (2016)
9. Babenko, A., Lempitsky, V.: Aggregating deep convolutional features for image retrieval. Computer Science (2015)
10. Yao, Y., Wang, J., Sheng, B., Tan, C., Mi, N.: Self-adjusting slot configurations for homogeneous and heterogeneous Hadoop clusters. IEEE Trans. Cloud Comput. **PP**, 1 (2017)
11. Li, J., Wang, J.Z.: Real-time computerized annotation of pictures. IEEE Trans. Pattern Anal. Mach. Intell. **30**, 985 (2008)
12. Yang, X., Qian, X., Xue, Y.: Scalable mobile image retrieval by exploring contextual saliency. IEEE Trans. Image Process. Publ. IEEE Signal Process. Soc. **24**, 1709 (2015)
13. Gordo, A., Almazán, J., Revaud, J., Larlus, D.: Deep image retrieval: learning global representations for image search. In: Leibe, B., Matas, J., Sebe, N., Welling, M. (eds.) ECCV 2016. LNCS, vol. 9910, pp. 241–257. Springer, Cham (2016). https://doi.org/10.1007/978-3-319-46466-4_15

Formal Specification of Concurrent Enforcement UCON Model with CTL Logic

Xie Lili[1(✉)] and Zhai Zhigang[2]

[1] School of Modern Posts and Institute of Modern Posts,
Nanjing University of Posts and Telecommunications, Nanjing 210003
Jiangsu, China
xielili@njupt.edu.cn

[2] Jiangsu Provincial Government Offices Administration,
Nanjing 210024, Jiangsu, China

Abstract. Usage Control (UCON) model has been considered as the next generation access control model, its distinguishing properties of attribute mutability and decision continuity were more suit for dynamic and open network environment. Just a single usage process was described in form of a state diagram in early formalization, it make it difficult to reason about the interactions of several concurrent usage control process. There were have many formal specifications of Usage Control model. But that formalization all are ambiguous about the interactions of several concurrent usage control process. In this paper we introduced the formal description of $UCON_{ABC}$ model and presented an alternative formalization of UCON using extended Computation Tree Logic (CTL) as the underlying formalism. The branching-time character of CTL makes it more naturally on the specification of concurrent enforcement and makes specify the usage control security policy better.

Keywords: Access control · Usage control · Formal specification · Concurrent enforcement · Computation Tree Logic

1 Introduction

Usage control model (UCON) [1] has been considered as the next generation access control model. As we know, the foremost innovations of UCON are the decision continuity and attribute mutability. This demands specific formal models to express the UCON system behavior and security policy statements. Formalization helps to identify possible system behaviors, whereas formal security policies govern the choices in the behaviors of the system.

To the best of our knowledge, the UCON model was firstly formalized and analyzed using an extension of TLA (Temporal Logic of Actions, TLA) by Zhang et al. [2, 3]. The UCON policy statement is represented in TLA as a logical formula. The logical

This work is partially supported by the Special topics for Jiangsu Education Science 13th Five-Year plan 2016(X-a/2016/08).

X. Sun et al. (Eds.): ICAIS 2019, LNCS 11633, pp. 627–641, 2019.
https://doi.org/10.1007/978-3-030-24265-7_54

formula is built from predicates and actions with logic connectors and temporal operators. But, the formal model focuses on a specification of a single usage control process, interactions between several concurrent usage control processes is not pointed.

An alternative approach to formalize the UCON model is documented by Janicke et al. [4, 5]. The term "distributed usage control" was introduced by Hilty et al. It addresses specific issues on the protection of digital information released by a provider to a remote consumer. The formal model of the distributed usage control is logic based OSL (Obligation Specification Language, OSL) [6]. Other formal descriptions of UCON models include LALR grammar to describe UCON policy [7], POLPA (POlicy Language based on Process Algebra, POLPA) [8], Petri net policy language [9]. "Metric first-order temporal logic" has been put forward by Basin et al. [10, 11], UseCON (Use-based Usage CONtrol, UseCON) [12] etc. Other attempts and studies by Gouglidis et al. adoption of multi-domain cloud systems [13], CH Zhou et al. think PAT is a really great tool for the systematic formal specification and security analysis of UCON [14], Gouglidis et al. express the high-level functional model of the UseCON [15] and Meijuan et al. proposes a data access control model based on XML (eXtensible Markup Language) [16].

So far, a usage control policy is specified either by logical formulae using temporal operators, or by process algebra statements, There is no complete description of the concurrent execution mechanism in UCON model, especially when multiple decisions are executed simultaneously. Considering the persistence of continuity of usage control decisions and the mutability of attributes, the concept of *interval* is very important in UCON model. By introducing the concept of *interval*, not only the concurrent execution of decision-making can be described, but also the authorization can be automatically controlled by *interval*. In addition, because of the uncertainties and concurrent execution of the decision, the state sequence is not sequential execution, and branching is necessary, while branching is a natural feature of CTL logic [17], so we think CTL logic can better describe the UCON model. Improving the syntax and semantic of a language can enhance its expressive ability and analytical skills [18]. In view of the specific situation of UCON model, we extend the CTL logic, give the syntax and semantics of the extended CTL, and formally describe the UCON model. The results show that CTL logic with the concept of *interval* can express the support for the concurrent execution mechanism of UCON model and provide automatic authorization control. And the support of attribute update can better express the security strategy of usage control.

Early formal descriptions of $UCON_{ABC}$ model were mostly based on a single usage process and did not support concurrent execution mechanisms in reality. This paper extends Computation Tree Logic (CTL), defines the grammar and semantics of extended CTL, defines the concurrent usage control process of $UCON_{ABC}$ model with extended CTL language, formally describes each sub-model of $UCON_{ABC}$ model, and shows its expressive ability by enumerating examples.

2 Formal Description of $\mathrm{UCON_{ABC}}$ Model

In Zhang Xinwen's definition, a usage control process is a system state transition graph [2, 3]. A system state is a set of values assigned by all attributes in the system, that is, assigning all attributes of subject and object. UCON model system state transition follows the following process: *initial*, *requesting*, *denied*, *accessing*, *revoked*, *end.* The session starts with the *initial* state, and the subject *s* applies for the right *r* of the object *o* by performing the *tryaccess (s, o, r)* operation, and the system goes to the *requesting* state. If the system refuses the access request, *denyaccess (s, o, r)* is executed, and if the attribute update is executed, the *preupdate* operation is executed. If this authorization is allowed and need attribute update beforehand, the *preupdate* operation is executed, and *permitaccess* (*s, o, r*) is executed, and the system goes to the *accessing* state. In the process of access execution, if the system checks that the access no longer meets the condition requirements, the *revokeaccess (s, o, r)* operation will be executed, and the *revoked* state will be entered, if there are attribute update, the *postupdate* operation will be executed. If there are no *revoke* operations and there are attribute update, perform the *onupdate* operation. At the end of the access, the subject *s* performs *endaccess (s, o, r)* operation, and the system enters the *end* state. If there are attribute update to perform the *postupdate* operation. at this point, a state transition to this end.

Zhang et al. used the extended TLA language to formalize the definition of UCON model [2, 3]. The basic concepts in TLA are "*Values*", "*Variables*" and "*States*", Basic expressions are "*Functions*", "*Predicates*" and "*Actions*", etc. The basic tense operations are □ (*Always*)", "◇ (*Eventually*)", "○ (*Next*)", "■ (*Has-always-been*)", "◆ (*Once*)", "Θ (*Previous*)"; operators are "*U (Until)*" and "*S (Since)*".

According to these preparations, the UCON model can be expressed as a five-tuple: $M = (S, P_A, P_C, A_A, A_B)$. Among them, *S* denotes the set of system state sequence; P_A denotes the finite set of subject and object attribute authorization predicates; P_C denotes the finite set of system attribute condition predicates; A_A denotes the finite set of usage control operations; A_B denotes the finite set of obligation operations.

The grammatical rules of the model are expressed as follows [2, 3]:

$$\emptyset ::= a|p|(\neg\emptyset)|(\emptyset \wedge \emptyset)|\emptyset \rightarrow \emptyset|\Box\emptyset|\Diamond\emptyset|\bigcirc\emptyset|\emptyset U\emptyset|\blacksquare\emptyset|\Diamond\emptyset|\Theta\emptyset|\emptyset S\emptyset|$$

a denotes operations, *p* denotes predicates, and ø denotes formulas.

There are several operations of the model, including system state transition operation and attribute update operation.

(1) *tryaccess* (*s, o, r*): make new requests for access (*s, o, r*), subject's request for execution.
(2) *permitaccess* (*s, o, r*): access requests (*s, o, r*) are allowed to be executed automatically by the system.
(3) *denyaccess* (*s, o, r*): denied access requests (*s, o, r*), which are automatically executed by the system.
(4) *revokeaccess* (*s, o, r*): revoke the executing access process (*s, o, r*), which is automatically executed by the system.
(5) *endaccess*(*s, o, r*): end the access process (*s, o, r*), executed by the subject.

(6) *preupdate* (*attribute*): update subject and object attributes or system attributes before accessing, which is executed automatically by the system.
(7) *onupdate* (*attribute*): update subject and object attributes or system attributes in the process of accessing, which is executed automatically by the system.
(8) *postupdate* (*attribute*): update subject and object attributes or system attributes after the end of the access, which is executed automatically by the system.

Based on this, a formal definition of the sub-model of UCON model is given. Control Rules (CRs) and Update Rules (URs) for the entire UCON model are described as follows [2, 3]:

CR1: $permitaccess(s, o, r) \rightarrow \Diamond\, (tryaccess(s, o, r) \wedge (\wedge_{ni} pa_{ni}) \wedge (\wedge_{nk} pc_{nk})) \wedge (\wedge_{nj} \Diamond\, ob_{nj})$
CR2: $\Box(\neg((\wedge_{ni} pa_{ni}) \wedge (\wedge_{nj}(pb_{nj1} \wedge \ldots \wedge pb_{njknj} \rightarrow ob_{nj})) \wedge (\wedge_{nk} pc_{nk})) \wedge (states(s, o, r) = accessing) \rightarrow revokeaccess(s, o, r))$

UR1: $permitaccess(s, o, r) \rightarrow \Diamond preupdate(attribute)$
UR2: $permitaccess(s, o, r) \rightarrow \Diamond(onupdate(attribute) \wedge \Diamond(endaccess(s, o, r) \vee revokeaccess(s, o, r)))$
UR3: $\Box(state(s, o, r) = accessing \rightarrow onupdate(attribute))$
UR4: $\Box((state(s, o, r) = accessing) \wedge p_{u1} \wedge \ldots p_{uj} \rightarrow onupdate(attribute))$
UR5: $endaccess(s, o, r) \rightarrow \Diamond\, postupdate(attribute)$
UR6: $revokeaccess(s, o, r) \rightarrow \Diamond\, postupdate(attribute)$

It should be noted that all the formal definitions and descriptions here are for a single usage control process in the model. This definition is limited in time. Several usage control processes are executed sequentially one after another. The interaction of several concurrent usage requirements is not considered, and even the sequence of usage control requirements is not considered. This complicates formal policy analysis. An alternative approach to formalize the UCON model is documented by Janicke et al. [4, 5]. They redefines the semantics of usage control process and request. Their approach deals mostly with continuous on-going usage scenarios. The proposed formal model assumes several usage control requests within one usage control process. The formalization is based on ITL (Interval Temporal Logic, ITL) and the semantics and syntax of ITL can be found in [4, 5]. The advantage of this method is that the definition assumptions are less, so the whole definition is simpler, which makes it more natural to define concurrent operations and sequence of operations.

The key notion of ITL is the *interval*. The *interval* is a (in)finite sequence of system states. The grammatical definitions in ITL are as follows [4]:

$$e ::= m|a|A|g(e_1, \ldots, e_n) \mid \bigcirc v|fin\ v$$
$$f ::= p(e_1, \ldots, e_n)| \neg f|f_1 \wedge f_2|\forall v \times f|\ skip\ |f_1;f_2|f^*$$

Here μ is an integer, a is a static variable, A is a state variable, v is a static variable or a state variable, g is a function symbol, p is a predicate symbol. See [4] for a detailed definition. A usage control process definition is used to do:

$$\begin{aligned} usage(s,o,r) \cong\ & tryaccess(s,o,r); \\ & (denyaccess(s,o,r) \oplus (preupdate(s,o,r) \wedge permitaccess(s,o,r); \\ & (((usage(s,o',r') \oplus idle(s))^{*} \oplus do(s,o,r)) \wedge onupdate(s,o,r)); \\ & (revokeaccess(s,o,r) \oplus endaccess(s,o,r)); \\ & postupdate(s,o,r))) \end{aligned}$$

This representation is not intuitive, and only describes the states that the same user opens multiple tasks, in fact, the user can only execute one decision at a time, when executing the current decision, other decisions will be in standby state, which is not really concurrent execution. The term "distributed usage control" was introduced by Hilty et al. It addresses specific issues on the protection of digital information released by a provider to a remote consumer.

Neither TLA nor ITL provides support for *post-obligation*. Distributed usage control refers to how to control data after publication. This definition of distributed usage control naturally supports *post-obligation.* In order to formally describe it, reference [6] proposes a universal Obligation Specification Language (OSL) to describe it. Describes distributed usage control, which can cover all kinds of usage control requirements. This concept of distributed usage control is different from UCON model, but it also provides support for decision continuity. The formal model of the distributed usage control is logic based OSL [6]. But OSL is for obligation operations, which must be performed after data is published, very different from the UCON definition. Moreover, the discussion of attribute variability in distributed usage control is insufficient. Reference [7] defines a LALR grammar to describe UCON policy. This grammar is simple and clear. It can be used to describe various access control strategies including DAC, MAC, RBAC and UCON. Another approach formalizing UCON in terms of process algebra named POLPA (POlicy Language based on Process Algebra, POLPA) [8], The grammar of the language is defined and the UCON model is formally described with the language. Katt et al. proposed a new policy definition language based on Petri nets to define UCON [9]. A policy definition language based on Colored Petri Nets (CP-net) was proposed. This strategy supports continuous control by defining Petri net like behavior definitions; and by defining *post-obligation,* supports the set of rule expression set of authorization and obligation; Supports concurrency control of shared resources. "Metric first-order temporal logic" has been put forward by David Basin et al. [10]. It adds timing control, tries to describe usage control, and simulates the implementation of China Wall strategy and separation of responsibilities. Temporal logic is applied to provide unambiguous semantics to functions supported by usage models, such as attribute mutability and continuity of decision [11]. UseCON (Use-based Usage CONtrol, UseCON) is a usage control model that provides enhanced expressiveness compared to existing access/usage control models and applicable in new computing paradigms [12]. Gouglidis et al. think the existence of an efficient management process for the enforcement of security policies among the participating cloud systems would facilitate the adoption of multi-domain cloud systems [13]. Zhou et al. think PAT is a really great tool for the systematic formal specification and security analysis of UCON [14]. Gouglidis et al. express the high-level functional model of the UseCON usage control model in the TLA+ formal specification language [15]. Wang et al. proposes a data access control model for individual users based on the semantic integration nature of XML data [16].

3 Syntax and Semantics of CTL

In previous formal descriptions of UCON models, it was assumed that if all paths satisfy a formal formula starting from a given state, then the state of the defined system satisfies this formal formula, where the universal quantifier of all paths is defined by default. This is not the case with UCON. Concurrent execution in the model can not be expressed entirely in this sequence. This is not really concurrent execution. We consider branches in CTL logic to describe concurrent execution mechanisms in UCON models. Before that, we first give the definition of *interval*.

Definition 1. Π is a set of non-spatial sequences (*intervals*) on the natural number N, I is an element in Π, denoted as $[c, d)$, where $c \in$ N, $d \in$ N $\cup$ $\{\infty\}$, and $c < d$, i.e. $[c, d)$: = $\{a \in \mathrm{N} \mid c \leq a<d\}$. i is an element in I, $i \in$ N.

In the case of the UCON model, I refers to a period of time; this period can be infinite or finite, mainly to represent the execution phase of the current use decision.

In order to save space, the definitions of state transition and predicate in UCON model are the same as those in reference [3]. State is to assign corresponding values to variables. Authorization and condition components are described by predicates and obligations are described by operations. CTL syntax does not include operations, there is no definition of thc "*Once*" operator, although the "*Once*" operator can be described by other operations, but for the sake of simplicity, we expand the CTL logic, adding the concept of operation, using the operator "*Once*" instead of the operator "*Next*", adding *interval* control, and so on. The improved CTL syntax is as follows (for simplicity, still call it CTL logic).

Definition 2. The syntax of CTL formulas is defined by the following recursive rules:

$$\begin{aligned}\emptyset ::= & \top|\bot|a|p|(\neg\emptyset)|(\emptyset\wedge\emptyset)|(\emptyset\vee\emptyset)|\emptyset\\ & \rightarrow\emptyset|AO_I\emptyset|EO_I\emptyset|AF_I\emptyset|EF_I\emptyset|AG_I\emptyset|EG_I\emptyset|A(\emptyset U_I\emptyset)|E(\emptyset U_I\emptyset)|\end{aligned}$$

where a is an action, p is a predicate symbol.

Informally, A and E mean "*along all paths*" and "*along at least one path*", respectively; whereas O, F, G and U refer to "*once state*", "*some future state*", "*all future states*", and "*Until*".

The semantic definition of CTL logic is as follows:

Definition 3. Let $M = (S, \rightarrow, L)$ be a model of CTL, S is an infinite state sequence, $s \in S$; "$\rightarrow$" is a transitional relation; L is a marker function $L{:}S \rightarrow P$, $L(s)$ is a set of atomic propositions accompanied by States s; and $i \in N$, is a point in I. ø is a CTL formula. $M, s, i \vDash ø$ are defined by structural induction.

1. $M, s, i \vDash \top$ for all states s;
2. $M, s, i \nvDash \bot$ for all states s;
3. $M, s, i \mid= a$ iff $s_i[[a]]s_{i+1}, i \geq 0$, $a \in A_A \cup A_B$, and s_{i+1} is the next state of s_i in s;
4. $M, s, i \vDash p$ iff $p \in L(s)$
5. $M, s, i \vDash \neg ø$ iff $M, s, i \nvDash ø$
6. $M, s, i \vDash ø_1 \wedge ø_2$ iff $M, s, i \vDash ø_1$ and $M, s, i \vDash ø_2$
7. $M, s, i \vDash ø_1 \vee ø_2$ iff $M, s, i \vDash ø_1$ or $M, s, i \vDash ø_2$
8. $M, s, i \vDash ø_1 \rightarrow ø_2$ iff $M, s, i \nvDash ø$ or $M, s, i \vDash ø_2$
9. $M, s, i \vDash \mathrm{AO_I}ø$ iff $M, s_{i-1}, i-1 \vDash ø$ for all states $s_{i-1}(i-1, i \in I)$ with $s_{i-1} \rightarrow s_i$.
10. $M, s, i \vDash \mathrm{EO_I}ø$ iff $M, s_{i-1}, i-1 \vDash ø$ for all states $s_{i-1}(i-1, i \in I)$with $s_{i-1} \rightarrow s_i$.
11. $M, s, i \vDash \mathrm{AG_I}ø$ iff for all paths $s = s_1 \rightarrow s_2 \rightarrow s_3 \rightarrow \ldots$, and all states s_j $(j \geq 1)$ along the path, we have $M, s_j, i \vDash ø$.
12. $M, s, i \vDash \mathrm{EG_I}ø$ iff there is some path $s = s_1 \rightarrow s_2 \rightarrow s_3 \rightarrow \ldots$, such that for all states s_j $(j \geq 1)$ along the path, we have $M, s_i, i \vDash ø$.
13. $M, s, i \vDash \mathrm{AF_I}ø$ iff for all paths $s = s_1 \rightarrow s_2 \rightarrow s_3 \rightarrow \ldots$, there is some state $s_j(j$ 1) along the path, for which $M, s_i, i \vDash ø$ in I.
14. $M, s, i \vDash \mathrm{EF_I}ø$ iff for some path $s = s_1 \rightarrow s_2 \rightarrow s_3 \rightarrow \ldots$, and some state s_j $(j \geq 1)$ along the path, we have $M, s_i, i \vDash ø$ in I.
15. $M, s, i \vDash \mathrm{A}[ø_1 \mathrm{U_I} ø_2]$ iff for all paths $s = s_1 \rightarrow s_2 \rightarrow s_3 \rightarrow \ldots$ there is s ome state s_j along the path, such that $M, s_j, i \vDash ø_2$ and $M, s_k, i \vDash ø_1$, for all $1 \leq k < j$ in I.
16. $M, s, i \vDash \mathrm{E}[ø_1 \mathrm{U_I} ø_2]$ iff for some path $s = s_1 \rightarrow s_2 \rightarrow s_3 \rightarrow \ldots$, there is some state s_j along the path, such that $M, s_j, i \vDash ø_2$ and $M, s_k, i \vDash ø_1$ for all $1 \leq k < j$ in I.

4 CTL Description of UCON Model

Definition 4. Subject and object are represented by *S* and *O* respectively, while *SYS* represents system; *ATT(S)*, *ATT(O)* and *ATT(SYS)* respectively represent subject attribute set, object attribute set and system attribute set; *s.a*, *o.a* and *sys.a* respectively represent some attribute of subject *s*, object *o* and system *sys*, such a *s.id* represents the identifier of subject *s*, *o.role* represents the role of object *o*, *sys.time* represents the system attribute of system time, and the assignment of attributes is expressed by *ent. att* = *value*, such as *s.id* = 192.168.0.1 for the IP address of subject *s* is 192.168.0.1.

Definition 5. *state* represents system state. A system state is actually a mapping of subject attribute, object attribute and system attribute at a certain time in the system, that is:

$$state \rightarrow 2^{ATT(S) \times ATT(O) \times ATT(SYS)}$$

Definition 6. *R* represents rights set, (*s, o, r*) represents a usage control process, That is, at some point, the subject *s* requests a certain right *r* over the object *o*. The right *R* here has a rich meaning. If it is in the database system, *R* includes *read, write, add, delete, modify* and other operations. In the operating system, in addition to the above operations, *R* also contains *execute, open, click* operations for files or entities. We often use *state* (*s, o, r*) to represent a usage control process in a system.

Definition 7. The predicate is a Boolean expression composed of variables, operators and constants. Variables include subject and object attributes, system attributes, etc. It is a mapping from system state to Boolean value, that is, system state satisfies a predicate, that is, the value of subject and object attributes and system attributes in the system state satisfies this predicate expression. For example, *s.clearance* ≥ *o.classification* denotes that the subject security level dominates the object classification.
In the formal description of the following model, the judgment of authorization policy and conditional policy is described by predicates, *pa* represents an authorization predicate, *pc* represents a conditional predicate.

Definition 8. Operations are a new feature of usage control models, including usage control operations and obligation operations; usage control operations include the following:

tryaccess (*s, o, r*): initiate an access control request, executed by the subject.
Permitaccess (*s, o, r*): allow an access control request to be executed by the system.
revokeaccess (*s, o, r*): revoke an access control request, executed by the system.
denyaccess (*s, o, r*): deny an access control request, executed by the system.
endaccess (*s, o, r*): end an access control request, executed by the subject.

According to the stages of usage control process, attribute updating operation includes *preupdate*(*attribute*), *onupdate*(*attribute*) and *postupdate*(*attribute*), which represent the updating of attribute before usage control process execution, the updating of attribute ongoing usage control process execution and the updating of attribute after usage control process execution. The attribute values include subject attribute, object attribute and system attributes.

Obligations operation is such operations as clicking buttons and opening windows. It is expressed by $ob(s_b, o_b)$. *ob* denotes the name of obligations operation. s_b denotes the subject of obligation and o_b denotes the object of obligation.

According to the syntax and semantics of the above CTL logic, the usage decisions of the UCON model are described below:

$$
\begin{aligned}
&usage(s,o,r) := (\mathrm{EO_{Ik}}(tryaccess(s,o,r) \wedge (\wedge_{\mathrm{ni}} pa_{\mathrm{ni}}) \wedge (\wedge_{\mathrm{nj}} pc_{\mathrm{nj}})) \wedge \mathrm{AO_I}(\wedge_{\mathrm{nl}} ob_{\mathrm{nl}}) \\
&\to permitaccess(s,o,r) \wedge \mathrm{EG_{Ik}}(preupdate(attribute) \vee \emptyset); \\
&\mathrm{EG_{Ik}}((state(s,o,r) = accessing) \wedge p_{u1} \wedge \ldots p_{uj} \to \mathrm{EG_{Ik}}(onupdate(attribute) \vee \emptyset)); \\
&\mathrm{AF_{Ik}}(\neg((\wedge_{\mathrm{ni}} pa_{\mathrm{ni}}) \wedge (\wedge_{\mathrm{nj}}(pb_{\mathrm{nj1}} \wedge \ldots \wedge pb_{\mathrm{njknj}} \to ob_{\mathrm{nj}})) \wedge (\wedge_{\mathrm{nl}} pc_{\mathrm{nl}})) \wedge (states(s,o,r) = accessing) \to \\
&(revokeaccess(s,o,r) \wedge \mathrm{EF_{Ik}}(onupdate(attribute) \vee \emptyset)); \\
&\mathrm{AF_{Ik}}(endaccess(s,o,r)) \to \mathrm{EF_{Ik}}(postupdate(attribute) \vee \emptyset)).
\end{aligned}
$$

Users can execute multiple usage control decisions simultaneously, which may be in the same *interval* or in different *intervals*. On the same object, there may also be multiple users performing access at the same time, occupying the same or different *intervals*. That is to say, whether the same user makes multiple usage control decisions at the same time, or multiple usage control decisions are executed on the same object at the same time, this description method can be used to describe. When a user submits an usage control request, it verifies whether the authorization predicate and condition predicate are valid, and verifies whether the obligation operation is performed. If all the requests are satisfied, it agrees to the usage control and performs attribute updating or not. In the process of accessing decision, the attribute is updated or not updated. If the authorization predicate or obligation operation is no longer satisfied or the condition predicate is no longer satisfied during the usage control process, the access is revoked and the attribute update operation or no operation is performed. After execution of the access decision, the attribute is updated or not updated.

The core components of the UCON model are Authorization, oBligation, and Condition. Combined with the two stages of the use of decision-making, it is used before and in use (expressed in *pre* and *ongoing*). Four states of attribute updating: no attribute updating, before updating, during updating and after updating (represented by 0, 1, 2, 3 respectively); The UCON model can be divided into 24 sub models. $\{\mathrm{A, B, C}\} \times \{\mathrm{pre, ongoing}\} \times \{0, 1, 2, 3\} = 24$,we are not going to formalize the 24 sub-models in detail, but to analyze the situation.

4.1 UCON$_{\mathbf{preA}}$

First, we must satisfy:

$$\bigcup_{k \in N, Ik \in II} \mathrm{EO}_{\mathrm{Ik}}\left(tryaccess(s,o,r) \wedge (p_1 \wedge \ldots\ldots \wedge p_j)\right) \rightarrow permit(s,o,r);$$

This is a prerequisite, that is, under certain *interval* conditions, to meet all the requirements of the authorization predicate premise, the subject has access to the object. If there are attribute updates, the following update operations are performed separately according to the attribute updates:*preupdate*(*attribute*), *onupdate*(*attribute*) and *postupdate*(*attribute*).

The pre-authorization sub-model is essentially no different from the traditional access control model. The traditional access control model can basically be simulated using this sub-model. We use several examples to show the expressive ability of the pre-authorization sub-model.

Example 1: MAC *L*: security level markers satisfying partial order relations
clearance: $S \rightarrow L$
classification: $O \rightarrow L$
ATT(*S*) = $\{clearance\}$
ATT(*O*) = $\{classification\}$

$$permitaccess(s,o,read) \rightarrow \mathrm{EO}_{\mathrm{Ik}}(tryaccess(s,o,read) \wedge (s.clearance \geq o.classification))$$
$$permitaccess(s,o,write) \rightarrow \mathrm{EO}_{\mathrm{Ik}}(tryaccess(s,o,write) \wedge (s.clearance \leq o.classification))$$

Example 2: DAC

N: is a set of identifiers
id: $S \rightarrow N$
ACL: $O \rightarrow 2^{N \times R}$
$ATT(S) = \{id\}$
$ATT(O) = \{ACL\}$

$$permitaccess(s,o,r) \rightarrow \mathrm{EO}_{\mathrm{Ik}}(tryaccess(s,o,write) \wedge ((s.id,\ r) \in o.acl))$$

Example 3: DRM

M: credit point value
credit: $S \rightarrow M$
value: $O \rightarrow M$
$\mathrm{ATT}(S) = \{credit\}$
$\mathrm{ATT}(O) = \{value\}$

$$permitaccess(s,o,read) \rightarrow \mathrm{EO}_{\mathrm{Ik}}(tryaccess(s,o,read) \wedge (s.credit \geq o.value)) \wedge \mathrm{EO}_{\mathrm{Ik}}(preupdate(s.credit))$$

preupdate (s, credit):*s.credit' = s.credit-o.value*

4.2 $\mathbf{UCON_{onA}}$

First, we must satisfy:

$$\bigcup_{k \in N, Ik \in II} \mathrm{AG}_{\mathrm{Ik}}(\neg(p_1 \wedge \ldots\ldots \wedge p_j) \wedge (state(s,o,r) = accessing) \rightarrow revokeaccess(s,o,r));$$

In the process of access decision execution, if an authorization predicate is no longer satisfied, the access process is revoked. This process may also be ended by the user itself:

$$\bigcup_{k \in N, Ik \in II} (state(s,o,r) = accessing) \wedge (\wedge_j p_j)\mathrm{AU}_{\mathrm{Ik}}(endaccess(s,o,r));$$

That is to say, the access execution process can be ended by the user, whether the authorization predicate satisfies the requirement after termination is not done.

Similarly, if there are attribute updates, the following update operations are performed separately according to the attribute updates: *preupdate(attribute)*, *onupdate (attribute)* and *postupdate(attribute)*.

Example 4: An example is given to execute revocation operations according to the use of idle time. At the same time, the number of subjects performing revocation operations on objects can not exceed 10. If more than 10 subjects are executed, the usage control process of subjects with the longest duration of idle time can be revoked automatically.

T: set of idle time satisfying partial order relation;
UN: number of subjects performing usage control operations on objects at the same time;
N: set of identifier;
idleTime: $S \rightarrow T$
accessMem: $O \rightarrow 2^S$
UN: $O \rightarrow |accessMem|$
ATT(*S*) = { *idleTime*, *status*}
ATT(*O*) = { *accessMem*, *UN* }

$Permitaccess(s,o,r) \rightarrow \mathrm{EO}_{\mathrm{Ik}}(tryaccess(s,o,r) \wedge preupdate(s.idleTime) \wedge preupdate(o.accessMem))$
$preupdate(s.idleTime) : s.idleTime' = 0$
$preupdate(o.accessMem) : o.accessMem' = o.accessMem \cup \{s\}$
$\mathrm{AG}_{\mathrm{Ik}}(\neg(o.UN \leq 10) \wedge (state(s,o,r) = accessing) \wedge (s.idleTime = Max_{idleTime}(o.accessMem))$
$\rightarrow revokeaccess(s,o,r))$
$\mathrm{AG}_{\mathrm{Ik}}((state(s,o,r) = accessing) \wedge (s.status = idle) \rightarrow onupdate(s.idleTime))$
$onupdate(s.idleTime) : s.idleTime' = s.idleTime + 1$
$endaccess(s,o,r) \vee revokeaccess(s,o,r) \rightarrow \mathrm{AG}_{\mathrm{Ik}} postupdate(o.accessMem)$
$postupdate(o.accessMem) : o.accessMem' = o.accessMem - \{s\}$

4.3 $\mathbf{UCON_{preB}}$

First, we must satisfy:

$$\bigcup_{k \in N, Ik \in II} \mathrm{EO}_{\mathrm{Ik}}\left(tryaccess(s,o,r) \wedge \mathrm{AO}_{\mathrm{Ik}}\left(\wedge_{\mathrm{j}} ob_{\mathrm{j}}\right)\right) \rightarrow permitaccess(s,o,r);$$

The premise of obtaining the right of access is that all obligation actions must be satisfied. Similarly, concurrent execution mechanisms are also supported here. If there are attribute update operations, add *preupdate(attribute)*, *onupdate(attribute)* and *postupdate(attribute)*.

Example 5: Give an example that access to a network resource must obtain third-party authentication consent:

OBS = *S*
OBO = {*license_agreement*}
OB = {*agree*}
getPreOBL (*s*, *o*, *r*) = {(*s*, *license_agreement*, *agree*)}
preFulfilled: $OBS \times OBO \times OB \rightarrow \{true, false\}$

$preB(s,o,r) = \wedge_{(obs,obo,ob) \in getPreOBL(s,o,r)} preFulfilled(obs,obo,ob)$
$permitaccess(s,o,order) \rightarrow \mathrm{EO}_{\mathrm{Ik}} tryaccess(s,o,order) \wedge \mathrm{EO}_{\mathrm{Ik}}(preB(s,license\_agreement,\ agree))$

4.4 $\mathbf{UCON_{onB}}$

The Ongoing obligation sub-model is the middle stage of decision execution, when the *permitaccess* has been executed and has entered the ongoing stage, then the strategy that must be met is:

$$\bigcup_{k \in N, Ik \in II} \mathrm{AG}_{\mathrm{Ik}}(\neg(\wedge_j (p_{j1} \wedge \ldots\ldots \wedge p_{jkj} \rightarrow ob_j)) \wedge (state(s,o,r) = accessing) \rightarrow revokeaccess(s,o,r));$$

Here, $p_{j1}, \ldots, p_{jkj}$ is a predicate about the attribute of subject and object, and ob_j is obligation action when $p_{j1}, \ldots, p_{jkj}$ for all states s that is, in a certain *interval*, when a obligation action that should be performed is not executed, the system automatically revokes the access.

Actually, the operation of obligation here is not necessarily related to the attributes of subject and object. If only the operation of obligation subject is considered, there are:

$$\bigcup_{k \in N, Ik \in II} \mathrm{AG}_{\mathrm{Ik}}(\neg(\wedge_j ob_j) \wedge (state(s,o,r) = accessing) \rightarrow revokeaccess(s,o,r));$$

That is to say, the implementation process in a certain *interval* in the decision-making, ongoing obligation sub-model, or all of the obligation action of operating system meet, or revoke access to execution.

Similar to the authorization sub-model, there are also situations where the user actively end the access:

$$\bigcup_{k \in N, Ik \in II} (state(s,o,r) = accessing) \wedge (\wedge_j ob_j) \mathrm{AU}_{\mathrm{Ik}}(endaccess(s,o,r));$$

Similarly, add operations such as *preupdate(attribute)*, *onupdate(attribute)* and *postupdate(attribute)* if an attribute is updated.

Example 6: Advertising windows must be kept active during accessing:

$OBS = S$
$OBO = \{ad\_window\}$
$OB = \{keep\_active\}$
$getOnOBL\ (s,\ o,\ r) = \{(s,\ ad\_window,\ keep\_active)\}$
$onFulfilled$: $OBS \times OBO \times OB \rightarrow \{true, false\}$

$$onB(s,o,r) = \wedge_{(obs,obo,ob)\in getOnOBL(s,o,r)} onFulfilled(obs,obo,ob)$$

$$\mathrm{AG_{Ik}}(\neg(onB(s,o,r)) \wedge (state(s,o,r) = accessing) \rightarrow revokeaccess(s,o,r))$$

4.5 UCON$_{\mathbf{preC}}$

In general, conditional constraints do not change the attributes of the subject and object, so there is no need to update operation, according to the access policy requirements, there are:

$$\bigcup_{k\in N, Ik\in II} permitaccess(s,o,r) \rightarrow \mathrm{EO_{Ik}}(tryaccess(s,o,r) \wedge (pc_1 \wedge \ldots\ldots \wedge pc_j));$$

pc_j is a conditional predicate, that is, in a certain *interval*, as long as all the conditional predicates are satisfied, access rights can be granted.

Similarly, add operations such as *preupdate(attribute)*, *onupdate(attribute)* and *postupdate(attribute)* if an attribute is updated.

Example 7: A data resource can only execute access control requests during daytime hours, that is, from 8 a.m. to 5 p.m.

$$ATT(sys) = \{currentTime\}$$

$$\mathrm{EO_{Ik}}(tryaccess(s,o,r) \wedge (8am \leq currentTime \leq 5pm)) \rightarrow permitaccess(s,o,r)$$

4.6 UCON$_{\mathbf{onC}}$

Similarly, the ongoing condition sub-model has nothing to do with the attributes of subject and object, so there is no problem of attribute updating, as long as the conditional strategy is satisfied:

$$\bigcup_{k\in N, Ik\in II} \mathrm{EG_{Ik}}(\neg(pc_1 \wedge \ldots\ldots \wedge pc_j) \wedge (state(s,o,r) = accessing) \rightarrow revokeaccess(s,o,r));$$

That is, in the process of access execution in a certain *interval*, if any condition predicate is no longer satisfied, the access is revoked.

Similarly, add operations such as *preupdate(attribute)*, *onupdate(attribute)* and *postupdate(attribute)* if an attribute is updated.

Example 8: As in the example above, if an executing access control requests finds that it is no longer working during the day, the access control request is revoked.

$$\mathrm{EG_{Ik}}(\neg(8am \leq currentTime \leq 5pm) \wedge (state(s,o,r) = accessing) \rightarrow revokeaccess(s,o,r))$$

5 Conclusion

As far as a security model is concerned, formal description is very important for analyzing the security and expressiveness of the model. This paper analyzes the advantages and disadvantages of previous formal descriptions of the UCON model, proposes an improved CTL logic, defines the grammar and semantics of improved CTL, points out that the improved CTL is more suitable for describing the UCON model, and gives a formal specification of concurrent enforcement UCON model, The expressive ability of the formal description is demonstrated by several examples.

References

1. Park, J., Sandhu, R.: The $UCON_{ABC}$ Usage Control Model. ACM Trans. Inf. Syst. Secur. **7** (1), 128–174 (2004)
2. Zhang, X.W., Park, J., Presicce, F.P., et al.: A logical specification for usage control. In: Proceedings of the 9th ACM Symposium on Access Control Models and Technologies, pp. 1–10. ACM, New York (2004)
3. Zhang, X.W., Presicces, F.P., Sandhu, R., et al.: Formal model and policy specification of usage control. ACM Trans. Inf. Syst. Secur. **8**(4), 351–387 (2005)
4. Janicke, H., Cau, A., Zedan, H.: A note on the formalisation of UCON. In: Proceedings of the 12th ACM Symposium on Access Control Models and Technologies, pp. 163–168. ACM, New York (2007)
5. Janicke, H., Cau, A., Siewe, F., et al.: Concurrent enforcement of usage control policies. In: Proceedings of the 2008 IEEE Workshop on Policies for Distributed Systems and Networks, pp. 111–118. IEEE Computer Society, Washington (2008)
6. Hilty, M., Pretschner, A., Basin, D., Schaefer, C., Walter, T.: A policy language for distributed usage control. In: Biskup, J., López, J. (eds.) ESORICS 2007. LNCS, vol. 4734, pp. 531–546. Springer, Heidelberg (2007). https://doi.org/10.1007/978-3-540-74835-9_35
7. Teigão, R., Maziero, C., Santin, A.: A grammar for specifying usage control policies. In: 2007 IEEE International Conference on Communications, pp. 1379–1384. IEEE Computer Society, Washington (2007)
8. Martinelli, F., Mori, P.: A model for usage control in GRID systems. In: Proceedings of the 3rd International Conference on Security and Privacy in Communication Networks, pp. 169–175. IEEE, Washington (2007)
9. Katt, B., Zhang, X., Hafner, M.: Towards a usage control policy specification with Petri Nets. In: Meersman, R., Dillon, T., Herrero, P. (eds.) OTM 2009. LNCS, vol. 5871, pp. 905–912. Springer, Heidelberg (2009). https://doi.org/10.1007/978-3-642-05151-7_11
10. Basin, D., Klaedtke, F., Müller, S.: Monitoring security policies with metric first-order temporal logic. In: Proceedings of the 15th ACM Symposium on Access Control Models and Technologies, pp. 23–33. ACM, New York (2010)
11. Lazouski, A., Martinelli, F., Mori, P.: Usage control in computer security: a survey. Comput. Sci. Rev. **4**(2), 81–99 (2010)
12. Grompanopoulos, C., Gouglidis, A., Mavridis, I.: A use-based approach for enhancing UCON. In: Security and Trust Management, pp. 81–96 (2013)
13. Gouglidis, A., Mavridis, I., Vincent, C.H.: Security policy verification for multi-domains in cloud systems. Int. J. Inf. Secur. **13**(2), 97–111 (2014)

14. Zhou, C.H., Chen, W.H., Liu, Z.F.: Formal specification and security verification of usage control model based on PAT. Chin. J. Network Inf. Secur. (2016)
15. Gouglidis, A., Grompanopoulos, C., Mavridou, A.: Formal verification of usage control models: a case study of UseCON Using TLA+. http://cn.arxiv.org/pdf/1806.09848v1. Accessed 2 Aug 2018
16. Meijuan, W., Jian, W., Lihong, G., et al.: Inverted XML access control model based on ontology semantic dependency. CMC: Comput. Mater. Continua **55**(3), 465–482 (2018)
17. Huth, M., Ryan, M.: Logic in Computer Science: Modelling and Reasoning about Systems, 2nd edn. Cambridge University Press, Cambridge (2004)
18. Suzhen, W., Lu, Z., Yanpiao, Z., et al.: Natural language semantic construction based on cloud database. CMC: Comput. Mater. Continua **57**(3), 603–619 (2018)

Design of Real-Time Resource-Aware Network Resource Allocation Mechanism Under SDN Background

Ningcheng Yuan[1], Zhe Zhang[2(✉)], Wenjing Li[2], Feng Qi[1], Shaoyong Guo[1], Xuesong Qiu[1], and Wenchen He[1]

[1] Beijing University of Posts and Telecommunications, Beijing, China
yuan_nc@qq.com

[2] State Grid Information Industry Group Co., Ltd., Beijing, China
zhangzhe@sgitg.sgcc.com.cn

Abstract. As the proportion of various types of multimedia services in the mobile Internet continues to increase, the traditional IP network architecture has been difficult to meet the business needs due to the high requirements in quality of service (QoS) for multimedia services. Software Defined Network (SDN) has received extensive attention as an important means of implementing network virtualization. In view of the problem of resource utilization efficiency and fault recovery capability in the network, and in order to meet the QoS requirements of different services, this paper proposes the network resource allocation and reliability guarantee mechanism of mobile core network. The Real-time resource-aware balanced allocation algorithm (RRBA) performs real-time monitoring on the utilization status of the substrate network resources, and preferentially allocates the services to the physical paths with more available resources, so as to achieve the balance of the network load as much as possible. In addition, in order to ensure the reliability of the network, a network mapping mechanism with backup is proposed. When the resource is allocated, the virtual network provides two network mapping results. In this way, when the original path fails, network traffic can be recovered faster. The simulation results show that on the basis of improving the efficiency of resource utilization, the reliability of the network is also guaranteed.

Keywords: SDN · Mobile network · Resource allocation · Network reliability

1 Introduction

Compared with other network services, multimedia services have higher requirements in terms of interactivity, integration and synchronization. QoS describes one aspect of multimedia service performance, and quantifies the quality of communication between the two parties in terms of delay and packet loss rate. The evaluation parameters of QoS mainly include transmission rate, transmission delay, delay jitter, arrival rate and security, etc. For different types of services, each parameter has different strict value ranges. The SDN-based network architecture makes it easier to realize the benefits of network virtualization. The basic idea is to centrally manage the network infrastructure

X. Sun et al. (Eds.): ICAIS 2019, LNCS 11633, pp. 642–652, 2019.
https://doi.org/10.1007/978-3-030-24265-7_55

hardware with software, and separate the control layer and the forwarding layer to make it programmable. In the context of SDN, network re-source allocation is an important part of the successful deployment of network services. At the same time, facing the physical path failure it's necessary to improve the survivability of the network and ensure the operation of the service.

The current research on resource allocation in the context of SDN has the following related research: in [1]. The proposed mechanism is driven by QoE, which can dynamically allocate network tasks to virtual network nodes and optimize end-to-end transmission quality. The best combination and collaboration between node functions provides users with optimized QoE quality. In order to ensure the final quality, adjacent nodes assist in the allocation of nodes. Especially for streaming media services, the method in this paper improves the quality of video. The SD-WAN architecture designed in [2] enhances the utilization efficiency of network resources and improves the quality of service of distributed services. Considering the demand of network services and the use status of network resources, the path planning problem is transformed into ILP problem. Finally, the Branch-and-Cut algorithm with polynomial time complexity is used to solve the target problem. Considering the network bandwidth, [3] can maximize the utilization efficiency of the network and improve the service completion. The simulation results show that under the background of the mechanism of optimizing bandwidth allocation proposed in this paper, even if SDN equipment is limited, it can still improve user satisfaction. Compared with other similar algorithms, the strategy in this paper takes more account of users' needs. The load balance problem of SDN method under the background of data center is pointed out in [4]. Because of the flow between the switch and the controller, the response time of the controller is prolonged. [5] studied wireless sensor networks, and proposed an algorithm based on Particle Swarm Optimization for network deployment. In this paper, a dynamic allocation algorithm for switches is proposed, which converts the problem into a one-to-many matching problem using game theory, so that each controller is limited to the minimum load. In addition, a stable matching algorithm between switch and controller is designed to maintain load balance and reduce delay.

Others have proposed other SDN-based virtual resource allocation algorithms [6–9]. However, in the current research situation of virtual resource allocation in the context of mobile core networks, the following problems still need to be solved: (1) the degree of utilization of substrate network resources is not balanced; (2) the reliability of the network is insufficient; (3) differentiated QoS requirements for different services is not considered.

2 System Model

2.1 System Overview

We first proposed a network virtualization system architecture based on SDN. The network control model of SDN is divided into physical plane, control plane and application plane from bottom to top. The physical plane is the substrate network resource. The SDN controller is a logically centralized entity that is responsible for transforming requirements from the application layer to the data path and providing the application with an abstract perspective of the network. The application plane is oriented to various business requests and passes the request to the control plane. In the SDN environment, the allocation of network resources is to allocate the available substrate resources provided by the physical layer to the virtual network, thereby truly providing network services for users (Fig. 1).

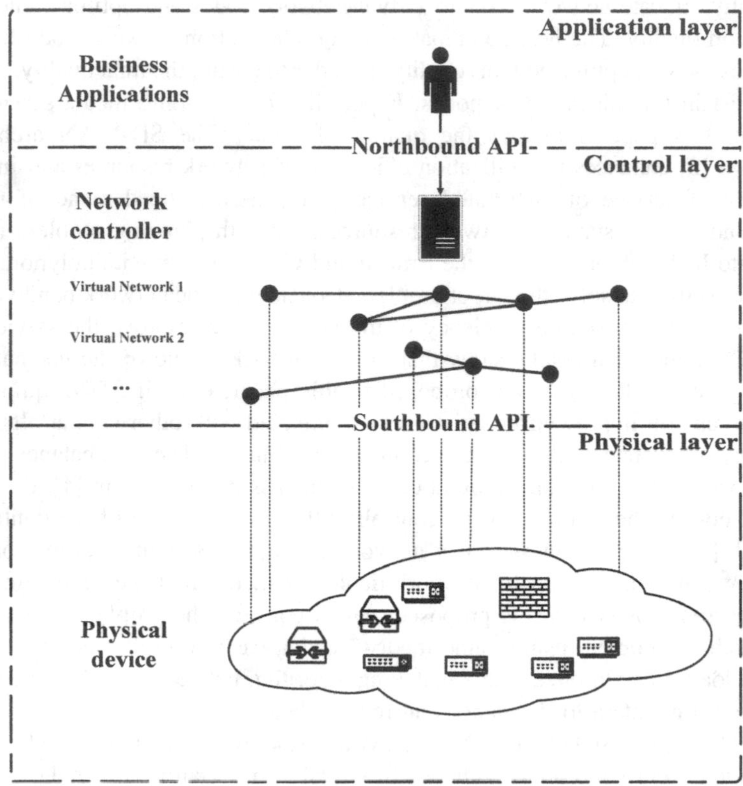

Fig. 1. Network virtualization system model architecture based on SDN

2.2 Substrate Network

Graph $G^p = (N^p, L^p)$ is used to describe the substrate network, in which N^p is the set of nodes and L^p is the links. Node $n_i^p \in N^p, i \in \{1, 2, \ldots, \mathrm{N}\}$. There are a total of N nodes. The service capability of node n_i^p is denoted as $Type(n_i^p)$, which represents the type of service the node can carry. The capacity of node n_i^p is C_i^p, and $C_i^p = \{C_i^p(CPU), C_i^p(Memory), \ldots\}$. If the substrate nodes n_i^p and n_j^p are connected, then binary variable $e_{ij} = 1$, otherwise $e_{ij} = 0$. The physical link connecting nodes n_i^p and n_j^p is expressed as $l^p(i,j) \in L^p | i \neq j; i,j \in \{1, 2, \cdots, N\}$ with bandwidth of $B^p(l^p(i,j))$ and delay of $T(l^p)$. $p(i,j) \in P$ represents all path starts from node n_i^p to n_j^p, where P is collection of all paths.

2.3 Virtual Network

The virtual network is represented as a weighted undirected graph $G^V = (N^V, L^V)$. The virtual node $n_q^V \in N^V, q \in \{1, 2, \cdots, M\}$, and M represents the number of nodes. The virtual network starts from n_1^V to $n_M^V \cdot n_q^V$'s capability requirement is $Type(n_q^V)$, capacity requirement is C_q^V. For the virtual link set L^V, $l^V(u,v) \in L^V | u \neq v, u, v \in \{1, 2, \ldots, M\}$ represents the virtual link connecting node n_u^V and n_v^V, the bandwidth requirement of $l^V(u,v)$ is $B(l^V(u,v))$. R_{ij}^{uv} is virtual link's traffic on substrate link $l^p(i,j)$. If it is 0, the virtual link isn't related to the substrate link $l^p(i,j)$.

2.4 Network Service

The service is denoted as $S(C, T_W, T_d)$, where C is the priority and T_t is the tolerance delay T_s is the time at which the service stays in the network.

2.5 Network Resource

Node Resource

Boolean variable x_i^λ is used to describe the mapping situation between virtual nodes and physical nodes. If the substrate node n_i^p is assigned to virtual node n_q^V, its value is set to 1, otherwise it is 0. The used capacity of the physical node is $C_{i\,used}^p = \sum_\lambda x_i^\lambda C_\lambda^V$. Thus, its available capacity is $C_{i\,avl}^p = C_i^p - C_{i\,used}^p$.

Link Resource Allocation

Boolean variable y_{ij}^{uv} is used to describe the mapping between virtual links and physical links. If the physical link $l^p(i,j)$ is assigned to virtual link $l^V(u,v)$, its value is taken as 1, otherwise it is taken as 0. $R_{ij}^{uv} = y_{ij}^{uv} \times B(l^v(uv))$, used bandwidth of $l^p(i,j)$ is $B_{used}^p(l^p(i,j)) = \sum_{uv} B^V(l^V(u,v)) \times y_{ij}^{uv}$, and whose available bandwidth is $B_{avl}(l^p) = B(l^p) - B_{used}(l^p)$.

Network Backup Mechanism

In multiple resource nodes, some resources may be unreliable, which will affect the execution and scheduling of business. There are many unsafe factors in cloud environment. If the network resource node in the cloud is attacked, it will directly affect the task execution on the node [10]. Considering the possibility of substrate network failure, it is necessary to allocate an alternate path for the service, so that the network can recover from the failure as soon as possible and improve network reliability. The mapping status of the primary path and the alternate path can be expressed by the binary variable $x_i^\lambda(m/b)$ and $y_{ij}^{uv}(m/b)$, if Physical node n_i is assigned as the main/backup node to the virtual node n_λ^V, $x_i^\lambda(m/b) = 1$; if physical link $l(i,j)$ is assigned as the main/backup path to the virtual link $l(u,v)$, $y_{ij}^{uv}(m/b) = 1$.

What's more, in order to improve the utilization efficiency of network resources, the backup resources of a certain path can also be used by other services when idle.

3 Problem Formulation

The main goal of network operating is to maximize its profits (i.e., the difference between the revenue generated by the network for business services and the operating costs of the network):

$$f : Max\{Rev - Co\} \tag{1}$$

Among them, Rev is the sum of the benefit of each service, $Rev = \sum_{W} rev(S)$. The revenue of a single service is related to the attributes of the business itself. $rev(S) = \mu \times C + \frac{\vartheta_1}{T_t + \eta_1} + \frac{\vartheta_2}{T_s + \eta_2} + \omega$, where μ, ϑ_1, ϑ_2 and η_1, η_2 are scale factors. ω is a constant.

Cost $Co = \kappa \times \sum_{i} C_q^V + \upsilon \times \sum_{ij} B^V(l^V)$, indicates the operating costs caused by the occupied link and node resources. Where κ and υ represent the cost of the unit node resource or bandwidth resource, respectively.

The objective function is subjected to the constraints below:

$$\mathrm{C}_{i\,avl}^{p} \geq x_i^q \mathrm{C}_q^V \tag{2}$$

$$Type(n_q^V) = \sum_{p} x_p^q \times Type(n_p) \tag{3}$$

$$\sum_{p} x_p^q = 1 \tag{4}$$

$$B_{avl}^p(l) \geq B^V(l^V) \tag{5}$$

$$\begin{cases} \sum\limits_{n_j \in A(n_i)} (R_{ji}^{(M-1)M} - R_{ij}^{(M-1)M}) = B^V(l^V(M-1, M)), \forall i, x_i^M = 1 \\ \sum\limits_{n_j \in A(n_i)} (R_{ji}^{12} - R_{ij}^{12}) = -B^V(l^V(1,2)), \forall i, x_i^1 = 1 \\ \sum\limits_{n_j \in A(n_i)} (R_{ji}^{(q-1)q} - R_{ij}^{(q-1)q}) = 0, \forall i, x_i^1 = 0 \,\&\, x_i^M = 0 \,\&\, x_i^q = 1, 2 < q < M \end{cases} \tag{6}$$

$$\begin{cases} x_i^\lambda = x_i^\lambda(m) + x_i^\lambda(b) \\ y_{ij}^{uv} = y_{ij}^{uv}(m) + y_{ij}^{uv}(b) \end{cases} \tag{7}$$

Where (2), (3) and (5) ensure that physical nodes (links) can meet the needs of virtual nodes (links). What's more, a virtual node can only be mapped to one substrate node, such as (4). According to (6), traffic flowing through nodes in the network is conserved. (7) indicates that the virtual network may not be mapped only if both the primary path and the alternate path fail.

4 Real-Time Resource-Aware Balanced Allocation Algorithm

In order to ensure that the network load can be as balanced as possible, the SDN controller needs to know the real-time resource status of the underlying network and adjust its allocation policy accordingly. It is considered to set the resource variable $\alpha_i = \frac{\varphi_1}{C_{iavl}(n_i) + \varepsilon_1} + \phi_1$ and $\beta_{ij} = \frac{\varphi_2}{B_{avl}(l) + \varepsilon_2} + \phi_2$ for the nodes and links, so that the physical paths with more available resources can be used preferentially. Among them, φ, ε and ϕ are constants. It can be seen that the resource coefficient and the size of the available resources are negatively correlated, and the more available resources, the smaller the weight of the path.

In Table 1, we initialize the network with the values defined above, and use RRBA algorithm to solve it. It can be seen that during the initialization, the proportion of the network resource state in the weight is maximized, so that the algorithm can maximize the balance of the network load.

Table 1. Algorithm 1

Algorithm1: Network parameter initialization

1. Input: Substrate Network G^p, business request w
2. Output: vectors x_i^λ and y_{ij}^{uv}
3. For (services) Do
4. Sort tasks in order of C, T_t and T_s
5. Link weights $W_{ij} = \gamma \times T(l)/T_W + \delta \times (\beta_{ij} + \frac{\alpha_i + \alpha_j}{2})$, where $\gamma = 0, \delta = 1$
6. RRBA(G)
7. End

The specific process of the RRBA algorithm is shown in Table 2. The RRBA algorithm selects the shortest path according to the link weight, and increases the weight of the delay in the weight step by step after the service allocation fails (lines 7–9).

Table 2. Algorithm 2

Algorithm 2: Real-time resource-aware balanced allocation (RRBA) algorithm

Node resource allocation
If (no available node)
    Return failed
Else
    For ($\gamma < 1$ & tolerance time up)
    find the shortest path (Floyd's algorithm)
    If (feasible paths<2)
        Increase γ
        Update w_{ij}
        If (link delay> T_t)
            Continue
        Else
            Get a feasible path
    Else
        Return vectors x_i^λ and y_{ij}^{uv}
Return failed
End

5 Performance Evaluation

5.1 Simulation Settings

We consider a 20-node substrate network where the resources of each node and link are random in (5,20). During the operation of the network, services with different parameters randomly arrive and request services. Services are abstracted into three representative businesses (Table 3):

Table 3. Business parameters

Services	Priority	Maximum delay/ms	Average bandwidth/(Mb/s)
E-mail	3	1	0.072
Live	2	0.75	10–50
Online game	1	0.25	100

In this environment, we compare our RRBA algorithm with the other two algorithms. One is the link-first allocation algorithm (LFA), which puts bandwidth requirements first, and allocates resources preferentially for services with high bandwidth requirements. If the task assignment fails, all the used physical resources are reclaimed for reallocation. Another is random node resource allocation algorithm (RNRA), the algorithm randomly allocates node resources, and selects links between nodes according to the shortest path algorithm. If the path resources are insufficient, the service request will be directly rejected.

5.2 Performance Analysis

Available Resource Variance

In the same network topology and service arrival, the variance of the network available resources is calculated under three algorithms respectively. It can be seen that since the RRBA algorithm considers using a path with more resources in the allocation, the available resources of the network are more balanced (Fig. 2).

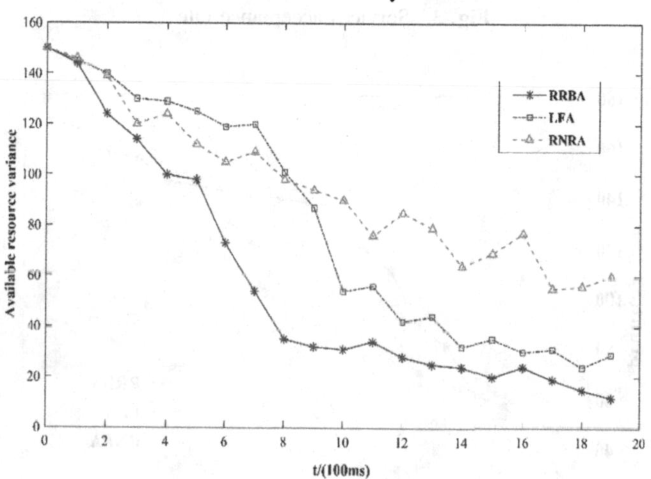

Fig. 2. Available resource variance

Services Acceptance Rate

The probability of different types of services being serviced is compared above. The service will leave the queue after the tolerance is exceeded. The acceptance rate of the business reflects the processing power of the network and the availability of resources. Because RRBA relatively guarantees the balanced load of the network, the available paths in the network are more, thus maintaining a higher service acceptance rate. At the same time, because the LFA algorithm may reclaim network resources for redistribution, the calculation time is doubled, which also leads to a higher rejection rate (Fig. 3).

Network Operating Profit

Intuitively, the more business the network successfully serves, the higher the profit earned. Since the RRBA algorithm guarantees the service rate of the service and especially guarantees the service rate of the high priority service, compared with the other two algorithms, my algorithm makes the network profit significantly improved (Fig. 4).

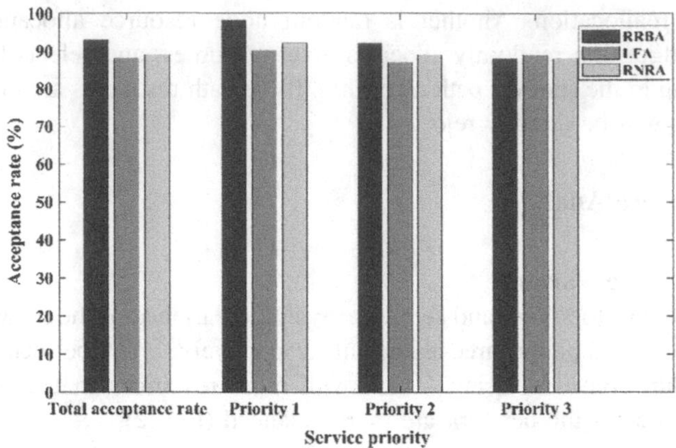

Fig. 3. Services acceptance rate

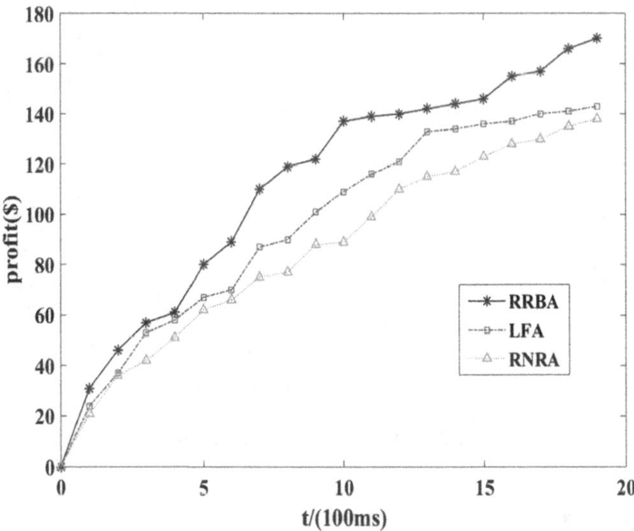

Fig. 4. Network operating profit

Network Reliability

Finally, compare the impact of the allocation of backup paths on network reliability. In a network with a backup path, services can be quickly transferred to the backup path after service interruption, which improves service survival. As a result, more business is successfully completed, and the profit is improved compared to the case of no backup (Figs. 5 and 6).

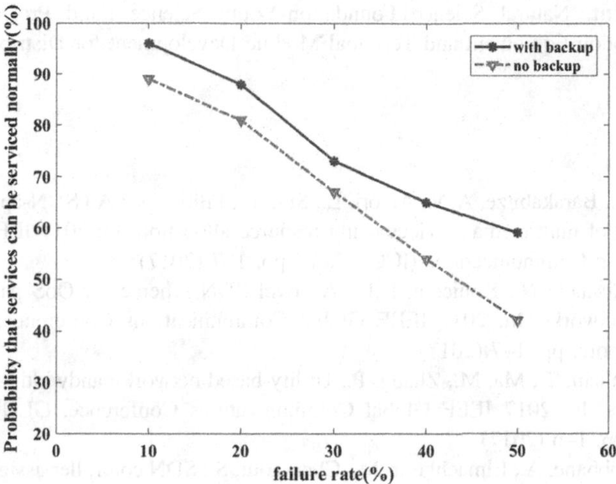

Fig. 5. The probability that a service can continue to be serviced normally under a certain probability of network failure

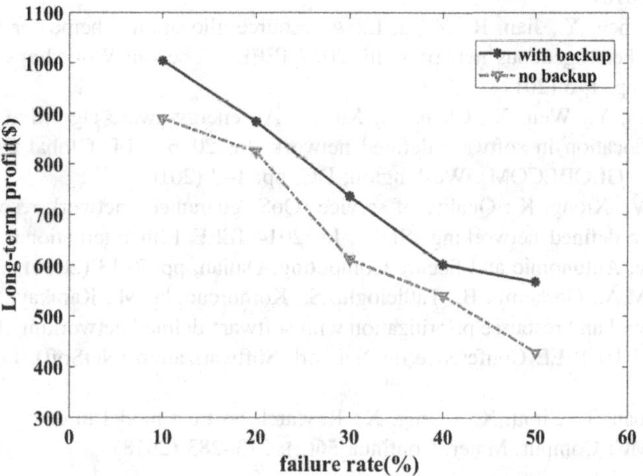

Fig. 6. Network profit in the case of a certain probability of failure arrival

6 Conclusion

Facing the multimedia application in the background of mobile core network, this paper proposes a network resource allocation mechanism to guarantee service QoS and resource utilization in the architecture model of SDN. The proposed algorithm formulates the mapping strategy of the virtual network according to the real-time utilization status of the network, and provides reliability guarantee for the service. The simulation proves the superiority of the algorithm in all aspects.

Acknowledgement. Natural Science Foundation-Youth Science Fund Project (61702048), Quantum Encryption Equipment and Terminal Module Development for Distribution Business.

References

1. Grigoriou, E., Barakabitze, A.A., Atzori, L., Sun, L., Pilloni, V.: An SDN-approach for QoE management of multimedia services using resource allocation. In: 2017 IEEE International Conference on Communications (ICC), Paris, pp. 1–7 (2017)
2. Fajjari, I., Aitsaadi, N., Kouicem, D.E.: A novel SDN scheme for QoS path allocation in wide area networks. In: 2017 IEEE Global Communications Conference, GLOBECOM 2017, Singapore, pp. 1–7 (2017)
3. Huang, X., Yuan, T., Ma, M., Zhang, P.: Utility-based network bandwidth allocation in the hybrid SDNs. In: 2017 IEEE Global Communications Conference, GLOBECOM 2017, Singapore, pp. 1–6 (2017)
4. Filali, A., Kobbane, A., Elmachkour, M., Cherkaoui, S.: SDN controller assignment and load balancing with minimum quota of processing capacity. In: 2018 IEEE International Conference on Communications (ICC), Kansas, MO, pp. 1–6 (2018)
5. Wang, J., Ju, C., Gao, Y., Sangaiah, A.K., Kim, G.: A PSO based energy efficient coverage control algorithm for wireless sensor networks. CMC: Comput. Mater. Continua **56**(3), 433–446 (2018)
6. Zhao, Y., Chen, Y., Jian, R., Yang, L.: A resource allocation scheme for SDN-based 5G ultra-dense heterogeneous networks. In: 2017 IEEE Globecom Workshops (GC Wkshps), Singapore, pp. 1–6 (2017)
7. Yu, B., Han, Y., Wen, X., Chen, X., Xu, Z.: An energy-aware algorithm for optimizing resource allocation in software defined network. In: 2016 IEEE Global Communications Conference (GLOBECOM), Washington, DC, pp. 1–7 (2016)
8. Akella, A.V., Xiong, K.: Quality of service (QoS)-guaranteed network resource allocation via software defined networking (SDN). In: 2014 IEEE 12th International Conference on Dependable, Autonomic and Secure Computing, Dalian, pp. 7–13 (2014)
9. Karaman, M.A., Gorkemli, B., Tatlicioglu, S., Komurcuoglu, M., Karakaya, O.: Quality of service control and resource prioritization with software defined networking. In: Proceedings of the 2015 1st IEEE Conference on Network Softwarization (NetSoft), London, pp. 1–6 (2015)
10. Xie, X., Yuan, T., Zhou, X., Cheng, X.: Research on trust model in container-based cloud service. CMC: Comput. Mater. Continua **56**(2), 273–283 (2018)

RSCM: A Reliability-Aware Service Chain Mapping

Guanjun Tang[1,2(✉)], Yonghua Chen[1,2], Shiguang Xu[1,2], Qian Chen[3], and Wenchen He[3]

[1] NARI Group Corporation (State Grid Electric Power Research Institute), Nanjing 211106, China
cqbupt@bupt.edu.cn

[2] NARI Technology Development Co. Ltd., Nanjing 211106, China

[3] Beijing University of Posts and Telecommunications, Beijing 100876, China

Abstract. As the development of Network Function Virtualization (NFV) technology, service is placed on a set of virtual network functions (VNFs), namely service chain. Operators provide differentiated services for users by managing and mapping placement and routing of VNFs. However, the existing mapping schemes lack comprehensive considerations of service reliability and QoS parameters such as latency, transmission rate. Besides, resource utilization efficiency also needs to be further improved. So, a reliability-aware service chain mapping (RSCM) algorithm is proposed. RSCM firstly gets reachable paths by improved breadth-first search (IBFS) algorithm and extends them in a cost-efficient manner to get routing scheme. Secondly, a P*Q replication method is proposed to guarantee reliability of services, where P VNFs are supported by Q replicas to improve resource utilization. The simulation result shows that our algorithm takes less time to generate service chain mapping scheme, which can reduce cost.

Keywords: NFV · Reliability · QoS · Service chain · Mapping

1 Introduction

In NFV-based network, failures of VNFs may be caused by various reasons [1,2]. One is that physical machines (PM) carrying network functions break down. The second is that virtual machines (VM) or software associated with VNFs fail. The failures of a single VNF will affect normal execution of entire service chain, resulting in serious data loss and resources waste. VNF replication is a common method to improve system reliability [3]. However, replicas may introduce additional overhead. At the same time, redundant VNFs increase the length of service chain. Additional links further increase end-to-end transmission latency of services. It is unacceptable for latency-sensitive services [4]. Therefore, it is an urgent to efficiently meet service reliability and QoS requirements with limited resources. In order to improve resource utilization, existing models have

X. Sun et al. (Eds.): ICAIS 2019, LNCS 11633, pp. 653–662, 2019.
https://doi.org/10.1007/978-3-030-24265-7_56

limitations and are difficult to handle a large number of services in a timely manner. In addition, consideration of QoS for services is insufficient.

In summary, the sharing of network function replications and latency requirements of extended links in mapping must be considered. Considering that possibility of VNFs' failures is mostly low, the method that P VNFs share Q replications can become feasible for maximal resource utilization. In the meantime, latency is an important indicator to measure whether mapping and replication schemes are reasonable, that is, service's end-to-end latency after being switched to new VNF must still meet requirements. In addition, in the process of links expansion, it is necessary to consider load balancing of links to avoid partial defects caused by excessive loads on links.

Therefore, this paper proposes a reliability-aware service chain mapping algorithm. The technical contributions of this paper are summarized as follows: (1) We propose a reliability-aware service chain mapping algorithm to complete service mapping in a cost-optimized manner. The latency is added to the pruning factor of the breadth-first search algorithm. We obtain an end-to-end reachable and cost-optimized path set through an improved breadth-first search (IBFS) algorithm, and then extend these paths to get the optimal path; (2) This paper proposes a P*Q replication algorithm to ensure the reliability of the service.

2 Related Work

Related works in area of guaranteeing QoS requirements of services generally focus on latency requirement. Authors in [5] present how latency rises when functions are completely virtualized and further affects VNF optimal placement. Considering above effects of latency, authors in [6] give a reliability-aware and latency-limited service chain joint optimization framework. This framework combines iterative backup selection and routing process in a subtle way, and considers single-route and multi-routing strategies to ensure reliability and guarantee end-to-end response latency. Authors in [7] focus on placement of VNFs, and aim to support different service demands amons users, as well as minimize the related VNF placement cost. However, resource utilization efficiency in these mapping schemes needs to be improved.

Specifically, considering reliability is of compelling criticality because the failure of any VNF of a particular network service chain can effect the entire chain and further cause suspension of service [8,9]. Authors in [10] propose to select a proper VNF to replicate, and select a server node with high reliability for VNF to maximize reliability with minimum cost. Authors in [11,12] propose security-aware virtual network embedding optimization problems, develop objective functions and mathematical constraints including resource and security constraints. However, the above solutions lack of consideration of replicas sharing.

In summary, those methods lack comprehensive considerations of latency, reliability in a cost-efficient manner. Our algorithm is able to map service chains in a high cost-effective manner while meeting latency and reliability requirements.

3 System Model and Problem Formulation

3.1 System Model

The weighted undirected graph $G = (V, L)$ is used to represent substrate network, and V and L are sets of physical nodes and links respectively. As for one server node n_i, its capacity to host VNFs is denoted as $cap(n_i)$, which represents physical resources such as CPU processing resource, memory and storage. For any physical link $l_{ij} \in L$ connecting n_i to n_j, transmission rate is denoted as b_{ij}, and transmission latency is denoted as d_{ij}. A service chain consisting of a series of VNFs. $V = \{v_1, v_2, ..., v_k\}$ represents a set of VNFs. $N(s_i)$ represents the number of VNFs in s_i, and M represents the number of service chains. VNF v_i requires physical resources $cap(v_i)$. VNF v_i has processing latency d_i and reliability r_i. Similarly, virtual link l^v_{uv} among VNFs is mapped to l_{ij}, while consuming transmission rate. The service has: transmission rate requirement B_{req}, latency D_{req}, and reliability requirement R_{req}.

3.2 Latency and Reliability

Services have different QoS requirements which typically include transmission rate and latency. Latency of service includes transmission latency and processing latency. It increases during expansion of links. If latency after extension exceeds latency requirement of service, existence of paths will become meaningless. Therefore, additional latency is a factor that must be considered in expansion process.

The reliability of one VNF is calculated by mean time between failures and average time to repair. The reliability of service is given as product of reliability of network functions, so reliability of a service chain is expressed as follow.

$$\begin{aligned} R_s &= \Pr[all\ VNFs\ are\ reliable] \\ &= \prod r \end{aligned} \tag{1}$$

In the case of complex network function failures, reliability of service is difficult to be guaranteed. Traditional one-to-one replication will lead to extra expenditure. Therefore, we propose an P*Q replication method, that is, P VNFs use Q replicas network functions. As shown in Fig. 1, it allows a VNF to have Q replicas, and greatly improves reliability. At the same time, Q replicas serve multiple VNF, which effectively improves resource utilization. Taking 3*2 as an example, when replicating the same number of VNFs, P*Q replication method is more reliable than one-to-one replication, and saves 33.3% of cost.

4 Reliability-Aware Service Chain Mapping Algorithm

4.1 Mapping Model

We design following binary auxiliary variables.

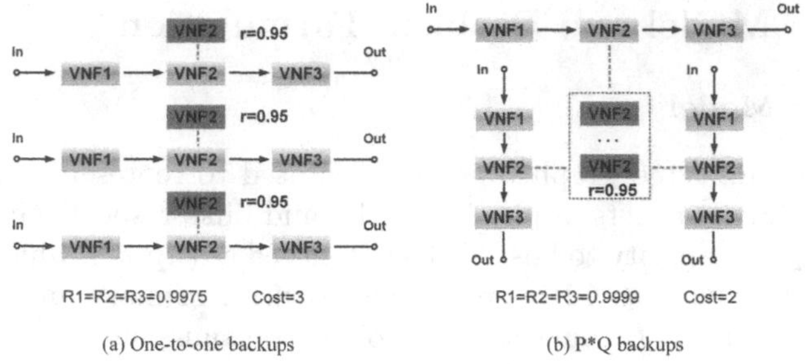

(a) One-to-one backups (b) P*Q backups

Fig. 1. Comparison of replication schemes.

- $x_{i,j}$: where $x_{i,j} = 1$ denotes that virtual network function v_j is replication for v_i.
- $y_{ij,uv}$: where $y_{ij,uv} = 1$ denotes that virtual link l_{uv}^v is mapped to physical link l_{ij}.
- $z_{i,j}$: where $z_{i,j} = 1$ denotes that VNF v_j is mapped to server node n_i.

The goal of mapping is to reduce network operator's capital expenditure and operation expenditure as much as possible while meeting requirements including reliability, transmission rate and end-to-end latency. The mapping cost can be expressed as follow.

$$cost = c_1 \sum_{i \in N} \sum_{j \in K} z_{i,j} + c_2 \sum_{i,j \in N} \sum_{u,v \in K} y_{ij,uv} B_{req} \tag{2}$$

The first item considers installation cost of network functions; the second item represents cost of consuming link transmission rate.

Constraints. Considering that embedding excessive network functions in one node does not help to improve reliability of services, we set a server node to carry a limited number of network functions.

$$C_1 : 1 \le \sum_{j \in K} z_{i,j} \le z_0, \forall i \in N \tag{3}$$

In the process of virtual link mapping, sum of directional traffic of other physical nodes is 0 except for source and destination nodes.

$$C_2 : \sum_{i,j \in N} y_{ij,uv} - \sum_{i,j \in N} y_{ji,uv} = \begin{cases} 1, & if\ z_{i,u} = 1 \\ -1, & if\ z_{j,v} = 1 \\ 0, & otherwise \end{cases} \tag{4}$$

Any primary VNF may have its replicas.

$$C_3 : \sum_{j \in K} x_{i,j} \le x_0, \forall i \in K \tag{5}$$

The scheme that one replica hosts excessive primary VNFs also does not help improve reliability of service chains. Therefore, we set that any replica can support a limited number of primary VNFs.

$$C_4 : \sum_{i \in K} x_{i,j} \leq d_0, \forall j \in K \tag{6}$$

Reliability of service chain cannot be less than its minimum reliability requirement.

$$C_5 : R_s = \prod r_i \geq R_{req} \tag{7}$$

Optimization Model. RSCM maps service chains with minimum cost while meeting latency and reliability requirements. So, optimization model is as follows.

$$\begin{aligned} &\min \quad cost \\ &\text{s.t.} \quad C_1 \sim C_5 \\ &x_{i,j}, y_{ij,uv}, z_{i,j} \in \{0, 1\} \end{aligned} \tag{8}$$

4.2 Reliability-Aware Service Chain Mapping Algorithm

Firstly, a reachable path set meeting latency requirement of service is calculated through improved breadth-first Search algorithm (IBFS). The algorithm classifies paths into $N(s_i) + 1$ based on the number of primary VNFs in these paths. Paths with greater than or equal to $N(s_i)$ primary VNFs are uniformly divided into Class $N(s_i)$. We select the lowest-cost path from each class to form original path set. Algorithm uniformly expands paths in original path set to $N(s_i)$ primary VNFs to meet service requirements. We refer to extended original path set as final feasible link set, and select path with the least cost from this set as final mapping scheme. The procedure of mapping is illustrated in Fig. 2.

In replication process, algorithm prefers to select the most cost-effective VNF to replicate. Cost performance is expressed as follow.

$$value = \frac{\Delta\, r}{cost} \tag{9}$$

Where $\Delta\, r$ represents improved reliability value of service chain after replicating this VNF. *cost* represents cost of replicating this VNF. The algorithm firstly selects existing replication functions within reachable range as its replicas. When there is no replication VNFs of same type in reachable range, a new replica is created for primary VNF. Since we consider P*Q backup, a primary VNF may have multiple replicas, which greatly increases backup links. Therefore, we do not reserve backup links for each replica. Instead, we use TDM approach to solve the problem of conflict between backup link and primary link during a fault. The reason for this feasibility is that there are Q replicas which can be selected when primary VNF fails. The TDM approach can effectively solve this problem. This is also the benefit of P*Q method. In addition, we consider load balancing as

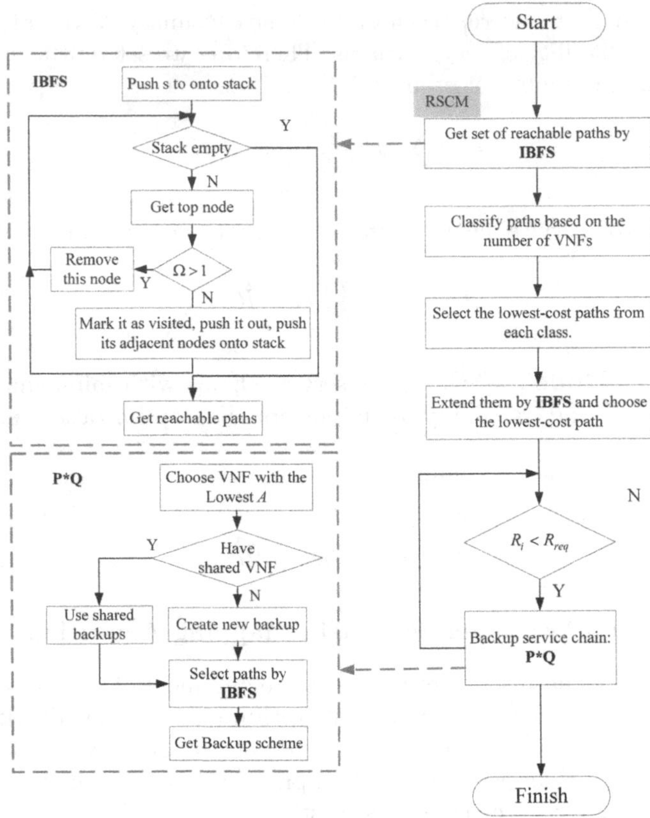

Fig. 2. Algorithm flow chart.

much as possible when determining backup links, to avoid the defects caused by excessive partial load of network.

This paper proposes IBFS to determine extended links. Algorithm pre-excludes infeasible paths on the basic of Ω. Definition of Ω is given by

$$\Omega = (\sum_{i\in K}\sum_{i\in N} z_{i,j}d_i + \sum_{i,j\in N}\sum_{u,v\in K} y_{ij,uv}d_{ij} \geqslant D_{req}) \tag{10}$$

5 Evaluation Analysis

5.1 Setting

We set a physical network including 20 server nodes and 50 switch nodes in experiment. Transmission rate are set to a random value (100–200 Mbps). Each service chain consists of 2–4 VNFs. Latency requirement varies from milliseconds to seconds.

To prove the effectiveness of three algorithms, two mapping algorithms are shown as comparisons. (1) Mincost algorithm: It chooses VNF with the lowest Cost-effectiveness, and replicate VNFs until reliability reaches requirement. (2) Single-path algorithm: The algorithm replicates all VNFs on original paths.

5.2 Result Analysis

(1) Cost: Fig. 3 presents expense of service chain orchestration possessing various reliability demands. Under five different conditions of reliability requirements, the solution cost of RSCM was lowest when comparing with other algorithms. A case study of 0.98 reliability requirement shows that compared with Mincost and Single-path, RSCM can save 17% and 32% cost respectively. As shown in Fig. 4, even with 0.999 reliability requirement, RSCM still keeps minimum cost, which is related to that final best path set is obtained by expanding paths in original path set instead of an original link with least coat when adopting RSCM algorithm. Additionally, our algorithm employing P*Q replication when replicating VNFs, which indicated that P VNFs can share Q replicas. Through improving the way of expanding path and utilization of resources, our algorithm shows an enormous advantage in the aspect of cost.

(2) Service acceptance rate: The 0.95 service acceptance rate of RSCM, Mincost and Single-path are 93.4%, 81.2% and 77.7%, respectively. And The 0.999 service acceptance rate of RSCM, Mincost and Single-path are 75.6%, 67.7% and 63.6%, respectively. Additional delay as a constraint condition guaranteed services of RSCM always meet delay demand. In addition, RSCM can use finite resource to obtain maximal reliability by P*Q replication method. RSCM also focus on keeping network load balance when selecting link. To sum up, the highest acceptance rate is achieved by RSCM rather than Mincost or Single-path.

(3) Average node usage rate: Fig. 6 exhibits average node usage rate with different algorithms. It is obvious that node load increased as traffic increases. Minimum cost is the basis of deploy of RSCM service chains. Resource utilization is improved effectively by maintaining a low resource occupancy rate. The quantity of VNF replicas is declined by P*Q replication method. Above factors make average node usage rate of RSCM lower than that of other two algorithms.

(4) Variance of link usage rate: the variance of RSCM is 17% and 65% below that of Mincost and Single-path respectively when the quantity of services increased to 800. A traffic-balancing index is set into path chose procedure and link cost calculation. In order to avert network congestion contributed to heavy local traffic load, RSCM tends to choose a link possessing a small load. As a result, network with balanced state can be guaranteed by RSCM (Figs. 5, 7).

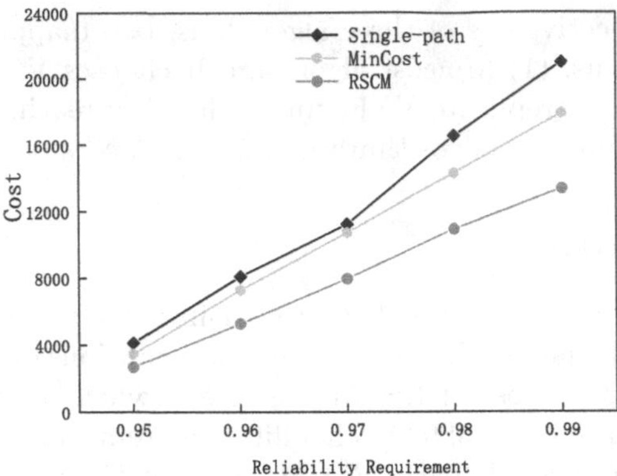

Fig. 3. Cost.

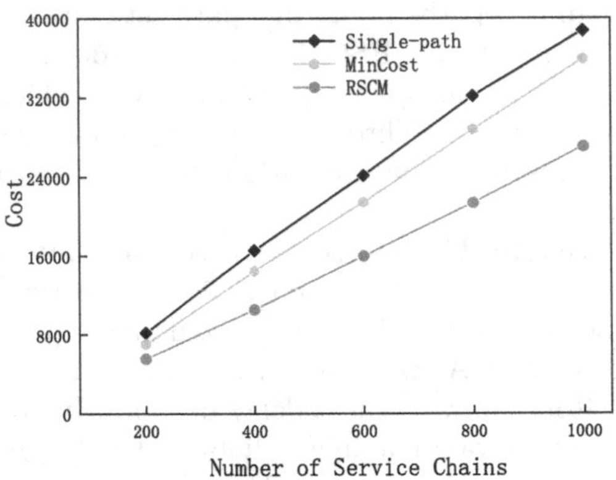

Fig. 4. Cost.

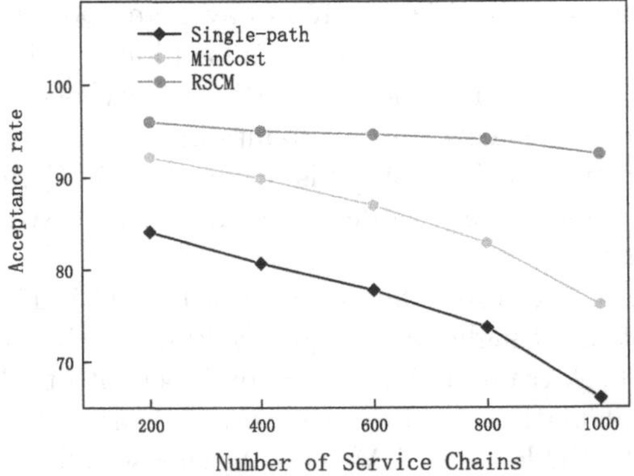

Fig. 5. Service acceptance rate.

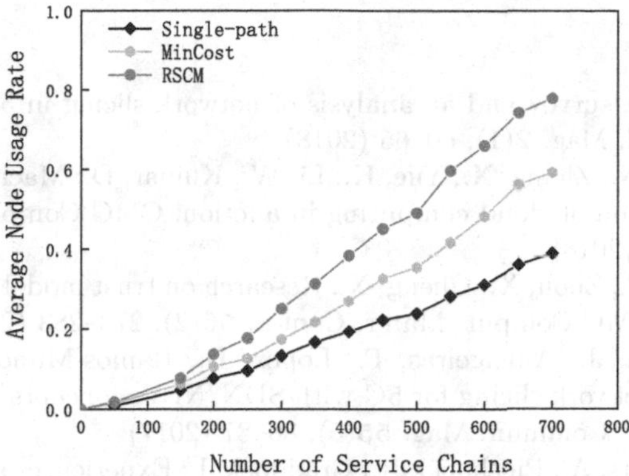

Fig. 6. Average node usage rate.

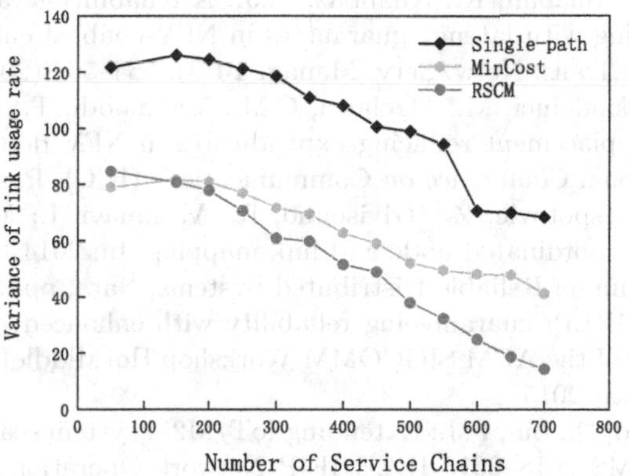

Fig. 7. Variance of link usage rate.

6 Conclusion

This paper proposes a reliability-aware service chain mapping (RSCM) algorithm. We consider latency and reliability requirements, and completes service chain deployment with the minimum cost. For VNF replication, this paper designs an P*Q replication scheme. We guarantee than RSCM can not only maximize resource utilization, but also meet the reliability requirements of the service chain. In addition, we consider selecting links with small load in process of expanding backup paths to ensure that network is always in a balanced state.

Acknowledgment. This paper is supported by SGCC Science and Technology Foundation "Core Technology and Development of Key Equipment for Power System Stable Control based on Multi Source Real Time Data Transfer Scheduling Mode" (Project NO: SGTYHT/15-JS-191).

References

1. Kaloxylos, A.: A survey and an analysis of network slicing in 5G networks. IEEE Commun. Stand. Mag. **2**(1), 60–65 (2018)
2. Zhang, J., Xie, N., Zhang, X., Yue, K., Li, W., Kumar, D.: Machine learning based resource allocation of cloud computing in auction. CMC Comput. Mater. Contin. **56**(1), 123–135 (2018)
3. Xie, X., Yuan, T., Zhou, X., Cheng, X.: Research on trust model in container-based cloud service. CMC Comput. Mater. Contin. **56**(2), 273–283 (2018)
4. Ordonez-Lucena, J., Ameigeiras, P., Lopez, D., Ramos-Munoz, J.J., Lorca, J., Folgueira, J.: Network slicing for 5G with SDN/NFV: concepts, architectures, and challenges. IEEE Commun. Mag. **55**(5), 80–87 (2017)
5. Fafoutis, X., Elsts, A., Piechocki, R., Craddock, I.: Experiences and lessons learned from making IoT sensing platforms for large-scale deployments. IEEE Access **6**, 3140–3148 (2018)
6. Qu, L., Assi, C., Shaban, K., Khabbaz, M.J.: A reliability-aware network service chain provisioning with latency guarantees in NFV-enabled enterprise datacenter networks. IEEE Trans. Netw. Serv. Manag. **14**(3), 554–568 (2017)
7. Vizarreta, P., Condoluci, M., Machuca, C.M., Mahmoodi, T., Kellerer, W.: QoS-driven function placement reducing expenditures in NFV deployments. In: 2017 IEEE International Conference on Communications (ICC), Paris, pp. 1–7 (2017)
8. Guerzoni, R., Despotovic, Z., Trivisonno, R., Vaishnavi, I.: Modeling reliability requirements in coordinated node and link mapping. In: 2014 IEEE 33rd International Symposium on Reliable Distributed Systems, Nara, pp. 321–330 (2014)
9. Fan, J. et al.: GREP: guaranteeing reliability with enhanced protection in NFV. In: Proceedings of the ACM SIGCOMM Workshop HotMiddleBox, London, U.K., pp. 13–18, August 2015
10. de la Bastidaand, D., Lin, F.J.: Extending IoT/M2M system scalability by network slicing. In: NOMS 2018–2018 IEEE/IFIP Network Operations and Management Symposium, Taipei, pp. 1–8 (2018)
11. Rahman, M.R., Boutaba, R.: SVNE: survivable virtual network embedding algorithms for network virtualization. IEEE Trans. Netw. Serv. Manag. **10**(2), 105–118 (2013)
12. Liu, S., Cai, Z., Xu, H., Xu, M.: Security-aware virtual network embedding. In: 2014 IEEE International Conference on Communications (ICC), Sydney, NSW, pp. 834–840 (2014)

Correction to: Prediction on Payment Volume from Customer Service Electricity Channel

Gong Lihua, Sheng Yan, Liu Kunpeng, Zhu Longzhu, and Zhang Yi

Correction to:
Chapter "Prediction on Payment Volume from Customer Service Electricity Channel" in: X. Sun et al. (Eds.): *Artificial Intelligence and Security*, LNCS 11633, https://doi.org/10.1007/978-3-030-24265-7_28

In the originally published version of chapter 28, the first affiliation included an error. The first affiliation has been corrected from "USA State Grid Corporation Customer Service Center, Tianjin 300000, China" to "State Grid Corporation Customer Service Center, Tianjin 300000, China".

The updated version of this chapter can be found at https://doi.org/10.1007/978-3-030-24265-7_28

X. Sun et al. (Eds.): ICAIS 2019, LNCS 11633, p. C1, 2020.
https://doi.org/10.1007/978-3-030-24265-7_57

Author Index

Printed in the United States
By Bookmasters